The Idea of the University
Volume 2

GLOBAL STUDIES IN EDUCATION

A.C. (Tina) Besley, Michael A. Peters,
Cameron McCarthy, Fazal Rizvi
General Editors

Vol. 18

The Global Studies in Education series is part of the Peter Lang Education list.
Every volume is peer reviewed and meets
the highest quality standards for content and production.

PETER LANG
New York • Bern • Berlin
Brussels • Vienna • Oxford • Warsaw

The Idea of the University

Contemporary Perspectives

Volume 2

Edited by
Ronald Barnett and Michael A. Peters

With the assistance of
Richard Heraud

PETER LANG
New York • Bern • Berlin
Brussels • Vienna • Oxford • Warsaw

The Library of Congress has catalogued the first volume as follows:

Names: Peters, Michael (Michael A.), editor. | Barnett, Ronald, editor.
Title: The idea of the university: a reader, vol. 1 / edited by
Michael A. Peters, Ronald Barnett.
Description: New York: Peter Lang, 2018.
Series: Global studies in education; vol. 17 | ISSN 2153-330X
Includes bibliographical references and index.
Identifiers: LCCN 2016023379
ISBN 978-1-4331-2191-3 (vol. 1, hardcover: alk. paper)
ISBN 978-1-4331-2190-6 (vol. 1, paperback: alk. paper)
ISBN 978-1-4539-1888-3 (vol. 1, ebook pdf)
ISBN 978-1-4331-3646-7 (vol. 1, epub) | ISBN 978-1-4331-3647-4 (vol. 1, mobi)
ISBN 978-1-4331-4978-8 (vol. 2, hardcover: alk. paper)
ISBN 978-1-4331-4979-5 (vol. 2, paperback: alk. paper)
ISBN 978-1-4331-4980-1 (vol. 2, ebook pdf)
ISBN 978-1-4331-4981-8 (vol. 2, epub) | ISBN 978-1-4331-4982-5 (vol. 2, mobi)
Classification: LCC LB2322.2.I33 | DDC 378—dc23
LC record available at https://lccn.loc.gov/2016023379
DOI 10.3726/978-1-4539-1888-3 (vol. 1)
DOI 10.3726/b11389 (vol. 2)

Bibliographic information published by **Die Deutsche Nationalbibliothek.**
Die Deutsche Nationalbibliothek lists this publication in the "Deutsche Nationalbibliografie"; detailed bibliographic data are available on the Internet at http://dnb.d-nb.de/.

The paper in this book meets the guidelines for permanence and durability of the Committee on Production Guidelines for Book Longevity of the Council of Library Resources.

29 Broadway, 18th floor, New York, NY 10006
www.peterlang.com

Printed in the United States of America

Table of Contents

Acknowledgements ix

Introduction: Overcoming Pessimism, Forging Possibilities
Ronald Barnett and Michael A. Peters 1

Part One: Addressing Neoliberalism **17**
Introduction by Michael A. Peters

Chapter One: University under Attack? Politics, Contestation and Agency beyond the 'Neoliberal University' 21
Jana Bacevic

Chapter Two: Defending Higher Education in the Age of Barbarism 37
Henry A. Giroux

Chapter Three: Academic Capitalism: Reflections on Higher Education in the United States and European Union 55
Sheila Slaughter and Brendan Cantwell

Chapter Four: Rethinking the Entrepreneurial University for the 21st Century 78
Wesley Shumar and Sarah Robinson

Part Two: The Global University 95
Introduction by Ronald Barnett

Chapter Five: The International University: Models and Muddles 99
Jane Knight

Chapter Six: The Anglo-American University: Support Structure for the 1 per cent 119
Simon Marginson

Chapter Seven: Freedom and Control in the Constrained Modern University 135
Francine Rochford

Chapter Eight: Displaced towards a Networked University 155
Nicolas Standaert

Part Three: European Ideas 171
Introduction by Michael A. Peters

Chapter Nine: The University and the State in Europe: The Uncertain Future of the Traditional Social Contract 175
Marek Kwiek

Chapter Ten: Forum Shifting and Shape Making in Higher Education Services 192
Susan L. Robertson, Joanna Tidy, and Janja Komljenovic

Chapter Eleven: The European University: Heartland to Periphery and Even Back Again? 216
Peter Scott

Chapter Twelve: The Nordic Idea of University 233
Jussi Välimaa

Chapter Thirteen: European Universities: Another Somewhat Lamenting—Yet Basically Hopeful—Account 252
Thorsten Nybom

Part Four: Regional Perspectives 269
Introduction by Ronald Barnett

Chapter Fourteen: The Idea of the University in the Evolving Higher Education Landscape in Africa 273
N'Dri Thérèse Assié-Lumumba

Chapter Fifteen: The Latin-American University: Past, Present and Future 292
Carolina Guzmán-Valenzuela and Andrés Bernasconi

Chapter Sixteen: Towards an African University in Becoming: Positive Risk, Hope and Imagination 311
Yusef Waghid and Nuraan Davids

Part Five: Knowledge and Research **329**
Introduction by Ronald Barnett

Chapter Seventeen: Citizenship and the University: The Consequences of Globalization 333
Gerard Delanty

Chapter Eighteen: Universities and the Knowledge Society Revisited 353
Alberto Amaral

Chapter Nineteen: Parting Ways: Analogue People in a Digital University 370
Robert Hassan

Part Six: Teaching and Students **389**
Introduction by Ronald Barnett

Chapter Twenty: Citizens of the World 393
Martha C. Nussbaum

Chapter Twenty-One: Trust in the University 412
Paul Gibbs

Chapter Twenty-Two: The University as Public Pedagogic Form 432
Jan Masschelein and Maarten Simons

Chapter Twenty-Three: Universities as Civic Spaces: In the Footsteps of Arendt and Jaspers 447
Jon Nixon

Part Seven: Possibilities **461**
Introduction by Michael A. Peters

Chapter Twenty-Four: The Idea(l) of a Paraversity 465
Gary Rolfe

Chapter Twenty-Five: The Platform University: The Destruction and Resurrection of Universities in the Auto-Industrial Age 483
Peter Murphy

Chapter Twenty-Six: The Fully-Functioning University 501
Tom Bourner

Chapter Twenty-Seven: Academic Citizenship beyond the Campus:
A Call for the Placeful University 522
Rikke Toft Nørgard and Søren Smedegaard Ernst Bengsten

Chapter Twenty-Eight: Do We Need an Academic Revolution
to Create a Wiser World? 539
Nicholas Maxwell

Chapter Twenty-Nine: Renewing the Idea of the University:
The Cosmopolitan and Postcolonial Projects 558
Michael A. Peters

Chapter Thirty: The Ecological University—A University Whose Time Has Come 575
Ronald Barnett

Contributor Biographies 591
Subject Index 597
Name Index 613

Acknowledgements

This volume forms part of a two-volume project on the idea of the university, of which Michael Peters and I conceived some time ago. (The parallel volume is a reader of extracts taken from historically important texts within the 200-year long canon on the very idea of the university.) Pulling off such a complex project has taken us longer than we originally anticipated and our acknowledgements must, in the first place, go towards our contributors, who have patiently awaited sight of their offerings.

We also gratefully acknowledge permissions to republish or rework earlier material as follows:

- Gerard Delanty's chapter 'Citizenship and the University: The Consequences of Globalization' was previously published as Chapter 30 in *The SAGE Handbook of Sociology* (2005), C. Calhoun, C. Rojek, & B. S. Turner (Eds.)
- Rikke Toft Nørgard and Søren Smedegaard Ernst Bengsten's chapter 'Academic Citizenship beyond the Campus: A Call for the Placeful University' was previously published in 2016 in *Higher Education Research & Development 35*(1), 6–14. Taylor & Francis. http://dx.doi.org/10.1080/07294360.2015.1131669

- Martha C. Nussbaum's chapter 'Citizens of the World' was previously published in 1997 in *Cultivating Humanity: A Classical Defense of Reform in Liberal Education* (Chapter Two, Citizens of the World) (pp. 50–84). Cambridge, MA: Harvard University Press. This chapter is an abridged version of the original chapter.

We also record our appreciation of the way in which the staff at Peter Lang—especially Sara McBride and Sara Bode—have shown much fortitude in persisting with this project, despite its occasional turbulent moments.

Lastly, but by no means least, Michael Peters and I warmly applaud the never-flagging and patient energies of our research assistant, Richard Heraud, who has helped considerably in keeping this particular show on the road in deftly engaging with the publishers, the contributors and, indeed, us.

Ronald Barnett

Introduction

Overcoming Pessimism, Forging Possibilities

RONALD BARNETT AND MICHAEL A. PETERS

Opening paths

This volume accompanies a separate volume consisting of readings from the 200-year long tradition of writings on the idea of the university. That lineage began in the writings of German philosophers at the end of the eighteenth century, was developed at the hands of English writers in the mid-nineteenth century, and was continued well into the twentieth century by authors from American, European and other traditions. Those writings have come to constitute a great tradition, increasingly cosmopolitan, with many books among that literature bearing the title 'The Idea of the University' or something very similar. So we find, for example, 'The Idea of a University' (Newman, 1976/1848), 'The Idea of the University' (Jaspers, 1960/1946), 'The Concept of a University' (Minogue, 1973), 'The Ideal of the University' (Wolff, 1997) and even 'The Idea of Higher Education' (Barnett, 1990). Recently, however, and alongside its hesitant continuation, that line of work has splintered, opening into perhaps *four* paths.

A first path opened from the middle of the twentieth century, consisting largely of an illumination of ways in which the university was unfolding. Works such as '*The Uses of the University*' (by Kerr, 1995/1963) which offered us the concept of the 'multiversity', '*Creating Entrepreneurial Universities*' (by Burton Clark, 1998) which bequeathed to us the idea of 'the entrepreneurial university' and '*Universities in the Marketplace*' (by Bok, 2003) which emphasised the ways in which the university was becoming attuned to the market, were insightful commentaries on the forms that the university was actually assuming. These were ideas of the university rooted in the university as a real institution in society.

We may note that there is here an axis opening, the poles of which are the *university as idea* and the *university as institution*. Writings at each of the poles have an interest in the idea of the university but that interest assumes a different balance at each of the poles. In the great tradition, from Kant and Newman onwards, we see an emphasis on *the idea of the university as such*. It was a distinctly *conceptual* approach. The very idea of the university captured the attention of the writers in this genre. Just what was it to be a university? To offer a space of reason? To bring forward the intellectual enlargement of the mind? At the other pole of this axis, we find an interest in *the university as an institution*, in the ways in which it was developing, and an effort to conceptualise the university on the basis of the new forms that the university as an institution was taking on. These latter writers, as it were, became—we might say—practical philosophers, intent on giving us new concepts, ideas and insights into the university but rooted in their understandings of the changes befalling the university qua institution. Through their writings, too, our concepts for understanding the university have been broadened, such that today we are unwittingly drawn into associating the university with ideas of its fragmented nature of a 'multiversity', of its entrepreneurial character and so moving in different directions, *and* of it having its very being in and open to the 'marketplace'.

A second path that has opened here over the last half century has taken the form of a critique of the contemporary nature of the university. Two such books stand out, *The Postmodern Condition* by Jean-Francois Lyotard (1984) and *The University in Ruins* by Bill Readings (1997). Strictly speaking, the former book is not actually about the university. It offers a commentary on the character of knowledge in the (then) contemporary world and it connects directly with the idea of the university. Explicitly, for 200 years or so, the university has been understood as an institutional space for systematic inquiry. However, in Lyotard's view, the concepts associated with this understanding of the university—of knowledge, truth, reason and so forth—have to be understood as constituting a grand narrative that warrants only 'incredulity'. This analysis—of the dissolution of the foundations of large ideas—pointed to knowledge and the university in the postmodern condition. Accordingly, the university had lost its legitimacy. If a new legitimation was possible, it could lie only in the idea of 'performativity', in which the test of knowledge could no longer lay in its truthfulness but rather as an answer to the question 'what use does it have'? (Lyotard, 1984, 51).

Readings, inspired by Lyotard, arrived at a similar endpoint. In his view, whereas the university had found its legitimation first in an inquiry for knowledge and truth and then subsequently in sustaining and developing a nation's culture, now the university had been reduced to falling back on a vacuous notion such as 'excellence', an empty signifier appropriated by neoliberals that quickly became essential to the prevailing mission statement for universities the world over. And, today, we might add the term 'world-class' here, the construction of 'the world-class university' as surely exhibiting the same emptiness as 'the university of excellence'. (We must return to this point about the emptiness of some ideas of the university.) For Readings, the university was 'in ruins'—a Romantic trope based on a kind of nostalgia—and the only possible foundation was that of understanding and realising the university as a place of, and a space for, 'dissensus'.

In short, these two analyses were remarkably alike in suggesting that the conceptual foundations of the university had crumbled and, in the process, any large story that had hitherto legitimised the university had also dissipated. Only weak and limited narratives were available through which the university could find any kind of serious justification. They were alike also in their analysis of the corruption of the form of the university by neoliberal capitalism—its structure and discourse—that became indistinguishable from any other corporation.

En passant, we may notice that other major contemporary figures who had come at the university through philosophical eyes had come to not-dissimilar positions. In their quite different ways, Alistair MacIntyre, Jacques Derrida and Jurgen Habermas had all noted that the university was in difficulty. MacIntyre (1985, 2011) argued that the university as a set of *practices* was being undermined by the university as an *organisation* and its characteristic inner virtues were being abandoned with the result that no longer could important questions be seriously pursued. Derrida (1992) wanted to reunite the university with a sense of its having 'responsibility' in the world but could only suggest that one could go forward and upward one step at a time, without any indication as to where those steps might lead. Habermas (1987) has been much more optimistic, seeing in the university resources of dialogical reason, which might foster societal learning processes.

Across all such recent philosophical accounts, there is little of substance in relation to the university's *possibilities in the world*. At best, we are offered—as we might term it—a debating society account of the university (Barnett, 2016). If disputes cannot be settled in any sure way, then at least the university can come to provide a place of dispute and argument and so help society to understand what collective learning might look like at its best. Inheritors of this position today offer accounts, for example, of the way in which internal activities of the university enjoy a particularly 'public' aspect, pointing to the collective exchange of views and the dialogic exposition of readings of the world (Masschelein and Simons, 2012).

A third position in understanding the idea of the university at the end of the twentieth century and beginning of the twenty-first century is implicit in the writings of critical sociologists. Concepts such as 'commodification' (Naidoo and Jamieson, 2005), 'academic capitalism' (Slaughter and Rhoades, 2004), universities 'for hire' (Reid, 1996), the 'corporate university' (Giroux and Myrsiades, 2001), and 'knowledge capitalism' (Peters & Besley, 2006) are examples of thick concepts, as the moral philosopher Bernard Williams puts it (Williams, 2006). They tell us something about the world—here, that the university's activities can be itemised and put into the knowledge economy to generate income, that academics themselves come to value their own activities in this way, that those activities are available at a cost to those who can purchase them, and that universities come to take on the character of a business that claims the allegiance of its employees—but these terms also secrete a *value element*. These terms are not just 'theory-laden' but actually cast the university in a poor light. The implication of such a vocabulary—which is frequently associated with a wider vocabulary of 'neoliberalism', 'profit', institutional 'competition' and the 'student-as-customer'—is that the university has fallen away from its true path. This sociology of higher education amounts, therefore, to an intensive and strong critique of the nature of the modern university as it has undergone a process of neoliberal globalisation.

There is, though, often to be found a third element in this sociological analysis, alongside its analyses and its value element. This is that these descriptions of the university are frequently associated with an unremitting bleakness. Not unusually, these accounts provide their analyses and, as stated, secrete their negative value elements and then conclude. The reader is often left with a of insights that is at once powerful and dismal. Its power derives from the topic in question—the student experience, the pedagogical relationship, the character of research (now termed 'knowledge production'), relationships with industry, the experience of international students or whatever it may be—being placed in a context of inescapable global forces at work. In this genre, there is, it appears, a tsunami composed of neoliberalism, performance management, the digital revolution, and cognitive capitalism. Its dismal character derives from a sense that nothing can contend against this tsunami. Accordingly, the fate of the university—on this perspective—is sealed. It has simply to accept its place as a cognitive and practical enterprise in the service of the knowledge economy.

We may note that this pessimism has its own virtues, not least in that it holds the university to account against its self-understandings and its public persona. The pessimism reminds its readers of the long-heralded associations of the university with openness, disinterestedness, equity, neutrality and academic freedom, and it finds the university wanting. The power of this pessimistic critique lies in its forensic excavations of the university as a hallowed and special space in the world. However, ultimately, this critique runs the risk of leaving things as they are, and even being judged on occasions to constitute 'an enemy of hope' (Tallis, 1999).

A fourth—and the last—path into which the philosophy of higher education has opened is, in contrast, constructive in that it seeks to open visions as to ways in which the university could plausibly develop in the twenty-first century. In this genre, we find, for example, Nicolas Maxwell (1987), who has been advancing for 40 years the idea of a university of wisdom, Jon Nixon (2008, 2011) and the idea of the virtuous and public university, Michael Peters with his invigoration of the open university (Peters and Britez, 2008; Peters, Liu, & Ondercin, 2012) and Ronald Barnett (2011, 2013) and his idea of the ecological university. Each of these philosophers of higher education couples together observations and a critique of the current state of affairs but none is content to rest there. To the contrary, each advances a positive idea of the university. What is more, each such idea is proposed as a feasible project: even given the global forces at work, each idea—so it is at least implied—could be realised. None is fanciful.

Patterns of possibilities

There are, then, at least four directions in which work on the idea of the university has recently been going. To re-present our preceding analysis, they are:

(1) commentaries that offer insights into the evolving nature of universities but which are largely endorsing the direction of travel;
(2) a placing of the university in the context of a wider dual social and philosophical undermining of the idea of the university, so leaving it with at best a residual idea;
(3) sociological critiques of the state into which the university has fallen, having been incorporated into agendas of powerful interests, especially but not only those of markets; and
(4) constructive efforts to discern feasible possibilities that both do justice to aspects of the historical idea of the university and are sensitive to the global forces at work that are subtly steering the university in the contemporary era.

Of course, this depiction of four paths is unduly neat. Approaches can be seen that criss-cross these paths. For example, the digital revolution has given rise to multiple trajectories of thinking. One trajectory, for example, offers a flight that underwrites individualised learning. This is a view that is (a) critical of the university—which it depicts as moribund in depending still on pedagogical relationships and technologies of yesteryear—and (b) is endorsing of the way the communications technologies are moving, and (c) purportedly is offering a brave new world for universities to embrace, but which is (d) actually serving the interests of the corporate world in its attempts to marketise learning, not least through the presence of for-profit universities built around individuals' online learning (Bradwell, 2009). Another quite different view sees here the possibilities for a 'socialist' learning, with both the material being freely available and the learning processes being 'open' and dialogical (Peters, Gietzen and Ondercin, 2012). These two sets of perceptions both see quite different possibilities in the 'same' situation *and* criss-cross the four paths—of the contemporary idea of the university—just identified.

This volume—and axes of the university

The structure of this volume works with the grain of these considerations. Part I contains critiques of neoliberalism, part II places the university in its global context, parts III and IV offer insights into the university in its regional and global contexts, parts V and VI set develop ideas of the university that focus in turn on its research and its teaching functions, and the final part turns to see if imaginative ideas of the university might be available which might help to carry the university forward and provide principles for its reconstruction. This volume, therefore, is testimony to the multiple avenues along which the idea of the university is currently being taken.

Broadly speaking, the contributions here tread the third and fourth paths of the contemporary idea of the university just identified here, being 'sociological critiques of the state into which the university has fallen' (especially in the context of markets) *and* offering 'constructive efforts to discern feasible possibilities ... in the contemporary era'. However, many of the offerings straddle these two camps, being both critical and constructive. Inevitably, too, some authors develop their analyses somewhat pessimistically, sensing that the contemporary forces at work are so powerful as to leave little room for manoeuvre such that only subversive activities are possible while others are more optimistic, sensing that there are at least opening spaces for new possibilities for the university; possibilities that do justice anew to such themes as social justice, freedom, wisdom and the idea of a public. Perhaps it might be observed, too, that the sociological mind tends to open itself to rather more pessimistic readings of the situation, while the philosophical mind—on the evidence here—tends to open itself to more optimistic readings. At least, that could be a matter for further reflection on another occasion.

Amid this conceptual and theoretical complexity, can anything be said with any assurance? That it cannot—we may observe—is precisely one of the planks of the stance of the second group of thinkers earlier identified, that of philosophers of the late twentieth century. It even led, we noted, to a situation in which Derrida (1992) rightly asked the question as to where lay the 'responsibility' of the university but then was unable to furnish us with a substantive answer. And that was understandable, for to have done so, to have come forward with a substantive idea of the responsibility of the university would have been implicitly to have identified firm foundations underpinning the university when just such foundations had been ruled as outré from the outset (of that deconstructionalist philosophy).

But yet some broad observations may be made of this situation. To begin with, we can observe that understandings of the idea of the university are rent with particular kinds of division. We can go even further than that for ideas of the university may be interrogated as to their position on a number of axes. These axes include the following:

(i) *The university as institution—the university as idea*: We encountered this axis earlier and it speaks for itself. Ideas of the university characteristically have their location in a conceptual space *or* are intimately connected with a sense of the university as a real institution in the world. Each approach has its strength and weakness. Ideas of the university that are seriously conceptual—perhaps developed say around the concept of reason, or the concept of academic freedom, or the concept of social justice—run up against the charge that they are 'not living in the real world'. They fail to observe the ways in which reason is being distorted, or that in some countries academics are being incarcerated or worse for speaking out or that claims for free 'public' higher education may act regressively upon the poor who end up subsidising the middle classes.

In contrast, ideas of the university that are based much more on the university as a real social institution underplay the intricacies that attach to concepts. Just what kind of reason might be associated with the university? Is it particular forms of knowledge or rather particular knowledge processes, or is it rather the university as a space in which reason might flourish? But what might that mean? Is there a significant difference between the university as a space of reason and the university as a space of reason*ing*? (cf. Bakhurst, 2011) On the one hand, those who favour a conceptual approach produce ideas of the university that are ontologically thin; on the other hand, those whose ideas of the university spring from an interest in the university as a social institution slide over fundamental issues, not merely of conceptual analysis but of matters that lie beneath concepts. Significant questions and, indeed, practical implications that arise from conceptual distinctions are neglected.

(ii) *Pessimism and optimism*: Ideas of the university may be given a kind of pessimism—or optimism—quotient. Pessimism and optimism, however, work somewhat differently here. Pessimism here denotes ideas of the university that spring from doleful readings of the situation in which universities find themselves. Depictions of the university as caught in webs of neoliberalism, competitive markets, judgemental audit regimes that subtly steer universities in particular directions, and processes in which universities take on the mantle of corporate organisations give rise all too easily to pessimism. Ideas of the university 'in crisis' (Moberly, 1949; Scott, 1984; Reeves, 1988) or 'in ruins' (Readings, 1997) or, less prosaically, as systematically falling short of their potential can all too easily generate a sense (even if not intended by their authors) that here, there is no alternative.

Optimism, however, shows itself not in a sense that the university *will* march on to happier times but rather a sense that a fuller realisation of the university is at least *plausible*. It is not that the university will find itself in a space in which it finds a new authenticity but that it is plausible to believe that it *could* do so. And theoretical readings may be advanced to back up such a more optimistic scenario. Spaces may be detected that are opening anew, or it might be possible to mount subversive forms of positive resistance, or entirely new ideas might be created that at once do justice to the world order and yet also reinvigorate earlier understandings of the university.

Another way of understanding this axis is via the ideas of *critique* and *construction*. For example, some deploy the concept of commodification as a powerful conceptual tool not just in understanding the contemporary university but also in critiquing it, especially under market conditions. Others, however, still argue a positive case for the university and do so with constructive and imaginative concepts. For example, Jan Parker (2005) has offered the idea of the theatrical university. This is certainly—to doff our caps to another concept in the armoury of critique—a performative university, but one in which the positive resources in the idea of performance are played up. Here, the university is envisaged as an institution with dramatic potential, capable of generating mystery, awe and wonder.

(iii) *Internalist–externalist conceptions*: A third axis on which ideas of the university are situated is that of internalist and externalist conceptions. Internalist conceptions are those that play up the internal goods or virtues of the university; externalist conceptions are those that are much more interested in the role of the university towards the wider society—or indeed, the wider world. Unsurprisingly, mainstream philosophers in the great tradition have tended to focus on *internal* construals of the idea of the university, variously seeing the university as a space of reason, or of inquiry, or of truthfulness, or as possessing certain kinds of inner virtue.

On the other hand, more recent voices of a philosophical orientation have tended to place the university much more in the context of the *external* world, and have sought to depict its potential thereto. Here, to return to earlier examples, we see Maxwell's idea of wisdom, whereby the university focuses on 'what is of value' in the world; Barnett's idea of the ecological university, which precisely picks up on the university's inevitable connections with various ecosystems in the world; and Peters' conception of the open university, which speaks to the possibilities of publicly open access and the ensuing 'socialist knowledge'. In parallel, contemporary efforts of social theorists to articulate new conceptions of the *public university* (Marginson, 2007) and the *engaged university* (Watson et al., 2012) are again explicitly driven by an interest in identifying the external benefits that the university offers.

(iv) *Superficiality and depth*: A fourth axis on which ideas of the university can be said to be placed has at its ends 'superficiality' and 'depth'. Among superficial ideas of the university, we find, as intimated, the university of 'excellence' and 'the world-class university'. These terms are empty signifiers, being devoid of content and yet they are in ubiquitous use (to be found in the websites of universities all over the world).

Among ideas of the university that have depth, and perhaps surprisingly, we may alight on the idea of 'the entrepreneurial university', if only to help in making the point. Much maligned and not without reason, this idea has depth for it gains its traction through resting on foundations of global forces at work, to which the entrepreneurial university is but a response. It was also given depth in being first articulated by Burton Clark (1998) on the basis both of serious cross-national empirical research and through his detailed theoretical exposition as to the institutional conditions of such a university.

The entrepreneurial university has added depth in that it sees itself as having its place in a world beset by globalisation, a worldly knowledge economy and the emergence of cognitive capitalism. The entrepreneurial university considers that its survival is dependent on its making its living by and for itself in such a turbulent world. It cannot be still. Its well-being depends on its wherewithal to propel itself forward through its own efforts. Accordingly, 'the entrepreneurial university' is nothing other than a term of art of the kind of university that is alleged to be necessary, given the depth and power of the forces that bestride it.

Narrowing the challenge

Contemporary ideas of the university may, then, be plotted along four axes: (i) the university as institution/the university as concept; (ii) pessimistic and optimistic conceptions of the university; (iii) internalist and externalist conceptions of the university; and (iv) ideas of the university that are superficial and those that have depth. Of course, this schema by no means exhausts the planes on which the idea of the university may be placed. Others would include *geographical range* (is an idea rather parochial or does it have global reach?), *conceptual scope* (does it spring from or has a sensitivity to *particulars* of the university and so views the university 'close-up'—interested, say, in the personal 'subjectivities' of its staff—or is it oriented towards large and even *universal* concepts, perhaps of freedom, of reason, of well-being, of justice or even of knowledge?), and its *temporal character* (is it concerned with contemporary matters or is it sensitive to the long historical sweep of the university or even to its potential future character?).

Accordingly, ideas of the university may then be interrogated with a multitude of conceptual and theoretical devices. An implication of this consideration is that the idea of the university is liable to shoot out in a myriad of directions. It might even be said that the idea of the university has before it an infinite 'lines of flight' (Deleuze and Guattari, 2007). The metaphor is powerful. It conveys a sense of trajectories, some ascending higher than others (perhaps reaching towards transcendent visions of the university as potentially lying in an ethereal space), some moving rapidly but perhaps rather lacking in direction (perhaps located in the superhighway of the Internet), and some motivated even by past traditions and so could be said to be retreating to earlier sentiments.

However, the metaphor of 'lines of flight' is surely too neat in the present context. As stated, the situation is at least of lines of flight that criss-cross and that even contest against each other (rather like an aerial dogfight). Some endorse contemporary paths of travel, others critique them; some are imaginative and constructive while others rest their laurels on their forensic and even critical commentaries; and some are addressed to market situations while others purport to be universal in character. Perhaps more liquid metaphors are called for. The university today is set in swirling and turbulent waters, and is pushed this way and that by severe underlying currents of massive force. Accordingly, so it might be felt, rather than taking on a rhizomatic form—with its rather static connotations—the university of the twenty-first century is taking on *squid-like* features. After all, this is an institution able to move quickly if need be, having the facility to range widely and possessing a long and even global reach, and to insert itself into the tiniest crevices, and yet possessing a hard shell.

Towards criteria of adequacy

Is this, then, the situation that confronts us here? That we can say little of substance about the university in the twenty-first century, with our only recourse being that of searching for metaphors that might just begin to do justice to a highly fluid setting, in which ideas of the university go hither and thither? Surely, we can do better than that.

We suggest that ideas of the university can be evaluated. After all, some ideas are going to bear more weight than others; and some are going to possess an ideological nature, acting as a cloak for large and hidden interests. We suggest, therefore, that ideas of the university can be put to a test, a test composed of various *criteria of adequacy* (Barnett, 2013). Our earlier discussion has surely intimated certain such criteria of adequacy. In these remaining paragraphs of this Introduction, let us edge towards just such a set of criteria by which ideas of the university might be judged.

Concepts are appropriate or not to their context, and the context of the university in the twenty-first century is not what it was in the eighteenth or nineteenth century. Perhaps the key consideration is that the university of the twenty-first century is deeply connected with the wider world. Willy-nilly, the university cannot escape this interconnectedness. Accordingly, adequate ideas of the university *have* to take on an externalist aspect. Adequate ideas are not going to be forthcoming where they are limited to interests and concepts of the university that have purely internalist leanings.

Further, across the world, the university has come to respond to a particular range of interests, especially those that frame the university in the service of cognitive capitalism (Boutang, 2011), and which play up institutional competition, the economic value of STEM (science, technology, engineering, mathematics) disciplines and the student as an economic subject. Ideas of the university, therefore, have a dual responsibility to heed this global context but to stretch it, and to seek spaces that widen the potential of the university in the world.

To say this is to say quite a bit. To call up some of our earlier distinctions, it is to *displace* internalist ideas of the university so as to encompass the university's *external* hinterland, and to put in a plea *additionally* for visionary and imaginative concepts that might widen the university's self-understanding in the world. It is to call attention—if it was needed—to the university as an *institution* as well as the bearer of ideas. It is to urge that philosophies of the university should adopt an explicitly *realist* aspect, being sensitive to the university as—*in part*—existing independently of ideas held of it, being in part steered by massive global forces that lie beyond immediate observation. It is to place a responsibility on those who might venture ideas of the university that they be *constructive* and not merely critical. And it is to be *optimistic*, not in the sense that matters will improve for the university but to sense that there is warrant for the imagination to do its work and that plausibly the university can be steered into a wider set of spaces; and there may even be embryonic examples of the university becoming other than its dominant forms suggest. It is to imbue the philosophy of the university with a hopeful spirit.

It is just possible, for instance (and to pick up some of the ideas on view here), to glimpse new kinds of *open universities*, of *socialist universities* that are determined to open themselves to participation by the wider world, of universities for which the attribute of *wisdom* is fitting, of universities that are embarked on a path of *engagement* with their surrounding communities, of *universities of culture* which are adorning their physical spaces with public art and encouraging all manner of cultural events and activities, of *cosmopolitan universities* that not only take advantage of their students-as-visitors from over a hundred countries but reach out into the world in a spirit that traverses cultures and communities and of *ecological universities* that are sensitive to their being embedded in manifold ecosystems and that are wanting to do all they can to enhance those ecosystems. The literature is, yes, ahead of, but in some ways, too, it is behind the university: in fact, in their interstices, universities across the world can be seen as stretching themselves into new constructive spaces in society, both by themselves and in association with other universities and with regional and global agencies.

In short, the idea of the university is not at an end. To the contrary, as this volume testifies, the idea of the university is alive and is being reinvigorated. New life is being breathed into it. But, as implied, we need not just new ideas of the university but we need robust ideas, ideas that will simultaneously:

i) lend themselves to implementation (through imaginative programmes of policy and action particular to each university),
ii) possess an ethical character, intent on furthering the well-being of the world—and, of course, understanding that well-being is itself a spacious concept that provokes dispute over its interpretation,
iii) open themselves to continuous reinterpretation in the light of particular circumstances,

iv) have emergent properties, that is, open themselves to practices and organisational forms that in turn will open again to *further* practices and institutional forms,
v) have conceptual and theoretical substance and range, *and* contend against the dominant ideologies of the age—and so have 'depth' rather than 'superficiality',
vi) be attractive to the widest set of audiences within the beyond the academy, and have elements of intrigue and even of mystery, and even contain seductive power, and
vii) be capable of helping to impart new energies to universities as organisations, such that they might come to be embodied by a new expansive spirit.

Together, these seven desiderata form a weighty set of *criteria of adequacy*. But they are necessary if ideas of the university are to prove their worth in a hostile and interest-laden world, with powerful forces at work that would callously steer the university in unduly limited ways. It is criteria such as these that will help to sift the conceptual wheat from the interest-laden chaff. Only through demanding criteria such as these can we hope to find ideas of the university that are going to help steer the university in new directions in which the university can sustain itself amid powerful global forces. And only through criteria such as these can ideas of the university emerge that are adequate to the situation in which universities find themselves in the twenty-first century across the world.

We believe that this volume of essays on contemporary perspectives does justice to these considerations. It shows critiques, empirically founded insights, conceptual accounts and imaginative ideas. There are even glimpses of utopia but they have an element of feasibility attached to them. Between them, the chapters offer a rich tapestry of interweaving themes and suggestions, which together—a bit like the Bayeux tapestry—forms a kaleidoscope of moving images, vistas and scenes. Together, they surely supply prompts for yet further thinking and action in relation to the idea of the university in the twenty-first century.

References

Bakhurst, D. (2011). *The Formation of Reason.* Chichester, Wiley-Blackwell.
Barnett, R. (1990). *The Idea of Higher Education.* Stony Stratford, Open University Press.
Barnett, R. (2011). *Being a University.* Abingdon and New York, Routledge.
Barnett, R. (2013). *Imagining the University.* Abingdon and New York, Routledge.

Barnett, R. (2016). *Understanding the University: Institution, Idea, Possibilities.* Abingdon and New York, Routledge.

Bok, D. (2003). *Universities in the Marketplace: The Commercialization of Higher Education.* Princeton and Oxford, Princeton University.

Boutang, Y. M. (2011). *Cognitive Capitalism.* Cambridge, England and Malden, MA, Polity.

Bradwell, P. (2009). *The Edgeless University: Why Higher Education Must Embrace Technology.* London, Demos.

Clark, B. R. (1998). *Creating Entrepreneurial Universities: Organizational Pathways of Transformation.* Oxford, Pergamon/IAU.

Deleuze, G. and Guattari, F. (2007/1980). *A Thousand Plateaus: Capitalism and Schizophrenia.* London and New York, Continuum.

Derrida, J. (1992). 'Mochlos; or, The Conflict of the Faculties', in R. Rand (ed.) *Logomachia: The Conflict of the Faculties*, Chapter 1, pp. 1–34. Lincoln and London, University of Nebraska.

Giroux, H. A. and Myrsiades, K. (eds.) (2001). *Beyond the Corporate University: Culture and Pedagogy in the New Millennium.* Lanham, MA and Oxford, Rowman and Littlefield.

Habermas, J. (1987). 'The Idea of the University: Learning Processes', *New German Critique*, 41, Spring–Summer, 3–22.

Jaspers, K. (1960/1946). *The Idea of the University.* London, Peter Owen.

Kerr, C. (1995/1963). *The Uses of the University.* Cambridge, MA and London, Harvard University.

Lyotard, J.-F. (1984). *The Postmodern Condition: A Report on Knowledge.* Manchester, Manchester University Press.

MacIntyre, A. (1985). *After Virtue: A Study in Moral Theory.* London, Duckworth.

MacIntyre, A. (2011). *God, Philosophy, Universities: A Selective History of the Catholic Philosophical Tradition.* Lanham, MA and Plymouth, Rowman and Littlefield.

Marginson, S. (ed.) (2007). *Prospects of Higher Educations: Globalization, Market Competition, Public Goods and the Future of the University.* Rotterdam, Sense Publishers.

Masschelein, J. and Simons, M. (2012). 'The University: A Public Issue', in R. Barnett, *The Future University: Ideas and Possibilities*, pp. 165-177. Abingdon and New York, Routledge.

Maxwell, N. (1987). *From Knowledge to Wisdom: A Revolution in the Aims & Methods of Science.* Oxford, Blackwell.

Minogue, K. (1973). *The Concept of a University.* London, Weidenfeld and Nicolson.

Moberly, Sir W. (1949). *The Crisis in the University.* London, SCM Press.

Naidoo, R. and Jamieson, I. (2005). 'Knowledge in the Marketplace: The Global Commodification of Teaching and Learning in Higher Education', in P. Ninnes and M. Hellstén (eds.) *Internationalizing Higher Education: Critical Explorations of Pedagogy and Policy*, pp. 37–51. Dordrecht, Springer.

Newman, J. H. (1976/1848). *The Idea of a University.* Edited by I. T. Ker. Oxford, Oxford University Press.

Nixon, J. (2008). *Towards the Virtuous University: The Moral Bases of Academic Practice.* New York and Abingdon, Routledge.

Nixon, J. (2011). *Higher Education and the Public Good: Imagining the University.* London and New York: Continuum.

Parker, J. (2005). 'A Mis-en-Scene for the Theatrical University', in R. Barnett (ed.) *Reshaping the University: New Relationships between Research, Scholarship and Teaching*, pp. 151-164. Maidenhead and New York, McGraw-Hill/Open University Press.

Peters, M. A. and Besley, T. (2006). *Building Knowledge Cultures: Education and Development in the Age of Knowledge Capitalism.* Lanham, Boulder, New York, Oxford, Rowman & Littlefield.

Peters, M. A. and Britez, R. (eds.) (2008). *Open Education and Education for Openness.* Rotterdam & Taipei, Sense Publishers.

Peters, M. A., Gietzen, G. and Ondercin, D. J. (2012). 'Knowledge Socialism: Intellectual Commons and Openness in the University', in R. Barnett (ed.) *The Future University: Ideas and Possibilities*, pp. 187-200. Abingdon and New York, Routledge.

Peters, M. A., Liu, T.-C., & Ondercin, D. (2012). *The Pedagogy of the Open Society: Knowledge and the Governance of Higher Education.* Rotterdam, Sense Publishers.

Readings, B. (1997). *The University in Ruins.* Cambridge, MA and London, Harvard University.

Reeves, M. (1988). *The Crisis in Higher Education: Competence, Delight and the Common Good.* Stony Stratford and Philadelphia, Open University Press/Society for Research into Higher Education.

Reid, I. (1996). *Higher Education or Education for Hire?* Rockhampton, Central Queensland University.

Scott, P. (1984). *The Crisis of the University.* Beckenham and Sydney, Croom Helm.

Slaughter, S. and Rhoades, G. (2004). *Academic Capitalism and the New Economy: Markets, State and Higher Education.* Baltimore and London, Johns Hopkins University.

Tallis, R. (1999). *Enemies of Hope: A Critique of Contemporary Pessimism.* Basingstoke, Macmillan.

Watson, D., Hollister, R. M., Stroud, S. E. and Babcock, E. (2012). *The Engaged University: International Perspectives on Civic Engagement.* New York and Abingdon, Routledge.

Williams, B. (2006/1985). *Ethics and the Limits of Philosophy.* Abingdon, Routledge.

Wolff, R. P. (1997). *The Ideal of a University.* New Brunswick and London, Transaction.

PART ONE

Addressing Neoliberalism

Introduction

Neoliberalism is a slippery label that began life as a left-wing negative description of a set of policies adopted and developed by Margaret Thatcher and Ronald Reagan. The idea had taken root in the 1930s and became the basis for a set of ideals that motivated the Mount Pelerin Society founded by Friedrich von Hayek in 1947. In the atmosphere of state phobia after the horror of Hitler's regime, Hayek and his colleagues committed themselves to a defence of the liberal state and its institutions including the free market and the rule of law.

It was during the decade of the 1980s that Hayek's political and economic philosophy was used by Thatcher and Reagan to legitimate the neoliberal attack on 'big government' and the bureaucratic welfare state with a policy mix based on 'free' trade and the establishment of the 'open' economy: economic liberalisation or rationalisation characterised by the abolition of subsidies and tariffs, floating the exchange rate, the freeing up of controls on foreign investment; the restructuring of the state sector, including corporatisation and privatisation of state trading departments and other assets, 'downsizing', 'contracting out', the attack on unions and abolition of wage bargaining in favour of employment contracts; and, finally, the dismantling of the welfare state through commercialisation, 'contracting out', 'targeting' of services, and individual 'responsibilisation' for health, welfare and education. In this view, there is nothing distinctive or special about education or health; they are services and products like any other, to be traded in the marketplace.

The university became a focus for many neoliberal reforms including the application of New Public Management reforms that emphasised a performance and audit culture, contestability of research funding, the introduction of student fees, the separation of management and council control with political appointments, and the realignment of the university as a service sector to the knowledge economy with its private/public partnerships, research parks, business start-ups and commercialisation of research. The transition to the neoliberal university represented a major shift from the traditional university based on the concept of the right to a free public higher education (HE) dedicated to student transformation and education for citizenship and democracy.

The five essays in this section take up these issues in different ways. Jana Bacevic in "University under siege?" investigates agency beyond the neoliberal university and begins by noting that while universities are centres of analysis and protests against neoliberalism, universities have been restructured according to neoliberal criteria. Bacevic explores the meaning and uses the term neoliberalism to investigate concepts of agency implied in the besieged university and the ways in which forms of political engagement and agency escape neoliberalism.

In ways not dissimilar, Henry Giroux defends HE in 'the Age of Barbarism' to explore the contemporary political economy threatening the notion of HE as a democratic public good, especially the huge and growing inequalities in wealth, income and power that have emerged under neoliberalism. He focuses on the loss of cultural democracy under a market-driven paradigm that has epitomised an age of high mass consumption and attacked labour relations creating a low-wage society and massive inequities in wealth and power. Giroux provides us with a clear and uncompromising picture of U.S. politics of HE and offers us a vision for reclaiming HE as a democratic public sphere.

Sheila Slaughter and Brendan Cantwell extend the now well-known thesis of 'Academic Capitalism' in the United States and European Union (EU) providing an up-to-date analysis of moves towards the market and the underlying notion of academic capitalism theory. Again, the emphasis falls on how the public nature of HE has been badly damaged. The chapter examines research that is still largely publicly funded and differences in narratives and discourses between the United States and EU that have been used to justify expanded managerial capacity and new funding streams. The authors detail an 'academic arms race' to enhance competition and reduce reliance on the state.

In the final chapter for this section, Wesley Shumar and Sarah Robinson rethink the entrepreneurial university for the twenty-first century, first, contesting the very concept of entrepreneurship that has traditionally been associated with small businesses and then unpacking its ideological significance within the neoliberal economic regime. Working from Scandinavian entrepreneurship education (EE), they attempt to break out of the neoliberal discourse in order to reimage the university in the tradition of *Bildung*, a form of EE 'where students are required to work *through* entrepreneurship by engaging with problems, stakeholders and potential customers in the real world and then reflect on the learning from these interactions.'

All five contributions are realistic and hard headed in recognising the pervasiveness and the neoliberal university and the ways it is locked into wider economic policy in an age of increasing massification and government cuts. Mostly they proceed from assumptions of political economy and together begin to provide a position analysis of ways in which universities can intelligently promote concepts of democracy and citizenship, while addressing traditional values of student transformation and questions of growing inequalities.

Michael A. Peters

CHAPTER ONE

University under Attack?

Politics, Contestation and Agency beyond the 'Neoliberal University'

JANA BACEVIC

Introduction: university under attack?

Anyone acquainted with the world of higher education and research could have hardly failed to notice a change in the ways we talk about universities. On the one hand, universities are promoted as drivers of economic growth, engines of innovation and promoters of social integration. On the other hand, universities across the world have become centres of protest against the privatisation and marketisation of higher education, rising tuition fees and the linking of higher education to economic competitiveness. The present moment seems to be defined by a crystallisation of different, and frequently opposing, views on what a university is and can be.

Many critics have taken these processes to mean that the university is 'in crisis'. Although 'crises' when it comes to universities are not particularly novel, there is a sense of a decisive and qualitative shift in what it means to *be* a university—in other words, in the ontology of the university (cf. Barnett, 2011; Delanty, 2001; Readings, 1996). The influential Anglo-American sociologist Michael Burawoy, for instance, writes that '[T]he university is in crisis, almost everywhere. In broadest terms, the university's position as simultaneously inside and outside society—both a participant in and an observer of society—has been eroded. With the exception of a few hold-outs the ivory tower has gone' (2011, p. 27).

The metaphor of the ivory tower, long used to depict the university as an institution somewhat isolated from the exigencies of its immediate environment, is now applied to signify the (crumbling) resistance in the face of an unknown external force. Some authors have likened this attack to a military conflict. For instance, in a recent book entitled *Universities at War*, Thomas Docherty writes: 'There is a *war* on for the future of the university as an institution (…) in many jurisdictions across the world, students and scholars are striving to find ways of responding adequately and appropriately to the disturbances that are afflicting societies in both the advanced and the developing economies' (Docherty, 2015, p. 5, emphasis mine). Others seem to equate it with a *force majeure*, as, for instance, in 'Most intellectuals are rendered passive and frightened by the *tsunami* around them. A central refuge for critique, the university, is under siege' (McKenna, 2013, p. 452, emphasis mine).

These narratives converge on the idea that there is an all-out attack on the university. Yet, where does this attack come from? The metaphor of the 'tsunami' seems to suggest that the university is besieged by a natural force, one that is, presumably, beyond human control. On the other hand, warfare seems to be a uniquely human phenomenon; it requires at least two clearly identifiable sides, with, presumably, mutually exclusive interests. Therefore, it would make sense to take a deeper look into the dynamics of the conflict, and to understand who or what is besieging the university.

Over the past years, this external threat has increasingly acquired a single diagnosis: neoliberalism. Canaan and Shumar argue that higher education is 'being pressured by a set of neoliberal practices and structures that are reshaping institutions and individuals, based on our growing recognition—as researchers, teachers and administrators—that the institutions to which we belong now are profoundly different from those in which we were educated largely during the 1970s and 1980s' (Canaan and Shumar, 2008, p. 3). Slaughter and Rhoades went further in pronouncing capitulation, saying that 'Public colleges and universities are exemplars of neoliberalism' (2000, p. 73). From academic discourse, the concept of neoliberalism as the main source and explanatory narrative for the global changes in knowledge production has 'trickled down' into mainstream media (e.g. Barkawi, 2013; Fish, 2009), and, further on, into the public sphere; it would not be an overestimation to say that neoliberalism has become one of the most influential frameworks used to explain the transformation of contemporary societies.

However, this does not necessarily mean that the growth of the popularity of neoliberalism as a diagnostic narrative has been followed by a matching analytical precision. A number of authors have suggested that neoliberalism has become a rather vague catch-all term. In Turner's words, 'What it stands for and what it explains is both confused and confusing' (Turner, 2008, p. 2). Peck finds it 'notable not only for its ubiquity, but also for its apparent *omnipotence*, as an alleged *first (or ultimate) cause of a bewildering array of contemporary developments*' (Peck, 2010, p. 14). This analytical vagueness has led some to dismiss the usage of neoliberalism 'a rhetorical tool and moral device for critical social scientists outside economics to conceive of academic economics and a range of economic phenomena that are otherwise beyond their cognitive horizons and which they cannot otherwise grasp or evaluate' (Venugopal, 2015, p. 183). Less radically, others question its validity as 'a sort of stand-in term for the political-economic zeitgeist, as a no-more-than approximate proxy for a specific analysis of mechanisms or relations of social power, domination, exploitation, or alienation' (Peck, 2010, p. 14).

This chapter aims to contribute to the critical exploration of the meaning and uses of neoliberalism as a term used to frame or explain the processes of transformation in contemporary universities. Given the limitations of space, the chapter does not aim to provide a comprehensive overview of the analytical figuration of the term in studies of higher education and research; rather, it will focus on the concepts of agency implied in the ideas of the contemporary university as 'under' attack or 'besieged' by neoliberalism. It will identify some of the ways in which dominant constructions of the 'neoliberal university' locate political power in relation to the university, and define those who can exercise it. I will argue that, in this process, such narratives redefine and renegotiate the boundaries of the university, and its relationship with the society. As an illustration, the chapter will briefly discuss the case of the firing of Professor Steven Salaita from the University of Illinois that happened in the autumn of 2014, in order to show the ways in which different actors are able to use and exercise agency in ways that are not completely covered by the metaphor of the 'neoliberal university'.

The objective of the text is not to argue that neoliberalism is 'over' (cf. Springer, 2015) or that it should be discarded as an analytical framework. However, rather than adopting it as a blanket term, I want to explore different political and social dynamics that play a role in contemporary university transformations. The concluding part, thus, will suggest some ways of thinking about the transformation of universities that take into account the myriad forms and manifestations of agency that permeate the institution we call the university, and its relationship with the 'outside world'.

Neoliberalism from nowhere?

If neoliberalism is used to define the external forces of change at universities, it makes sense to try to understand both where it comes from, and how it is manifested. Olssen and Peters define neoliberalism as '... a politically imposed discourse, which is to say it constitutes a hegemonic discourse of Western nation-states' (2005, p. 314). Therefore, neoliberalism is created by the nation-state as a political framework and imposed on universities. Furthermore, 'Within higher education neoliberalism has introduced a new mode of regulation or form of governmentality' (2005, p. 314). The emphasis here is on neoliberalism as a technique of governance. As such, neoliberalism seeks to redefine the relationship between the universities and the state.

Contrary to what is sometimes assumed of its 'cousin' or predecessor, classical liberalism, however, neoliberalism does not argue for a complete withdrawal of the state from public services. Instead, it entails a reconfiguration of its role through mechanisms of measurement that put an emphasis on productivity and performance: '... For neoliberal perspectives, the end goals of freedom, choice, consumer sovereignty, competition and individual initiative, as well as those of compliance and obedience, must be constructions of the state acting now in its positive role through the development of the techniques of *auditing*, *accounting* and *management*' (2005, p. 315).

In this sense, 'units' of measurement—that is, universities—are put in competition against each other, and for public funding. The emphasis on measuring productivity means that those that can demonstrate success in these forms of competition are recognised as 'excellent', 'outstanding', 'world class', etc. Within this framework, it comes as no surprise that academics, as knowledge producers, experience the shift in their own work environment as one of the most prominent features of the changing conditions of knowledge production. For instance, Giroux writes that 'Central to [the] neoliberal view of higher education in the United States and United Kingdom is a market-driven paradigm that seeks to eliminate tenure, turn the humanities into a job preparation service, and transform most faculty into an army of temporary subaltern labor' (Giroux, 2013).

The emphasis on academics' experience of the changes in the working environment at universities has become one of the foci of the research on contemporary changes in higher education. On the more formal side, work of the academic profession has attempted to operationalise the impact of the broader socioeconomic changes on the identities and self-perception of academics (Gordon and Whitchurch, 2010; Gornall, Cook and Daunton, 2014; Kehm and Teichler, 2013; Teichler and Höhle, 2013). From a more qualitative side, a number of studies have drawn on Foucault (1972) and studies of discourse to examine the interaction between the neoliberalisation of knowledge production and the construction of subjectivity among academics. Studies applying the concept of 'audit culture', for instance, have argued that techniques of measurement institute a new 'sense of the self' for academics, teaching them to be continuously productive and competitive

(Posecznick, 2014; Shore and McLauchlan, 2012; Shore and Wright, 2000). A related strand, focusing on the notion of performativity, has underlined the effects of the policies seeking to measure academic productivity on academics' subjectivities (Ball, 2003; Ball and Olmedo, 2013; Leathwood and Read, 2013).

However, there is a difference between experiencing a shift in the working conditions within universities in the context of the changing nature of global capitalism, and constructing a causal link between the two (cf. Santiago and Carvalho, 2008). While few would deny that working conditions of academics have substantially changed over the past decades, it makes sense to pay closer attention to the mechanisms of political power that make such shifts possible. In other words, we need to examine what kind of political actors are awarded and exercise power in the 'neoliberal university'.

The metaphor of the 'university under siege' assumes that the university is an *object* or *target of attack* by the forces of neoliberalism. Primary political agency, in this sense, is located outside the university. If neoliberalism is understood as a mode or tool of governance, political agency is primarily exercised by governments, through the implementation of neoliberal policies. In some cases, of course, the nation-state is supplemented (or perhaps even superseded) by supranational entities and processes—most notably, in the case of Europe, by the European Union and the Bologna Process. And while there is a growing body of literature on the transformations of political agency in relation to different scales of states, supranational entities and regions, what these approaches share is that they attribute agency to the relatively 'classical' group of political actors: governments, international governmental or non-governmental organisations, agencies, representative bodies, trade unions, etc. Policies, in this sense, are conceptualised as influencing universities from the *outside*.

This, however, does not mean that universities are completely devoid of agency (cf. Barnett, 2016). Still, the paradigm of the 'neoliberal university' assumes that most things happen at universities as a consequence of implementation of the aforementioned neoliberal policies. Secondary political agency, in this sense, is exercised by managers or administrators, who are seen as chief implementers or translators of neoliberalism into universities. Halffman and Radder, for instance, write: 'Universities are occupied by management, a regime obsessed with "accountability" through measurement, increased competition, efficiency, "excellence," and misconceived economic salvation. Given the occupation's absurd side-effects, we ask ourselves how management has succeeded in taking over our precious universities' (2015, p. 165). Here, we encounter a modification of the metaphor of the 'siege'—universities are under occupation, and management is the occupier. The management acts as the chief conduit for neoliberalism at universities.

Furthermore, the management is clearly perceived as *external*, as an 'intruder': the sentence '*our* precious universities' suggests that the universities rightfully belong to the academics, and that managers and administrators are a foreign, occupying force.

While identifying managers as agents of neoliberalism arguably offers a more nuanced notion of political agency, it still reproduces the image of the university as isolated from the world of politics. Namely, managers are seen as 'outside intruders', implementers of neoliberal techniques of governance. This is particularly curious given that, despite the trend of professionalisation of university management, most managers at universities are, actually, academics or former academics (e.g. Deem, 2006). In that sense, the boundaries between the two professional groups are more nuanced than might appear at first. What plays out here, thus, is a sort of 'turf war' where academics are positioned (or position themselves) against managers in the battle 'for' the university. In this sense, the metaphor of the university 'under siege' by the forces of neoliberalism is actually being used by academics to assert their right to control and decide what a university is and how it should function.

This, of course, is not to deny the existence of power disparities at universities, nor to negate the trend of the concentration of power in the hands of university administration. Yet, attributing power to university managers has important consequences for the understanding of the political dynamics at contemporary universities. On the one hand, it frames political agency as happening outside 'proper' academia. In this sense, academics are framed as *reactive*; in other words, their agency is seen as happening to a great extent as a consequence of external drivers. On the other hand, this sort of framing means that almost anything academics do is understood as 'opposition' or 'resistance' to the forces of neoliberalism. This legitimises academic agency as almost by definition *defensive*; in other words, whatever academics stand for or do is automatically justified if it can be described as a reaction to external political pressure.

Locating the source of political agency beyond the walls of the ivory tower, in turn, redraws the boundary between the university and the 'surrounding' society. Academics are presented as being on the 'inside', where they presumably need to remain insulated from the exigencies of politics and economy, in order for knowledge to flourish. Administrators and managers are represented as 'agents' that jeopardise this process by transferring political pressure into the ivory tower. Students and academics, in turn, have no choice beyond compliance or resistance; that is, their forms of political agency are reduced to reacting to the 'external' threat.

At the end of the day, thus, the boundary between the university and the 'outside world' is reinforced. Politics is seen as something that needs to remain 'outside' of the university in order to ensure its survival. Attempts at governing the university, including from a distance, are interpreted as attacks on the ivory tower, and threats to the principles of university autonomy and academic freedom. And while these should not be taken lightly, it makes sense to examine, for a moment, the historical context of the relationship between the university and the state and, more broadly, the university and the world of politics.

We were never an ivory tower?

To a great extent, the history of the modern university can be read as the history of its evolving relationship with the political community that surrounds it. In the eighteenth and nineteenth centuries, when European universities developed as semi-autonomous, self-governed communities of scholars helping to ground the principles of academic freedom and university autonomy, they did so under the patronage of the state—most famously, in the case of the University of Berlin, the Prussian Empire—and with the explicit understanding that in order for them to thrive, the state needed to abstain from direct interference in matters of learning and research (e.g. Ash, 2006). Importantly, thus, the freedoms embedded in what came to be known as the 'Humboldtian' model of the university were both instrumental (that is, oriented towards a specific outcome), and granted (that is, given by the state). In this sense, the isolation from the world of 'outside' politics was never absolute; on the contrary, the relationship between the university and its surrounding political community was fundamental to both.

This social contract was significantly challenged in the 1960s and the 1970s. In this period, universities in different parts of the world became centres of protest movements. To a great extent, these movements arose as reactions to the political and historical context. In the United States, there was the prolonged involvement in the Vietnam War, and the blossoming civil rights movement that sought to challenge racial, gender and social inequalities embedded in the society. In France, there was the growing disillusionment with the post-war legacy of De Gaulle's regime and especially with the ways it approached the independence movements in former colonies. Yet, there are also important socio-demographic factors that help explain why universities could come to play such a central role in these movements.

Especially in the industrialised nations, the period after World War II was characterised by the rapid expansion of higher education, both in terms of the growth in absolute numbers of students, and, even more importantly, in the broadening of the social base from which they were recruited (e.g. Rüegg and Sadlak, 2011). Consequently, members of social groups that would have been previously most likely excluded from higher education began enrolling into universities.

This meant that, over a relatively short period of time, the political significance of higher education was radically altered. From one-time highly selective institutions designed to educate the intellectual, political and economic elite, they were turning into places with mass attendance, where people from different walks of life could become exposed to (and generate) ideas critical of the established order. Of course, this doesn't mean that the role of universities in social stratification or selection was lost. Many institutions remained highly selective and rather conservative. But, in the popular imaginary, universities became associated with left-wing and politically progressive views. This, in turn, strengthened their position on the 'boundaries' of the society: they needed to be close enough to day-to-day politics to comment on it, but far enough to prevent the world of politics from interfering with the way in which universities are run.

Understanding contemporary debates about higher education requires acknowledging the extent to which the legacy of this particular historical period informs the idea of the university and of its relation with the society. There is hardly a discussion on university autonomy or academic freedom that does not bring up the 'Spirit of the 1968' in some capacity, usually as an argument towards 'guarding' the university from undue 'outside' influence. However, the assumption that universities are inherently critical of the establishment has other, equally relevant, implications both for policy and practice. On the one hand, it fuels the notion of academics as, almost by definition, anti-hegemonic, egalitarian, and progressive. On the other hand, it reinforces the idea that universities must somehow be 'controlled', that is, kept in line with the political and economic concerns of the state; and that, failing this, they are bound to spin out of control.

Neoliberalism, from this perspective, is simultaneously used to describe the contemporary setting in which these tensions are played out, and to criticise its potential consequences. The fact that, as Peck (2010) notes, it is almost never used by the 'other side'—that is, although favoured by academics, it is rarely picked up by politicians and policy-makers—signals that it has political significance as a self-defensive term used to justify the 'special' status of universities and the right of academics to define the terms under which they want to engage with the society. While, in and of itself, this does not mean 'neoliberalism' has no heuristic value, it makes sense to think about the limitations of using it to explain different aspects of change taking place at universities today.

In order to illustrate this point, this chapter will include a vignette that shows that political agency is constructed and performed through universities in ways that cannot be completely explained as either reaction or resistance to neoliberalism. It concerns the case of Professor Steven Salaita, who was offered and then refused tenure at the University of Illinois in 2014, ostensibly over a tweet critical of Israel's campaign in the Gaza Strip. The event, which caused prolonged public controversy, points to multiple political frameworks relevant for understanding the dynamics of contemporary knowledge production.

University outside itself? The Salaita Case

The 'Salaita Case', as it will probably be remembered, concerns a controversy surrounding the appointment of Professor Steven Salaita to the University of Illinois at Urbana–Champaign. In September 2013, Salaita was offered a tenured position in Native American Studies, which he accepted and was due to start teaching in the Fall Semester of 2014. However, in August 2014, the Board of Trustees withdrew the offer, citing Salaita's 'incendiary' posts on Twitter concerning the, at the time ongoing, escalation of Israeli military offensive in the Gaza Strip as a reason[1].

Together with the greater part of the American academic left, Salaita was (and is) a vocal critic of Israel's policy in this regard, and has repeatedly called for an academic boycott of Israel. He is also a widely recognised authority on Native American Studies. The Board's decision was eventually harshly criticised both by the American Association of University Professors and different non-governmental and civil society organisations for what was framed as a violation of academic freedom. Salaita sued the University of Illinois, eventually receiving settlement.

The Salaita case is usually framed as a clash between the principles of academic freedom and the legal right of university boards to decide on appointments. In particular, Professor Salaita's activity on Twitter was defended as the right to free speech and freedom of expression. Salaita is quoted saying: 'Like any American citizen, I have the right to express my opinion on pressing human rights concerns, including Israeli government actions, without fear of censorship or punishment. … The University's actions have cost me the pinnacle of academic achievement—a tenured professorship, with the opportunity to write and think freely. What makes this worse is that in my case the University abandoned fundamental principles of academic freedom and shared governance, crucial to fostering critical thought, that should be at the core of the university mission' (Fulton, 2015). Against the principles of academic freedom, as a part of the reactions asserted, were the interests of the (anonymous) donors to the University of Illinois, whose expressed dissatisfaction with Salaita's activity on Twitter was seen as instrumental to the Board's decision to refuse his appointment. One of the attorneys representing Salaita stated: 'Only donor pressure, or sheer pride, can explain the administration's stubborn refusal to revisit a decision that has done so much harm to Dr. Salaita and to constitutional and other principles that academics hold dear … The administration has something to hide, and through this lawsuit we intend to expose it' (Flaherty, 2015).

Most defenders of the University of Illinois' decision reiterated the legal argument concerning the right of the Board to revoke offers of tenure. Where arguments delved into questions of academic freedom, Salaita's critics argued that the principle should not apply beyond the university walls; in other words, that Salaita's tweet was a public statement, and as such should not be protected under the auspices guarding academics' freedom of expression. Some of the criticism ostensibly came from students, who found Salaita's statements 'offensive' or politically biased. This, again, brought attention to the issue of regulating academics' communication—on or off-campus—as well as the question of the legality of using a perceived violation of its principles as grounds for dismissal (Dorf, 2014 offers a good legal analysis of the issue).

The way in which the debate played out reflects quite closely some of the main elements of the 'ivory tower under siege' metaphor. Although neoliberalism is not always brought up, the sides in the conflict are constructed as 'academics' vs. 'managers' or, even more radically, as the principles of academic freedom vs. the interests of capital, the latter being personified in the anonymous donors of the university. The professoriate, thus, is portrayed as defending the university against the interference from the 'outside', standing up for core academic values against those oriented towards profit. While the Salaita case certainly points to multiple problematic aspects related to the governance of contemporary universities, I would like to devote some space to pointing to other relevant aspects of the case that are not reducible to the 'administration vs. academics' or 'capital vs. academic freedom' dynamics.

Most obviously, the Salaita case reflects the complex position of the United States towards Israel/Palestine, and, more importantly, the ways in which this relationship has been reflected in American higher education. Though it would be difficult to give an exhaustive overview of different aspects of this here, it makes sense to remember that Jewish émigrés fleeing Nazi persecution played a significant role in the constitution of American academia and, more broadly, public life (e.g. Ash, 2006; Hollinger, 1998). While this does not by any means imply that all of these intellectuals were or are necessarily or uncritically supportive of Israel as a political project, it does make the discussion of Israel/Palestine conflict particularly sensitive in academic contexts. On the other hand, most intellectuals on the left side of the political spectrum are very critical of the State of Israel, and support the Palestinian struggle. During the past decade, this line of division in became particularly relevant the discussions surrounding proposals for the boycott of Israeli universities.

A significant number of scholars and academic associations have argued that U.S. institutions of higher education should boycott different forms of academic cooperation with Israel on the grounds of its violation of human rights in Palestine, including those of Palestinian academics (Butler, 2006). During Israel's military campaign in 2013, there was a renewed public call for the boycott. Those opposed to it, including the influential American Association of University Professors, stated that banning Israeli academics from cooperation would, of itself, constitute a violation of academic freedom that cannot be justified through appeals to solidarity with those whose rights are violated (Fish, 2014). And while academic freedom and freedom of speech constitute the crux of most of these discussions, their political context is, of course, much broader.

On the one hand, it concerns the issue of the role of the United States in the Middle East, and its foreign policy overall. While debates in the academia are far from being crucial in this sense, they are still considered capable of influencing popular opinions and shaping the public sphere. Therefore, it is also about the public role of universities and political engagement of intellectuals; or, rather, about the negotiation between the 'boundaries' of academic agency and the society. This brings in another aspect of the political context of the case, which is the question of the transformation of the public sphere in relation to the rise of social media, including Twitter. Namely, one of the main issues in the application of the concept of academic freedom was whether it extends beyond the more-or-less traditionally conceived boundaries of the university; in other words, when academics voice their opinions in social media, especially if not on their field of specialisation. Twitter is a particularly salient example, as it clearly transgresses the boundary between the private and the public; in this sense, whether Salaita criticised Israel as a scholar or as a private person remains an open question.

This aspect brings in again the question of the role of the academia—and of academics—in the society. The concept of 'public intellectuals' assumes that academics should, in principle, be able to voice their opinions on matters of general interest, and that they should be able to do so publicly. Furthermore, academics are increasingly encouraged to be 'present' and visible in social media—for instance, the number of Twitter followers can be taken as a measure of an academic's public influence, which contributes to their 'public engagement' or 'service' portfolio—which is, in turn, becoming increasingly important for career progression within the academia itself (Carrigan, 2016; Baert and Booth, 2012). While, from this perspective, it is clearly possible to see academics' engagement in the new social media as a *consequence* of the changing conditions of academic labour and new expectations related to the communication and public visibility of their work, it also makes sense to acknowledge that academics may seek this sort of attention independently from the system of incentives and rewards immediately tied to promotion or tenure (e.g. Freese, 2009).

On the other hand, especially in the past decade, there has been growing pressure on academics in the United States to present 'balanced' political opinions on campus—the movement that came almost as a direct reaction to what was perceived as 'oversaturation' by 'leftist' views in the academia. 'Silencing' Salaita can, in this sense, be seen as part of the movement that claims students have the 'right' to be exposed to the broadest possible array of opinions. While this view is tied to the concept of students as consumers and thus can be classified within the neoliberal paradigm of higher education, it is also—and, I would argue, more importantly—part of a longer and more complex history of the tensions between progressive and conservative intellectuals in the American academia, which continues to shape politics both on and off-campus.

Clearly, thus, the Salaita case is about much more than neoliberalism in higher education, a turf war between academics and administrators, or the interests of scholarship and interests of capital. Although there is no denying that university competition, and the related expectation from academics to be publicly engaged and thus justify public spending on higher education and research, played a role in setting the stage for the Salaita case, the specific ways in which it was (and continues to be) played out, as well as the forms of agency, social identities and boundaries it entails, cannot be explained or attributed to the 'war on universities' alone. If nothing else, there is a multitude of other conflicts that 'feed' into it—the Israeli–Palestinian one being just the tip of the iceberg. Most importantly, however, it is about the positioning of academics vis-à-vis the society and, at the same time, about the ways in which those working at universities construct their roles and the institution they work at. All of this points to the conclusion that conceiving of the university as only or even most importantly 'under siege' by forces of neoliberalism can conceal a complex network of political forces that all play a role in the construction of university–society relationships—a process in which, it warrants emphasising, academics have more power than it may appear at first.

Conclusions: the university—an assemblage of political (f)actors?

What does all of this suggest about the ways in which we can think of the contemporary university? The analysis here aspired to demonstrate that constructing universities as being 'under attack' by forces of neoliberalism, while it may elicit sympathies or recognition in academic circles, is somewhat questionable as an analytical strategy. Firstly, it dislocates political power from the university, placing it primarily in the hands of 'classical' political actors such as nation-states, supra-national entities or private shareholders. Secondly, it draws an artificial division line between academics (usually framed as good and just) and managers or administrators (usually framed as evil agents of neoliberalism). Correspondingly, the agency of academics is almost by default defined as 'resistance', or oppositional to the perceived neoliberal policies. Thirdly, the metaphor of ivory tower under siege denies the historicity of university–society relationships, and the interplay of political powers that gave rise to the concepts of academic freedom and university autonomy. Rather than being universal, these are historically and sociologically situated, and the ways in which they are used today very much reflects this background—though not always in explicit ways.

A critical analysis of the transformation of the contemporary idea of the university, therefore, also needs to take into account the political contexts in which autonomy and academic freedom are brought up, and the intricacies of the relationships between different actors in situations where this happens. The story of Steven Salaita, in this context, serves as an example of multiple social and political backgrounds that all informed the controversy surrounding his appointment-then-dismissal. Although not disconnected from, for instance, the processes of socioeconomic transformation of academic labour, the case represents a situation where the idea of universities as being 'under attack' by forces of neoliberalism cannot fully explain either the specific sequence of events or their outcome.

Of course, all of this is not to suggest that neoliberalism as an explanatory framework or diagnostic narrative is wrong or methodologically incorrect. But attributing causality to (ill-defined) neoliberalism both removes political agency from the university and offers a rather partial view of power, omitting to perceive its manifestations that are happening alongside—but not always in direct relation to—neoliberal transformations. In part, I would argue that this occurs because—as Bourdieu noted in *Pascalian Meditations* (Bourdieu, 2000)—it is difficult for academics to perceive the conditions of their own reproduction from *within*, that is, from inside of the walls of the academia. In part, however, it might also happen because portraying the university as a hapless victim of neoliberal oligarchy serves as a self-justificatory narrative that also takes the conversation away from the examination of academic privilege, or, more broadly, the reproduction of social inequality *in* and *through* universities. The construction of a powerful external threat, at the end of the day, concentrates the 'ranks' and shifts attention from forms and exercise of power that take place *within* them.

Universities are and should be uniquely equipped to discuss contemporary transformations, remain reflexive and retain a critical edge despite (though not *in spite of*) being a part of the society. The challenge, thus, is how to think and talk about what is going on at and around universities, without sliding either into an apology of neoliberalism or into ivory tower nostalgia. Contemporary transformations of knowledge production, while in many ways questioning the 'traditional' definition of a university, also provide an opportunity for a careful reconsideration of its role and purpose, and its relationship with the society. This text hopes to have made a small contribution in that direction.

Note

1. One of the Tweets widely publicized as an example of 'incendiary' language is "Zionists, take responsibility: if your dream of an ethnocratic Israel is worth the murder of children, just fucking own it already."

References

Ash, M. G. 2006. Bachelor of What, Master of Whom? The Humboldt Myth and Historical Transformations of Higher Education in German-Speaking Europe and the US. *European Journal of Education* 41 (2), 245–267.

Baert, P. and J. Booth. 2012. Tensions Within the Public Intellectual: Political Interventions from Dreyfus to the New Social Media. *International Journal of Politics, Culture, and Society* 25 (4), 111–126.

Ball, S. 2003. The Teacher's Soul and the Terrors of Performativity. *Journal of Education Policy* 18 (2), 215–228.

Ball, S. and A. Olmedo. 2013. Care of the Self, Resistance and Subjectivity under Neoliberal Governmentalities. *Critical Studies in Education* 54 (1), 85–96.

Barkawi, T. 2013. Neoliberal Assault on the Academia. *Al Jazeera*, 25 June 2013, http://www.aljazeera.com/indepth/opinion/2013/04/20134238284530760.html

Barnett, R. 2011. *Being a University*. London: Routledge.

Barnett, R. 2016. The University as Agent. In: *Understanding the University: Institution, Idea(s) and Possibilities*. London: Routledge, 158-169.

Bourdieu, P. 2000. *Pascalian Meditations*. Cambridge: Polity Press.

Burawoy, M. 2011. Redefining the Public University: Global and National Contexts. In: Holmwood, J., ed. *A Manifesto for the Public University*. London: Bloomsbury, 27–41.

Butler, J. 2006. Israel, Palestine and the Paradoxes of Academic Freedom. *Radical Philosophy* 135, 8–17.

Canaan, J. and W. Shumar, eds. 2008. *Structure and Agency in the Neoliberal University*. London: Routledge.

Carrigan, M. 2016. *Social Media for Academics*. London: Sage.

Deem, R. 2006. Changing Research Perspectives on the Management of Higher Education: Can Research Permeate the Activities of Manager-academics? *Higher Education Quarterly* 60 (3), 203–228.

Delanty, G. 2001. *Challenging Knowledge: the University in the Knowledge Society*. Buckingham: Open University Press.

Docherty, T. 2015. *Universities at War*. London: SAGE.

Dorf, M. 2014. Academic Freedom in the Salaita Case. https://verdict.justia.com/2014/08/13/academic-freedom-salaita-case [accessed 1 July 2015].

Fish, S. 2009. Neoliberalism and Higher Education. *New York Times*, 8 March 2009, http://opinionator.blogs.nytimes.com/2009/03/08/neoliberalism-and-higher-education/ [accessed 1 July 2015].

Fish, S. 2014. *Versions of Academic Freedom: From Professionalism to Revolution*. Chicago: University of Chicago Press.

Flaherty, C. 30 January 2015. "Steven Salaita's Long-Anticipated Lawsuit Against Illinois University Includes a Twist". https://www.insidehighered.com/news/2015/01/30/steven-salaitas-long-anticipated-lawsuit-against-u-illinois-includes-twist [accessed 1 July 2015].

Foucault, M. 1972. *The Archaeology of Knowledge*. London: Routledge.

Freese, J. 2009. Blogs and the Attention Market for Public Intellectuals. *Society* 46 (1), 45–48.

Fulton, D. 29 January 2015. http://www.commondreams.org/news/2015/01/29/uncivil-professor-sues-university-free-speech-rights [accessed 1 July 2015].

Giroux, H. 2013. Public Intellectuals against the Neoliberal University. http://www.truth-out.org/opinion/item/19654-public-intellectuals-against-the-neoliberal-university [accessed 1 July 2015].

Gordon, G. and C. Whitchurch, eds. 2010. *Academic and Professional Identities in Higher Education: The Challenges of a Diversifying Workforce*. New York: Routledge.

Gornall, L., C. Cook, L. Daunton, et al., eds. 2014. *Academic Working Lives: Experience, Practice and Change*. London: Bloomsbury.

Halfmann, W. and H. Radder. 2015. The Academic Manifesto: From an Occupied to a Public University. *Minerva* 53 (2), 165–187.

Hollinger, D. 1998. *Science, Jews, and Secular Culture: Studies in Mid-Twentieth-Century American Intellectual History*. Princeton, NJ: Princeton University Press.

Kehm, B. M. and U. Teichler, eds. 2013. *The Academic Profession in Europe: New Tasks and New Challenges*. Dordrecht: Springer.

Leathwood, C. and B. Read. 2013. Research Policy and Academic Performativity: Compliance, Contestation and Complicity. *Studies in Higher Education* 38 (8), 1162–1174.

McKenna, B. 2013. Paulo Freire's Blunt Challenge to Anthropology: Create a Pedagogy of the Oppressed for Your Times. *Critique of Anthropology* 33 (4), 447–475.

Olssen, M. and M. A. Peters. 2005. Neoliberalism, Higher Education and the Knowledge Economy: From the Free Market to Knowledge Capitalism. *Journal of Education Policy* 20 (3), 313–345.

Peck, J. 2010. *The Constructions of Neoliberal Reason*. Oxford: Oxford University Press.

Posecznick, A. 2014. Introduction: On Theorizing and Humanizing the Politics of Complicity in Higher Education. *Learning and Teaching: The International Journal of Higher Education in the Social Sciences* 7 (1), 1–11.
Readings, B. 1996. *The University in Ruins*. Cambridge, MA: Harvard University Press.
Rüegg, W. and J. Sadlak. 2011. Relations with Authority. In: Rüegg, W., ed. *History of University in Europe*, Vol. IV. Cambridge: Cambridge University Press, 73–123.
Santiago, R. and T. Carvalho. 2008. Academics in a New Work Environment: The Impact of New Public Management on Work Conditions. *Higher Education Quarterly* 62, 204–223.
Shore, C. and L. McLauchlan. 2012. 'Third Mission' Activities, Commercialisation and Academic Entrepreneurs. *Social Anthropology* 20 (3), 267–286.
Shore, C. and S. Wright. 2000. Coercive Accountability: The Rise of Audit Culture in Higher Education. In: Strathern, M., ed. *Audit Cultures: Anthropological Studies in Accountability, Ethics and the Academy*. London/New York: Routledge, 57–89.
Slaughter, S. and G. Rhoades. 2000. The Neo-Liberal University. *New Labor Forum* 6, 73–79.
Springer, S. 2015. Postneoliberalism? *Review of Radical Political Economics* 47 (1), 5–17.
Teichler, U. and Höhle, E. A. (eds). 2013. *The Work Situation of the Academic Profession in Europe: Findings of a Survey in Twelve Countries*. Dordrecht: Springer.
Turner, R. 2008. *Neo-liberal Ideology*. Edinburgh: Edinburgh University Press.
Venugopal, R. 2015. Neoliberalism as Concept. *Economy and Society* 44 (2), 165–187.

CHAPTER TWO

Defending Higher Education in the Age of Barbarism

HENRY A. GIROUX

Donald Trump's ascendancy in American politics has made visible a scourge of oppressive stupidity, manufactured deceptions, a corrupt political system, and a contempt for reason that has been decades in the making; it also points to the withering of civic attachments, the undoing of civic culture, the decline of public life, and the erosion of any sense of shared citizenship. Galvanizing his base of true-believers in post-election demonstrations, the world is witnessing how Trump's history of unabashed racism and politics of hate is transformed into a spectacle of fear, divisions, and disinformation. Under President Trump, the plague of mid-20th century authoritarianism has returned not only in the menacing spectacle of populist rallies, fear-mongering, unchecked bigotry, and humiliation, but also in an emboldened culture of war, militarization, and extreme violence that looms over society like a rising storm.

The reality of Trump's election may be the most momentous development of the age because of its apocalyptic irrationality and the shock it has produced. The whole world is watching, pondering how such a dreadful event could have happened. How have we arrived here? What forces have undermined education as a democratic public sphere making it incapable of producing the formative culture and critical citizens that could have prevented such a catastrophe from happening in an alleged democracy? We get a glimpse of this failure of civic culture, education, and civic literacy in the willingness and success of the Trump administration to empty language of any meaning, a practice that constitutes a flight from historical memory, ethics, justice, and social responsibility. Under such circumstances and with too little opposition, the United States government has taken on the workings of a disimagination machine, characterized by an utter disregard for the truth, and often accompanied, as in Trump's case, by "primitive schoolyard taunts and threats." In this instance, Orwell's "Ignorance is Strength" materializes in the Trump administration's weaponized attempt not only to rewrite history, but also to obliterate it. What we are witnessing is not simply a political project but also a reworking of the very meaning of education both as an institution and as a broader cultural force.

Higher education in our politically desperate age is threatened by a legacy that it does not dare to name and that inheritance has an eerie resonance with an authoritarian past that asserts itself, in part, with a growing belief among the American public that education is "bad for America" and that it is at odds with Trump's vision of making America great again. The Trump administration needs education to fail in a very particular way. Hostile to its role as a public good and democratic sphere, it is attempting to reshape education according to the market-driven logic of neoliberalism with its emphasis on privatization, commodification, deregulation, fear, and managerialism. In this reactionary view, education is defined in economic terms and is beholden to the assumption that only corporations and market driven interests have the right to define both the purpose of education and what type of education is needed by students. Under such circumstances, higher education is threatened for its potential role as a public sphere capable in educating students as informed, critical thinkers capable in not only holding power accountable but also fulfilling the role of critical agents who can act against injustice and resist diverse forms of oppression. The modern loss of faith in the merging of education and democracy needs to be reclaimed, but that will only happen if the long legacy of struggle over education is once again brought to life as part of a more comprehensive understanding of education being central to politics itself.

Today, political parties, anti-public intellectual pundits, and mainstream news sources view the purpose of higher education largely as a workstation for training a global workforce and generating capital for the financial elite. Hence, it is not surprising that many of them also view the more progressive ideals of higher education as a significant threat to the power of the surveillance state, the ultrarich, and religious fundamentalists. Under such circumstances, it becomes more difficult to reclaim a history in which the culture of business is not the culture of higher education. This is certainly not meant to suggest that higher education once existed in an idyllic past in which it only functioned as a public good and provided a public service in the interest of developing a democratic polity. Higher education has always been fraught with notable inequities and antidemocratic tendencies, but it also once functioned as a crucial reminder of both its own limitations and the potential role it might play in attacking social problems and deepening the promise of a democracy to come. As difficult as it may seem to believe, John Dewey's insistence that "democracy needs to be reborn in each generation, and education is its midwife" was once taken seriously by many political and academic leaders.[1] Today, it is fair to say that Dewey's once vaunted claim has been either willfully ignored, forgotten, or has become an object of scorn.[2]

We now live at a time in which institutions that were meant to limit human suffering and misfortune and protect the public from the excesses of the market have been either weakened or abolished, especially under the presidency of Donald Trump.[3] The consequences can be seen clearly in the ongoing and ruthless assault on the social state, workers, unions, higher education, students, poor minorities, and any vestige of the social contract. Free market policies, values, and practices with their emphasis on the privatization of public wealth, the elimination of social protections, and the deregulation of economic activity now shape practically every commanding political and economic institution in the United States.

Public spheres that once offered at least the glimmer of progressive ideas, enlightened social policies, non-commodified values, and critical dialogue and exchange have been increasingly commercialized—or replaced by private spaces and corporate settings whose ultimate fidelity is to increasing profit margins. For example, higher education is defined more and more as simply another core element of corporate power and culture, viewed mostly as a waste of taxpayers' money, and denied its value as a democratic public sphere and guardian of public values. What has become clear is that the attack on the social state, workers, and unions is now being matched by a full-fledged assault on higher education. Such attacks are not happening just in the United States but in many other parts of the globe where casino capitalism is waging a savage battle to eliminate all of those public spheres that might offer a glimmer of opposition to and protection from market-driven policies, institutions, ideology, and values.

We live at a time when it is more crucial than ever to believe that the university is both a public trust and social good. At best, it is a critical institution infused with the promise of cultivating intellectual insight, the imagination, inquisitiveness, risk-taking, social responsibility, and the struggle for justice. In addition, higher education should be at the "heart of intense public discourse, passionate learning, and vocal citizen involvement in the issues of the times."[4] Underlying this vision of the university are some serious questions about its relationship to the larger society. For instance, how might the university's responsibility be understood with respect to safeguarding the interests of young people at a time of violence and war, the rise of a rampant anti-intellectualism, a devastating gap in income and wealth, the rise of the surveillance state, and the threat of ecological and nuclear devastation?

What might it mean to define the university as a pedagogical space that disrupts, disturbs, inspires, and energizes young people to be individual and social agents rather than as an institution that redefines itself in terms of market values and reacts mostly to market fluctuations? It is in the spirit of such considerations that I first want to address those larger economic, social, and cultural interests produced largely by the growing inequalities in wealth, income, and power that threaten the notion of higher education as a democratic public good.

As higher education's role as a center of critical thought and civic engagement is devalued, society is being transformed into a "spectacular space of consumption" and financial looting. One consequence is an ongoing flight from mutual obligations and social responsibilities and what Tony Judt has called a "loss of faith in the culture of open democracy."[5] This loss of faith in the power of politics, public dialogue, and dissent is not unrelated to the diminished belief in higher education as central to producing critically engaged, civically literate, and socially responsible citizens. At stake here are not only the meaning and purpose of higher education, but also civil society, politics, and the fate of democracy itself. And, yet, under the banner of right-wing reforms, the only questions being asked about knowledge production, the purpose of education, the nature of politics, and the future are determined largely by market forces. In this discourse, education is reduced to training, public values are transformed into crude instrumental values, and, public and higher education are reduced to operating systems, posing problems that can only be solved through quantification, effective programming, high stakes testing, and an obsession with numerical data. This is a form of neoliberal or corporatized education wedded to market-driven values that lacks any vestige of a democratic vision and makes clear "the contradiction between democratic values and market fundamentalism."[6]

The mantras of the new market fundamentalism are now well known: government is the problem; society is a fiction; governance is market-driven; deregulation and commodification are vehicles for freedom; long-term thinking and planning is a hindrance; "individuals have to seek, find and practice individual solutions to socially produced troubles"[7]; and higher education should serve corporate interests rather than the public good. In addition, the yardstick of profit has become the only viable measure of the good life while civic engagement and public spheres devoted to the common good are viewed by many politicians and their publics as either a hindrance to the goals of a market-driven society or alibis for government inefficiency and waste.

Missing from neoliberal market societies are those public spheres—from public and higher education to the mainstream media and digital screen culture—where people can develop what might be called the civic imagination. Tied largely to instrumental ideologies and measurable paradigms, many institutions of higher education are now committed almost exclusively to economic goals, such as preparing students for the workforce—all done as part of an appeal to rationality, one that eschews matters of inequality, power, public values, and the ethical grammars of suffering.[8] Many universities have not only strayed from their democratic mission, they also seem immune to the plight of students who face a harsh new world of high unemployment, the prospect of downward mobility, and debilitating debt.

The question of what kind of education is needed for students to be informed and active citizens in a world that increasingly ignores their needs, if not their future, is rarely asked.[9] In the absence of a democratic vision of schooling, it is not surprising that some colleges and universities are increasingly opening their classrooms to corporate interests, standardizing the curriculum, instituting top-down governing structures that mimic corporate culture, and generating courses that promote entrepreneurial values unfettered by social concerns or ethical consequences.

Central to this view of higher education in the United States is a market-driven paradigm that seeks to eliminate tenure, turn the humanities into a job preparation service, and transform most faculty into an army of temporary subaltern labor. For instance, in the United States, out of 1.5 million faculty members, 1 million are "adjuncts who are earning, on average, $20K a year gross, with no benefits or health care, and no unemployment insurance when they are out of work."[10] The indentured service status of such faculty is put on full display as some colleges have resorted to using "temporary service agencies to do their formal hiring."[11] A record number of adjuncts are now on food stamps and receive some form of public assistance. Given how little they are paid this should not come as a surprise, though that does not make it any less shameful.[12] As Noam Chomsky has argued, this reduction of faculty to the status of subaltern labor is "part of a corporate business model designed to reduce labor costs and to increase labor servility."[13]

While it has been clearly recognized that the ideal of shared governance between faculty and administrators has broken down, what has not been analyzed is how the Walmart model of power and labor relations—in both the university and the larger society—is connected to the massive inequality in wealth and income that now corrupts every aspect of American politics and society. No democracy can survive the kind of inequality in which "the 400 richest people … have as much wealth as 154 million Americans combined, that's 50 percent of the entire country [while] the top economic 1 percent of the U.S. population now has a record 40 percent of all wealth and more wealth than 90 percent of the population combined."[14] On a global scale, according to a study by anti-poverty charity

Oxfam, it reports that "Eight men own the same wealth as the 3.6 billion people who make up the poorest half of humanity."[15]

Higher education will not fare well as a public good under such massive inequities in wealth and power. Reduced to consumers, students will fare no better and will be treated as either clients or as restless children in need of high-energy entertainment. Within such iniquitous conditions of power, access, and wealth, education will not foster a sense of organized responsibility fundamental to a democracy. Instead, it encourages a sense of organized irresponsibility—a practice that underlies the economic Darwinism and civic corruption at the heart of a debased politics.

Higher Education and the Crisis of Legitimacy

What has become clear is that universities are losing their sense of public mission, just as leadership in higher education is being stripped of any viable democratic vision. In the United States, college presidents are now called CEOs and move without apology between interlocking corporate and academic boards. With few exceptions, they are praised as fund-raisers but rarely acknowledged for the quality of their ideas. It gets worse. As Adam Bessie points out, "the discourse of higher education now resembles what you might hear at a board meeting at a No. 2 pencil-factory, The emphasis here is on: productivity, efficiency, metrics, data-driven value, [all of] which places utter, near-religious faith in this highly technical, market-based view of education [which] like all human enterprises, can (and must) be quantified and evaluated numerically, to identify the 'one best way,' which can then be 'scaled up,' or mass-produced across the nation, be it No. 2 pencils, appendectomies, or military drones."[16]

In this new Gilded Age of money, greed, selfishness, and profit, academic subjects gain stature almost exclusively through their exchange value on the market. For example, BB&T Corporation, a financial holdings company, gave a $1 million gift to Marshall University's business school on the condition that *Atlas Shrugged* by Ayn Rand (Congressman Paul Ryan's favorite book) be taught in a course. What happens to education when it is treated like a corporation? What are we to make of the integrity of a university when it accepts a monetary gift from powerful corporate interests or rich patrons demanding as part of the agreement the power to specify what is to be taught in a course or how a curriculum should be shaped? Some corporations and universities now believe that course content is not an academic decision but a market consideration. In addition, many disciplines are now valued almost exclusively with how closely they align with what might be euphemistically called a business culture.

One egregious example of this neoliberal approach to higher education is on full display in Florida where Governor Rick Scott's task force on education attempted to implement a policy that would lower tuition for degrees friendly to corporate interests in order to "steer students toward majors that are in demand in the job market."[17] Scott's utterly instrumental and anti-intellectual message is clear: "Give us engineers, scientists, health care specialists and technology experts. Do not worry so much about historians, philosophers, anthropologists and English majors."[18] In Wisconsin, Governor Scott Walker drew up a proposal to remove the public service philosophy focus from the university's mission statement which states that the university's purpose is to solve problems and improve people's lives. He also scratched out the phrase "the search for truth" and substituted both ideas with a vocabulary stating that the university's goal is to meet "the state's work force needs." But Walker's disdain for higher education as a public good can be more readily understood given his hatred of unions, particularly those organized for educators. How else to explain his egregious comparison of union protesters to the brutal terrorists and thugs that make up ISIS. In 2016, Walker not only cut 250 million dollars from the education budget, he also effectively passed legislation that eliminated tenure at state universities.[19]

Walker represents a new breed of politician waging war on higher education, the public good, and any viable notion of the welfare state. Like many of his politically extremist colleagues, he epitomizes an era in which there is near zero tolerance for economic and racial justice and "infinite tolerance for the crimes of bankers and government embezzlers which affect the lives of millions."[20]

What both Scott and Walker make clear is not only that their brand of free market fundamentalism undermines both civic education and public values but that it also confuses education with training. Moreover, this market fundamentalism wages a war on what might be called the radical imagination. For instance, thousands of students in the United States are now saddled with debts that will profoundly impact their lives and their future, likely forcing them away from public service jobs because the pay is too low to pay off their educational loans. Students find themselves in a world of massive inequality in which heightened expectations have been replaced by dashed hopes and a world of onerous debt.[21] Struggling to merely survive, the debt crisis represents a massive assault on the imagination by leaving little or no room to think otherwise in order to act otherwise. David Graeber is right in insisting that "student loans are destroying the imagination of youth." As he puts it, "If there's a way of a society committing mass suicide, what better way than to take all the youngest, most energetic, creative, joyous people in your society and saddle them with, $50,000 of debt so they have to be slaves?"[22]

In a market-driven system in which economic and political decisions are removed from social costs, the flight of critical thought and social responsibility is further accentuated by what Zygmunt Bauman calls "ethical tranquillization."[23] One result is a form of depoliticization that works its way through the social order, removing social relations from the configurations of power that shape them, and substituting "emotional and personal vocabularies for political ones in formulating solutions to political problems."[24] Under such circumstances, it becomes difficult to provide conditions within institutions of schooling that expand the capacities of students to think critically and teach them how to take risks, act in a socially responsible way, and connect private issues with larger public considerations. The current attack on higher education, teachers' unions, women's reproductive rights, voting rights, low income people, and minority youth suggests that we are witnessing the breakdown of democracy, the infantilization of thought, the disappearance of critical intellectuals, and what C. Wright Mills once called "the collapse of those public spheres which offer a sense of critical agency and social imagination."[25] This is a particularly important insight in a society where the free circulation of ideas is not only being replaced by mass mediated ideas but where critical ideas, if not dissent itself, are increasingly viewed or dismissed as either too liberal, radical, or even seditious.

As educators, we need to recognize that the most important forms of domination are not only economic but also intellectual and pedagogical, and lie on the side of belief and persuasion. This suggests that educators bear an enormous responsibility for challenging this form of domination. Nor should the relevance of education being at the heart of politics be lost on those of us concerned about inviting the public back into higher education and rethinking the purpose and meaning of higher education itself. Democracy places civic demands upon its citizens, and such demands point to the necessity of an education that is broad-based, critical, and supportive of meaningful civic values, participation in self-governance, and democratic leadership.

Dreaming the Impossible

Reclaiming higher education as a democratic public sphere begins with the crucial recognition that education is not solely about job training and the production of ethically challenged entrepreneurial subjects, but also about matters of civic engagement, critical thinking, civic literacy, and the capacity for democratic agency, action, and change. It is also inextricably connected to the related issues of power, inclusion, and social responsibility.[26] If young people are to develop a deep respect for others, a keen sense of social responsibility, as well as an informed notion of civic engagement, education must be viewed as a cultural, political, and moral force that provides the knowledge, values, and social relations to make such democratic practices possible and connect human agency to the idea of social responsibility and the politics of possibility. In this instance, teaching needs to be rigorous, self-reflective, and committed not to the dead zone of instrumental rationality but to the practice of freedom, to a critical sensibility capable of advancing the parameters of knowledge, addressing crucial social issues, and connecting private troubles and public issues. What we don't need are modes of governance that reduce faculty to clerks, forms of pedagogy rooted in modes of infantilization, conformity, and repression. Instead of models of governance that vacate egalitarian and democratic principles, we need pedagogical practices that create leaders, people capable of envisioning a more just and democratic world and willing to struggle for it.

Before his untimely death, Edward Said, himself an exemplary public intellectual, urged his colleagues in the academy to confront directly those social hardships that disfigure contemporary society and pose a serious threat to the promise of democracy.[27] He urged them to assume the role of public intellectuals, wakeful and mindful of their responsibilities to bear testimony to human suffering and the pedagogical possibilities at work in educating students to be autonomous, self-reflective, and socially responsible. Said rejected the notion of a market-driven pedagogy that lacking a democratic project was steeped in the discourse of instrumental rationality and fixated on measurement. He insisted that when pedagogy is taken up as a mechanistic undertaking, it loses any understanding of what it means for students to "be thoughtful, layered, complex, critical thinker[s]."[28] For Said, the educational obsessions with mathematical utility and instrumental rationality were antithetical to a pedagogy rooted in the practice of freedom and attentive to the need to construct critical agents, democratic values, and modes of critical inquiry. On the contrary, he viewed the obsession with methods and practicality as a mode of training more suitable to creating cheerful robots and legitimating organized recklessness and legalized illegalities.

In opposition to such a debased view of educational engagement, Said argued for what he called a pedagogy of wakefulness—that is cosmopolitan and imaginative—a public affirming pedagogy that demands a critical and engaged interaction with the world we live in mediated by a responsibility for challenging structures of domination and for alleviating human suffering. This is a pedagogy that addresses the needs of multiple publics. As an ethical and political practice, a public pedagogy of wakefulness rejects modes of education removed from political or social concerns, divorced from history and matters of injury and injustice. Said's notion of a pedagogy of wakefulness includes "lifting complex ideas into the public space," recognizing human injury inside and outside of the academy, and using theory as a form of criticism to change things.[29] This is a pedagogy in which academics are neither afraid of controversy nor the willingness to make connections between private issues and broader elements of society's problems that are otherwise hidden.

I believe that Said was right in insisting that intellectuals have a responsibility to unsettle power, trouble consensus, and challenge common sense. This is a view of education that should disturb, inspire, and energize. The very notion of being an engaged public intellectual is neither foreign to nor a violation of what it means to be an academic scholar, but central to its very definition. According to Said, academics have a duty to enter into the public sphere unafraid to take positions and generate controversy, functioning as moral witnesses, raising political awareness, making connections to those elements of power and politics often hidden from public view, and reminding "the audience of the moral questions that may be hidden in the clamor and din of the public debate."[30]

The view of higher education as a democratic public sphere committed to producing young people capable and willing to expand and deepen their sense of themselves, to think the "world" critically, "to imagine something other than their own well-being," to serve the public good, take risks, and struggle for a substantive democracy has been in a state of acute crisis for the last thirty-five years.[31] When faculty assume, in this context, their civic responsibility to educate students to think critically, act with conviction, and connect what they learn in classrooms to important social issues in the larger society, they are hounded by those who demand "measurable student outcomes," as if deep learning breaks down into such discrete and quantifiable units. Or, even worse, they are derided by politicians such as Rudy Giuliani who believes that any attempt to hold established power accountable amounts to not loving one's country, and, of course, not loving Rudy and his friends. What do the diverse faculties of higher education amount to if they do not teach the practice of freedom, especially at a time when training is substituted for education?

In a society that remains troublingly resistant to or incapable of questioning itself, one that celebrates the consumer over the citizen, and all too willingly endorses the narrow values and interests of corporate power, the importance of the university as a place of critical learning, dialogue, and social justice advocacy becomes all the more imperative. As part of a broader discourse of excellence, equity, and democracy, we must defend the distinctive role that faculty play in this ongoing pedagogical project of shaping the critical rationalities through which agency is defined and civic literacy and culture produced, along with support for the institutional conditions and relations of power that make them possible.

Higher education represents one of the most important sites over which the battle for democracy is being waged. It is the site where the promise of a better future emerges out of those visions and pedagogical practices that combine hope, agency, politics, and moral responsibility as part of a broader emancipatory discourse. Academics have a distinct and unique obligation, if not political and ethical responsibility, to make learning relevant to the imperatives of a discipline, scholarly method, or research specialization. But more importantly, academics as engaged scholars can further the activation of knowledge, passion, values, and hope in the service of forms of agency that are crucial to sustaining a democracy in which higher education plays an important civic, critical, and pedagogical role.

C. Wright Mills was right in contending that academics in their roles as public intellectuals ought to transform personal troubles and concerns into social issues and problems open to critique, debate, and reason.[32] Matters of translation, connecting private troubles with larger systemic considerations, were crucial in helping "the individual become a self-educating [person], who only then would be reasonable and free."[33] Yet, Mills also believed, rightly, that criticism is not the only responsibility of public intellectuals. As Archon Fung points out, they can "also join with other citizens" to address social problems, aid popular movements, develop broad-based unions, and organizations in their efforts to advance justice, and sometimes work with governments "to construct a world that is more just and democratic."[34]

We live at a time in which public values, social provisions, and public goods are under attack, just as power is being concentrated more and more in the hands of the upper 1 percent. Higher education is under siege along with faculty, students, and unions and as such democracy itself is on life support. But history is open and there is a new spirit of resistance emerging in both the United States and around the globe. Educators must be at the forefront of such resistance, because education is central to overcoming both the crisis of ethics, public memory, and agency itself. Let me conclude by suggesting a few things that educators might do as part of this struggle to reclaim higher education in the service of democracy rather than in the service of the agents of privatization, deregulation, commodification, and the concentration of power in the hands of the few.

First, educators must go on the offensive in defending higher education as a public good. This means fighting back against a conservative-led campaign "to end higher education's democratizing influence on the nation."[35] This means defending higher education as a public good in order to reclaim its egalitarian and democratic impulses. Higher education should be harnessed neither to the demands of the warfare state nor to the instrumental needs of corporations. Clearly, in any democratic society, education should be viewed as a right, not an entitlement. This suggests that higher education in public colleges should be free. According to government figures, tuition at public colleges in 2012 was about 62.6 billion. As *Think*

Progress points out, "That's less than what the government already spends to subsidize the cost of college through grants, tax breaks, and work-study funds, which comes to about $69 billion. It spends another $107.4 billion on student loans. That means that with the money it already spends to make college affordable, the government could instead subsidize public college tuition, thereby making it free for all students. This would not just mean anyone could attend a higher education institution without worrying about cost, but it could incentivize private ones to reduce their costs in order to compete with the free option."[36] This suggests a reordering of state and federal priorities in order to make that happen. In addition, much needed revenue can be raised by putting into play even a limited number of reform policies in which, for instance, the rich and corporations would be forced to pay a fair share of their taxes, a tax would be placed on trade transactions, and tax loopholes for the wealthy would be eliminated. It is well known that the low tax rate given to corporations is a major scandal. For instance, the Bank of America paid no taxes in 2010 and "got $1.9 billion tax refund from the IRS, even though it made $4.4 billion in profits."[37]

While there is a growing public concern over rising tuition rates along with the crushing debt students are incurring, there is little public outrage from academics over the money squandered on the military budget, and billions of dollars wasted on military projects like the F-35 Stealth Fighter jet (average cost for three variants is $178 million), which over the lifetime of the project [55 years] is expected to cost $1.5 trillion dollars—and by the way they can't fly in the rain. Democracy needs a Marshall Plan in which funding is sufficient to make all levels of education free, while also providing enough social support to eliminate poverty, hunger, inadequate health care, and the destruction of the environment. There is nothing utopian about the demand to redirect money away from the military, powerful corporations, and the upper 1 percent.

Second, addressing these tasks demands a sustained critique of the transformation of a market economy into a market society along with a clear analysis of the damage it has caused both at home and abroad. Power, particularly the power of the largest corporations, has become more unaccountable and "the subtlety of illegitimate power makes it hard to identify."[38] Disposability has become the new measure of a savage form of casino capitalism in which the only value that matters is exchange value. Compassion, social responsibility, and justice are relegated to the dustbin of an older modernity that now is viewed as either quaint or a grim reminder of a socialist past.

As the welfare state is defunded and dismantled, the state turns away from enacting social provisions and becomes a punishing and surveillance state more concerned about personal security than social welfare. In this script, fear replaces compassion, and a survival of the fittest ethic replaces any sense of shared responsibility for others. This suggests—as Angela Davis, Michelle Alexander, and others have argued—that there is a need for academics and young people to become part of a broader social movement aimed at dismantling the repressive institutions that make up the punishing state. The most egregious example of which is the prison-industrial complex, which drains billions of dollars in funds to put people in jail when such funds could be used to fund public and higher education. We live in a country in which the police have become militarized, armed with weapons from the battlefields of Iraq and Afghanistan. The U.S. prison system locks up more people than any other country in the world, and the vast majority of them are people of color. Moreover, public schools are increasingly modeled after prisons and are implementing policies in which children are arrested for throwing peanuts at a school bus or violating a dress code. The punishing state is a dire threat to both public and higher education and democracy itself. The American public does not need more prisons; it needs more schools, free health services, and a living wage for all workers.

Third, academics, artists, journalists, and other young people need to connect the rise of what we might call the Wal-marting of the labor force, in both the university and the larger society, to the massive inequality in wealth and income that now corrupts every aspect of American politics and society. For instance, the Koch brothers made 3 million an hour on their dividends in 2012. Moreover, they "made enough money in one second to feed one homeless woman on food stamps for an entire year."[39] And they along with their billionaire friends are corrupting politics by buying candidates, shaping legislation with an army of lobbyists, and turning higher education into an outpost of corporate power.

The current state of inequality in higher education is most pronounced not simply in rising tuition and the growing exclusion of working and middle-class students as serious as these issues are, but in the transformation of over two-thirds of faculty positions into an army of exploited, overworked, and powerless academic labor force. This shameful Wal-marting of academic labor needs to be challenged and changed as soon as possible. Higher education will lose its critical focus and ability to teach students how to think critically and learn how to take risks as long as a large number of faculty are relegated to the status of part-time workers who are struggling just to make ends meet financially. Clearly, the call to take back higher education from the corporations and religious and political fundamentalists will not take place unless faculty are provided with full-time positions, tenure, benefits, and the power to influence the meaning, purpose, and operation of higher education. Faculty need to take back the university and reclaim modes of governance in which they have power while denouncing and dismantling the increasing corporatization of the university and the seizing of power by administrators and their staffs who now outnumber faculty on most campuses.

Fourth, academics need to fight for the rights of students to be given a formidable and critical education not dominated by corporate values, and to have a say in the shaping of their education and what it means to expand and deepen the practice of freedom and democracy. Young people have been left out of the discourse of democracy. They are the new disposables who lack jobs, a decent education, hope, and any semblance of a future better than the one their parents inherited. They are a reminder of how finance capital has abandoned any viable vision of the future, including one that would support future generations. This is a mode of politics and capital that eats its own children and throws their fate to the vagaries of the market. If any society is in part judged by how it views and treats its children, American society by all accounts has truly failed in a colossus. How else to explain the fact that over half of all public school children live in poverty and thousands of students will not have access to higher education because of rising tuition costs.

Finally, there is more at stake here than making visible the vast inequities in educational and economic opportunities and the corruption of the political process; there is also the corrosion of democracy itself. Multinational corporations have abandoned the social contract and any vestige of supporting the social state. They plunder labor and perpetuate the mechanizations of social death whenever they have the chance to accumulate capital. This issue is not simply about restoring a balance between labor and capital; it is about recognizing a new form of serfdom that kills the spirit as much as it depoliticizes the mind. The new authoritarians do not ride around in tanks, they have their own private jets, they fund right-wing think tanks, lobby for reactionary policies that privatize everything in sight while filling their bank accounts with massive profits. They are the embodiment of a culture of greed, cruelty, and disposability. Democracy in the United States is on life support and as a recent Princeton University study noted, democracy has been hijacked by a free-floating class of ultrarich and corporate powerbrokers and has been transformed into an oligarchy "where power is effectively wielded by a small number of individuals."[40]

Conclusion

The promise of educated citizens along with the enduring character of critical reflection and the search for economic, political, and racial justice lives on in the demonstrations of workers, unions, and young people all across America who are not just protesting police brutality but also marching in order to have their voices heard as part of the promise of a radical democracy along with the arrangements that give it and them a meaningful and just life. Teachers are demonstrating in Detroit, Seattle, Philadelphia, and Chicago against a barbarous neoliberalism that strips them of power, dignity, and creativity. Students are reduced to numbers and metrics and subjected to pedagogies of repression while schools are increasingly modeled after prisons. Against this dystopian vision, teachers, educators, and other cultural workers are fighting for a notion of education that is linked to hope, justice, and the promise of empowerment. At its best education is dangerous because it offers young people and other actors the promise of racial and economic justice, a future in which democracy becomes inclusive, and a dream in which all lives matter. Universities should be subversive in a healthy society; they should push against the grain, and give voice to the voiceless, the unmentionable, and the whispers of truth that haunt the apostles of unchecked power and wealth. These may be dark times, as Hannah Arendt once warned, but they don't have to be, and that raises serious questions about what educators are going to do within the current historical climate to make sure that they do not succumb to the authoritarian forces circling the university, waiting for the resistance to stop, and for the lights to go out. Resistance is no longer an option, it is a necessity.

Notes

1. John Dewey cited in E. L. Hollander, "The Engaged University," *Academe* (July/August, 2000). Online: http://www.aaup.org/publications/Academe/2000/00ja/JA00Holl.htm
2. This position has been developed fully in the works of a number of educators. See especially, Kenneth Saltman, *The Failure of Corporate School Reform* (Boulder: Paradigm, 2012); Alexander J. Means, *Schooling in the Age of Austerity: Urban Education and the Struggle for Democratic Life* (New York: Palgrave, 2013); Diane Ravitch, *Reign of Error: The Hoax of the Privatization Movement and the Danger to America's Public Schools* (New York: Vintage, 2014). See also Henry A. Giroux, *Schooling and the Struggle for Public Life* (Boulder: Paradigm, 2005).
3. This theme is take up powerfully by a number of theorists. See C. Wright Mills, *The Sociological Imagination* (New York: Oxford University Press, 2000); Richard Sennett, *The Fall of Public Man* (New York: Norton, 1974); Zygmunt Bauman, *In Search of Politics* (Stanford: Stanford University Press, 1999); and Henry A. Giroux, *Public Spaces, Private Lives* (Lanham: Rowman and Littlefield, 2001).

4. The Homeless Adjunct (Debra Leigh Scott), "How The American University was Killed, in Five Easy Steps," *The Homeless Adjunct Blog* (August 12, 2012). Online: http://junctrebellion.wordpress.com/2012/08/12/how-the-american-university-was-killed-in-five-easy-steps
5. Tony Judt, "I Am Not Pessimistic in the Very Long Run," *The Independent* (March 24, 2010). Online: http://www.independent.co.uk/arts-entertainment/books/features/tony-judt-i-am-not-pessimistic-in-the-very-long-run-1925966.html
6. Lani Guinier and Anna Deavere Smith, "Rethinking Power, Rethinking Theatre: A Conversation between Lani Guinier and Anna Deavere Smith," Theater (Winter 2002), 34–35.
7. Zygmunt Bauman, *Liquid Times* (London: Polity Press, 2007), p. 14.
8. Frank B. Wilderson III, *Red, White, & Black* (London: Duke University Press, 2012), p. 2.
9. Stanley Aronowitz, "Against Schooling: Education and Social Class," *Against Schooling* (Boulder: Paradigm Publishers, 2008), p. xii.
10. The blog of Junct Rebellion, "How The American University was Killed, in Five Easy Steps," *The Homeless Adjunct* (August 12, 2012). Online: http://junctrebellion.wordpress.com/2012/08/12/how-the-american-university-was-killed-in-five-easy-steps/
11. Scott Jaschik, "Making Adjuncts Temps—Literally," *Inside Higher Ed* (August 9, 2010). Online: http://www.insidehighered.com/news/2010/08/09/adjuncts
12. Stacey Patton, "The Ph.D. Now Comes with Food Stamps," *The Chronicle of Higher Education* (May 6, 2012). Online: http://chronicle.com/article/From-Graduate-School-to/131795/
13. Noam Chomsky, "How America's Great University System is Being Destroyed," *Alternet* (February 28, 2015). Online: http://www.alternet.org/corporate-accountability-and-workplace/chomsky-how-americas-great-university-system-getting
14. David DeGraw, "Meet the Global Financial Elites Controlling $46 Trillion in Wealth," *Alternet* (August 11, 2011). Online: http://www.alternet.org/story/151999/meet_the_global_financial_elites_controlling_$46_trillion_in_wealth
15. Editorial, "Just 8 men own same wealth as half the world," Oxfam International (January 16, 2017).Online:https://www.oxfam.org/en/pressroom/pressreleases/2017-01-16/just-8-men-own-same-wealth-half-world
16. Adam Bessie, "The Answer to the Great Question of Education Reform? The Number 42," *Truthout* (October 15, 2013). Online: http://truth-out.org/opinion/item/19356-the-answer-to-the-great-question-of-education-reform-the-number-42
17. Lizette Alvarez, "Florida May Reduce Tuition for Select Majors," *New York Times* (December 9, 2012). Online: http://www.nytimes.com/2012/12/10/education/florida-may-reduce-tuition-for-select-majors.html?_r=0
18. Ibid.; Lizette Alvarez, "Florida May Reduce Tuition for Select Majors."
19. Rebecca Schuman, "The End of Research in Wisconsin," *Slate* (March 21, 2016). Online: http://www.slate.com/articles/life/education/2016/03/university_of_wisconsin_and_the_aftermath_of_destroying_professor_tenure.html
20. Alain Badiou, *The Rebirth of History*, trans. Gregory Elliott (London: Verso, 2012), pp. 18–19.
21. See Steve Fraser, "The Politics of Debt in America: From Debtor's Prison to Debtor Nation," *TomDispatch.com* (January 29, 2013). Online: http://www.tomdispatch.com/

dialogs/print/?id=175643. On the history of debt, see David Graeber, *Debt: The First 5,000 Years* (New York: Melville House, 2012).
22. Alexander Reed Kelly, "David Graeber: 'There Has Been a War on the Human Imagination'," *Truthdig* (August 12, 2013). Online: http://www.truthdig.com/avbooth/item/david_graeber_there_has_been_a_war_on_the_human_imagination_20130812/
23. Gerry McCarthy, "*The Social Edge* Interview: Zygmunt Bauman." *The Social Edge* (February 2007). Online: http://webzine.thesocialedge.com/interviews/the-social-edge-interview-sociologist-and-author-zygmunt-bauman/.
24. Wendy Brown, *Regulating Aversion: Tolerance in the Age of Identity and Empire* (Princeton, NJ: Princeton University Press, 2006), p. 16.
25. C. Wright Mills, The Politics of Truth: Selected Writings of C. Wright Mills (New York: Oxford University Press, 2008), p. 200.
26. On this issue, see the brilliant essay: Susan Searls Giroux, "On the Civic Function of Intellectuals Today," in Gary Olson and Lynn Worsham, eds. Education as Civic Engagement: Toward a More Democratic Society (Boulder: Paradigm Publishers, 2012), pp. ix–xvii.
27. I have used this example in other pieces, and I use it again because of its power and insight.
28. Cited in Matthew Cunningham-Cook interviews Patricia William, "Re-imagining Dissent," *Guernica Magazine* (March 1, 2013). Online: http://www.guernicamag.com/interviews/re-imagining-dissent/
29. Said, *Out of Place,* p. 7.
30. Edward Said, "On Defiance and Taking Positions," *Reflections on Exile and Other Essays* (Cambridge: Harvard University Press, 2001), p. 504.
31. See, especially, Christopher Newfield, *Unmaking the Public University: The Forty-Year Assault on the Middle Class* (Cambridge: Harvard University Press, 2008).
32. C. Wright Mills, *The Sociological Imagination* (New York: Oxford University Press, 2000), p. 181.
33. Ibid.; Mills, "On Politics," p. 186.
34. Archon Fung, "The Constructive Responsibility of Intellectuals," *Boston Review* (September 9, 2011). Online: http://www.bostonreview.net/BR36.5/archon_fung_noam_chomsky_responsibility_of_intellectuals.php
35. Gene R Nichol, "Public Universities at Risk Abandoning Their Mission," *The Chronicle of Higher Education* (October 31, 2008). Online: http://chronicle.com/weekly/v54/i30/30a02302.htm
36. Bryce Covert, "How the Government Could Make Public College Free for All Students," *Think Progress* (January 12, 2014). Online: http://thinkprogress.org/education/2014/01/12/3151391/cost-public-college-free/
37. Michael Snyder, "You Won't Believe Who Is Getting Away with Paying Zero Taxes While the Middle Class Gets Hammered," *InfoWars.com* (February 19, 2013). Online: http://www.infowars.com/abolish-the-income-tax-you-wont-believe-who-is-getting-away-with-paying-zero-taxes-while-the-middle-class-gets-hammered/
38. Susan George, "State of Corporations: The rise of Illegitimate Power and the Threat to Democracy," in Transnational Institute and Occupy.com. *State of Power 2014: Exposing the Davos Class* (February 2014). Online: http://www.tni.org/sites/www.tni.org/files/download/state_of_power-6feb14.pdf

39. Paul Buchheit, "4 Ways the Koch Brothers' Wealth Is Incomprehensible," Salon (November 27, 2013). Online: http://www.salon.com/2013/11/27/4_ways_the_koch_brothers_wealth_is_incomprehensible_partner\
40. Tom McKay, "Princeton Concludes What Kind of Government America Really Has, and It's Not a Democracy," *Popular Resistance* (April 16, 2014). Online: http://www.policymic.com/articles/87719/princeton-concludes-what-kind-of-government-america-really-has-and-it-s-not-a-democracy

CHAPTER THREE

Academic Capitalism

Reflections on Higher Education in the United States and European Union

SHEILA SLAUGHTER AND BRENDAN CANTWELL

Introduction and theoretical considerations

In this chapter, we compare the way the United States and the European Union (EU) are moving higher education toward the market using the theory of academic capitalism as our analytical focus (Cantwell & Kauppinen, 2014; Slaughter & Cantwell, 2012; Slaughter & Leslie, 1997; Slaughter & Rhoades, 2004; Slaughter & Taylor, 2015). The comparison is merited given that the EU has indicated it hopes to surpass the United States in research by 2020.[1] The theory of academic capitalism teases out the ways in which new institutional and organizational structures that link state agencies, corporations, and universities developed to take advantage of the openings provided by the neoliberal state to move toward the market.

Segments of all sectors—state agencies, nongovernmental organizations (NGOs), corporations and universities—are involved. Universities are not simply acted upon by outside forces. Segments of the university, including faculty, administrators, and students, embrace market activity, while other segments are resistant (or neglected). *New circuits of knowledge* that link state agencies, corporations and universities in entrepreneurial research endeavors are developed. *New funding streams* support these knowledge constellations and *interstitial organizations*—organizations that emerge from other organizations within universities to facilitate entrepreneurial activity—facilitate the new knowledge circuits. *Intermediating networks*—or linking organizations that form intersections between the higher education sector and other domains in the political economy—then stabilize the new circuits of knowledge. At the same time, universities build *extended managerial capacity* that enables them to function as economic actors. *Narratives, discourses,* and *social technologies* that justify and normalize these changes are developed, elaborated and articulated by all the players, and deployed via social technologies. There is no particular order in which these phenomena occur. They can take place sequentially, simultaneously, independently, and always recursively. They explain how universities become marketized not only in science and engineering fields, but across a variety of fields.

A note on theory and concepts

There has been considerable interest in the topic of markets in higher education since at least the 1990s. Retrenchment of public funding, the rise of new managerial ideologies, increased revenue seeking by universities, and heightened competition in the sector all fuelled this interest. Nevertheless, in most countries, public investment still provides the bulk of funds for tertiary education. In 2011, on average, 69.2% of all higher education expenditures are financed publically, and among the EU21 countries, the share of public support is even higher (78.6%) (OECD 2014, Table B3.1). There are, however, market outliers including the UK (30.8%)—which has undergone radical market reforms since the Great Recession—and the United States (34.8%) whose higher education systems are only about one-third funded publically. And the Organisation for Economic Co-operation and Development (OECD) and EU trend is toward increased privatization as the share of funding that is derived from public sources has dropped since 2000 in nearly all countries (OECD, 2014, B3.2c).

This chapter gives greatest, though not exclusive, attention to activities related to academic research and development (R&D). Academic R&D is one area of university activity that remains largely publically funded in most academic systems, yet in the United States and increasingly in EU countries, research funds are not distributed directly to universities but are instead allocated through market-like mechanisms which require universities to compete for funds (Slaughter & Cantwell, 2012). This is to say, much of the discussion about market activity in higher education refers to market-like activity that is promoted by the state. While discussion of markets is still commonplace in higher education studies, it is perhaps more accurate to think about higher education markets as "quasi-markets," or competitive spaces crafted by policy rather than spontaneous economic processes

(Le Grand, 1991; see also Marginson, 2013; Taylor, Cantwell, & Slaughter, 2013). The term quasi-market was not used in the foundational work on academic capitalism (Slaughter & Leslie, 1997; Slaughter & Rhoades, 2004), but it is nonetheless consistent with academic capitalism theory, which has always theorized a central role for the state. For the sake of ease we use the term "market" synonymously with "quasi-market."

Before proceeding to our analysis it is useful to clarify the relationship between academic capitalism and related work. Burton Clark's (1998) concept of the *entrepreneurial university* has been widely influential. Clark argued a turbulent environment with competing demands required that universities to strengthen their administrative core in order to engage in activities that increase new sources of revenue, decrease reliance on the state, and craft new missions that meet environmental demands. Similarly, the concept of "third mission" activities has been influential in Europe and Latin America and describes efforts by universities to generate revenue and respond to social demands (Laredo, 1997). These concepts differ from the theory of academic capitalism because they tend to be based on institutional theory, do not attend clearly to power relations, and do not attend to the structural relations that draw together higher education, the state, and market sectors.

Analysis and comparison of EU and U.S. moves toward the market

Intermediating organizations

Over time, the term neoliberalism has been so widely used as to have lost some of its analytic power, and often requires specification to indicate what aspects of neoliberalism are important for any given analyses. In this chapter, we see neoliberalism as a preference on the part of individuals, nonprofits, corporate leaders, and the state to use markets to attain wage growth, innovation, economic stability, and policy goals, including social welfare platforms, such as universal higher education. In neoliberal states, intermediating organizations span public, nonprofit, and for-profit organizations, working across them to shape policy, and soften and redraw boundaries, reconfiguring these spaces so they are more amenable to the market. In the United States, such intermediating organizations proliferated from the late 1970s. With regard to research policy, examples are the Carnegie Commission on Science, Technology and Government, the Belfer Center for Science and International Affairs, the Brookings Institution, the American

Enterprise Institute, and the Council on Competitiveness. A classic example in the United States is the Business-Higher Education Forum, which deliberately brought together chief executive officers (CEOs) from industry and academe to craft policy narratives that specified the way tertiary education should contribute to competitiveness. Started in the late 1970s, the Forum saw the private sector as the engine of social progress: "*Thus, the Forum makes only one overall recommendation: as a nation, we must develop a consensus that industrial competitiveness is crucial to our social and economic well-being*" (italics in the original, Business-Higher Education Forum, 1983). The proper work of government was to create a "climate for competitiveness" (Business-Higher Education Forum, 1986; Slaughter, 1990). The Business-Higher Education Forum produced position papers and lobbied Congress to create Bayh-Dole type legislation, which, like the namesake U.S. law, allow universities and private entities to benefit financially from publically funded research discoveries, as well as tax-free financial instruments called individual education accounts to which people could contribute funds that could later be withdrawn to pay for educational programs designed to retrain workers for jobs in the new economy.

The EU competitiveness trajectory had some similarities with the United States. Beginning in the 1980s, groups of European political and business elites began to lobby and operate within European institutions in order to enact neoliberal polices and establish a discourse on European global competitiveness (Bieler & Morton, 2001). For example, the European Round Table of Industrialists (ERT), a group comprised of around 50 CEOs and chairmen from large European corporations, convened to influence the European policy agenda. ERT lobbied heavily before and after the Treaty of Maastricht to establish EU-wide consensus for public institutions to aid the private sector in the efficient allocation of labor within the common European market (van Apeldoorn, 2000).

In February 2008, the EU held the first meeting of a newly created Higher Education-Business Forum. The Forum brought together university administrators, European Commissioners, representatives from chambers of commerce, and business executives, to network and coordinate the activities of academia and industry in order for Europe's educational institutions to better serve the smart economy. In justifying the forum, European Commissioner Juan Figel explained, "Europe has been too weak for too long in bringing the worlds of university academia and business enterprise together, to achieve successful commercial exploitation of academic excellence" (Europa, 2008).

Intermediating organizations span public, nonprofit, and for-profit sectors, and realign the boundaries among states, state agencies, nonprofits, and for-profits. The professionals who staff these intermediating organizations circulate among the various sectors carrying discourse, narratives, and ideologies. Sometimes they represent corporate elites, as in the case of the Business-Higher Education Forum in the United States as well as the Higher Education-Business Forum and EIT in Europe. At other times they are composed largely of professional organizations, some of which are not directly related to the economy, as is the case with the EC's expert committees and U.S. organizations such as the National Academy of Sciences. Although diverse, the participants in intermediating organizations represent a rather limited segment of society. For the most part, they are business elites, middle to high-ranking government officials, and/or professionals with advanced degrees. They usually see advantage from rearranging the traditional, distinct sectors of state, nonprofits, and for-profits to create new opportunities configured in a neoliberal frame.

Narratives, discourses and social technologies

Beginning in the 1980s, human capital and competitiveness discourses were among the major narratives that circulated around and through intermediating organizations, research universities, and various policy groups in the United States and Europe. As they gained strength, in great part because of the way they slotted into neoliberal market narratives, social technologies such as audit exercises, league tables, and varieties of rankings and benchmarks were used to assess the success of universities in various aspects of competition. These social technologies were made possible by quantitative developments that depended on information technology, such as citation indices and patent data, which in turn reinforced certain types of social science.

The discourses in the United States and EU are somewhat different. In the United States, human capital was the higher education discourse that intersected broader competitiveness narratives. As is typical in the United States, the human capital narrative emphasized the role of the individual, thereby converting higher education into a private good (Becker, 1964; Leslie & Brinkman, 1988; McMahon, 2009). Complementing human capital discourses were competitiveness narratives, which were initiated by corporate leaders and nonprofit think tanks in the 1980s (Bruno, 2009; Slaughter, 1990; Slaughter & Rhoades, 2005) to deal with the stiff competition the United States faced from Germany and Japan. Students' investment in human capital was represented as serving not only individuals' ends, but societal needs for a highly educated labor force to build a strong economy. In other words, societal goods were conceived of in economic terms, rather than social goods or social justice. Like human capital discourses, competitiveness narratives were also taken up by the intermediating organizations discussed above, as well as by some university staff, some academic disciplines and some faculty, many of whom demonstrated their closeness to the market through patenting, technology transfer, and product and technology innovation. The competitiveness and human capital narratives stress investment in education that contributes to productivity, economic growth, health, environmental issues, and national defense. These types of education create a "scientifically literate" population and are predicated on a workforce versed in STEM fields. The humanities, arts, and social science fields not concerned with social technologies are, by and large, not mentioned.

During this period, human capital theory also became prominent among international organizations and trading blocs in Europe. Building on legal architecture established by the Treaty of Rome, the European Community organized the Education Committee in 1974 with a near-exclusive focus on vocational education and training. Cooperation in market-oriented training was expected to boost the Continent's stock of human capital, thereby reducing unemployment and increasing labor mobility. Hence, a market development narrative and legal framework undergirded the establishment of a European educational space (Ertl, 2006).

The Lisbon Agenda elaborated on the EU competitive narrative. Using language of the academic capitalist knowledge/learning regime, the often cited Lisbon Agenda aims were to make Europe the most competitive region in the world (European Commission, 2000). Higher education was integral to the Lisbon Agenda, which calls for economic competitiveness through the interaction between the state, industry, and universities in networks of innovation driven by application and production of knowledge. Lisbon goals include expanding public and private funds for R&D, industry–university partnerships, establishing EU-wide networks of lifelong learning, and boosting tertiary participation, especially in science and technology fields. In 2006, the EC made the case that "European universities have enormous potential, but this potential is not fully harnessed and put to work effectively to underpin Europe's drive for more growth and more jobs" (European Commission, 2006, p. 3) and a detailed plan for "modernizing" Europe's universities, which largely focused on further market reforms, was announced.

Human capital and competitiveness narratives and discourses are often developed in intermediating organizations that span public, private and non or linking organizations that form intersections between the higher education sector and other domains in the political economy profit organizations, and reconfigure those sectors in ways that promote individuals, markets, and competition in spaces designed to foster the success of knowledge economy corporations. Science and engineering located in universities are often targets of the narratives.

The discourses, narratives, and social technologies underline the opportunities available to faculty and nonfaculty professionals for engaging in competition for external resources, cooperation with industry, attainment of bench or linking organizations that form intersections between the higher education sector and other domains in the political economy marks, and success in rankings. Some social sciences provide the methods, theoretical frameworks, and concepts (which are simultaneously discourses and narratives themselves) for social technologies such as bibliometrics (the analysis of academic article citations), rankings and league tables, soft law and Open Method of Coordination (OMC) that turn the attention of faculty and fields to the narratives by providing incentives designed to gently nudge professionals' activities in line with policy goals.

Interstitial organizations

Groups within universities often intersect intermediating organizations and the opportunities they provide through interstitial organizations, which then become bearers of the narratives and discourses of human capital and competitiveness. Interstitial organizations emerge from the interstices of existing organizations within the university (Mann, 1986, Slaughter & Rhoades, 2004). Obvious interstitial organizations are those that deal with research commercialization or technology transfer. These began to expand in the United States following the passage of the Bayh-Dole Act in 1980. Over the 1980s and 1990s, research universities across the United States established technology transfer offices that supported the process of patenting research discoveries and developing spin-off companies. For the most part, personnel within universities developed and pursued these initiatives. For example, technology transfer offices were often staffed by scientists, engineers, and lawyers initially lodged in more traditional units, as were the managers of university-sponsored business incubators and research parks that followed. These units enjoyed substantial state and institutional investment, and their purpose was to produce patentable intellectual property and innovative technologies, generating revenues from university science and technology and building the economy (Link, 2006).

In the United States, interstitial organizations emerged spontaneously from within universities to intersect incrementally opportunities such as those created by Bayh-Dole at the state and national levels. In the EU, the development of interstitial organizations often seems not to have occurred through spontaneous adaptations to regulatory opportunities. Rather, states and universities frequently worked together to develop economic strategy to set the agenda for establishing intersecting structures through which innovation and commercialization occur. As knowledge transfer units (similar to U.S. technology transfer offices) were created, they began to develop a dense web of networks across a number of European countries.

The European Commission Frameworks programs encouraged university and national efforts to stimulate knowledge transfer by providing "systematic procedure[s]" for setting R&D and technology transfer agendas, policies, and infrastructure. Beginning with the Third Framework from 1991 to 1994 research, technology and development policy has been placed at the forefront of European innovation and competition. The Seventh Framework and Lisbon agreements amount to a more concerted effort to establish a European Research Area (ERA) in which trans-EU university/industry collaboration and innovation are central to the Commission's stated goal of making the EU the most competitive innovation region in the world (Breschi & Cusmano, 2004). The commission incentivised the development of technology transfer organizations by funding trans-sector research networks, intending the institutionalization of knowledge transmission and innovation.

These interstitial organizations act like switching devices, chanelling energy, effort, and revenues to the new circuits of knowledge. They create new careers and a host of new rewards. Because these opportunities emerge interstitially, they often built on or related to the activities that were core to organizations and offices out of which they grew. However, they switch the activities to entrepreneurial circuits, recruiting energies of faculty and nonacademic professionals within universities, committing them to academic capitalist knowledge/learning regimes.

Expanded managerial capacity

At the same time that interstitial organizations emerged from the interstices of traditional organizations such as departments, centers, and institutes, the managerial structures of universities were changing rapidly to enable universities to conform with and participate in shaping relations with neoliberal states. Although there is great diversity in management modes among and between universities in the United States and EU, there is a general trend toward increased corporate-like governance of higher education through three interrelated processes. First, interstitial organizations are being institutionalized, contributing to expanded managerial capacity. Second, university management is expanding on a number of dimensions and the new managers are shifting the human resources profile within higher education intuitions. Third, universities are expanding managerial capacity to monitor, incent, and discipline the increasing and highly differentiated numbers of faculty and nonacademic professionals that make up the growing tertiary education workforce.

In the United States, expansion of managerial capacity is presided over by boards of trustees or regents working closely with "executive management" (presidents, chancellors, provosts, vice presidents). These governing boards, whether public or private, are designed to provide universities some autonomy. The trustees or regents are largely comprised of corporate CEOs and professionals external to academe—for example, senior partners in law or medical firms—who are responsible for management of the universities and their endowments. Many of the trustees of private American Association of University members are CEOs of Fortune 500 corporations and sit on the boards of directors of other Fortune 500 corporations (Pusser, Slaughter, & Thomas, 2006). Historically, these trustees or regents had fiduciary responsibility, which meant they were held legally to a very high standard of trust. However, in keeping with broader changes in the neoliberal state, that responsibility was altered in 1998, at which point the Supreme Court declared that trustees of institutions of higher learning will be held to the same (and lower) standard of conduct as trustees of corporations (Kavanaugh, 2010). Since the 1980s, trustees/regents and executive management have governed and managed in ways that make universities a space that supports marketization, ranging from faculty intellectual property to recruitment of full fees–paying overseas students.

Trustees often delegate to university executive managers, who in turn have utilized successions of management systems that are similar to New Public Management, which stressed marketization of state and supranational agencies, including national university systems, to improve economy and efficiency (Deem, 2001, 2004; Deem, Mok, & Lucas, 2008). Generally, these management systems privilege management authority over decisions by faculty collegiums, asserting the rights of managers to assess, reward, and regulate academic work.

U.S. university managers have changed the human resources profile of universities, so they resemble the human resources profile of "smart" economy corporations. Colleges and universities are increasingly moving away from a human resources profile of relatively large numbers of full-time permanent faculty who make decisions through vehicles like faculty senates to a managerial model comprised of increasing numbers of contingent faculty and researchers managed by growing numbers of nonacademic professionals and managers (Schuster & Finkelstein, 2006). Thirty-five years ago, 75% of faculty were eligible for tenure and only 25% were adjunct or contingent or non-track. Today those trends are reversed (Bousquet, 2008). By 2007, part-time faculty accounted for nearly half of all academics (National Center for Educational Statistics, 2009), with full-time, tenured, or tenure-eligible faculty members rapidly becoming a minority among the ranks of U.S.-based academics.

However, U.S. university human resources profiles differ from corporate profiles in an important respect. U.S. universities have greatly expanded the number of nonacademic professionals, so their management structures are far from lean. Tertiary institutions in the United States now have more nonacademic professionals than faculty members. In fall 2007, at the national postsecondary level, professional staff (nonacademic professionals) without faculty status constituted a greater share (53%) of full-time professional employees than faculty members (47%). These nonacademic professionals make approximately the same salaries as faculty, and like faculty, the salaries are highly differentiated (Knapp, Kelly-Reid, Ginder, & Miller, 2008).

Many European countries are seeking to give universities more autonomy and create stronger executive management. The justification for reform is that universities need to be more competitive in terms of excellence indicators, to be more attractive with regard to international student mobility, to create universities that are better able to prepare students for work in the knowledge economy, thus promoting economic development, and to better intersect new funding streams from the European Research Council (ERC) and U.S. funding agencies (European University Association, 2009). Autonomy usually involves greater separation of the university from the state, for example, through eliminating employee civil service status. Universities are increasingly engaging in corporate-like financial management that involves investment, leverage, and the acquisition of financial risk (Cantwell, in press), that sometimes have "satellite" legal entities, and "arms-length" foundations and boards that are able to engage in a wide variety of market transactions. European universities are beginning to shift toward "CEO type leader[s]" with executive management groups that exercise enhanced decision-making power as well as greater authority over budget and decision-making regarding staffing patterns. However, salary differentiation among staff has occurred slowly. The trend for boards is toward dual systems, which are now more widespread than traditional unitary boards. The boards include external "stakeholders," who sometimes have a full role in decision-making (Estermann & Nokkala, 2009).

University management has expanded dramatically. Executive managers hired large numbers of nonacademic professionals as interstitial organizations focused on market opportunities were institutionalized. At the same time, management created new human resource profiles, in which the full-time faculty numbers decreased relative to broadly increased contingent academic labor. In the United States, this shift is more marked than in Europe, and has contributed to the growth of salary disparity within fields, with savings from contingent labor being concentrated on fields close to the market.

Like U.S. universities, European university managers are using their executive authority to alter human resource profiles. The numbers of contingent faculty in the EU-15 are growing, as are the numbers of nonacademic professionals (Ackers & Gill, 2005; Rhoades & Sporn, 2002) and now account for approximately 43%

of academic staff (Eurostat, 2010a, 2010b). Although Eurostat does not collect data on nonacademic professionals, studies from individual countries suggest that numbers of nonacademic professionals are increasing. For example, in Norway, the number of nonacademic middle management professionals has increased substantially (Gornitzka & Larsen, 2004).

At the EC level, national efforts toward competition and "excellence" are promoted through "soft law" and OMC that use social technologies such as framework implementation and various rating systems as well as grants competitions to steer national systems in the directions outlined above. As is the case with managers of neoliberal states, university management is now able to act in public, nonprofit, and for-profit venues. They can deploy activities among these sectors for strategic advantage. For example, relatively "autonomous" U.S. public universities can often borrow in private bond markets for building loans and direct their students toward student aid loans from private corporations, while nonprofits like Harvard or Yale can draw on the resources of the state to guarantee bonds, receive aid for their students from state and federal governments, and of course compete for federal research funds, all while not paying taxes. Both public and nonprofit universities can create arms-length nonprofit appendages, such as advisory boards, whose membership is often drawn from corporations with research interests in the colleges, centers, and institutes they advise. They can also create for-profit arms-length foundations or satellite entities that handle for-profit activity, executing contracts and granting licenses through technology transfer offices. Both public and nonprofit universities have endowments to which private citizens and corporations can make donations, greatly reducing their income tax.

In short, universities are increasingly managed as neoliberal institutions. As NGOs with industrial interconnections, universities have access to public funds that can be used to generate commercializable knowledge. Public support for universities can act as inverse redistribution, that is a reverse "Robin Hood" process, when public funds are chanelled through universities in the service of commercial interests.

New circuits of knowledge and new funding streams

New circuits of knowledge are characterized by increased intensity and frequency of activities that generate revenue, are markers of success in R&D quasi-markets, or facilitate knowledge economy innovation and development. Examples include publishing, especially the results of applied scientific research, patenting, licensing, start-ups and other entrepreneurial activities, such as university funding of research parks and incubators. New funding streams are often discussed in the narratives and discourses about entrepreneurial science as if they are tightly coupled and market-related. For example, revenues for patents are represented as contributing substantially to university general funds, and successful innovations based on academic discoveries are presented as an enticement for industry to contribute more funding to academic R&D. However, patents have not provided substantial revenue streams for most universities, and industry contributions to academic R&D have fallen off. In many instances, funds for entrepreneurial science are not market-derived. Rather, new circuits of knowledge are funded primarily by redirecting and expanding government funding streams for academic research, or by new government funding streams. Moreover, government research funding in the United States and EU is increasingly concentrated on STEM fields, directing resources to areas where there are relatively few undergraduate students. Resources for entrepreneurial science are also funded by diversion of traditional resource flows—for example, rapidly increasing undergraduate tuition has paid part of the rising costs of research. Fee-paying international students, usually undergraduates, are an exception, providing fresh revenue streams from private markets for the United States and EU.

In the United States, research universities' circuits of knowledge began to be reformatted in the 1980s. Before 1981, fewer than 250 patents were issued to U.S. universities each year. Between 1991 and 1999, annual college and university invention disclosures increased 63%, to 12,114. New patents filed increased 77% to 5,545, and new licenses and options executed by universities increased by 129% to 3,914. Between 1980 and 2001, at least 3,807 new companies were formed based on licenses from academic institutions (National Science Board, 2008). When similar statistics are reviewed for 2003 and 2007, invention disclosures grew from 13,700 in 2003 to 17,700 in 2007. Patent applications increased from 7,200 to 10,900. By 2009, there were 3,148 cumulative operating start-ups associated with U.S. university patenting and licensing activities (National Science Board, 2002, 2008, 2010). Despite broad reformatting of research university circuits of knowledge to strengthen entrepreneurial science, funding streams from technology transfer activity continue to be highly concentrated in a small number of institutions. In 2007, many university technology transfer offices reported negative income (National Science Board, 2010).

In large part, the federal government and academic institutions themselves have supported the research that makes possible patents, licenses, and start-ups. Currently, the federal government accounts for about 63% of academic R&D, and institutions about 19%. At its peak, industry contributed 7–8% of funding for academic R&D, and currently is down to about 3–5%. The relatively small and declining portion of academic R&D funded by industry in the United States demonstrates industry collaborations do not serve as a funding panacea as promised in narratives on entrepreneurial science. State support remains central for academic science, though state funding patterns have shifted.

Overall, federal academic R&D funds are concentrated in STEM fields, which account for roughly 96% of all funding. The social sciences experienced the largest decrease of any fields in share of R&D funds over the past three decades, dropping by more than half from 7.5% in 1975 to 3.6% in 2006. The humanities are excluded from U.S. academic R&D statistics altogether (National Science Board, 2010).

Similar patterns are emerging in Europe. The EU new circuits of knowledge linking industry with academe were initiated in the late 1980s and have grown over the past 25 years, most recently with support from the European Commission. The European Centre for Strategic Management of Universities (ESMU)—a think tank linking university managers with commercial sectors and the state—was established in 1986. From 1987 to 1995, ESMU administered the Commission-funded COMETT I and COMETT II programs designed to bring university technologies to market. The COMETT programs resulted in over 200 industry–academy partnerships placed over 35,000 students in industrial employment and facilitated the exchange of over 1,000 technology transfer personnel between universities and firms. ESMU is a hub for integrating circuitry through which industrial knowledge transfer occurs but also serves as circuitry through which norms and practices related to the management of universities in knowledge economies flows. European circuits of innovation span university–government–industry sectors but are knit tightly around science and technology interests.

The newly created European Research Council has made new streams of research funds available for the ERA through the Seventh Framework. Over the period 2007–2013, the ERC awarded 7.5 billion in research grants. Investigators can win up to 2 million per grant, which may last up to 5 years (European Research Council, 2008). Grants are made through two streams, one for advanced investigators and one for starting investigators who completed their Ph.D. within the last 9 years in life sciences, physical science and engineering, social sciences and humanities "domains." The ERC (2007) prioritized projects in information technology, "innovative" medicine, nano-electronics, embedded systems, aeronautics and air transport, hydrogen and fuel cells, and global monitoring for the environment. As is the case in the United States, research funds are concentrated in STEM fields, and especially the biomedical sciences, although not so heavily.

The number of patents originating in EU universities has increased substantially over recent decades, but the absolute numbers remain small. In 1990, there were 96 EU patents, by 2003 this number increased by 33% to 127. Although there has been an annual ebb and flow, universities accounted for about 9% of all European patents approved from 1990 to 2003 (Eurostat, 2009). However, 80% of patents with an academic inventor did not originate in universities, suggesting that European companies do not rely on university technology transfer offices for knowledge transfer and that laws conferring ownership of knowledge discovered in academe on universities are not yet widespread in Europe.

In the United States, federal academic R&D funding was not the only new or expanded revenue stream for entrepreneurial universities. Rapidly increasing tuition fees have also been a growing source of revenues for U.S. colleges and universities. In recent years, the price of tuition has increased much faster than the rate of inflation (Ehrenberg, 2000). Universities have seen increasing fees as an easy way to boost revenues and students have tolerated these increases in part because of readily available federally guaranteed loans. Some tuition revenues have been diverted to entrepreneurial science and technology, suggesting that instruction suffers relative to research.

International students represent an important and growing source of income for U.S. universities. Overall, the graduate and undergraduate international student market generated over $13.3 billion in 2007. However, overseas fees do not benefit all fields equally. International students are concentrated in a handful of fields and many universities' financial policies allow colleges and departments to retain a portion of international students' tuition fees. International students prefer business, science, and engineering.

New funding streams in EU countries include direct state investment as well as tuition fees from both EU and overseas students. While the Bologna process focuses on intra-European mobility, Lisbon sets out an agenda to market the European higher education area to fee-paying students from outside of the region. The Lisbon agreement calls for member countries to change funding formulas so that student fees represent a greater share of university revenues.

Recruiting international students is an integral part of the Lisbon strategy. Large higher education systems in the region have indeed attracted substantial and increasing numbers of international students. Unlike the United States where around one-quarter of international students are funded by their host institution (Institute for International Education, 2009), mostly as teaching and research assistants at the graduate level, nearly all international students from outside the EU (graduate and undergraduate) at European universities are full fees–paying students relying on personal or home country resources. These high fee–paying students have provided substantial new funding streams for universities in these countries. However, 72.8% of all international students in the EU are concentrated in three countries—the UK, Germany, and France—which enjoy substantial revenues from international student fees. And most are in social science and business or STEM fields.

In sum, new funding streams emerged in the United States and EU that contributed to reformatting circuits of knowledge. Although the narratives and discourses surrounding entrepreneurial science suggest that new circuits of knowledge will generate new revenue streams from for-profit markets for universities, for the most part that has not happened. The majority of funding for academic R&D, entrepreneurial or other, continues to be governmental. Moreover, the way the academic R&D funding streams are channeled benefits elite research universities in the United States, and wealthy countries with strong research universities in Europe (UK, Germany, France), and STEM fields, that, at the undergraduate level have relatively few students. Ironically, marketization of research, technology, and innovation has occurred primarily through state funding.

Implications and conclusion

The implications of these transatlantic moves are many, and to be fully understood require situated case studies that tease out consequences. Nonetheless, our analysis is suggestive of broad implications for states, intuitions, and academic disciplines. Implications of moves to the market include endless competition, uneven development, and increased exposure to market failure.

Endless competition in academic outputs is likely in the vision of smart economies articulated by those who see universities as central to national competition. Academic arms races are not new—the unbridled pursuit to amass nuclear weapons during the Cold War was driven by armies of physicists and engineers. Contemporary competition between the EU and United States to become first in the smart economy may not risk mutually assured destruction but does imply a (possibly endless) ratcheting-up of rhetoric, costs, and governance technologies. Given that there is no finish line in a race to be most excellent and most innovative, competitors are compelled to maintain a drive to excellence. And resources are needed to keep the throttle down and competition agendas rattling forward.

In the United States, where expenditures on higher education and R&D account for a greater share of gross domestic product (GDP) than in most EU countries, new funding streams emerged in the form of targeted state investment and increased private spending (mostly in the form of tuition fees). High fees have led to high debt; in just the 2008–2009 academic year students in the United States borrowed $75.1 billion to finance the cost of higher education (Chaker, 2009). These high expenditures are rationalized by the need to maintain excellence and global competitiveness but place high debt burdens on young workers and may have long-term impacts on the national economy.

Despite increased federal funding, the U.S. share of articles and article citation has declined. Between 1998 and 2008, the U.S. share of world articles declined from 34% in 1998 to 29% in 2008, while its share of total citations in science and engineering articles declined from 47% to 38%. The decline is likely explained by increased competition from other countries, many of which are new entrants in the world class university game. The United States continues to have the highest number of highly cited articles, but maintenance of the U.S. position is costly.

In Europe, the Commission has generated new streams of funding, yet calls to nations within the EU to substantially increase the share of GDP for higher education have not been fully met. There are two paths to stay in the higher education arms race, and both are challenging. One is for states to substantially increase higher education expenditures, which has not happened yet and seems unlikely for many EU countries given the fiscal restraints they are experiencing. The second option is to continue to introduce and increase tuition (student) fees across the continent in order to raise private higher education expenditures. While this approach appears likely, it is unclear to what extent students and their families will tolerate increased tuition fees given the pushback countries like Germany experienced.

Uneven development is a hallmark of neoliberal economic organization. The United States experienced growing income inequality since the 1980s (Saez, 2009), and the gap between the rich and poor in European countries appears to have been expanding since the 1990s (Harjes, 2007). Academic moves to the market are also associated with patterns of uneven development. Individual institutions and academics, as well as fields of study, have entered new circuits of knowledge and have tapped into new funding streams while others have been left behind. At the institutional level this gap is most apparent in the United States with the growing inequality of resources and faculty salaries between well-to-do nonprofit universities (which receive substantial public support) and public universities (Alexander, 2000; Taylor, in press), but is also apparent within universities, where faculty in innovative STEM fields on average make substantially more than faculty in the fine arts and/or humanities. In the EU, institutional stratification is occurring through differential state funding structures including performance-based funding models, which have employed assessment technologies (e.g., Research Assessment Exercise in the UK; Centers of Excellence initiative in Germany) in resource distribution. These research performance funding systems, which have been introduced in a number of EU countries, appear to be associated with initial surges in research production, but in the medium and long terms will concentrate resources in a relatively few institutions, and are therefore unlikely to achieve production efficiencies, and consequently may inhibit innovative activities most likely to benefit society (Geuna & Martin, 2003).

Increased exposure to market failure is another likely implication of the market moves we have described. Exposure to market failure can be understood in at least three ways. First, increased managerial capacity, targeted funding streams, and exclusive knowledge circuits, all nested within narratives that extol the value of science and engineering in knowledge economies, have led to heightened investment and managerial focus on a limited array of academic pursuits. Moreover, these few and privileged academic activities are increasingly reliant on private markets through industry–academy collaborations, commercialized knowledge, and spin-off firm development. If the markets connected to these activities—biotechnology, energy, information technology, for example—were to collapse like the dot-com industry in the 2000s, many universities may be exposed to limited returns on their investments and erosion of legitimacy, with few other assets to fall back upon. In other words, there are risks to putting all the eggs in one basket. Even if entrepreneurial activities represent only a fraction of institutions' income at most universities, singular devotion to such pursuits exposes institutions to risk in the eventuality that these activities fail to bear fruit. Second, universities are also exposed to failure in the market. There is no guarantee that efforts to compete in academic enterprise will be successful, either in traditional academic measures such as publication output or in market measures including patent and technology transfer income.

Universities are encouraged to become market facing in order to diversify funding streams and reduce reliance on the state. And while academic capitalism has heralded new funding streams, the number of these streams has proved limited and many institutions compete for the same rather narrow band of resources such as overseas student fees, patent royalties, partnerships with publishers, and industry funding for research. In only a few areas, such as overseas students, has the market expanded much and in most cases a large number of organizations are competing for a limited set of rewards. As institutions increasingly concentrate their efforts in a narrow array of academic markets, the chances of any individual competitor to experience success would appear to decline. We suspect that a likely outcome of moves to the market is those institutions already most successful in knowledge economies will extend their advantage over institutions less well positioned to compete. Substantial investment in market activities is a losing proposition for many universities.

Third, the neoliberal state and deregulated market economy may pose the largest risk of market failure for universities. So long as the economy was expanding, universities were able to compete for increased funds for innovation, but large bank and corporate failures that set off the deep market crisis of 2009 have slowed universities. In the United States, the effects are reaching down to the states in 2010—most dramatically California, Arizona, Nevada, and Florida—as tax receipts drop dramatically. In the EU, Greece, Spain, Ireland, Portugal, and even the UK (where demand for higher education vastly exceeds capacity) now face deep structural deficits. Though the European context is more complicated and may not be attributed entirely to deregulation, the boom and bust cycles of neoliberal capitalism have clearly contributed to the financial calamity. Despite the market rhetoric, public funds, whether from regional, local, federal, or supranational state agencies, provide the greatest revenue source for research universities. Ironically, they may have to tap their largest clientele—undergraduate students—with prices close to the real cost of higher education to keep meeting classes.

Initially, the theory of academic capitalism focused on four mechanisms: new circuits of knowledge (patenting, start-ups), interstitial bodies (technology transfer offices, research parks), intermediating organizations (the Business-Higher Education Forum, IET) and expanded managerial capacity (Slaughter & Rhoades, 2004). Slaughter and Cantwell (2012) added new funding streams, narratives, discourses, and social technologies. Currently, we argue that mechanisms promoting academic capitalism are proliferating, concomitantly intensifying competition, and becoming more common in the EU.

Over time, many organizations that emerged interstitially became *institutionalized*. These organizations also have tended to expand managerial capacity, allowing changes to be made more thoroughly and quickly, intensifying activity surrounding many mechanisms and developing new ones. *Repurposing* existing organizations is yet another mechanism for strengthening the academic capitalist knowledge/learning regime. For example, the busar's office at U.S. colleges and universities traditionally was, as McPherson and Schapiro (1998) famously put it, little more than a charitable organization directing limited institutional funds to needy and deserving students. Over time, however, this office has morphed into "enrollment management" enterprises, with multiple professional staff focused on "bringing in the class" that has the right mixture of high tuition–paying students, high scoring students, students representing targeted segments of the general population, and "legacies," students whose parents have attended the university in question, often for generations, and who are likely to give generously.

In sum, mechanisms for moving universities ever more deeply into competitive spaces are proliferating and deepening. These changes reinforce and accelerate academic capitalist processes. Examples include new funding streams, changing narratives and discourses, emerging social technologies, expanding managerial authority, and the repurposing of existing organizations. These mechanisms embody actors, organizations and opportunity structures, and have opened up large spaces that do not focus on the interaction of faculty and students in classrooms or research laboratories. Rather than focusing directly on educational activities—indeed, sometimes at the expense of operational efficiency and effectiveness—they often support competitions for external revenues. Indeed, the standard practice of research universities in this new environment is to ratchet up competition in the areas that "count"—success in research, entrepreneurial engagement with industry and finance and endowment management. Research universities accumulate these resources by deploying academic capitalist mechanisms early and often.

The chapter has described in some detail the ways in which policy and other mechanisms draw universities into market-facing positions, encouraging higher education to be more entrepreneurial and entangling the sector in a dense set of ties that link the academy with the state and market. As discussed at the start of the chapter, in the 1990s there was a great deal of interest in higher education markets. This reflected real shifts in policy and organizational behavior in the sector, but also both the neoliberal market exuberance that followed the fall of the Soviet Union and the powerful critiques leveled at utopian market ideologies and policy regimes. While understanding university–market connections remains important, it is no longer sufficient to claim that marketization is occurring without engaging in careful and nuanced consideration of the contradictions of higher education markets, not least of which is that they are primarily state sponsored.

The market project has been uneven. In the UK, for example, market reforms have dominated higher education policy while in Germany, and perhaps more extremely Chile, such reforms have met stiff resistance and have been peeled back. The market for overseas students is robust but only a few countries have been able to substantially cash in on overseas revenue. Similarly, transfer of university-derived technology to the private market is a common policy goal but the overall track record of market success in this endeavor has been mixed. As the case of the EU suggests, it may be now that the modus operandi of academic capitalism is to make a profit, which is after all the ultimate objective of capitalist economic systems, but to support political and economic interests related to national and regional competiveness.

Does this indicate the arrival of a post-marketization period in higher education? We see this as an interesting proposition but one that can only be assessed through careful conceptualization and rigorous empirical analysis. One of the major contributions of the theory of academic capitalism has been to provide a set of conceptual and empirical tools for tracing relations between higher education, the state, and market actors, as well as the mechanisms that initiate and regulate these relations (Cantwell & Kauppinen, 2014). As capitalist societies and economies change so will universities, which are important social intuitions. Future research into academic capitalism will be most fruitful not when it makes singular and absolute claims about the pitfalls or benefits of marketization but when it builds upon existing conceptual and empirical tools to understand the mechanisms that shape the relationship between universities and the societies in which they exist.

Note

1. This chapter is a condensed and updated version of Slaughter and Cantwell (2012).

References

Ackers, L., & Gill, B. (2005). Attracting and retaining early career researchers in English higher education. *Innovation: The European Journal of Social Science Research*, *18*, 277–299.

Alexander, F. K. (2000). The silent crisis: The relative fiscal capacity of public universities to compete for faculty. *Review of Higher Education*, *24*(2), 113–129.

Becker, G. S. (1964). *Human capital: A theoretical and empirical analysis, with special reference to education*. National Bureau of Economic Research, General Series, no. 80. New York, NY: Columbia University Press.

Bieler, A., & Morton, A. D. (Eds.). (2001). *Social forces and the making of the New Europe: Restructuring European social relations in the global political economy*. Basingstoke: Palgrave Macmillan.

Bousquet, M. (2008). *How the university works: Higher education and the low-wage nation*. New York, NY: New York University Press.

Breschi, S., & Cusmano, L. (2004). Unveiling the texture of a European research area: Emergence of oligarchic networks under EU framework programmes. *International Journal of Technology Management*, *27*(8), 747–772.

Bruno, I. (2009). The "indefinite discipline" of competitiveness benchmarking as a neoliberal technology of government. *Minerva*, *47*, 261–280.

Business-Higher Education Forum. (1983). *America's competitive challenge: The need for a national response*. Resource document. Business-Higher Education Forum.

Business-Higher Education Forum. (1986). *An action agenda for American competitiveness*. Resource document. Business-Higher Education Forum.

Cantwell, B. (2016. The new prudent man and financial academic capitalism. In Slaughter, S. & Taylor, B. J. (Eds.), *Stratification, privatization and vocationalization of higher education in the US and EU: Competitive advantage*. Springer Books.

Cantwell, B., & Kauppinen, I. (Eds.). (2014). *Academic capitalism in the age of globalization*. Baltimore, MD: Johns Hopkins University Press.

Chaker, M. (2009, September 4). Students borrow more than ever for college: Heavy debt loads mean young people can't live the lives they expected. *Wall Street Journal*. http://www.online.wsj.com/article/SB10001424052970204731804574388682129316614.html. Accessed 3 March 2010.

Clark, B. R. (1998). *Creating entrepreneurial universities: Organizational pathways of transformation*. New York, NY: Elsevier Science.

Deem, R. (2001). Globalisation, new managerialism, academic capitalism and entrepreneurialism in universities: Is the local dimension still important? *Comparative Education*, *37*, 7–20.

Deem, R. (2004). The knowledge worker, the manager-academic and the contemporary UK university: New and old forms of public management? *Financial Accountability and Management*, *20*, 107–128.

Deem, R., Mok, K. H., & Lucas, L. (2008). Transforming higher education in whose image? Exploring the concept of the "world-class" university in Europe and Asia. *Higher Education Policy*, *21*(1), 83–97.

Ehrenberg, R. G. (2000). *Tuition rising: Why college costs so much*. Cambridge, MA: Harvard University Press.

Ertl, H. (2006). European Union policies in education and training: The Lisbon agenda as a turning point? *Comparative Education*, *43*(1), 5–27.

Estermann, T., & Nokkala, T. (2009). *University autonomy in Europe I: Exploratory study*. Resource document. European University Association. http://www.eua.be/Libraries/Publications/University_Autonomy_in_Europe.sflb.ashx. Accessed 1 March 2010.

Europa. (2008, February 28). Commission organises forum to foster university—business cooperation (Press release IP/08/343). http://www.europa.eu/rapid/pressReleasesAction.do?reference=IP/08/343&format=HTML&aged=1&language=EN&guiLanguage=en. Accessed 16 February 2010.

European Commission. (2000). *Presidential conclusions: Lisbon European Council 23 and 24 March 2000*. Resource document. http://www.europarl.europa.eu/summits/lis1_en.htm. Accessed 20 May 2010.

European Commission. (2006). Delivering on the modernization agenda for universities. http://ec.europa.eu/education/policies/2010/lisbon_en.html. Accessed 17 May 2010.

European Research Council. (2007). The European Research Council awards its first grants (Press Release MEMO/07/586). http://www.europa.eu/rapid/pressReleasesAction.do?reference=MEMO/07/86&format=HTML&aged=1&language=EN&guiLanguage=en. Accessed 1 March 2010.

European Research Council. (2008). *ERC advanced grant competition 2008: Statistics*. Brussels: ERC.

European University Association [EUA]. (2009). Mission statement. http://www.eua.be/about-eua/what-wedo/mission/. Accessed 5 May 2009.

Eurostat. (2009). Patent statistics. European Commission. http://www.appsso.eurostat.ec.europa.eu/nui/setupModifyTableLayout.do. Accessed 1 May 2010.

Eurostat. (2010a). *Education and training statistics*. European Commission. http://www.epp.eurostat.ec.europa.eu/portal/page/portal/education/data/database. Accessed 1 May 2010.

Eurostat. (2010b). Science, technology and innovation: Gross domestic expenditure on R&D. European Commission. http://www.epp.eurostat.ec.europa.eu/portal/page/portal/science_technology_innovation/introduction. Accessed 1 May 2010.

Geuna, A., & Martin, B. (2003). University research evaluation and funding: An international comparison. *Minerva*, *41*(4), 277–304.

Gornitzka, Å., & Larsen, I. M. (2004). Towards professionalisation? Restructuring of administrative work force in universities. *Higher Education*, *47*(4), 455–471.

Harjes, T. (2007). Globalization and income inequality: A European perspective (Working Paper WP 07/196). International Monetary Fund, Paris, France and Brussels, Belgium.

Institute for International Education [IIE]. (2009). *Open doors*. New York, NY: Author.

Kavanaugh, M. (2010). Interests in conflicts: A legal analysis of university conflicts of interest (Doctoral dissertation). Institute of Higher Education, University of Georgia.

Knapp, L. G., Kelly-Reid, J. E., Ginder, S. A., & Miller, E. (2008). Employees in postsecondary institutions, fall 2006, and salaries of full-time instructional faculty, 2006–2007 (NCES 2008–172). Washington, DC: National Center for Education Statistics.

Laredo, P. (1997). Revisiting the third mission of universities: Toward a renewed categorization of university activities? *Higher Education Policy*, *20*(4), 441–456.

Le Grand, J. (1991). Quasi-markets and social policy. *The Economic Journal*,101 (408), 1256–1267.

Leslie, L., & Brinkman, P. (1988). *The economic value of higher education*. New York, NY: American Council on Education/Macmillan Series on Higher Education.

Link, A. (2006). *Public/private partnerships: Innovation strategies and policy alternatives*. New York, NY: Springer Science and Business Media.

Mann, M. (1986). *The sources of social power*. Cambridge: Cambridge University Press.

Marginson, S. (2013). The impossibility of capitalist markets in higher education. *Journal of Education Policy*, *28*(3), 353–370.

McMahon, W. (2009). *Higher learning, greater good: The private and social benefits of higher education*. Baltimore, MD: Johns Hopkins University Press.

McPherson, M. S., & Schapiro, M. O. (1998). *The student aid game: Meeting and rewarding talent in American higher education*. Princeton, NJ: Princeton University Press.

National Center for Educational Statistics. (2009). Chapter 3 postsecondary education. Digest of Educational Statistics. http://www.nces.ed.gov/pubs2010/2010013_3a.pdf. Accessed 1 March 2010.

National Science Board. (2002). *Science and engineering indicators 2002*. Arlington, VA: National Science Foundation (NSB-02-1).

National Science Board. (2008). *Science and engineering indicators 2008*. 2 vols. Arlington, VA: National Science Foundation (volume 1, NSB 08-01; volume 2, NSB 08–01A).

National Science Board. (2010). *Science and engineering indicators 2010*. Arlington, VA: National Science Foundation (NSB 10-01).

OECD. (2014). *Education at a glance 2014: OECD indicators*. Paris: Author.

Pusser, B., Slaughter, S., & Thomas, S. L. (2006). Playing the board game: An empirical analysis of university trustee & corporate board interlocks. *Journal of Higher Education*, 77(5), 747–775.

Rhoades, G., & Sporn, B. (2002). New modes of management and shifting modes of cost of production: Europe and the United States. *Tertiary Education and Management*, *8*, 3–28.
Saez, E. (2009). Updated tables from Saez, E. & Piketty, T. (2003). Income inequality in the United States, 1913–1998. *The Quarterly Journal of Economics*, *118*, 1–39. Updated tables. http://www.econ.berkeley.edu/*saez/TabFig2008.xls. Accessed 17 May 2010.
Schuster, J. H., & Finkelstein, M. J. (2006). *The restructuring of academic work and careers: The American faculty*. Baltimore, MD: The Johns Hopkins University Press.
Slaughter, S. (1990). *The higher learning and high technology: The dynamics of higher education policy formation*. Albany, NY: SUNY Press.
Slaughter, S., & Cantwell, B. (2012). Transatlantic moves to the market: Academic capitalism in the US & EU. *Higher Education*, *63*(5), 583–606.
Slaughter, S., & Leslie, L. L. (1997). *Academic capitalism: Policies, politics and the entrepreneurial university*. Baltimore, MD: Johns Hopkins University Press.
Slaughter, S., & Rhoades, G. (2004). *Academic capitalism and the new economy: Markets, state and higher educatio*n. Baltimore, MD: Johns Hopkins University Press.
Slaughter, S., & Rhoades, G. (2005). From endless frontier to basic science for use: Social contracts between science and society. *Science, Technology and Human Values*, *30*(4), 1–37.
Slaughter, S., & Taylor, B. J. (Eds.). (2016). *Higher Education Stratification, privatization and workforce development: Competitive advantage in Europe, the US and Canada*. Switzerland: Springer International Publishing.
Taylor, B. J. (2016). The field dynamics of stratification among US research universities: The expansion of federal support for academic research, 2000–2008. In Slaughter, S. & Taylor, B. J. (Eds.), *Higher Education Stratification, privatization and workforce development: Competitive advantage in Europe, the US and Canada*. Switzerland: Springer International Publishing, 59-80.
Taylor, B. J., Cantwell, B., & Slaughter, S. (2013). Quasi-markets in US higher education: The humanities and institutional revenues. *The Journal of Higher Education*, *84*(5), 675–707.
van Apeldoorn, B. (2000). Transnational class agency and European governance: The case of the European Round Table of Industrialists. *New Political Economy*, *5*, 157–181.

CHAPTER FOUR

Rethinking the Entrepreneurial University for the 21st Century

WESLEY SHUMAR AND SARAH ROBINSON

Introduction

There is a deep concern about how higher education worldwide has become more narrowly focused on the economy, on qualification and credentialing. Central to this concern is the notion of the "Entrepreneurial University". Touted by policy makers, university administrators, and politicians as the model for the future, entrepreneurial is seen as a synonym for the marketized and economized university, an institution where economic rationality determines research directions, curricular content, pedagogical theory, and services. Critics of the entrepreneurial university regard this market-oriented focus as destructive to the pursuit of knowledge, the well-being of citizens and society. These arguments have been developed in literature on the commodification of the university (Shumar 1997), the market mantra of neoliberalism on education (Blum & Ullman 2012), and the growth of the knowledge society (Hargreaves 2003). But one thing they share with the conservative advocates of the entrepreneurial university is an ideology of what is meant by "entrepreneurial." Ronald Barnett (2013) suggests that agreement around what constitutes the term entrepreneurial, coupled with the fact that supporters and critics alike feel we cannot escape the entrepreneurial university, creates an ideology that "forecloses the possibility of other imaginations of the university."

There are a number of recent works that are attempting to complicate this story of the entrepreneurial and open up a discussion of how to think about creativity, and individual innovation, even though these potentialities are pressured by neoliberalism and global consumer capitalism (Lundvall 2002, Peters, Marginson & Murphy 2009). In the spirit of this work and Barnett's call to open ourselves up to other forms of imagination, we would like to suggest a very different conception of the entrepreneurial, which comes from the work in entrepreneurship education (EE) in Scandinavia. The present climate has produced a legitimacy crisis in that the only knowledge that is socially valued is knowledge that is already seen to have economic value. But Scandinavian EE sees entrepreneurship as an opportunity for purposeful education, notions which are more in line with young progressives when they think about the entrepreneurial, whether it be social entrepreneurship or an alternative craft industry.

Traditionally, the pursuit of knowledge is understood to be good for the individual and in turn good for the society (Jaspers 1959). The growth of the individual might lead to new discoveries, among other things, that then turned out to be good for society and more specifically for the economy. Furthermore, we know from prior history that often economic value is discovered later after the pursuit of basic knowledge. But now, with the emphasis on producing "valuable knowledge" and credentials, the order has become reversed—higher education is supposed to be for the good of the economy, and in addition, the individual and society may benefit (Apple 2001). We question whether this approach to higher education under neoliberal reform is likely to stimulate individuals. From the standpoint of the individual, pursuing qualifications for credentials is alienating and discourages engagement and creativity (Biesta 2009). If individuals do not grow and develop, then they are less likely to contribute to a creative and growing economy and society.

Throughout the history of the (higher) education institution there is evidence of diverse agendas for the purpose of education; an example of one agenda is the focus on what is easy to teach and to learn, where learning is remembering facts, not for their application but for their reproduction instead. This agenda, requiring passive learners and a focus on detachment, has been strengthened recently by the knowledge society movement. Another agenda, and one that gained strength throughout the 1960s and 1970s, is one that was labeled "progressivism" or constructivism. Here learning is developed through active engagement by learners and is much more difficult to plan and to assess as individuals make their own learning journeys. However, this approach may result in making education meaningful for the individual. This alternative agenda brings us close to terms that have been used in education philosophy in Europe, in Germany—*bildung*, in

Scandinavia—dannelse. Both these terms can be broadly understood to mean the self-actualization of the individual, linking purpose to the goal of education. Furthermore, we believe that the current "audit" approach to creating and measuring educational quality is bankrupt. Audit has a tendency to disempower faculty and students and move the discourse from process (becoming educated) to product (performativity) (Shore & Wright 2000).

Drawing on these arguments we suggest that a broader definition of EE, as imagined in Scandinavia, could ironically bring higher education back to a more genuine foundation of the pursuit of knowledge that helps the individual grow and also builds a strong society. We argue that this approach resonates with the 18th-century notion of 'bildung' (or the notion of 'dannelse' in Scandinavia), which develops the idea of an educated individual who actualizes his/her potential through education. In this chapter, we argue for a particular framing of EE that promises a contemporary return to purposeful education.

Contesting the concept of entrepreneurship

We begin with a discussion of the term entrepreneurship and the multiple ways in which this concept is being imagined. Very narrowly, entrepreneurship is defined as creating a business or venture for the purpose of making money or creating value. And traditionally the term entrepreneur has been associated with small businesses. But beyond this most basic definition, the term entrepreneurship has been imagined in both a politically rightward and leftward direction. For the right, it is imagined that small businesses flourish when the market is as free and open as possible so that entrepreneurship becomes a way of talking about neoliberalism. The fantasy is that all small businesses have the potential to grow into large profit-making institutions in the free market. Not that all will, but the market will make sure that some do. Further, if governments, and schools, and other social services are encouraged to be more entrepreneurial, this implies that they become "economized" to run like a business with a focus on efficiency, cost savings, value for dollar, and contribute to the larger economy. It is this notion of entrepreneurial, as it has come to the university that critics on the left are most concerned with.

The leftward understanding of entrepreneurship has more to do with social justice and other forms of value creation. It is most often captured with the term social entrepreneurship. This is a concept that is particularly embraced by younger progressives, but it indicates an interesting shift in thinking. First, it is an effort to avoid direct conflict with more mainstream thinking. Today, young environmentalists would rather be called social entrepreneurs because it suggests bringing creativity to environmental problems and constructing something of value, not just fighting the status quo. But social entrepreneurs are also aware that the top-down forms of welfare, be they national or international, often do not work because they do not connect with people's lives. One must engage with a group of people to figure out how to create value, in order to help people improve their lives.

Researchers in EE in Scandinavia realize that these two notions of entrepreneurship do not themselves need to stand in contrast. If we broaden our sense of value creation, and if we broaden our understanding of venture creation, and if we see entrepreneurship as creating value in the process of solving human problems, then we have a progressive notion of entrepreneurship that can create all forms of value including the monetary. In his classic work on the "theory of practice," Pierre Bourdieu (1977) suggested that this kind of ideological work around a term like entrepreneurship is tricky. Bourdieu argues that in the social universe of discourse that he called the "doxa," there would be heterodox and orthodox positions, and that the more orthodox positions would be dominant. These are the definitions of entrepreneurship as neoliberalism and social entrepreneurship we have sketched out above. So it is not surprising that so many see entrepreneurship equating with neoliberalism as for Bourdieu, in the doxa that is the dominant position. The position we are arguing for, coming from Scandinavian EE, is to break out of this discourse and reimagine what it might mean to be entrepreneurial (Barnett 2013).

In order to explore these ideas, we begin with a brief history of the role of the university in society going back to (forgotten) terms that dominated the European model for the university. We then focus on the changes that have taken place over the last two centuries. Then drawing on insights from our research in EE with a group of entrepreneurship educators in Scandinavia since 2012, we argue that taking the broad definition of EE provides an opportunity to imagine a 21st–century entrepreneurial university that allows for a (re)turn to a more purposeful education, one which seems to have been forgotten.

The purpose of education—*bildung*?

In Germany, much of the philosophical debate around the modern university, its organization, and its role in society were centered around the founding of the University of Berlin (Kwiek 2006, O'Boyle 1983, Wittrock 2004). Called the Humboldt University, it is a discourse that involved Kant, Fichte, Schelling, Schleirmacher, Humboldt, and Hegel as its main interlocutors (Kwiek 2006: 14). Our focus here is on the three essential functions of the modern university that Humboldt defined. First, the modern university would involve a unity of teaching and research; second, there would be academic freedom; and third, philosophy (the liberal arts) would be the core of the university (Kwiek 2006, O'Boyle 1983,

Wittrock 2004). Kwiek (2006) and others spell out the implications of these three features of the modern university in great detail. The combination of teaching and research essentially unified faculty and university students in the process of doing research together and that research was the core of the university. Knowledge production and its dissemination was the key activity of the university, while a possible effect was really the responsibility of other (and lesser) institutions. Academic freedom implied that it is extremely important that university intellectuals, faculty and students, pursue truth and knowledge wherever it took them and that there should be no impediments to the seeking of truth and knowledge.

Science, the systematic approach to knowledge, was seen as the supreme form of enlightenment at this stage and the salvation of humanity. Furthermore, the pursuit of sciences was the pursuit of truth. This truth was the salvation for society and so universities needed to be free to go wherever truth took them. That curiosity-driven nature of knowledge seeking and knowledge production was as important for students as it was for faculty and of course the idea was that students and faculty were locked together in a pursuit of knowledge. Over time, our focus has moved academic freedom to primarily a faculty issue.

Drawing on the 19th-century German tradition of "bildung," our modern education systems, both in Northern Europe and the United States, built on a definition of education that draws on an actualization of self at a higher plane of existence. John Dewey, inspired by the Hegelian tradition of bildung, focused on education and experience. For Dewey, learning was a central part of being human; what we do as human beings is learn. For Dewey, the way to do this was to provide a context for students where they have educative experiences that build on prior learning and called the individual to a higher state of understanding. This thinking is not only consistent with the German humanistic notion of bildung but it is also consistent with a Hegelian notion of dialectical movement.

Post World War II—from elitism to massification

After World War II, we see two trends coming together. It is the peak of this enlightenment notion of higher education, and it is the beginning of the massification of higher education in many societies. The postwar brought establishment of the welfare society where health and education were seen as a social good and a "right" for all. Further, there was a move toward more equity—the notion that success can be achieved by hard work and not by position and social standing. The model of the Humboldt University paid off in the postwar period and there was expansion of science and technology that created the possibility for new products in a growing industrial economy. There was also the beginning of the consumer economy and growth and expansion of social sciences that supported the development of technologies of consumption and social control. There were signs that the modern university, with its focus on curiosity and individual interests, benefited the modern consumer economy too. And so began the shift of focus toward the economic benefit that education could provide.

As the economy of the postwar expanded in the United States, Europe, and Asia, higher education expanded too. Many nations experienced a "boom" of higher education throughout the 1960s. The UK saw the development of many new universities and new polytechnics during this period of time as did the rest of Europe. It is during this growth period that the rhetoric about progressive education unfolded (Labaree 2005). Many progressives saw this growth as a sign that basic education, with a focus on the learning of the individual, was truly good for the economy. A progressive strand of this work is still evident today in more collaborative, student-centered, dialogic and social learning models.

However, this more progressive side of the contemporary educational movement collided with dominant discourses that shaped what educators did and how they did it and which were politically driven. Indeed, many educators also began to worry about credentialing and making sure that outcomes were somehow measured. These discourses were driven by a need to streamline educational administration to make it efficient—for society and for the economy (Labaree 2005: 281). In addition, this discourse was linked to the rise of professionalism and the pressures on universities to "credential" new professional groups (Collins 1979). The expansion of university education across many nations in the post-WW II era results in shifts from the original vision of the German enlightenment and ideas of bildung toward a more technical focus on professionalization and workplace competencies. Pressures on universities are directly linked to the pressure on nations; this is something that the German enlightenment thinkers well understood—the fate of the university and the fate of the nation are tied.

Marketization and the growth of a knowledge economy

The period of economic growth came to an end in the 1970s as the Fordist/Keynsian economic system, and the welfare state began to experience stress and contradictions. Overall, global consumption stagnated in the 1970s with high levels of inflation and declining economic growth. As the global economy begins to go into a series of crises from the late 1970s up to the current era of debt-crisis post 2008, many nations make a series of related moves, which include passing the cost of education on to the public, and moving to transform education into a commodifiable knowledge. As the welfare system comes into crisis, we begin to see the first movement of what will later be called neoliberalism. Early on, the movement of free market economics was simply a strategy to free up the financial system to create a little movement in the global economy and the "illusion" of growth. But as neoliberalism continues, it becomes a deeply ingrained political ideology as well as global economic policy and ideology.

The United States, with its complex system of public and private universities, was on the leading edge of these market changes. As early as the 1970s, as state support for higher education began to decline in the United States, universities were forced to turn to the market to survive. They became neoliberal before the moment of neoliberalism. Students began to be imagined as customers, admissions offices began to see themselves as marketing departments and education as their product. University administrations began to imagine faculty as workers, and dream of being able to have a more efficient and rational workforce. Further, in the 1990s and 2000s, we see the Federal and State governments moving to undermine public higher education; in several states, the percentage of the university budget coming from a public source has dwindled to 10–15% (Newfield 2008).

In this new world of the university, education has become a commodity. But in the world of commodity exchanges, commodities take on a dual function, a use-value and a sign function. In *Critique of Commodity Aesthetics*, Wolfgang Haug (1986) explores the irony of the Marxian split of use and exchange value and thinks about how exchange value sets us up for a world of signification. The distance between use and exchange value can be great. For instance, when many organizations are looking for a credential for their workers, there is not always a clear relationship between the credential and true knowledge and skill acquisition. Many times the university degree legitimates, through the exchange value of the degree, a skill that the worker already has.

Increasing numbers of American universities begin to market education as a product, where the skills that are sold will improve consumers' position in the marketplace. Commodification became the way that higher education is expanded in the United States in the contemporary period. And that expansion was not built on a broader and deeper set of educational relationships between teachers and students pursuing knowledge together for the greater good. It was built upon the credentials that universities offered that may or may not have had real useful knowledges and skills associated with them.

While the United States pursued its own unique path to the commodification of the university, marketization has taken a much more rapid route in the UK, Europe, Australia and New Zealand, and many other places. In the *Great University Gamble*, Andrew McGettigan (2013) discusses the rapid marketization of universities in Great Britain and the undermining of the public resource through a rather shadowy and undemocratic process of finance and loan schemes. This rapid move to transfer the financial burden of supporting the university from the state to students (families), without being really clear about the process is fascinating. It also comes on the heels of the UK's very draconian audit and accountability schemes. The effects of these policies will be to further benefit the elite institutions and further damage non-elite institutions.

During this moment, universities turn their attention toward survival and away from basic progressive ideas about learning, knowledge production, the good of the individual, and the good of society. In fact, the whole vision of higher education in industrialized nations begins to change. The massification of the university in the postwar, especially in the 1960s, led to questions about how the state can pay for university education. There was increasing agreement that individuals and families should shoulder some percentage of the cost of higher education. The uneven development of this idea hit many nations differently. As mentioned above, in the United States, this process began very early in the 1970s and led to the commodification of the university (Shumar 1997, Slaughter & Leslie 1997, Slaughter & Rhoades 2004). Commodification was a distributed response on the part of higher education administrations to the decline in state funding and the decline in traditional aged students in the 1970s and 1980s. The pressures for accountability came much later.

In the UK, Europe, and parts of Asia, audit and accountability came first followed by marketization. Perhaps this makes sense as in Europe, the UK, and other parts of the world, higher education was more reliant on state funding. As Shore and Wright (1999, 2000) point out, the mechanisms introduced to justify teaching and research performance, as well as to account for effective institutions are justified in the name of being responsible to the public purse, but are means for social control and an example of neoliberal governmentality (Ong 2006). In New Zealand, the process was quick as neoliberal ideology marketized the university and changed university education from a social good to a commodity almost overnight (Shore 2010). In the UK, the shift toward marketization was slower, beginning in the 1990s and culminating in full fees in the last few years (Ainley 1994, Canaan & Shumar 2008, McGettigan 2013). Although some nations and institutions continue to resist these pressures, maintaining university education as a social good and a welfare right, there is tremendous pressure on them to change.

Another movement happening during this period of time, which could be thought of as another phase of the commodification or marketization of the university, brought about a broader set of social changes. The information revolution and the growing global economy brought about an emphasis on the "knowledge economy" among leading industrialized nations. This movement became merged in part with the consumer economy and a lifestyle economy. Led by the computer and software industries of the 1980s and 1990s, a process described by Ritzer and Jurgenson (2010) as "prosumption" began to develop. Prosumption is the merging of production and consumption. Computer programmers working on Microsoft's campus, resembling a university campus, sip espresso, play games, ride their bikes, all while working on the development of new products. This movement presented universities with an opportunity to be central to, and even drivers of, regional economic development in a knowledge economy (Shumar 2008).

While there are positive things about the university becoming central to the knowledge economy, this fact, coupled with the marketization pressures mentioned above, has led to a complete transformation of a university education and the purpose of academic knowledge. Neoliberal economic ideology suggests that market efficiency is the best model for all human social behavior and that the economizing of all ideas and activities is a worthwhile goal. Of course the economic is very important, but this emphasis tends to lower the value of human life and activity. Rather than in the 19th-century Hegelian sense where knowledge and learning should call the individual upward, neoliberalism calls the individual and the society down to earth, limiting the vision of what life can be and reducing our sense of value and what goodness is (Nussbaum 2010). Ironically, this emphasis will, in the long run, be bad for the economy too, because new ideas tend to come from unexpected places as people were following their interests and concerns in the quest for new knowledge. Peters, Marginson, and Murphy (2009), also very aware of the tensions at the current moment, suggest that the information revolution and an entrepreneurial spirit can foster creativity and innovation in universities. But at the same time, these forces are governed by the logic of "cognitive capitalism" where knowledge is one of the key commodities in the global marketplace. For them as for us, the tensions revolve around how ideas like "creative" and "entrepreneurial" are defined and in whose interests the university is being reinvented.

The development of the entrepreneurial university

The term entrepreneurial university was introduced in 1998 in Clark's book entitled *Creating Entrepreneurial Universities: Organizational Pathways of Transformation*. Higher education institutions have since interpreted the rhetoric and discourses in a variety of ways. The significance of these discourses is that there appears to be a new relationship between academia and business. There is a burgeoning literature on the entrepreneurial university, which is generally divided into two camps. One camp, mainly higher education researchers, critiques the rhetoric and discourses and warns of the demise of the university, a degradation of its mission and loss of academic freedom (Shore & McLauchlan 2012, Slaughter & Leslie 1997). The other camp presents a more positive take on what entrepreneurial institutions can achieve. Mautner (2005: 103) describes these camps as a polarization of the frameworks and describes them as believers and nonbelievers. In brief, the believers regard the vision of an entrepreneurial university as a good that will result in the restructure of a stuffy hierarchical organization. The development from being the keeper and transmitter of knowledge to "an originator of knowledge" is the goal of the entrepreneurial university (Etzkowitz 2013: 487). This trend, however, is not new, as partnerships between research departments and industry and regional development were in fact fostered in the postwar period (Etzkowitz 2013). The goal is to link the entrepreneurial university to society through government and industry. So the classic linear development of research to practices now becomes cyclical as problems in practice are tackled by those working in research environments that lead to an academic enterprise. Citing Marques et al. (2006), Sam & van der Sijde (2014) suggest that the modern university is the melting pot for human capital (graduates), knowledge, and spaces for innovation.

The entrepreneurial university is then positioned to identify and exploit opportunities by providing the environment in which experimentation and risk-taking can take place (Sam & van der Sijde 2014). On the other hand, the nonbelievers warn of the dangers of the marketization of the university and the loss of academic freedom. These discourses are a response to (i) cuts in government funding, (ii) de-regulation, (iii) open competition and internationalization, and (iv) new managerialism. Whichever side we choose, these discourses seem to have taken hold and, as Mautner (2005: 96) maintains, entrepreneurship has become both an "activity and discourse." It is a dominant "activity and discourse" that focuses on how universities primary mission is the support of wealth creation.

Again what is true about both of these opposing perspectives on the entrepreneurial university is that there is ideological closure around what the term entrepreneurial and entrepreneurship mean. As stated above, this instrumental and narrow definition of entrepreneurship is not helpful for moving the university forward. It also limits us from seeing that each perspective does offer some things of value.

Entrepreneurship education

There has, in the past decade, been a surge in courses, both curricular and extra-curricular, promoting entrepreneurship, value creation, enterprise, entrepreneurial mind-set, etc., for a diverse group of students, for a variety of purposes. The curricular courses usually take one of three forms. Firstly, there are those that focus on producing students who know *about* 'entrepreneurship' and can reproduce theory and knowledge. Secondly, students are provided with tools *for* entrepreneurship and are required to demonstrate that they know how to apply what they have learned, e.g. a business model or marketing tool. There is a third type of course where students are required to work *through* entrepreneurship by engaging with problems, stakeholders, and potential customers in the real world and then reflect on the learning from these interactions. The third type of course is the most effective type if the university is to produce budding entrepreneurs; however, these courses are also the most difficult to design and to assess (Pittaway & Edwards 2012). Therefore, the locus of courses is on the 'about' and for 'types'. What is common to all three types is that they resonate with the narrow market-focused definition that policy makers and governments adhere to and seek to promote. These courses will focus on entrepreneurship as wealth creation and profit-making, which is a probable explanation for why most people, on hearing the word entrepreneurship, immediately assume it is about business/start-up.

Alongside the growth in these courses is an increasing research interest into entrepreneurial learning—in how entrepreneurs learn to do what they do successfully and how this can be transferred to the classroom. Cope (2005) describes entrepreneurial learning from three perspectives—the functional-economic, the personal, and the behavioral. While these approaches are interesting, they tend still to focus on the intended outcome as one of starting a business and economic gain. Gibb (2002) argues that real understanding of entrepreneurial behavior is unlikely to come from business schools and that an organizational revolution is required. He further argues that the competences that entrepreneurs have are not ones that are just for business development but are required throughout society. He concludes that rather than relegating entrepreneurship to the business school, it may be better to allow the university as a whole to meet this challenge.

Our studies in the Scandinavian context demonstrate how the dominant discourses on business/start-up are challenged by a different definition, and what we regard as, capable of broadening the idea of pursuing knowledge. This group of researchers and educators advocate conceptualizing entrepreneurship as everyday practice (Blenker et al. 2012). They focus on what EE is and what its purpose should/could be. They argue that "engaging in entrepreneurial processes is fruitful for solving a broad spectrum of social problems and for creating a better life in general, by empowering people and setting them free to pursue value creation for themselves and others" (Blenker et al. 2012: 419). The research group combine Spinosa, Flores and Dreyfus's (1999) perspective of "disclosive spaces" with the work of Shane and Venkataraman (2000) who suggest that entrepreneurship happens in the nexus between the individual and potential opportunity in the larger social world. They conceptualize 'entrepreneurship' as being sensitive to one's own environment and practices. In *Disclosing New Worlds*, Spinoza, Flores, and Dreyfus (1999) look at the ways that entrepreneurship is similar to democratic action and the cultivation of solidarity. The authors suggest that entrepreneurship is practical action that is about dealing with the limitations we experience in our current world and imagining solutions to problems that bring about a new world. This process of bringing a new world into being is both highly creative and produces potential value for all involved. Further, it is not abstract knowledge but rather Bourdieu's (1990) "sens practique." For Spinoza, Flores and Dreyfus, entrepreneurs are central individuals in the reconfiguration of their worlds. This notion of entrepreneurship is one that is shared by many young entrepreneurs who see no contradiction between the idea of entrepreneurship and actively creating a better world for all people. Dealing with problems in the everyday requires skills to negotiate, understand, and to solve, and are competences that can be taught and fostered through educational practices.

This notion of entrepreneurship does not take its starting point with the economic but instead allows for a broader definition of entrepreneurship that could bring education back to meaning in the sense of self-actualization described above. Robinson and Blenker (2014: 90) suggest that "an understanding of enterprise education as a radical way of regaining intellectual freedom in academia and on classical ideas of self-directed learning, activism and emancipation" is in fact a way to open up for more meaningful participation in learning.

Summing up

We have described how the university imaginary has gone through a massive transformation where faculty were once very different kinds of citizens who had a very special role in society. While this older imaginary of the university was itself riddled with contradictions, there were many benefits to this model that are still being reaped today. First, distance from the economy is good for the economy. There are three ways in which universities were distant from the economy. The first was the insistence on basic research and seeing curiosity-driven research not as a problem but an ideal. Second, they were distant from the economy in that they were educating citizens and not training workers primarily. The third way in which they were distant is that they were literally not near most businesses and so the instrumentality of the business life did not permeate the university atmosphere. This provided an environment that allowed for freedom that sparks interest and motivation and inspires inquiry, and leads to discovery and the production of new forms of knowledge. It led not just to new technologies that then ended up benefiting our advanced economy, but it also led to the flourishing of art, literature, culture, and democratic conversation. In short, the modern university led to the expansion of the Habermasian lifeworld (Habermas 1989).

Ironically, with its emphasis on accountability and measurable outcomes, the neoliberal university has become an environment that is less creative than the corporation, not more. Universities are developing tremendous amounts of effort toward rationalizing the teaching process, creating formula that people can reuse, measuring learning and outcomes. These tasks not only take a lot of time, but they also involve experts in measurement, evaluation, rationalization, etc. Often these experts are not experts in learning or creative thinking. All of this grows out of a concern about control over the activities of teachers, researchers, and students (Shore 2010, Shore & Wright 1999, 2000). There is a double or triple reification going on here. Not only has learning and knowledge become a commodity, but the learning relationship has become quantifiable and regarded as if it were a thing. Likewise, knowledge production has become quantified and regarded as if it were a thing too.

Our premise in this chapter is that conceptualizing entrepreneurship (education) in a broader way can provide an opportunity to return purpose and meaning to education. We have discussed how a traditional view of entrepreneurship is about starting a business. But even in this very everyday sense of the term, starting a business is bringing something into being that does not yet exist.[1] Let us imagine something more complex—how might we solve a problem that many people have, where the solution currently does not exist? In this case, the bringing into being of a product, or service, or institution, might genuinely change the world in ways that we cannot yet imagine. Following the thinking of the scholars/teachers we worked with, the value that gets created might not initially be monetary, but something else. Or it might be a combination of a monetary value and other forms of value. In addition, it relates to a progressive vision of the kind of world we might imagine for our children and ourselves.

This broad definition of EE is difficult to teach and to learn because we are limited in the language we have for articulating future-oriented scenarios. A broader definition of EE presents both an opportunity and challenge. The image of the entrepreneur as the lone hero is well ingrained in society alongside the image of profit-making from entrepreneurial ventures. These narrow definitions are damaging, not only for our education system, but also for society and the economy. Surely it must be better to teach students how to realize their own potential, to understand their opportunities in relation to others, and how to examine and explore their everyday practices to create value that goes beyond the monetary to the social, environmental, and human. The notion that universities should allow for unfettered exploration of knowledge by individuals who direct their own pathways and journeys may provide an opportunity to develop new knowledge rather than reproducing the knowledge we already have. In this way there is the potential to create something of value with others for others and for society as a whole.

There is an opportunity here to make learning natural, engaging, and authentic. EE presents an opportunity that may return us to education that is more purposeful and meaningful. With a firm basis in present forms of knowledge and disciplines and coupled with an approach that does not delineate boundaries but instead opens up for curiosity and possible new worlds, we argue that EE is an approach that fosters exploration and examination of ourselves and others and our everyday practices. It is a developing pedagogy that has something important to offer in higher education. We suggest that the Scandinavian definition of entrepreneurship moves us toward an "educational entrepreneurship" (Lakeus 2015: 13) that provides us with the opportunity to move our students from passive receivers of knowledge to activists capable of creating not only new knowledge but value for others. It is not so far from Dewey's notion of educative experiences that build on past learning and call the individual to a higher state of understanding. Potentially students and teachers become activists and givers. Surely that engagement in itself is enough to make meaning where there was none before. EE could make it possible to combine individual learning with collaborative learning in explorative and/or experimental environments where attention is given to sense making, thereby creating value for the individual and for society.

Acknowledgment

The research reported in this chapter is part of a larger study (2012–2016) into "Promoting a Culture of Entrepreneurship" (PACE), a project that has been made possible by the Danish Innovation Fund (Grant ref. no. 11-115735).

Note

1. And there are a number of groups now imagining how we could reinvent the university for the future. For example, see Boden, Ciancanelli and Wright (2012) and Wright, Greenwood and Boden (2011)).

References

Ainley, P. (1994). Degrees of Difference: Higher Education in the 1990s. London: Lawrence & Wishart Ltd.

Apple, M. (2001). Comparing neo-liberal projects and inequality in education. *Comparative Education* 37 (4): 409–423.

Barnett, R. (2013). Imagining the University. Milton Park, Abingdon, Oxon, and New York: Routledge.

Biesta, G. J. J. (2009). Good education in an age of measurement; on the need to reconnect with the question of purpose in education Educational Assessment. *Evaluation and Accountability* 21 (1): 33–46.

Blenker, P., Frederiksen, S., Korsgaard, S., Müller, S., Neergaard, H. & Thrane, C. (2012). Entrepreneurship as everyday practice; towards a personalized pedagogy of enterprise education. *Journal of Industry and Higher Education* 26 (6): 417–430.

Blum, D. & Ullman, C. (2012). The globalization and corporatization of education; the limits and liminality of the market mantra. *International Journal of Qualitative Studies in Education* 25 (4): 367–373.

Boden, R., Ciancanelli, P. & Wright, S. (2012). Trust universities? Governance for post-capitalist futures. *Journal of Co-operative Studies* 45 (2): 16–24.

Bourdieu, P. (1977). Outline of a Theory of Practice. Cambridge: Cambridge University Press.

Bourdieu, P. (1990). The Logic of Practice. Stanford: Stanford University Press.

Canaan, J. & Shumar, W. (Eds.) (2008). Structure and Agency in the Neoliberal University. New York: Routledge.

Clark, B. R. (1998). Creating Entrepreneurial Universities: Organizational Pathways of Transformation. Oxford, UK: Pergamon Press.

Collins, R. (1979). The Credential Society: An Historical Sociology of Education and Stratification. New York: Academic Press.

Cope, J. (2005). Toward a dynamic learning perspective of entrepreneurship. *Journal of Entrepreneurship, Theory and Practice* 29 (4): 373–397.

Etzkowitz, H. (2013). Anatomy of the entrepreneurial university. *Social Science Information* 52 (3): 486–511.

Gibb, A. (2002). In pursuit of a new 'enterprise' and 'entrepreneurship' paradigm for learning: creative destruction, new values, new ways of doing things and new combinations of knowledge. *International Journal of Management Reviews* 4 (3): 233–269.

Habermas, J. (1989). The Structural Transformation of the Public Sphere: An Inquiry into a Category of Bourgeois Society. Cambridge: Polity Press.

Hargreaves, A. (2003). Teaching in the Knowledge Society; Education in the Age of Insecurity. New York: Teachers College.

Haug, W. F. (1986). Critique of Commodity Aesthetics: Appearance, Sexuality, and Advertising in Capitalist Society. Minneapolis: University of Minnesota Press.

Jaspers, K. (1959). The Idea of the University. Boston: Beacon Press.

Kwiek, M. (2006). The Classical German Idea of the University Revisited, or on the Nationalization of the Modern Institution. Center for Public Policy Research Paper Series. Vol. 1. http://www.cpp.amu.edu.pl/pdf/CPP_RPS_vol.1_Kwiek.pdf.

Labaree, D. (2005). Progressivism, schools and schools of education: an American romance. *Pedagogica Historica: International Journal of the History of Education* 41 (1–2): 275–288.

Lakeus, M. (2015). Two flavours of entrepreneurial education; happiness empowerment versus meaningful creativity. Working paper presented at Doctoral Course 'Fostering the entrepreneurial self' with Karin Berglund Stockholm, May 2015.

Lundvall, B.-Å. (2002). Innovation, Growth and Social Cohesion: The Danish Model. Cheltenham, UK: Edward Elgar Publishers.

Marques, J. P. C., Caraça, J. M. G., & Diz, H. (2006). How can university–industry–government interactions change the innovation scenario in Portugal?—the case of the University of Coimbra. Technovation, 26(4), 534–542.

Mautner, G. (2005). The entrepreneurial university; a discursive profile of a higher education buzzword. *Critical Discourse Studies* 2 (2): 95–120.

McGettigan, A. (2013). The Great University Gamble: Money, Markets and the Future of Higher Education. London: Pluto Press.

Newfield, C. (2008). Unmaking the Public University: The Forty Year Assault on the Middle Class. Cambridge, MA: Harvard University Press.

Nussbaum, M. C. (2010). Not for Profit: Why Democracy Needs the Humanities. Princeton and Oxford: Princeton University Press.

O'Boyle, L. (1983). Learning for its own sake: the German university as nineteenth-century. *Comparative Studies in Society and History* 25 (1): 3–25. Published by Cambridge University Press. Stable URL: http://www.jstor.org/stable/178570. Accessed: 28/11/2014, 13:50.

Ong, A. (2006). Neoliberalism as Exception: Mutations in Citizenship and Sovereignty. Durham, NC: Duke University Press.

Peters, M. A., Marginson, S. & Murphy, P. (2009). Creativity and the Global Knowledge Economy. New York: Peter Lang Publishing.

Pittaway, L. & Edwards, C. (2012). Examining practice in entrepreneurship education. *Journal of Education and Training* 54 (8/9): 778–800.

Ritzer, G. & Jurgenson, N. (2010). Production, consumption, prosumption: the nature of capitalism in the age of the digital prosumer. *Journal of Consumer Culture* 10 (1): 13–36.

Robinson, S. & Blenker, P. (2014). Tensions between rhetoric and practice in entrepreneurship education; an ethnography from Danish higher education. *European Journal of Higher Education* 4 (1): 80–93.

Sam, C. & van der Sijde, P. (2014). Understanding the concept of the entrepreneurial university from the perspective of higher education models. *Higher Education* 68: 891–908. DOI: 10.1007/s10734-014-9750-0.

Shane, S. & Venkataraman, S. (2000). The promise of entrepreneurship as a field of research. *The Academy of Management Review* 25 (1): 217–226.

Shore, C. & Wright, S. (1999). Audit culture and anthropology: neo-liberalism in British higher education. *The Journal of the Royal Anthropological Institute* 5 (4): 557–575. Published by Royal Anthropological Institute of Great Britain and Ireland. Stable URL: http://www.jstor.org/stable/2661148. Accessed: 16/12/2013, 15:34.

Shore, C. & Wright, S. (2000). Coercive accountability: the rise of audit culture in higher education. In M. Strathern (Ed.), Audit Cultures: Anthropological Studies in Accountability, Ethics and the Academy (pp. 57–89). London: Routledge.

Shore, C. N. (2010). Beyond the multiversity: neoliberalism and the rise of the schizophrenic university. *Social Anthropology* 18 (1): 15–29. DOI: 10.1111/j.1469-8676.2009.00094.x; URL: http://hdl.handle.net/2292/10824.

Shore, C. N. & McLauchlan, L. (2012). 'Third mission' activities, commercialisation and academic entrepreneurs. *Social Anthropology* 20 (3): 267–286. DOI: 10.1111/j.1469-8676.2012.00207.x.

Shumar, W. (1997). College for Sale; A Critique of the Commodification of Higher Education. Oxon: Routledge Falmer.

Shumar, W. (2008). Space, place and the American university. In J. Canaan & W. Shumar (Eds.), Structure and Agency in the Neoliberal University (pp. 67–83). New York: Routledge.

Slaughter, S. & Leslie, L. (1997). Academic Capitalism: Politics, Policies and the Entrepreneurial University. Baltimore, MD: Johns Hopkins University Press.

Slaughter, S. & Rhoades, G. (2004). Academic Capitalism and the New Economy; Markets, State and Higher Education. Baltimore, MD: John Hopkins University Press.

Spinosa, C., Flores, F. & Dreyfus, H. L. (1999). Disclosing New Worlds: Entrepreneurship, Democratic Action, and the Cultivation of Solidarity. Cambridge, MA: MIT Press.

Wittrock, B. (2004). The transformation of European universities: disciplines and professions in England, Germany and Russia since 1870. *Contemporary European History* 13 (1): 101–116. Published by Cambridge University Press. Stable URL: http://www.jstor.org/stable/20081195. Accessed: 25/11/2014, 14:09.

Wright, S., Greenwood, D. & Boden, R. (2011). Report on a field visit to Mondragón University: a cooperative experience/experiment. *Learning and Teaching: The International Journal of Higher Education in the Social Sciences (LATISS)* 4 (3): 38–56.

PART TWO

The Global University

Introduction

Universities are now global, and in several ways. They are located in global movements of knowledge, of the global economy, and worldly movements of staff and students. These global circuits affect universities, often in unanticipated ways. A government may decide to change its policy in relation to its incoming international students and suddenly find that its policy moves are interpreted such that its inflow from a particular country may fall off quite markedly. World rankings are exerting considerable influences both institutionally and even discursively, as states look to bring on 'world-class' universities. Academic life is increasingly shaped by worldwide, if tacit, standards and expectations. And research is unevenly distributed, with published papers increasingly exhibiting large groups of researchers working together characteristically across leading universities on an international basis.

There are, in all of these movements, diffuse flows, spaces and networks, exhibiting varying degrees of agency and structure. Knowledge moves haphazardly in the spaces of the Internet, being taken up 'transgressively' (Nowotny, Scott and Gibbons, 2001: 21) across disciplines and countries. Universities seek new ventures, perhaps opening campuses overseas. Trans-national agencies and collectives form, in research, development and teaching, that opens possibilities but also constrains. Universities, accordingly, offer a pointed illustration of Castells'

(1996) phrasing of a 'space of flows'. In turn, new and incoherent relationships form between universities and states: states characteristically wish to steer their universities but their universities are no longer simply 'theirs', for universities are now compelled to work with international horizons and reach out beyond their host nation.

Jane Knight's chapter, on 'The International University: Models and Muddles', builds on her own programme of research over more than a decade and takes up several of these considerations. Key to the chapter is the contention that internationalization can be understood as a response to globalization and that, therefore, as globalization takes on changing forms, so too does the internationalization of universities. And this internationalization is exhibited both in institutional forms and practices and in the very language through which those forms and practices are understood and steered. Knight discerns three models of international universities—classical, satellite and internationally co-founded/co-developed. The last, and most recent, has a particular significance in that such institutions exist in a global space of their own. Internationalization is becoming a zone in which traditional values of 'cooperation, exchange [and] partnership' are challenged by 'competitiveness and commercialization'. In such a dynamic situation, there are bound to be 'risks and unintended consequences' which 'illustrate that nothing unfolds entirely as planned'. In consequence, the values attaching to what it is to be a university are now unclear.

Simon Marginson's chapter, 'The Anglo-American University: support structure for the 1%', examines issues of global significance with specific reference to the United States and the UK. In countries across the world, for half a century, it has been an assumption and a legitimation of higher education that universities aid social opportunity and are, thereby, a major instrument of 'occupational merit'. The chapter traces the evolution of the U.S. and UK systems and shows how that, 'since the 1970s, the University's chosen function of social merit and mobility has played out in a setting in which Anglo-American societies ... have become significantly more unequal'. In that context, dramatic class differences can be observed in access to elite universities. Cultural capital and social networking form additional elements to this pattern, enabling elites 'to secure entry to the upper echelons of the graduate labour market'. However, low social mobility in the US and UK does not mean that the University itself is the driver of 'low social mobility and high social inequality', when placed against wider social, political and economic horizons. 'The University ... cannot and will not trigger the development of a more egalitarian society on its own.'

Francine Rochford, in her chapter on 'Freedom and Control in the Constrained Modern University', examines subtle changes where, in the context of their commercialization, 'universities abandon the posture of inquiry and lock their teaching and research priorities to specific, narrow and uncontested priorities'. One of the changes that Rochford identifies is that of a change in the landscape of legitimation. 'Critique of the "idea of the modern university" ends up sounding like advocacy of social inequality'. Opportunities for alternative ideas of the university are limited, therefore, both materially and discursively, a situation exacerbated by the way in which in the very marketization of knowledge; universities now find themselves in competition with providers in the corporate and private sectors. 'The university, locked into the capitalist market framework, becomes complicit in this process because it can't afford to resist it'. In turn, nice questions arise over matters of academic freedom and institutional values in what has become a contested terrain and in which universities, both separately and collectively, are entangled. At present, it appears that the systematic and uncritical integration of external systems and goals is having a perverse effect, not least on universities as spaces of academic freedom.

Nicolas Standaert, in his chapter on 'Displaced towards a Networked Society', takes up the metaphor of 'network' in an examination of the university in modern society. The metaphor works at two levels, those of society and of universities as institutions: universities are themselves networks within a networked society. The networked university is a relatively new form of the university, having emerged from former 'pyramid' and 'pillar' formations. The network form reaches into the interstices of the university, not least in the way in which knowledge processes becomes more diffuse and are much less associated with tight disciplinary boundaries. More generally, as well as being an assembly of places, universities become a set of fluid spaces; and there emerge dynamic interplays between places and spaces, a matter exacerbated by the digital world. Bodily presence is less significant in communication. 'Thus the challenge for the university is how and to what extent "to connect" the place of speaking with the place of listening and understanding, even at a local level'. In navigating this terrain, Standaert introduces the concept of 'in-between', which takes on real form in the context of 'encounters'. Accordingly, 'Universities should make a fresh effort to create new, mobile "spaces of encounter"'.

Ronald Barnett

References

Castells, M. (1996). *The Rise of the Network Society.* Chapter 6. Malden, MA and Oxford: Blackwell.

Nowotny, H., Scott, P. and Gibbons, M. (2001). *Re-Thinking Science: Knowledge and the Public in an Age of Uncertainty.* Malden, MA and Cambridge: Polity.

CHAPTER FIVE

The International University

Models and Muddles

JANE KNIGHT

Introduction

It is impossible to reflect on the 'idea of a university' without looking at the international imperatives and dimensions of higher education. Universities have been active internationally for centuries through academic collaboration and the mobility of scholars and knowledge around the world. The fact that 'universe' is the root concept for university is clear evidence of its internationality. But the role, priorities and strategies of universities have twisted and turned over the years in response to the environment in which they operate.

There remains little doubt that globalization, interpreted to mean the worldwide movement of ideas, people, economies, trade, values, services and technology, has had a profound impact on higher education. More importantly, the internationalization of universities has itself substantially changed over the last three decades in response to, or as an agent of, the forces and opportunities of globalization. For example, the bifurcation of internationalization into two interdependent pillars: 'at home' and 'abroad' is evidence of this change. Academic mobility has moved from student and scholar mobility to programme and policy mobility. Cross-border education has gradually shifted from a development cooperation approach to a commercial competitive orientation. The international dimension of the curriculum has progressed from an area studies and foreign language approach to the integration of international, global, intercultural and comparative perspectives into the teaching/learning process and programme content. New information and communication technologies have introduced innovations in distance and online learning including the recent introduction of worldwide massive open online courses (MOOCs). Universities are establishing branch campuses in other countries, academic cities and hubs are being established and new independent universities are being co-founded by international partners. As the twenty-first century progresses, the internationalization of higher education is becoming increasingly important and at the same time, more complex (Altbach and Knight 2007).

Recent developments such as increased privatization and commercialization of higher education, the knowledge economy, for-profit education providers, new quality assurance and accreditation regulations, global higher education ranking systems, international research networks, and increased emphasis on learning outcomes and skill development have all influenced how the tertiary sector has interpreted and promoted the international dimension of higher education. There have been multiple benefits of internationalization, some risks, and, as internationalization matures, many unintended consequences as well. The purpose of this chapter is to explore the contemporary phenomenon of higher education internationalization in an applied sense, examine different models of the so-called 'international university', and identify critical trends and consequences.

The chapter is divided into three parts. The first part analyses the meaning of higher education internationalization, changing rationales, and new developments related to internationalization on campus and abroad. The second part focuses on the current interpretation—some say confusion—of what constitutes an international university by looking at three models or generations of international higher education institutions. The final part returns to the broader issues of higher education internationalization and examines the benefits, risks and unintended consequences. Important to note is that any examination of higher education internationalization needs to take into account the differences among countries and regions of the world recognizing that priorities, rationales, approaches, risks and benefits differ between east and west, north and south, sending and receiving, developed and developing countries and their higher education institutions.

Internationalization—A Complex and Changing Process

Internationalization is a term that is being used more and more to discuss the international dimension of higher education and, more widely, tertiary education.

Because it means different things to different people, it is used in a myriad of ways. Most often it is described in terms of international activities such as academic mobility for students, researchers and teachers; international linkages, partnerships and projects; new international academic programmes and research initiatives. For others it means delivering education to other countries using a variety of face-to-face and distance techniques and new types of arrangements such as branch campuses or twinning and franchise programmes. To many, it means including an international, intercultural, and/or global dimension in the curriculum and teaching learning process. Still others see international development projects or, conversely, commercial cross-border education as internationalization. And others focus on the international makeup of the student, teacher and scholar population and the development of a multi-ethnic or international culture on campus. Finally, it is also being used to describe regional education hubs, zones, hotspots, education cities and knowledge villages.

Clearly the internationalization of higher education is interpreted and used to describe a vast array of issues, strategies and new developments around the world. Yet, there is concern that internationalization is becoming a catch-all concept for anything that is related to the international dimension of higher education. Perhaps the elasticity of the concept may have stretched too far when internationalization is described as a university's ranking in international league tables. The current obsession by higher education institutions around the world about their global standing and brand is a sign of the times. Definitely, there is an appetite for international and regional rankings of institutions but one needs to seriously question whether this is part of the internationalization process or part of a university's international marketing and public relations campaign.

It is revealing to see how the terminology used to describe international dimension of higher education has evolved over the past fifty or more years. Table 5.1 illustrates how vocabulary reflects the priorities and trends over the years. Who would have guessed that in the 1960s when the emphasis was on scholarships for foreign students, international development projects and area studies that today we would be discussing branding, cross-border education, global citizenship, international rankings, franchising, and education visa factories. International education has been a much used term throughout the years and still is a preferred term in many countries, but the processes of internationalization, globalization, regionalization, and now planetization, are actively debated concepts and central to promoting and sustaining the international dimension of higher education (Knight 2012).

Table 5.1: Evolution of International Education Terminology.

Recent Terms (Last 15 years)	*New Terms (Last 25 years)*	*Existing Terms (Last 35 years)*	*Traditional Terms (Last 50 years)*
Generic Terms			
-regionalization -planetization -glocalization -global citizenship -education hubs -edu-glomerates -global rankings -academic cities -int co-founded university	-globalization -borderless education -cross-border education -transnational education -virtual education -internationalization 'abroad' -internationalization 'at home'	-internationalization -multicultural education -intercultural education -global education -distance education -offshore or overseas education	-international education -international development cooperation -comparative education -correspondence education
Specific Elements			
-MOOCs -international competencies -degree mills -visa factories -joint, double, multiple degrees -branding, status building	-education providers -corporate universities -liberalization of educational services -networks -virtual universities -branch campus -twinning and franchise programmes	-international students -study abroad -institution agreements -partnership projects -area studies -binational cooperation	-foreign students -student exchange -development projects -cultural agreements -language study

Source: Knight (2012), updated by author 2015.

Internationalization—A Working Definition

The purpose in trying to develop a clear and comprehensive definition of internationalization is to help clarify the current confusion and misunderstanding of what it means or involves. It is appropriate that there will never be one universal definition but the challenging part of developing a definition is the need for it to be generic enough to apply to many different countries, cultures and education systems.

In the past three decades various definitions of internationalization have been proposed (Arum and Van de Water 1992, Van der Wende 1997, de Wit 2002, Hudzik 2011) but their universal application has been severely curtailed by the inclusion of specific rationales, actors, strategies and outcomes embedded in the description. It is contrary to the spirit of internationalism to have a definition biased towards a particular country or cultural perspective or activity. Recent debates about whether internationalization is a 'western' or 'eastern' or 'northern' construct reflect the ongoing concern that internationalization is interpreted as westernization, Americanization, Europeanization or modernization (Odin and Mancias 2004, Dzulkifli 2010). These debates often focus on the driving rationales and the implementation strategies which reflect national/cultural norms. That is precisely why a definition of internationalization of higher education needs to be neutral and void of motivations, benefits, activities and results as these vary enormously across nations, and from institution to institution. The working definition proposed for this chapter is the following. Internationalization at the national/sector/institutional levels is defined as:

> the process of integrating an international, intercultural or global dimension into the purpose, functions or delivery of post-secondary education. (Knight 2004, p. 11)

This is intentionally a neutral definition of internationalization. Many would argue that the process of internationalization should be described in terms of rationales, strategies or outcomes such as promoting cooperation and solidarity among nations, improving quality and relevance of higher education, developing international understanding and intercultural competences in students, or contributing to the advancement of research. While these are noble intentions and internationalization can contribute to these goals, a definition needs to be objective enough that it can be used to describe a phenomenon which is in fact universal, but which has different purposes and outcomes, depending on the actor, stakeholder and context. Central to understanding internationalization is to see it as an 'ization' or a process and not an 'ism' or an 'ideology'. Internationalism is different from internationalization even though both stress the concept of 'between and among nations' (Knight 2012).

Rationales Driving Internationalization

Traditionally, the rationales driving internationalization have been presented in four groups: social/cultural, political, academic and economic (Knight and de Wit 1999). This provides a useful macro view but as internationalization becomes increasingly complex and widespread, a more up-to-date set of motives is needed to reflect current realities. Furthermore, it is important to distinguish between rationales at different levels of actors/stakeholders, especially individual, institutional, national and regional levels. Table 5.2 juxtaposes the four categories of rationales first defined in the late 1990s, but still relevant, with the rationales at the institutional, national and regional levels reflecting current trends and realities. Of particular interest is the relationship of higher education institutional rationales as compared to the national and regional actors and environments. Whether the rationales of universities converge or diverge from national priorities depends on the country and region of the world and merits serious examination.

Table 5.2: Changes in Rationales Driving Internationalization.

Four Categories of rationales (Knight and de Wit 1999)	Levels of Rationales (Knight 2015a)
Academic International Dimension to Research and Teaching Institution Building Profile and Status Enhancement of Quality International Academic Standards	*Individual Level* Develop worldview Enhance career Intercultural understanding and skills Knowledge of national/international issues Develop international network
Economic Revenue Generation Competitiveness Labour Market Financial Incentives	*Institutional Level* International branding and profile Student and staff development Strategic alliances Knowledge production Income generation
Political Foreign Policy National Security Peace and Mutual Understanding National Identity Regional Identity	*National Level* Human resources/skill development Increased access to higher education Commercial trade Nation building Social-cultural development Diplomacy and soft power
Social National cultural identity Intercultural understanding Citizenship development Social and community development	*Regional Level* Alignment of national systems Regional identity Geopolitical alliances Regional competitiveness

Source: Knight (2012), updated by author 2017.

Internationalization: 'At Home' and 'Cross-Border'

A significant and interesting development in the conceptualization of internationalization at the institutional level has been the division of internationalization into 'internationalization at home' and 'cross-border education'. A fundamental assumption is that these two pillars are separate but closely linked and interdependent. Cross-border education has significant implications for campus-based internationalization and vice versa.

At Home—Campus-Based Internationalization

The 'at home' concept has been developed to give greater prominence to campus-based strategies given the recent heightened emphasis on international academic mobility. These 'at home' strategies can include the intercultural and international dimension in the teaching learning process, research, extracurricular activities, relationships with local cultural and ethnic community groups, as well as the integration of foreign students and scholars into campus life and activities. There is also a realization that the number of domestic students who have some kind of study abroad or international research or field experience is frustratingly low in most countries around the world, with Europe being the exception. This requires that more attention be paid to campus and curriculum based efforts to help students live in a more interconnected and culturally diverse world. Students and faculty need increased understanding of international and global issues and greater intercultural understanding and skills even if they never leave their community or country (Deardorff 2006). Such is the world we live in now and even more so in the future. Universities thus have the responsibility and challenge to integrate international, intercultural and comparative perspectives into the student experience through campus-based and virtual activities in addition to international academic mobility experiences. Table 5.3 provides a framework of the major categories of activities involved in internationalization 'at home'.

Table 5.3: Framework for Internationalization 'At Home'.

Internationalization 'at home'—campus based
Curriculum and programmes -new programmes with international theme -infused international, cultural, global or comparative dimension into existing courses -foreign language study -area or regional studies -joint or double degrees

(*Continued*)

Table 5.3: (*Continued*)

Internationalization 'at home'—campus based
Teaching/learning process -active involvement of international students, returned study abroad students and cultural diversity of classroom in teaching/learning process -virtual student mobility for joint courses and research projects -use of international scholars and teachers and local international/intercultural experts -integration of international, intercultural case studies, role-plays, problem-solving scenarios, project-based learning, teams, learning communities, resource materials -integration of global learning outcomes and assessment
Research and Scholarly Activity -area and theme centres -joint research projects -international conferences and seminars -published articles and papers -international research agreements -research exchange programmes -international research partners in academic and other sectors -integration of visiting researchers and scholars into academic activities on campus
Co-curricular activities -international/global leadership development programmes -interdisciplinary seminars and think tanks -international in-service learning -distinguished speaker seminars
Extracurricular activities -student clubs and associations -international and intercultural campus events -language partners, friendship programmes, student speaker programmes -liaison with community-based cultural and ethnic groups -peer support groups and programmes
Liaison with local community-based cultural/ethnic groups -involvement of students in local cultural and ethnic organizations through internships, volunteering, placements and applied research -involvement of representatives from local cultural and ethnic groups in teaching/learning activities, research initiatives and extracurricular events and projects

Source: Knight (2012), updated by author 2017.

Cross-Border Education

Cross-border education refers to the movement of people, programmes, providers, policies, knowledge, ideas, projects and services across national boundaries.

Delivery modes range from face-to-face to virtual. Cross-border education can be part of development cooperation projects, academic partnerships or commercial trade. It includes a wide variety of arrangements ranging from study abroad to twinning to franchising to branch campuses. It is a term that is often used interchangeably with transnational, offshore and borderless education which causes some confusion and misunderstandings (Knight 2008).

The demand for international education is forecast to increase from 1.8 million international students in 2000 to 7.2 million international students in 2025 (Boehm et al. 2002). By all accounts these are staggering figures and present enormous challenges and opportunities. It is not known what proportion of the demand will be met by student mobility but it is clear that there will be exponential growth in the movement of programmes and institutions/providers across national borders.

Table 5.4 provides a schema to understand the nature of cross-border education and illustrates two significant trends. The first trend is the vertical shift downwards from student mobility to programme mobility to provider mobility to policy mobility. It is important to note that the numbers of students seeking education in foreign countries is still increasing; however, there is growing interest in delivering foreign academic courses and programmes to students in their home country. The second shift is from left to right signifying substantial change in orientation from development cooperation to competitive commerce, or in other words—from aid to trade.

Cross-border mobility of providers can be described as the physical or virtual movement of an education provider (institution, organization, company) across a national border to establish a presence in order to offer education/training programmes and/or services to students and other clients. The difference between programme and provider mobility is one of scope and scale in terms of programmes/services offered and the local presence (and investment) by the foreign provider.

This section has discussed internationalization of higher education as a process of integrating international, intercultural or global dimensions into the goals, functions (i.e. teaching/learning, research and service to society) and delivery of higher education. Changes in the rationales driving internationalization during the past fifteen years were examined and the key strategies for at home internationalization and cross-border education have been identified. The next section focuses on the often used term—international university. Three different types or models of international higher education institutions are proposed and the key characteristics identified.

Table 5.4: Framework for Cross-Border Education.

Category	*Forms and Conditions of Mobility*
	Development Cooperation → Educational Linkages → Commercial Trade
People Students Professors/scholars Researchers/ Experts/consultants ↓	Semester/year abroad Full degrees Field/research work Internships Sabbaticals Consulting
Programmes Course, programme sub-degree, degree, post graduate ↓	Twinning Franchised Articulated/Validated Joint/Double Award Online/Distance
Providers Institutions Organizations Companies ↓	Branch Campus Virtual University Merger/Acquisition Independent Institutions
Projects Academic projects Services ↓	Research Curriculum Capacity Building Educational Services
Policies Academic Management Institutional and National ↓	Quality Assurance Degree Levels Credit Accumulation and Transfer Degree Recognition Academic Mobility

Source: Knight (2012), updated by author 2017.

International University—Three Models or Approaches

In the first part of the twenty-first century it is commonplace for a higher education institution, which is nationally founded, registered and often funded, to call itself an international university. But what does the term 'international university' actually mean? The definition of an international university is both comprehensive and evasive. The expression 'international' or 'internationalized university' is now so commonplace that it has become a catch-all phrase for any hint of international activity at an institution of higher education and thus has also become almost meaningless. It does illustrate, though, how attractive and important it is for a university to describe itself as international. To complicate the understanding of the concept of an international university, different labels such as multinational, cosmopolitan, transnational and global are being used interchangeably and without consistency with the term international university (Knight 2015b).

The purpose of this section is to introduce three generic models of international universities—Classic, Satellite, Co-founded—in an attempt to clarify the confusion around the use of the term international university. The intent is to examine the defining characteristics of each model. The discussion focuses on the distinguishing characteristics of the three generic types and does not attempt to dissect the differences between the terms international, multinational, binational or global. Such an exercise is important to undertake but is complex due to the nuances of meaning according to different disciplines, the biases of the English language, and the difficulty of translating subtle differences into other languages. Thus, 'international university' is the operative term and for the purposes of this chapter a proxy for the others.

Important to note is that terms describing higher education institutions as 'world class' or 'internationally recognized' universities are not addressed because they deal more with perception and branding issues than the substantive nature of an international university. The term 'world class' is closely linked to global ranking and league tables. For instance, the Times Higher Education (THE) has prepared its own ranking of the top 100 most international universities in the world (Crook 2015). The ranking is based on three specific measures of what THE calls an 'international outlook'. The indicators are (1) the proportion of international students at each university, (2) the proportion of international faculty and (3) the proportion of an institution's research papers that are published with at least one author from another country. While these are relevant indicators, they represent an extremely narrow approach to defining an international university and do not represent the richness and diversity of activities undertaken by higher education institutions to become more international and intercultural. This categorization of an international university has very limited use.

Three Models of International Universities

Classic Model

Today, a common characteristic of universities is collaboration with international partner universities and research centres. These partnerships span a diversity of academic and management initiatives including: academic student/scholar mobility, joint programme development and delivery, collaborative research projects, benchmarking, professional development, etc. The number of these bilateral or network-based arrangements has soared in the last few years. A 2013 worldwide survey of higher education institutions indicates that the international imperative and activities continue to grow in importance and number (Egron-Polak and Hudson 2014).

Most of the partnerships are motivated by academic benefits, yet there are some which are driven by status building or commercial rationales. Nevertheless, for whatever reason, it is common practice for universities to have both international students and staff and be engaged with multiple foreign partners for a diversity of activities both on campus and abroad. These are labelled the Classic Model of an International University and constitutes by far the most common interpretation and use of the term international university. This Classic model aligns closely with the examination on the meaning and strategies of internationalization of higher education as discussed in the previous section.

Satellite Model

An important new development in cross-border education is the number of universities that are establishing a presence in other countries of the world through (1) satellite research centres, (2) branch campuses and (3) contact offices for alumni support, recruitment of students and professors, development of projects, fund/friend raising and other related activities.

The international branch campuses are primarily devoted to providing undergraduate or graduate degree programmes in a different country but the courses are designed and quality assured by the parent institution in the home country. The teaching can be done by local, expatriate faculty locally based or by fly-in faculty from the parent institution. International branch campuses are stand-alone independent brick and mortar campuses or can be located in rental premises in an 'education city' type of arrangement. On the other hand, the contact/representative offices are often embedded in a local partner institution, or co-located in the offices of an international education office or embassy from the home/sending country.

The main feature of this model is that the university has strategically planned and developed a series of research, teaching or management offices in targeted countries around the world

The growth of international branch campuses (IBCs) over the last decade has been steady and impressive. The most recent report from the Observatory on Borderless Higher Education (OBHE 2012) indicates that in 2004 there were only 24 reported IBCs, but by 2009 the number jumped to 162, and by 2011 there were 200 operating around the world with another 37 planned. Furthermore, it is a common assumption that not all IBCs have been included in the OBHE report and the actual number of IBCs is much higher. The landscape of satellite operations is changing rapidly and the scenario may look quite different in the next five years.

There is significant variation in how universities establish and operate their satellite academic, research or management offices (Wilkins and Huisman 2012). A university with three or more campuses or offices is often referred to as an international networked university. For example, New York University calls itself a 'Global Networked University' with branch campuses in Shanghai, Abu Dhabi and New York and 11 research centres around the world.

Thus, the second model, known as the Satellite model focuses on cross-border education and setting up a presence in other countries. Worth noting is that the Classic and Satellite models are not mutually exclusive. Many of the Satellite models would have a full range of international activities and could also be seen as a Classic model, but the converse is not true. Not all Classic model international universities have established satellite operations in other countries even though they may have multiple international partnerships.

Internationally Co-founded/Co-developed Model

A more recent and bold development is the founding of new stand-alone universities involving one or more foreign partner institutions. This type of international higher education institution differs significantly from the IBC model because they are not operating as satellite operations of a parent institution. These are independent, internationally co-founded or co-developed institutions licenced by the host country but developed through international collaboration among partner institutions (Knight 2015b).

There are many examples: Singapore University of Design and Technology is co-founded by MIT, Zheijang and Singapore authorities; Nazarbeyev University in Kazakhstan has developed its academic programme universities in the United States, UK and Singapore; German University of Technology in Oman; the Sino-British University; and the Xi'an Jiaotong Liverpool University in China. While each example is slightly different, a common element is that existing universities from different countries have been deeply involved in the establishment of a new institution and its academic programmes.

Apart from the common challenges facing most universities such as funding, improving quality, responding to the needs of community and labour market, student and staff recruitment, research funding, there are other issues which are more specific to the co-founded model of international universities (Zhuang 2009). These include governance models, intercultural partnerships, accreditation, awarding of qualifications, staffing, language, host country regulations and sustainability.

As discussed and illustrated, much confusion exists as to what an international university actually means. In fact, the term is less important than the model used to meet the needs and objectives of the participating higher education institutions. There is no standardized model of an international university, nor should there be. A 'cookie cutter' approach to international universities neglects the critical importance of the cultural, social, economic, political and academic context of the host country and the nature of the international academic partnerships.

The next section of the chapter looks at the benefits, risks and unintended consequences linked to the complex and changing phenomenon of higher education internationalization.

Benefits, Risks and Unintended Consequences

As internationalization changes to meet new challenges, it is important to examine some of the unexpected developments and results. While the benefits of internationalization are many and varied, there are clearly risks and also unintended consequences which need to be addressed and monitored (Knight 2009).

Student Mobility; The Brain Drain—Gain-Train

Little did we know twenty-five years ago that the highly valued and beneficial international academic mobility for students, scholars and professors would have the potential to grow into a very competitive international recruitment business. Several countries are investing in major marketing campaigns to attract the best and brightest talent to study and work in their institutions in order to supply the 'brain power' for innovation and research agendas. The difficulties and challenges related to academic and professional mobility should not be underestimated. Nor should the potential benefits. But, it is impossible to ignore the latest race for attracting international students and academics for 'brain power' and for 'income generation'. The original goal of helping students from developing countries study in another country to complete a degree and return home is fading fast as nations compete for retaining needed human resources.

While 'brain drain' and 'brain gain' are well-known concepts, research is showing that international students and researchers are increasingly interested in taking a degree in country A, followed by a second degree or perhaps internship in country B, leading to employment in country C and probably D, finally returning to their home country after 8–12 years of international study and work experience. Hence, the emergence of the term 'brain train'. In the final analysis, whether one is dealing with brain gain, brain drain or brain train, this phenomenon is presenting benefits, risks and new challenges for both sending and receiving countries (Knight 2012). From a policy perspective, higher education is becoming a more important actor and is now working in closer collaboration with immigration, industry and the science and technology sectors to build an integrated strategy for attracting and retaining knowledge workers. The convergence of an ageing society, lower birth rates, the knowledge economy and professional labour mobility is introducing new issues and opportunities for the higher education sector and producing some unanticipated results and challenges in terms of international academic mobility.

Quality, Accreditation and Credential Recognition

The increase in student, programme and provider mobility is intended to increase access to higher education and meet the appetite for foreign credentials, but there are serious issues related to the quality of the academic offer, the integrity of the new types of providers and the recognition of credentials. The increase in the number of foreign degree mills (selling 'parchment'-only degrees) and accreditation mills (selling bogus accreditations for programmes or institutions), and rogue for-profit providers (not recognized by national authorities) are realities that students, parents, employers and the academic community now need to be aware of. Who would have guessed two decades ago that international education would be struggling to deal with issues such as i) fake degrees and accreditations; ii) academic credentials that are earned but not recognized; and iii) non-regulated 'fly-by-night' institutions?. Of course, it is equally important to acknowledge innovative developments by bona fide new providers and traditional universities who are delivering high-quality programmes and legitimate degrees through new types of international arrangements and partnerships (franchise, twinning, branch campus). The perpetual challenge of balancing cost, quality and access significantly impacts the benefits and risks of cross-border education.

Double and Joint Degrees—Twice the Benefit or Double Counting?

Improvement in the quality of research, the teaching/learning process and curriculum has long been heralded as the positive outcome of international collaboration. Through exchange of good practice, shared curricular reform, close research cooperation and mobility of professors/students, there is much to be gained through internationalization. A recent trend has been the establishment of collaborative programmes between institutions in different countries that lead to double (or multiple degrees) and in some cases joint degrees—although the latter face steep legal constraints (Kuder et al. 2013).

Collaborative programmes are intended to provide a rich international and comparative academic experience for students and to improve their opportunities for employment. But, with all new ideas, come questionable adaptations and unintended consequences. For instance, in some cases, double degrees can be nothing more than double counting one set of course credits. Situations exist where two/three credentials (one from each participating institution) are conferred for little more than the workload required for one degree. While it may be very attractive for students (and potential employees) to have two degrees from institutions in two different countries, the situation can be described as the thin edge of academic fraud if course requirements for two full degrees are not completed or differentiated learning outcomes not achieved. It is important to point out that there are many excellent and innovative joint and double degree programmes being offered, but one of the unanticipated consequences is the potential misuse or abuse of degree granting and recognition protocols.

Intercultural Competence for Academic Staff and Students

One of the key factors involved in the success and sustainability of international education and research partnerships is effective and respectful communication and shared decision-making. While this may be obvious, it is not always evident in the relationship. Many reasons account for this. The motivations driving the education partnership are not always academic in nature and secondly, the intercultural competence of academics is often limited. This is a particular challenge with senior professors and scholars who believe that knowledge of the discipline and research area is the number one priority and that 'science' is an international language, thereby diminishing the importance of what is perceived to be the soft skill of intercultural competence. This is an ongoing risk and challenge in international education partnerships.

In terms of the design and delivery of collaborative education programmes, the situation of intercultural competence is more critical and complex. There are multiple challenges involved in designing appropriate curriculum but a more fundamental factor is the intercultural dimension of teaching/learning in multicultural situations. Not only do you have faculty coming from different cultural, linguistic and disciplinary backgrounds, the same is true for the students. To complicate matters further, the language of instruction is often not the native tongue of the instructors or learners. Thus the role of intercultural awareness and competence is as important in the teaching/learning process as the recognition of cultural norms and practices in the design of curriculum. While there is increasing awareness of the intercultural realities and challenges in education partnerships, the importance attached to this issue and the professional development opportunities available for staff to improve their intercultural competence are unfortunately limited.

Commodification and Commercialization—For-Profit Internationalization

For many educators, the heart of the debate about increased commercial cross-border education is the impact on the purpose, role and values of higher education. The growth in new commercial and private providers, the commodification and market orientation of education, and the prospect of new trade policy frameworks are catalysts for stimulating serious reflection on the role, social commitment and funding of public higher education institutions in society. The trinity of teaching/learning, research, and service has traditionally guided the evolution of universities and their contribution to the social, cultural, human, scientific and economic development of a nation and its people. Is the combination of these roles still valid, or can they be disaggregated and rendered by different providers?

Cultural Diversity or Homogenization?

The impact of new forms of international academic mobility on the recognition and promotion of indigenous and diverse cultures is a subject that evokes strong positions and sentiments. Many believe that modern information and communication technologies and the movement of people, ideas and cultures across national boundaries present new opportunities to promote one's culture to other countries and to enhance the fusion and hybridization of cultures. Supporting their position is the assumption that this flow of culture across borders is not new at all; only the speed has been accelerated and the modes broadened.

Others see both the movement and the speed as alarming. They contend that these same forces are eroding national cultural identities and that, instead of creating new hybrid cultures, indigenous cultures are being homogenized, which in most cases means Westernized. Because education has traditionally been seen as a vehicle of acculturation, these arguments focus on the specifics of curriculum content, language of instruction (particularly the increase in English) and the teaching/learning process in international education.

Branding and Competition—World Rankings

International and regional rankings of universities have become more popular and problematic in the last five years. The heated debate about their validity, reliability and value continues (Hazelkorn 2011). But at the same time university presidents declare in their strategic plan that a measurable outcome of internationalization will be the achievement of a specific position in one or more of the global ranking instruments. Internationalization is perceived by some institutions as a means to gaining worldwide profile and prestige. Is this really internationalization or is it international marketing and branding? The intense competition for world rankings would have been impossible to imagine a mere twenty years ago when international collaboration among universities through academic exchanges and development cooperation projects were the norm. Of course, these types of activities still occur, but the factors driving internationalization are becoming increasingly varied, multifaceted and competitive. Is international cooperation becoming overshadowed and trumped by competition for status, bright students, talented faculty, research grants, membership in elite global networks and rankings?

Last Words—Focus on Values

These new developments and unintended consequences illustrate that nothing unfolds entirely as planned and it is necessary to stay alert to unexpected bumps and diversions along the road of internationalization. With innovation and a more globalized world come new opportunities, successes and also threats. It is imperative that the international, intercultural and global dimensions of higher education continue to be proactive, responsive and innovative while keeping a close watch on unanticipated spin-offs, misconceptions and implications.

Serious reflection and debate are needed about the direction that internationalization is taking. Academics and organizations are calling for a new conceptualization, definition or term for internationalization. But are new words enough? How can we avoid a scenario where words might change but actions and understandings do not?. Practice and policy need to be closely examined in terms of what values and purposes are driving internationalization. No one could have predicted that the era of globalization would have changed internationalization, from what has been traditionally considered a process based on values of cooperation, partnership, exchange, mutual benefits and capacity building, to one that is increasingly characterized by competition, commercialization, self-interest and status building (Knight 2013). In other words, have the values related to economic-, political- and status-related rationales trumped the importance and values related to academic and social-cultural purposes and benefits of higher education internationalization?

Internationalization and even the term 'international university' have always meant different things to different people, institutions and countries. They always will. Internationalization has been guided by the principles that it must be linked to local context and purpose, that there isn't one way or a right way to internationalize, and that it is a means to an end not an end unto itself. The challenge of strengthening and reinforcing the values of cooperation, exchange and partnership over the current emphasis on competitiveness and commercialization is front and centre.

*This chapter is adapted from Knight's articles from 2012, 2013, 2015a and b listed below.

References

Altbach, P. G. and Knight, J. (2007). The internationalization of higher education: Motivations and realities. *Journal of Studies in International Education* 11(3–4): 290–305.

Arum, S. and Van de Water, J. (1992). The need for a definition of international education in U.S. universities. In C. Klasek (Ed.), *Bridges to the future: Strategies for internationalizing higher education*. Carbondale, IL: Association of International Education Administrators, pp. 198–206.

Boehm, A., Davis, D., Meares, D. and Pearce, D. (2002). *The global student mobility 2025 report: Forecasts of the global demand for international education*. Canberra, Australia: IDP.

Crook, R. (2015). *The 100 most international universities in the world 2014*. http://www.timeshighereducation.co.uk/news/the-25-most-international-universities-in-the-world/2010783.article

de Wit, H. (2002). *Internationalization of higher education in the United States of America and Europe: A historical, comparative and conceptual analysis*. Westport, CT: Greenwood Press.

Deardorff, D. (2006). Identification and assessment of intercultural competence as a student outcome of internationalization. *Journal of Studies in International Education* 10(3): 241–266.

Dzulkifli, A. R. (2010). *Is internationalization a Western construct*. Presentation at British Council Going Global 4 Conference, London.

Egron-Polak, E. and Hudson, R. (2014). *Internationalization of higher education: Growing expectations, fundamental values*. IAU 4th Global Survey, International Association of Universities. http://www.iau-aiu.net/sites/all/files/IAU-4th-GLOBAL-SURVEY-EXECUTIVE-SUMMARY.pdf

Hazelkorn, E. (2011). *Rankings and the reshaping of higher education: The battle for world class excellence*. Basingstoke: Palgrave Macmillan.

Hudzik, J. (2011). *Comprehensive internationalization: From concept to action*. Washington, DC: NAFSA, Association of International Educators.

Klasek, C. (Ed.) (1992). *Bridges to the future: Strategies for internationalizing higher education.* Carbondale, IL: Association of International Education Administrators, pp. 198–206.

Knight, J. (2004). Internationalization remodeled: Definitions, rationales, and approaches. *Journal for Studies in International Education* 8(1): 5–31.

Knight, J. (2008). *Higher education in turmoil: The changing world of internationalization.* Rotterdam, the Netherlands: Sense Publishers.

Knight, J. (2009). New developments and unintended consequences: Whither thou goest, internationalization? In R. Bhandari and S. Laughlin (Eds.), *Higher education on the move: New developments in global mobility.* New York: Global Education Research Reports. Institute for International Education, pp. 113–125.

Knight, J. (2012). Concepts, rationales, and interpretive frameworks in the internationalization of higher education. In D. Deardorff, H. De Wit and J. Heyl (Eds.), *Handbook of international higher education.* Thousand Oaks, CA: Sage Publishers.

Knight, J. (2013). The changing landscape of higher education internationalization for better or worse? *Perspectives: Policy and Practice in Higher Education* 17(2): 84–90.

Knight, J. (2015a). Meaning, rationales and tensions in the internationalization of higher education. In S. McGrath and Q. Gu (Eds.), *2015 Routledge handbook on international education and development.* London: Routledge.

Knight, J. (2015b). International universities: Misunderstandings and emerging models. *Journal for Studies in International Education* 19(2): 107–121.

Knight, J. and de Wit, H. (Eds.) (1999). *Quality and internationalization in higher education.* Paris, France: Programme on Institutional Management in Higher Education (IMHE) of the Organization for Economic Cooperation and Development (OECD).

Kuder, M., Lemmens, N. and Obst, D. (2013). *Global perspectives on international joint and double degree programs.* New York: Institute of International Education.

OBHE (2012). *International branch campuses: Data and developments.* Authored by W. Lawton and A. Katsomitrous. London: Observatory of Borderless Higher Education.

Odin, J. and Mancias, P. (Eds.) (2004). *Globalization and higher education.* Honolulu, Hawaii: University of Hawaii Press.

OECD (2004). *Quality and recognition in higher education. The cross-border challenge.* Paris, France: Centre for Educational Research and Innovation, OECD.

Van der Wende, M. (1997). Missing links: The relationship between national policies for internationalisation and those for higher education in general. In T. Kalvermark and M. Van der Wende (Eds.), *National policies for the internationalisation of higher education in Europe.* Stockholm, Sweden: National Agency for Higher Education, pp. 10–31.

Wilkins, S. and Huisman, J. (2012). The international branch campus as transnational strategy in higher education. *Higher Education* 64(5): 627–645.

Zhuang, L. (2009). The challenges facing Sino UK transnational education: An institutional experience. *Journal of Knowledge-Based Innovation in China* 1(3): 243–255.

CHAPTER SIX

The Anglo-American University

Support Structure for the 1 per cent

SIMON MARGINSON

Introduction

This chapter reflects on the vicissitudes of the central idea that has animated social and policy expectations about the university in the era of mass higher education, in which the university became the 'Multiversity' (Kerr 2001a). The idea is that of society organised on the basis of educational and occupational *merit*, in which schooling and the university are guarantors for equality of social opportunity. Rather against the odds—given the taken-for-granted domination of the university by a restricted social elite, not to mention the ongoing inequality of Anglo-American capitalist societies—in the 1960s the idea of meritocracy became installed on a lasting basis as the principle of system organisation, as manifest in the 1960 Master Plan in California (Kerr 2001b) and the Robbins (1963) report in Great Britain—both of which retain some relevance today.

The 1960s meritocratic ideal had two faces that spoke to different modalities of government: the notion of higher education as human capital, as economic progress; and the notion of higher education as equality of opportunity, as social justice. Despite certain tensions between them, each was essential to the meritocratic ideal, and each has since proven resilient, though their discursive trajectories have been heterogeneous. Each of these founding norms imagines that the university has a great role in making society, in which merit conquers all, though in reality the university has little control over the economic and social settings that constitute its possibilities and limits.

The chapter explores what happened in the 1960s and after, not just in the context of public policies and the practices of the university, but in the context of the larger society and economy, and implications for the role of the university in social allocation.

The 1960s and the heyday of merit

The historical understanding of social selection, merit and equality in Anglo-American societies has been advanced by Piketty's *Capital in the Twenty-first Century* (2014). Social competition is always partly zero-sum. But Piketty shows that special circumstances after 1945 opened the way to greater social mobility and a larger role for social allocation by the university in the US and UK, and other countries.

Before World War I, inherited wealth and capital incomes retarded the potential for upward social mobility through work and education. The World Wars and the Depression evacuated many of the great fortunes, providing more space for upward movement after 1945. The politics also changed. There was a widespread determination to create a more democratic and humanist order, alongside continuing faith in the efficacy of state intervention. The US was shaped by the 1930s New Deal, the UK by the welfare state launched by the 1942 Beveridge report. For a time after 1945 there was continued support for the wartime instruments of state planning. Progressive income tax and inheritance taxes, used to mobilise resources for the war effort, continued into the post-war era, reducing the intergenerational transfer of wealth (Piketty 2014, p. 374). For the next generation, until the 1970s, savings from labour were to be the main source of wealth. Throughout the 1950s/1970s period, the top tax rates were high and managers' salaries were restrained. High and stable economic growth and the expanding functions of the state facilitated the spread of home-ownership by what Piketty calls the 'patrimonial middle class', including teachers, public servants and academics. There was more room at the top and (partly because of that) more room in the middle of society.

In the 1950s to 1970s the Anglo-American countries came closer to becoming meritocratic than before or since. 'During the decades that followed World War II, inherited wealth lost much of its importance, and for the first time in history, perhaps, work and study became the surest routes to the top' (Piketty 2014, p. 241). It was widely, though not universally, agreed that the best means of sorting the competition for social position was the university, and the education/work nexus.

Aspirations for education boomed. Credentials multiplied. Governments financed the growing social demand for education, even in the US, providing infrastructure and tuition costs.

Equality of opportunity and human capital theory

Governments built bigger education systems to provide for expanding opportunity. The planners wanted to combine excellence and equality, consistent with the existing social and institutional hierarchies, while providing broader pathways for movement into those hierarchies. Here Robbins and the Master Plan did not create social mobility, they facilitated it. Arguably, the 1960s and 1970s saw the peak of the university's role in social allocation in the English-speaking countries. The secondary school and the university were both more open in themselves, and more able to facilitate social mobility. It is no coincidence that the most progressive education policy, and the greatest willingness of states and taxpayers to finance opportunity, combines with maximum openness in the social structure. The mistake educationists often make is to assume that education policy and practice alone can prise open society to expand upward mobility.

The UK Robbins report declared it axiomatic that 'higher education should be open to all those who are qualified by ability and attainment' and 'who wish to' enrol (Robbins 1963, p. 8), though the expansion of opportunity should not compromise academic excellence (Robbins 1966, p. 107). The pool of ability was much larger than often thought, it stated. It was impossible to identify a limit (Robbins 1963, p. 49). The number of places should be regulated by social demand for them, a policy implemented in the UK only in 2015, though adopted earlier in California. The 1960 Californian Master Plan adopted the principal of open access, with the bulk of expansion to take place in two-year community colleges. Above them were the state universities, and then the top tier, the multi-site University of California, the world's strongest system of science universities. However, the democracy of the Master Plan, its reconciliation of institutional hierarchy with universal opportunity, rested on the promise of broad pathways for upward transfer between lower and upper tiers (Parry 2011). Likewise, the Robbins Report (1963, p. 9) stated: 'We attach great importance' to the transfer function. In the outcome transfer was to be largely forgotten. In the UK there was little interface between further education and the university. In the US, upward transfer routes became centred on a few community colleges captured by middle-class families.

Meanwhile, human capital theory was also being born, not in California but in Chicago (Mincer 1958; Schultz 1959, 1960, 1961; Becker 1964). Human capital theory is pure 1960s. While it conflicts with liberal self-determined learning, it is as meritocratic and optimistic as equality of opportunity. Piketty (2014, p. 385) notes that Gary Becker's mathematisation of human capital theory is permeated by the belief that capital other than human capital has lost its determining importance. In the human capital universe, when students acquired the right educated attributes—the embodied productivity required by graduate employers—salary and success would follow. Providing graduates were 'employable', there was no end to the social wealth that the university could generate by this mechanism, until saturation participation was reached. This notion of open potential for growth and enrichment is a long way removed from Bourdieu's (1984, 1993) zero-sum competition for social position, where the prospects of each person are limited by the positions and trajectories of others. While there were broad opportunities for upward mobility, human capital theory seemed to work. In the longer run it created impossible expectations. The university became responsible not just for personal development and social justice, but for universal career success, private enrichment and collective economic growth. It also took a larger role in the social order. Merit as a learned and portable ability had a legitimating power. Human capital theory, floating free of other forms of capital, implied that those with social advantages had succeeded not because of their birth and connections, but because of their abilities and powers of application (Hennessy 2014, pp. 1 and 34). In this curious backhand way, human capital theory modernised (meritified) privilege, and made social scientists complicit in privilege, though their own normative commitment was to equality of opportunity.

Human capital theory rested on the notion of the student not as a democratic rights-bearing citizen but as *homo economicus*, the economic subject, the central figure in an economic market. In imagining education as a form of economic investment in the self-as-enterprise, it offered a new power to the student/graduate, of a particular kind (Foucault 2008, p. 226), while subordinating the same graduate to labour market forces. It also constituted a point of purchase for governments that sought to deploy education as a condition of the market economy, and could calculate its economic efficiency on the basis of rates of return to the investment. There were tensions between the notions of the graduate-in-society with multiple potentials, and the graduate-in-economy as human capital; but as Foucault states in his 1978–1979 lectures at the College de France, these notions were combined within the ensemble of liberal government.

> *Homo economicus* and civil society are therefore two inseparable elements. *Homo economicus* is, if you like, the abstract, ideal, purely economic point that inhabits the dense, full, and complex reality of civil society. Or alternatively, civil society is the concrete ensemble within which these idea points, economic men, must be placed so that they can be appropriately managed. So, *homo economicus* and civil society belong

> to the same ensemble of the technology of liberal governmentality. (Foucault 2008, p. 296. For the fuller argument, see pp. 291–313)

Since the 1960s these two meritocratic paradigms have dominated policy language and research on higher education. Social scientists still focus on widening equal opportunity, on the barriers to equality, and on issues affecting the participation of subpopulations. Other researchers still focus on the disjointed passage between education and work, including tens of thousands of studies of private rates of return.

Social and economic inequality after 1980

However, since the 1970s, the university's chosen function as the engine of social merit and mobility has played out in a setting in which Anglo-American societies—though not all societies, or not to the same extent—have become significantly more unequal.

Trends in inequality are readily quantified only in relation to incomes and wealth. Income inequality is the aggregation of inequality of income from labour and inequality of income from capital in the form of financial holdings and property. More than 99 per cent of people earn the majority of income from labour. Both labour and capital incomes are affected by taxation policy, which can either decrease or increase inequality. In general, societies that are relatively equal in their distribution of income and wealth are also societies in which intergenerational social mobility is maximised (Piketty 2014), which, as noted, provides the greatest scope for the allocative role of the university. Piketty and others show that in the Anglo-American countries, the concentration of wealth and income in the hands of the top 10 per cent, top 1 per cent and top 0.01 per cent have increased sharply since 1980 (Saez 2013; Stiglitz 2013; Dorling 2014; OECD 2014; Piketty 2014). There is no debate about the continuing empirical trend to greater inequality in the US and UK (Piketty 2014, pp. 315–316). It is clear and dramatic.

In 1970s Scandinavia, the most equal of the modern societies, the top 1 per cent received 7 per cent of all income. In Europe in 2010, the top 1 per cent received 10 per cent of income. In the US in 2010, the top 1 per cent received 20 per cent of all income, the same level as in the aristocrat-led societies of late nineteenth-century Europe. However, in 2010, the top 1 per cent in the USA achieved 20 per cent of income more through labour income and less through inherited capital than was the case in old Europe. This greater element of apparent merit is legitimating, but as elite graduate recruitment shows, the competition for high paid jobs is not a level playing field.

Since the 1980s, economic inequality has increased in about two-thirds of countries. Nowhere has income inequality increased by more than in the US and UK. There has been an explosion in the value of top managerial salaries in the US, UK and to a lesser degree in Canada, Australia, Japan and European countries, much of it in the finance sector. Finance, which received 40 per cent of US profits prior to 2008 (Stiglitz 2013, p. 120), has twice the proportion of very high salaries than is suggested by its sector share of total economic production (Piketty 2014, p. 303). Managers often set their own remuneration, including bonuses, or negotiate that remuneration with boards of like-minded folk on which they themselves sit (Stiglitz 2013). Again we find that inequality takes a more modern quasi-meritocratic form, centred on control over work rather than inheritance, and normatively grounded in the 'shareholder value conception of the firm' in which managers are seen to contribute disproportionately to value (Hanley 2011, p. 904).

Between 1980 and 2010, in the US, the income share held by the top 0.1 per cent rose from 2 per cent to nearly 10 per cent. Income in the US is now 'about as unequally distributed as has ever been observed anywhere' (Piketty 2014, pp. 256 and 319). Piketty expects that by 2030, the top 1 per cent in the US will receive 25 per cent of all income, compared to 20 per cent in 2010, and the bottom 50 per cent's share will have fallen from 20 to 15 per cent (p. 249). In the UK, between 1980 and 2010, the income share of the top 1 per cent moved from 6 to 15 per cent, reaching the highest level since the 1930s. In Canada, it was 12 per cent in 2010, in Australia, 10 per cent (p. 316).

Salary inequality is partly balanced by the patrimonial middle class, though in the US the decline in the market value of many homes, and the slippage in the middle class share of wages, indicates the position of the 'middle middle' and lower middle class is declining (Stiglitz 2013). In the next generation, when today's super manager salary is tomorrow's inheritance, the more traditional form of inequality will return. Society will become more closed at the top, reducing meritocratic mobility into and within the elite, while income shares continue to decline at the middle and bottom of the pyramid.

Piketty argues that the trend to inequality and the attenuation of social mobility are endogenous to the capitalist economy, unless corrected by policy. The endogenous trend has been the starting point for the political developments of the last three decades, in the neo-liberal era. Societies relatively static in terms of social mobility, in which social elites are rapidly concentrating their economic power, are vulnerable to the plutocratic capture of politics, and the implementation of political ideologies and fiscal and monetary policies crafted to advance the interests of the elite. This has happened in the US and UK, and arguably also in Australia. The problem of plutocratic capture of the Anglo-American polity is much discussed in the inequality literature, including that of the global policy agencies and global NGOs (e.g. Cingano 2014 for OECD, Oxfam 2014). Plutocratic capture has been linked to financial deregulation and the 'financialization' of the economy (e.g. Hanley 2011, p. 908; Tridico 2012; Bentele 2013, p. 29; Stiglitz 2013, pp. xxiii, 43, 120, and 308; Wisman 2013, p. 939; Dorling 2014, pp. 55 and 83–90; OECD 2014, p. 9; Piketty 2014, pp. 193–194, 303 and 376); and political symbiosis between central government regulation—particularly in Treasury-dominated polities such as the UK and Australia—and the private finance sector (Stiglitz 2013, pp. xxiii and 311).

Plutocratic capture of the polity is illustrated by tax policy. There is a close numerical relationship between the growth of the income shares of the top 1 per cent and 0.1 per cent, and the reductions in the rate of tax on capital and labour incomes (Stiglitz 2013, p. xxxi; Dorling 2014, p. 77). The anti-tax posture now mandatory in Anglo-American politics acts to protect the rich. Piketty remarks: 'Taxation is perhaps the most important of all political issues. Without taxes, society has no common destiny, and collective action is impossible' (2014, p. 493). However, it is now impossible for any political party to take government without conforming to the finance sector policy templates, including deregulation and low tax. In the context of elite capture of the Anglo-American polity, the fact that it is exceptionally difficult to secure increases in university funding, and the regulation of schooling in the interests of elite 'stakeholders', becomes easier to understand. The neglect of state schools; the fostering and funding of private schools, which encourages some families to invest in privileged treatment for their own children at the expense of others; the policy failure to secure greater social equality in access to Oxford, Cambridge and the American Ivy League universities; the nurturing of positional hierarchies through competition and league tables; and in the US the lucrative federal subsidisation of the for-profit colleges despite their low quality, and poor student completion rates and the poor employment standing of their degrees (Mettler 2014, pp. 87–110)—these are minor aspects of the much larger plutocratic political project. Yet this political project not only violates equality of opportunity in education, it also tears the meritocratic mask away from human capital theory.

Social and educational inequality after 1980

Equality of opportunity in the full sense is unrealisable, because of the persistence of irreducible differences between families in economic, social and cultural resources. Policy can partly compensate for economic differences, but can scarcely eliminate the potency of the family in cultural capital and social networks (Corak 2006; Mountford-Zimdars and Sabbagh 2013). One outcome of these starting social differences is that families and students have differentiated expectations. Students from low socio-economic status (SES) backgrounds, and in remote locations, tend to underestimate their own academic potential, are less willing to take risks, and are less familiar with performance and application strategies (e.g. Thomsen et al. 2013, pp. 457, 471 and 474). These difficulties can be tackled by extensive identification and tailored assistance, for example by locating the strongest teachers in districts with the highest proportion of disadvantaged students, as in Finland. In the Anglo-American education systems, the energy for large-scale compensatory measures, potent in the 1960s/1970s, diminished in the Reagan and Thatcher years in the 1980s, though minor programmes continued.

Hoxby and Avery (2012) provide a census-level study of all 2008 applicants to higher education in the United States. They found that the vast majority of low-income high achievers do not apply to any selective American university or college, despite the lower price of tuition in selective HEIs due to financial aid. Low-income high achievers opt for more uniformly safe choices than do their high-income colleagues. Typically the former are from districts too small for selective high schools or a mass of high achievers, and unlikely to encounter a teacher who attended a selective college. They make application decisions without fully knowing their own capabilities. In another large-scale study, in the UK, Boliver (2011, 2013) identifies continued and dramatic class differences in access to elite UK universities:

> Applicants from lower class backgrounds and from state schools remained much less likely to apply to Russell Group universities than their comparably qualified counterparts from higher class backgrounds and private schools, while Russell Group applicants from state schools and from Black and Asian ethnic backgrounds remained much less likely to receive offers of admission from Russell Group universities, in comparison with their equivalently qualified peers from private schools and the White ethnic group. (Boliver 2013, pp. 344–345)

Those 'schooled in the state sector remain just half as likely to apply to a Russell Group university as those from private schools' (Boliver 2013, pp. 344–345). UK students must file applications before their final school results are known, increasing what Hoxby and Avery call the 'undermatching' effect (Hoxby and Avery 2012, p. 4; Borgen 2015, p. 34). Worse, however, Boliver shows that inequality of opportunity is also built into the university admissions process. In the case of students with equivalent qualifications, 'applying to a Russell Group university from a private school rather than a state school, or from a White ethnic background rather than a Black Caribbean/African or Pakistani/Bangladeshi one, increases the odds of admission to a Russell Group university by at least as much as having an additional B-grade A-level' (Boliver 2013, p. 358). Findings that the merit principle itself is violated might have caused an outcry in the 1960s, but the university of the 2010s is less likely to be held to public account.

One legacy of the Thatcher/Reagan years is that structured hierarchies of value, such as that between state and private schools, or between different university tiers, have been normalised. In stratified systems, those with prior social advantages are best placed to compete for the places conferring high positional advantages. The social hierarchy becomes matched to the hierarchy of educational sectors, institutions and programmes, varied on the basis of selectivity. In the US, financial barriers have accentuated the prior social differences though, in the UK, income contingent tuition loans tend to soften the regressive social effects of high student charges.

The post 1990 turn to quasi-market competition in system organisation is associated with the accentuation of stratification between institutions. Research by Davies and Zarifa (2012), using Gini coefficients and other measures of the stratification of higher education in the US and Canada, and focused on institutional resources, shows that the vertical 'stretch' in both countries has increased—the US system is considerably 'steeper' than that of Canada, and the Ivy League is peeling away from the rest. Davies and Zarifa note that in competitive systems a process of cumulative advantage operates, whereby top institutions leverage their resources and status to further lift their relative position. These trends are not an inevitable outcome of growth per se. Nordic education shows that policy, regulation and funding together can limit to modest levels the resource and status differences between schools and between universities, so that formal education tends to reduce rather than reproduce or increase overall social and economic inequality. However, a certain threshold level of trust and equality of respect is needed to establish and maintain such systems (Gärtner and Prado 2012).

Inequality of opportunity becomes especially concentrated when the above factors intersect, for example, in cultural capital and social networking within elite structures. In a qualitative study of students at the University of Oxford and at Sciences Po in Paris, Tholen and colleagues (2013) show how these students use networked connections to secure entry to the upper echelons of the graduate labour market. One student distinguishes between 'good' and 'bad' networks: good networks are grounded in the quick-wittedness and adaptability of the student and academic merit; bad networks solely in family and ambition (p. 148). The merit principle is still normative but here it plays out within restricted circles, legitimating elite trajectories, rather than underpinning whole-of-system organisation. This is more obvious in Rivera's (2011, 2012, 2015) research on the hiring practices of leading Northeastern banks, consulting and law firms in the US. These firms recruit not simply from selective schools, but solely from Harvard, Yale, Princeton and Stanford, and Wharton at MBA level. It is not the content of Ivy League education they value but its prestige. They attribute superior qualities to these graduates because they had been selected into top universities, regardless of academic performance once there. Further, following a process also used in Ivy League admissions, at point of hire the elite firms perform a strong secondary screen on candidates' extracurricular accomplishments. They favour high-status, resource-intensive activities typical of white upper-middle-class culture, to achieve cultural fit between graduates and other employees of the firm.

These studies, quantitative and qualitative, indicate the extent to which the university has fallen short of the 1960s' meritocratic ideal. There is an unmistakable class-based and location-based patterning of outcomes. The extreme case is the US, where 64 per cent of the students of Tier 1 institutions are from the top 10 per cent American families in terms of income. Some leading public universities do better. The University of California Berkeley's intake is as academically strong as that of the Tier 1 private universities, yet it enrols as many low-income students, and students from under-represented minorities, as the whole Ivy League. Only 28 per cent of its intake is from the top income decile (Soares 2007, pp. 166–167). But this is an egalitarian drop in the sea of inequality. Equality of opportunity is further reduced in the US by informal quotas that limit the number of Asian-Americans entering prestige universities, despite superior academic performance (Unz 2012).

Attenuated social mobility

In the US, the rate of participation in tertiary education by the school-leaver age cohort is close to 90 per cent, one of the highest levels in the world, but many students drop out and others complete only two-year diplomas with little market power. In 2013, 77 per cent of persons in the top US family income quartile had completed a degree by age 24 years. The graduation rate had almost doubled from 40 per cent in 1970. In the bottom quartile the graduation rate also rose, but from 6 per cent in 1970 to 9 per cent in 2013. In the second bottom quartile the graduation rate was 17 per cent in 2013 (The PELL Institute 2015, p. 31). Reflecting on this, in *Degrees of Inequality* (2014), Suzanne Mettler argues that: 'Over the past thirty years … our system of higher education has gone from facilitating upward mobility to exacerbating social inequality'. Higher education fosters a society that 'increasingly resembles a caste system: it takes Americans who grew up in different social strata and it widens the divisions between them and makes them more rigid'.

It 'stratifies Americans by income group rather than providing them with ladders of opportunity' (Mettler 2014, pp. 4–5, 8).

Comparative data on social mobility indicate that in terms of intergenerational patterns of earnings, mobility in the US is relatively low (Corak 2012). Stiglitz (2013, p. 20) finds a stronger link between parental education and children's economic, educational and socio-economic outcomes in the USA than in the other English-speaking countries as well as Europe; again indicating relatively low mobility in the US. Using an intergenerational incomes comparison, Stiglitz states that in Denmark, of those in bottom fifth in terms of family income, 25 per cent of children stay in bottom fifth. In UK that figure is 30 per cent, in USA 42 per cent, with almost two-thirds staying in the bottom 40 per cent. While in Denmark 14 per cent of children of the bottom income quintile get into the top 20 per cent, in the USA that figure is 8 per cent (pp. 22–23). Likewise, Blanden and colleagues (2005) find that the USA had the lowest social mobility of countries in their comparison. Mobility in the UK was also low, Germany was in the middle of the comparator group, while Canada and the Nordic countries exhibited relatively high levels of intergenerational mobility (p. 159), as in other studies.

However, low social mobility in the US and UK does not mean the university *itself* is the driver of low social mobility and high social inequality. And even in the Nordic world, after half a century of equality of opportunity policies, there is some disappointment in the role of the university as an engine of social mobility. Across the world, research into the growth of participation finds that as systems expand, social inequalities in access to elite universities and career outcomes are not reduced (Arum et al. 2007, p. 3). 'Qualitative differentiation replaces inequalities in the quantity of the education obtained' (Arum et al. 2007, p. 4). Stratification effects trump the equalisation of educational quantity through growth, except in unusual times of high social mobility such as the US in the 1960s/1970s. The national case studies in *Stratification in Higher Education* (Shavit et al. 2007) demonstrate that as higher education expands, affluent families dominate the elite institutions. Newly participating social layers are largely confined to the sub-elite institutions where participation alone is not enough to generate strong social outcomes. Piketty remarks:

> Did mass education lead to more rapid turnover of winners and losers for a given skill hierarchy? According to the available data, the answer seems to be no: the intergenerational correlation of education and earned incomes, which measures the reproduction of the skill hierarchy over time, shows no greater trend toward greater mobility over the long run, and in recent years mobility may even have decreased. (Piketty 2014, p. 484)

Conclusions: The university and Anglo-American inequality

In the English-speaking world, the rapid growth of inequality is taking place in societies in which formal participation in the university and other higher education institutions is at a historic high. If universities produce human capital, which determines marginal productivity, and that determines rates of return, then education-determined inequality of skills and productivity is responsible for the growing income inequality. Yet the university is largely decoupled from the surge in top incomes (Piketty 2014, pp. 315 and 330). The theory of marginal productivity, human capital theory, cannot explain large variations in graduate incomes over time. Nor does it explain differences between earnings, and patterns of income distribution, in countries whose higher education is relatively similar (p. 308).

It is clear that the social allocation function of the university is not a constant but is conditioned by the larger social, economic and political setting. Nor is this function necessarily constant across a single population. William Deresiewicz (2014) and Roger Geiger (2015) suggest that in the US, elite universities play a primary role in distinguishing the upper middle class—those nestling the top 1 to 5 per cent—from the more beleaguered American 'middle middle' class, and execute fine-grained allocations to elite tracks within the upper-middle-class group. Here something like 1950s/1970s social allocation plays out. However, above and below the middle layer, it is different. For Americans in the bottom two income quartiles, the university's role in social allocation is limited, as less than 15 per cent have degrees at age 24 years, as discussed. Above the level of the upper middle class, university as such again becomes less important. Though the apparent returns to education are maximised, more than the university is driving those returns. As private fortunes grow, especially as inheritance returns to a primary role in wealth generation, the university becomes less essential—notwithstanding its meritocratic legitimation function, and the prestige consumption of Ivy League and Oxford/Cambridge degrees. In the US, Joseph Soares finds that 22 per cent of the children of high-income professional families enrol in Tier 1 institutions, and 14 per cent of children from high-income non-professional families. In fact, 19 per cent of the children of all high-income professional families, and 36 per cent from other high-income families, attend no college at all (Soares 2007, pp. 173–179).

The paradox is that the university is potent in creating new prospects for individuals from low SES backgrounds lacking family capital, even while it fails to redistribute opportunities, especially in elite institutions, on a social scale. Brand and Xie (2010) and Dale and Krueger (2011) finds that students from under-represented social groups gain the largest benefits from the university, relative to their compatriots who do not participate. Conversely, socially advantaged students depend on the university the least for access to social status, income and professional work. Yet they participate at the highest rate. What the university cannot do on its own, despite the promise of human capital theory, is expand the number of high value positions in society, so as to enable expanded mobility into the middle and upper echelons of society. In the absence of absolute growth in opportunities—or what was always more unlikely, a redistribution which would reduce the opportunities to some families from the middle and/or upper layers of the SES distribution—competition into and within the university can only become more intense, as middle-class families jostle for position and bring every possible asset to bear on the competition to secure advantage. Until the political economy changes, that is the future for the Anglo-American university.

The university can facilitate meritocratic social allocation and intergenerational mobility when the right social order is in place, as in the Nordic countries. But it cannot and will not trigger the development of a more egalitarian society on its own. In the Nordic countries, as elsewhere, it is part of a much larger circuit of institutions and processes that shape income distribution, equality and mobility. Universities should set aside the self-fulfilling hubris that they are the principal maker of society. In aggregate, what happens with incomes, wealth, labour markets, taxation, government spending, social programmes and urban development is overwhelmingly more important. Christening the social realm a 'knowledge economy' or 'innovation society' will not change this. If there is to be a new opening and equalising of educational opportunity, the preconditions lie in changes in the distribution of economic rewards, a reduced tolerance for social hierarchy, and the re-democratisation of politics and policy.

References

Arum, R., Gamoran, A. and Shavit, Y. (2007). More inclusion than diversion: Expansion, differentiation and market structures in higher education. In Y. Shavit, R. Arum and A. Gamoran (eds.), *Stratification in Higher Education: A Contemporary Study* (pp. 1–35). Stanford: Stanford University Press.

Becker, G. (1964). *Human Capital: A Theoretical and Empirical Analysis with Special Reference to Education.* Chicago, IL: University of Chicago Press.

Bentele, K. (2013). Distinct paths to higher inequality? A qualitative comparative analysis of rising earnings inequality among U.S. States, 1980–2010. *Research in Social Stratification and Mobility*, 34, pp. 30–57.

Blanden, J., Gregg, P. and Machin, S. (2005). *Intergenerational Mobility in Europe and North America.* London: Centre for Economic Performance, London School of Economics.

Boliver, V. (2011). Expansion, differentiation, and the persistence of social class inequalities in British higher education. *Higher Education*, 61, pp. 229–242.

Boliver, V. (2013). How fair is access to more prestigious UK universities? *The British Journal of Sociology*, 64 (2), pp. 344–364.

Borgen, N. (2015). College quality and the positive selection hypothesis: The 'second filter' on family background in high-paid jobs. *Research in Social Stratification and Mobility*, 39, pp. 32–47.

Bourdieu, P. (1984). *Distinction: A Social Critique of the Judgment of Taste*. Trans. R. Nice. London: Routledge and Kegan Paul.

Bourdieu, P. (1993). *The Field of Cultural Production*. Trans. Various. New York: Columbia University Press.

Brand, J. and Xie, Y. (2010). Who benefits most from college?: Evidence for negative selection in heterogeneous economic returns to higher education. *American Sociological Review*, 75, pp. 273–302.

Cingano, F. (2014). Trends in income inequality and its impact on economic growth. *OECD Social, Employment and Migration Working Papers*, No. 163. Paris: OECD.

Corak, M. (2006). *Do Poor Children Become Poor Adults? Lessons from a cross country comparison of generational earnings mobility*. IZA Discussion Paper No. 1993. Bonn: Institute for the Study of Labor.

Corak, M. (2012). *Inequality from Generation to Generation: The United States in comparison*. Ottawa, Canada: Graduate School of Public and International Affairs, University of Ottawa.

Dale, S. and Krueger, A. (2011). *Estimating the Return to College Selectivity over the Career Using Administrative Earnings Data*. NBER Working Paper 17159. Cambridge, MA: National Bureau of Economic Research.

Davies, S. and Zarifa, D. (2012). The stratification of universities: Structural inequality in Canada and the United States. *Research in Social Stratification and Mobility*, 30, pp. 143–158.

Deresiewicz, W. (2014). *Excellent Sheep: The Miseducation of the American Elite and the Way to a Meaningful Life*. New York: Free Press.

Dorling, D. (2014). *Inequality and the 1%*. London: Verso.

Foucault, M. (2008). *The Birth of Biopolitics: Lectures at the College de France 1978–1979*. Houndmills: Palgrave Macmillan.

Gärtner, S. and Prado, S. (2012). *Inequality, Trust and the Welfare State: The Scandinavian model in the Swedish mirror*. Högre seminariet, 7 November. Ekonomisk-historiska institutionen, Göteborgs universitet.

Geiger, R. (2015). Does higher education cause inequality? Essay review on Mettler (2014) and Armstrong and Hamilton (2013). *American Journal of Education*, 121 (2), pp. 299–310.

Hanley, C. (2011). Investigating the organizational sources of high-wage earnings growth and rising inequality. *Social Science Research*, 40, pp. 902–916.

Hennessy, P. (2014). *Establishment and Meritocracy*. London: Haus Publishing.

Hoxby, C. and Avery, C. (2012). The missing 'one-offs': The hidden supply of high-achieving, low-income students. NBER Working Paper No. 18586. Washington: The National Bureau of Economic Research.

Kerr, C. (2001a/1963). *The Uses of the University*. 5th edition. First edition 1963. Cambridge, MA: Harvard University Press.

Kerr, C. (2001b). *The Gold and the Blue: A Personal Memoir of the University of California, 1949–1967. Volume 1: Academic Triumphs*. Berkeley: University of California Press.

Mettler, S. (2014). *Degrees of Inequality: How the Politics of Higher Education Sabotaged the American Dream*. New York: Basic Books.

Mincer, J. (1958). Investment in human capital and personal income distribution. *Journal of Political Economy*, 66 (4), pp. 281–302.

Mountford-Zimdars, A. and Sabbagh, D. (2013). Fair access to higher education: A comparative perspective. *Comparative Education Review*, 57 (3), pp. 359–368.

Organisation for Economic Cooperation and Development (OECD) (2014). *United States: Tackling High Inequalities, Creating Opportunities for All*. Paris: OECD.

Oxfam (2014). *Even It Up: Time to End Extreme Inequality*. Oxford: Oxfam GB.

Parry, G. (2011). Mobility and hierarchy in the age of near-universal access. *Critical Studies in Education*, 52 (2), pp. 135–149.

The PELL Institute (2015). *Indicators of Higher Education Equity in the United States*. Co-published with PennAHEAD, Graduate School of Education, University of Pennsylvania. http://www.pellinstitute.org/downloads/publications-Indicators_of_Higher_Education_Equity_in_the_US_45_Year_Trend_Report.pdf

Piketty, T. (2014). *Capital in the Twenty-first Century*. Trans. A. Goldhammer. Cambridge, MA: Belknap Harvard University Press.

Rivera, L. (2011). Ivies, extracurriculars, and exclusion: Elite employers' use of educational credentials. *Research in Social Stratification and Mobility*, 29, pp. 71–90.

Rivera, L. (2012). Hiring as cultural matching: The case of elite professional service firms. *American Sociological Review*, 77 (6), pp. 999–1022.

Rivera, L. (2015). *Pedigree: How Elite Students Get Elite Jobs*. Princeton, NJ: Princeton University Press.

Robbins, L. (1963). *Higher Education: Report*. London: Her Majesty's Stationery Office.

Robbins, L. (1966). *The University in the Modern World*. New York: St Martin's Press.

Saez, E. (2013). *Striking It Richer. The evolution of top incomes in the United States*. Berkeley: Department of Economics, University of California. http://eml.berkeley.edu//~saez/saez-UStopincomes-2012.pdf

Schultz, T. (1959). Investment in man: An economists' view. *Social Service Review*, 33 (2), pp. 109–117.

Schultz, T. (1960). Capital formation by education. *Journal of Political Economy*, 68 (6), pp. 571–583.

Schultz, T. (1961). Investment in human capital. *American Economic Review*, 51 (1), pp. 1–17.

Shavit, Y., Arum, R. and Gamoran, A. (2007). *Stratification in Higher Education: A Comparative Study*. Stanford: Stanford University Press.

Soares, J. (2007). *The Power of Privilege: Yale and America's Elite Colleges*. Stanford: Stanford University Press.

Stiglitz, J. (2013). *The Price of Inequality*. Penguin: London.

Tholen, G., Brown, P., Power, S. and Allouch, A. (2013). The role of networks and connections in educational elites' labour market entrance. *Research in Social Stratification and Mobility*, 34, pp. 142–154.

Thomsen, P., Munk, M., Eiberg-Madsen, M. and Hansen, G. (2013). The educational strategies of Danish university students from professional and working class backgrounds. *Comparative Education Review*, 57 (3), pp. 457–480.

Tridico, P. (2012). Financial crisis and global imbalances: Its labour market origins and the aftermath. *Cambridge Journal of Economics*, 36, pp. 17–42.

Unz, R. (2012). The myth of American meritocracy. *The American Conservative*, December, pp. 14–51.

Wisman, J. (2013). Wage stagnation, rising inequality and the financial crisis of 2008. *Cambridge Journal of Economics*, 37, pp. 921–945.

CHAPTER SEVEN

Freedom and Control in the Constrained Modern University

FRANCINE ROCHFORD

Introduction

The ideal conception of the university, rarely effected, places such 'glittering generalities' as academic freedom (Riddiford, 2009) at its centre. The independence of thought necessary to the 'advancement of truth' (Association of American Colleges and Universities, 1940, p. 3), however insecure it may have been in the past, appears almost tokenistic in the modern university environment. The familiar constraints on the university—a highly competitive global market, the compromises required in an 'enabling regulatory environment' with 'appropriate financial incentives' (World Bank, 2002, p. 83)—have an impact on the activities of the individual academic. Whereas the first 'academic revolution' integrated research into the academic mission (Rodrigues, 2011) the 'second academic revolution' has imposed on universities a '"new third mission"—contributing to the economy' (Ylijoki, 2003, pp. 307–308). There are two aspects to this: universities must demonstrate 'their relevance to labour market conditions and prospects' (Olssen & Peters, 2005, p. 326). Secondly, universities must demonstrate their own role in socio-economic development. To do this, universities have typically adopted the strategies and tools of commercial entities. Thus, universities have deployed the internal management systems of private corporations, and have deployed the external relationship management strategies of marketers.

Thus, management, and research management in particular, share characteristic audit and accounting mechanisms across university systems, imposing parallel homogenising systems (Olssen & Peters, 2005, p. 327). The university academic (or academic-turned administrator) remains iconoclastic at their peril, because they must account for their priorities, their outcomes and their time using accounting and audit tools. Conversely, universities deploy marketing strategies to demonstrate the 'difference' of their university as an employer and as an undergraduate destination. The problem with this, however, is that universities can't afford to align themselves with people, attitudes or arguments that have become, in the 'post-democratic' space, 'beyond dispute'. Contention, argument and conclusions relating to important questions have already occurred in public discourse, short-circuiting moderating processes of hypothesis, testing, enquiry and counter-enquiry.

This chapter explores one of the consequences of this process by interrogating the role of the university in facilitating the emergence of a 'post-democratic political configuration' (Swyngedouw, 2010) in which universities abandon the posture of enquiry and lock their teaching and research priorities to specific, narrow and uncontested priorities. This occurs when universities are compelled to adopt marketing and branding techniques suitable to a highly competitive market. Once these techniques have been deployed, they begin to exercise control on core aspects of the university—the curriculum and research—and rewrite internal controls so that consistent branding and management of the university 'message' to the market dominates the obligation of the individual scholar to engage the discipline.

The co-option of the university in the process of marketisation would not be significant if it did not occur at a system level; the abandonment of the critical position in favour of a market-friendly consensus is problematic. It minimises the key point of difference between the university and other research- and teaching-able institutions. By allowing this to occur, the university is collaborating in its own devaluation.

The implications of systemic co-option have been identified by academics, particularly in scientific disciplines (Evans & Packham, 2003). The consequences of 'entanglement' (Ylijoki, 2003) are felt within the university, as 'the fundamental norms and values of the scientific community turn upside down', replacing scientific commons with commercialisation of results and disinterested enquiry with political or profit motive (Ylijoki, 2003, p. 308). Along with these discipline concerns, however, there have been contentious high-profile outcomes of this process. The political decision to fund an Australian Consensus Centre at the University of Western Australia, and a subsequent decision by the University to 'cancel the contract and return the money to the government' in the face of 'strong opposition' to the Centre (Johnson, 2015), emphasises the pressure placed on universities by government incentives, and other, sometimes contrary pressures on universities arising as a result of their exposure to market forces.

This chapter will first canvas the constraints on a modern university in the context of massification and the shift to New Public Management and managerialism as the modern governance style (Rochford, 2006). It will then attempt to conceptualise the way in which these changes have modified universities' relationship with the creation and transmission of 'knowledge'. It will then consider whether this challenges the claims of universities to 'academic freedom'—a historical ideal and 'key legitimating concept' (Menand, 1996). It will consider if, in fact, universities can articulate a new set of meanings with claims to legitimacy in the new public sphere—the 'post-political' or 'post-democratic' domain in which claims to truth have already been canvassed and concluded in a noisy and unmoderated public discourse—or if the adoption of those conclusions in their marketing strategies, values and visions precludes further engagement in certain topics of concern.

The university ideal

The *cri de coeur* in university common rooms—or more commonly now, corridors—is the loss of meaning of academic vocations and of universities in general. That '[t]he current model of the Australian university is broken' (Murphy, 2013), that there is 'a crisis of confidence' (Moses, 1995), that the system 'has lost its way and is rudderless in a sea of change' (Department of Employment, Education, Training and Youth Affairs, 1997); that '[u]niversities are in crisis' (Bauman, 1997). This is not limited to Australian universities: in the United States, Zusman notes that crisis and change 'have been the rule, not the exception' (Zusman, 2005). These assertions are not always disinterested, and nor do they hold particular cogency other than as expostulations or tools of emphasis. The significance of such arguments may be that they suggest a meta-dialogical framing of the subject of the university.

It is possible that the continuing atmosphere of unease and 'general conceptual loss' (Gaita, 1997) that characterise academic accounts of the role of the university may arise from a sense of powerlessness which may differ from the gripes of those on the factory floor against 'management'. In itself this would be not be problematic if the historic university ideal held—that the university is the sum of its scholars and students, and that academic work was insulated from pressures that could corrupt academic enquiry. However, if scholars and students are personifications of the university and are free of improper pressure to write and teach as they considered appropriate, why would distinguished academics be 'powerless' to contend with the forces that were shaping the new idea of the university?

Although several causes of disquiet—public sector reform and correlative introduction of managerialism and the corporate model (Coaldrake, 1995), the Dawkins reforms (in Australia) (Ashenden, 2012) and equivalent trends overseas (Shattock, 1996), 'massification' (Schapper & Mayson, 2004), reduced government funding per student (Davis, 2017), the corporate model (Marginson & Considine, 2000)—can be readily identified, there is little likelihood that a reversal of the trend is imminent. These are interrelated, causally dependent, deeply embedded responses to external pressures. They also tend to be homogenous across jurisdictions (Kelsey, 1998).

The societal and economic imperatives that create these pressures are not all negative—who, for instance, would wish for a decline in economic fortunes so that students would not aspire to a more prosperous future? How many would own to a desire that a smaller portion of the population would obtain a higher degree? Many of the concerns relating to massification and consequent pressure to adopt corporate forms can be attributed to a sense that nomenclature is problematic. 'Modern universities' are not what traditional universities were. This is, in fact, historically accurate. Many post-secondary institutions in Australia are amalgamations of universities and other higher education providers as a result of the Dawkins 'revolution' (Watts, 2006) and its equivalent in other western university systems. The end of the binary system was only one of the reforms instituted by the reform process, at the end of which a whole range of courses which would not necessarily have been offered by traditional universities are offered to students who would not have achieved a place at a traditional university.

The accompanying press of students and rising costs of the expanded sector required additional funding and answerability for that funding, consistent with the premises of transparency and accountability of New Public Management. Accordingly, funding has been accompanied by a suite of regulatory mechanisms which apply a series of brakes on the activities of academics and demand a growing managerial class. This generates academic pushback, but counter-critique is readily deployed to respond to the concerns of academics: Watts posits that the subtext of many critiques of regulatory control 'is the concern about governments pursuing justice and access objectives, leading to the destruction of universities' capacity to insist on rigorous selection standards. Critique of the "idea of the modern university" ends up sounding like advocacy of social inequality' (Watts, 2006, p. 253). In other words, academic critique of the modern university is portrayed as reactionary and elitist. It could be argued that this is one of those 'short-circuited' arguments in the post-democratic public domain in which 'ivory tower' becomes the ad hominem fallacy that concludes the argument.

The government strategies which have transformed universities in these characteristic ways can be broadly considered manifestations of neo-liberalisation that enable 'governance at a distance'. Rather than occupy the policy domain, governments of all persuasions have abandoned it in favour of technocratic management (Swyngedouw, 2010). 'In line with the notions of remote government control, self-regulatory systems, and a model of government supervision instead of stringent planning and control' (de Boer & Goedegebuure, 1995), government policy planning in relation to universities is apparently market-based. It is supplemented by accountability mechanisms that in themselves place financial pressure on universities. In turn, universities adopt complex and costly accountability controls, by which the university administration effects governance of academics. In place of discipline-based academic governance, teaching and research decisions are the result of institution-wide strategies and plans, which reward on-target outcomes with a mix of cross-subsidisation, grants and penalties.

The university in the knowledge economy

What further insights can be gained in this heavily contested domain? This account does not attempt to repeat the extensive literature attributing cause, postulating effect or apportioning blame. Rather, it highlights a tendency apparent in wider society and becoming identifiable in universities—channelling of matters considered appropriate for critical enquiry through the multiplicity of accountability and performance management tools now deployed by the modern university.

Often this phenomenon is masked by the identification of the 'entrepreneurial' (Philpott, Dooley, O'Reilly, & Lupton, 2011) aspect of the modern university, by the 'dominant market ethos' (Lam, 2010), or discussion of the 'third mission' or 'triple helix' of university–industry–government relations (Etzkowitz, Webster, Gebhardt, & Cantisano Terra, 2000). However, what is becoming apparent is a change in the cultural understanding of knowledge itself prompted by the dual developments of an increasingly proprietary attitude towards knowledge 'products' on the one hand and a democratisation of knowledge on the other. It is argued that '[t]he collegial community that in the past was mainly interested in producing a free and widespread product, i.e. knowledge, ... is now driven by the necessity to reach high levels of revenue' (Barnabe, 2004, p. 3).

It is trivially obvious that many types of knowledge are saleable; and conversely, the manipulation of legal instruments to ensure economic rewards for intellectual endeavour is of long standing. The enactment of the *Statute of Anne* (1710, 8 Ann c,19) was recognition of the societal benefits of vesting ownership of intellectual property in works (Zimmerman, 2010). The concomitant disadvantage—the cost to society of the creation of monopoly interests—was balanced by the necessity to value intellectual work; otherwise none would choose to perform it. Other intellectual property regimes—particularly patent protection—attempted to balance the cost of vesting a monopoly in an inventor with the public benefit of promulgation of research by registration of patents (Scotchmer, 1991). The balance between the constraints of monopoly and the benefits of knowledge creation is in perpetual flux, but tends towards the utilitarian or at least economic justification (Scotchmer, 1991).

The university is neither the sole creator of knowledge nor its primary repository. Historically it has been in receipt of public funding; again, often for utilitarian reasons. For instance, traditionally one of the arguments for the public funding of university research, particularly in areas with potential industrial applications such as pharmaceuticals, has been the potential for underinvestment in 'basic research' (Aghion, Dewatripont, & Stein, 2008). However, the modern university competes in the knowledge economy both with those exploiting the economic value of knowledge and those willing to create and disseminate intellectual property freely—and with increasing ease. The university–industry–government interaction sees institutions increasingly 'take the role of the other' (Etzkowitz, 2003, p. 295), superseding the 'traditional match of institution to function' (Etzkowitz, 2003, p. 295). The changing relationship between the university and knowledge has seen a complex shift in the expectations of the university by government and industry, and in the expectations within the university of its staff. The entrepreneurial university requires academics to take on a new role—that of 'promoting innovation' (Etzkowitz, 2003, p. 300).

Conversely, 'industry' is incorporating academic characteristics to incubate new knowledge, and take on many of the traditional functions of the university. Universities are now in direct competition with 'industry' in knowledge creation. However, in many modern economies they are required to demonstrate that they do not enjoy competitive benefits denied to private investors, and respond to economic and policy settings with largely the same suite of legal and market instruments as other competitors. The Australian *Competition Policy Reform Act* 1995 (Cth) applies to commercial activities of universities to eliminate competitive advantages experienced by government businesses when competing with the private sector.

One of the manifestations of the 'knowledge economy' is the crowded market for the *supply* of knowledge products—a market in which the university had once occupied a privileged position. In the competition for students, institutions with the appellation of 'university' are increasingly required to differentiate themselves from privately funded and non-university competitors. In the pursuit of government funding, universities respond to national priorities or projected course demand. Thus, they enact the imperatives of capitalism and the market economy, reorganise their branding and teaching focus and restructure their operations, targeting courses and subjects with low enrolment. Short-term, vocational and government policy priorities have more force than disciplinary concerns. As Coetzee notes, '[a]ll over the world, as governments retreat from their traditional duty to foster the common good and reconceive of themselves as mere managers of national economies, universities have been coming under pressure to turn themselves into training schools equipping young people with the skills required by a modern economy' (Coetzee, 2013). In that space, however, non-accredited training institutes, technical colleges and online providers can provide cost advantages not available to universities who are also obliged to research and provide a community service (Byon, 2015).

Universities are obliged to distinguish themselves as providers of attractive and relevant education for students, employers and funding providers, whilst proving themselves high-quality research institutions within complex and technical government parameters (Trounson, 2015). They have adopted commercial forms of governance but are constrained by legislation and are required to comply with burdensome audit and accountability regimes (PhillipsKPA, 2012). Many have historical advantages in real estate, equipment or expertise, but they are not necessarily permitted to take advantage of them because of the requirement of competitive neutrality. In their primary roles of creating and disseminating knowledge, universities have few remaining natural advantages over their competitors, and are increasingly constrained from utilising those advantages.

Academic freedom in uncontested terrain

One of the few remaining advantages inherent in the university—one of the key areas in which it can be distinguished from the other creators and disseminators of knowledge—is in the university's adherence to academic freedom. Indeed, '[a]cademic freedom is generally considered a *sine qua non* for the proper functioning of modern universities' (Vrielink et al., 2011, p. 118)—whatever academic freedom actually means (Rochford, 2003).

Universities and governments provide rhetorical adherence to the premise of academic freedom. The influential American Association of University Professors has declared that academic freedom is fundamental to both research and teaching in pursuit of the 'common good', and the common good—rather than the interest of the individual teacher or institution—is the aim of Institutions of Higher Education (Association of American Colleges and Universities, 1940). Recent case law in the United States has reassured proponents of academic freedom that it is still protected (Demers v Austin, 2014). In Australia, it is legislatively supported, if obliquely. A Senate Standing Committee on Education, Employment and Workplace Relations conducted an enquiry into academic freedom in 2008, in which the principle of academic freedom was assumed rather than asserted (Senate Standing Committee on Education, Employment and Workplace Relations, 2008). The Committee made particular reference to the Australian Universities Quality Agency submission, which stated that '[a]cademic freedom is a necessary pre-condition in the development of a knowledge society and in the foundation of knowledge institutions such as universities' (Australian Universities Quality Agency, 2008). Reference to 'the values of a university relating to teaching, research, independence and academic freedom' appears in the requirements of Council membership in Victorian legislation creating universities (see, for instance, the *Deakin University Act* 2009 (Vic), the *Victoria University Act* 2010 (Vic), the *Swinburne University of Technology Act* 2010 (Vic) and the *University of Melbourne Act* 2009 (Vic)).

Fixing upon concrete outcomes for academic freedom of the slew of external and internal pressures on academics is problematic, however. It is common to cite the risk of proxies such as grant applications or grant success in designated fields becoming the goals of university research, thus acting as a constraint on research direction rather than as a constraint on academic freedom per se. Those pressures are likely to impact on more junior researchers and those without tenure, potentially creating risks for the coming generation of researchers. However, if it is to be effective, academic freedom is not merely a right inherent to an individual, but an attitude and environment afforded to the university and enjoyed by the university as an institution (Vrielink et al., 2011). The pressure on the institution, and the way in which it resists those pressures, is both the measure of academic freedom and its merit. University autonomy is required to create the conditions in which academic freedom can be practised. Is the university autonomous—that is, capable of providing real critique—when it is conjoined to industry by grant priorities? The 'post-democratic' global context, described as one in which the politics of consensus arguably replaces real political dissent, has as its organising principle the capitalist market.

Research into the consequences of new models of academic engagement with industry suggests a series of consequences, both positive and negative (Perkmann et al., 2013). External engagement with industry is reported to result in change to the choice of research topics in some cases, and in any event tends to arise from individual characteristics—'analytically, commercialisation is more akin to an entrepreneurial act … involving an emphasis on the aspects of opportunity recognition and individual economic incentives' (Perkmann et al., 2013, p. 430). Each scholar has his or her own motivation for engaging in industry collaboration or commercialisation. If, in response to government priorities, universities prioritise this type of 'applied' research, it results in the selection and promotion of individuals with particular motivations and interests. Over time, universities, particularly those most vulnerable to funding constraint, will not risk 'frontier researchers', but will seek those engaged in external collaboration. University policy settings in promotional criteria and teaching load calculations lead to that outcome. There is limited research on the intra-organisational factors that surround commercialisation and external collaboration. Government policy settings and university responses to those settings mandate collaboration with industry. However, '[e]xtant analyses have neglected to consider its impact on educational outputs, such as time devoted to teaching, curriculum and courses development, and teaching quality. Insights into this aspect of engagement would be highly valuable in extending our knowledge of the benefits or costs of "third stream" activities within the context of universities' other missions' (Perkmann et al., 2013, p. 431).

Post-political public engagement

More problematically, universities have been motivated to make strong alignments between key government priorities, themselves borrowed from post-democratic discursive frames, and universities' own value sets and external orientations. What this means is that the powerful or controlling elements of universities, which subscribe to the model of 'consensus politics' and assume the values of the capitalist market, have to avoid the political and reputational risk they would incur if they transgressed populist mores. A cogent example of Australian universities' desire to avoid 'transgression' of consensus mores arose in the decision of the University of Western Australia to decline to host the 'Australia Consensus Centre' which was to 'undertake detailed cost benefit analysis into many of Australia's biggest challenges' (Johnson, 2015). The centre was unpopular because of the involvement of Bjorn Lomborg, who has been described as '"infamous" for his views on climate change' (Milman, 2015). Despite the Vice Chancellor's assurance that the centre was 'not a centre to study climate change' (Johnson, 2015), the involvement of Bjorn Lomborg generated the hostility of staff and students to such an extent that the university withdrew from the arrangement. More recently, (South Australian) Flinders University was invited to host the centre, but the South Australian government has opposed it 'on "ideological" grounds' (Owen, 2015). This complex example demonstrates the pressures placed on universities. The offer of government funding, aligned with the (Federal) Liberal party, was an incentive for the university, but the high profile of the climate change movement enabled such a response that the university risked its reputation in key marketing demographics if it agreed to host the centre.

It could be argued that universities, pressed into new shapes by these multiple external pressures, have conceded to a new relationship with knowledge. Knowledge, as a marketable product, is to be measured, costed, valued and utilised jealously in the development of the university's reputation. Knowledge, as a reputational risk, must be assessed, guarded, finessed and repackaged. As universities take their place in this post-political public space, they are increasingly tempted to constrain their activities. Capitalism and the market economy have reformatted the internal governance and networks of the university, replacing flat, collegial, non-hierarchical systems with 'technocratic management and problem-focused governance, sustained by populist discursive regimes' (Swyngedouw, 2010, p. 215).

The subjects of consensus, those themes that dominate the post-political public domain, may be co-produced by—or rather, within—universities. The way these themes are elevated to discourses which 'forge, configure and entrench' the public domain (Swyngedouw, 2010, p. 216) is another process altogether. A 'matter of fact' becomes a 'matter of concern' in the new public domain through modern, short-circuited processes. Knowledge was once, to a great degree, moderated by expertise. Now, unprecedented access to techniques of mass communication, the capacity to initiate instantaneous worldwide unmoderated commentary and sophisticated but accessible film and music production software sideline the role of the expert. This short-circuited process is not within the control of the university and uses techniques that target non-rational responses—rhetoric, performance, gesture—to manipulate discourse (Swyngedouw, 2010, pp. 217–218). The university, locked into the capitalist market framework, becomes complicit in this process because it can't afford to resist it.

Mission and value statements

Of course, compliance with uncontested truths does not always occur through the use of directive behaviour, at least in relation to the academic operations of institutions. In the Lomborg example, the university's actions have been described as 'soft-censorship' (Wilson, 2015). But it is rare that events reach this pitch of emotion. Rather, internal techniques of governance at a distance signal the uncontested norms within which academic enquiry will be funded. Universities' control over unfunded research is less complete; even there, however techniques can be deployed. The use of key accountability techniques such as performance management and promotional matrices constrains the creation and promulgation of knowledge.

So, acting within the capitalist framework and adapting to the apolitical movements that have been mobilised and have assumed an entrenched position, universities deploy techno-managerial tools to harness the dominant message and use it to market advantage. The creation of Vision and Mission statements and integration of 'Values' into the decision systems in the university organisation create a discursive matrix operating as an internal and an external statement of meaning—performative gestures for consumption. Typical values packaged in this way are the pursuit of excellence, service to the community and rigour in scholarship and academic freedom. The codification of statements of values such as these acts as 'instructions' for organisational members to assist them to 'distinguish between activities that conform to institutional imperatives and those that do not' (Morphew & Hartley, 2006, p. 457). Conversely, they purport to 'communicate ... characteristics, values and history to key external constituents' (Morphew & Hartley, 2006, p. 457). However, critics also note that mission statements exist because they are expected to exist. They are a manifestation of the techno-managerial tools of modern capitalism and demonstrate university compliance with the rules of the now uncontested domain. 'Institutional theorists point to organizational artefacts like mission statements and knowingly describe them as ritualistic or mythological ... they serve a legitimating function' (Morphew & Hartley, 2006, p. 458).

The normative prescription of mission statements has the supplementary requirement that the mission statement should 'incorporate the elements commonly understood to form the basis for a higher education mission' (Morphew & Hartley, 2006, p. 458). The adoption of 'vague and vapid goals' (Morphew & Hartley, 2006, p. 459) does not challenge the institution to perform, but rather act as a symbol of alignment with uncontested norms. Modern mission and value statements, however, go beyond the claims of excellence, the search for knowledge, teaching and service to the community. Many universities lay claim to uncontested 'matters of concern' such as 'sustainability', 'globalisation', 'equity', 'inclusiveness', 'participation', 'relevance', 'connectivity', 'innovation' or 'regionalism.' It has been argued that universities make claims to values to 'signal key external constituencies that the institution in question shares these groups' values and goals' (Morphew &

Hartley, 2006, p. 466). In particular, these values and goals signal to the key government constituency which is the source of research funding and which sets the policy environment in which teaching is funded.

Because of this core constituency, there is a high degree of homogeneity in the values asserted by Australian institutions. This can be illustrated by a comparison between a 'Group of Eight' institution (a leading research-focused university, broadly comparable with the ancient or 'sandstone' universities in the United Kingdom), the 'Innovative Research Universities' (IRU) (technology-focused universities, comparable to the 1994 Group in the United Kingdom), and the 'Australian Technology Network', primarily composed of universities which were previously institutes of technology. Despite their radically different history and student and staff composition, these three groups of institutions make claims to similar sets of values and goals, aligning themselves with stated government priorities. These clusters of common interest may result in different behaviour, interests and outcomes, particularly in industry engagement although possibly for more complex reasons (Perkmann et al., 2013).

The Universities of Melbourne, Sydney, Adelaide, Queensland, New South Wales and Western Australia, Australian National University and Monash Universities form the Group of Eight (or Go8), and typify the institutions first created as universities in Australia, being the oldest universities and as a consequence having a marked advantage in position, bequests and research funding. Exemplifying the vague stated goals of this type of institutions is the University of Melbourne which cites three core strategic objectives: globally competitive research, provision of internationally recognised degree programmes and external engagement: the 'triple helix' (The University of Melbourne, 2011). The University of Sydney states its values as 'Engaged enquiry' and 'Mutual accountability' (The University of Sydney, 2010). Equity and participation is an explicit aim in these universities, despite historically lower levels of participation amongst students of low socio-economic status (Koshy, 2014), partly because those values are aligned to government funding mechanisms. Thus, the Go8 group aims, *inter alia* to 'expand opportunities for domestic and international students, regardless of background, to participate in higher education at the frontier of world practice' (Group of Eight Australia, n.d.).

The IRU in Australia are a network made up of Charles Darwin, James Cook, Griffith, Flinders, La Trobe and Murdoch Universities. These universities tended to be founded in the period of expansion of university education in the 1960s and 1970s, and although they may have had to combine with Colleges of Advanced Education as a consequence of the Dawkins Reforms, they were already established as research universities. The aims of the IRU are to 'build profile and a strong voice with government and other influential bodies', to 'enhance quality' and to 'create opportunities' (Innovative Research Universities, 2015). Again, the language of equity is assumed, although it has a different focus.

The 'Australian Technology Network' is made up of universities which were, historically, linked with industry or were institutes of technology. This group is made up of Curtin University, Queensland University of Technology, Royal Melbourne Institute of Technology (or 'RMIT University'), the University of South Australia and the University of Technology, Sydney. It signals claims to 'innovation' and 'enterprise', practicality, partnerships with industry and professional education (Australian Technology Network of Universities, 2004). These universities are signalling that they are relevant to the needs of the economy and enterprise.

The mission and value statements of each university alone must align with that of the group. In turn these statements must signal alignment with key stakeholder (particularly government) priorities. Universities, however, are faced with a high degree of homogeneity in Australian policy settings across states and constituencies, making it difficult for universities to differentiate themselves. Value statements speak to the fact that 'institutions include in their mission what their benefactors value' (Morphew & Hartley, 2006, p. 467) rather than what the institutions actually believe, and in the small, consensus-framed Australian society, this leads to depressing sameness.

The development and use of mission and value statements may serve to legitimate the university's continued operation and to signal compliance with the neoliberal environment in which it operates. It also signals acceptance of a range of other normative or global assumptions. Thus, there will typically be acceptance of the benefits of globalisation, of diversity, of openness, of inclusiveness and of 'opportunity for all'. These sentiments appear unexceptional, but ignore their political content. Globalisation, to take one commonly espoused value or mission, could readily be reinterpreted as a euphemism for anti-protectionism, colonialism (Altbach, 2004), cultural diffusion and reinforcement of inequality. There is a sense in which universities appear to be stating the obvious when they make claim to the benefits of globalisation, but there is also a clear tendency to strip the term of its political or contentious meanings. Universities make value statements which align with government policy, and government policy may be aspirational or a statement of the inevitable. By incorporating such sentiments in university planning and publicity statements, then aligning its internal research and teaching with these statements, the university is both adapting to the post-political space and facilitating its emergence. What should be highly charged political concepts are neutered and harnessed for marketing purposes—does that render them beyond dispute within the university? At the very least, if required to choose between a research project funded because it aligned with the espoused goal of the institution and the project which was not aligned, a researcher with an eye to promotion, or even a positive performance management review, would choose an aligned project.

Along with these political concepts, universities have become complicit in rendering other facts 'beyond dispute' (Ylijoki, 2003, p. 217). The value sets or norms encompassed in university mission and value statements align with external institutions, such as funding bodies, and make claims to authority. Although there may be a 'lack of coherence among competing scientific understandings' (Sarewitz, 2004), the underlying 'variety of normative lenses' (Sarewitz, 2004), and the short-circuiting of the value-formation process, which would have identified those different lenses, renders sets of 'facts' uncontestable.

Articulating the meaning of the university

When a university accedes to the consensus, and allows a matter of fact to become a matter of concern, it triggers soft-censorship. The university as employer has both directive power and technocratic tools of governance and deploys these against academic staff. Apart from internal funding, a primary technique of governance is the 'performance management' of staff (Meriac, Gorman, & Macan, 2015). Where 'performance effectiveness indicators' have to be assigned to academic staff, the integration of the external projection of the university's values with its internal values gives rise to the potential for 'soft-censorship'.

Morphew and Hartley note that 'one of the primary points of institutional theory, [is] that an organization such as a university succeeds when everyone inside and outside the organization agrees that it is a university' (Morphew & Hartley, 2006, p. 458). A university's statement of values, or mission statement, articulates the meaning the university wishes to project—the point of difference between the university and other organisations. Where a value statement is a reflection of an internal culture, the integration of that value is not of great moment. However, where the value statement is externally focused, market oriented or directive, then significant work must occur to ensure alignment within the university. This is a particular problem in the higher education sector, as 'higher education remains an institution one of whose outstanding features is an immense and omnipresent organisational memory—a feature shared by few other social institutions, with the obvious exception of the churches, the law courts and the legislature' (Neave & Van Vught, 1991, p. ix).

The formation of a value set in itself may occur through a variety of processes. Early research into the adoption of mission statements by universities in the United Kingdom found that '[d]rafting mission statements is considered to be a top level management activity and little participation from the wider staff, student or stakeholder body is invited' (Davies & Glaister, 1996, p. 291). In an environment in which the academic function has been sidelined by the managerial systemic function, this can render the co-option of 'values' a hollow process of echoing norms generated in the post-political public space and rendered consensual and uncontestable by their elevation to matters of concern.

How problematic is the alignment of institutional goals to the protection of an environment of academic freedom? Alignment with a new set of values occurs through a suite of mechanisms—collectively, aspects of 'performance management' which 'improve organisational performance by linking and aligning individual, team and organisational objectives and results' (ANAO, 2004–05; Morris, Stanton, & Young, 2007). One of the characteristics of New Public Management, performance management is easily justified as an exemplary manifestation of accountability for public funds. Successive government reports in multiple jurisdictions required the adoption of these techniques, and universities' reliance on public funding demanded their adoption (Hoare, 1995). The result has been called the 'Evaluative State' (Neave, 1988).

Performance management in Australian universities is largely a product of the 1990s, and in its modern form adopts developmental or control (or judgemental) tools (sometimes undistinguished). The success of implementation of those tools depends on the credibility of the process (Morris, Stanton, & Young, 2007). Ironically, given the necessity of 'agreement' or alignment between university values and performance management processes, the implementation of system-wide processes seems, in many cases, to be achieved by importing external consultants and off-the-shelf or bespoke information technology systems and applying them with apparently minimal modification. The use of these tools of remote governance is not value free. Their use implies acceptance of a framework within which values are developed, integrated and devolved (for instance, the value sets of modern capitalism). Moreover, the articulation of value statements in itself, where utilised as assertion of product differentiation in a marketing process, risks rendering contestable statements beyond dispute.

As the trend to use of these tools is relatively recent, there is little longitudinal research on its effects. Recent studies on the effect of performance management tools suggest that their emphasis on 'objective' measures is just a 'relocation' of subjectivity. More problematically, these tools could damage creativity in both teaching and research as scholars 'play it safe' (ter Bogt & Scapens, 2012).

However, in a relatively optimistic account, Sarrico notes that performance management, if it takes a developmental (rather than financial, operational or stakeholder) perspective, may empower the academic 'to take shared responsibility and the initiative for quality ... and take care of the processes in line with it. This means that the university should not only be accountable to the state and the market, but also to academia itself' (Sarrico, 2010, p. 155).

Conclusion

Echoing Kerr, it is possible to assert that Australia, like the United States, has relied utterly on education for solutions to a wide range of problems (Kerr, 1991, p. 21). Universities have become 'sandwiched between the state and the market' (Sarrico, 2010, p. 153). In doing so, they have adopted the dominant neoliberal paradigm—indeed, in an environment of funding constraint, they had little choice. In itself the paradigm is contestable, but the primary concern of this chapter has been the effect of implementation of the various accountability mechanisms arising from the adoption of this paradigm. The potential for techniques of governance to narrow fields of research, to emphasise 'mainstream' issues at the expense of developing or contentious areas, the homogenisation of the university sector and the (self-) suppression of creativity by both scholars and their institutions should cause universities to be on their guard. Further, the societies served by universities should be on their guard against institutions which have so wholeheartedly embraced the common ground.

This chapter interrogated the sustainability of the notion of a 'university' in the current political, social and economic environment. It has asserted that the features that denoted a traditional university have been compromised to such an extent that serious thought must be given to realigning institutions. There is room for retreat to the less nuanced epithet 'higher education provider' in appropriate instances, but those institutions that intend to assert the characteristics of a university face serious challenges. Utilisation of techniques of corporate governance shift universities into a post-democratic, post-political space, borrowing values from stakeholders and customers and retrofitting the techniques of corporate accountability onto the university. The systemic integration of systems of accounting and control, the alignment of goals within the university, cedes control of the articulation of the 'values' of the institution by creating a self-selecting bias towards those acceding to particular performance demands, those compliant with external goals and those willing to tolerate uncontested norms. This, in an institution seeking to preserve academic freedom—that is, in a university—is a perverse outcome.

References

Aghion, P., Dewatripont, M., & Stein, J. C. (2008). Academic freedom, private-sector focus, and the process of innovation. *RAND Journal of Economics* 39(3), 617–635.

Altbach, P. G. (2004). Globalisation and the university: myths and realities in an unequal world. *Tertiary Education and Management* 10(1), 3–25.
ANAO. (2004–05). *Audit Report No 6.* Canberra: Australian National Audit Office.
Association of American Colleges and Universities. (1940). *Statement of Principles on Academic Freedom and Tenure.* Retrieved January 20, 2010, from AAUP: http://www.aaup.org/AAUP/pubsres/policydocs/contents/1940statement.htm
Ashenden, D. (2012, 22 November). *Decline and Fall?.* Retrieved 26th February 2015, from: Inside Story: http:/inside. org.au/decline-and-fall.
Australian Technology Network of Universities. (2004). *About ATN.* Retrieved March 18, 2015, from Australian Technology Network of Universities: http://www.atn.edu.au/About-ATN/
Australian Universities Quality Agency. (2008). *Submission to the Senate Standing Committee on Education, Employment and Workplace Relations.* Commonwealth of Australia.
Barnabe, F. (2004). From ivory towers to learning organisations: the role of system dynamics in the 'managerialization' of academic institutions. In *Proceedings 22 System Dynamics International Conference* (pp. 40–59). Oxford.
Bauman, Z. (1997). The present crisis of the universities. In J. Brzezinski & L. Nowak (Eds.), *The Idea of the University* (pp. 47–54). Amsterdam: Rodopi Press.
Byon, J. (2015, July 29). Students already carry share of load. *The Australian iPad edition.*
Coaldrake, P. (1995). Implications for higher education of the public sector reform agenda. *The Australian Universities' Review* 38(1), 38–40.
Coetzee, J. M. (2013, November 1). *Universities Head for Extinction.* Retrieved March 11, 2015, from Mail & Guardian—Africa's best read: http://mg.co.za/article/2013-11-01-universities-head-for-extinction/
Davies, S. W., & Glaister, K. W. (1996). Spurs to higher things? Mission statements of UK universities. *Higher Education Quarterly* 50(4), 261–294.
Davis G. (2017). Australia: Why I Support the Deregulation of Higher Education. In: Mihut G., Altbach P. G., Wit H.. (eds) Understanding Global Higher Education. Global Perspectives on Higher Education. SensePublishers, Rotterdam.
de Boer, H., & Goedegebuure, L. (1995). Decision-making in higher education: a comparative perspective. *The Australian Universities' Review* 38(1), 41–47.
Demers v Austin, 746 F.3d 402 (9th Circuit Washington January 29, 2014).
Department of Employment, Education, Training and Youth Affairs. (1997). *Learning for Life—Review of Higher Education Financing and Policy.* A policy discussion paper.
Etzkowitz, H. (2003). Innovation in innovation: the Triple Helix of university-industry-government relations. *Social Science Information* 42(3), 293–337.
Etzkowitz, H., Webster, A., Gebhardt, C., & Cantisano Terra, B. R. (2000). The future of the university and the university of the future: evolution of ivory tower to entrepreneurial paradigm. *Research Policy* 29(2), 313–330.
Evans, G., & Packham, D. (2003). Ethical issues at the university-industry interface: a way forward? *Science and Engineering Ethics* 9(1), 3–16.
Gaita, R. (1997). Truth and the idea of the university. *Australian Universities' Review* 40(2), 13.
Group of Eight Australia. (n.d.). *Go8 Strategic Plan.* Retrieved March 18, 2015, from Group of Eight Australia: https://go8.edu.au/

Hoare, D. (1995). *Report of the Committee of Inquiry: Higher Education Management Review.* Canberra: Australian Government Publishing Service.

Innovative Research Universities. (2015). *Our Purpose and History*. Retrieved March 18, 2015, from Innovative Research Universities: http://www.iru.edu.au/

Johnson, P. (2015). *Message from the Vice-Chancellor on the Australian Consensus Centre.* Retrieved from the University of Western Australia: http://www.news.uwa.edu.au/201505087564/message-vice-chancellor-australian-consensus-centre.

Kelsey, Jane. 1998. 'Privatizing the Universities.' 25 *Journal of Law and Society* 51.

Kerr, C. (1991). *The Great Transformation in Higher Education, 1960-1980.* Albany: State University of New York Press.

Koshy, P. (2014). Student Equity Performance in Australian Higher Education: 2007-2012. *National Centre for Student Equity in Higher Education*. Perth.

Lam, A. (2010). From 'Ivory Tower Traditionalists' to 'Entrepreneurial Scientists'? Academic scientists in fuzzy university-industry boundaries. *Social Studies of Science* 40(2), 307–340.

Melbourne University Act 1958 (Vic). (n.d.).

Marginson, S., & Considine, M. (2000). *The Enterprise University*. Cambridge: Cambridge University Press.

Menand, L. (1996). The limits of academic freedom. In Menand, L. *The Future of Academic Freedom* (pp 3-20). Chicago: University of Chicago Press.

Meriac, J., Gorman, P, Allen, C., & Macan, T. (2015). Seeing the forest but missing the trees: the role of judgments in performance management. *Industrial and Organizational Psychology*. 102-108.

Milman, O. (2015, July 28). Bjorn Lomborg's $4m centre rejected by Flinders University academics. *The Guardian online.*

Morphew, C. C., & Hartley, M. (2006). Mission statements: a thematic analysis of rhetoric across institutional type. *The Journal of Higher Education* 77(3), 456–471.

Morris, J., Stanton, P., & Young, S. (2007). Performance management in higher education—the great divide. *Association of Industrial Relations Academics of Australia and New Zealand*, 18–32.

Moses, I. (1995). Tensions and tendencies in the management of quality and autonomy in Australian Higher Education. *The Australian Universities' Review* 38(1), 11–15.

Murphy, P. (2013). The rise and fall of our bureaucratic universities. *Quadrant* 57(5), 48–52.

Neave, G. (1988). On the cultivation of quality, efficiency and enterprise: an overview of recent trends in higher education in Western Europe. *European Journal of Education* 23(1/2), 7–23.

Neave, G., & Van Vught, F. A. (1991). *Prometheus Bound—The Changing Relationship between Government and Higher Education in Western Europe.* Oxford: Pergamon Press.

Olssen, M., & Peters, M. A. (2005). Neoliberalism, higher education and the knowledge economy: from the free market to knowledge capitalism. *Journal of Education Policy* 20(3), 313–345.

Owen, M. (2015, July 29). State's rebuff of $4m Lomborg policy centre slammed as 'bizarre'. *The Australian* iPad edition

Perkmann, M., Tartari, V., McKelvey, M., Autio, E., Brostrom, A., D'este, P., et al. (2013). Academic engagement and commercialisation: a review of the literature on university-industry relations. *Research Policy* 42(2), 423–442.

PhillipsKPA. (2012, December). *Review of Reporting Requirements for Universities.* Retrieved December 18, 2013, from LH Martin Institute: http://www.lhmartininstitute.edu.au/userfiles/files/news-media/FinalReportReviewofReportingRequirementsForUniversities.pdf

Philpott, K., Dooley, L., O'Reilly, C., & Lupton, G. (2011). The entrepreneurial university: examining the underlying academic tensions. *Technovation* 31(4), 161–170.

Post, R. (2006). The structure of academic freedom. In B. Doumani (Ed.), *Academic Freedom After September 11.* MIT Press, Cambridge, MA. (p. 61).

Riddiford, M. (2009, October 14). *Academic freedom a political football.* Retrieved December 4, 2009, from The Australian: http://www.theaustralian.com.au/higher-education/opinion-analysis/academic-freedom-a-political-football/story-e6frgcko-1225786422196

Rochford, F. (2006). Is there any Clear Idea of a University? *Journal of Higher Education Policy and Management* 28(2), 147-158.

Rochford, F. (2003). Academic freedom as insubordination: the legalisation of the academy. 15(4) *Education and the Law* 249-262.

Rodrigues, C. (2011). Universities, the second academic revolution and regional development: a tale (solely) made of "techvalleys"? *European Planning Studies* 19(2), 179-194.

Royal Melbourne Institute of Technology Act 1992 (Vic). (n.d.).

Sarewitz, D. (2004). How science makes environmental controversies worse. *Environmental Science and Policy* 7(5), 385–403.

Sarrico, C. S. (2010). On performance in higher education: towards performance governance. *Tertiary Education and Management* 16(2), 145–158.

Schapper, J. M., & Mayson, S. E. (2004). Internationalisation of curricula: an alternative to the Taylorisation of academic work. *Journal of Higher Education Policy and Management* 26(2), 189–205.

Scotchmer, S. (1991). Standing on the shoulders of giants: cumulative research and the patent law. *The Journal of Economic Perspectives* 5(1), 29–41.

Senate Standing Committee on Education, Employment and Workplace Relations. (2008). *Allegations of Academic Bias in Universities and Schools: Report.* Canberra: Commonwealth of Australia.

Shattock, M. (ed) (1996). *The Creation of a University System.* Oxford: Blackwell Publishers

Swinburne University of Technology Act 1992 (Vic). (n.d.).

Swyngedouw, E. (2010). Apocalypse forever? Post-political populism and the spectre of climate change. *Theory Culture Society* 27(2-3), 213–232.

ter Bogt, H. J., & Scapens, R. W. (2012). Performance management in universities: effects of the transition to more quantitative measurement systems. *European Accounting Review* 21(3), 451–497.

Trounson, A. (2015, July 29). 'Pedantic' assessment slammed. *The Australian iPad edition.*

University of Ballarat Act 1993 (Vic). (n.d.).

The University of Melbourne. (2011). *The University Plan 2011-2014.* Melbourne: The University of Melbourne.

The University of Sydney. (2010). *Strategic Plan 2011—2015.* Sydney: The University of Sydney.

Vrielink, J., Lemmens, P., Parmentier, S., & Rights, L. W. (2011). Academic freedom as a fundamental right. *Procedia Social and Behavioural Sciences* 13, 117–141.

Watts, R. (2006). The politics of discourse: academic responses to the Dawkins reforms of higher education, 1945–1991. *Melbourne Studies in Education* 47(1-2), 235–267.

Wilson, T. (2015, May 11). Soft censorship wins out over public policy. *The Australian online.*

World Bank. (2002). *Constructing Knowledge Societies: New Challenges for Tertiary Education.* Washington DC: World Bank.

Ylijoki, O.-H. (2003). Entangled in academic capitalism? A case-study on changing ideals and practices of university research. *Higher Education* 45(3), 307–335.

Zimmerman, D. L. (2010). Statute of Anne and its progeny: variations without a theme. *Houston Law Review* 47, 965–1011.

Zusman, A. (2005). Challenges facing higher education in the twenty-first century. In P. G. Altbach, R. O. Berdahl, & P. J. Gumport (Eds.), *American Higher Education in the Twenty-first Century* (pp. 115–160). Baltimore: The Johns Hopkins University Press.

CHAPTER EIGHT

Displaced towards a Networked University

NICOLAS STANDAERT

Introduction

The birth of a 'network society' appears to be a fundamental paradigm shift in the present world. It greatly affects the way society and also education will be organised in the future. As such, a whole new world enters into universities: web-thinking, accessibility, Internet, linking, nodes, hubs, clusters, hotspots, open source, open access, virtual, free, space, distant learning, are keywords of this shift.

A central question emerging from this shift is: What are the new or alternative ways of organising, practising and conceptualising university life in a network society? This question forms the background of the present contribution, which takes the 'networked university' as its main focus. Yet, the concept of 'network' is taken here as a challenge for universities, rather than an ideal.

In the following pages, I will first trace a short history of the university on the basis of the images of 'pyramid', 'pillar' and 'web'. Next, I will argue that by paying attention to 'displacements between spaces' one can start to frame the university of the future. As such, a networked university may come into being.

I will raise questions rather than provide answers. This is due to the fact that in a period of transition there are no immediate or ready-made answers. I will mainly use visual images or metaphors. In an article entitled '"Metaphoric Imaginings": Re-/Visions on the Idea of a University', Susan Robertson (2009) insisted on the importance of metaphors and showed how new metaphors are driving a set of alternatives to education which offer a refreshing change to what was before. As has been proven in practice, images also help more profound reflection on certain essential aspects. I hope in this way to stimulate reflection on new ideas about the university, which is the objective of this book.

First Metaphor: Pyramid, Pillar and Web—Three Forms of Academic Practice

In the history of the university and of the sciences, there has so far been one major paradigm shift: from renaissance to modernity. This transition occurred gradually and took about two hundred years before resulting in the university structure with which we are acquainted today. One could represent these two structures with the images of 'pyramid' and 'pillar'. The question that is raised today is whether we face a new paradigm shift which could quite radically influence the structure of the university and of scientific practice. The image of the new structure is that of a 'web'. In order to understand the present situation, it is helpful to look back at the characteristics of the medieval-renaissance and of the modern university.

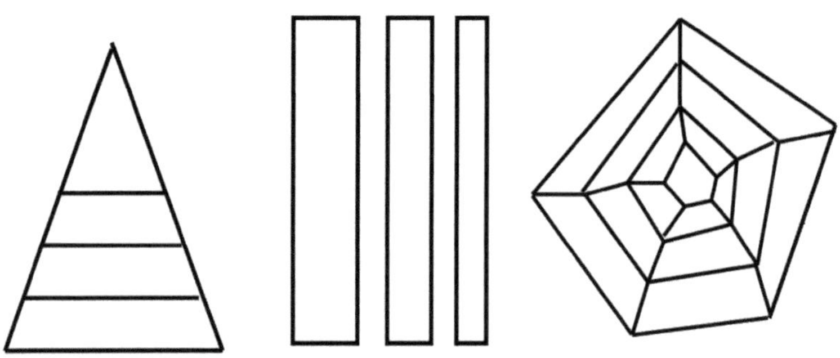

Figure 8.1: Pyramid, Pillar, Web.
Source: Author (2009).

Pyramid

As an image of the medieval-renaissance university, one can adopt the form of a 'pyramid'. Universities emerged at a time when both secular and religious society in Europe was organised like a pyramid: a hierarchical society of stratified social classes going from lower levels to the top (king or pope), the ultimate reference points in an all-embracing organisation.

Education was organised in a similar way and one can find this reflected in the classification of sciences. At the bottom were the *artes serviles* (agriculture, surgery, military sciences), which were usually not taught at universities; next came the *artes liberales* consisting of the *trivium* (grammar, rhetoric, dialectics) and the *quadrivium* (geometry, arithmetic, astronomy and music, all different disciplines belonging to mathematics), which were the foundation for the *artes superiores:* (Aristotelian) physics, ethics, metaphysics and theology respectively. Theology, as a speculative science concerning the coherence of things, was considered the 'Queen' of the sciences, while the other sciences were her ladies-in-waiting. Noteworthy is that the acquisition of knowledge was consecutive: one first had to study the *artes liberales* (at least partially) before proceeding to the higher sciences. One also has to underscore the place of mathematics in Aristotelian philosophy: it was an essential preparation to theology.

The social structure of the medieval university was not as unequivocal as the image of a pyramid suggests. The organisation of a university consisted in the fact that it was a *universitas magistrorum et scholarium*, a community of study, a *studium*, a guild of teachers and students, which formed the core of the relationship between teachers and students and which was spatially expressed in the colleges where the students and teachers lived. The *studium* was characterised by principles of autonomy and free research. As it was believed that there was one all-encompassing and ultimate truth, which formed the common ground, any particular truth could be put into question during an academic exercise, such as a debate. Pedagogy consisted of a culture of debate (*disputatio*) in which students entered at least once a week in a public and often controversial debate with each other. Finally one can point out that the *ius ubique docendi* (the right to teach everywhere) broke through the territorial demarcation of a particular university.

Pillar

As a result of developments during the Renaissance and the Enlightenment, a new structure came into place. During this transition, which took circa two hundred years, secular society moved away from the pyramid model towards a pillar (or silo) model, in which different entities no longer belong to one all-embracing structure but manifest themselves separately and independently from each other. This happened in society as a whole: Church and state were separated; independent nation-states were created; and different political parties, trade unions and Christian denominations were established. In academic life, the Enlightenment and the birth of 'modern' science radically changed the former pyramidal structure. We are the heirs of this shift and the existing system can still be described in terms of pillars.

One important evolution was the autonomous place that mathematics acquired. This resulted in a conflict with theology which ended with the lady-in-waiting knocking the 'Queen' from her throne and becoming queen herself, or even better, all former sciences becoming queens. From that time onwards, they were to a large extent separated from each other, working in a parallel way. Characteristic of these 'new' sciences is a specialised way of knowledge acquisition. In the structure of a modern university, theology, philosophy, language and literature, mathematics, physics are all separated from each other in distinct faculties and departments with their own study programmes adapted to their own discipline.

The relationship between teachers and students also underwent a significant change: a vertical transmission of knowledge (increasingly specialised) replaced the previous layered acquisition of knowledge: now omniscient teachers could proclaim all wisdom and knowledge in their field. Truth no longer belongs to theology alone: each science has its own (ultimate) truth. The pedagogical consequence was the replacement of the medieval debate by a one-way instruction in many European (mainly Catholic) countries. In terms of territorial demarcation the creation of the nation-state consolidated this pillar system since the international character of the *universitas magistrorum et scholarium* (with its *ius ubique docendi*) was abandoned. Universities were increasingly distinguished on the basis of their national character: empirical in Great Britain, rational in France, idealistic in Germany. Professors only taught in their own national language at their own university.

Web

The thesis of this contribution is that a new transition is taking place, one that is at least as revolutionary, if not more, than the one that led us into modernity. We are quickly moving towards the realisation of the 'network society', which will tremendously influence the way both secular society and education as a whole will be organised in the future (Castells, 1996; Grewal, 2009). This new reality, which mirrors the 'Internet', is driven by networks, interdisciplinary connections, real and virtual meeting points and collaborations, both at a local as well as at an international (global) level. This so-called web model also entails fundamental structural changes from a vertical towards a more horizontal approach and away from the current linear structures towards multidimensional ones.

In the new structure of classification, the sciences still have their own discipline but become organically linked to each other within one space (cf. an ecosystem). This shift already appears in new names: e.g. 'life sciences' for medicine, agriculture, health, ecology, pharmacy and biology. Sciences themselves become dynamic spaces ('tissues'). Medicine, for example, had a hierarchical structure of body and head during the Renaissance; in modernity it differentiated various limbs with their own specialisation and students had to get acquainted with them separately. The new programmes in medicine now use dynamic terms: 'anatomy' becomes 'blood and blood cell–producing organs'; 'gynaecology' and 'paediatrics' become 'reproduction and development'. Moreover, new forms of acquisition of knowledge consist of not remaining enclosed within one's own discipline but to search for multidisciplinary, interdisciplinary and even transdisciplinary links with other sciences. Methodologically speaking, the mode of 'analogy' plays an important role: how changes in other sciences can be analogically applied to one's own discipline. In the structure of a university, the classrooms and separate spaces interconnect and form open networks.

In the relationship between teachers and students, exchange and communication become central and both parties are encouraged to treat each other as equals. In the acquisition of knowledge and its evaluation, the principle of authority is transferred to the peer group. The principle of a single absolute truth is put into question (cf. postmodernism). In the search for truth, one uses converging principles. In terms of pedagogy, one uses interactive methods and education itself becomes a process (project education, life-long learning). All kinds of Internet programmes allow new forms of teaching. Territorially speaking, strict demarcations are no longer respected. In Europe, Erasmus-Socrates programmes allow students and teachers to establish border crossing networks with colleagues.

If the rough sketch is correct, if indeed we are in a transitional period, then the question is how to deal with this new situation. Yet, this short historical overview has shown that a new system builds on a previous system and that the answers always preserve the essential characteristics of a university.

Second Metaphor: Displacements between Spaces

In the subsequent section I will review some of the previous questions related to the shift to a network society on the basis of a new set of images. The underlying metaphors are those of 'place' and 'space'. At first, it can be observed that the notions of 'place' and 'space' are constitutive of the present-day discourse on universities and education, since in such a context one often uses a topographic vocabulary: e.g. expressions such as teaching *environments*, knowledge *spaces*, the European Higher Education or Research *Area*, a global higher education *landscape*, etc. (Weymans, 2009). At the same time there is also a 'crisis of place', since the importance of place, as an integrative and stabilising force in human experience, is waning. Indeed, our experiences of time, space, work, communication and social relations are increasingly becoming mediated by a series of devices and systems (especially communication and information networks) that diminish the impact and meaning of place (Verschaffel, 2009: 133). This also has its impact on an institution such as a university. When investigating networks from the perspective of place and space, I also want to look at their dynamic aspect by extending these metaphors to the one of 'displacement'.

Place, space and in-between

Terms such as 'place' and 'space' are not only used by geographers, but also by observers of culture. Michel de Certeau, for instance, made the following distinction between place (*lieu*) and space (*espace*). 'A place is an instantaneous configuration of positions. It implies an indication of stability. By contrast, a space exists when one takes into consideration vectors of direction, velocities, and time variables. Thus space is composed of intersections of mobile elements. (…) In short, space is a practised place' (de Certeau, 1988: 117). These concepts gain a new significance in a network society, in which, according to Manuel Castells, another important observer of contemporary culture, 'spaces of flows' form part of the network society, i.e. the material organisation of time-sharing social practices that work through flows (exchanges and interaction between social actors) (Castells, 1996: ch. 6, esp. 441ff. and 453ff). Castells registers the motion, and retains its stable, but static, trace, which he calls 'space of places'. Yet, the relationships between the 'space of flows' and 'space of places', between simultaneous globalisation and localisation, are not predetermined in their outcome.

These concepts gain a new significance for universities in this network society. In the story of universities in such a network society, the opposition between 'place' and 'space' will thus rather refer to two sorts of determinations (following de Certeau): the first, a determination through objects that are ultimately reducible to the being-there; such as the concrete university buildings, labs, teaching halls, offices; the second, a determination through operations by the actions of the subjects involved, the students, the professors, the administrative and technical personnel. Subsequently, their stories result in an interplay between places and spaces, which constantly transform places into spaces and spaces into places. This, of course, has always been the case, but in the present-day Internet society we often tend to communicate without 'place', even within one particular institution. This is because, as pointed out by Bart Verschaffel, communication networks entail that the act of speaking is disconnected from a specific place: 'the place occupied by the speaker in reality (that is, where his or her body is) has no bearing on the speaking or listening, and does not determine the distance over which the voice carries. Virtual contact and virtual ubiquity result in the body being left behind on the edge of the network, as well as in new types of relations, unconnected to bodily presence, substituting for place-bound relations' (Verschaffel, 2009: 133–134).

Thus the challenge for the university is how and to what extent to 'connect' the place of speaking with the place of listening and understanding, even at a local level. But following Castells, there is also the opposition between the global and the local: the former is dominated by the space of flows, constituted by circuits of electronic exchanges of e.g. scientific material, databanks, and by nodes and hubs of important academic centres, international conference halls, etc.; the latter is dominated by the space of places, with the concrete local dynamics, such as academic power relations or the teaching or scientific experience in a given local university. Here the challenge for the university is how and to what extent to 'link' the local to the global. But in both cases concrete encounters 'between' the actors involved are the result of 'travelling or walking': they transform places into spaces.

Here I want to introduce the concept of 'in-between', because it is at the centre of the 'encounter' that take 'place' in 'spaces', as is well reflected in the earlier image of the web. 'In-betweenness' or 'the between' draws the attention to one particular aspect of space: instead of focusing on oppositions, on either/or, on Self or Other, the focus moves to the 'between', to the search for the 'interaction' in space 'between' the opposites, to various forms of encounter and conversation ('*entre-tien*' in French). Attention to in-betweenness means attention to intervals, gaps, cracks, in-between moments or zones in culture and human life (Standaert, 2015). This notion of in-betweenness shows that many human activities come into being due to the existence and creation of space 'between' the Self and the Other, or between the transmitter and the receiver, between the teacher and the student, etc. This space acts both as that which allows an encounter to take place (leading to interaction and communication) and as that which is produced by the encounter as such. Encounters 'between' persons result in stories that take the form of a text, image, research project, social network, community. The interaction is considered a permanent tension: between the possibility of understanding (and being understood) and the impossibility of such an understanding, between the local and the global. The interaction therefore causes the partners to readjust, rethink and reformulate ideas of themselves and of others. Thus in-betweenness is the space in which an encounter can take place (for de Certeau on in-between, see Standaert 2017).

All these concepts may appear rather abstract, but they become concrete when applied to universities, especially since universities in the future will not only be places of knowledge 'production' or of 'virtual communication' but also spaces of encounters. One challenge for networked universities is to become in new ways such privileged spaces of encounters. This supposes an ethos of a renewed attention to 'in-betweenness', to concrete places where the actors (teachers, students, researchers) encounter each other by treating each other as subjects. Many universities are already searching for such alternatives. For sure, many of these alternatives are often rather local and still waiting for a language and opportunity to manifest themselves, but they indicate how universities actively search a place in the network society.

The networked university as a space

In an essay in a recent book entitled *Rethinking the University after Bologna*, Ronald Barnett takes the networked university fully into account. Universities have their being in networks, he says, both intentionally and unwittingly. It was always so, but today, networks are a vital part of what it is to be a university in the twenty-first century. 'The networked university' has emerged. Thus the question is not whether universities have the choice of becoming networked universities or not, but rather what kind of networked universities they will become. Barnett raises several questions in this regard: What is the ethical basis of these networks? To what ends is the university involved in these networks? Is it engaging thus for its own ends? Or is it reaching out to others—other institutions and organisations—to help to bring about a better world?

In the next series of questions Barnett raises, the metaphor of 'space' is central: What spaces, what new networks, might universities open out and be part of? (…) What spaces (…) are now available to the university? Are there other kinds of spaces that will encourage forward an alternative set of knowledge interests? In response to such questions, 'the ecological university', as he terms it, prompts itself. 'The ecological is none other than a university that takes its networks and its networking seriously. That is to say, it understands that it lives amid networks and that, therefore, the responsibility arises as to which networks are to claim its primary allegiance. (…) The networked university becomes the ecological university when it intends deliberately not merely to safeguard the public realm but actively to enhance it. (…) This, then, is a university that has a care for the wider society, for the unequal life chances of its people, and for the severe challenges that society faces. (…) The ecological university, accordingly, may also be termed (…) "the public university"' (Barnett, 2009: 114–115).

The concepts of 'place', 'space' and 'public' occupy an important position in the article by Jan Masschelein and Maarten Simons in the same book. They first observe that present-day universities are places that permanently and relentlessly *mobilise* researchers, lecturers and students. Through the well-developed systems of quality control, excellence financing, rankings, etc., they are all asked to mobilise their intellectual (human) capital. Next, they plead for a 'world-university': by the space called 'the world' they mean the place and time where things are made public. Paradoxically the proposal for a world-university is a proposal to slow down the construction of a common world, to create a space (one amongst others) for hesitation. Their proposal aims precisely to disrupt this mobilisation and thus requires a different *ethos*. And they continue: 'One could think, then, of the world-university as the place where we are not mobilised, but slowed down and provoked to think, and where this provocation finds (its) place (and the university as this place), the place where research is put on the table (made present) and its protection (by methods and theories) undone'.

In their eyes, the world-university is, too, the place where teaching is stripped off its protections (by teaching methods, didactic devices) and is no longer instruction but becomes what they like to call lecturing, i.e. 'precisely not teaching a lesson but making things public, reading them before an audience, exposing them (and being in the presence of), making them speak as it were, giving them a presence that calls a thinking public into existence. Making things public, then, is not only making them known, but making them present and inviting us to explore new ways of relating to them (i.e. to the matter and to ourselves)' (Masschelein & Simons, 2009: 95–97).

Despite the differences between the approaches of these authors, they share the conviction that networked universities will be public spaces with attention to the world, to hesitation, to fragility, to the uncertain and unknown.

In this context, one may draw further attention to the metaphor of 'displacement'. While the images of pyramid and pillars are linked to 'stability' or minimal mobility within the pyramid or pillar, the images of web, space and place are associated with mobility: circulating from one hub to another, or better 'between' the nodes. 'Displacement' means that one moves from one (physical) place to another, thus creating new spaces for encounter. Yet, displacement not only takes place through one's own *self* initiative; it also happens when one is moved by initiatives *by others*. That is why we are often reactively 'displaced', for instance by metaphors, rather than that we actively displace ourselves. The search for new forms of university life supposes this kind of displacements. These deregulate, but next allow reconfiguration. In this context, one can discern different types of displacements: mental and physical, though they most often operate together.

Mental displacements

The landscape of classification of sciences (Standaert, 2009: 46–48) presents a challenge that a knowledge culture addresses to the university and to broader society: the acknowledgement of, and respect for, different approaches to knowledge, its development and its type of evaluation. Therefore, the variety of sciences and disciplines contains an invitation to a first—mental—'displacement' within the landscape of knowledge. Can we, in our own research and our evaluation of it, move to the places occupied by other sciences? Even more important is whether we can allow ourselves to be displaced. Such a displacement may lead to new discoveries. The engagement with other sciences may also lead to the discovery of the space where we lose control over what we think we master. Such an in-between space is present in any science. Indeed, the drive for knowledge has its roots precisely in what we do *not* know (Vest, 2005: 99). The more we know, the more we want to know, but a displacement within the field of knowledge confronts us with vulnerability and lack of control.

At present there is a tendency towards strengthening the pillars, even within the classification of sciences, instead of moving towards nodes between them, illustrated by the image of the web where the sciences are interlinked with each other. I am of the opinion that the major challenge is to search for new ways as to how different disciplines can meet each other: in other words, how can one create new nodes in the web of sciences? This call of displacement is not a return to the premodern system, in which one could cover several sciences, but a challenge of a different kind. The main reason is that, in contrast with the Renaissance period, modern sciences have reached such a high degree of specialisation that it is no longer possible to cover all sciences. Thus the question becomes, given that specialisation is inevitable for research, how to prevent specialisation in one field from enclosing itself into itself, which is entrenching the pillar system. Is the simple accumulation of various specialisations the only alternative? Or is the challenge to search for ways of combining in-depth knowledge of one field with a more comprehensive view that takes in sciences beyond one's own? This problem still needs to be explored, but it may require a kind of 'horizon' perspective: this means the more in-depth mastering of one's field should not lead to a further confinement to one's field, but rather to a greater perspective on other fields. In a time of fragmentation there is need of rediscovering the whole. Thus, academic research and teaching will be more networked, if one's own specialised research is 'linked' to a wider context, a new type of *universitas*.

This is also true for the polarisation between the so-called measurable and hermeneutic sciences. In the transition between renaissance and modernity, 'measurable' sciences, which express and process their data arithmetically and statistically, came to be opposed to sciences that try to understand (hermeneutically), that search for meaning, or that at times express a judgement of value about what it true, good, beautiful or important, though the latter sciences are at the foundation of what the university is (Illich, 2010). The measurable sciences are cumulative, since any invention or discovery forms the basis for the next scientific development. They tend to univocality: one language (English) and one exclusive method (mathematics/statistics). The hermeneutic sciences are cyclical because they reread and reinterpret previous knowledge over and over. They are multivocal: they avail themselves of and publish in different languages and employ a variety of methods. The former seek to 'explain' (*Erklären*) phenomena in terms of cause and effect; in contrast, the latter seek to 'understand' (*Verstehen)* in terms of the relations of the part to the whole (as pointed out by Wilhelm Dilthey). Yet today, at least in the dominant discourse, a break is established between the two, with the measurable sciences (based on 'counting' or 'reckoning') almost excluding the other (based on 'recounting' or 'narrating'). I am of the opinion that the major challenge today is to search for new ways how the two can meet each other: in other words, how can one create new nodes at the centre of the axis of knowledge? Here the issue is also whether language should not perform a new role, which is how 'counting and recounting' could meet each other and forge a new narrative? In a certain sense, the intrinsic link that exists between both terms in various European languages should be restored: *compter* and *(ra)conter* (French), *zählen* and *zählen* (German), *tellen* and *vertellen* (Dutch). In fact, the whole operation of 'counting' not only requires a 'recounting' but also finds its origin in a broader narrative; it is only when this link is established that the results can be accounted for and estimated. As such they will become more universal and public.

In the meeting of 'reckoning' and 'narrating', of 'measurable' and 'hermeneutic' sciences at this level of language, analogy and metaphor will play an important point as nodes or contact points. In scientific discoveries, metaphors make us travel and be displaced from one scientific discipline to another. In this respect, Alan Lightman, who is both physicist and novelist, points out that one distinction that can be made between physicists and novelists, and between the scientific and artistic communities in general, is what he calls 'naming'. Roughly speaking, the scientist tries to name things and the artist tries to avoid naming things. And he goes on to show (with examples from Isaac Newton, James Clerk Maxwell and Georges Lemaître) that analogies and metaphors are aids to scientific discovery. 'In doing science, even though words and equations are used with the intention of having precise meanings, it is almost impossible not to reason by physical analogy, not to form mental pictures, not to imagine balls bouncing and pendulums swinging. Metaphor is part of the process of science' (Lightman, 2005: 50). Likewise, analogies with biomedical or exact sciences help processes of understanding in hermeneutical sciences. By such metaphorical displacements, encounters 'between' sciences are established. The use of imagination also leads to a greater universality, thus *universitas*. Very often academics see their problems or solutions as absolute, but by confronting them with problems and solutions in other places, they are put in a universal perspective.

Physical displacements

At present, the weblike structuring of universities still needs to be invented, since most universities are still organised into faculties and disciplinary departments that reflect the pillar system; and the financing, recruitment (of staff and students) is organised likewise. It is not yet clear what a more network-like structuring of universities should look like. In the transition period there is probably need for 'nomadic' practices within a university.

One can observe that the most creative search is situated in these nomadic practices. Stef Langmans, a student in pedagogy at the University of Leuven, for instance, made a survey of such alternative practices which he found on the web and brought them together under the title 'publiversity'. They are oriented towards the university space and its 'public' role. His blog devoted to this topic brings together 175 examples of academic initiatives intended to create public practices (http://publiversity.wordpress.com/). These examples were brought together on the basis of keywords such as 'free, open, public, mobile, nomad, informal, invisible, interdisciplinary', which indicate the movement between places, and arranged under the headings 'art & social, educational, knowledge system, publishing & archiving, research, student, organisational'. These examples reveal that at least the following aspects enter into play in the reconfiguration of academic practice in a network society: *space* (Is it concrete, virtual, mobile?), *access* (Is the public gaining access to the organisation or is the organisation stepping towards the public? Is it focused on an elite or a broad public?), *values* (Are activities oriented towards excellence and submitted to quality control? Is any university rank required for teaching? Is research fundamental or society oriented?), *outcome* (Do the institutions provide a diploma or is knowledge spread for its own sake? Are there any (public) knowledge repositories?), *interrelation* (What is the level of cooperation, interactivity in workshops, Internet forums, community service?).

Langmans' survey shows a large variety of displacements and nomadic practices by which institutions and individuals look for new ways of organising, practising and conceptualising university life. They search for alternatives in different directions: new practices inside the university as well as practices outside the institution and at its edges, which might inspire university institutions. They point at examples that created new links, that made students work together in a transdisciplinary way, that have made research publicly accessible, that opened spaces in which creativity could bloom or where researchers could meet each other not only to count but also to recount. There are also many institutional examples in which displacement is at the forefront: *Barefoot University* works with the marginalised, impoverished and poor in South Africa (http://www.barefoot-university.org.za/); *Communiversity* is an adult education programme taught by volunteer teachers of the University of Missouri, Kansas City (http://www.umkc.edu/commu/); *Campus for Peace* of the Universitat Oberta de Catalunya is at the service of NGOs (http://www.campusforpeace.org/). This search is open-ended, many initiatives are experimental and their outcome is unpredictable.

One concrete example of education through physical displacements is the course on 'world-forming education' organised by Jan Masschelein at the University of Leuven. During the last several years, he travelled with students to post-conflict cities (Sarajevo, Belgrade, Tirana, Bucharest, Kinshasa) and non-tourist megacities in China (Shenzhen, Chongqing) for 10–14 days. Students were asked to walk day and night along arbitrary lines drawn on city maps: lines starting and leading nowhere particularly, lines without plan, crossing at random neighbourhoods, buildings, or areas. Every day, during long talks, he asked each of them very simple questions: What have you seen? What have you heard? What do you think about it? What do you make of it? At the end of the travel they had to present in the streets somewhere in the city their 'look at the city'. He calls these travels experiments in 'e-ducating the gaze': it is not getting at a liberated or critical view, but about liberating or displacing our view. Walking, in his eyes, is the physical activity of displacing one's gaze (i.e. leaving one's position, one's ex-position) along an arbitrary line, a trajectory that at the same time exists (and is recaptured) and is paved anew, a way for new perspectives, and so not leading to somewhere given before, but somewhere without a destination or familiar kind of orientation. This opening our eyes is the opening of an existential space, a space for practical freedom (Masschelein, 2009, 2010).

This walking through cities raises the question of the territorial demarcation of a university, which is directly related to its place, in the physical and stable sense. The changes of the network society are obvious, since many places are transformed into virtual spaces (through Internet), that connect subjects without having to change places. They enhance virtual displacements. But, as Jean-Claude Guédon points out, networks also grow as the physical displacement (mobility) increases: students, researchers and professors move now increasingly from one place to another to build new networks. The obvious advantage of this networked, connected, perspective is that it immediately transcends traditional boundaries, be they political, institutional or based on disciplines. He concludes: 'As space would grow as networks grow, it would also bring us back to de Certeau's notion of a space that develops even as the individual walks and interprets' (Guédon, 2009: 72).

Yet, this transcendence raises a new tension: that is the one of local embedding, to which is related the physical place of universities.

The present-day physical emplacement of European universities and its architecture are built on a tradition, which is to a large extent the reflection of the pillar system of the universities: buildings are organised according to different disciplines, usually each discipline in its own building or floor within a building. The space of a networked university still has to be invented. On the one hand, the university as institution needs architecture, as pointed out by Bart Verschaffel: 'an actual, real space, and bodies who feel they are really in the game because they are in the building. (…) These institutional spaces provide—as long as they last—unique conditions to talk and think about what is happening "outside", in the streets, the new virtual communication spaces, and the world' (Verschaffel, 2009: 145–146). On the other hand, there is need for a new architecture, where buildings are interconnected, and hubs and meeting places are created across disciplines. There is a need for spaces where researchers belonging to different sciences can encounter each other and exchange forms of 'counting and recounting'. Universities should make a fresh effort to create new, mobile 'spaces of encounter'. For instance, one could create new meeting centres to which scholars could be invited to be displaced for the duration of one semester. All participants would have their office and administrative support in that place, while continuing their normal academic activities of teaching and research. However, they could try to share free time together: informal meetings and also formal seminars. In these seminars they could explain to the other members (who are not specialised in their own field) in a comprehensible way their research and the methodology required for it. This might be a creative way of travelling through the landscape of knowledge. Thus by moving to new places within a given university, participants would create new spaces of interaction. It is to be expected that this is a way in which new networks are likely to be formed, which possibly might result in new insights.

Conclusion: Open Space

Central to this chapter has been the use of metaphors. They are mobile forces of imagination that displace us and that make educational creativity and scientific development possible. The mobility of displacement also belongs to the essential power of a metaphor itself. With regard to the meaning of 'metaphor', Michel de Certeau points out that in modern Athens, the vehicles of mass transportation are called *metaphorai*. To go to work or come home, one takes a 'metaphor'—a bus or a train (de Certeau, 1988: 115). Thus by their power of imagination, metaphors displace us. In a transition period of university life such as the one in which we are living, the university is both displaced from its previous forms and is displaced into a new set of open spaces which in turn opens possibilities. In this contribution we argued that it is fruitful to being displaced by the metaphor of a 'networked university', not only because it is at the image of the 'network society', but also because of the multiple characteristics it embodies: the interdisciplinary connections, real and virtual meeting points (hubs), the interplay between places and spaces, or the in-betweenness at the centre of encounter. Thus metaphors also help to stimulate reflection on the possibilities facing the university in the twenty-first century. In contrast with the present-day tendency that expects concrete results on the basis of preset objectives and clear benchmarks, also in universities, the image of a networked university still needs to be discovered, by slowing down, by being hesitant, by becoming attentive to how the network society presents itself. The image of the web shows the open space at the centre of any web: it is the space of the *non-dit* of our hopes, desires and drives. It is the space of what is uncertain, vulnerable, uncontrollable or incomprehensible that is the mainspring of human action. It is the in-betweenness that makes people encounter each other and that may constitute an essential part in the search towards a networked university.

References

Barnett, Ronald, 'Knowledge Interests and Knowledge Policies: Re-thinking the University in the Twenty-First Century', in *Rethinking the University after Bologna*, 2009, pp. 105–119.

Castells, Manuel, *The Rise of the Network Society*. Oxford: Blackwell, 1996.

de Certeau, Michel, *The Practice of Everyday Life*, trans. Steven Rendall. Berkeley: University of California Press, 1988.

Grewal, David Singh, *Network Power: The Social Dynamics of Globalization*. New Haven/London: Yale University Press, 2009.

Guédon, Jean-Claude, 'Between Excellence and Quality: The European Research Area in Search of Itself', in *Rethinking the University after Bologna*, 2009, pp. 57–79.

Illich, Ivan, 'Le texte et l'université: idée et histoire d'une institution unique', *Esprit* 367 (août-septembre 2010), pp. 172–184.

Lightman, Alan, *A Sense of the Mysterious: Science and the Human Spirit*. New York: Vintage Books, 2005.

Rethinking the University after Bologna: New Concepts and Practices beyond Tradition and the Market. By Ronald Barnett, Jean-Claude Guédon, Jan Masschelein & Maarten Simons, Susan Robertson, and Nicolas Standaert, Antwerpen: UCSIA, 2009.

Masschelein, Jan, 'The World "Once More": Walking Lines', *Teachers College Record* (June 2009), art.nr. ID Number: 15647. http://www.tcrecord.org.

Masschelein, Jan, 'E-ducating the Gaze: The Idea of a Poor Pedagogy', *Ethics and Education* 5(1) (2010), pp. 43–53.

Masschelein, Jan & Maarten Simons, 'The University as a Matter of Public Concern: Thinking about and of a World-University', in *Rethinking the University after Bologna*, 2009, pp. 83–99.

Robertson, Susan, '"Metaphoric Imaginings": Re-/Visions on the Idea of a University', in *Rethinking the University after Bologna*, 2009, pp. 25–37.

Standaert, Nicolas, 'Pyramid, Pillar and Web: Questions for Academic Life Raised by the Network Society', in *Rethinking the University after Bologna*, 2009, pp. 39–53.

Standaert, Nicolas, 'Towards a Networked University', in Ronald Barnett (ed.), *The Future University: Ideas and Possibilities*. New York: Routledge, 2012, pp. 87–100.

Standaert, Nicolas, 'Don't Mind the Gap: Sinology as an Art of In-Betweenness', *Philosophy Compass* 10(2) (2015), pp. 91–103.

Standaert, Nicolas, 'Attention à l'écart: l'art de l'entre-deux', in Luce Giard (ed.), *Michel de Certeau: Le voyage de l'œuvre*. Paris: Éditions Facultés jésuites de Paris, 2017, pp. 207-231.

Verschaffel, Bart, 'Semi-public Spaces: The Spacial Logic of Institutions', in Raf Geenens & Ronald Tinnevelt (eds.), *Does Truth Matter?* Dordrecht: Springer, 2009, pp. 133–146.

Vest, Charles M., 'What We Don't Know', in C. Vest (ed.), *Pursuing the Endless Frontier: Essays on MIT and the Role of Research Universities*. Cambridge, Mass.: MIT Press, 2005.

Weymans, Wim, 'From Coherence to Differentiation: Understanding (Changes in) the European Area for Higher Education and Research', in Robert Cowen & Andreas M. Kazamias (eds.), *International Handbook of Comparative Education*. Dordrecht: Springer, 2009, pp. 569–585.

PART THREE

European Ideas

Introduction

Europe is home to the idea of the modern university and is a continuing source of innovation and change with a greater emphasis on regional networking, quality assurance mechanisms, standardization and recognition of qualifications in the EU since the Bologna process established the European Higher Education Area. In 2015, Education Ministers agreed on four priorities: enhancing the quality and relevance of learning and teaching; fostering the employability of graduates throughout their working lives; making our systems more inclusive; and implementing agreed structural reforms.

In the Foreword to the first volume of *A History of the University in Europe*, Walter Rüegg writes:

> The University is a European institution; indeed, it is the European institution par excellence. … It is moreover the only European institution which has preserved its fundamental patterns and its basic social role and functions over the course of history. … No other European institution has spread over the entire world in the way in which the traditional form of the European university has done. (p. xix)

He goes on to discuss "contradictory lines of development" of "Governmentally organized education system perfected by Napolean … [and] inspired by von Humboldt [as involving]—research without practical ends" (p. xxiv).

In the fourth and final volume *A History of the University in Europe. Vol. IV: Universities Since 1945* (Rüegg, 2011), the remarkable expansion of European universities is commented on—the existing 201 universities in 1945 in 50 years had grown by over 600. Rüegg (2011) traces developments in terms of humanism (Bildung), liberal reform, expansion and democratic reforms, entrepreneurial reforms, globalization, and finally Americanization. The four major themes discussed are reform, destruction of ivory tower, provincialization, and loss of world dominance. One might argue that in terms of world competition the European university has been a victim of its own success, especially in the American era, soon to be followed by Chinese dominance.

In this section, there are five chapters that address many of the issues facing European universities. Marek Kwiek examines the relationship between the university and the state charting an uncertain future for the social contract noting that state-funded higher education formed one of the bedrocks of the European welfare system and arguing that changes wrought by globalization over the past 30 years have led to renegotiation of the social contract.

In Chapter 10, Susan Robertson, Joanna Tidy, and Janja Komljenovic investigate the shifting forums that now shape higher education services in light of global market pressures. The authors examined a series of post-GATS "forum shifting" strategies such as the EC's Directive on Services 2006, the Trans-Pacific Partnership (TPP) and the Transatlantic Trade and Investment Partnership (TTIP) that have introduced regulatory changes affecting both regional and national scales.

In a chapter entitled "The European University: Heartland to Periphery and Even Back Again?", Peter Scott begins by scrutinizing the claim that Europe is the home of the university tradition focusing on its fading dominance and its revival after the signing of the Bologna Declaration in 1999. He charts the emergence of a "common architecture" with the Bologna process and its extension leading to the creation of the European Higher Education Area.

In "The Nordic Idea of University," Jussi Välimaa starts from the assumption that the university is a political institution and provides an account of how universities are defined by Nordic welfare states noting that this does not imply that there does not exist a homogenous form or idea. He discusses the significance of the idea of equality and equal educational opportunity as common values that are now under pressure through globalization and neoliberal management in the name of economic efficiency.

In the final chapter of this section, Thorsten Nybom begins from the premise that European universities should initiate a change by admitting that present-day universities *are nothing like* what they still were in the 1970s, that today they function under a completely different set of conditions. Admitting mistakes made between 1965 and 1985 which have resulted in the disintegration of the European higher education systems, makes it possible to describe the nature of the confluence of cultural, intellectual, economic and political forces that have conditioned higher education change during the last twenty years, for which Nybom provides an itemized critique of key problems.

Michael A. Peters

References

Ridder-Symoens, H. (1992) (ed.): *A History of the University in Europe. Vol. I: Universities in the Middle Ages*, Cambridge, Cambridge University Press.

Rüegg, W. (2011) (ed.): *A History of the University in Europe. Vol. IV: Universities since 1945*, Cambridge, Cambridge University Press, ISBN 978-0-521-36108-8.

CHAPTER NINE

The University and the State in Europe

The Uncertain Future of the Traditional Social Contract

MAREK KWIEK

Introduction

Europe is witnessing general attempts at a reformulation of the postwar social contract which gave rise to the welfare state (with public higher education as we know it). I argue here for a strong thesis according to which Europe is facing the simultaneous renegotiation of the postwar social contract concerning the welfare state and the accompanying renegotiation of a smaller scale, by comparison, modern social pact between the university and the nation-state.[1] The renegotiation of the (nation) state/university pact is not clear outside of the context of the changing welfare state contract, as state-funded higher education formed one of the bedrocks of the European welfare system in its major forms, and state-funded higher education remains one of its foundations.

I am following here Stephan Leibfried and colleagues who argue that "competitive pressure to lower tax rates undermines the state's resources and has the potential to unleash financial crises that, in turn, trigger cuts in welfare spending" (Hurrelmann et al. 2007: 7). Consequently, what they term "the golden-age constellation" of the four components of the state (the territorial state, the constitutional state, the democratic welfare state, and the interventionist state) is currently threatened: "different state functions are threatened to a greater or lesser degree, and subjected to pressures for internationalization of varying intensity"

(Hurrelmann et al. 2007: 9). I argue here that higher education policies, and especially public funding for universities, are one of the dimensions of the "golden-age constellation" under renegotiations in Europe today: they come under the "interventionist state" and its functions in Leibfried's formulation.

Higher education has been largely publicly funded in its traditional European forms and its period of largest growth coincided with the development of the postwar welfare state. The massification processes in European higher education were closely linked to the growth and consolidation of (major models of) European welfare states (on Central European welfare states, see Kwiek 2013, 2014). We are currently witnessing the growing significance of knowledge production, acquisition, dissemination, and application in our societies and economies on the one hand—and the rapidly changing roles of European higher education systems on the other.

Despite—as it seems—radical changes in the functioning of European universities that have been taking place for the last twenty to thirty years, both European societies and, especially, European policymakers are thinking about further structural changes. On reading national governmental and international reports, transnational and EU visions of the functioning of universities and of the whole public services sector in the future, we can conclude that profound transformations of the higher education sector, and of its narrow sector of research universities, are still ahead of us. Universities, throughout their history, change as their environments change, and the early twenty-first century is not exceptional. Despite relatively homogeneous cross-national arguments for reforms—often linked to the ideas of New Public Management—there are different actual directions of current and projected reforms in different national systems (Gornitzka and Maassen 2011, Mazza et al. 2008, Paradeise et al. 2009).

Education, including higher education, is viewed in this chapter as a significant component of the traditional welfare state (following Joseph Stiglitz from *Economics of the Public Sector* and Nicolas Barr from *Economic Theory and the Welfare State*). Transformations to the state, and the welfare state in particular, affect—both directly and indirectly—public higher education systems in Europe. This chapter sees the institution of the university and the institution of the state as closely linked (following Becher and Kogan 1980, Kogan et al. 2000, Kogan and Hanney 2000): problems (and real and perceived failures) of the latter inevitably bring about problems (and real and perceived failures) of the former, as historically, in the postwar period in Europe, the success of the latter led to the success of the former.

Thus I view the modern university and the modern state closely linked throughout the last two centuries, from the very beginning in the Humboldtian ideas of the research university from the early 1800s (Kwiek 2006: 81–138, Kwiek 2008b, Wittrock 1993). This way of thinking about the university and the state can be found in the ideas of new institutionalism in organization studies, especially those emerging in the last three decades in political sciences. Institutions, the arguments go, do not undergo their transformations in isolation: institutions operate in parallel, and in parallel they change (see Aldrich 2008, Brunsson and Olsen 1993, Hannan and Freeman 1989, March and Olsen 1989). There is a complex interplay of influences between institutions and their environments, and universities are perfect examples of powerful connectedness between changes in institutions and changes in the outside world from which they draw their resources, founding ideas, and social legitimacy. Without high levels of resources, strong and widely socially accepted founding ideas, and powerful social legitimacy, institutions begin to falter. Resources follow founding ideas, embedded in social legitimacy; the danger is that decreasing legitimacy and weak founding ideas may lead to declining (especially public) resources. This is especially relevant for countries in which there is a strong cross-sectional competition for scarce public funding between competing claimants, such as the competition between healthcare, pensions, and higher education spending in Central and Eastern Europe in the last quarter of a century, combined with cross-generational conflicts in rapidly aging societies (see Kwiek 2013). The institution of the university in Europe, in its different national embodiments, is clearly undergoing a fundamental transformation today—along with the traditional institution of the state in general, and the welfare state in particular. First, I shall discuss the modern university in the context of the changing welfare state, and then in the context of the changing nation-state; then conclusions will follow.

The Modern University and the Welfare State

In the new global order (Djelic and Quack 2003, Hale and Held 2011, Held and McGrew 2007, Slaughter 2004), universities as institutions are striving for a new social, cultural (and perhaps especially economic) place as they are increasingly unable to maintain their traditional roles and tasks. Universities cannot afford the frustration associated with potentially declining institutional prestige and potentially dwindling financial resources across Europe. Universities as institutions need to remain key social institutions in contemporary knowledge-based societies, as they have been so at least since the early 1800s of the Humboldtian and the Napoleonic reforms in Prussia and France. Currently, their institutional prestige is on the rise in all major European systems, and public spending in higher education, in most Continental European countries, has outpaced growth in student numbers, despite the recent financial crisis.

The social and economic environment of universities has been changing radically in the last two to three decades (as scrutinized in Amaral et al. 2009, Bonaccorsi and Daraio 2007, Mazza et al. 2008, Paradeise et al. 2009). The positions taken by their most important stakeholders have been evolving too (primarily those taken by the state and, to a lesser extent, students and labor markets). Market opportunities for the functioning of universities have been growing, as most European economies have been getting more and more market-oriented with respect to public sector services in general, and as, increasingly, students and their families have been having increasingly marketized and customer-like demands (see Teixeira et al. 2004). Higher education quasi-markets emerged, first in England and later on in the Continental Europe. "Academic entrepreneurialism," or seeking noncore non-state income through risk-taking activities, became an important part of the higher education landscape, as various recent empirical studies show (Kwiek 2013, Shattock 2009, Williams 2004, 2009). The "entrepreneurial university" became a topic for both academics (see Kwiek 2008a) and transnational organizations (see, for instance a joint 2014 initiative of the European Commission and the OECD: *heinnovate*, a web-based tool to measure the degree of entrepreneurialism of academic units and universities along seven major dimensions, from "leadership and governance" to "organizational capacity, people and incentives" to "entrepreneurship development in teaching and learning," www.heinnovate.eu). Both the official discourse of the emergent European Higher Education Area and European Research Area, as well as a large part of academic debates accompanying their formation, increasingly emphasize the belief that universities should play a stronger role of effective engines for economic growth in the emergent knowledge-based economies (Kwiek 2010, 2012).

In this way, the university in the European context, basically without any large-scale public and academic debates about its fundamental principles, seems to be opening a new chapter in its history. In contrast, such public and academic discussions accompanied the formation of its Humboldtian model in the early nineteenth century in Berlin, and accompanied the most important twentieth-century debates on "the idea" of the university, on the occasion of publications devoted to the issue of the university such as prewar works by Ortega y Gasset and Max Weber and postwar works by Karl Jaspers and Jürgen Habermas (see Gasset 1944, Habermas 1971, Jaspers 1959, Weber 1973, as discussed in Kwiek 2008b).

The public university is increasingly viewed as merely one among many types of public sector institutions and its traditional claims to social (as well as economic and political) uniqueness are increasingly falling on deaf ears across Europe. A current Europe-wide discourse on the university as a key institution for economic growth, in the version consistently promoted by the European Commission and the OECD, questions all its aspects and criticizes it to its very foundations. The long-term problem is, as shown by theories of institutional change (Dryzek 1996: 104), that

> no institution can operate without an associated and supportive discourse (or discourses). Discourses may best be treated as institutional software. Institutional hardware exists in the form of rules, rights, operating procedures, customs, and principles.

The European university is not an exception. Its strength in the last two hundred years resulted from the power of the accompanying discourse of modernity in which the university held a central, highlighted, specific (and carefully secured) place in European societies (Delanty 2001, Rothblatt and Wittrock 1993, Wittrock 2003). A new social and economic location of the institution requires a new discourse which legitimizes and justifies it and sustains public confidence, without which, in the long run, it is impossible to maintain a high level of public trust (and, consequently, a high level of public funding). Therefore, the struggles over a future form of the institution are also, and perhaps above all, the struggles over a form of a discourse which legitimizes its place. In the new century, those struggles have intensified and for the first time became global, with the strong engagement of international and transnational organizations and institutions. To a large extent, the future of European universities will depend on the social and political acceptance of legitimizing discourses currently emergent around them. Supportive discourses for universities seem to be still in the making, amid the transformations of their environments. The strength of supportive discourses shall indirectly determine the social and economic location of universities in the future. And the supportive discourses for universities unavoidably clash with supportive discourses for other competitive public resources in our aging societies (Poland is a good example: Kwiek 2012). New cross-sectoral competition for higher social legitimacy emerges as public spending on the two major claimants to the public purse is on the rise: healthcare and pension schemes.

Consequently, reforms of the public sector are underway across Europe, and the university has been subject to them, despite its traditional, historical exceptionality. It seems better to be able to steer the changes rather than to drift with them, though. Often new quasi-market rules operate alongside more traditional rules linked to the modern university (Kwiek 2009b). Current debates about the future of the university are more central to public policy and wider public discussions than ever before: European universities consume annually hundreds of billions of euros on teaching and research and produce millions of students and graduates. The future of average European citizens has never been so closely linked to the performance of European universities. It is hardly possible to view the transformations to the institution of the university without viewing the transformations to the social fabric in which it has been embedded. The modern university is under the very same pressures as other modern institutions and other social arrangements. The possible decline of its historical exceptionality (at least compared with the postwar period, if not with the two hundred years of the materialization of Wilhelm von Humboldt's ideas) results from the same pressures as those affecting other modern institutions—including the institutions of the state and its agencies, public services, and institutions of the private corporate world (see Campbell 2004, Djelic and Quack 2003, Held and Young 2011).

Political scientists often stress the idea that the economic space of the nation-state and national territorial borders no longer coincides. Examples include Fritz Scharpf (a former director of the Max Planck Institute for the Studies of Societies in Köln) and John G. Ruggie of Harvard University (see also Beck 2005, Held et al. 1999, Held and McGrew 2007). Consequently, the postwar "embedded liberalism compromise"—the social contract between the state, market, and labor—does not work anymore as it was designed to work within closed national economies (see Hays 2009: 150–158). Scharpf argues that in the history of capitalism, the decades following the Second World War were "unusual in the degree to which the boundaries of the territorial state had become coextensive with the boundaries of markets for capital, services, goods and labor" (Scharpf 2000: 254; see also Scharpf 2010: 91–126, 221–246). At the moment of the emergence of classic European welfare states, investment opportunities existed mainly within national economies and firms were mainly challenged by domestic competitors. At the time, however, when major European welfare state regimes were being constructed, it was not fully realized how much the success of market-correcting policies depended on the capacity of the territorial nation-states to control their economic boundaries. Under the forces of globalization, though, this controlling capacity was lost. Therefore, "the 'golden years' of the capitalist welfare state came to an end" (Scharpf 2000: 255; see also Kwiek 2007, Mishra 2011, Scharpf and Schmidt 2000).

The social contract which had allowed the nation-states in advanced capitalist countries to be accompanied by a welfare state originated right after the Second World War. With the advent of globalization, the social contract is eroding, or is at least under powerful pressures, though, to different extent in different countries. The compact between state and society in postwar territorially bounded national democracies was intended to mediate the deleterious domestic effects of postwar economic liberalization. Now it is under question, in theory, in practice, or both (Blyth 2002, Held and McGrew 2007).

This postwar compromise assigned specific policy roles to national governments—which governments seem increasingly unable, or unwilling, to perform. One of the indirect effects of globalization on the state is its impact on the ability of the state to "live up to its side of the postwar domestic compact" (Ruggie 1997: 2). The emergence of global capital markets posed entirely new policy problems. As Castles and colleagues summarize recent changes (see also Pestieau 2006: 1–8, Swank 2002: 274–289, Seeleib-Kaiser 2008: 1–13):

> Now there is marked tendency to perceive social investment as a dead weight on the economy rather than as a factor providing a boost off the starting blocks in a "race to the top". In a nutshell, the transformation of the international political economy decreased the autonomy and sovereignty of the nation-state—but did not support the evolution of functionally equivalent higher authorities at the international level. (Castles et al. 2010: 11)

The existing systems of supervision and regulation, systems of taxation and accounting, were created for a "nation-based world economic landscape" (Ruggie 1997: 2). Economic policies are becoming increasingly denationalized and the state is increasingly unable, or unwilling, to keep its promises from the Golden Age of the welfare state. As Leibfried and Obinger (2001: 2) stress, "the welfare state is now seen as a part of the problem, not as part of the solution, as it was in the earlier Keynesian view." The whole idea of the welfare state is under renegotiations, and the access to and eligibility for tax-based public services are under discussions, increasingly related to possible individual contributions. And the welfare state has traditionally been one of the main pillars in the appeal of the nation-state construction.

The power of the nation-state, and the power of the loyalty of its citizens, has rested, *inter alia*, on a firm belief in (historically unprecedented) welfare rights. When the Keynesian welfare state was formed, the role of the state was to find a fair balance between the state and the market—which had fundamentally transformed postwar social relations in all the countries involved in this social experiment (mostly advanced Western democracies). The task of this postwar institutional reconstruction was to devise a framework which would safeguard and aid the quest for domestic stability without triggering the mutually destructive external consequences that had plagued the interwar period.

Science, and public funding for science, was in a state of perpetual expansion in the "Golden Age" (1950–1975) of the postwar Keynesian welfare state in Europe (Bush 1945, Kwiek 2013, Ziman 1994). The massification of higher education was in full swing in Europe. The stagnation which started in the mid-1970s in Europe was perhaps the first symptom that the welfare system in the form designed for one period (the postwar reconstruction of Europe) might not be working in a different period. The social conditions have changed considerably; the postwar social contract was related to an industrial economy in a period of considerable growth, the male breadwinner model of work, and closed, national economies with largely national competition for investment, goods, products, and services. Since the 1970s, the marriage of the nation-state and the welfare state has been under powerful internal and external pressures. The social agenda of the 1980s and 1990s changed radically: after the policies of the golden age of expansion, European welfare states have been shaped by what Paul Pierson termed "politics of austerity" (Pierson 2001). Increasingly, the changing conditions affect universities.

The Modern University and the Modern Nation-State

It is the overall argument of the present chapter that current transformations to the state under the pressures of globalization (and Europeanization) will not leave the university unaffected, and consequently it is useful to discuss the future tasks and mission of the university in the context of the current global transformations of the state. The legitimacy of, and loyalty toward, modern liberal democratic welfare states is under severe stress today and the whole idea of a (European) postwar "social contract" between the state and its citizens is threatened. The sovereignty of the state has traditionally meant also the sovereignty of national educational policies and full state support for nation-state–oriented universities (from their inception as modern institutions bound by a "pact" with modern nation-states, as shown excellently by Bill Readings in his *The University in Ruins*, 1996). The university used to provide the modern nation-state with "a moral and spiritual basis" and, along Humboldtian lines, professors, as Gerard Delanty argues in *Challenging Knowledge: The University in the Knowledge Society*, "constructed themselves as the representatives of the nation" (Delanty 2001: 33, 34; see Kwiek 2009a). Not any more, though.

As I argued elsewhere (Kwiek 2006), national education systems were created as part of the state-forming process which established the modern nation-state. They were born when states based on absolutistic or monarchical rule gave way to the modern nation-state: as Andy Green stresses in his *Education, Globalization, and the Nation-State*, the history of "national education" is thus very much the history of the "nation state in formation" (Green 1997: 131). National education systems contributed to the creation of civic loyalties and national identities and became guardians for national languages, cultures, literatures, and consciousness. The modern university and the modern nation-state went hand in hand, or were parts of the same wider process of modernization (and I mean here two Continental models: the Humboldtian and, to a lesser extent, the Napoleonic one). Consequently, reconfigurations of the modern nation-state today (mostly, but not exclusively, under the pressures of globalization) are bound to affect the modern institution of the university. State-sponsored mass education was in modernity the primary source of socialization facing the individual as citizen of a nation-state (Spybey 1996). European nation-states were engaged in authorizing, funding, and managing education systems, including higher education, to construct unified national policies.

The crucial step in the historical development of European universities is what Guy Neave termed the process of their "nationalization"—bringing the university formally into the public domain as a national responsibility. With the rise of the nation-state, the university was set at the apex of institutions defining national identity (Neave 2001: 26). The emergence of the universities in Berlin and in Paris marked the termination of the long process for the incorporation of the university to the state (Neave 2001: 25). The process of the "nationalization" of the university settled the issue of what the role and responsibilities of the modern institution in society should be. The emergent nation-state defined the social place of the emergent modern university and determined its social responsibilities. The nation-state determined the community to which the university would be answerable: it was going to be the national community, the nation. The services and benefits the unitary and homogeneous nation-state gradually, and over the passage of time, placed at the disposal of society went far beyond education and included, for example, generous healthcare systems and old-age pension schemes. Nowadays, as the redefinition of material foundations of the welfare state in general progresses smoothly (through new legislation) in most parts of Europe, social contracts with regard to these (and possibly other) areas of state benefits and state-funded services may have to be renegotiated, significantly changing their content, range, and the validity of the contract itself.

Increasingly, at the beginning of the nineteenth century, culture in the sense of *Bildung* (until then more related to the development of the individual as the individual and not to the individual as the nation-state citizen) became mixed with political motivations and aspirations, focused around the notion of the German national state (Wittrock 1993).[2] In a global age, these motifs have been put under pressure. Forging national identity, serving as a repository of the nation's historical, scientific or literary achievements, inculcating national consciousness and loyalty to fellow-citizens of the nation-state do not serve as the rationale for the existence of the institution of the university any more. At the same time, the disinterested pursuit of truth by curiosity-driven scholars in the traditional sense of the term is no longer accepted as a general *raison d'être* for the institution either.

Consequently, regardless of whether we focus more on the cultural unity of the nation or on the political unity of the nation as the two distinct driving forces behind the development of the modern university, both motifs are not working in post-national and global conditions. Neither serving truth nor serving the nation (and the nation-state) can be the guiding principles for the lavish public subsidization of the institution today, and neither of them are even mentioned in current debates at global or European levels. What increasingly counts is the economic "relevance" of universities, and their possible contribution to economic growth (see Brennan 2007, Pinheiro et al. 2012, Välimaa and Ylijoki 2008). Traditional missions of the modern university are subject to far-reaching renegotiations. Massified European universities, open to millions of students, with millions of graduates, with huge annual operating budgets, seem no longer able to follow traditional "ideas of the university" discussed in Volume 1 of this publication.

Conclusions

There are four tentative conclusions. Firstly, traditional relationships between higher education and the state are changing, and the main forces driving the change are globalization-related (and, in Europe, Europeanization-related). Globalization processes affect the institution of the university mainly indirectly while the processes of European integration affect it mostly directly (the best example being the Bologna Process). Higher education is likely to be strongly affected by these globalization-related processes mainly through the impact of the ongoing transformations to the state. As Peter Scott argues about the threats of globalization to universities, consistently with arguments in this chapter,

> as the welfare state struggles to preserve core services—for example, in basic education, health, and social security—universities may find that their current funding base is increasingly eroded. ... The autonomy traditionally enjoyed by universities, and their consequent semi-detachment from state bureaucracies, have made them especially vulnerable to these new experiments in "semi-detachment" (in other words, reduced availability of state subsidy). The upward pressure on tuition fees in "state" universities is perhaps an example of this phenomenon. (Scott 2005: 48)

Secondly, public higher education worldwide is a much less exceptional part of the public sector than it used to be a few decades ago (before the ideas of New Public Management became prevalent): either in public perceptions, or in organizational and institutional terms (governance and funding modes), or both. This disappearing—cultural, social, and economic—exceptionality of the institution of the university will heavily influence its future relations with the state which, on a global scale, is increasingly involved in reforming all its public services (see Krücken and Meier 2006, Musselin 2007, Kwiek 2011). General reform ideas in higher education become similar to general reform ideas in the public sector, cost-sharing/co-funding being a good example of similar lines of thinking.

Thirdly, further reforms of higher education in Europe are inevitable, as the forces behind ongoing changes are global in nature and similar in kind throughout Europe. The forces of change are similar, although their current influence varies from country to country (the room of manoeuvre of individual institutions, perhaps except for high globally ranked research universities, seems to be very small in Europe due to their dominant reliance on public funds in both teaching and research missions. Exceptions include universities in England—in contradistinction to the rest of the UK—which apply strong cost-sharing mechanisms and operate in a strong higher education "quasi-market": the level of private funding available is more changeable and potentially more based on individual institutional strategies). In Europe, the forces of change are structurally similar, although they act through various "national filters" (Gornitzka and Maassen 2011). The creation of mass higher education is no longer a dominant goal of states and governments as it has already been achieved: there are many other, competing, social needs today, though.

And fourthly, it is increasingly difficult to understand the dynamics of future transformations of universities without understanding the transformations of the social fabric in which they are embedded, including transformations to the welfare state and the nation-state.

New ideas about the functioning of the state indirectly give life to new ideas about the functioning of universities—which in Continental Europe have traditionally been heavily, directly or indirectly, dependent on public funding. One can summarize briefly changes in European welfare state models: things will never be the same (see Greve 2012, Palier 2010, Pestieau 2006). Presumably, the same refers to European universities, keeping in mind the multidimensionality of transformations, their powerful embodiment in the cultural traditions of particular European nation-states, and their strong dependence on the pace of changes taking place across all public sector services.

Finally, the traditional social contract between the university and the state is faltering because the state across Europe is under unprecedented pressures. The ongoing renegotiation of this contract will determine the future of European universities for decades to come: a major role of national academic communities today is to understand the change process and to assist in defining terms and conditions of a revised contract for the benefit of both the society and their institutions. If they do not push for a revised "idea of the university" themselves (as integral part of an emergent contract), new ideas stemming entirely from the outside of academe may prevail. In Continental Europe, the "idea of the university" is in the making, right before our eyes. Just as the European Union and its "jewel in the crown," the European welfare state, is globally unique, so are European universities. As large-scale and empirically based global comparative studies demonstrate (see Teichler et al. 2013), the governance and funding patterns in (Continental) European universities are worlds apart from global patterns. A new European–global hybrid in university funding and organization may be emergent today: while European universities are powerfully affected by global trends (as are European welfare states), they are bound to retain their distinctiveness. The degree to which this European–global hybrid will be more "European" than "global," that is to say, the degree to which traditional elements of the university/state social contract will be retained in the future, depends to a large extent on the academic profession. The form of the revised social contract can still be influenced, and there is still enough time to consider its long-term implications, including implications for the academic profession as the core of the whole academic enterprise. Let us academics be not caught by surprise.[3]

Notes

1. For the origins of the social pact between states and universities in France (see Weisz 1983); in Germany (see McClelland: 1980); see also such classics as Ringer (1990) on Germany, Sanderson (1999) on Great Britain, Ben-David (1992) on Britain, France, and Germany, and Rothblatt and Wittrock (1993) on the emergence of the "modern university."
2. I present detailed arguments combined with reading of the relevant works by Wilhelm von Humboldt, Johann Gottlieb Fichte, Friedrich Schleiermacher, and Friedrich W. J. Schelling as well as the discussion on the German "idea" of the university between Jürgen Habermas and Karl Jaspers in Kwiek (2006: 80–136), in a Chapter: "The Idea of the University Revisited (the German Context)."
3. I would like to express my gratitude for highly useful comments I received from Michael Peters and Ronald Barnett. All limitations of the chapter are clearly mine, though. This chapter draws from my book, *Knowledge Production in European Universities. States, Markets, and Academic Entrepreneurialism* (Frankfurt and New York: Peter Lang, 2013). The

author also gratefully acknowledges the support of the National Research Council (NCN) through its MAESTRO grant DEC-2011/02/A/HS6/00183.

References

Aldrich, Howard E. (2008). *Organizations and Environments*. Stanford: Stanford University Press.

Amaral, Alberto, Guy Neave, Christine Musselin, Peter Maassen, eds. (2009). *European Integration and the Governance of Higher Education and Research*. Dordrecht: Springer.

Barr, Nicholas, ed. (2001). *Economic Theory and the Welfare State. Volume I: Theory*. Cheltenham: Edward Elgar.

Becher, Tony, Maurice Kogan (1980). *Process and Structure in Higher Education*. London: Heinemann.

Beck, Ulrich (2005). *Power in the Global Age. A New Global Political Economy*. (K. Cross, trans.). Cambridge: Polity.

Ben-David, Joseph (1992). *Centers of Learning: Britain, France, Germany, United States*. New Brunswick: Transaction Publishers.

Blyth, Mark (2002). *Great Transformations: Economic Ideas and Institutional Change in the Twentieth Century*. Cambridge: Cambridge University Press.

Bonaccorsi, Andrea, Cinzia Daraio, eds. (2007). *Universities and Strategic Knowledge Creation. Specialization and Performance in Europe*. Cheltenham: Edward Elgar.

Brennan, John (2007). "The Academic Profession and Increasing Expectations of Relevance." In: Maurice Kogan, Ulrich Teichler (eds.), *Key Challenges to the Academic Profession*. Kassel: INCHER. 19–28.

Brunsson, Nils, Johan P. Olsen (1993). *The Reforming Organization*. Copenhagen: Fagbokforlaget.

Bush, Vannevar (1945). *Science: The Endless Frontier*. A Report to the President on a Program for Postwar Scientific Research. Reprinted July 1960, Washington, DC: National Science Foundation.

Campbell, John L. (2004). *Institutional Change and Globalization*. Princeton: Princeton University Press.

Castles, Francis G., Stephan Leibfried, Jane Lewis, Herbert Obinger, Christopher Pierson (2010). "Introduction." In: Francis G. Castles, Stephan Leibfried, Jane Lewis, Herbert Obinger, Christopher Pierson (eds.), *The Oxford Handbook of the Welfare State*. New York: Oxford University Press. 1–15.

Delanty, Gerard (2001). *Challenging Knowledge. The University in the Knowledge Society*. Buckingham: SRHE and Open University Press.

Djelic, Marie-Laure, Sigrid Quack, eds. (2003). *Globalization and Institutions: Redefining the Rule of the Economic Game*. Cheltenham: Edward Elgar.

Dryzek, John S. (1996). "The Informal Logic of Institutional Design." In: Robert E. Goodin (ed.), *The Theory of Institutional Design*. Cambridge: Cambridge University Press. 103–125.

Gasset, José Ortega y (1944). *Mission of the University*. Princeton: Princeton University Press.

Gornitzka, Åse, Peter Maassen (2011). "University Governance Reforms, Global Scripts and the 'Nordic Model'. Accounting for Policy Change?" In: J. Schmid, K. Amos, J. Schrader, A. Thiel (eds.), *Welten der Bildung? Vergleichende Analysen von Bildungspolitik und Bildungssystemen*. Baden Baden: Nomos Verlagsgesellschaft. 149–177.

Green, Andy (1997). *Education, Globalization and the Nation-State*. London: Macmillan Press.

Greve, Bent, ed. (2012). *The Times They Are Changing? Crisis and the Welfare State*. Chichester: Wiley-Blackwell.

Habermas, Jürgen (1971). *Toward a Rational Society*. London: Heinemann.

Hale, Thomas, David Held, eds. (2011). *Handbook of Transnational Governance: Institutions and Innovations*. Cambridge, Malden: Polity Press.

Hannan, Michael T., John Freeman (1989). *Organizational Ecology*. Cambridge, Mass: Harvard University Press.

Hays, Jude C. (2009). *Globalization and the New Politics of Embedded Liberalism*. Oxford: Oxford University Press.

Held, David, Anthony McGrew, eds. (2007). *Globalization Theory. Approaches and Controversies*. Cambridge: Polity Press.

Held, David, Anthony McGrew, David Goldblatt, Jonathan Perraton (1999). *Global Transformations: Politics, Economics and Culture*. Cambridge: Polity Press.

Held, David, Kevin Young (2011). "Crises in Parallel Worlds: The Governance of Global Risks in Finance, Security, and the Environment." In: Craig Calhoun, Georgi Derluguian (eds.), *The Deepening Crisis: Governance Challenges after Neoliberalism*. New York and London: Social Science Research Council and New York University Press. 19–42.

Hurrelmann, Achim, Stephan Leibfried, Kerstin Martens, Peter Mayer (2007). "The Golden-Age Nation State and its Transformation: A Framework for Analysis." In: Achim Hurrelmann, Stephan Leibfried, Kerstin Martens, Peter Mayer (eds.), *Transforming the Golden-Age Nation State*. Basingstoke: Palgrave Macmillan. 1-23.

Jaspers, Karl (1959). *The Idea of the University*. (H.A.T. Reiche, H. F. Vanderschmidt, trans.). Boston: Beacon Press.

Kogan, Maurice, Marianne Bauer, Ivar Bleiklie, Mary Henkel (2000). *Transforming Higher Education: A Comparative Study. London: Jessica Kingsley Publishers.*

Kogan, Maurice, Stephen Hanney (2000). Reforming Higher Education. London: Jessica Kingsley Publishers.

Krücken, Georg, Frank Meier (2006). "Turning the University into an Organizational Actor." In: G. S. Drori, J. W. Meyer, H. Hwang, eds., *Globalization and Organization. World Society and Organizational Change*. Oxford: Oxford University Press. 241-257.

Kwiek, Marek (2006). *The University and the State. A Study into Global Transformations*. Frankfurt a/Main and New York: Peter Lang.

Kwiek, Marek (2007). "The University and the Welfare State in Transition. Changing Public Services in a Wider Context." In: D. Epstein, R. Deem et al. (eds.), *World Yearbook of Education 2008*. New York: Routledge. 32–50.

Kwiek, Marek (2008a). "Academic Entrepreneurship vs. Changing Governance and Institutional Management Structures at European Universities." *Policy Futures in Education* 6(6). 757–770.

Kwiek, Marek (2008b). "Revisiting the Classical German Idea of the University (on the Nationalization of a Modern Institution)." *Polish Journal of Philosophy* 2(1). 55–78.
Kwiek, Marek (2009a). "Globalisation: Re-Reading Its Impact on the Nation-State, the University, and Educational Policies in Europe." In: M. Simons, M. Olssen, M. E. Peters (eds.), *Re-Reading Education Policies. A Handbook Studying the Policy Agenda of the 21st Century*. Rotterdam: Sense. 195–215.
Kwiek, Marek (2009b). "The Changing Attractiveness of European Higher Education: Current Developments, Future Challenges, and Major Policy Issues." In: Barbara Kehm, Jeroen Huisman, Bjorn Stensaker (eds.), *The European Higher Education Area: Perspectives on a Moving Target*. Rotterdam/Boston/Taipei: Sense Publishers. 107–124.
Kwiek, Marek (2010). *Transformacje uniwersytetu. Zmiany instytucjonalne i ewolucje polityki edukacyjnej w Europie*. Poznań: Wydawnictwo Naukowe UAM (in Polish).
Kwiek, Marek (2011). "Universities and Knowledge Production in Central Europe." In: P. Temple (ed.), *Universities in the Knowledge Economy. Higher Education Organisation and Global Change*. New York: Routledge. 176–195.
Kwiek, Marek (2012). "Changing Higher Education Policies: From the Deinstitutionalization to the Reinstitutionalization of the Research Mission in Polish Universities." *Science and Public Policy* 39. 641–654.
Kwiek, Marek (2013). *Knowledge Production in European Universities. States, Markets, and Academic Entrepreneurialism*. Frankfurt and New York: Peter Lang.
Kwiek, Marek (2014). "Changing Higher Education and Welfare States in Postcommunist Central Europe: New Contexts Leading to New Typologies?" *Human Affairs* 24(1). 48–87.
Leibfried, Stephan, Herbert Obibnger (2001). "Welfare state futures. An introduction". In: Stephan Leibfried (ed.), *Welfare State Futures*. Cambridge: Cambridge University Press. 1-13.
March, James G., Johan P. Olsen (1989). *Rediscovering Institutions. The Organizational Basis of Politics*. New York: The Free Press.
Mazza, Carmelo, Paolo Quattrone, Angelo Riccaboni, eds. (2008). *European Universities in Transition: Issues, Models and Cases*. Cheltenham: Edward Elgar Publishing Limited.
McClelland, Charles E. (1980). *State, Society and University in Germany 1700–1914*. Cambridge: Cambridge University Press.
Mishra, Ramesh (2011). "The Logic of Globalization: The Changing Context of the Welfare State." In: Pete Alcock, Martin Powell (eds.), *Welfare Theory and Development. Volume IV*. London: SAGE. 55–73.
Musselin, Christine (2007). "Are Universities Specific Organizations?" In: G. Krücken, A. Kosmützky, M. Torka (eds.), *Towards a Multiversity? Universities between Global Trends and National Traditions*. Bielefeld: Transcript Verlag. 63–86.
Neave, Guy (2001). "The European Dimension in Higher Education: An Excursion into the Modern Use of Historical Analogues." In: Jeroen Huisman, Peter Maassen, Guy Neave (eds.), *Higher Education and the State. The International Dimension of Higher Education*. Amsterdam: Pergamon Press. 13–75.
Palier, Bruno, ed. (2010). *A Long Goodbye to Bismarck? The Politics of Welfare Reform in Continental Europe*. Amsterdam: Amsterdam University Press.

Paradeise, Catherine, Emanuela Reale, Ivar Bleiklie, Ewan Ferlie, eds. (2009). *University Governance. Western European Comparative Perspectives*. Dordrecht: Springer.

Pestieau, Pierre (2006). *The Welfare State in the European Union: Economic and Social Perspectives*. Oxford, England: Oxford University Press.

Pierson, Paul (2001). "Coping with Permanent Austerity: Welfare State Restructuring in Affluent Democracies." In: P. Pierson (ed.), *The New Politics of the Welfare State*. Oxford: Oxford University Press. 410-456.

Pinheiro, Rómulo, Paul Benneworth, Glen A. Jones, eds. (2012). *Universities and Regional Development: A Critical Assessment of Tensions and Contradictions*. London: Routledge.

Readings, Bill (1996). *The University in Ruins*. Boston: Harvard University Press.

Ringer, Fritz K. (1990). *The Decline of the German mandarins: The German Academic Community, 1890–1933*. Hanover and London: University Press of New England.

Rothblatt, Sheldon, Björn Wittrock, eds. (1993). *The European and American University since 1800: Historical and Sociological Essays*. Cambridge: Cambridge University Press.

Ruggie, John Gerard (1997). "Globalization and the Embedded Liberalism Compromise: The End of an Era?" Max Planck Institute for the Studies of Societies. Working Paper 97/1.

Sanderson, Michael (1999). *Education and Economic Decline in Britain, 1870 to the 1990s*. Cambridge: Cambridge University Press.

Scharpf, Fritz W. (2000). "Negative Integration: States and the Loss of Boundary Control." In: Christopher Pierson, Francis G. Castles (eds.), *The Welfare State Reader*. Cambridge: Polity Press. 223—235.

Scharpf, Fritz W. (2010). *Community and Autonomy: Institutions, Policies and Legitimacy in Multilevel Europe*. Frankfurt, New York: Campus Verlag.

Scharpf, Fritz W., Vivien A. Schmidt, eds. (2000). *Welfare and Work in the Open Economy. Volume 1. From Vulnerability to Competitiveness*. Oxford: Oxford University Press.

Scott, Peter (2005). "The Opportunities and Threats of Globalization." In: G. A. Jones, P. L. McCarney, M. L. Skolnik (eds.), *Creating Knowledge, Strengthening Nations: The Changing Role of Higher Education*. Toronto: University of Toronto Press. 42–55.

Seeleib-Kaiser, Martin (2008). "Welfare State Transformations in Comparative Perspective: Shifting Boundaries of 'Public' and 'Private' Social Policy?" In: Martin Seeleib-Kaiser (ed.), *Welfare State Transformations: Comparative Perspectives*. Basingstoke: Palgrave Macmillan. 1–13.

Shattock, Michael (2009). *Entrepreneurialism in Universities and the Knowledge Economy. Diversification and Organizational Change in European Higher Education*. Maidenhead: Open University Press and SRHE.

Slaughter, Anne-Marie (2004). *A New World Order*. Princeton: Princeton University Press.

Spybey, Tony (1996). *Globalization and World-Society*. Cambridge: Polity Press.

Stiglitz, Joseph E. (2000). *Economics of the Public Sector*. Third Edition. New York: W. W. Norton & Company.

Swank, Duane (2002). *Global Capital, Political Institutions, and Policy Change in Developed Welfare States*. Cambridge: Cambridge University Press.

Teichler, Ulrich, Akira Arimoto, William K. Cummings (2013). *The Changing Academic Profession. Major Findings of a Comparative Survey*. Dordrecht: Springer.

Teichler, Ulrich, Ester Ava Höhle, eds. (2013). *The Work Situation of the Academic Profession in Europe: Findings of a Survey in Twelve Countries.* Dordrecht: Springer.

Teixeira, Pedro, Ben Jongbloed, David Dill, Alberto Amaral, eds. (2004). *Markets in Higher Education. Rhetoric or Reality?* Dordrecht: Kluwer.

Välimaa, Jussi, Oili-Helena Ylijoki, eds. (2008). *Cultural Perspectives on Higher Education.* Dordrecht: Springer.

Weber, Max (1973). *On Universities. The Power of the State and the Dignity of the Academic Calling in Imperial Germany.* (E. Shils, trans.). Chicago: The University of Chicago Press.

Weisz, George (1983). *The Emergence of Modern Universities in France, 1863–1914.* Princeton: Princeton University Press.

Williams, Gareth, ed. (2004). *The Enterprising University. Reform, Excellence and Equity*, London: Open University Press and SRHE.

Williams, Gareth (2009). "Finance and Entrepreneurial Activity in Higher Education in a Knowledge Society." In: M. Shattock (ed.), *Entrepreneurialism in Universities and the Knowledge Economy: Diversification and Organizational Change in European Higher Education.* Berkshire: SRHE & Open University Press. 8–32.

Wittrock, Björn (1993). "The Modern University: the Three Transformations." In: Sheldon Rothblatt and Björn Wittrock (eds.), *The European and American University since 1800: Historical and Sociological Essays.* Cambridge: Cambridge University Press. 303–362.

Wittrock, Björn (2003). History of Social Science: Understanding Modernity and Rethinking Social Studies of Science. In: Bernward Joerges, Helga Nowotny (eds.), *Social Studies of Science and Technology: Looking Back, Ahead.* Dordrecht: Kluwer Academic Publishers. 79-101.

Ziman, John (1994). *Prometheus Bound. Science in a Dynamic Steady-State.* Cambridge: Cambridge University Press.

CHAPTER TEN

Forum Shifting and Shape Making in Higher Education Services

SUSAN L. ROBERTSON, JOANNA TIDY, AND JANJA KOMLJENOVIC

Introduction

Beginning in mid-1980s, proponents have not only sought to open up new markets in sectors protected from trade and advance their expansion as part of global trade rules,[1] but also create mechanisms that protect these arrangements into the future from (particularly national) politics.[2] Over time, they have engaged in a complex game of 'forum shifting' (Sell, 2009) involving multiple scales and strategies to advance their agendas. In the 1980s, the U.S.-based Coalition of Service Industries pressed the U.S. Department of Trade to advance the negotiation of a services and intellectual property agreement at the global level which paralleled the postwar General Agreement on Tariffs and Trade as part of what is known as the Uruguay Round.[3]

The eventual emergence of the World Trade Organization (WTO) in 1995 and its ongoing rounds of negotiations, however, have failed to deliver on what is widely referred to as the Doha Development Round (DDR)[4]–because of the controversial nature of many services, the highly uneven distribution and deployment of power in the trade negotiations causing considerable dissent by the 'global south', the difficulties in negotiations around agriculture and other key sectors, and as a result of organized protest.

In this chapter, we explore the ways in which a series of post-General Agreement on Trade in Services (GATS) 'forum shifting' strategies have been deployed resulting in significant regulatory changes at both regional and national scales via a new set of market-making actors, strategies, and instruments aimed at including higher education as a services sector. A first wave of scalar strategies includes the EC's Directive on Services launched in 2006 (European Parliament and Council, 2006), the strategic targeting of national governments and agencies by edu-investor firms to open up new spaces for market activity, the use of the 2006 EC's Directive in Services to claim tax exemptions making it more viable to enter national education sectors, and the explosion of Bilateral and Preferential Trading Agreements. From 2011 onwards, spurred on and legitimated by the 2008 Financial Crisis and poor economic development, a second wave of scalar strategies has emerged that includes the Trans-Pacific Partnership (TPP),[5] the Comprehensive Economic Trade Agreement (CETA) the Transatlantic Trade and Investment Partnership (TTIP), and the Trade in Services Agreement (TISA).[6] In these negotiations and agreements, education is included as a services sector (EC, 2013a, 2013b)—though precisely what aspects, and what conditions, are still not entirely clear in large part because these are 'closed door' negotiations and several of these agreements are yet to be properly concluded. We reflect on the longer-term consequences for education being included; the likely implications of closing down sub/national education policy spaces through binding future measures; the potential for 'regulatory hopping' by investors to secure the best deal; and the implications of multiple, overlapping, agreements for governing higher education.

'First wave' Post-GATS Trade Agreements

In this section, we explore in detail three 'first wave' post-GATS trade agreements: the EU's Directive on Services launched in 2006 (European Parliament and Council, 2006); the strategic targeting of national governments and agencies by education-investor firms to open up new spaces for profitable market activity; and the expansion of Preferential Trading Agreements on a bilateral basis. these latter agreements also involve new regulatory mechanisms that did not feature in quite the same way in the GATS, in particular the Investor Dispute mechanisms. Each move has created new opportunities for further opening up the education sector to trade that has also advanced mechanisms to lock in these agreements in ways that work in the interests of edu-investors.

Creating a New Forum—the EC's Directive on Services 2006

The *Directive on Services* in the internal market (commonly referred to as the Bolkestein Directive), ratified by the European Parliament in 2006, is aimed at establishing a single market for services within the European Union (EU). The

Directive was regarded as an important kick-start to the stalling of the Lisbon Agenda initially launched in 2000—a strategy backed by the Member States to make the EU '... the world's most dynamic and competitive economy' by 2010 (EC, 2001). By 2003, economic growth in Europe had slowed. This coincided with ongoing challenges in the WTO, and a shift within the European Commission by putting into place intra-EU trade policies to ensure European competitiveness (Hay, 2007).

As Hay points out, a very particular view of competitiveness now underpinned the Commission's *Directive on Services*; that there would be efficiency gains arising from heightened economic integration, and also that '... all markets for goods and services are analogous to those for cheap consumer goods—that is, both highly price sensitive and highly demand price elastic. This assumption led the EU to privilege strategies of costs and price containment to the detriment of other strategies for enhancing competitiveness ...' (Hay, 2007: 26; see also Jessop, 2008). This version of competitiveness also threatens the viability of the distinctive social and economic paradigm that underpinned the European social model (Hay, 2007).

The European Commission has used the Directive on Services to police European member states regulations over what it views as protectionist and out of step with the Directive. In a case directly relevant to education, the European Commission issued a statement to the Cypriot government in November 2009, on their 'provision of education services'. We quote:

Cyprus—provision of education services

> The European Commission has decided to send a reasoned opinion to Cyprus in relation to certain provisions of the law regulating the establishment and operation of institutions of tertiary education.
>
> Under this law private institutions of tertiary education in Cyprus are prohibited to 'allow, by any means, to foreign educational institutions the possibility to award their own degrees in the Republic'. This prohibition renders impossible the provision of services entailing the award of foreign degrees by educational institutions in Cyprus (such as services under validation, franchising or similar agreements), where recipients of such services are private institutions of tertiary education in Cyprus. The Commission considers this a restriction on the freedom to provide services and a restriction on the freedom of establishment which cannot be justified.
>
> In addition, in accordance with the law in question, a company having as a shareholder or a member of its board a person who is neither a Cypriot citizen nor a citizen of a EU Member State cannot establish a private institution of tertiary education in Cyprus. As this prohibition precludes the recognition of companies duly formed in accordance with the law of another Member State, the European

> Commission considers it a restriction on the freedom of establishment which cannot be justified.
>
> —EUROPEAN COMMISSION (2009)

In short, under the 2006 Directive on Services, Cyprus cannot deny the right of other EU countries to establish higher education institutions in Cyprus, and award their own degree. The 2006 Directive on Services offers the EC and its industry backers, such as the European Business Roundtable, a different spatial strategy to advance the liberalization of trade in services. As a result, new structural selectivities favoring other nations and edu-investors are now embedded in national territorial spaces in turn challenging national sovereignty (as we see with the case of Cyprus).

Creating New Forums and Mechanisms

One forum where investor agreements have been advanced is through growth in the number of Bilateral and Preferential Trade Agreements (BTA/PTA) and International Investment Agreements (IIA). Horn et al. (2010) show that PTAs have grown in number since 1995 when the World Trade Organization was launched—from 50 active PTA in 1995, to around 200 active agreements in 2008. A large part of this expansion involves agreements where either the United States or the EC are at the center of the partnership. However, these newer PTAs are different to those formed prior to 1995; the earlier group largely focused on trade in goods. With services and intellectual property now part of the multilateral trade negotiations, post-1995 PTAs now include the regulatory aspects of services and trade-related intellectual property—the two areas that have been particularly difficult to achieve under the DDR (Sauvé, 2014).

Commentators argue what is notable about this new generation of PTAs is that they go much further in the coverage of regulatory issues than under the WTO/GATS, and include provisions and mechanisms such as; '… investment protection, competition policy, labour standards and protection of the environment' (see Horn et al., 2010: 1566). This has led some to argue that though the EC and United States account for no more than 40% of world GDP and world trade, they account for 80% of the rules that regulate the functioning of world markets, and thus can be regarded as 'regulators of the world' (2010).

In their 2014 *Trade and Development Report*, the United Nations Conference on Trade and Development (UNCTAD) signalled their concern over this steady erosion of national 'policy space' as a result of PTAs and International Investment Agreements, '… some of which contain provisions that are more stringent than those covered by the multilateral trade regime, or they include additional provisions that go beyond those of the current multilateral trade agreements' (UNCTAD, 2014a: 19). They go on to argue that provisions in PTAs

> have become ever more comprehensive and many of them include rules that limit the options available in the design and implementation of comprehensive national development strategies. Even though these agreements remain the product of (often protracted) negotiations and bargaining between sovereign States, there is a growing sense that, due to the larger number of economic and social issues they cover, the discussions often lack transparency and the coordination—including amongst all potentially interested government ministries. (UNCTAD, 2014a: 19)

International Investment Agreements have been steadily growing: by 2013, there were some 3,236—giving rise to major concerns over the loss of national policy space particularly in those partnerships which share major asymmetries of power (Bhagwati et al., 2015). UNCTAD (2014a: 20–21) notes that when these agreements were being concluded in the 1990s, a common view was this was a small price to pay for increased foreign direct investment (FDI). However, by 2000, this view had changed in that it was evident investment rules could also obstruct a wide range of public policies—including the policy areas we are concerned with in this chapter—education, and related sectors such as industrial policy, and its implications for labor markets and employment.

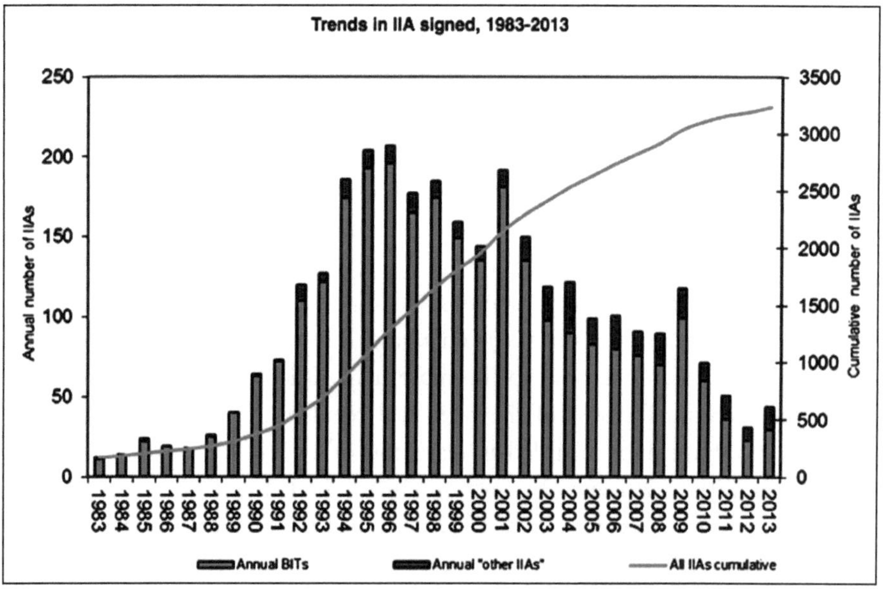

Figure 10.1: Trends in International Investment Agreements Signed 1983–2013.
Source: UNCTAD [2014b], IIA database.

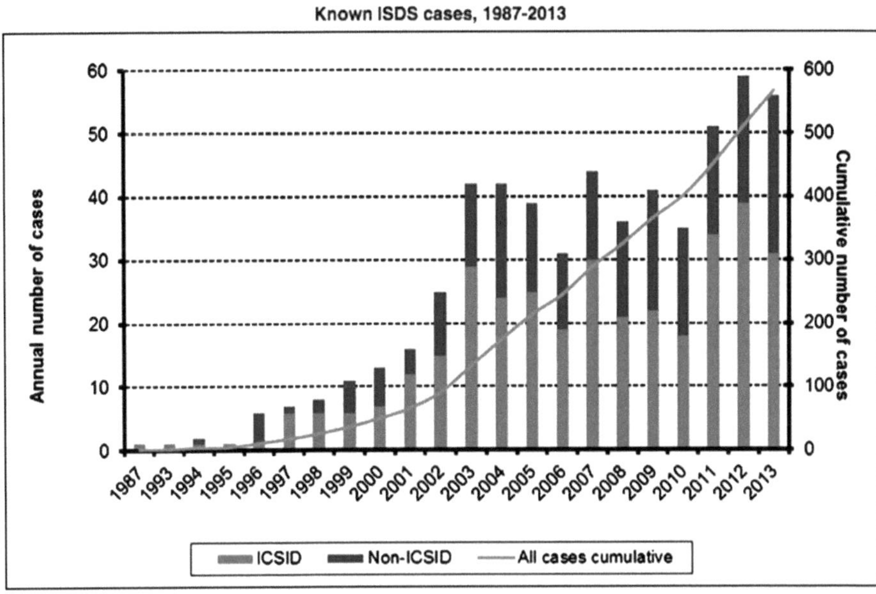

Figure 10.2: Known Investor State Dispute Settlement Cases 1983–2013.
Source: UNCTAD [2014b], IIA database.

Others have called for the *elimination* of ISDS mechanisms in that they are antithetical to sustainable development (Friends of the Earth, 2014). Even *The Economist*, not known for its anti-investor stance—reported in October 2014:

> Multinationals have exploited woolly definitions of expropriation to claim compensation for changes in government policy that happen to have harmed their business. Following the Fukushima disaster in Japan in 2011, for instance, the German government decided to shut down its nuclear power industry. Soon after, Vattenfall, a Swedish utility that operates two nuclear plants in Germany, demanded compensation of 3.7 billion ($4.7 billion), under the ISDS clause of a treaty on energy investments. This claim is still in arbitration. And it is just one of a growing number of such cases. (Economist, October 11, 2014)

The Economist goes on to argue the sharp rise in contentious arbitrations is the result of companies having learnt how to exploit ISDS clauses, going as far as buying firms in jurisdictions where they apply simply to gain access to them. Arbitrators are also paid $600–700 an hour, giving them little incentive to dismiss cases out of hand; the secretive nature of the arbitration process and the lack of any requirement to consider precedent allows plenty of scope for creative adjudications (Economist, 2014).

Shopping around for firms in jurisdictions where they can make a claim is not just a case of 'forum shopping'—a term used to describe firms who look around for agreements that will give them most 'return' regarding potential investor payouts—but also what we have argued elsewhere is 'place hopping' (Robertson and Komljenovic, 2016); that is, looking for those places, or jurisdictions, that enable the launch of a more lucrative claim—much as capitalists have used tax havens and states with a low taxation floor. This uneven terrain is the result of different degrees of economic and political liberalization operating vertically and horizontally, as well as overlapping and competing spaces and places regarding trade rules. My purpose in bringing this 'actually existing' regulatory landscape into view is because it feeds into the ongoing trade negotiations as part of the 'game is never really over' (in this case TPP, TTIP, CETA and TISA).

Enter a 'Second Wave' of Spatial Strategies

We now examine a second wave of trade negotiations that gained momentum from 2010 onwards. In the interests of space, we will focus only on TPP, TTIP and TISA—recognizing nonetheless that there is much to be learned from negotiations, such as CETA, regarding the likely scope, form, and content of these negotiations. In all these cases the negotiations have taken place in secret, giving rise to considerable unease among the wider public. In the case of TISA, negotiation takes place in Geneva, but outside the WTO structures.

TPP

The TPP agreement was a U.S.-led regional trade agreement involving 12 Asia-Pacific countries (Australia, Brunei, Canada, Chile, Japan, Malaysia, Mexico, New Zealand, Peru, Singapore, the United States, and Vietnam)—though it needs to be pointed out that following the election of Donald Trump to the US Presidency, the US has withdrawn from the TPP. The TPP negotiations were launched in 2010 and concluded toward the end of 2015. The TPP was finally signed by all members in Auckland, New Zealand, on February 4, 2016 and goes into force once it has been ratified by six countries representing 85% of its economic activity.

Notionally, the United States, Australia, Canada, Malaysia, Mexico, Peru, and Vietnam were acceding to a predecessor agreement: the Trans-Pacific Strategic Economic Partnership Agreement which involved Chile, New Zealand, Singapore, and Brunei, and concluded in 2005. This formed the basis of TPP. However as Kelsey (2008: 239) points out: 'In reality, the United States does not accede to other countries' agreements. The U.S. Trade Representative (USTR) has dominated the negotiations, reportedly seeking to extend the rules in existing U.S. Free Trade Agreements (FTAs), and to supplement them with new proposals'.

As an economic strategy, TPP brings together 12 states representing 700 million people, with a combined GDP of $28bn, and 40% of the world's gross domestic product. Taken together, TPP constitutes one of the largest trade agreements globally, include trade in goods and services, with attention particularly now on *nontariff* barriers. For the United States, the other 11 TPP countries have a combined population of around 486 million, and generate around 15% of global trade. They are therefore a critical market for the United States. What is of particular interest to the United States is a growing middle class in the Asia-Pacific as a potential profitable market. 'By 2030, Asia's middle class is projected to reach 3.2 billion people, and those consumers will drive demand for everything America is great at making, from autos and airplanes, to agricultural goods, movies, software and services ... TPP puts America at the centre of the world's fastest-growing region and help us become the world's premier place to set up shop, make things, and sell them to the world' (United States Department for Trade and Industry, 2016a: 2–3).

Like other commentators, Kelsey has pointed to the profoundly geopolitical nature of the TPP; as the economic limb of a two-pronged strategy to reinvigorate U.S. leadership in the Asia-Pacific region, the other limb a renewed military presence in the region as a counter to China's growing ascendency. In short, the Obama administration has heralded the TPP as a strategic agreement that underpins its rebalancing of the Asia-Pacific to ensure that China cannot write the rules on regional economic issues—but that it was the United States seeking to write the rules of trade in the fastest growing region of the world, with China faced with being a rule-taker rather than a rule-maker. As such, it is more than *just* trade negotiations.

But it is not only that the TPP is about geostrategic interests. Rather, it is that this 'groundbreaking' agreement (to use the words of the USTR, Michael Froman) has the capacity to reach further into domestic economies and domestic policy settings than conventional trade agreements. It does this through '... framing how governments make their domestic policy and regulatory decisions as a complement to more extensive rules that constrain the substance of those decisions' (Kelsey, 2008: 237). Its use of the 'negative list' parallels other FTAs; that is, any exclusions need to be stated in advance—with all else both now and into the future regarded as in. The TPP also includes Investor State Dispute Settlement mechanisms—allowing investors to sue governments if policy changes or court rulings substantially affect the value of their investment.

For the most part, the TPP has split its proponents and critics largely around what free trade really means and delivers. Proponents in the United States argue that the TPP will diversify consumer choice, increase U.S. exports, protect intellectual property rights, and level the playing fields for American companies through lowering the barriers to trade in participating countries. The opponents, on the other hand, argue that the TPP will work in the interests of the corporations and result in a further erosion of jobs from the United States. They point to the ways in which the FTA have perpetuated a global race to the bottom as many countries seek to remain competitive in the global marketplace, and maintain low labor costs by ignoring or interfering with fundamental labor rights. In short, though the FTAs do have labor chapters, the United States has not taken any interest in insisting on International Labor Organization (ILO) level standards in its partner countries. That Mexico, Malaysia, Vietnam, and Brunei all show a very low level of compliance with ILO standards (forced labor, economic inequality, and so on) suggests that the outcomes are likely to be very different.

Our interest in this chapter is on education as a services sector. And indeed the TPP promises to increase opportunities for American service providers in the Asia-Pacific region. As it states:

> Services industries account for four out of five jobs in the United States, the world's largest services exporter. In 2014, U.S. services exports of $710 million supported an estimated 4.6 million jobs and expanded the U.S. services trade surplus to $233 billion. American service workers are in industries that include the Internet, information, and software services; professional services; financial services; media and entertainment; express delivery and logistics; scientific research and development, telecommunications, and others. Securing liberalized and fair access to foreign services markets will help U.S. service suppliers, both small and large, to increase exports to TPP markets and support more jobs at home (International Trade Administration, 2016: 1).

While education is not directly referenced, in its unbundled form, it is clearly implicated in Internet services, scientific research and development, professional services, financial services, and so on. Howard Davies (2016: 2) also draws the conclusion that '… education is likely to feature prominently: Australia in particular, will look to extend its delivery of HE services (online programmes, branch campuses) notably to Malaysia and Vietnam, as well as to make government procurement bids to all signatory countries'.

Joseph Stiglitz, Nobel Laureate and former Chief Economist of the World Bank, has been forthright about the challenges the TPP represents, arguing that it is only one aspect of a larger problem; '… our gross mismanagement of globalization' (2014: 1). In essence, Stiglitz is pointing to the globalization of neoliberal policies that have generated unprecedented inequalities around the globe—of which the current round of trade deals are seen to be a part because of their focus upon nontariff barriers—which in effect is a neologism for 'regulations'. And while the corporations complain that what is at issue are inconsistent regulations that make business costly, in effect they are regulations to protect workers, the consumer, the economy, and the environment.

The TPP has galvanized the EU into action in the region. It began bilateral talks with Australia and New Zealand in 2016. It also completed a FTA with Vietnam toward the end of 2015, which will come into force in 2018. The EU's memorandum promises EU access to a broad range of services, which according to an internal European Services Forum document includes higher education (Davies, 2016: 2). However the bulk of the EU's efforts have been consumed in the TTIP and CETA negotiations—the latter of which was concluded between the EU and Canada, which went to the Council and Parliament in 2016, and came into force in 2017. In the following section, I look more closely at the emergence of TTIP and its likely implications for education.

TTIP

The Transatlantic Trade and Investment Partnership (TTIP) emerged out of recommendations of the final report of the joint *High level Working Group (HLWG) on Jobs and Growth* following a EU–U.S. summit held in Washington in November 2011. The HLWG was directed by EU and U.S. leaders to identify policies and measures to increase transatlantic trade and investment so as to boost growth following the 2008 global financial crisis.

The Transatlantic Economic Council established in 2007 had tried to manage some of these issues but with little success. However, '… concerns over slow economic growth, job creation, and increased competition from emerging markets promoted calls by public and private stakeholders for a renewed intensive focus on eliminating or reducing tariff and nontariff barriers to US-EU trade and investment' (Akhtar and Jones 2014: 3). According to the European Commission (2013a), reforming services matters as they account for as much as 60% of the global economy. The United States and Europe account for nearly half of global GDP, about 30% of global exports and have $3.7 trillion in each other's economies, but EU firms still face major hurdles when they try to sell their services in the U.S. marketplace.

The justification for the TTIP negotiations is that the two economies have not maximized their economic relationship, and there continue to be major regulatory and tariff barrier challenges (Akhtar and Jones, 2014) and that TTIP represents—in the words of the UK Prime Minister—David Cameron, a 'once-in-a-generation' prize

(Cameron, 2013) allowing the EU and the United States to boost their economies by eliminating barriers to trade and setting global standards (Siles-Brügge, 2014: 1).

The purpose of TTIP is to increase market access through: (i) the elimination of barriers to trade and investment on goods, services, agriculture, and government market procurement; (ii) enhancing regulatory coherence; and (iii) developing new rules, especially in the area of Foreign Direct Investment (FDI), intellectual property, labor, and emerging new trade areas, such as data flows. TTIP is the largest FTA ever negotiated by the United States. Akhtar and Jones note the EU and United States have also '... expressed an interest in using the TTIP to present common approaches for the development of globally-relevant rules and standards in future multilateral trade agreements' (2014: 3).[7]

On February 11, 2013, the HLWG released a final report, and in February this was used to launch preparations for the TTIP negotiations. In March 2013, the Obama administration notified Congress of its intent to negotiate under the procedures of the Trade Promotion Authority (TPA) (otherwise known as the Fast Track), though Davies (2015: 2) reports that this was not given the green light in 2015, largely as the Democratic Party have been deeply opposed to TTIP. TTIP negotiations began in July 2013.

On the EU side, the EC agreed to draft a concept paper (European Commission, 2013a) to establish a mandate for the TTIP negotiations, which was then sent to the Council of Ministers for approval by the Member States. Though not formally required to do so, the European Parliament (by simple majority) passed a resolution supporting TTIP, while at the same time noted sensitivities, particularly around the ISDS mechanisms and some services sectors. By June 14, 2013, the Council of Ministers approved the mandate for the EC to negotiate TTIP. It should be noted that since the Lisbon Treaty, the Parliament's role in EU trade policy has increased a great deal and is thus an important forum regarding rules for engagement. The EU Parliament is therefore an increasingly important space for contestation for member states.

There have now been 11 rounds of negotiations (EC, 2015: 1). However, like other forums such as the WTO, TTIP has become increasingly mired in controversy and buffeted by the volatility of global politics (Davies, 2014a). As in the WTO/GATS process, guiding the negotiations forward has been particularly tricky. It has not helped that the process is conducted in secret, with only leaked documents—often via Wikileaks, and growing public opposition through organized protest and the use of social media. This has led to a great deal of speculation and guessing; the CETA between the EU and Canada is often referred to as a potential prototype.

Within the European Parliament, the Chair of the influential International Trade Committee (INTC), Bernd Lange, has been critical of the lack of transparency in the TTIP process.[8] In particular, Lange has raised doubts over the EC's commissioned 'impact assessment' of TTIP conducted by the Centre for European Policy Studies (CEPS) (see Pelkmans et al., 2014). CEPS is a pro-business think tank located in Brussels. INTC have commissioned its own review of CEPS' impact assessment and which raises doubts about CEPS' methodology, and whether an impact assessment is actually feasible (Raza et al., 2014) (see a longer and wider discussion of this in Robertson and Komljenovic, 2016).

This leads to the next question of *how* are these barriers to be eliminated. That is, what will be the regulatory mechanisms used to achieve the elimination of Non-Tariff Barriers (NTBs): harmonization, mutual recognition, or national treatment? Harmonization refers to a common Trade in Services Agreement (TISA) regulatory space between the United States and the EU. Mutual[9] recognition means that the regulatory frameworks in the United States and Europe respectively are recognized (this gives primacy to the market, and assumes a level of common identity—whether or not this is the case). National treatment means that the foreign investor is treated like a local firm or organization (thus national politics holds sway). TTIP is promoting mutual recognition (MR) of standards (as more feasible) rather than the harmonization or national treatment. In other words, the standards (labor, safety, worker protection, qualifications, and so on) of the 'home' country will be recognized.

This is likely to lead to the exploitation of uneven development by investors, giving rise to even further uneven development as place-based actors try to use their less demanding regulatory environment to attract investors. De Ville and Siles-Brügge (2015) show that the combination of the assumptions built into the Computational General Equilibrium (CGE), the regulatory mechanism to be used, and the capacity to liberalize across the board, ends up exaggerating the potential economic benefits of TTIP while underplaying other likely outcomes—such as where bilateral MR without a minimum floor of harmonization may lead to a race to the bottom in social, educational, and environmental standards.

For those not only skeptical but deeply opposed to TTIP, the inclusion of an Investor State Dispute Settlement mechanism has been particularly controversial. Like those opposed to the ISDS mechanisms in TPP, they argue this will give foreign companies the right to sue national and regional governments for compensation whenever their access to markets is impeded by what they see as unfair legislation, or whenever their expectations as legitimate inward foreign investors is thwarted. For its own part, the EC Trade Commissioner and Chief Negotiator for TTIP has, until recently, argued that the inclusion of ISDS in regional and preferential trade agreements has not placed any pressure on national sovereignty. However, this view is not widely shared and indeed UNCTAD has become increasingly concerned about the limits on national policy spaces.

Perhaps as a means of easing the difficulties still facing TTIP, in the 2015 Report on the 10th TTIP Round held in July 2015, the European Commission has referred to a State-to-State Dispute Settlement (SSDS) mechanism as opposed to an ISDS. They state that discussions on the SSDS have, '… focussed on the rules of procedure, the EU's proposal for a voluntary and complementary mediation mechanism, and on the compliance phase' (EC, 2015: 5). But quite what this means in practice is too early to say. However, it does suggest that TISA negotiators have had to respond to public demand that the investor-driven dispute mechanism be dropped. However, we also note that the EU's Directive on Services with its investor dispute mechanism in place opens up the possibility for investors to use that as a mechanism to dispute regulatory changes.

TISA

TISA refers to a self-styled 'Really Good Friends of Services' (RGFSs) group of 25 countries[10] with the European Union representing its 28 Member States—bringing this to a total of 52. Like the TPP and TTIP, TISA has also been conducted in secrecy.

A TISA arose out of these discussions in July 2012, led by the United States and Australia. Their aim was for a stand-alone agreement on trade in services that would advance the Doha Development Agenda (DDA) negotiations among willing WTO members. The participants in this initiative, calling themselves the 'Really Good Friends of Services', were an ad hoc coalition of all those WTO members who had putatively shown willingness to advance services negotiations. Since these first discussions, participation has expanded from 16 to 25 parties, with the European Union representing its 28 Member States, making up a total of 52 WTO Members. The 25 TISA parties (as of August 2015) comprise: Australia, Canada, Chile, Chinese Taipei, Colombia, Costa Rica, European Union (representing its 28 Member States), Hong Kong, Iceland, Israel, Japan, Liechtenstein, Mauritius, Mexico, New Zealand, Norway, Pakistan, Panama, Paraguay, Peru, Republic of Korea, Switzerland, Turkey, the United States, and Uruguay. Most TISA parties are also forum shoppers; many of them participate in often more than once Preferential Trade Agreement (PTA) in services among themselves (Marchetti and Roy, 2013), along with inclusion in other pluri-lateral negotiations.[11]

We can get a good sense of the overall aims of TISA by examining the European Commission's communication to the European Council (European Commission, 2013b) when seeking a mandate to negotiate. The main elements were:

- An agreement compatible with the General Agreement in Trade in Services (GATS) agreement to be later multilateralized;

- comprehensive in scope with no exclusions of services sectors at the outset or mode of supply (this means education is included); commitments should reflect reality on the ground (hence very liberalized education sectors would need to remain so, and from there go further);
- new and better rules to be developed to cover new economic developments—including e-commerce, data, and so on;
- a combination of positive[12] and negative[13] lists (WTO/GATS only works with a positive list);
- national treatment that applies horizontally to all service sectors and modes of supply; and
- the future elimination of discriminatory measures to be locked in (i.e., there is no return to a different regulatory environment; the so-called 'ratchet clause).

Despite the mix of developed and developing countries, what is striking in TISA is the dominance of OECD members. TISA parties collectively account for around 70% of global trade in services, and it is argued that for these economies, services is both a significant and rising component of domestic output and employment particularly for the developed economies. As Sauvé (2014) shows, among the TISA participants, the EU (36.4%) and the United States (26.9%) dominate in terms of share of world services trade.

Yet more than 30% of world trade in services is still among WTO members outside the TISA process. This matters in that, like with TTIP, while the argument is that the negotiators of the TISA architecture will attempt to align it with the WTO GATS. Sauvé (2014) points out this will be particularly challenging in that there will be little appetite to take on a set of rules that have been negotiated in secret.

Of the top 20 services exporters/importers globally, China, India, Singapore, Russia, Brazil, Malaysia, Saudi Arabia, United Arab Emirates, and Indonesia are not currently in TISA (Marchetti and Roy, 2013). This would have major implications for sectors like education, where international student flows and international branch campuses occur from, or are located within, countries not included in the TISA negotiations (Marchetti and Martin, 2013: 21). In other words, there are more markets of interest for TISA members *outside* (judging by WTO requests received and requests sponsored) rather than *inside* TISA. But their exclusion is also political, and there is a widely shared view that the EU and the United States are attempting to create a set of rules for the global economy that work in their interests rather than in those of the developed and developing worlds (cf. Bhagwati et al., 2015).

Much discussion on TISA, as with TTIP, also concerns the way in which the negotiations are being conducted—yet with ambitions to anchor it in the WTO architecture in the future—with invitations to others to join once the rules for engagement have been worked out. Sauvé (2014: 7), a veteran WTO negotiator, remarks that TISA is proceeding without the formal ascent of the broader WTO membership, negotiations are taking place in Geneva, but outside of the perimeter of the WTO, it is at arm's length to the WTO secretariat, and the Really Good Friends (RGFs) of services do not allow observers, including the WTO.

This exclusive 'club mind-set' of TISA is viewed as problematic; it reduces the overall legitimacy of the agreement and it is unlikely to get buy-in from a very significant group of developing countries much as with the WTO negotiations. The ultimate outcome, in Sauvé's (2014: 5) view, is that TISA is likely to face the very same fate of the services negotiations under the Uruguay and Doha Rounds.

A key issue with TISA are the regulatory mechanisms being developed. Currently TISA offers around *market access* will take a positive list approach, while national treatment will take a negative list approach (remember a negative list means listing all exemptions, otherwise all else is in; a positive list means listing all inclusions for offer with the rest remaining outside trade rules). Those skeptical or opposed to the TISA negotiations have called for a positive list only, much as under the WTO/GATS round of negotiations which avoided the need to list all nonconforming measures. The argument here is that a negative list assumes all exemptions can be known now and into the future (surely madness) as all new services not known now will be deemed to be included. Equally as important is that this also places TISA at odds with any potential GATS architectural alignment, in the same way that TTIP is not aligned with GATS.

TISA is also promoting a 'ratchet clause'; a mechanism currently found in the Canada-EU Comprehensive Trade Agreement (CETA) that requires the parties to automatically bind any autonomous liberalization. Those concerned with wider social and economic issues view the ratchet clause as undermining social and other equity goals (see ETUCE, 2014; Scherrard, 2014). Sauvé (2014: 19–20) calls for a more flexible approach to rule making; one that is less binding and more experimental in approach to the regulatory architecture so as to '… acknowledge the increasing diversity of collective preferences'. He goes on: 'Concluding plurilateral outcomes in an open setting that allows for economies of scale and learning is not the same thing as negotiating behind closed doors. History has not been kind to the latter initiatives' (2014).

A New Geometry of Education and the Loss of Policy Space?

There are important dynamics at work that are giving shape to this new power geometry of education: these include (but are not limited to) (i) the ways in which the negotiations are conducted in secret to limit wider social and political engagement in the negotiations; (ii) what counts as public education and thus a possible basis for exemption; (iii) being able to anticipate the future and to place limits on progressive liberalization; (iv) processes of ratification in multi-scalar governing systems; and (iv) the dangers inherent in deploying mutual recognition as a basis for regulation. Taken together, they represent the potential loss of policy space, and thus a basis for viewing education as part of democratic processes.

On the question of secrecy, across all of the different negotiating spaces, this is the new politics. As a result, those concerned with not *whether* but *how* education will be included as a services sector can only guess at what the final outcomes might be. Concerned bodies, including UNISON (2015), Public Services International (2014), the European Universities Association (2015), Education International (ETUCE, 2014), and Universities College Union/UK (Scherrard, 2014), have all been monitoring developments, holding meetings, making public statements, and leading demonstrations.

Davies has produced a series of updates on TTIP and TISA for European University Association (EUA) that also includes EUA's statement on the matter (2014a, 2014b, 2014c, 2015, 2016), but these implications are very often inferred. What is clear, however, is that the EU negotiating mandate in TTIP aims to bind the EU and the United States to the highest degree of service liberalization envisaged as part of the WTO's GATS, much as TISA appears to be doing, and TPP seems to have done. This kind of approach to negotiation (secret) to sectors (including public services) favors those corporations who would benefit most from getting rid of regulations so as to enhance profits. As Stiglitz (2015: 2) observes: 'These high stakes are why it is especially risky to let trade negotiations proceed in secret. All over the world trade ministries are captured by corporate and financial interests. And when negotiations are in secret, there is no way that the democratic process can exert the checks and balances required to put limits on the negative effects of these agreements'.

As a result, getting a sense of what might emerge from the negotiations is rather like playing a game of 'waiting' with little to no space to influence the outcomes, unless of course you happen to be the United States, the EC's Department for Trade, or an interest group like the European Services Forum. That said, Member States do have some space for exerting leverage. In the case of the TTIP negotiations, while 12 EU Member States have set no limits to higher education services, the Commission was nervous about the number of reservations made by the remaining 16 Member States and was asking them to think again as a result of pressure from the USTR.

Second, the issue of whether education is 'public' continues to sit at the heart of competing interpretations around its status. Like under GATS, only those services that are truly 'public'—that is services supplied in the exercise of 'governmental authority'—see Article 1.3 (WTO Secretariat, 1999)—can be exempted in both TISA and TTIP. Yet in many countries all levels of education have become so thoroughly marketized over the past two decades—with countries like the UK actively pursuing a free-market model of governance in the sector. Most other systems across Europe would therefore find it extremely difficult to show that they are not some kind of hybrid—public private system—with the end result being that there is no basis for complete exemption—aside from political pressure.

Third, the 'negative list' principle for national treatment adopted by TISA and TTIP, along with the ratchet effect, will lock in a future that works in the interests of the corporations rather than the interests of any nation and its society. For instance, the assumption with a negative list is that all services sectors foreign providers will be treated in a manner no less favorable than domestic providers, unless explicitly stated. This assumes a capacity to second guess the future, and be able to state that future exemption.

Fourth, where and by whom ratification might take place. Specifically, can the EU strike agreements covering policy areas in which it has only complementary competence—such as in education? Davies (2016: 3) notes that the ratification of what is viewed to be a 'mixed agreement' is unclear, though according to the EU Trade Commissioner, this decision is made by the Commission itself on a case by case basis. In essence, this will result in the lobbying of the Commission by those pressing for a stronger trading position and keen to export education services, and those seeking to oppose their extension. That this is likely to happen at a scale (regional) removed from daily political life (national/subnational) further erodes the space for political accountability.

A fifth issue concerns how different regulatory regimes might be made compatible. These might involve harmonization, the recognition of equivalences, or mutual recognition. Given the challenges of the first two, it is highly likely that mutual recognition will prevail as a preferred strategy. Myant and O'Brien (2015: 22) note 'that mutual recognition could lead to different levels of regulation competing with each other ... with companies moving their operations to a lower level of regulation'. More than this, Myant and O'Brien point out that while the EU Treaty contains a provision to prevent a race to the bottom, there is no such provision in TTIP. The same also applies to the TPP.

In sum, it can be concluded that education is likely to be affected in multiple ways. First, through the easing of the conditions of entry into the sector of commercial firms seeking the liberalization and marketization of higher education—using those Member States of the EU with a very low regulatory floor—such as England or the United States—as the place from which to claim mutual recognition. This will result in growing fragmentation and diversification in the sector. It will likely sever the relationship between the idea of a university and research often used as a basis for recognition as a higher education institution, as research is viewed as a nontariff barrier to trade. It will result in the conservative use of policy in national regulatory environments, for as UNISON (2015: 5) states—the investor dispute mechanism and ratchet effects create '… a "regulatory chill" that stays the hand of governments to regulate in the public interest for fear of litigation'. Academic autonomy and other conditions of work will be viewed as nontariff barriers that should be done away with, while quality assurance and other mechanisms are regulatory mechanisms that place undue burden on the provider.

It is also as yet unclear how the differences and synergies between the competing agreements will play out. The move by TTIP toward a Regulatory Cooperation Council versus the Investor State Dispute Settlement mechanism, currently part of TISA and most PTAs, will create a proliferation of uneven development spaces that will also encourage forum shifting and place hopping. This in turn may well lead to the shaping of education sectors in ways that will place limits on the capacity to respond politically, culturally, or socially to a highly unequal present, and an unknown future.

Concluding Thoughts

We began by noting the proliferation of trade agreements involving Europe and education as a services sector in what we have been calling the post-GATS era—and suggested it is possible to identify a game of cat and mouse staging of spaces for brokering trade rules in two waves: a first wave shaped by national strategies, and regional and bilateral negotiations; and a second wave which now includes the TISA, and the TTIP.

Our argument is that two distinct clusters of rescaling strategies have been advanced that are shaping the trade in education landscape, as those actors/institutions seeking to advance trade rules have strategically developed new spaces and relations that in turn have resulted in the reshaping of the education regulatory space. This proliferation of regulatory spaces creates opportunism, as we see with the ways in which investor claims can then be advanced. On the other hand, they create a new layering of differently regulated spaces that means that there is unlikely to be, as Siles-Brügge, describes it, one big deregulatory 'big bang' (2014: 1).

At one level, the overall unevenness of the spaces being negotiated, the overlaying of multiple regulatory regimes, the sheer difficulty for Member States to make all of the appropriate reservations both now and into an as yet unknown, and unknowable, future that constitutes the basis of a negative list, will bring its own pressures and tensions. Add to this the likely tendency to 'forum shop' and 'place hop'—an outcome of the proliferation of negotiations and their uneven development—means it will also be a space full of frictions, and one that is difficult to stabilize.

That said, the rules of the trade negotiation games, as they begin to be played out across a range of these different forums, are all aimed at constraining the regulatory autonomy of the state and its citizens, by entrenching competition as the dynamic shaping the sector (with no concessions as to whether it is for car making, chemical production, or providing learning), and to put downward pressure on those nontariff barriers (such as standards) that chews into and erodes both profit margins and flexibility. And while final deals will have to be approved by the various ratifying bodies—from national parliamentary systems to Congress, the European Council (national governments) and European Parliament, these bodies are not able to make amendments to an agreement; they can only accept or reject the final deal (UNISON, 2015). Much depends, of course, on the mood of national governments, and on how (if at all) this is sold to the public.

And it is those investors in the developed economies, and most particularly the OECD countries with Europe and the United States as major players, who have aggressively advanced what some see as an antidemocratic and antidevelopment post-GATS agenda in each of these waves. When linked to the dominance of the United States and Europe in the rapid expansion of PTAs, and their roles in TTIP and TISA, it is clear trade is also being politically used to contain the rise of China and the (Brazil, Russia, India and China) 'BRICs' especially around rules driving the global economy.

What is at stake for education is its incorporation into binding trade rules; it ceases to be an arena for national/local contestation, on the one hand, and a space of democratic possibility, on the other. Given the sub/national state's role in the provision of welfare and other public services, and in the area of education an obligation under the Universal Declaration of Human Rights (United Nations, 1948) to provide free public education, it is of utmost importance that any trade agreement and its regulatory apparatus do not privilege the rights of capital to make claims about future returns by placing serious limits on the sovereignty of sub/national states to deliver on this. Equally as important is the expectation that citizens have the possibility to imagine a different world, and to implement these policies so as to bring this about.

Notes

1. The U.S.-based Coalition of Service industries began pushing for the liberalization of services in the 1980s, and was an important advocate for their inclusion in the agenda of the World Trade Organization that was launched as a new multilateral organization in 1995 (see Robertson et al., 2002).
2. Regional agreements like the North American Free Trade Agreement include mechanisms that enable investors to claim future lost earnings if public policy decisions were to be unfavorable toward their ongoing operations.
3. The Uruguay Round was the eighth round of Multilateral Trade Negotiations (MTN) conducted within the framework of the General Agreement on Tariffs and Trade (GATT), spanning from 1986 to 1994, and embracing 123 countries as 'contracting parties'. The Round led to the creation of the World Trade Organization, with GATT remaining as an integral part of the WTO agreements. The broad mandate of the Round was to extend GATT trade rules to areas previously exempted as too difficult to liberalize (agriculture, textiles) and new areas previously not included (trade in services, intellectual property, investment policy trade distortions). The Round came into effect in 1995 with deadlines ending in 2000 (2004 in the case of developing country contracting parties) under the administrative direction of the newly created World Trade Organization (WTO).
4. The Doha Development Round or Doha Development Agenda (DDA) is the current trade-negotiation round of the World Trade Organization (WTO) that commenced in November 2001. Its objective was to lower trade barriers around the world, and thus facilitate increased global trade. Since 2008, talks have stalled over a divide on major issues, such as agriculture, industrial tariffs and nontariff barriers, services, and trade remedies. The most significant differences are between the developed nations, led by the European Union (EU), the United States (USA) and Japan, and the major developing countries led and represented mainly by India, Brazil, China, and South Africa. There is also considerable contention against and between the EU and the USA over their maintenance of agricultural subsidies—seen to operate effectively as trade barriers.
5. The Trans-Pacific Partnership (TPP) is a trade agreement among twelve Pacific Rim countries (Brunei, Chile, New Zealand, Singapore, Australia, Canada, Japan, Malaysia, Mexico, Peru, the United States, and Vietnam) which was signed on February 4, 2016 in Auckland, New Zealand. TPP has not yet entered into force; it needs to be ratified by each signatory country. In the case of the USA this means gaining the support of Congress. The 30 chapters of the TPP Agreement concern many matters of public policy and a stated goal to '...promote economic growth; support the creation and retention of jobs; enhance innovation, productivity and competitiveness; raise living standards; reduce poverty in our countries; and promote transparency, good governance, and enhanced labour and environmental protections'.
6. While there are a range of other trade negotiations taking place, including in the Balkans region, these are the two key ones. TTIP parallels the Trans-Pacific Partnership, involving the USA and the Pacific region (includes Australia).
7. It should be noted, however, that the regulatory mechanisms are different making it difficult to anchor in WTO (Sauvé, 2014).

8. National governments and MEPs from the European Parliament's Trade Committee have only limited access to documents. MPs at Westminster have no access to the texts being negotiated. Both the European Court of Justice and the European Ombudsman have criticized the high level of secrecy and the European Commission has been forced to publish some negotiating texts (UNISON, 2015: 2).
9. The United States has not ratified a number of the most important ILO Conventions, including the rights to freedom of association and collective bargaining. The United States has also passed the 'Right to Work' legislation in 24 states, meaning a union's capacity to organize is limited. This will encourage a firm to set up in one jurisdiction in the United States, and operate using these regulations in Europe.
10. The 25 TISA countries comprise Australia, Canada, Chile, Chinese Taipei, Colombia, Costa Rica, European Union, Hong Kong, Iceland, Israel, Japan, Lichtenstein, Mauritius, Mexico, New Zealand, Norway, Pakistan, Panama, Paraguay, Peru, Republic of Korea, Switzerland, Turkey, the United States, and Uruguay.
11. For example, the Trans-Pacific Partnership Agreement (TPP), the Regional Comprehensive Economic Partnership Agreement (RCEP), the Pacific Alliance (PA), and Transatlantic Trade and Investment Partnership (TTIP).
12. A positive list refers to only those measures and regulations that are listed concerning modes of supply/categories within a sector are included.
13. A negative list means all measures and regulations are covered, unless specifically listed for exclusion.

References

Akhtar, S., and Jones, V. (2014). *Proposed Transatlantic Trade and Investment Partnership (T-TIP): In Brief*, Congressional Research Service, June 11, 2014.

Bhagwati, J., Krishna, P., and Panagariya, A. (2015). Where is the world trade system heading? *Adephi Review*, pp. 17–38. doi:0.1080/19445571.2014.1019714

Cameron, D. (2013). *G8 Summit: US and EU Trade Summit*, speech delivered to the G8 Summit, Lough Erne, June 17, 2013.

Davies, H. (2014a). *Transatlantic Trade and Investment Partnership (T-TIP)*, EUA Background Paper, January, Brussels: European University Association.

Davies, H. (2014b). *Transatlantic Trade and Investment Partnership (T-TIP)*, Update No. 2, August, Brussels: European University Association.

Davies, H. (2014c). *Transatlantic Trade and Investment Partnership (T-TIP)*, Update No. 4, August, Brussels: European University Association.

Davies, H. (2015). *EUA Statement on TTIP and TISA* January, Brussels: European University Association.

Davies, H., (2016). *EUA Special Update on EU Trade Agreements and on the Recognition of Professional Qualifications*, Brussels: EUA.

De Ville, F., and Siles-Brügge, G. (2015). The Transatlantic Trade and Investment Partnership and the role of Computable General Equilibrium Modelling: an exercise in 'managing fictional expectations', *New Political Economy*, 20 (5), pp. 653–78.

Economist (2014). The arbitration game: investor-state dispute settlement, [https://www.economist.com/news/finance-and-economics/21623756-governments-are-souring-treaties-protect-foreign-investors-arbitration—last accessed 14 November, 2017].

European Commission. (2001). *European Governance: A White Paper.* COM/2001/0428 final. [http://eur-lex.europa.eu/legal-content/EN/TXT/HTML/?uri=CELEX:52001DC0428&from=EN].

European Commission. (2009). *Free Movement of Services: Commission Takes Action against Germany (Care Insurance) and Cyprus (Education Services)*, IP/09/1761, Brussels, 20 November [http://europa.eu/rapid/press-release_IP-09-1761_en.htm?locale=en—last accessed August 12, 2015].

European Commission. (2013a). *Concept Paper: Investment in TTIP and Beyond: The Path to Reform*, Brussels: European Commission.

European Commission. (2013b). *Negotiations for a Plurilateral Agreement on Trade in Services*, Europa Communiqué de Presse, Memo/13/107, Brussels: European Commission (15 February) [http://europa/ed/rapid/press-release MEMO-13-107 en.htm—last accessed August 14, 2015].

European Commission. (2015). *Report of the Tenth Round of Negotiations for the Transatlantic Trade and Investment Partnership, Brussels: European Commission* [http://trade.ec.europa.eu/doclib/docs/2015/july/tradoc_153667.pdf—last accessed August 3, 2015].

European Commission and Parliament (2006). Directive 2006/123/EC on services in the internal market 12 December 2006, [http://eur-lex.europa.eu/legal-content/EN/TXT/PDF/?uri=CELEX:32006L0123&from=EN – last accessed November 14, 2017].

European Trade Union Committee for Education. (2014). *Statement on the Transatlantic Trade and Investment Partnership*, Brussels: Education International.

Friends of the Earth. (2014). The Hidden Cost of EU Trade Deals, Friends of the Earth Europe [https://www.foeeurope.org/hidden-cost-eu-trade-deals—last accessed August 12, 2015].

Hay, C. (2007). What doesn't kill you can only make you stronger: the Doha Development Round, the Services Directive and the EU's conception of competitiveness, *Journal of Common Market Studies*, 45, pp. 25–43.

Horn, H., Mavroidis, P., and Sapir, A. (2010). Beyond the WTO? An anatomy of EU and US preferential trade agreements, *The World Economy*, 33 (11), pp. 1565–88.

International Trade Administration (2016). *Washington: Expanding Exports and Supporting Jobs through Trade Agreements*, [https://www.trade.gov/mas/ian/build/groups/public/@tg_ian/documents/webcontent/tg_ian_005360.pdf - last accessed 15 November, 2017]

Jessop, B. (2008). A cultural political economy of competitiveness and its implications for higher education, in B. Jessop, N. Fairclough and R. Wodak (eds) *Education and the Knowledge-Based Economy in Europe*, Rotterdam: Sense.

Kelsey, J. (2008). *Serving Whose Interests? The Political Economy of Trade in Services Agreements,* London and New York: Routledge.

Marchetti, J., and Roy, M. (2013). *The TISA Initiative: An Overview of Market Access Issues, WTO Staff Working Paper*. No. ERSD-2013–11.

Myant, Martin and O'Brien, Ronan, The TTIP's Impact: Bringing in the Missing Issue (January 16, 2015). ETUI Working Paper 2015.01 [https://ssrn.com/abstract=2554355 or http://dx.doi.org/10.2139/ssrn.2554355 - last accessed 15 November, 2017].

Pelkmans, J., Lejour, A., Schrefler, L., Mustilli, F., and Timini, J. (2014). *The Impact of TTIP: The Underlying Economic Model and Comparisons*, No. 93, October 2014. Brussels: Centre for European Policy Studies.

Public Services International. (2014). *Global Trade in Services Forum* [http://www.world-psi.org/en/presentations-global-trade-services-forum—last accessed August 15, 2015].

Raza, W., Grumiller, J., Taylor, L., Tröster, B., and von Arnim, R. (2014). ASSESS_TTIP: *Assessing the Claimed Benefits of the Transatlantic Trade and Investment Partnership*, Policy Note, Austrian Foundation for Development Research (ÖFSE), No. 10/2014.

Robertson, S., Bonal, X., and Dale, R. (2002). GATS and the education service industry, *Comparative Education Review*, 46 (4), pp. 472–96.

Robertson, S. and Komljenovic, J. (2016). Unbundling the university and making higher education markets, in Verger, A., Lubienski, C., Steiner-Kamsi, G. (eds). *The Global Education Industry* (Vol. 2016). (World Yearbook in Education). London: Routledge.

Robertson, S., Verger, A, Mundy, K., and Menashey, F. (2012). *Global Governance, Private Sector Partnerships and Education for Development,* Cheltenham: Edward Elgar.

Sauvé, P. (2014). *A Plurilateral Agenda for Services? Assessing the Case for a Trade in Services Agreement (TISA),* Geneva: NCCR Trade Regulation.

Scherrard, J. (2014). *Transatlantic Trade and Investment Partnership: A Threat to UK Education*, London: University College Union.

Sell, S. (2009). *Cat and Mouse: Forum Shifting in the Battle over Intellectual Property Enforcement*, paper presented to the American Political Science Association Meeting, September 3–6, Toronto.

Siles-Brügge, G. (2014). *'Race to the bottom' or Setting Global Standards? Assessing the Regulatory Impact of the Transatlantic Trade and Investment Partnership*, ARI 42/2014 Elcano Real Instituto, [http://www.realinstitutoelcano.org/wps/portal/web/rielcano_en/contenido?WCM_GLOBAL_CONTEXT=/elcano/elcano_in/zonas_in/ari42-2014-siles-brugge-assessing-regulatory-impact-ttip#.Vct6bvmgva8—last accessed August 12, 2015].

Stiglitz, J. (2014). On the wrong side of globalization, *The New York Times*, 15 March, [https://opinionator.blogs.nytimes.com/2014/03/15/on-the-wrong-side-of-globalization].

Stiglitz, J. (2015). *The secret corporate take-over*, Project Syndicate Blogsite, [https://www.project-syndicate.org/commentary/us-secret-corporate-takeover-by-joseph-e--stiglitz-2015-05?barrier=accessreg – last accessed 15 November, 2017].

Tuerk, E. (2014). *Preparatory Process for the Third International Conference on Financing for Development, Presentation to Trustee Council Chamber, United Nations*, New York, 10 December.

UNCTAD. (2014a). *Trade and Development Report, 2014*, Overview: Geneva: UNCTAD.

UNCTAD. (2014b). *Investor-State Dispute Settlement: UNCTAD Series on Issues in International Investor Agreements II*, Geneva: UNCTAD.

UNISON. (2015). *TTIP, CETA AND TISA: What You Need to Know about EU Trade Agreements*, London: UNISON.

United States Department for Trade and Industry (2016). *The Trans-Pacific Partnership*, [https://ustr.gov/sites/default/files/TPP-Economic-Benefits-Fact-Sheet.pdf – last accessed 14 November, 2017]

United Nations. (1948). *Universal Declaration of Human Rights*, Geneva: United Nations [http://www.un.org/en/documents/udhr/—last accessed August 14, 2015].

World Trade Organization Secretariat (1999). *General Agreement on Trade in Services*, [http://www.wto.org/english/news_e/pres99_e/pr149_e.htm - last accessed 15 November, 2017]

CHAPTER ELEVEN

The European University

Heartland to Periphery and Even Back Again?

PETER SCOTT

Introduction

The preeminent role of the European university within the university tradition is beyond doubt—or so it has always seemed. Indeed it can be argued that the European university tradition *is* the university tradition, in the sense that its contemporary rivals in North America and now East Asia are branches of the European root—or, if more than branches, grafts taken from that root. The twenty-first–century university is the European university written large—and, maybe, differently. Its origins are plain. Europe is the heartland of the university, at any rate in a historical sense.

There are a number of difficulties with this claim. The first is that it may be another, unjustifiable, expression of Orientalism, the belief that there is something special, even universal, about the path that has been taken by European societies (and their transoceanic plantations) since the eighteenth century. Reason, Enlightenment, secularism, liberalism, nationalism, industry, capitalism, even Revolution are for all—and for all time. Once that belief appeared to be difficult to challenge, due to powerful forces of darkness in the shape of imperialism but also due to forces of light in terms of the extraordinary creativity of European culture in the nineteenth and early twentieth centuries. The European university was reflected in, and magnified by, the bright light of Goethe and Dostoyevsky, Beethoven and Monet, Freud and Einstein. The crisis of 1914–1945 (perhaps until 1989 in central and eastern Europe) extinguished that bright light. Inevitably, the European university lost some of its lustre, and prestige.

The second difficulty is that the special claim of the European university to be the archetype, even if it can be sustained, is derived from its organisational form more than its intellectual or cultural power. As such, this is a more limited claim to preeminence. The *universitas*, or *studium generale*, as it emerged in the high Middle Ages in southern and western Europe, was new and special because of its corporate form (Gieysztor 1992, Pedersen 1997). It shared this organisational principle with merchants' guilds, fraternities, religious orders and even parliaments. Its novelty lay in its separate status and its legal privileges, which were more difficult to envisage in more centralised, and more theocratically inclined, societies. In few other senses could it be regarded as superior to earlier proto-universities such as Plato's Academy or Bede's Jarrow; and it was markedly inferior in its own time to Averroes' Córdoba or Avicenna's Bukhara (Makdisi 1990). Medieval scholasticism has left little behind; other, less firmly institutionalised, intellectual traditions retain their charisma even today.

The third difficulty is that this claim implies a sequential relationship between the European and other university traditions for which there is little warrant. Europe did not come first, with the rest of the world following. For example, the reform (in effect, the re-foundation) of the German university after 1810 and the establishment of the civic universities in Victorian Britain later in the nineteenth century were contemporary with the transformation of American east-coast colleges into great universities and the creation of land-grant universities after 1864. Ideas and values, and the institutions in which they flourished, were two-way traffic—like trade and commerce (Rothblatt and Wittrock 1993). Only a handful of universities existed in Europe, in any substantial sense, before 1800. The European university is not so much an ancient as a modern institution. It developed alongside the (north and Latin) American university, and only slightly ahead of universities in the rest of the world.

The fourth difficulty is that there has never been a single European university tradition. At its birth there was a significant divergence between the student-led collectives that developed in medieval Italy and the scholars' corporations, under royal tutelage, more characteristic of northern Europe. Of much greater contemporary relevance in the nineteenth century there developed a variety of separate traditions—the Humboldtian tradition based on respect for *wissenschaft*, *bildung* and *lernfreiheit*; the French tradition of *grandes écoles* beginning with the foundation of the *École Polytechnique*; the Anglo-Saxon tradition of liberal education (celebrated perhaps more in the breach than the observance);

the Scottish 'philosophical' tradition; the many strands of professional and higher technical education (Gellert 1994). This intra-European variety is probably greater than any contrast between universities in Europe and other world regions. It may even have been exacerbated by a particular tendency to draw an oversharp distinction between British universities and universities in the rest of Europe. All emerging higher education systems contained similar strands of traditions and institutions. Exchanges—of people and practices—were intense and intensive between Europe and the United States and Latin America and, through European colonies, with much of the rest of the world. As a result, the extent to which it is possible to regard the European university tradition as distinctive, except in terms of geographical location, is open to question.

Nevertheless, there is a strong case for emphasising, and celebrating, the contribution made by European universities to the development of worldwide higher education, in terms of values but also exemplars. The first reason is that many of the ideas that have gone to form the wider university tradition have been incubated in Europe, even if not exclusively so. While steering clear of Orientalist prejudices, it is still reasonable to argue that over the long haul Europe has exported much more than it has imported, even if the balance of trade shifted decisively westwards across the Atlantic during the twentieth century. It is also possible to argue that in the past two decades European universities have recovered their self-confidence mainly as a result of the Bologna process (which will be a major topic of this chapter), and they are once more in a stronger position of global influence. The second reason is that, even confined within the geography of the continent, the fortunes of European universities are of wider significance. The European Union, even the battered Eurozone countries that are at its heart, is the world's largest integrated economy. It includes not only countries of world historical significance, for good and ill, but also many of the world's most progressive societies in which human, legal and democratic rights (and academic freedom) are most securely respected. The European university, and wider higher education systems, play a key role in this economy and in these societies. Put simply, what happens to the European university matters.

The remainder of this chapter is divided into two main sections. The first considers 'what went wrong', the reasons why the European university, battered by war and revolution, found it difficult quickly to recover its past poise even with peaceful and prosperous times after 1945. The second focuses on the revival of the European university that has gathered pace since the signing of the Bologna Declaration in 1999—and which may have given higher education in Europe a coherence that it never possessed in the past (actually as opposed to rhetorically).

Fading domination

In the course of the nineteenth century, universities in Europe established a dominance within the world higher education that has never been recovered—and never really can be recovered because of the global economic and geopolitical shifts that have taken place over the past 150 years. They played a key role in the modernisation of society (and the economy) as well as spreading a culture of modernity. Not only did they produce the administrative and professional elites without which the modern state could not operate; they also became primary sites for the production of science, technology and other forms of expert knowledge (at any rate, by the end of this period). Of course, this was not solely a European achievement in a strict geographical sense; universities were established throughout the European diaspora from Harvard in the 'other' Cambridge and other American universities and across Asia, Africa and Australasia. Other modernising societies, notably Japan, eagerly espoused European (and American) models. But, if global league tables had existed in 1900, there can be little doubt that universities located in Europe would have dominated the top positions.

That European dominance came to an end—slowly and inexorably as the balance of economic power (and political influence) shifted to other regions; but also dramatically as a result of the collapse of European civilisation in the years between 1914 and 1945. The former was a process that could be accepted and managed; the latter led to an almost existential crisis that eroded the normative base of the European university. How could the philosopher Martin Heidegger, as rector of Freiburg, come to reach even the most transitory accommodation with the Nazi regime? Other changes, although not existential threats, were also far-reaching. After 1914, British universities cut their former intimate links with Germany, although refugees from Germany and eastern Europe immeasurably enriched them between the two world wars, and reoriented themselves westwards, outside Europe to the Empire and the United States. The process of academic emigration accelerated as intolerance spread. Isaiah Berlin, Ludwig Wittgenstein, Karl Popper, Nils Bohr—the list of exiled, and therefore appropriated, talent is a long one. Initially the focus was on England as a safe haven, but ultimately the major flows were to the United States (and even, in Popper's case, as far as New Zealand) (Coser 1984). It may be too fanciful to claim that the U.S. (and, to a lesser extent, UK) dominance of league tables of the world's leading universities in the twenty-first century can be largely attributed to these violent shifts between 1914 and 1945. But this is where it began—and the losers were universities in (continental) Europe, their progress set back by the devastating impact of world war and revolution.

What is perhaps more difficult to explain is the slow recovery of the European university after 1945, not so much in material as in moral terms (although the reputation, and resources, of British universities had been increased rather than diminished by the experience of war). This is in sharp contrast with the fact that most European societies (at any rate, west of the Elbe) staged a remarkable economic recovery, and an even more remarkable social reconstruction, even social transformation. The *trentes années glorieuses* that France enjoyed after 1945 did not lead to any substantial reform of higher education until the end of that period, the 1968 reforms associated with Edgar Faure (and the trigger was the pseudo-revolutionary 'events' of that year on the streets of Paris rather than the dynamics of modernisation). It seems a paradox that France appeared definitively and irrevocably to have embraced modernity without much help from its universities and other higher education institutions. Nor was France alone. Reform, as opposed to expansion, seemed to be slow to take hold in many other European countries. The explicit, and closely examined, engagement with mass higher education so evident in the United States was absent—with the possible exception of Scandinavia. Instead, universities just grew bigger and, their conservative critics insisted, more disorganised. Efforts to embrace higher technical education and professional schools within integrated higher education systems were limited. Instead, divisive—and unstable—'binary' systems were maintained. In the absence of conceptual innovation, structural change was often seen as just too difficult. As a result, the language of mass higher education, its theoretical formulations, was an American import—and perhaps still is today.

However, this contest between the root-and-branch modernisation of most (western) European societies after 1945, often leaping ahead even of the United States in terms of social liberalism or popular culture, and the reluctance to abandon older forms of higher education remains puzzling. One explanation may be that the wider modernisation of these societies was not as thorough as it may have appeared at the time; certainly the recent revival of more conservative and even nationalistic impulses (as a backlash to immigration and multiculturalism) may suggest that such modernisation had its limits. Another may be that, for a mixture of ideological and structural reasons, the reform of the European university was not—initially—regarded as a central component of this wider modernisation. The higher education reforms that did take place were often forced, imposed by wider social pressures, rather than as a result of internal dynamics or as part of well-articulated proactive plans. Outer forms were forced to change but inner values and beliefs often proved to be more resistant. As a result, the European university perhaps came to be regarded as a poor instrument for promoting modernisation, as opposed to responding unwillingly to its effects.

A third explanation, paradoxically, may be found in the Atlanticist orientation of much of postwar western Europe (with the, limited, exception of France under De Gaulle). The Marshall Plan, although mightily reviving Europe's shattered economies, may have been accompanied not only by an ideological subordination but by a wider cultural fascination that may have made it more difficult to rediscover an authentically distinctive European voice. This pervasive Atlanticism encouraged bilateral transatlantic engagements, perhaps at the expense of collective conversations within Europe. The strains of the Cold War intensified these effects, crudely so at its height as covert agencies funded cultural projects. The Cold War also, of course, divided the continent. Universities in central and eastern European were frozen in a totalitarian time-warp until 1989. There the university was subordinated to vocational higher education—thus, paradoxically, preserving it from some of the social pressure to which universities in western Europe were exposed.

Of course, it would be misleading to exaggerate. Much was achieved. The Faure reforms effectively re-established the French universities as unified institutions, after more than a century as disaggregated Faculties. In Germany, some comprehensive universities, combining the functions of the traditional universities and the *fachhochschulen*, were established—for example, in Kassel. Experimental universities, such as Konstanz, were also founded. In Britain, new campus-based universities were also established, dedicated at least initially to drawing up 'new maps' of knowledge (although American models were clearly very influential) (Briggs 1991). In Britain, a better articulated 'binary' system was also developed, as vocational institutions were grouped into more powerful polytechnics, leading eventually to a unified system. All this represented progress. It would be wrong to suggest that European higher education slumbered through the second half of the twentieth century, unregarding and unreformed.

However, the—comparative—lack of dynamism of the European university, certainly compared with the dynamism of the enveloping European society, still raises interesting questions. One explanation is simply that reform was simply delayed. Between the 1950s and, certainly, the 1970s, the focus of educational reform in most European countries was on primary and secondary schools. A second, already mentioned, is that perhaps only when the Cold War was over could its pervasive Atlanticism, with its instinctive focus on American models, be challenged. In this less constrained environment, the unity of European higher education could be recovered. A third is that the particular forms taken by the postwar development of higher education, which saw reform through the (American) lenses of mass higher education and, later, the entrepreneurial university, did not resonate so persuasively with the European tradition and experience (Trow

1993, Clark 1998). This suggests that, despite the setbacks experienced by the European university between 1914 and 1945 (and its slow and uncertain recovery in the postwar years), tradition represented something more than, in Metternich's famous phrase about Italy, a 'geographical expression', a residue of values and practices that could be built upon when European higher education entered a more dynamic phase in the 1990s.

Revival and recovery

The revival of the European university in the late twentieth century can be attributed to three main strands. The first was an accumulation of national reform programmes. The Faure reforms in France have already been mentioned. But there were few European countries, at any rate in the north and west of the continent, which did not embark on more or less radical reforms. Notable was the root-and-branch reform of higher education in Sweden from the 1960s; a system that has once been close to, and even modelled on, the German system was reoriented towards a more American pattern; the two-phase bachelors-masters pattern of courses and awards was adopted and the idea of an integrated, if not fully unified, system was developed. Far-reaching reforms were also introduced in other Nordic countries, the Netherlands, Germany (to a more limited degree) and Spain (after the recovery of democracy). In the UK, the expansion of higher education was accompanied by, initially, the establishment of much larger non-university institutions, the polytechnics, and then the development of a fully integrated system after 1992. The tempo of these national reform programmes increased during the 1990s, especially in central and eastern Europe, and 2000s (Scott 2000). But what was important was the increasing tempo of more explicit policy borrowing between European systems. These policy borrowings made an important contribution to the sense that a Europe-wide process of reform was underway.

The second strand was the growth of much stronger European institutions. The most powerful and prominent, of course, was the European Community (and then European Union) itself. Through the Erasmus programme of student (and staff) mobility, and associated programmes such as Tempus and Leonardo, and through successive Framework programmes for research, the EU became a key contributor to the articulation of more explicitly European perspectives and policies on higher education (European Commission 2013a). Even in the notoriously 'mid-atlantic' UK system, there was unambiguous evidence of this shift towards Europe as Erasmus students flowed into UK institutions (although not balanced by an equivalent outward flow) and UK institutions competed successfully for European research grants.

Accompanying this strengthening of the EU's role in higher education and research was an equivalent strengthening of other European organisations, several of which paradoxically took advantage of the global dominance of English as their *lingua franca*. For example, the European University Association was created by a merger of two much weaker organisations, the Conference of European Rectors and the Confederation of European Rectors Conferences. Later more informal groupings such as the League of European Research Universities were established. This growing momentum at the European level was linked to two new developments in the wider 'architecture' of Europe. The first was the Maastricht Treaty—the commitment to 'ever closer union', however controversial at the time and since. The creation of the Euro as a common European currency in the core European states was also a key development; the difficulties that have arisen since the 2008 banking crisis were not, and could not have been, foreseen. The second was the enlargement of the EU to include much of central and eastern Europe. This development paradoxically was supported most strongly by those countries most sceptical about the benefits of closer union. But its effect made a powerful contribution to the revival of European identity, as these post-Communist regimes aspired both to go back (by re-engaging with older European traditions) and forward (by dismantling rigid state structures) (Scott 2006).

The third strand, of course, was the so-called Bologna process itself on which most attention has focused (Crosier and Parveva 2013). However, the success of Bologna needs to be seen in the wider context of the two other strands, the intensification of policy borrowing between European countries (which has been strengthened by the regular round of Bologna meetings) and the strengthening of European institutions (Olsen and Maassen 2007) The development of the Bologna process can be divided into five main phases—(i) its beginnings, including the Sorbonne Declaration which preceded it and the (mixed) motives of the European states that signed the declaration in Bologna in 1999; (ii) a second phase when the emphasis was very much on harmonising the architecture of European higher education systems; (iii) an extension phase when its scope was widened to include doctoral courses and it first acquired a distinctive 'external face'; (iv) its culmination in the establishment of the European Higher Education Area (and more explicit links research policies across Europe); and (v) the current phase of retrenchment—and, possibly, retreat.

Beginnings

The Bologna Declaration was signed by ministers of 27 European countries in the summer of 1999 (Bologna Declaration 1999). However, the groundwork had been laid the previous year when the Sorbonne Declaration had been signed by ministers from just four countries—France, Germany, Italy and the UK. The Bologna Declaration was essentially a scaled-up version of this earlier initiative. Its intentions were limited and practical, despite subsequent enthusiasm for its role in the wider 'European project'. Bologna grew out of three distinct agendas. The first was student (and, to a lesser extent, staff) mobility which was already well established; it was felt that, in the absence of some harmonisation of the architecture of European higher education, the ambitious goals that had been set for the proportion of students who were able to study in more than one European country—one in ten—would be difficult to achieve. The second agenda also had deep roots but had been given a new urgency by the commitment to 'ever closer union'—free movement across the EU, especially for the highly skilled with academic and professional qualifications; once again, it was felt that a greater degree of harmonisation was needed. The third agenda was a medley of national agendas. For example, in Germany, a European initiative was seen as easing the path to reform, in particular by reducing the length of 'initial' higher education qualifications, while in France such an initiative was regarded as helping to break down the barriers between universities and other higher education institutions including the grades écoles. The primary motive of the UK appears to have been to establish a watching brief (to ensure that the process of Europeanisation remained limited in scope, perhaps).

Another sign that the Bologna process was initially regarded as limited was that it was an intergovernmental rather than European initiative. One reason was the reluctance to treat education (except for professional training) as within the competence of the European Community/Union, which went back to the reservations entered by Denmark when it had become part of the EC two decades earlier. Another reason was the resistance encountered in many countries to the ambitious integrationist goals of the Maastricht Treaty, combined within a degree of irritation especially in France and the UK about the performance of the current European Commission. The concern that higher education should not simply be swept up in the movement towards an 'ever closer union' reinforced the conviction that it should remain the responsibility of individual member states, albeit acting in concert, rather than of the Brussels bureaucracy. A third, and more fundamental, reason was the recognition that Europe extended far beyond the frontiers of the EU. In retrospect, given the plain desire to control and limit the Bologna process, it is paradoxical that the fact it was not confined to existing members of the EU provided its subsequent momentum and dynamism.

A common architecture

The immediate goal of the Bologna process was to create a common structure of courses across Europe based on a two-cycle pattern of bachelor's and master's degrees. In some European countries this was straightforward. Higher education in the UK, the Netherlands and most Scandinavian countries was already organised according to the two-cycle pattern (although the UK had to work hard to secure acceptance of three-year rather than four-year bachelor's and one-year rather than two-year master's, on the grounds that they had equivalent learning outcomes). In countries that had already embarked on wider reforms this change did not pose great difficulties either, which may explain why it was more readily accepted in Spain than in Italy or Greece. In central and eastern European countries too there were few obstacles to the (formal) adoption of the two-cycle pattern, because the collapse of Communism after 1989 had opened the way to (often chaotic) reform. In France, a two-cycle pattern already existed in principle, although on rather different principles. In Germany and Austria, this new pattern presented a greater challenge because many employers, especially in engineering, felt a strong commitment to the longer *Diplom*. However, across the continent, at any rate formal adoption of the two-cycle pattern, despite the taint of its Anglo-American origins, proceeded more smoothly than many early critics and opponents had expected (Reichert and Tauch 2005; Wächter 2006).

Another Bologna goal, almost as important, was to encourage a much stronger 'quality culture' in European higher education; in other words, the adoption of more explicit quality assurance arrangements. This presented greater difficulty because such arrangements were sparse in many European countries (once again, outside the UK, the Netherlands and Scandinavia). In theory, academic awards were made on behalf of the State, although in practice, universities in particular were largely free from peer scrutiny as opposed to bureaucratic regulation. However, the early years of the Bologna process coincided with moves in many parts of Europe to devolve greater administrative responsibility to institutions. This loosening of the formal bureaucratic ties between the State and universities strengthened the case for arguing that the latter must also take greater responsibility for policing their own academic quality and standards. Against this background, the development of a more explicit 'quality culture', underpinned by formal quality assurance arrangements based on peer review, became easier to accept.

Although the Bologna process remained (and remains) an intergovernmental initiative, it quickly became clear that some degree of organisational structure was needed to carry it forward. Brussels, if not the European Commission directly, would need to become more directly engaged. This has happened mainly through the Bologna Follow-Up Group, which provided the continuity between the biannual ministerial meetings (by both preparing the ground for subsequent meetings and, as its title suggests, monitoring progress towards the goals that had been endorsed). The driving force behind the Bologna process became a coalition of officials in national ministries responsible for European matters and European institutions such as the EUA and the European Students Association. Although Bologna was not 'captured' by the Commission, it—inevitably—came to reflect, and depend on, the dynamics of Brussels.

Extending Bologna

In the third phase, the scope of the Bologna process was extended in two main ways. First, it was extended to embrace the third cycle of doctoral education alongside the first two cycles. This has not been straightforward because PhD students are treated in different ways across Europe. In some countries such as the UK they are still regarded as students, although many take on some teaching responsibilities of graduate teaching assistants. In other countries such as the Netherlands they are treated as apprentice researchers, and as junior university employees. Perhaps for that reason some of the most interesting debates have been about the future of doctoral education in which broader academic as opposed to simply structural and administrative issues have been raised. The extension of the Bologna process to embrace doctoral education also brought stronger links with research, both at European and institutional levels (Keeling 2006). Because research is such an important part of the mission of most European universities, this extension made the Bologna reforms more central to the development of European higher education. The links between university-based research, technology, innovation and economic development were also made explicit in the 2005 Lisbon Declaration (European Council 2000).

Secondly, Bologna became more outward-looking. New programmes were developed, such as Erasmus Mundus, designed to promote student mobility between Europe and other world regions (European Commission 2013b). However, the growing coherence of European higher education, a product of the Bologna reforms, also enhanced its distinctive as a model of development. Instead of being regarded as over-traditional and ripe for modernisation, European institutions now appeared to be entering a more dynamic phase (Muche 2005). Other countries that had historically looked to Europe, for example Francophone Africa and Latin America, were encouraged to embark on similar reforms. Also the almost exclusive focus on the United States as a model for development, which had become entrenched after 1960, came to be questioned. The scale of—two-way—policy borrowing increased. Of course, there was considerable controversy about this new European model. Critics of Bologna persisted in their belief that the principal aim of these reforms was to encourage universities to behave in more 'entrepreneurial' ways, and they continued to associate the Bologna process with neoliberal ideology. Supporters of Bologna emphasised instead the way in which this emerging model of higher education valued and respected the 'social dimension', although the precise meaning of that phrase remained unclear.

European Higher Education Area

The Bologna process culminated in the establishment of the European Higher Education Area (EHEA) in 2010 at the ministerial meeting in Budapest and Vienna, to mirror the earlier creation of the European Research Area (ERA) (European Commission. 2012). The geographical extent of the EHEA was impressive, stretching from (notionally) Greenland to the Russian Far East. It was—and is—the largest higher education bloc in the world. The original 27 signatories of the Bologna Declaration had grown in 13 years to 43. Only Belarus and Monaco remain outside. As indicated already, the influence of Bologna, and the EHEA, was not confined to its members. The geopolitical significance of the Bologna reforms, and the revival of the European university, were underlined by the establishment of the EHEA.

The EHEA has had several functions:

- First, it has brought together not only the structural and other reforms that had been directly promoted through the Bologna process but also many of the other European programmes and initiatives that were relevant to higher education. It created a framework in which all these various reform strands could, potentially, be coordinated. Not surprisingly the Bologna process had led to a proliferation of activities and initiatives, for which the EHEA provided an umbrella (European Commission 2011).
- Secondly, the EHEA was an instrument for the consolidation of the Bologna reforms. The various policy instruments that had been developed since 1999, and also the organisational structures (both formal such as regular ministerial meetings and the work of the Bologna Follow-Up Group and less formal occasions such as semi-regular meetings of higher education researchers across Europe and the explosion of Bologna-themed enquiries, reports and conferences), acquired a new solidity within the EHEA.

- Thirdly, the EHEA reinforced the global ambitions of European higher education. It made a statement about Europe's reviving self-confidence and ambitions. Following the 2012 Bucharest ministerial meeting, equal emphasis was placed on 'public responsibility' (a statement that not only embraced a commitment to public funding but also embraced a determination to protect and promote the 'social dimension' more broadly) and 'global mobility' (signalling Europe's positive engagement with globalisation in its widest sense). These two themes have come to define the essence of the EHEA's ambitions. They stand in stark contrast to the more modest and limited goals agreed at Bologna.

On the defensive?

The final, and current, phase of the Bologna process is perhaps a footnote. There appears to have been a degree of political disinvestment. For example, officials have sometimes replaced ministers at regular ministerial meetings. The number of countries represented by their ministers at the latest meeting in Yerevan in April 2015 is smaller than at the previous meeting in Bucharest in 2012. There are probably several reasons for this apparent reluctance to engage in Bologna meetings at the highest political level—the economic stagnation in the Eurozone following the banking crisis of 2008 (and, in particular, the economic difficulties faced by Greece, Spain and Italy); the rising tide of opposition to immigration (which compromises the outward-facing stance of European institutions in global higher education); a certain disenchantment with European institutions (and criticisms of their lack of democratic accountability, a charge that can also be laid against the Bologna reforms also despite the fact that they are an intergovernmental process); and tensions and even armed conflict within Europe. The optimism of the 1990s, and the drive to 'ever closer union', lie—temporarily perhaps—firmly in the past.

Another factor may have been the rise of the 'entrepreneurial university', at any rate as a policy discourse (Clark 1998). At first sight this may have seemed a setback to the ambition of European universities to establish a distinctive presence, separate from those of the once (and still) dominant U.S. and rapid emerging East Asian presences. The idea of the 'entrepreneurial university' may have been a U.S.-Europe co-production with as many European as American case studies, but it perhaps reflected American experiences and ambitions most strongly. However, the notion of 'entrepreneurialism' was quickly absorbed into European thinking and later studies of the 'entrepreneurial university' have been conducted on a transatlantic basis. On balance, as with the worldwide dominance of the English language, European coherence was strengthened by this new policy language. Europe was now confident enough to absorb and modify non-European ideas and models.

Yet the Bologna process itself is unlikely to be seriously affected. What began as a top-down political initiative in 1999 has now been taken possession of by the institutions themselves. The reforms have been internalised (Scott 2012). Bologna has also acquired a wider resonance, both with regard to research and innovation policies within Europe and globally applicable models of higher education development. Most powerfully perhaps Bologna has become a symbol of the revival of the European university—again in a variety of perspectives, not all consistent with each other; in central and eastern Europe it has become a rallying cry for a return to 'normality' after the years of Communist rule while in parts of western Europe it has come to represent a process of reform and modernisation designed to promote global competitiveness. Yet its cumulative meanings have given the Bologna process a resilience that is likely to overcome temporary political dislocations.

Conclusion

The argument presented in this chapter has been that, after a period of (relative) decline in the middle years of the last century, the European university has experienced a revival since the 1990s that has been associated with, and accelerated by, the Bologna process. The first part of this argument is unlikely to be contested, although it is important to emphasise that the decline was relative not absolute; it was during this period that modern systems of higher education were developed in Europe and the research and scholarly achievements of the leading European universities were second only to those of American universities. The second part of the argument is more open to debate (Ritzen 2009). Although the Bologna process has had a transformative impact of the higher education systems emerging from decades of totalitarian rule, whether in the Iberian Peninsula or central and eastern Europe, its impact has been more muted in other parts of Europe. Scandinavian universities were already committed to a path of modernisation before Bologna, and the development of higher education in the UK (especially England) appears to owe little to wider European models and influences, despite the major contributions UK institutions have made in European research programmes. At best, therefore, the case for the transformative effects of Bologna is non-proven.

It can also be argued that, despite the extension of the Bologna process described in the preceding section, its impact on higher education has still largely been structural and systemic rather than normative. The Bologna process and associated national reform agendas have offered some tantalising glimpses of a distinctive vision of the European university in the twenty-first century—but nothing more. Key perhaps has been the pregnant phrase, the 'social dimension', coupled with continuing emphasis on the 'public responsibility' of universities. While some have argued that European higher education has also embraced the market-inclined agendas and neoliberal ideologies that have become established as the global 'standard' (and, indeed, that this is the drive behind Bologna-mediated reforms), such language suggests a reluctance fully to embrace such a future.

According to a pessimistic view, the European university has been slow to adapt and although it may now be catching up, it remains a laggard—still struggling in the wake of the more entrepreneurial American system and also being rapidly overtaken by the dynamic systems of East Asia. However, according to a more optimistic view, the European university has been more successful than these other systems in establishing a balance between the imperatives of modernisation, the drive to create more entrepreneurial and managerially robust institutions, and a reviving sense of how the ideals of 'public' higher education and a more traditional academic culture can be sustained even under these new conditions.

On balance, the revival of the European university over the past two decades, triggered to some degree and certainly symbolised by the Bologna reforms, perhaps offers more evidence to support the latter, more optimistic, view. It may even be possible to discern the emergence of a new model of the university focused on democracy, human rights and social justice (extensions of the European commitment to protecting and enhancing the 'social dimension') and also characterised by a growing scepticism about the unalloyed benefits of consumption-led economic growth, a heightened awareness of the possible limitations, and even perversions of technology and new ecological concerns. Although European universities may perhaps be better placed to articulate such a model than American or East Asian universities, it would clearly be going too far to align such broad movements with the development of higher education in any particular world region. But one benefit of the European university's recovery may indeed be that it has produced a more open and balanced future for higher education, no longer constrained by a single-path there-is-no-alternative pattern of development.

References

Bologna Declaration (1999). *The European Higher Education Area: Joint Declaration of the European Ministers of Education*, Bologna, June 19, 1999.

Briggs, Asa (1991). 'A Founding Father Reflects', *Higher Education Quarterly*, 45: 4, 311–331.

Clark, Burton (1998). *Creating Entrepreneurial Universities: Organizational Pathways of Transformation*, Oxford: Pergamon.

Coser, L. (1984). *Refugee Scholars in America: Their Impact and Their Experience*, New Haven: Yale University Press.

Crosier, David and Teodora Parveva (2013). *The Bologna Process: Its Impact on Higher Education Development in Europe and Beyond*, Paris. UNESCO International Institute for Educational Planning.

European Commission (2011). *A New Agenda for the Modernisation of Europe's Higher Education Systems*, Brussels: European Commission.

European Commission (2012): *The European Higher Education Area in 2012: Bologna Process Implementation Report*. Brussels. Statistical Office of the European Communities/ Eurydice.

European Commission (2013a). *The Erasmus Programme*, Brussels: European Commission, ec.europe.eu/lifelong-learning-programme/erasmus_en.htm.

European Commission (2013b). *Erasmus Mundus*, Brussels: European Commission, e.europe.eu/lifelong-learning-programme/mundus_en.htm.

European Council (2000). *Lisbon European Council: Presidency Conclusions*, Brussels: European Council, www.consilium.europa.eu/uedocs/cms_data/docs/pressdata/en/ec/00100-rl.en0.htm.

Gellert, Claudius (1994). 'Structural and Functional Differentiation: Remarks of Changing Paradigms of Tertiary Education in Europe', in C. Gellert (ed.) *Higher Education in Europe*, London: Jessica Kingsley.

Gieysztor, Aleksander (1992). 'Management and Resources', in H. De Ridder-Symeons (ed.) *A History of the University in Europe: Volume 1 – Universities in the Middle Ag*es, Cambridge: Cambridge University Press.

Keeling, Ruth (2006). 'The Bologna Process and the Lisbon Research Agenda; The European Commission's Expanding Role in Higher Education Discourse', *European Journal of Education, Research, Development and Policy*, 41: 2, 203–223.

Makdisi, George (1990). *The Rise of Humanism in Classical Islam and the Christian West*, Edinburgh: Edinburgh University Press.

Muche, Franziska ed. (2005). *Opening up to the Wider World. The External Dimension of the Bologna Process*, Bonn: Lemmens.

Olsen, Johan and Peter Maassen (2007). 'European Debates on the Knowledge Institution: The Modernization of the University at European Level', in P. Maassen and J. Olsen (eds.) *University Dynamics and European Integration*, Dordrecht: Springer.

Pedersen, Olaf (1997). *The First Universities: Studium Generale and the Origins of University Education in Europe*, Cambridge: Cambridge University Press.

Reichert, Sybille and Christian Tauch (2005). *Trends IV: European Universities Implementing* Bologna, Brussels: European University Association (www.eua.be).

Ritzen, Jo (2009). *A Chance for European Universities: Or, Avoiding the Looming University Crisis in Europe*, Amsterdam: Amsterdam University Press.

Rothblatt, Sheldon and Björn Wittrock eds. (1993). *The European and American University since 1800: Historical and Sociological Essays*, Cambridge: Cambridge University Press.

Scott, Peter (2000). *Ten Years on: Higher Education in Central and Eastern* Europe, Bucharest: UNESCO-CEPES.

Scott, Peter (2006). 'The European University; What is it Future', in Flather Paul (ed.) *The Future of European Universities*, Oxford: Europaeum (www.europaeum.org), 17–22.

Scott, Peter (2012). 'Going Beyond Bologna: Issues and Themes', in Andrej Curaj, Peter Scott, Lazar Vlasceanu and Lesley Wilson (eds.) *European Higher Education at the Crossroads: Between the Bologna Process and National Reforms*, Dordrecht: Springer.

Waechter, Bernd (2004). 'The Bologna Process: developments and prospects', *European Journal of Education*, 39: 3, 265–273.

CHAPTER TWELVE

The Nordic Idea of University

JUSSI VÄLIMAA

Introduction

University is a political concept, and universities are political institutions, because of great variations in the purposes and goals of universities among disciplines, academics and students. Universities are also political institutions concerning their relationships with societies because of the variety of conflicting definitions on the purposes and goals of universities and their roles in societies (see Pusser 2015). Often these different expectations and objectives for universities are discussed in and through the idea of a university. In these discourses, the idea of a university aims to define the 'true nature' of university thus hiding the political motives behind the arguments. Classical examples of this kind of discourses are both the Humboldtian idea of university which was developed as late as the beginning of the 20th century to defend institutional autonomy when Wilhelm von Humboldt unfinished memo from the beginning of the 19th century was found by a German historian (Nybom 2007). The same was true with Cardinal Newman's ideas which emphasised liberal (elite) education as the main purpose of a university. Being a political concept, the idea of a university is often used to promote interests of certain groups of people whether they be academics, students, political actors or entrepreneurs or civic society organisations. The idea of a university is also a relative concept because the definitions of a university and its purposes have changed over time (Välimaa 2015).

In this chapter I will discuss the Nordic idea of university keeping in mind the political nature of university as an institution by approaching the topic from a societal perspective. In other words, I will analyse how universities are defined in contemporary Nordic Welfare states, and how universities are related to Nordic societies through their system of higher education. These two aspects are inseparable because the idea of a university is always a socially constructed concept evolving in the contexts of their societies.

However, the concept of a Nordic idea of university is a rather problematic one to be used because there does not exist a homogenous Nordic idea of a university. This may be a bit paradoxical statement because the Nordic higher education seems to be a rather homogenous social entity when it is approached from outside the Nordic countries. However, inside the Nordic region, we can see the differences better. The main reason for the lack of a monolithic Nordic idea of university is related to the fact that there are variations between the systems of higher education in Nordic countries and, consequently, between their universities. Therefore, I need to approach the topic at a rather high level of abstraction in order to reflect on common starting points for Nordic ideas of universities in Nordic welfare societies. Nordic welfare state is a crucial concept here, because it helps to explain why education and higher education are seen important in all Nordic countries. I will discuss the concept below.

Nordic countries refer here to Denmark, Finland, Norway and Sweden which are located in the European mainland and which are all small nation states as for their population but geographically big—with the exception of Denmark. They are also tied together by rather similar historical developments and social structures, whereas Iceland is a significantly smaller country with different social dynamics at work in the island. Therefore, Icelandic higher education is left out of the analysis even though Iceland is also a Nordic country. For the sake of clarity, I will take examples from the Finnish higher education which I know the best.

Similarities in Nordic welfare societies

A number of similarities can be found among all Nordic countries. According to Esping-Andersen (1990), Scandinavian countries belong to the same—universal version of welfare regimes where all welfare benefits are provided to all citizens. This model, or a way of seeing the role of the state in relation to market and family, is related to the fact that all Nordic countries share a strong tradition of equality. It is defined both in relation to gender, socio-economic status, ethnicity and geographical location. Policies promoting equality (in health, education, economy and politics) have been rather successful because according to Gender Gap Index, the least unequal countries in 2014 were: (1) Iceland, (2) Finland, (3) Norway, (4) Sweden and (5) Denmark out of 142 countries evaluated (World Economic Forum 2015). In the field of education, equality is normally defined as equal educational opportunities for all citizens.

According to Abrahamsson (1994 in Lin 2004), 'Scandinavian welfare societies' are combined by existing strong bonds of mutual obligation between the state and citizens. It has been argued that the common social understandings concerning the social role of state, citizens and government begun to develop at the time of the Reformation in the 16th century (Alestalo and Kuhnle 1987). It has also been explained with the help of the 19th century processes of modernisation, the structures of pre-industrial rural communities with strong traditions of the division of labour between men and women, the rise of socialism and nationalism emphasising national unity, and the rise of Social democracy in the 1930s. However, according to Kettunen, Kuhnle and Ren (2014, 16), 'instead of making a choice between these different proposals, it is reasonable to re-interpret the divergent "origins" as temporal layers in the Nordic welfare state. Mediated through mentalities, traditions, values, epistemic practices and social movements, these layers are present in the formal and informal rules and norms of the Nordic model'. In this historically developed understanding of a beneficial state, public authorities are normally seen as helping their citizens in all spheres of life.

An important social basis for all Nordic welfare societies is trust meaning that the resources of society are less used to control citizens but more to treat citizens equally. In social and economic life trust also helps to save transaction costs because interpersonal relationships become easier. According to sociological research, there are two hypotheses on trust. The first one, institution-centred hypothesis, emphasises the role of the institutions of society in supporting trust, whereas the society-centred hypothesis emphasises the importance of civic engagement in associations and social interaction taking place at the grassroots level of society (see Kouvo 2014). According to empirical evidence, the first hypothesis explains better the nature of trust and just and well-functioning public institutions. Furthermore, impartial and objective taxation seem to be very important in reinforcing trust in fellow citizens. It has been suggested that universal welfare policies in the Nordic countries are the key factor behind the high trust levels in these countries. According to Kouvo (2014, 5), 'in addition to contacts with welfare state institutions, their assumed generosity might also serve as significant societal sources of interpersonal trust in the nation itself'. Therefore, the universal (Nordic) welfare state is an important ingredient of the trustful society (Kouvo 2014). As for higher education, trust can be seen in the Nordic ideas of evaluation, especially in Finland, which aims to use evaluation as an instrument of enhancement rather than as an instrument of control (Hämäläinen et al. 2001). Trust also can be seen in the Nordic convictions that universities should be autonomous institutions which are publicly funded.

As for Finnish higher education, Finnish science barometer (2013), based on questionnaires, tells that the most trusted social institutions in Finnish society are (in this order): (1) police, (2) defence forces, (3) universities, (4) system of legislation, (5) state technical research centres and (6) science and academic community out of 20 Finnish institutions measured. The ranking order of institutions has not changed during the last ten years. Therefore, it is fair to say that universities, academic communities and research have a high status in Finnish society. It may even be that the appreciation of universities as societal institutions can be found behind the Nordic idea of universities.

Similarities and differences among Nordic systems of higher education

Nordic systems of education have similar basic structures. They all have both universities and vocationally oriented and more regional higher education institutions (HEIs) which may be called either as University Colleges in Denmark, Norway and Sweden or Universities of Applied Sciences (UAS) in Finland. In addition to the public HEIs, there can be found a number of private educational establishments which focus on first or second cycles of qualifications or have a limited focus in their curriculum (often theology or business) in Norway, Denmark and Sweden. In Finland, the situation is a bit different because all UAS were run by either by private foundations, or by public corporation owned by cities, or by alliance of cities before 2015 (Välimaa and Neuvonen-Rauhala 2010). Now all Finnish UAS are run, funded and regulated by the Ministry of Education and Culture (MEC), in other words, by the Finnish state. Despite their numbers, the educational significance of the independent institutions remains quite low in terms of student numbers. Interestingly, these independent institutions are not referred to as private HEIs in public Nordic documents but as independent institutions. They also are regulated and/or controlled by the corresponding Nordic ministries of education making them part of the publicly steered systems of higher education. Therefore, it is fair to say that private sectors of higher education are insignificant in Nordic countries.

Nordic countries have rather similar sized systems of higher education, even though Finland is slightly above others both concerning actual and relative student numbers and gross enrolment rates. The level of education of the whole population is also higher in Scandinavian countries than the OECD average. Namely, tertiary level education has been reached by 40% of the population in Finland followed by Sweden (36%), and Denmark and Norway (35%) whereas the OECD average is 32%. The gross enrolment ratios are also above OECD average, varying between 70% (Sweden) and 94% (Finland) (OECD 2014).

Table 12.1: The Number of Universities, University Colleges (UC) or Universities of Applied Sciences (UAS) and Independent Higher Education Institutions; Number of Higher Education Students (Percentage of Women) in Finland, Denmark, Norway and Sweden in 2011/2012.

Country	Universities	University colleges (UC)/UAS	Independent HEIs	He students (female %)	Public funding (%)	Odds ratio
Finland	14	26 + 1 UAS	–	307 059 (53%)	95.9	1.4
Denmark	12 (8 uni + 4 art academies)	7 UC	9 profess. academies	132 400 (uni) + 91 469 (colleges) = 223 869 (57%)	94.5	3.0
Norway	8	25 UC	23	235 840 (60%)	95.9	2.0
Sweden	17	17 UC	13	301 300 (59%)	89.5	2.3

Sources: OECD 2014 and national databases.

Equality and equal educational opportunities

Typical of all Nordic welfare societies is the strong emphasis put on equality and high investment in education, especially higher education. The 'odds ratio', which 'reflects the relative likelihood of participating in tertiary education of individuals whose parents have upper secondary or tertiary education' (OECD 2014, 93) reveals the successfulness of educational policies aiming to provide equal educational opportunities. Again, all Nordic countries are clearly better than the OECD average (odds ratio 4.5). This means that in Finland it is only 1.4 times more likely to have access to higher education if one's parents have tertiary level education, followed by Norway (odds ratio 2), Sweden (odds ratio 2.3) and Denmark where it is three twice times more likely (see Table 12.1). When saying this we should remember, however, that there are huge socio-economic differences in the students' backgrounds according to disciplines. The majority of students in the field of medicine normally come from the highest strata of society (Ahola 2015).

Equality is one of the strongest common values in all Nordic societies. In the field of higher education it is translated into policy principles of providing equal educational opportunities for the whole population irrespective of gender, socio-economic background or geographical location of the citizens. According to the Development Plan for Finnish Education (2011–2016):

> Equal opportunity in education is the underpinning of Finnish welfare. For educational equality to be realised, it is imperative that everyone gains a solid basis for learning already in early childhood and in basic education and that pupils and students with special needs and at risk of exclusion have access to a diverse range of supportive action. Measures must also be taken to alleviate differences and heredity in post-compulsory education. (http://www.minedu.fi/OPM/Koulutus/koulutuspolitiikka/asiakirjat/Kesu_2011_2016_fi.pdf)

The second important principle in all Nordic countries is free education. This principle provides good support for the students in higher education. In Finland, state support for students is about 440 euros a month for 9 months in a year for 5 years (target time to a degree) in addition to state-guaranteed loans. The sums and forms of state support have changed over the years, but the principles of tuition-free education and state support have not been seriously challenged despite some neo-liberal attempts to introduce tuition fees for Finnish students. As for international students, both Denmark (in 2007) and Sweden (in 2011) have introduced tuition fees, and the Finnish Parliament has decided that Finland will follow the suit in 2017. Only Norway has declined this suggestion.

The third common principle in Nordic countries is the strong role the nation state plays in funding, in legislation, and consequently, in steering higher education. Ethically and politically, education, including higher education, is normally understood and defined as a public service and a civil right rather than a consumer good. This understanding has its consequences. First, in Nordic countries, the proportion of public funding of HEIs is among the highest of all OECD countries with the average public funding being 69%. Finland, Norway and Denmark are predominantly funded through public sources (95–97%), whereas in Sweden the bigger proportion of private funding (10.5%) is mainly through strong private foundations which fund Swedish research activities (see Table 12.1). Secondly, Nordic countries invest much in public education. According to the OECD, 'at the tertiary level, public expenditure per student on both public and private institutions averages USD 9,221 in OECD countries, but varies from about USD 2000 in Chile to more than USD 17,000 in Denmark, Finland, Norway and Sweden, four countries in which the share of private expenditure is small or negligible' (OECD 2014, 243).

Finally, education and research are seen as important for the national identities and national economies and the well-being of societies. The role of education has been essentially important in the building of the Nordic Welfare States, because education has been seen as one of the major processes in the making of more equal societies. It even seems that the political project of making the welfare society brought together cultural, societal and economic motives to develop societies through equal access to education, including higher education. During the 1960s and the 1970s, HEIs were seen as important for economic development through manpower planning. From the 1990s onwards, HEIs have been seen as crucially important for the development of knowledge society and knowledge-based economies (Välimaa et al. 2016).

On the definitions of universities in Nordic countries

In order to analyse Nordic understandings of universities, I will now focus on official documents, more precisely, university and/or higher education acts. My assumption is that the analysis of these documents helps to understand how Nordic societies define the idea of a university. When saying this, I am aware that these documents do not necessarily help to illuminate the realities of universities because higher education policy makers also use other steering instruments (funding, performance discussion and ordinances) together with the fact that every HEI acts in different socio-economic and regional contexts. However, university acts provide an equal level of abstraction for the analysis of the idea of university across Nordic countries.

In what follows, I will pay special attention to the definitions of universities, the definitions of their governance structures and their relationships with the nation state and society. The analyses are based on unofficial English translations of national laws which provide, however, enough reliable material for the purposes of this academic analysis.

Denmark

The Danish (Consolidation) Act no. 960 of 14 August 2014 on Universities (hereafter the University Act; https://www.retsinformation.dk/Forms/R0710.aspx?id=168797) begins by the definition of universities:

> The universities are government-financed independent institutions under public sector administration overseen by the Minister for Higher Education and Science. (1§, 2)

It then continues by defining the objectives of the universities:

> The university is tasked with performing research and offering research-based education at the highest international level in the disciplines it covers. The university must ensure a balanced relationship between research and education; strategically select, prioritise and develop the fields of research and study in which it is active; and disseminate knowledge of scientific and scholarly methods and results. (2§, 2)

These objectives are followed by the definition of academic freedom:

> The university enjoys freedom of research. The university must defend and uphold both scientific ethics and the freedom of research of the individual researcher as well as of the university as a whole. (2§, 2)

It is quite important that academic freedom is defined by the Danish legislators as an institutional obligation rather than as an individual academic right. Therefore, universities are empowered to defend academic freedom. Typical of the Nordic way of thinking is also the fact that legislators see no contradiction in defining universities as government-financed and independent institutions overseen by the Ministry. This relationship is not seen as a paradoxical matter but as a normal state of affairs.

The Danish University Act also describes how universities should interact with their society by saying that:

> The university must collaborate with the society of which it is a part and contribute to the development of international collaboration. The results achieved by the university in the areas of research and education must contribute to promoting growth, welfare and development in society. As society's central repository of culture and knowledge, the university must exchange knowledge and competences with the society it belongs to and encourage its staff to take part in public debate. (2§, 33)

Again, important is the definition of universities as part of civic society because of their responsibility to take part in public debates and contribute to the potential of economic and social growth. This is, in fact, a unique definition of the tasks of universities to be found in Nordic countries. However, it describes quite well the social roles of universities and the values of openness, transparency and social responsibility to be found in other Nordic societies as well. However, these values are challenged by the corporatisation of universities, especially in Finland where universities have begun to develop corporate brands being increasingly concerned about their reputation (Välimaa 2012).

As for the governance of universities, the Danish University Act says that:

> The board is the highest authority of the university. The board safeguards the university's interests as an institution of education and research and determines guidelines for its organisation, long-term activities and development. The board's work must be performed with the greatest possible degree of openness and transparency. (10§, 1–2)

Danish legislator also has decided that:

> the board is to be composed of external members and members representing the academic staff of the university, including salaried PhD students, the technical and administrative staff and the students. The majority of board members must be external members. The board elects a chairman from among its external members.(12§, 1)

This is a rather popular composition of university boards in all Nordic countries consisting of both the representatives of academics and students and external members. The Danish legislation also describes what it means by institutional autonomy: the university is responsible for organising its internal management. However, the proper operation of the university is safeguarded by the possibility of state interferences. Thus:

> the board is answerable to the minister regarding the activities of the university, including the administration of the university's total resources. If the board disregards orders from the minister concerning the rectification of unlawful conditions, the minister may order the board to resign so that a new board can be appointed. If the board's actions jeopardise the university's continued existence, the minister may order the board to resign immediately, and in this connection install an interim governing board until such time as a new board is appointed. The board or the minister may decide to bring an action against members of the board, the rector, any university accountants or other parties in the event of losses suffered by the university. (11§, 1–4)

This section indicates quite accurately that institutional autonomy is allowed to take place in the frames regulated by the nation state. This means that the possibility for state intervention should be taken into account if trust is jeopardised by the university boards.

Finland

I have translated the Finnish Universities Act which can be found in the database finlex (yliopistolaki 558/2009 http://www.finlex.fi/fi/laki/alkup/2009/20090558). The Finnish act describes quite briefly, and at the highest level of abstraction of all Nordic countries, the relationship between universities and state and society and the internal governance structures of universities. This was a conscious decision made by the Finnish legislators based on the conviction that universities will decide more precisely on their internal management and administration structures following the general principles mentioned in the Universities Act (Välimaa 2012).

The Finnish Universities Act begins by defining two different forms of public universities in Finland. These are the universities run by foundations (two universities) under the Foundations Act (109/1930) and universities as corporations under public law defined as independent legal entities (12 universities). This is a new formulation in Finnish legislation and it was introduced with the universities act. However, all universities have similar governance bodies and public responsibilities irrespective of their legal statuses.

According to Finnish legislation:

> The objectives of the universities are to advance free research and scientific and artistic bildung (education and culture); to provide highest teaching based on research, and to educate students to serve their fatherland and humanity. When taking care of these duties universities must promote life-long learning, interact with the rest of the society and promote the impact of research outcomes and artistic activities on society. (2§)

Part of this definition can be understood in relation to the history of previous university acts because the act repeats the formulation for the University of Helsinki from the 19th century when the aim of the (then Imperial Alexander) university was 'to educate students to serve their fatherland and czar'. Finnish legislators also refer to the third mission of universities (service function) and lifelong learning which is one of the structuring principles in all levels of the Finnish system of education.

Finnish legislation continues by stating that:

> Universities must organize their functioning so as to assure high international standards in research, education and training, and in artistic activities respecting ethical principles and good scientific practices. (2§)

The reference to ethical codes and principles can be found only in Finnish and Danish university acts. However, this does not mean that the same principles would not be followed in other Nordic countries as well. In the Finnish case, this means that legislators need to bear in mind the ethical nature of academic work by making universities responsible for maintaining (and controlling) high ethical principles in research and teaching.

The Finnish Universities Act also defines the autonomy of universities by stating that:

> The universities have autonomy which secures the freedom of science, arts and highest teaching. Autonomy includes the right to make decisions on matters concerning internal administration. Universities also shall have the right to be heard when drafting legislation concerning universities. (3§)

The Act also declares that:

> The freedom of research, teaching and arts prevails in universities. However, a teacher must follow existing rules and regulations when organising teaching and training. Instruction in the universities shall be public. The access to teaching can be restricted with good reasons. (6§)

Important here is that Finnish universities have institutional autonomy which is also mentioned (and thus guaranteed) in the Finnish constitution (1999/731, 123§). Finnish legislation also emphasise academic freedom in research and teaching in universities. Rules and regulations refer to national ordinances and institutional regulations. The Universities Act also declares that studying is free of charge for everybody living permanently in Finland.

As regards governance, Finnish universities have wide internal autonomy exercised by the *University Collegium*, *University Board* and *the Rector* (University Act 13§). The university collegium consists of the representatives of academic staff and students. It accepts the budget and nominates members of the University Board (7, or 9–14 members, 40% of whom can be external members) (14§–22§). In fact, the Universities Act introduced a strong line organisation into Finnish universities by ordering that the rector is appointed by the Board, and rector appoints deans who, in turn, appoint department heads. Before 2010, all these actors were elected by academics and students (Välimaa 2012). *De jure,* Finnish universities are separated from the state machinery because they have fiscal and internal autonomy and staff members are no longer civil servants. However, *de facto,* the majority of the funding comes from budget of the Ministry of Education and Culture (MEC) (64%) and the rest of the funding from other, predominantly, public sources.

This situation described the trend of changes in other Nordic countries as well because all of them have adopted governance elements from the business world in order to make universities more efficiently managed organisations in the spirit of new public management (see Fägerlind and Strömquist 2004). However, according to a recent study, the overall autonomy of Nordic universities remains relatively high even though there are differences between countries (Nokkala and Bladh 2104).

Norway

The Norwegian Higher Education act covers both universities and university colleges (see: https://www.regjeringen.no/globalassets/upload/KD/Vedlegg/UH/UHloven_engelsk.pdf). The Norwegian legislation describes the objectives and activities of the universities and university colleges in a rather detailed manner. It states that universities should:

> a) provide higher education at a high international level; b) conduct research and academic and artistic development work at a high international level; and c) disseminate knowledge of the institution's activities and promote the understanding and application of scientific and artistic methods and results in public administration, cultural life and business and industry. (chapter 1, section 1–1).

This means that universities (and other HEIs) should:

- provide higher education on the basis of the foremost within research, academic and artistic development work and empirical knowledge;
- conduct research and academic and artistic development work;
- efficiently manage resources provided and actively seek provision of external resources;
- help to disseminate the results of research and of academic and artistic development work;
- contribute to innovation and value creation on the basis of the results of research and academic and artistic development work;
- make provisions for participation in public debate by the institution's staff and students;
- help to ensure that Norwegian higher education and research participates in the front line of international research and development of higher education provision;
- cooperate with other universities, university colleges and corresponding institutions in other countries, local and regional civic and working life, public administration and international organisations;
- provide continuing and further education in the institution's field of operation. (chapter 1, section 1–3)

This comprehensive list of activities mentioned in the Higher Education act shows that universities are assumed to play an active role in the Norwegian society from culture to politics to economy. The list also reveals that Norwegian universities are seen as national cultural institutions being important for all spheres of society (see also Vabo 2002). This matter of fact is made quite clear by the description of national responsibilities:

> (1) Universities and university colleges have a special responsibility for fundamental research and research training in the fields in which they award doctorates. (2) The University of Bergen, the University of Oslo, the University of Tromsø and the Norwegian University of Science and Technology have a special national responsibility for building up, managing and maintaining museums with scientific collections and public exhibitions. (3) The Ministry may assign individual institutions a special national responsibility for research or teaching in specific fields. In the same way, the Ministry may assign individual institutions special national responsibility for building up, managing and maintaining research libraries, knowledge repositories and databases as well as museums with scientific collections and public exhibitions for specific fields. (4) The Ministry may, in consultation with the institution concerned, place the management of a common national responsibility at a specific institution without the institution's own governing body being made responsible for the academic activities involved.

This section describes the power of the Ministry of Education to decide on matters which are seen as nationally important. A similar way of thinking can be found in Denmark, Finland and Sweden.

The Norwegian Universities Act describes institutional autonomy in an original way by stating how universities cannot be instructed by the state:

> Universities or university colleges may not be instructed regarding a) the academic content of their teaching and the content of research or artistic or scientific development work. b) individual appointments. (chapter 1, section 1–5)

Norwegian legislators also admit that HEIs have institutional autonomy because:

> institutions accredited as universities have the authority to decide themselves which study programmes and disciplines the institution shall provide, and which shall form part of the basis of a degree or professional training course established. (chapter 3, section 3–3)

Sweden

The Swedish Higher Education Act (Högskolelag 1992, 1434) Swedish Code of Statutes (SFS) No. 1992:1434/) is both the most global and the most detailed in its approach (see: http://www.uhr.se/sv/information-in-english/laws-and-regulations/the-swedish-higher-education-act/#Chapter%201).

The Swedish Higher Education Act makes the rules of the game clear in the first section:

> This act contains provisions relating to higher education institutions for which the accountable authority is the Government. As the accountable authority, the Government shall establish higher education institutions for the provision of: 1) courses and study programmes based on scholarship or artistic practice and on proven experience, and 2) research and artistic research as well as development work. The mandate of higher education institutions shall include third stream activities and the provision of information about their activities, as well as ensuring that benefit is derived from their research findings. (chapter 1, sections 1 and 2)

The Swedish legislation sees the responsibility of universities in a broad picture by stating that:

> in the course of their operations, higher education institutions shall promote sustainable development to assure for present and future generations a sound and healthy environment, economic and social welfare, and justice. (chapter 1, section 5).

The Swedish legislatoon also wants to make clear that 'in their operations higher education institutions should promote understanding of other countries and of international circumstances'. (chapter 1, section 5). These sections which look more like political declarations than exact sections of a law are unique to Sweden, even though the same kind of mentality can be found in other Nordic countries as well. The sections indicate that these values are felt to be very important in the Swedish society. In a similar vein, the Swedish Act is the only one which mentions gender equality and affirmative action even though these values are important in all Nordic countries:

> Equality between women and men shall always be taken into account and promoted in the operations of higher education institutions. Higher education institutions shall also actively promote and widen recruitment to higher education. (chapter 1, section 5).

The Swedish Parliament has recognised academic freedom by emphasising the freedom of research. The Swedish legislation declares that the following principles apply to research:

> 1) research issues may be freely selected, 2) research methodologies may be freely developed, and 3) research results may be freely published. (chapter 1, section 6).

As a contrast to a quite general, or even global, approach in defining the goals for universities, the Swedish law describes the relationship between the state and the

HEIs in a rather detailed way. It starts by stating that the Parliament (Riksdag) 'decides which public-sector higher education institutions shall exist'. Secondly, it says that 'the board of governors of a higher education institution shall supervise all of its operations and assume responsibility for the fulfilment of its mandate' (chapter 2, sections 1 and 2). However, important and interesting is the fact that the Swedish Government:

> shall appoint the chair of the board of governors of a higher education institution. The vice-chancellor (... being responsible for the management and appointed by the Board ...) shall be a member of the board of governors. Teachers and students at the higher education institution shall be entitled to representation on the board of governors. Regulations on who is to appoint such representatives are laid down by ordinance. The Government appoints other members of the board of governors. (chapter 2, section 4)

This is clearly the most detailed description of the state intervention to universities to be found in any Nordic country because of the state-appointed members of the board. It shows that the Swedish state is interested in close-range steering of universities which are, however, defined as autonomous institutions. It therefore seems that the attitude of social engineering of HEIs characterises the Swedish Universities Act.

Conclusions and discussion on the dimensions of a Nordic idea of university

The analysis of Nordic legislations shows that there are differences in wordings and approaches to universities and their autonomy. Sweden has the most detailed steering of universities in the spirit of social engineering, whereas Finnish and Norwegian legislations give more procedural autonomy to universities (see Nokkala and Bladh 2014). Danish legislation takes the middle ground with clearly set conditions for potential state interference in universities. However, common to all Nordic societies is the concern that universities should be efficiently managed organisations. One of the indicators of this argument is the influence which neo-liberal policies have had in all Nordic countries (Fägerlind and Strömquist 2004).

Despite differences, four common dimensions of a Nordic idea of university can be found. First comes the notion that universities are autonomous institutions. Universities enjoy good institutional autonomy in their internal matters. The Nordic idea of university also emphasises the academic freedom of academics. Academic freedom is nurtured and supported both by universities as institutions and by academics themselves. It is therefore both an institutional and an individual quality. Nordic legislation is very clear with its emphasis of academic freedom as fundamental right and as a starting point for high-quality international research and teaching. According to a recent study, Nordic universities have more institutional autonomy than continental universities (Nokkala and Bladh 2014). This seems to speak to the trust in universities as autonomous institutions. Academic freedom, which is conceptually connected with institutional autonomy, is seen as natural in Nordic states which are characterised by trust between welfare states and their citizens—including academics working in HEIs.

Secondly, Nordic legislators would like to see their universities as international and internationalising institutions in two ways. Universities are both encouraged to collaborate internationally with other universities and to contribute to international research communities. Universities are also expected to reach the highest international standards in their research and teaching activities.

Thirdly, the most important relationship defining the Nordic idea of university is the relationship with the nation state. As organisations, universities are strongly steered by benevolent nation states which wish to guarantee their operational basis as public institutions through public funding, steering and legislation. This relationship seems to be based on trust on universities as societal and civic institutions, but trust with a condition: the state is willing to interfere if universities misuse their institutional autonomy. It reflects Stensaker's observation (2004, 349) that, 'the state is an important actor for the whole system, both as the resource provider and as the actor that regulates and steers the system'. This argument describes the underlying idea of the Nordic higher education systems, even though the quotation is about Norway.

The fourth evident conclusion is that universities are seen as socially responsible institutions of civil society. This is related to the fact that higher education is understood as a public service rather than as a consumer good. Universities and academics are seen as active partners and actors of their societies in order to make them better and more equal. Education and research are seen important for civil societies through the expectations that universities and academics should contribute to public debates, cultural life and economic activities for the benefit of Nordic welfare states. Nordic societies (especially Finland and Norway) share a tradition of defining universities as national cultural institutions, even though this tradition has been defined somewhat differently in each country.

All these dimensions are helpful when reflecting on the nature of universities as political institutions in Nordic societies. First, a crucial matter for the nature of Nordic universities as political institutions is the strong relationship with the nation state. Institutional autonomy is defined mainly in relation to the legislator and funder of the universities, in other words, the nation state but not in relation to students, or board of trustees (which do not exist) or to the business world. This definition comes close to the German approach to institutional autonomy which often emphasises the relationship with the state (see Nokkala and Bladh 2014). Secondly, universities are also political institutions because of their assumed strong relationship with civil society and national economy. Universities are expected to contribute both to political life (especially in Denmark) and to the economic advancement of national economies. Therefore, the loyalties and responsibilities of universities and their academics are assumed to be related both to citizens and NGOs (civil society), to businessmen and workforce (economy), and to the nation state and its institutions. Finally, Nordic legislators also see universities as political organisations which should include both their students, members of academic communities and representatives of society in their political decision-making processes. Strong student representation in the university decision-making is a typical Nordic tradition (Nokkala and Bladh 2014). Through these ways universities exercise their roles as political institutions both in their internal administration and in their relationships with society.

Naturally, it is unclear whether this balance between different political roles will remain in the future because of the strong challenges related to economic globalisation and the neo-liberal pressures for both management efficiency and instrumental, economic usefulness of universities. However, what seems to be probable is the continuation of the strong power the Nordic nation states are willing to use as the regulators of their systems of higher education. This will, in itself, counterbalance the influence of the market forces in the Nordic region.

References

Abrahamsson, P. (1994). The Scandinavian Model in a Time of Change, in W. Cave & P. Himmelstrup (eds.) *The Welfare Society in Transition: Problems and Prospects of the Welfare Model.* Copenhagen: Danish Cultural Institute, 93–144.

Ahola, S. (2015). Suomalaisen korkeakoulukentän sosiaalinen ulottuvuus. The Social Dimension of the Finnish Field of Higher Education. Presentation on November 2nd, 2015, Helsinki.

Alestalo, M. & Kuhnle, S. (1987). The Scandinavian Route: Economic, Social and Political Developments in Denmark, Finland, Norway and Sweden, in R. Erikson et al. (eds.) *The Scandinavian Model: Welfare States and Welfare Research.* New York & London: Sharper, 3–38.

Esping-Andersen, G. (1990). *The Three Worlds of Welfare Capitalism.* New Jersey: Princeton University Press.

Fägerlind, I. & Strömquist, G. (2004). *Reforming Higher Education in the Nordic Countries – Studies of Change in Denmark, Finland, Iceland, Norway and Sweden.* Paris: UNESCO and International Institute for Educational Planning.

Finnish Science Barometer (2013). *Finnish Society for Scientific Information.* Helsinki: Yliopistopaino.

Hämäläinen, K., Haakstad, J., Kangasniemi, J., Lindeberg, T. & Sjölund, M. (2001). *Quality Assurance in the Nordic Higher Education.* Helsinki: ENQA Occasional Papers 2.

Kettunen, P., Kuhnle, S. & Ren, Y. (2014). Introduction. The Development and Diffusion of Welfare Systems and Policies in the Nordic Countries and in China, in P. Kettunen, S. Kuhnle & Y. Ren (eds.) *Reshaping Welfare Institutions in China and the Nordic Countries.* Helsinki: NordWel Studies in Historical Welfare State Research 7.

Kouvo, A. (2014). *Luottamuksen lähteet. Vertaileva tutkimus yleistynyttä luottamusta synnyttävistä mekanismeista [The Sources of Generalized Trust—A Comparative Study].* Annales Universitatis Turkuensis C 381.

Lin, K. (2004). Sectors, Agents and Rationale. A Study of the Scandinavian Welfare States with Special Reference to the Welfare Society Model. Sage: *Acta Scociologica*, 47, 141–157.

Nokkala, T. & Bladh, A. (2014). Institutional Autonomy and Academic Freedom in the Nordic Context –Similarities and Differences. *Higher Education Policy*, 27, 1–12.

Nybom, T. (2007). A Rule-Governed Community of Scholars: The Humboldt Vision in the History of the European History, in P. Maassen & J. P. Olsen (eds.) *University Dynamics and European Integration.* Dordrecht: Springer, 55–80.

OECD (2014). Education at Glance. http://www.oecd.org/education/eag.htm

Pusser, B. (2015). A Critical Approach to Power in Higher Education, in A. M. Martínez-Alemán, B. Pusser & E. M. Bensimon (eds.) *Critical Approaches to the Study of Higher Education.* Baltimore: Johns Hopkins University Press, 59–79.

Stensaker, B. (2004). The Blurring Boundaries between Accreditation and Audit: The Case of Norway, in S. Schwarz & D. F. Westerheijden(eds.) *Accreditation and Evaluation in the European Higher Education Area.* Dordrecht: Kluwer, 347–370.

Vabo, A. (2002). *Mytedannelser i endringsprosesser i akademiske institusjoner.* Academic Dissertation. University of Bergen.

Välimaa, J. (2012). The Corporatization of National Universities in Finland, in B. Pusser, K. Kempner, S. Marginson, & I. Ordorika (eds.) *Universities and the Public Sphere. Knowledge Creation and State Building in the Era of Globalization.* New York: Routledge, 101–120.

Välimaa, J. (2015). Yliopistot keskiajan sosiaalisena innovaationa: Paavi, Ruhtinas ja Kaupunki. [Universities as Medieval Social Innovations: The Pope, The Prince and The City]. *Kasvatus ja aika,* 3, 244–256.

Välimaa, J., Brennan, J. L., Rhoades, G., Teichler, U., & Hoffman, D. M. (2016). Main Findings and Discussion, in D. M. Hoffman & J. Välimaa (eds.) *Re-Becoming Universities? Higher Education Institutions in Networked Knowledge Societies.* Dordrecht: Springer.

Välimaa, J. & Neuvonen-Rauhala, M.-L. (2010). "We are a Training and Development Organisation" –Research and Development in Finnish Polytechnics, in S. Kyvik & B. Lepori (eds.) *The Research Mission of Higher Education Institutions outside the University*

Sector. Striving for Differentiation. Higher Education Dynamics 31. Springer: Dordrecht, Heidelberg, London, New York, 135–154.

Websites visited 30.11.2015

Ministry of Education and Culture, The Development plan of Education for 2011–2016:
http://www.minedu.fi/OPM/Koulutus/koulutuspolitiikka/asiakirjat/Kesu_2011_2016_fi.pdf
OECD (2014) Education at a Glance:
http://www.oecd.org/education/eag.htm
Danish University Act:
https://www.retsinformation.dk/Forms/R0710.aspx?id=168797
http://www.au.dk/fileadmin/www.au.dk/Regelsamlingen/2014/EN_Bekendtgoerelse_af_lov_om_universiteter_367.pdf
Finnish University Act:
http://www.finlex.fi/fi/laki/alkup/2009/20090558
Norwegian higher education law:
https://www.regjeringen.no/globalassets/upload/KD/Vedlegg/UH/UHloven_engelsk.pdf
Swedish higher education law:
http://www.uhr.se/sv/information-in-english/laws-and-regulations/the-swedish-higher-education-act/#Chapter%201
World Economic Forum 2015:
http://www.weforum.org/reports/global-gender-gap-report-2014

CHAPTER THIRTEEN

European Universities

Another Somewhat Lamenting—Yet Basically Hopeful—Account[1]

THORSTEN NYBOM

Introduction

Even if my deliberations will be personal and my "conclusions" will be contestable—to put it mildly—they are nevertheless founded in my fairly extensive experience, reading, writing, discussion, and a wee bit of thinking with respect to the specific field of study and social practice we usually call higher education and research policy.

As far as I am concerned, the starting point for any discussion today of the position, organization, and tasks of the European universities must be that the university no longer has the same, self-evident, and undisputed legitimacy that it had just 30 years ago.

First, because today practically all European research and higher education systems are in flux, regardless of their organization, structure, historic roots, and funding principles.

Second, and perhaps even more seminal, because the traditional European universities are plagued by deep social, economic, and intellectual uncertainty, and this goes to the very core of the institutions. In short, the university has, so to speak, to renegotiate its "social contract" with regard, not only to its funders and students, but also to society at large.

Paradoxically, the crisis the universities are presently facing can at least partly be seen as a consequence of the emergence of what is called the *knowledge society*, because this has meant not only a rise in the *demand* for higher education, professional skills, and sophisticated knowledge, but also to an enormous growth in the *supply* of such services. Fifty years ago, the university still had a virtual monopoly on the production and distribution of qualified knowledge and research. Today, one can find producers and transmitters of knowledge just about everywhere and in a number of alternative, institutional arrangements—in industry, in public and private bureaucracies, in the arts and the entertainment sector, and even in the media.

As a result, in the eyes of funders, students, and prospective employers, the university, is only *one* of several possible alternatives or options. This competitive situation, in turn, has resulted in growing demands for accountability and external scrutiny. Clearly, it has become gradually more or less impossible and irresponsible to go on trying to defend the—both economically and intellectually speaking—somewhat "uncommunicative" higher education systems that existed in Europe until the 1980s.

It is thus high time that we at the European universities start admitting that the present-day universities *are nothing like* what they still were in the 1970s. We are doing more—and different—things than we did then, and under totally different conditions. To begin with, there is a different student body. The student–faculty ratio has changed dramatically. The principles, level and sources of funding have changed radically. The distance between high-quality research and undergraduate education has become almost insurmountable; in many cases, cutting-edge research has left the university altogether.

Yet another paradox is that accompanying a deep and widespread uncertainty about the future tasks and institutional organization of the higher education and research system, there remains an implicit belief in the salutary effects of research and higher education—most notably, among the chattering political classes. This belief presupposes an immediate connection between the volume of research and higher education, on the one hand, and economic development, on the other.

This is a fairly dubious assumption; at very least, it must be supplemented by considerable reservations. The only thing we historians can really say regarding the interrelation between the educational level of a nation and its economic performance is that a connection of this kind *does exist.* But to proceed from this reasonable supposition to categorical statements as to what this connection *actually looks like* and how it should be institutionalized, organized, and funded is hazardous, irresponsible, and really just plain silly.

Historical Mistakes: The Disintegration of the European Higher Education System(s) 1965–1985

In the late 1960s and early 1970s, as a consequence of genuine demographic, democratic, and economic pressures, institutions of higher learning in Continental Europe were transformed from rather exclusive institutions to institutions of mass instruction. In contrast to the United States 20 years earlier, this reaction to very real pressures was implemented without a simultaneous restructuring of the existing higher education system. This blatant sin of omission on the part of both ignorant politicians and arrogant academics had a number of more or less critical and long-term effects and consequences:

1. The universities in some parts of Europe have sometimes virtually ceased to function as proper institutions of higher learning (Southern Europe).
2. In other parts of Europe, institutions of higher education were "reconstructed" through heavy-handed bureaucratic means, which eventually led to even greater uniformity instead of a necessary differentiation (Sweden).
3. As a consequence of 2), wherever it has been possible, a substantial part of qualified research has tried to decouple itself from the comprehensive university, either through different forms of "inner emigration" (Sweden) or by simply leaving the university in favor of independent extramural research institutes (Germany).
4. Politicians no longer honour the 200-year-old contract between the state and the university system. Instead, there has emerged a fundamental lack of trust between the two parties.

The first two points (and indirectly, the third, as a consequence of the second) are directly tied up with a sharp and continuous rise in student enrollment during the last 30 years. Several of the European higher education systems have evolved from mass university systems to become more or less *universal* higher education systems. In most cases on the European continent, this has happened without any fundamental structural and institutional changes in the existing, often unitary and inflexible, state-controlled higher education systems. Accordingly, this growth has caused substantial structural, institutional, and intellectual dysfunctions and deficits. To make matters worse, the rapid growth of the student body has been accompanied by unchanged or, in many cases, reduced levels of per-capita state funding.

Regarding the fourth point, the lack of trust between the university and the state may be seen as a clear indication of the massive retreat on the part of the European states and central governments from their traditional "Humboldtian" obligation of being the ultimate guardian angel of their national institutions of higher education. Further, they abandoned the block grant funding system in which resources were allocated directly to the universities and research in favor of a system where so-called "competitive funding" became the standard operating procedure. This meant that the material conditions for long-range planning at the university level were eviscerated, leading to a radically diminished capacity to function as autonomous institutions. Thus, I maintain, during the last 15 years, European central governments have become just another—albeit more powerful—"stakeholder" in the university, which treats the universities not as a public good *as such*, but rather as just another political means for achieving all sorts of political ends the present government has on its agenda.

Paradoxically, although to an historian certainly unsurprisingly, this "New Public Management"-inspired "withdrawal by the state" and deregulation were almost everywhere accompanied by a general trend of increased *politicization* of higher education and research, which in some cases has led to a redefinition of the ultimate role and mission of higher education institutions. The most obvious example of this dual development is England, but the trends are visible almost all over Europe—not least in my own country. Universities are no longer considered to be invaluable national academic institutions and *cultural* centers. They are primarily seen as instrumental *means*; they function as "development or innovation centers" in national or even regional economic policy. Moreover, this process has been accompanied by an almost explosive expansion of evaluations and accountability schemes, which have turned the traditional European system of exclusive and strict "input control" (*Abitur* and peer-review) into different schemes of "output control" in which practically "everything that moves is measured."

Finally, in a European "étatist" university context and tradition, precious few of the present European central governments (with the possible exception of Switzerland, Denmark, and the Netherlands—whatever the actual outcome) can be said to have articulated, much less pursued, any form of conscious or even consistent national science and higher education policy in last four decades. Instead, practically every European politician is standing on the ruins of his/her crumbling university system, delivering one statement after the other—in Brussels and elsewhere—regarding the strategic importance of knowledge, research, innovation, education, etc.

Against this background, one could very well start wondering if the euphoria over the alleged unlimited possibilities opened up by the implementation of the Bologna process in European higher education, especially among European politicians and higher education bureaucrats, has *anything* to do with a serious will on part of its academic and political protagonists to promote the pursuit of qualified knowledge. A more cynical observer would perhaps rather detect a hidden political agenda behind the massive enthusiasm among national and European politicians, bureaucrats, and lobbyists, which might indicate that the main advantage of the Bologna scheme is that it gives these politicians an opportunity to avoid the risk of having to take responsibility for a number of necessary but presumably very controversial reforms on the *national* level concerning a) funding (fees); b) differentiation; c) access (master's level); and d) marketization. Instead, unpopular undertakings can be presented as "unavoidable and logical consequences" of Bologna.

This type of argumentation is sometimes called the TINA syndrome (There Is No Alternative) and is frequently used by politicians, bureaucrats, and economists—not only concering higher education. In the worst of all possible scenarios, the politicians—together with their allies in academia—in particular, the European Association of Universities (EAU)—will succumb to the illusion, or at best maintain the unfounded belief, that Bologna will, in itself, *both* raise the quality of higher education and research *and* at the same time take care of the constantly growing needs for qualified vocational training and lifelong learning structures.

The Confluence of Internal and External Forces of Change since 1995

But it is certainly not only politics and political decisions that have had far-reaching consequences for the university and institutionalized research. It is possible to distinguish a number of fundamental and partly concurring structural processes that to high degree will define the decisive parameters for European higher education and research systems at present and in the future. What is extraordinary about today's situation is not the fact that the systems are changing. On the contrary, more or less dramatic change has characterized the universities ever since they emerged 1000 years ago. The exceptional in the present development—just as 200 years ago—is that we are facing something close to a Cultural Revolution. By this I mean that the ongoing and coming changes will have significant consequences at almost every level and for every actor and activity within the higher education and research system:

(1) The shift from mass higher to universal tertiary education and to life-long learning

As a consequence of the European systems' adaptation to an ever increasing array of tasks and a more heterogeneous student body, they are moving toward a more or less unplanned vertical stratification (with the exception of Germany, which has intentionally taken steps in this direction), rather than toward functional horizontal differentiation that characterizes the higher education system in the United States. Admittedly, the United States higher education system is characterized by an overt and forceful vertical dimension (regarding mission and excellence), but an equally important dimension of that system is horizontal institutional differentiation, which promotes not only institutional competition but also cooperation, i.e., without the confessional, liberal arts, and technical colleges, no Harvard or UC Berkeley!

(2) The uncontrolled growth of qualified knowledge

When discussing the massive and rapid growth in higher learning, we tend to concentrate almost exclusively on student numbers and rising overall costs. Almost as significant and potentially as transformative is the enormous growth in knowledge production. This perpetual expansion has at least two fundamental consequences for traditional institutions of higher education and research: a) the universities can no longer maintain the illusion of being the sole provider of qualified knowledge in society; b) this process of knowledge-flooding, which per definition includes a growing heterogeneity of the institution's knowledge production and knowledge transfer, puts an additional strain on the internal coherence and the common value system of the universities.

(3) The continuous advance of institutional heterogeneity

The higher education sector is neither capable of nor interested in acting as a combined political force in higher education and research policy. The most obvious example here is, once again, England, where a number of different so-called "mission groups" among the universities are certainly not engaged in any "common course," but rather actively combat each other. This dissolution process is also visible in other European countries.

As of today—and in the foreseeable future—there will be, at least, five ideal-typical forms of institutional orders or agencies that will be operating in the sector of higher—or better tertiary—education. In real life, there will eventually emerge an almost endless flora of different varieties and combinations of these ideal-typical forms:

- For-profit providers—on- and off-line.
- Multi-versities
- Professional Schools
- Research Universities
- Elite Colleges

This ongoing and accelerating process of differentiation and diversification has already had and will continue to have deep going implications and consequences on practically every dimension of higher education systems: national policy, internal governance and decision-making, staff recruitment, societal affiliations, number and types of students, norm systems and academic standards, working conditions, level of academic freedom, funding, basic mission, etc.

For-Profit Tertiary Education (10–15%)
Mission: *Generate an optimal rate of profit*
Central Task: *Semi-professional vocational training*
Strategic Competence: *Market adaptability*
Governance: *Business management*
Recruitment of Staff: *Market driven; short term*
Volume: *Unrestricted, demand-pull*
Community: *"GLO-cal"*
Academic Freedom: *Irrelevant or non-existing*
Educational Ideology: *"Employability"*
Student Role: *Customer = Purchaser of a private good*

- Ideal Type: University of Phoenix

Multi-Versity (40–50%)
Mission: *Mass higher education and semi-professional training*
Central Task: *Undergraduate education, lifelong learning*
Strategic Competence: *Educational efficiency*
Governance: *Bureaucratic hierarchy: (state) regulated*
Recruitment of Staff: *Inclusive demand pull/policy push*
Volume: *Unrestricted: demand-pull/supply-push*
Community: *Regional (and national)*
Academic Freedom: *Restricted*
Educational Ideology: *Comprehensive; Vocational*
Student Role: *Consumer = User of a public good*

- Ideal Type: California State Univ. System

Professional School (15–20%)
Mission: *Training of professional elites—excellence in applied research*
Central Task: *Research-based professional graduate training*
Strategic Competence: *Professional excellence*
Governance: *Professional hierarchy: semi-autonomous*
Recruitment of Staff: *Exclusive, market/policy driven*
Volume: *Restricted and competitive*

Community: *National and international*
Academic Freedom: *High, but regulated*
Educational Ideology: *Specialized and in-depth*
Student Role: *Apprentice*

- Ideal Type: MIT; Grandes Écoles; Eth

Research University (15–20%)
Mission: *Training of academic elites; Basic research*
Central Task: *Masters- and PhD-training*
Strategic Competence: *Academic excellence*
Governance: *Collegiate "Iroquois-League" with strong "chief"*
Recruitment of Staff: *Exclusive and meritocratic; Tenured*
Volume: *Restricted and supply driven*
Academic Freedom: *Optimal*
Community: *International*
Educational Ideology: *Academic and in-depth*
Student Role: *Collaborator*

- Ideal Type: Harvard, Cambridge

Elite College (1–2%)
Mission: *Training of academic and social elites*
Central Task: *Excellence in undergraduate education*
Strategic Competence: *Pedagogical excellence*
Governance: *Collegial: Autonomous*
Recruitment of Staff: *Exclusive and meritocratic; Tenured*
Volume: *Supply-driven and restricted*
Community: *National and international*
Academic Freedom: *High but conditional*
Educational Ideology: "*Bildung*"
Student Role: *Client ("in loco parentis")*

- Ideal Type: Amherst, Swarthmore

(4) ICT and the (probable) coming of a cognitive, pedagogical, and logistic revolution

The long-term impact of this process in the life and organization of the university remains as yet to be seen. There will be some major con-sequences, including, but not limited to, questions of curricula and pedagogy, but the consequences will probably not be the ones described in the proselytizing campaigns of today's "MOOC-zealots."

(5) The simultaneous processes of globalization, individualization, and "marketization"

These are, of course, general developments with extensive ramifications and important implications for all spheres of modern society. Nonetheless, I believe that their impact on the European higher education systems will be relatively more profound for the simple reason that those systems were considered, until the 1980s, to some extent to "live in a world of their own."

(6) The dissolution of the historical nexus between the nation-state and the higher education and research system

In addition to the more direct and obvious consequences discussed earlier, this process has also created something of an ideological crisis, that is, a feeling of deep uncertainty among European universities regarding who their actual owners and principals really are.

(7) Chronic public underfunding and the retreat from political responsibility: "The New Public Management" revolution

As noted above, NPM-advocates almost nowhere seem to have recognized—or cared—that uncontrolled deregulation of a bureaucratic rule-governed system invariably leads either to anarchic marketization or to increased political interventionism. In Sweden, the former has been the case in the elderly care sector, whereas the latter has characterized the higher education and research system, in Sweden as elsewhere in Europe.

(8) New relations between knowledge, industry, and society: "Triple-Helix", "Mode 2," "Entrepreneurial Universities," etc.

Potentially, this process of integration between the activities of the university and the demands and expectations of external "stake-holders" could have considerable consequences, not only on curricula, training, funding, and research output, but also on university management, governance, and steering. As the university is increasingly subsumed under the "innovation system," albeit as its perceived motor, the rationale for academic self-legislation, for instance, loses its relevance.

(9) Growing tensions between education as a public and a private good

This is perhaps the most fundamental and momentous ideological shift during the last 30 years. First of all, this shift strikes at the very heart of the ethos and self-understanding of the classical university. Secondly, this shift affects the role and behavior of the students, gradually turning them into customers. And, where there are customers seeking private goods, there will certainly also be a number of prospective profit-seeking private providers of such "goods"—in many cases, of dubious quality.

(10) The conflation between information and knowledge

Commentators and self-appointed experts routinely use "the information society" and "the knowledge society" as synonymous and interchangeable concepts. This tendency to conflate information and knowledge is not merely sloppy or thoughtless. In point of fact, it reveals a fatal misunderstanding. The information society is and will remain at odds with anything that might be rightly called the knowledge society. Knowledge is achieved through laborious effort and ingenuity; information is merely dispersed, collected, and disseminated. If we fail to make this distinction, we may very well face a future in which mediatized information may come to pose the greatest threat to institutionalized science and knowledge production.

(11) The dissolution of traditional academic values and a subsequent crisis of legitimacy and rationality in research and research funding

During the period discussed here, research funding has undergone a period of massive bureaucratization and instrumentalization, as is made manifest by the ever-increasing importance—direct and indirect—of the so-called EU "Framework Programmes." It has also largely become a dominant trend in science policy and research funding on the national level. The "Policy for Science" that characterized the first three decades after the Second World War, the Vannevar Bush formula, has been abandoned for something that rightfully could be labelled "Politicized Science."

The ominous development really started to accelerate in the early 1980s. From then on there has also been a constantly growing gap between the United States and Europe when it comes to the pursuit of excellence in scientific research. Considering the natural delay of causes and effects in research practice and research policy planning, there are good reasons to believe that something happened in European and/or American research policy in the 1970s, and it most certainly did. Starting in the 1970s, many European countries gradually replaced the existing Vannevar Bush model for science policy and research funding, and it is not only possible but even instructive to divide this process of fundamental change into three distinct chronological phases of research policy, which have had deep and lasting consequences on the well-being of the European university.

The first phase, which could be labeled "the technocratic phase," started in the mid-1960s and lasted roughly until the late 1970s. This development constituted no immediate threat to the primacy of basic research and to traditional academic values. Instead, it was seen as a complementary but supposedly more socially relevant form of knowledge production, which was funded and administered outside the traditional research sector, but, nevertheless, often under the qualitative supervision of academic research. It could, perhaps, a little simplistically, be regarded as an attempt to fulfill the old social democratic dream of the good society governed by a scientifically based and enlightened form of social engineering.

The second phase, through the 1980s and into the early 1990s, could be characterized as a massive effort of political interventionism under the abovementioned labels of deregulation and marketization. This did not just include a fundamental shift in the funding of research and higher education, it also entailed the introduction of full-scale political steering and earmarking of research funding, where some ministers and government bureaucrats started to usurp what had hitherto been considered to be an exclusive academic function and prerogative, previously, usually carried out by different types of research council bodies. Furthermore, in many countries, the traditonal research council organizations were transformed from academic to politically dominated governmental bodies.

Accordingly, during this phase, the attacks on peer-reviewing and disciplinary-based research became open and sometimes even aggressive. These procedures were increasingly accused of being anti-innovative, conservative, and ill-adjusted to the real social and economic problems. This anti-academic, and I would say anti-intellectual, offensive was soon also eagerly supported by an array of postmodern representatives from within the traditional academic community, who had an equally immediate and equally vested interest in subverting traditional academic norms and values.

The third phase, over the last ten years, could be described, I would say, as an almost deadly combination of the bureaucratic rule of the first, and the ideological interventionism of the second, and has been even more disastrous. The new system was introduced on a super-national level in the form of the EU Framework programmes, which among other things, also constituted blatant breaches with traditional forms and principles of science policy planning. Instead, we actually got something almost similar to the old Soviet bureaucratic five-year plans in science policy.

One consequence is the growing tendency in research funding to replace the traditional criterion of genuine academic excellence with more nebulous criteria with an array of labels: "strategic significance," "social and economic relevance," "mode 2," "the production of socially robust knowledge." The list of terms in this Orwellian science policy newspeak would seem endless. The terminology is intimately bound up with politically controlled earmarking, in which pork-barreling and "strategic" allocation of resources have become the rule rather than the exception. (Significantly enough, the laudable establishment of the European Research Council [ERC]—a small step back toward the Vannevar Bush-principle of research funding—was by no means an initiative taken by the Bruxelles research bureaucrats or even by European university leadership; it was initiated and carried through by a handful of independent European research foundations and academies of science, despite fairly heavy resistence.)

The ramifications of the development sketched above are enormous, and have yet to be fully grasped. They have to do with the internal life of science and the university, including the self-understanding and professional ethos among scientists and scholars and their relationship to their disciplines. Thus it is no exaggeration to predict a gradual demise of the university as an institution. But what even those who acknowledge and perhaps even accept the disappearance of the classical university fail to notice is this: as goes the university, so go the disciplines and the research and teaching which define them. Even if the traditional disciplinary structure is still well anchored in academic life and its prestige structure, it has nevertheless by degrees lost its special position in the research policy hierarchy. There is no reason to assume that this trend will be reversed any time soon, if no explicit effort is made to turn the tide.

It is commonly assumed that what I have described is merely a matter of evolution, that is, a more or less natural consequence of the alleged widening gap between academic basic research and the acute problems the world is facing and will be facing in years to come. But this is only true in part. The insistence on interdisciplinary approaches, for instance, is not always clearly motivated by the alleged lack of relevance of contemporary science; rather, it has turned into an ideological or political tool—*not least inside academia*—to undermine academic autonomy and its traditional value system. The repercussions for the health and welfare of the European university, by which I mean its teaching and research, can hardly be overestimated.

(12) The breakthrough of global one-dimensional excellence criteria and rankings and the introduction of "opportunistic instrumentalism" at universities

Before concluding these perhaps not too original deliberations, let me at least touch upon three of the most frequently used buzzwords in the present higher education debate: internationalization, excellence, and ranking, since these dimensions are usually discussed in either fairly simplistic terms, be they enthusiastic or dismissive.

Internationalization is almost always presented as one of the key features of higher education and research that should have top priority. In principle, this is all well and good, but one must also realize that internationalization, like everything else in human life, carries with it certain risks and drawbacks. Hence, the internationalization of research and graduate education can lead to growing unease and even disintegration at the local level. When a person joins—or is admitted into—"the international tribe of top 'gypsy-scholars'", her first loyalty will be toward that particular tribe. The home university/ department and local colleagues will quite naturally tend to become less interesting—or even unimportant. So, in these days of *Festreden* over the infinite blessings of internationalization, one should still remember the sobering words of Jürgen Mittelstrass regarding a dilemma that existed at least until quite recently: "there is nothing more international than modern elite research, and probably nothing more national than the European university systems."

One should also be aware of the fact that the internationalization euphoria, and the media exposure that frequently accompanies it, is not exclusively connected to elite- or cutting-edge research. The intensified international exchange has also opened the door to "unconventional" academic careers and research-related entrepreneurship, where "visibility" and "performance" have largely superseded documented and solid research achievements as viable "intellectual capital." There are numerous examples, in Sweden and elsewhere, of individuals and entire institutes who have chosen this alternate route to fame and fortune. If the international academic community is not prepared to combat this torrent of *Geschäft*, it runs the risk of irrevocably compromising the scholarly endeavor and lowering the scientific spirit.

Concerning the issue of excellence, or centers of excellence, the small European nations—and in research and science we are all small compared to the United States—must realize that if we are going to create real centers of excellence in research and research education, we can very seldom do so on a local or even national level. We have to think, behave, and act like MIT or UC Berkeley. To create genuine centers of excellence one has to look for competence, literally, everywhere. So, if my former university, Uppsala, decides to become a center of excellence in almost any field of study, nine times out of ten, only a minority of the researchers would—or should—come from Uppsala. This, together with the fact that the establishment of centers of excellence would require substantial resources, and put severe organizational, financial, and cultural pressure on the internal and national funding systems.

Finally, I would like to say something about rankings. In the course of the last two decades, various sorts of rankings, preferably in the form of league tables, have become a more or less regular, although still controversial, element in higher education and research policy. Regardless of the actual motives behind this worldwide deluge of rankings, there is hardly any reason for higher education representatives to moralize over the present state of affairs. Instead, it is high time that universities contemplate how their own negligence and irresponsibility have actually promoted or at least contributed to a situation where externally initiated rankings today are not merely viewed as news and information commodities, but are perceived as entirely legitimate and relevant evaluations of academic quality by an increasing number of societal actors, who—with or without justification—consider themselves to be legitimate stakeholders when it comes to deciding upon the size, quality, efficiency, resources, and missions of the higher education system.

What is the actual impact of rankings on higher education institutions so far? According to recent studies, the impact of rankings for the individual student's actual institutional and educational choice, for very good reasons, seems thus far to be extremely limited. The best guess put forward is that students from more privileged social strata (and their parents) probably have a more pronounced tendency to study the rankings than fellow students coming from more deprived socio-academic conditions. The same differences might possibly be observed between those students who have an international perspective, and those who have a local perspective in their educational choices. But with the gradual introduction of almost North-American Ivy League levels of tuition fees in some European countries, the impact of rankings might in time become quite palpable, and eventually play an increasingly important role when students, especially the ones coming from overseas, choose their institutional affiliation and academic career.

There are, however, at least three levels or areas of higher education and research policy planning where rankings have had an obvious and distinct impact: politics, university boards, and university leadership/management. When it comes to politics, I will only state as my firm conviction that the German *Exzellenz-Initiative* (or any other comparable European excellence scheme, for that matter) would probably never have come about without the impact of the Shanghai Jaio Tong- and Times Higher Education-rankings.

Not surprisingly, it seems to be university boards that are most likely to ascribe immediate policy relevance to ranking results. To a sometimes lay-dominated university board, often recruited from the quarterly-report-obsessed business sector or from the vote-seeking political sphere, and with often rather rudimentary knowledge of university life, changes in the ranking can be perceived as almost the only unambiguous and "objective" evidence of institutional success or decline. League tables then tend to become the bottom line in the "balance sheet" of the "company." Whenever a university board starts showing signs of unease, an insecure and academically weak university leadership is prone to feel pressed to take urgent and "radical" steps. Eventually, management-inclined university executives may be tempted to carry out relatively extensive and expensive "quick fixes," primarily in order to affect some simple but important rankings indicator, although such actions will have precious little, if anything at all, to do with the actual quality of teaching and research of the institutions. The effects with regard to the balance of power within the institution, on the other hand, may be pervasive and permanent.

Concluding Remarks and a Few Very Modest Proposals[2]

In my view, during the last three or four decades, the European higher education systems have undergone a process of disorientation, brought about by the confluence of several simultaneous cultural and intellectual, as well as economic and political, forces. The development in science policy, research organization, and higher education has also had a lack of focus and has actually led to a crumbling of the value system and self-confidence of the traditional European university. I would go so far as to compare the current period to that of the era of turbulence and decline that preceded the foundation and development of a university that gradually transformed virtually all universities, i.e. the creation of the so-called Humboldtian university.

Having stated this, I would nevertheless urge us all at long last, to take a definite if certainly affectionate and grateful farewell to Wilhelm von Humboldt, and instead turn for guidance to other, more recent authorities. We certainly do not need any more pompous declarations by European prime ministers or ministers of education, or even by representatives of the EAU, about the glorious future of the European universities in 20XX. Instead, we need to devote all our intellectual efforts, and a substantial portion of our economic and human resources, to rebuild our education systems in general, and our damaged higher education systems in particular.

In my opinion, the position and future development of the European university systems calls for rethinking on a systematic level comparable to what occurred in California in the 1950s and early 1960s, even if, as the Californians appear to feel, no fundamental change can ever be permanent. The California model, it is clear, is in trouble, but that does not mean that the issues it confronted are not issues that Europeans should be confronting today

One crucial message we should take away from the California Master Plan and its instigator Clark Kerr's vision is the urgent need to make a serious effort to figure out how quality universities, educating and training talented young people at the highest level, with support from the public purse and with rigorous critical standards, can be combined with a system of mass access to higher education. The crucial issues remain those of *system differentiation*. This means that we need to address the following questions: a) how do we construe a workable higher education system, that is, one that can adequately execute the steadily growing number of diversified tasks and obligations placed upon it?; b) how do we define the characters and number of institutions actually needed in each category or segment of that system?; c) how do we secure the continued existence and flourishing within this system of the delicate species called the research university with its particular qualities?, and d) how can we best fund and finance such a diversified system?

Without such reflection and planning, I fear that a research and educational system will eventually emerge that bears no resemblance to that particular and peculiar *Lebenswelt* that was the European research university for the last 150 years; the latter will sooner or later suffer from a gradual loss of creativity, competence and, in the end, legitimacy. In short, I would like to see a discussion of how the European university of the past may be *reconstituted* to serve the present by regaining its historical strengths—not by nurturing its obvious weaknesses.

The European governments and responsible ministers initiating such a long overdue discussion would certainly be worthy of our unreserved respect and praise. They would also have started the long and cumbersome road "back to business." The days of quick fixes and flashy one-liners in European higher education and research policy should definitely be over. Accordingly, it would perhaps be not only proper but even wise if concerned European actors in all sectors of academia and research policy planning reminded themselves of the academic sincerity, administrative ingenuity, political wisdom and, most especially, the intellectual and moral integrity that characterized the way and works of the late Clark Kerr. It would of course be both improper and even pointless to compare Professor Clark Kerr with Wilhelm *Freiherr* von Humboldt, but he is at the end of the day the closest we have come in the last century.

Notes

1. An extended version of an essay published in Knowledge Cultures 3(6) 2015.
2. Since I have seen no obvious reason to change my mind radically in the last year or so, this concluding passage is an almost verbatim quotation from Thorsten Nybom, "The Disintegration of Higher Education in Europe, 1970–2010: A Post-Humboldtian Essay" in Sheldon Rothblatt (Ed.) *Clark Kerr's World of Higher Education Reaches the 21st Century: Chapters in a Special History*. Springer, Dordrecht 2012, pp. 179–180.

PART FOUR

Regional Perspectives

Introduction

Across the world, nations are struggling to develop their higher education systems against the background of a number of challenges and pressures. *The challenges* include those of past colonial systems of government that either suppressed higher education or looked to it to develop elites who could be co-opted so as to maintain those regimes; dictatorships, who again were fearful of higher education or which, somewhat paradoxically, built it up but through a privatisation of higher education that worked in tandem with the economically powerful; a legacy of an underfunding of systems differentiated by class and ethnicity and lacking in a research capability; and the sheer expense of high-quality higher education systems at a time when there are so many other calls on the budgets of developing nations.

The pressures include those of a global knowledge economy in which developing countries face a prospect of an ever-weakened position; the emergence of world rankings of universities that tacitly seem to favour the already powerful nations; clamourings from within that higher education should manifestly be seen to be playing a significant part in social reconstruction; and the sheer need to invest in universities so as to support economic regeneration. This is a formidable set of challenges and pressures that play out differently in different regions of the world, depending on the historical, cultural, economic and geopolitical background.

The chapter by Assié-Lumumba offers a synoptic overview of Africa as a whole. The theme of colonialisation is strong but, perhaps not often realised, as the chapter observes, university systems in some parts of Africa can be traced back to two thousand years. The historical picture, therefore, is complex, with an interweaving of Arab and Islamic traditions with (later) Christian and Western traditions and then with colonial interests. Emerging from periods of colonisation, African universities found themselves in difficult situations. They tended to be educating small proportions of the population, and characteristically exhibited states of poor financial health and yet were faced with expanding demands that they were unable to meet.

Perhaps not surprisingly, the private sector of higher education—which includes both sectarian and secular institutions—has witnessed a massive expansion even during the start of the present century. These latter institutions, intent on securing their income base, have rarely shown an interest in the research function of universities. Consequently, issues of the public good and mission of Africa's universities constitute a huge practical and political matter; and raise in turn the further matter of university governance. But behind these issues lurk, too, the issues of the relationship between universities and the state: to what extent and in what ways can a nation's universities be brought explicitly to play their part in a country's development? Can a 'framework of partnership' be developed to which all universities can be seen to be making an active contribution?

The chapter by Guzmán-Valenzuela and Bernasconi offers another synoptic study but, here, of Latin America. Although not of the longevity of some African universities, it is nevertheless observed that Latin American universities have five hundred years of history behind them. Again, too, a dominant part of the story here is one of colonisation by European powers. An additional important concept is that of imperialism, such that the story of higher education in Latin America can be seen against the background of the 'north–south' relationships, markedly with the imposition of Western ideas of the university and evaluation systems. A yet further key concept is that of oligarchy, where society is dominated internally by elites. Latin American universities have, accordingly, often evinced a critical function in society, combating social inequalities and dictatorship regimes.

The story of Latin American universities is complex, and not only because of inevitable differences across countries. With independence from colonial powers, the state took on responsibilities for universities and so academic autonomy became a key issue. Subsequently, an era of reform emerged in which, notably, students acquired significant agentic powers of their own, marked especially by the Cordoba movement in 1918. More recently, a period of massification has ensued, made possible largely through the proliferation of private institutions, often during dictatorships (which have been more oriented to market models of public services). Perhaps unsurprisingly, Latin American universities remain especially characterised by inequalities of access and resources. Now, post-dictatorships, Latin American universities find themselves faced with globalisation processes, world rankings (in which these universities are largely invisible), and extreme forms of privatisation that have led—especially in Chile—to a new student protest movement. Accordingly, Latin American universities are on a cusp, on the one hand faced with calls to fall in with a global mantra of 'world-class universities' (and all that goes with such aspirations) and a desire to work out new models and ideas of the university that are appropriate to the region and its socio-economic-political struggles.

The chapter by Waghid and Davids focuses on South Africa, which makes for a fascinating case study of the playing out, in one nation, of matters of colonialisation, race, social transformation and citizenship. In the turbulent situation of South Africa, in which many expectations are invested in its universities, much is at stake. Not only is the 'emancipatory transformative discourse of the university' at risk but so too is the university's claim to advance social justice itself. Again, in South Africa too, we have seen students taking on agentic roles, in disturbing the social and political situation, not least in calling attention to the ways in which its universities continue to harbour or reflect forms colonialism but also in seeking fairer systems of finance and access to higher education.

Inequality, access and exclusion continue to be dominant themes in public and political debate over higher education in South Africa. But these issues play out against a wider horizon of concerns about, and interest in, the potential of South African universities to assist in the social reconstruction of the nation, post-Apartheid. Perhaps the largest concept present here is that of democracy. But more especially, so argue Waghid and Davids, critique, hope and imagination can also be powerful concepts in helping to reshape universities for the challenges that they and South Africa face. Here arises the idea of a 'positive risk', to identify possibilities, to struggle for a 'pedagogy of risk', in which universities might work for that which is, as yet, invisible.

Ronald Barnett

CHAPTER FOURTEEN

The Idea of the University in the Evolving Higher Education Landscape in Africa

N'DRI THÉRÈSE ASSIÉ-LUMUMBA

Introduction

With only a few exceptions, the oldest among the contemporary African universities are postcolonial institutions. These universities were conceptualized by the first generation of postindependence African leaders, beginning in the late 1950s. These universities were assigned the responsibility of training highly competent graduates to help propel African countries out of underdevelopment. In general, they strove to ensure excellence in the areas of teaching, research, and service. Although they apparently emulated the institutional traditions of the colonial powers and the industrialized world in general, national sovereignty was an important marker for these institutions.

More than half a century after the creation of postindependence universities, it is worth taking stock of their progression (Assié-Lumumba, Mazrui and Dembélé 2013). Among the questions to be addressed are: What has been the evolution of the thoughts, vision, and mission articulated by the leadership? What have been the changes, if any, in interest groups and the relative power and authority of the different agents in defining the domestic higher education policy? What have been the patterns of the relationships between the local and global dynamics?

In 1960, there were barely 100 higher education institutions that could be identified. As of 2015, there are nearly 1,500 colleges and universities (http://ranking.journalsconsortium.org, last accessed on October 19, 2015). There are various issues regarding the quality of the curricula provided to learners, and whether or not this positions learners and institutions well to appropriately participate in knowledge production. In spite of the seemingly big increase in the number of institutions, demand continues to outweigh supply across Africa. The growth in numbers also connotes an increase in the diversity of these institutions.

Remarkably, most universities immediately after independence had an almost exclusively public status. Currently, however, there has been an increase in the number of private universities, both secular and confessional. In most countries, there was usually one university while some countries had none. The earlier universities were also associated with extreme selective and elitist characteristics. Furthermore, they were located in urban settings, especially in the capital cities, often in particular neighborhoods with socioeconomic and sociopolitical features. In recent years, there have been growing numbers of universities in different neighborhoods in major cities, in smaller towns, and in rural communities. With the exception of the Ahfad University for Women in Sudan, a private women's university created in 1966, the earlier institutions were basically coeducational with a few de facto (by their enrollment patterns) and legally males' institutions. Recently, there have been a few colleges and universities for women in Kenya and Zimbabwe for instance. This adds to the complex set of indicators that reflect the changing landscape of institutions of higher learning in Africa. One of the main concerns in this chapter is how the new types of institutions relate to the postcolonial idea, public policy, and the role of the university in the national development agenda.

This chapter is a reflection on the evolution of higher education institutions in Africa with a focus on the universities. Using historical approaches, it analyzes the meanings of the university, starting with earlier experiences and then shifting focus to postcolonial Africa. The main focus is the analysis of critical questions related to the agency of the national authorities in framing the role of higher education institutions in the national development agenda. The chapter also critically examines the conceptualized, expected, and actual role of the university in framing and ensuring the fulfillment of the role of higher education.

The chapter is structured under three headings. The first section recalls the historical background of higher education in Africa to better locate the recent progression, and the nature of the issues involved. The second section discusses the idea of the university in the early postcolonial national development agenda. The third section critically examines the surge in demand, the emergence and escalation of neoliberalism, and the articulation of the new vision of policies of national development, as well as the treatment of higher education. Two dimensions of the implication of the liberalization and privatization will be analyzed as to how the idea of the university as an institutional instrument to promote a national development agenda has fared in the new context. The conclusion will wrap up the main arguments of the chapter.

Historical Background of Higher Education and Universities in Africa

The university is one category in a wide range of institutions of higher learning (International Association of Universities 1977). Of all of them, the university in its classical definition covers a wider scope of educational and societal missions. The information available in statistical data bases often does not disaggregate these institutions by type, but rather classifies them as tertiary or higher education institutions. However, it is only fair to argue that the university in Africa has experienced wide and profound changes that can be articulated within different historical moments. While these recent historical periods are defined within the colonial experience, it has been argued authoritatively that institutionalization of higher education in Africa has ancient indigenous roots in different socio-geographic spheres. As stated by Ajayi, Goma and Johnson (1996:4), it has been established "that indigenous education involved far more than an inward-looking process of socialization" and included an array of institutional arrangements from what could be considered basic education to the highest levels of learning. Century-old and newly unearthed evidences of these learning arrangements provide an indication that indeed "indigenous higher education produced and transmitted new knowledge necessary for understanding the world, the nature of man (sic), society, God and various divinities, the promotion of agriculture and health, literature and philosophy" (Ajayi, Goma and Johnson 1996:5).

Citing specific examples in Africa, it has been argued that "the roots of the University as a community of scholars, with an international outlook but also with responsibilities within particular cultures, can be traced back to two institutions that developed in Egypt in the last two or three centuries B.C. and A.D." with two models, namely the Alexandria model and the monastic system with complex and sophisticated knowledge production (Ajayi, Goma and Johnson1996:5, Lulat 2005). This earlier Egyptian case can be fully articulated only in the broader framework of the Nile Valley Civilizations organically connected to the Upper Nile regions, including Ethiopia. The old Alexandria model stands out in terms of its secular and religious components as well as its deep roots in a civilization of universal reach, while being nurtured primarily from the African land and intellectual contributions.

With the expansion and firm establishment of Islam in North and West Africa as well as on the Eastern Coast of the continent, new types of reputable higher education institutions were created by Islam within broader African cultural settings. These institutions included universities that were created, such as Karawiyyinn in Fez (Morocco) in 859 A.D., Al-Azhar in Cairo (Egypt) in 970, and Sankore in Timbuktu from the 12th century. Today, Al-Azhar is considered the "oldest continuously operating University in the world" (Arab Information Center 1966:282). In this context, the dissemination of learning led to the appropriation of key elements by the Africans. Of great significance was the transcription of African languages using Arabic (Hassane 2008, Kane 2011, Sy 2014). Ali A. Mazrui (2012:6) argues that:

> While Euro-colonial and post-colonial American branches have been important stages towards the emergence of the global university, we should bear in mind the real origins of the global university. Muslim Africa virtually invented the global university in its simpler form. The standing monuments to that Muslim African invention consist today of Al-Azhar University in Cairo and the Qarawiyin Center of Learning in Morocco, both of which are over a thousand years old. These two Afro-Muslim institutions are centuries older than Oxford and Cambridge in England, and certainly even more ancient than than arvard, Yale and Princeton.

These African Muslim institutions are also older than those created in Medieval Europe as sites of Western intellectual development. The Parisian elitist and selective model and subsequent development of Sorbonne was dominated by the Christian religious congregations, especially the Jesuits and Oratorians, while the Bologna model had a participatory framework where students played central roles.

A characteristic of the early "Afro-Muslim institutions" (Mazrui 2012:6) was their reliance on Arabic as the language of instruction. It was used directly or indirectly through Ajami in which an Arabic script was used to transcribe African languages (Hassane 2008, Kane 2011). As argued by Ousmane Kane in his book Non-Europhone Intellectuals (2011:23), "Arabic has been for many of the Islamized peoples the equivalent of Latin for the peoples of Western Europe, *mutatis mutandis*. Learned people in the Islamized world not only learnt Arabic and contributed to Arab intellectual history, but they appropriated the Arabic characters in order to promote their own languages."

The use of one language for broader intellectual pursuit was also a model used in early European universities, as Latin was first the predominant language until it was supplanted in the modern and contemporary periods by English. Through historical processes, English is today the dominant and still growing language in institutions of higher learning globally, even in countries that were not colonized by Great Britain. This is also the case of Ethiopia, which ironically has its own written languages including a lingua franca Amharic.

The other key characteristic is the centrality of religion. Initially, European universities extended the scope of education to provide specialized trades for the expanding and more complex economy in addition to Christian education. The early Afro-Muslim as well as Judeo-Christian–based European institutions had in common spirituality and morality as constituting critical importance in the education they conceptualized and provided. Institutions that grew from the European context were successful in expanding considerably their secular mission and components that have led to contemporary universities in Europe and their extension across the globe. The United States, through its economic hat, is now leading this development, thus translating into cultural dominance with formal education, and mainly higher education as the driving force.

However, the pioneering achievements on the African continent did not lead to substantive and robust intellectual development in the contemporary period. A wide range of disciplines of study and the transformation of the Afro-Islamic institutions into secular institutions of higher learning responding to the challenges of the modern period did not occur in any significant way. As a result, the overwhelming majority of the contemporary institutions of higher learning in Africa derive from the colonial experience as a European legacy and the impact of the European extensions, especially in North America, with the leading role played by the United States.

Ironically, in essence, the European establishment in Africa in the context of the 19th century/early 20th century colonial domination was incompatible with the development of higher education. Colonial policies of education had to be compatible with the colonial project that required total domination and control of the colonized. Even the proclaimed assimilationist French model (Assié-Lumumba 1984) was marred with contradiction that could not be resolved in favor of the colonized and the humanist ideal of equality. Assimilation in essence assumes equality of all populations under the assimilationist policy. However, under colonial rule, the citizens of the metropolitan country and the colonized under the native law did not enjoy equal rights. Higher education was historically, and by the time of early colonial rule, reserved for the nobility and the clergy destined to rule. In essence, higher education could not logically and practically be made available to the colonized, even under the French assimilationist policy. Through indirect rule, the British developed in their colonies institutions which evolved into postsecondary and even universities at the time of independence.

Indeed, in the British colonies, several colleges were created between the end of the 19th century and the 1920s. Pursuant to the studies and recommendations of committees and commissions including the British Advisory Committee on Education in the Colonies and the Phelps Stokes Commission, new appreciation of local demand led to future development of education in the British colonies. Gordon Memorial College in Khartoum (Sudan), Makerere Government College in Kampala (Uganda), Yaba Higher College in Lagos (Nigeria), Princess of Wales

School and College in Achimota (Ghana), and Fourah Bay College in Freetown (Sierra Leone) constituted the foundation of the institutions of higher learning that gradually evolved into universities around the time of independence.

The idea that higher education is an important factor in the development of nations is now embedded in the African social fabric and shared over several decades after the period of colonization. This was the rationale for holding the 1961 Addis Ababa Conference when the process of decolonization was still topical, while searching for the most effective means to achieve socioeconomic development. The centrality of education, especially university education in development, has been reaffirmed over more than six decades, as remarked by Teferra and Altbach (2003) and as reiterated by many (Bloom, Canning and Chan 2005).

Since the era of independence, the university has been conceptualized as central to national and continental development. The idea and its impact on the type of higher education and unity are analyzed next.

The University in the Colonial and Early Postcolonial Eras and the Agenda for Development

As indicated above, colonization and higher education in Africa constituted an oxymoron. Thus, for instance, despite the stated French assimilation policy and its proclaimed openness and universalistic reach, it took longer to introduce higher education in the French colonies than in the British. To understand the nature, types, and evolution of the development of higher education institutions in African countries today, the processes of their creation in the African contexts and the main features of the different colonial and cultural traditions, including some regional/inherited specificities, it is useful to provide an historical background of the new higher education landscape.

Egypt has a unique situation as, in addition to the earlier sophisticated institutions dating back to time of the Pharos, and home of the oldest running institution of higher learning, it was not colonized in a conventional way and earned relative autonomy between the two world wars while powers were consolidating their grip across the continent. Today, it has an estimated 127 universities and ranks second only to Morocco, which has 149 institutions of higher learning (http://ranking.journalsconsortium.org, last accessed on October 19, 2015).

Ethiopia has an exceptional history too, having averted colonization by defeating the Italians in 1896. Ethiopia built a solid foundation for its modern higher education system in the middle of the 20th century. The University College of Addis Ababa (UCAA) was established along with other smaller and specialized colleges that were merged into Haile Sellassie I University in 1961. While UCAA had American influence, it had a practice of no "commitment to any single foreign culture, system, or doctrine." Although the incorporation of different educational traditions and influences including American, British, and German, into a single institution created serious "problems of integration," at the same time "it offered rich opportunity to develop an Ethiopian institution under Ethiopian leadership" (Wodajo 1973).

Liberia was founded in 1821 by the American Colonization Society (ACS) with a direct involvement of the American government, to accommodate formerly enslaved Africans in America who wanted to return home. The country became independent in 1847 as the first modern state in Africa, especially in the context of restructuring by force of the political units that existed prior to the Berlin Conference. The Liberia College created in 1862 made Liberia the first African state to have the foundation of a Westernized higher education institution, which became the University of Liberia in 1951. The Episcopal Church created Cuttington College earlier in the 19th century, which experienced a dormant period until it reopened in 1949. Crippled for years by civil war, it is reviving its long tradition of higher education.

In the Democratic Republic of Congo (formerly Belgian Congo) and also Burundi and Rwanda (under the status of trusteeship territories administered by Belgium), there was a policy of mass enrollment at the basic level without any possibility for higher education (except students in seminary schools destined to become priests). While Portugal declared its colonies of Africa overseas territories in the1950s, it did not set up higher education institutions. Universities were created after independence in the mid-1970s.

In South Africa, the structural inequality of apartheid was reflected in the education system as a whole and particularly in the provision of higher education along racial lines. Universities for whites and/ or coloreds were well funded and continue to thrive in the 21st century, for example, University of Cape Town, University of Pretoria, University of the Witwatersrand, while the institutions for the Blacks were/are struggling. By and large, some of them are incorporating many innovations such as indigenous knowledge systems (IKS) in institutions such as the University of Venda.

For former British colonies in general, a policy for the use of African languages in the schools was discussed and in 1939, the Governors of West African colonies agreed on the creation of a West African university. They insisted on the importance of making sure that this institution (at Achimota) would be "West African in spirit and reality as well as in name, and not a mere colourless imitation of a British University" (quoted by Ajayi, Goma and Johnson 1996:52). It is important to note a contradictory component of the decision by the Governors as they requested that it be made a prerequisite that African universities be necessarily affiliated with one or several British universities to ensure quality for these institutions. If the British made such a request, it was a sign of the postcolonial dependence that would follow. This is important, as it became a key element in the dependency trap in the postcolonial era. As Ajayi, Goma and Johnson (1996:52) commented:

> How affiliation with a British University was to produce a University that was truly West African and no colourless imitation, was not explored. Perhaps they set it as a conundrum to put off their critics. Perhaps it was an admission that they had run out of arguments to defend colonial obstructions to educational development in the colonies.

Sierra Leone presented an interesting historical case with the historic "Freetown debate," in which James Johnson and Edward Blyden argued for a liberal-arts–classical education that would link contemporary Africa with ancient civilization and the period in which African achievement loomed large. Johnson and Blyden criticized the missionary education that they viewed as Eurocentric and limiting, in part because the content of education starting with the transatlantic enslavement did not offer any critical insight and was considered as rather defined by the "race poison" (Ajayi, Goma and Johnson 1996:20). Blyden also played a role in the development of Liberia College.

Following Italian occupation of Libya, British occupation expressed less resistance to the development of education at large, although enrollment was limited. The University of Libya (now Al-Fateh University), which grew out of colleges set up in the 1950s, was established after independence. However, the ongoing chaos since the invasion and assassination of Kaddafi in 2011 has left the institutions dysfunctional.

In the French colonies, by and large, offering higher education was not considered a possibility. Ajayi, Goma, and Johnson captured this situation when they stated that "for the Africans, the French policy aimed to leave the mass uneducated, and to groom a select few as évolués, co-opted as loyal upholders of French culture and colonial rule, encouraged to complete their education in France and to feel more at home in Paris than in Africa" (Ajayi, Goma, Johnson 1996:39). Even close to the independence period, only a few *Instituts des Hautes Études*, constituted a semblance of institutions of higher learning in very few locations, namely Dakar, Tananarive and Abidjan. In North Africa, the precolonial century-old universities (Ez-Zitouna in Tunisia and Karawiyyinn in Morocco) were not dismantled because of the religious power and authority vested in them, while a university such as the *Institut des Hautes Études* (Tunisia) created after the respective independence of these countries, only functioned "under the patronage of the University of Paris" and acquired its status as a university by decrees in 1960 and 1961 (Arab Information Center 1966:260), respectively.

This chapter does not cover the many problematic and outright destructive postindependence regimes that emerged in many dysfunctional African states ruled by tyrants. The point to be made here is that regardless of their actual records, all African leaders officially declared their commitment for socioeconomic development using education, especially the university, as the unavoidable institutional base for training the needed human resources. The independence euphoria that characterized African states embodied bold decisions toward self-rule, nation building, and socioeconomic development. This undertaking involved the establishment of universities that were run by African governments. Domatob (1996:29) articulates the nature of early postindependence universities as modeled after European universities, which developed organically in European-wide social structures and embodied their economic, political, and broader cultural contexts.

The role of formal education in Africa, especially higher education, was articulated within the framework of the national strategies of development at a time when several development theories—modernization theory, human capital theory, Marxist theory, dependency theory—were being articulated in industrial and other Third World countries. In Africa, there was a realization that formal education inherited from the colonial experience was the *sine qua non* for individual and collective advancement in the context of Europeanizing and further westernizing African societies. For the individual it was a guarantee for upward mobility. Private and social rates of return and correlation coefficients between education and earnings were calculated to support human capital theory. There is a memory as well as learned experiences from former colonial powers, as Crawley (2000:29) in "The Myth of a European Identity: the Role of the Universities in the Formation of European Citizens" explains, in the case of the role of universities in the formation of European citizens:

> The university is that place in our society where we come to an understanding of ourselves as individuals committed to specific projects within a community having a recognisable culture and a shared identity. This is the role, not so much for which the university was designed, but which it created for itself. From its origin in medieval society the university enacted a place to theorise the contingencies of the human situation, to assemble theory into the coherence and unity of science, and to initiate the next generation of scholars and citizens into the discourse appropriate to the engagements of society. Higher learning entails, in part, coming to see the commitment to individual projects as a form of participation in the expression and development of a society's culture.

While universities are considered to be repositories of values that may have universalistic dimensions, Clark (1983:250) points out that:

> In developing countries, the state wants from the higher education system: socioeconomic relevance defined in terms of practicality and professionalization, cultural relevance referring to cultural revival and national identity, and political relevance defined as good citizenship and commitment to political goals.

In analyzing the universities in the post-apartheid period, Higgs (2002) argues that it is misguided to define the role and mission of the university in utilitarian terms of economic development and nation building. For him the university provides service to society as "a community of reason." Waghid (2002) challenges this view as he considers that it is possible, and perhaps even necessary, for the university to remain "a community of reason" and at the same time play a social role in nation building.

Despite the discourses and policies, the African continent remains the world region with the lowest proportion of its predominantly youthful and university-aged population actually enrolled. Tapping into these population segments with rising demand, new agents have created universities that are neither owned nor managed by governments (Johnstone, Arora and Experton 1998:3). They include privately owned universities. Therefore, there is a changing landscape, which is an important issue about the nature of the new institutions and their roles in the national policies.

The Nexus of Demand and Neoliberal Turning Point: New Higher Education Landscape and the Imperative of National Agenda

In the history of the modern world, higher education institutions in a given societal context relate to the broader society in a dialectical framework. Thus, in one of his seminal works on universities, namely *Universities: British, Indian, African,* Eric Ashby (1966:3) stated:

> An institution is the embodiment of an ideal. In order to survive, an institution must fulfill two conditions: it must be sufficiently stable to sustain the ideal which gave it birth and sufficiently responsive to remain relevant to the society which supports it. The university is a medieval institution which fulfills both these conditions. The ideal—the disinterested pursuit of learning—which drew scholars to Oxford seven centuries ago still unites a guild of scholars in that city, and similar guilds flourish in hundreds of other cities. Yet the university has kept pace with the mutations of society; a college in California is as relevant to modern American society as the studium generale in ancient Paris was relevant to church and state in the Middle Ages.

African countries offer a multiplicity and complexity of national contexts for the functioning of educational institutions. In the past six decades, there have been generations of institutions corresponding to different moments: 1) euphoria of the early independence era and unquestionable belief in human capital theory; 2) double shock of the economic crisis and the anti-university stance of the international financial institutions; 3) the awakening and resurgence of demand; and 4) the acceleration of the liberal globalization, increasing demand, and the emergence of alternative institutions.

(1) *The euphoric belief in, and demand for, education supported by national stakeholders and international assistance in the 1960s and 1970s and the creation of African universities with public funding*: The notion of the caring state with the responsibility of promoting education as public good also helped actualize national development agendas. The universities were public with an overwhelming proportion of their revenues provided by the state (Negrao 1995). Many of them were national single-campus and multi-campus institutions that encompassed all the disciplines and fields of study. They also accorded considerable importance to research. Some countries like Côte d'Ivoire had positions for full-time researchers who taught only a few courses besides the professorial staff with more teaching responsibilities while also conducting research.
(2) *The shock of the economic crisis, subsequent policies of international financial institutions, and the decline by stagnation or decline in enrollment rates in many countries*: This new phenomenon was in sharp contrast with the educational expansion of the two previous decades. The latter experienced constant enrollment growth, although only a few of them (e.g., Congo, Tanzania) reached universal primary enrollment during those two decades. During this period, higher education in general was openly under attack by international organizations at that time, especially by World Bank and some industrial countries referred to as the "donor community." African universities were considered to be bankrupt and a source of development problems rather than an instrument promoting progress. Despite these critiques from various actors and institutions, it was not possible to dismantle the universities.
(3) *The renewed high demand at the national levels and stated commitment at the global level minus the economic resources of the first phase*: During this period, demand increased and the international institutions, led by the World Bank, reversed its position as illustrated by the 2000 joint task force with UNESCO on Higher Education and Society entitled *Higher Education in Developing Countries: Peril or Promise*. Ironically, some of their own shortsighted policies had been contributing to the increased demand as a result of their policies emphasizing basic education which increased the pool of university applicants. Families and students of modest origins realized

that education remained the main avenue in their aspiration for upward mobility.

The main issue to be tackled at that juncture was how and what institutional capacity to put in place to meet the high demand. This situation was unfolding in the broader context of the liberal globalization shaping institutions of higher learning.

From the late 1980s through the 1990s, new institutions were being created. Even countries that had previously engaged in expansion of their higher education systems, for instance in North Africa with the striking cases of Algeria and Morocco, had supply shortages. Beside the expansion of existing system a wave of new universities started. In the case of Mali, for instance, where the socialist regime of Modibo Kéita decided at independence to create specialized institutions of higher learning, but no university succumbed to the pressure, and so created by law in 1993 the University of Bamako with many subsequent campuses after it became functional in 1996.

Unlike in the first generation of postcolonial universities, many new universities had disciplinary foci, with various combinations of science, technology, and agriculture. A new critical factor was the tendency to expect these universities to respond to focused and sometimes narrowly defined labor market needs, with the expectations that they would help to meet human resource needs for the economy and that the graduates would achieve more easily desired socioeconomic attainments. Another type of institution in this period was the distance-learning university that had only three older versions, namely the University of South Africa (UNISA) created in 1946 and three postcolonial cases of Zimbabwe Open University and the Open University of Tanzania.

(4) The fourth historical moment was characterized by increased globalization and liberalization with the General Agreement on Trade in Services (GATS) of the World Trade Organization (WTO) policies and their impact on higher education (Gossa 2008). There have been implications of the liberal globalization and privatization of African higher education. One of the critical areas of concern is the challenge of pursuing the idea of the university as an institutional instrument to promote a national development agenda when the private component is increasing, as shown in Figure 14.1 below.

Even at the dawn of the 21st century, the proportion of the private institutions and student enrollment was still modest for most countries. The aggregate data for the continent captured in the Figure 14.1 show a general trend of increase amid

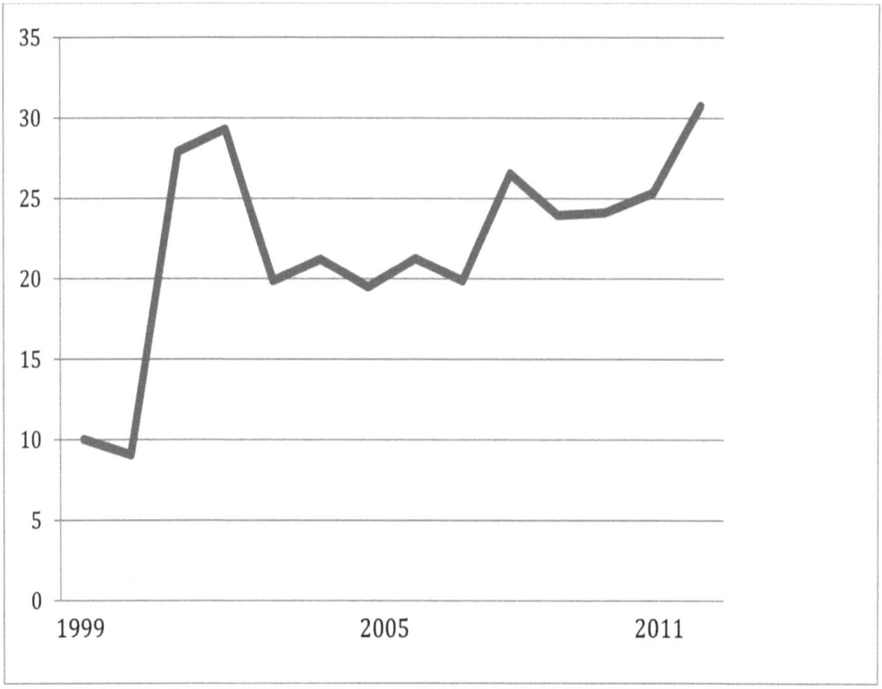

Figure 14.1: Percentage of Students Enrolled in Private Institutions of Higher Education: 1999–2011.
Source: Compiled from UNESCO Institute of Statistics, 1999–2011.

growing liberal globalization despite the critique as summarized in Economic Commission for Africa of the United Nations (1989:19):

> [T]he presumptive superiority of private over public enterprises has no theoretical foundation. There is also the incorrect assumption in the argument for privatization that the indigenous private sector is strong enough to take over state enterprises. In African countries, where this generally is not true, privatization could lead to the takeover of these public enterprises by transnational corporations, thereby deepening further their external dependence. What is worse is the substitution of the profitability criterion for the social welfare criterion in vital areas such as water supply in a continent where the majority of the population have no access to potable water.

The private universities include sectarian and secular institutions. Some of them are comprehensive while others are very focused and specialized in selected fields. It is the case with the University for Islamic Sciences of Constantine in Algeria with the interface of science and religion. It is also important to highlight

Table 14.1: Number of Religiously Affiliated Universities by Denominations.

Christian Denomination	N	Countries
Anglican	8	Kenya, Liberia, Nigeria, Tanzania, Uganda
Baptist	3	Ghana, Nigeria, Tanzania
Catholic	31	Angola, Cameroon, Congo, Ghana, Kenya, Malawi, Mozambique, Nigeria, Rwanda, Sierra Leone, South Sudan, Tanzania, Uganda, Zambia, Zimbabwe
Evangelical	9	Congo, Ghana, Kenya, Nigeria,
Inter-denominational	1	Kenya
Lutheran	2	Tanzania
Methodist	7	Angola, Ghana, Kenya, Liberia, Nigeria, Zimbabwe
Pentecostal	8	Ghana, Nigeria
Presbyterian	6	Ghana, Kenya, Malawi, Tanzania

Source: World Higher Education Database, International Association of Universities (http://www.whed.net/home.php).

that the surge of private institutions originating from religious institutions have a predominance of the various Christian denominations as shown in Table 14.1. They are often connected to broader global networks, hence are well funded and tend to exhibit relatively higher quality. Some of the religious-based universities form a new Islamic trend.

Public institutions can be local, regional, national (in single-state countries or in federal systems) institutions, or transnational. Private institutions can also have a similar basis of differentiation. Many other factors such as gender (coeducational versus single-sex institutions), the commonly called elite/selective versus popular institutions (directly or indirectly associated with social class) are important bases in the effort to find a typology of higher education institutions. Private institutions also encompass all these variables as well.

In recent years, eUniversities or open and mega-universities have increased. Some among these eUniversities consist of a dual mode in which distance learning is designed as a component of the regular face-to-face learning within traditional brick-and-mortar institutions, while an increasing number of single-mode programs of distance learning—for instance in open- and mega-universities—operate entirely as virtual institutions.

A new development worth mentioning is the emergence of rural/village universities, especially in East African countries such as Kenya and Uganda. However, questions about the quality of education have been raised. This rural phenomenon is in contrast to the urban institutions in the capital cities and most lavish neighborhoods of the earlier periods. A version of this was developed under apartheid.

A fundamental question regarding the raison d'être of the growing number of institutions of higher learning in Africa concerns the type of higher education institution in the quest for renewal of structural change toward social progress. For instance, earlier postindependence universities were expected to cover critical areas of their institutional and social mission including research. Knowledge production was part of the universities' programs. Even if the budget for research has been consistently negligible, the importance of research was at least acknowledged. Yet, one of the main features of the new private universities, specifically for-profit institutions, is the lack of incorporation of research in their programs and expectation of the teaching staff to conduct research.

In *Knowledge Matters: the Public Mission of Research Universities*, Diana Rhoten and Craig Calhoun (2011) argue that, as the title of the book indicates, research universities ought to be committed to the production of public good, including research, regardless of their legal statuses. It is interesting that Japan has been viewed by African countries in general as a model of socioeconomic success as, despite all its natural challenges, it rose to become the world's second most powerful economy and has been displaced by China only recently and still holds its third position. Considering these challenges and limited natural resources, Japan's stature has led to the reference to its achievements as a "miracle." Those who want to explain this success story in identifying the contributions of education as an investment tend to refer to the Meiji Restoration and the legal and actual treatment of education as a duty and a source for generating national wealth. The type of education and institutional priorities and mission are not always fully acknowledged and analyzed, particularly by political and educational leaders. However, one of the key policies in the Japanese goal of emerging to a prominent level concerned the role of research.

Philip G. Altbach and Jorge Balán (2007:vii) argue that "research universities are central to almost all the world's academic systems. … In the knowledge-based world of the 21st century, research universities are of great importance. Not all countries can afford 'world-class' universities, but most can—and must—have universities that fully participate in the world of research and development." Concerning Africa, Altbach and Balán (2007:2–3) assert that "Africa's traditionally strong universities are seeking to improve their quality in an effort to achieve research university status, with assistance from external funders, although it is, in general, behind levels of academic development on the other continents."

In *Providing Global Public Goods: Managing Globalization*, Kaul et al. (2003:Inside page of the front cover) articulate the notion of "the triangle of publicness" as "The first is *publicness in consumption*: is a good consumed by all? The second is *publicness in net benefits*: are the good's net benefits equitably distributed? The third is *publicness in decision-making*: who decided to place this good in the public domain?"

How can the private universities that derive from the liberal globalization help achieve these goals for the individuals, groups, communities and nation-states in Africa? In the case of Nigeria, Bako (2002) has argued that, considering about 212 higher education institutions then and accounting for half of the African university students with higher numbers of private universities, "the rather phenomenal but unplanned expansion of higher education in Nigeria in the past two decades has now landed the country into some intractable quagmire" (Bako 2002:1).

The fundamental question is ownership and consistency in designing domestic policies for higher education committed to the advancement of African societies and countries. There are examples of economically advanced countries in the world with major research universities of private status that play a vital role. Precisely in part because of their developmental missions, these institutions receive considerable amounts of public funds. In the United States for instance, many leading private universities receive huge amounts from the federal government and individual states through mega grants. However, considering the abject conditions of African countries, while they may contribute to some private universities, many others have financial autonomy that limit the state's authority and power as a central authority that shapes and controls national development agendas. The states in these situations are not in a position to influence these private institutions to make them respond to the national development agendas.

The institutions of higher learning, especially the universities, can play their central roles only within a national development framework. African institutions of higher learning are confronted by various aspects of the globalization phenomenon, especially with the agenda of the GATS, are set to speed up the process of guided internationalization of higher education institutions in the framework of liberalization. Ali Mazrui used the analogy of multinational subsidiaries when he articulated "The African University as a Multinational Corporation: Problems of Penetration and Dependency" (Mazrui 1975). Nevertheless, as contradictory as it may be, it was within the public universities that the idea and domestic policies were formulated. The African leaders were able to officially articulate the African university as an institution that must promote national development. However, the GATS and the new form of competition have been compromising the few spaces of relative autonomy of the African higher education institutions.

In the edited book *African Universities in the Twenty-first Century*, Zeleza and Olukoshi (2004) and the contributors articulate powerfully the negative aspects of globalization and of the fast-paced technological change in terms of their impact on

African universities and their institutional and societal missions to teach, produce knowledge that is relevant to the African societies, as well as to provide services toward social progress in Africa. There are new roles and missions that African institutions of higher learning must play to advance the national development agenda. They tackled the quandary of competing demands for, and effort to strike, a positive balance between Africanization/indigenization, while at the same time participating in the international and global scholarship. This is in part to promote equity while striving for excellence and efficiency toward equal opportunity and social progress. The questions addressed include what type of system can be imagined to structurally transform the existing institutions and creating more relevant ones within a new philosophy of education that can help meet the many challenges including increasing demand while fostering and sustaining social progress.

Conclusion

African higher education is in apparent need for reconceptualization as a public good. Such an articulation can be effective and meaningful only if the people and a caring state accomplish it on the grounds of domestication and ownership while forging constructive and empowering partnerships with the outside world. The national project requires agency and a framework within which the national and international institutions must function. Without a national agenda for development that institutions are required to support and contribute to actualize, African countries will again become new frontiers for activities without accountability and responsibility for the well-being of the people.

Private higher education institutions that are created in Africa with the sole purpose of making financial profit and/or advancing religious agendas, while meeting the high demands may not help advance the major national policies of development that require concerted coordination for structural transformation. Within national frameworks, new tools such as the information and communication technologies can be fruitfully used and contribute to achieving new goals of social progress.

Some institutions make genuine efforts to addressing the numerous challenges. And many institutions, especially the secular ones, are subsidized by the state partly in recognition of their contributions in addressing, for instance, the issue of basic access. However, numerous issues that are generated by the rise of private universities constitute hindrances to national development. Besides not supporting research, there are issues regarding the disciplines that are offered in relation to the present and projected job market. Issues of questionable quality and lack of equivalency agreements for the diplomas and certificates, the type of gender representations, and so forth, are of critical importance. A framework of partnership within the national development agenda may contribute to enhancing their complementary role. Some may even play leading roles as models. It is the case of institutions such as Ashesi University College in Ghana, among many others, considering institutional philosophy, curriculum and sheer excellence.

Despite their constraints, many public universities that survived the difficult period of the previous decades are also involved in innovations and transformative changes. The national development project still requires coordination and national policies that the operating institutions must take into account so that the substantial change in the landscape of African universities can translate into partnership for social progress.

References

Ajayi, J. E. A., Lameck K. H. Goma, G. Ampah Johnson; with a contribution by Wanjiku Mwotia. 1996. *The African Experience with Higher Education.* Accra: The Association of African Universities; London: James Currey; Athens, Ohio: Ohio University Press.

Altbach, P. G. and Jorge Baláneds. 2007. *World Class Worldwide: Transforming Research Universities in Asia and Latin America.* Baltimore: Johns Hopkins University Press.

Arab Information Center. 1966. *Education in the Arab States.* New York: Arab Information Center.

Ashby, E. in association with Mary Anderson. 1966. *Universities: British, Indian, African; a Study in the Ecology of Higher Education.* Cambridge, MA: Harvard University Press.

Assié-Lumumba, N. T. 1984. Colonialisme et Assimilationisme: la Politique Educative de l'Administration Coloniale Française en Afrique. Paper presented at the 5th World Congress of Comparative Education, Paris, France.

Assié-Lumumba, N. T., Ali A. Mazrui and Martial Dembélé. 2013. The Owl of Minerva on a Baobab Tree, Schooling, and African Awakening: Half a Century of Post-Colonial Education for Development in Sub-Saharan Africa. Special issue of *African and Asian Studies* 12: 1–2.

Bako, S. 2002. Union, State and the Crisis of Higher Education: The Latest Phase of Struggle for and against Restructuring and Deregulating the Nigerian Universities. Paper prepared for the 10th CODESRIA General Assembly taking place in Kampala, Uganda 8–12 December.

Bloom, D., D. Canning, and K. Chan. 2005. Higher Education and Economic Development in Africa. Research Commissioned by the World Bank (AFTHD), http://www.worldbank.org/afr/teia/Higher_Education_Economic_Growth_in_Africa.pdf

Clark, B. 1983. *The Higher Education System: Academic Organization in a Cross-national Perspective.*

Crawley, F. P. 2000. The Myth of a European Identity: the Role of the Universities in the Formation of European Citizens. In F. P. Crawley, P. Smeyers, and P. Standish (eds.) *Universities Remembering Europe: Nations, Culture, and Higher Education.* New York: Berghahn Books.

Domatob, J. K. 1996. Policy Issues for African Universities. *Issues*, 24.

Economic Commission for Africa (ECA). 1989. *African Alternative Framework to Structural Adjustment Programmes for Socio-Economic Recovery and Transformation (AAF-SAP)*. United Nations, Economic Commission for Africa.

Gossa, Jose. 2008. *Power, Politics, and Higher Education in Southern Africa: International Regimes, Local Governments, and Educational Autonomy*. Amherst, NY: Cambria Press.

Hassane, M. (2008). Ajami in Africa: The Use of Arabic Script in the Transcription of African Languages. In Sahamil Jeppie and Souleymane Bachir Diagne (eds.), *The Meanings of Timbuktu*. Dakar: Council for the Development of Social Science Research in Africa, 109–121.

Higgs, P. 2002. Nation Building and the Role of the University: A Critical Reflection. *Southern Africa Journal of Higher Education*, 16 (2).

International Association of Universities. 1977. *Differing Types of Higher Education*. Paris: International Association of Universities.

Johnstone, D. B., A. Arora, and W. Experton. 1998. *The Financing and Management of Higher Education: A Status Report on Worldwide Reforms*. Washington, DC: World Bank.

Kane, O. 2011. *Non-Europhone Intellectuals*. Dakar: Council for the Development of Social Science Research in Africa.

Kaul, I., et al. (eds). 2003. Providing *Global Public Goods*: Managing *Globalization*. New York: Published for the United Nations Development Programme [by] Oxford University Press.

Lulat, Y. G.-M. 2005. *A History of African Higher Education from Antiquity to the Present: A Critical Synthesis*. Westport, Connecticut and London: Praeger.

Mazrui, A. A. 1975. The African University as a Multinational Corporation: Problems of Penetration and Dependency. *Harvard Educational Review*, 45: 191–210.

Mazrui, A. A. 2012. From Euro-Colonial Colleges to the Global University: Transitions in Muslim ad African Experience (second Draft). Paper written at the invitation of the International Institute of Islamic Thought, Herndon, Virginia. U.S.A.

Negrao, J. 1995. *Adequate and Sustainable Funding of African Universities*. Accra: Association of African Universities.

Rhoten, D. and Craig Calhoun. 2011. *Knowledge Matters: The Public Mission of the Research University*. New York: Columbia University Press.

Sy, J. H. 2014. L'Afrique, Berceau de l'**Écriture.** Et ses manuscrits en peril, Des origines de l'écriture aux manuscrits anciens (Egypte pharaonique, Sahara, Sénégal, Ghana, Niger). Paris: l'Harmattan.

Teferra, D. and P. G. Altbach. (eds.). 2003. *African Higher Education: An International Reference Handbook*, Bloomington: Indiana University Press.

Waghid, Y. 2002. Rationality and the Role of the University: A Response to Philip Higgs. *Southern Africa Journal of Higher Education*, 16 (2).

World Higher Education Database, International Association of Universities, http://www.whed.net/home.php

Zeleza, P. T., and A. Olukoshi. (eds.). 2004. *African Universities in the 21st Century. Volume 1: Liberalisation and Internationalisation*. Dakar, Senegal: CODESRIA.

CHAPTER FIFTEEN

The Latin American University

Past, Present and Future

CAROLINA GUZMÁN-VALENZUELA AND
ANDRÉS BERNASCONI

Introduction

The first universities were established in Hispanic America barely half a century after Columbus landed in Hispaniola. Since then, thousands of universities have opened, evolved, prospered or withered, some ceasing to operate, responding both to local developments and worldwide intellectual currents concerning the idea of the university. Thus, even the newer Latin American (LA) universities are steeped in history, their structures, functions and missions shaped by local, regional and global structural forces that include political, cultural, social and financial features. Long hatched tendencies, as well as sudden events became milestones that have projected their influence across different countries creating a kind of 'domino effect' in the region across the centuries.

Thus, although LA universities retain a rich diversity in governance structure and control, funding schemes, mission and scope of activity, they share a common historical background and tend to be linked to each other by the influence some of them exert over the higher education field as a whole. In effect, the most prestigious of these universities have, through their discourse and action, created patterns followed by other universities in the region even into the present age. While these patterns of discourse and action encompass various themes and motifs, crucial mainstays have been the involvement of the university in national politics, their leading role in construction and critique of ideology, and the struggle to preserve their autonomy notwithstanding their profound participation in the political life of their nations and the ideological disputes that colour them.

This chapter stresses that which LA universities have in common, both in their historical roots, and the ideas about the university as an institution that nowadays predominate in shaping their identities and missions. We are mindful, however, that universities in LA are many and diverse, and that commonalities discussed here may give the impression that there is more homogeneity than really exists. This is not our intention, but we cannot give much space to differentiation in a work devoted to common features. However, there is one very consequential source of diversity in LA higher education since the late nineteenth century which deserves mention at the outset: the private or public nature of the university (Levy, 1986; Bernasconi, 2008). Not only are public universities different from private universities in many aspects discussed here, but diversity also exists within the private and the public sectors of higher education in LA. Typically, however, when 'the Latin American university' is discussed as a construct, it is the subsector of the large public universities, the national 'flagships', that serves as the source of the evidence on which generalizations are made.

We will, in all likelihood, be guilty of the same sin, as this chapter is based on secondary sources which overwhelmingly rest on the histories and present situation of the public national universities. We therefore hasten to warn that what we will describe here as representing the university in LA pertains mostly to public universities, especially the older, most prestigious ones, which occupy the apex of their national systems of higher education and from that position influence the rest.

Building an identity of LA universities: ideologies and historical processes

The LA university has been building its identity through a differentiating process that throughout the early nineteenth century involved the rejection of colonialism (Jiménez, 2007). The concept of *colonialism* is understood here in a broad sense, namely, as a process through which a dominant culture or country imposes its political, religious, financial, cultural, etc. system to other regions or countries. As we will see, the LA university resisted initially the heritage of the Catholic Church and the Spanish monarchy and, currently, partakes in the critique of a globalization based on neo-liberal ideas and policies.

A second concept that helps us to understand the construction of the LA university is the concept of *imperialism* (Bodenheimer, 1971; Larraín, 2000). Imperialism involves a process of division between capital and work through which some groups, countries or regions hold the major part of the capital (money, privileges, social and cultural capital, best qualified jobs and so on) to the detriment of other groups that suffer from exploitation and impoverishment. In the literature, it is usual to refer to the concept of imperialism as the 'north–south' domination (Petras, 1990; Quijano, 1993; Connell, 2007; Mignolo, 2013; Brunner, 2013; de Sousa Santos, 2014). Imperialism involves the binomial dominant-dominated that, in the case of LA universities, is reflected in the dominance of a western model of the university (Acosta, 2002): in the past, the Spanish colonial model, then the French Napoleonic idea, and currently, a model coming from the United States and Europe based on the notion of a 'world class' university (Altbach, 2004; Salmi, 2009; Altbach & Salmi, 2011).

A third concept useful for our analysis is the concept of *oligarchy*. Oligarchy, as imperialism, involves domination, but in this case, by some elites usually associated with wealthy and powerful political groups within a country or region. The oligarchical structure of societies in LA has led to permanent internal fights between social classes in LA countries (Larraín, 2000; Keen & Haynes, 2012) which have given birth to revolutions (for example, in Cuba or Mexico). These political processes have had an impact upon the university—especially public ones—which have often given birth to or harboured revolutionary or leftist political parties and social movements, protected persecuted dissidents, challenged dictatorships, educated political leaders and strengthened trade unions (Arocena & Sutz, 2005).

It is also possible to distinguish historical stages or cycles that describe the becoming of the LA university (Albornoz, 1986). The concept of historical cycles denotes connected elements: an event or process that takes place in an interval of time, which repeats itself several times, and so becomes a pattern. According to Albornoz (1986), there are three historical stages in the LA university: repression, expansion and contraction. These three stages are not always consecutive and respond to structural powers. The stage of *repression* involves the imposition of an authoritarian model, for example, during the colonial period, then during several dictatorships in the region, or nowadays, when a model of a marketized university jointly with public policies inspired by the New Public Management strengthen the executive power of presidents or rectors to the detriment of collegial government (Acosta Silva, 2009; Ordorika, Martínez & Ramírez, 2012). The stage of *expansion*—that includes the development and growing of universities in the region—has taken place in several moments of history, slowly during the colonial age and after independence, but with breakneck speed since the 1970s, when the massification of the university occurred as a global phenomenon. Finally, the stage of *contraction*, from a financial point of view (Albornoz, 1986; Didriksson et als, 2008), refers to the retreat of the state and the decrease of public funds in the mix of resources available for universities. Most contemporary universities in the world—and not only in LA—are experiencing this stage in parallel with a growing privatization of the sector (OECD, 2014).

In the following sections, we will describe the diverse periods through which the LA university has passed and which show the historical stages described above, as well as the ideals of autonomy that the LA university has tried to maintain during its history.

The colonial period: initial contests to gain autonomy

The way universities developed during the colonial period can be retrospectively read as a first instance of a pattern of universities challenging external models of governance and organization.

Historically, most of what we now know as Latin America was under the regime of the Spanish crown, closely connected to the Catholic Church (Arocena & Sutz, 2005), for around three centuries, from the beginning of the sixteenth century until the beginning of the nineteenth. The connection between the Spanish crown and the Catholic Church framed a political-religious role of universities in Latin America (Jiménez, 2007) with consequences spanning to the present. Indeed, universities in LA required acts of establishment from both the Pope and the Spanish king to be legally founded.

Initially, in the sixteenth century, the Spanish crown organized the government of America in two vice-royalties 'virreinatos', which were territorial, financial and administrative entities representing the Spanish crown in the new lands: New Spain (comprised, broadly, by Central America and Mexico) and Peru (comprised by the territories in South America). Later, in the eighteenth century, two new vice-royalties were established: New Granada or Santa Fe, currently, Venezuela, Colombia, Ecuador and Panama) and River Plate (Virreinato del Río de la Plata), currently, Argentina, Paraguay and Peru. The three oldest universities in the region were linked to the first two vice-royalties[1]: the Universidad Santo Tomás de Aquino (founded in Santo Domingo, currently the capital of the Dominican Republic, in 1538) which disappeared at the beginning of the nineteenth century, the Universidad Mayor Nacional de San Marcos (established in Lima, Peru, in 1551)—known then as 'Universidad de Lima', and the Royal and Pontifical University of Mexico (created in 1551). All three universities were run by the Catholic Church through different religious congregations (Dominican and Franciscan). Their model was Spain's University of Salamanca.

By the end of the colonial era, there existed some 25 universities in LA, and many more seminaries (Levy, 1986: 29). Over time, Catholic congregations lost power as secular members of the university strengthened their influence. Particularly, academics set up a process of secularization of the Universidad de Lima that represented the search for autonomy through which secular rectors, jointly with both academics and students, sought the governance of the university. Independence from Spain (or Portugal, in the case of Brazil) was achieved by the newly formed countries at different times between 1810 and the mid-1820s. During the nineteenth century, most of the colonial universities were turned into state universities, purging from them the religious mission and most of the clergy. A few disappeared, and fewer still remained operating as Catholic universities. Additionally, some of the new republics established state universities from scratch. The inspiration for these reformed or new institutions was no longer service to the church and the colonial bureaucracy, but the training of the professional and technical cadres required for nation building, following the Napoleonic idea of the Imperial University as a branch of the public administration for service to the state.

This idea, of course, clashed with the notion of university autonomy. It is precisely the value of autonomy that would become a banner of reform movements at the beginning of the twentieth century, as will be discussed in the next section.

First decades of the twentieth century: the emergence of student movements

The years between 1908 and 1929 are considered as 'the years of the university reform in Latin-America' (Van Aken, 1971; Marsiske, 2004: 161). Students were key in this reform (Van Aken, 1971; Arocena & Sutz, 2005). University reforms in Uruguay began with student pressure in 1908, and an important student movement in Córdoba, Argentina, in 1918, had impact over the following decades on universities as far away as Mexico and Cuba. To some extent, all ensuing national university reform movements were connected to ideals of university autonomy and political nationalism first articulated during these formative years of the LA model of the university (Marsiske, 2004; Bernasconi, 2008). Since then, in LA countries, universities have become important spaces for the political formation of students and the development of political ideas and cadres (Van Aken, 1971) who have promoted the modernization of the university and have fought against the predominance of certain groups of power and social classes.

The Córdoba University student movement was a crucial milestone. Students pursued co-governance of the university (by academics, students and graduates) in order to guarantee the modernization of the university, seeking pedagogical, professional and scientific renovation through processes which we, nowadays, would consider as quality assurance. At the same time, ideals of democracy, academic freedom, widening participation and social responsibility were important components of autonomy as defined by reformers.[2] The Córdoba Manifesto (Van Aken, 1971) became an ideological expression of students' claims and it included their main demands. Student strikes had such an impact in Argentina that they led to a legal reform that welcomed students' demands. Something similar happened in Peru where legal reforms originated after student protests promoted university autonomy through student participation in governance processes, academic freedom and non-mandatory class attendance. In Peru, students' movements were, further, linked to working-class political parties who fought against the oligarchy. One strategy lay in the creation of popular universities open for working-class citizens.[3]

In Mexico, the university reform was different as it was crossed by the Mexican Revolution that struggled against aristocracy—another expression of oligarchy—and in favour of the working and rural classes. In this context, the Mexican university led processes of literacy aiming to bring the university closer to the working classes. In 1929, a student strike put on the table the issue of autonomy in processes of examination. This strike was the precursor of a national legal modification that freed the universities from state control.

In Cuba, student movements antagonized political and social powers to promote social change. In this country, again, there was a link between student movements and political parties close to the working classes and the Communist Party. An important issue here was the struggle against imperialism and the influence of the United States that crystallized in a conflict between students and university authorities when the latter awarded a representative of the American President a *honoris causa* degree. Subsequently, students demanded autonomy of the university in financial, political and administrative terms. Another outcome of the university reform in Cuba was the creation of popular open universities for working classes.

So far, in this section, we have described a diversity of processes of activism and resistance led mainly by university students. These processes sought university autonomy through different expressions, but all of them understood autonomy as self-governance in academic, financial and administrative matters. Probably, the student movement was the purest in Argentina, in the sense that it was not explicitly crossed by political parties and union fights. Meanwhile, in Peru, Mexico and Cuba, there was a kind of blending of interests and agendas coming from the university with others carried by trade unions and left-oriented parties.

The 1980s and 1990s: a convulsed period

In this section, we will briefly examine a more recent historical period characterized by diverse elements that have had an impact upon the LA university and that simultaneously illustrates the stages of repression, expansion and contraction identified by Albornoz (1986); a sequence that comprises the massification of the university, the backlash from the generalized irruption of military dictatorships in the region and the resistance of universities against them, the financial crisis of the 1980s, and the globalization of the university in current times (Acosta, 2002).

Massification

Following global processes of mass access to universities in the 1960s and 1970s in the western world, many higher education systems in the LA region went from elite to mass enrolments. Public universities in countries such as Argentina, Mexico and Brazil expanded considerably to become 'mega universities' (García-Guadilla, 2003),[4] as institutions with enrolments over 100,000 are known in the region. Partly due to the impossibility of the public system to absorb the soaring demand for higher education, the private sector expanded and strengthened (Villanueva, 2010).[5] The private sector in most countries in the region has been growing exponentially (Didriksson et als, 2008), especially in Brazil, Colombia, Chile, El Salvador and the Dominican Republic, facilitated by lax regulations and the absence of planning that has begun to be addressed only recently (Villanueva, 2010). The case of Chile—with over 80% of private funding in the overall expenditures for the higher education system (OECD, 2014)—is particularly interesting since it has become an outlier in the privatization of the higher education system in OECD countries, where the average of private expenditure in higher education is approximately 30%, the rest coming from the state (OECD, 2014).

Nevertheless, mass access and the creation of thousands of new private universities since the 1980s in the region have not redressed the equality deficit typical of LA societies. Higher education has become as socially segmented as the nations they serve. It is possible to distinguish, for example, elite and prestigious universities on the one hand (research-oriented and predominantly public, together with older, consolidated private universities) and second or third tier universities (mainly new private, teaching-oriented universities, although some public universities with the same profile also exist) on the other. And this segregation leads to a phenomenon of inverted poles in which tuition-free public universities are selective and elitist and usually receive students of affluent classes who have the upper hand in the competitive admission processes by which students are selected, while some private universities receive mainly students of lower classes whose families assume the financial burden[6] (Villanueva, 2010).

Dictatorship regimes

Since independence, LA countries have been a favourite stage for military coups and dictatorships, but in the decades of the 1970s and the 1980s these regimes received more attention and analysis probably because of their repressive violence and consequences in the political landscape. Countries such as Argentina, Bolivia, Brazil, Chile, Ecuador, El Salvador, Guatemala, Haiti, Honduras, Nicaragua, Panama, Paraguay, Peru and Uruguay were shaken by military regimes, usually favouring nationalistic discourses and right-wing agendas. In some of these countries, universities acted as important counter forces, especially through the action of academics and mobilized students. Lest it appears as if universities always took the way of martyrdom in the face of repression, it has to be pointed out that silence and accommodation were also found as reactions to *de facto* regimes.

In general, the social sciences and the humanities were hit hardest. Academics suspected of leftist leanings were purged from the university and forced to seek exile. Some were killed. Universities were required by the military rulers to ensure their compliance with the new regime. Autonomy was obliterated and universities became battlegrounds between the military regimes and their resistance. By the 1990s, democracy had been restored throughout the region, but this change in the political landscape did not bring the hardships of universities to an end: the economic crisis of the 1980s had left them impoverished and further behind in capital investment and faculty salaries.

Financial crisis and greater regulation

In the aftermath of the financial crisis—the 'lost decade' of Latin America in the 1980s (Easterly, 2001; Saxonhouse & Stern, 2003)—discourses of quality assurance as well as accountability were driven by the UNESCO and the World Bank around the world not only in the higher education system but also in the primary and secondary levels of education. In the region, after a period of political instability in the 1970s and 1980s provoked by several coups d'état and a severe economic recession, states initiated a period of rationalization of public resources and, along with that, processes of evaluation and accountability were implemented (Acosta, 2002).

The 1990s are known as 'the decade of evaluation' in universities in LA (García-Guadilla, 2003; Acosta, 2002; Villanueva, 2010). During this period, most of the countries of the region introduced legal reforms to regulate the higher education system, established accreditation agencies (Chile, El Salvador and Colombia, for example) or quality evaluation systems (Argentina, Brazil, Mexico, Costa Rica and Cuba), and set up new institutions to administer funds for scientific research and to generate information on the systems (Bernasconi, 2008). All these evaluation mechanisms were oriented to improve quality, especially in undergraduate programmes, but were not oriented to a more ambitious rearrangement of the higher education systems (Acosta, 2002, 2009; Ordorika, Martínez & Ramírez, 2012).

Processes of globalization

In the 1990s, the LA University was also influenced by discourses and practices of globalization, internationalization, technologization (and the growth of both virtual undergraduate and postgraduate courses, as well as virtual universities), and commercialization of knowledge and research capacities in an era of financial and economic growth, with several international agreements for commerce such as the Mercosur and the 'Free Trade Area'. As a result, there was an explosion in the offer of postgraduate degrees as well as the creation of research networks with Europe (such as the Alfa and Columbus programs). At the same time, there were several publications and conferences dedicated to analyse and compare the higher education systems across Latin America, especially regarding research (Brunner et al., 1994; Kent, 1997).

Despite these efforts of articulation and organization in the region, there have been disparate developments of the university in diverse countries as well as different strategic missions and actions that make it difficult to compare cases and establish generalizations. This disparity can be seen when analysing, for example, the cases of Brazil, Chile and Colombia, in contrast to countries such as Venezuela and Argentina. Universities in the former countries show receptiveness to the horizon of world-class universities, and seek to strengthen their research capabilities and output, while universities in the latter countries seem to continue to be heavily involved in national politics that have instrumentalized the university and may have distracted it from attention to their main tasks, namely, teaching and research.

The era of the marketized university and its discontents

The marketized university (Molesworth, Scullion & Nixon, 2011) represents a contemporary prevailing global model of the university. The marketized university is an entrepreneurial university (Clark, 1998, 2004; Etzkowitz, 2004) strategically impelled to generate income and produce marketable outcomes in a context of privatization of the higher education system, competition and the retreat of the state (Acosta, 2002; Guzmán-Valenzuela & Barnett, 2013a, 2013b). There are two milestones here that we want to analyse briefly: the Chilean student protests on the one hand, and a reluctance to identify with academic rankings on the part of academics on the other. Both show the rejection, by sectors of academics and students, of global models in force in the international setting that respond to neo-liberal practices and academic capitalism (Slaughter & Leslie, 1997, 2001; Slaughter & Rhoades, 2004; Rhoades & Slaughter, 2006).

The Chilean students' movement

Processes of massification together with the configuration of a highly selective system at the top, which produced a segmented higher education system, with a few elite universities providing for their graduates the best employment opportunities and social prestige, along with institutions of dubious educational quality having a feeble impact on the social mobility of their graduates (Albornoz, 1986), became a breeding ground for student discontent. In Chile, the year 2011 became a milestone in the history of the higher education system, with immediate impact on the student-led neutralization of the Colombian government higher education reform initiative the same year, and ripple effects on several other countries in the region. The Chilean protest movement was a result of the privatization of the higher education system and the perception of poor quality of education in both state and private universities, partly as a result of an inadequate state regulation system (Guzmán-Valenzuela, 2016). Students claimed 'free access to the university and an education of quality for everybody' (Bernasconi, 2012, 2014; Espinoza & González, 2012; Bellei, Cabalin & Orellana, 2014).

As a consequence of this movement, a reform agenda has been brought forward in the Chilean Congress by a newly elected government (Bernasconi, 2014). Before her election, President Bachelet was under pressure to attend to student demands, and her willingness to make room for them in her election plank was a key factor in the new government's electoral success. It is interesting to notice that the Chilean student movement was echoed especially in countries with high rates of privatization in the higher education system, such as Colombia, Mexico and Brazil. It also received media attention in other OECD countries with high levels of privatization in the higher education sector, especially the United States, or where tuition fees are a hot political issue, such as the United Kingdom.

The rejection of rankings and the underlying world-class university model

In 2012, in an annual meeting in Mexico supported by UNESCO, a statement was issued by a group of rectors of LA universities grouped in UDUAL (The Union of Latin American Universities, an association of the region's most recognized public universities, and some well-regarded privates) to the effect that academic rankings are not valid in evaluating performance in universities in Latin America because any set of performance indicators will be appropriate in some but not all countries (Bernasconi, 2013). The LA rectors considered that the dominant rankings were inadequate in measuring performance in relation to 'those responsibilities and tasks that are beyond those traditional ones in Anglo-Saxon universities'.[7] They added that these rankings are distant from the LA context since they are based on productivity indicators linked to Thomson Reuters and Scopus indexes, with most of them published in English and in the disciplines of the 'hard' sciences. Rankings are considered by the rectors present in this meeting to be part of a model of the university that is being imposed upon the region, which, in the end, can be seen as a renewed form of ideological colonization.

The paucity of LA universities in the first several hundred positions in international rankings shows that LA universities are having problems in competing with global universities and in adapting to a world-class model that is predominant in the contemporary global university system. There are several factors that are present here and that point to various deficiencies (Bernasconi, 2013): lack of proper financing from state funds; insufficient academic preparation among faculty, especially as measured by the proportion of academics who have earned a doctorate and academics who can obtain and conduct competitive research projects, and the scarce limited capability of academics in using English to publish their research findings in a way that facilitates publication in international journals (Guzmán-Valenzuela, 2017).

Nevertheless, there are different positions being taken in regard to this world-class university model both across the region and among universities within a particular country. In some universities in countries such as Chile, Brazil and Colombia, there is an emerging model of a research university with a new generation of scholars educated abroad, pushing for internationally valid research, as opposed to the LA scholarly tradition of publishing scholarly essays without peer review (Balbachevsky, 2015). The few research-capable universities stand out above the others and usually conduct most of the research in the country and receive the majority of the public research funds. They, or their most internationally embedded academic units, have chosen to follow the world-class university model. A large majority of universities in the region, though, oppose this model because they have neither the financial resources nor the human capabilities to embark on this venture. The stand a university takes in this matter depends largely on the profile of its faculty. Teaching-only institutions see the notion of a world-class university flying way above their heads. Universities populated by academics who interpret research as the publication of learned essays in non–peer-reviewed books and journals denounce indexing and citation counts (unavailable to their scholarship) as Yankee imperialism.

In search of the Latin-American University: looking at the past to project a future

LA universities have played an important role across the history of the continent not only in developing a doctrine of autonomy for themselves but also in developing political transformations both nationally and in the region. LA universities have been trying to keep at bay external powers in order to govern themselves and, at the same time, have been participating in wider political processes that have helped to change the political landscape of their countries. Both actions (inwards and outwards) have a combative stance that encloses a paradox: the university reclaims the right to intervene in national politics as it sees fit, but it resists the attempts of governments—democratic governments these days—to dictate higher education policy. There are even those who would oppose any such form of accountability to society at large as an infringement of academic freedom and institutional autonomy.

The tension between equal opportunity and access on the one hand, and excellence in education, on the other—as Clark (1960) has described—illustrates this uneasy relationship between universities and higher education policy. The relationship between Labor Party governments in Brazil and the federal universities is a case in point. The government is demanding that universities be more responsive to black and mulatto populations, who cannot gain entrance via admission tests, and cannot study full time for they need to work to sustain themselves. Racial quotas and evening programmes have been demanded of federal universities, encountering resistance from universities, who feel such openness would compromise their autonomy and their academic quality.

The higher education policies of democratically elected governments are a new phenomenon throughout the region: if universities oppose them, they need to argue beyond the discussion-stopper reference to autonomy, for autonomy entails no exemption from rational deliberation in a democratic society wherein sovereignty is vested not in the university, but in Congress and the Administration. Thus, universities need to engage in serious discussion of such academic issues that concern society at large as student retention and time to graduation, employability of graduates, productivity of the faculty or mechanisms for inclusion of underserved populations.

Also, universities, as knowledge institutions, need to discuss what they are doing in relation to their main tasks of teaching and research. An important issue here is monitoring and increasing the quality of teaching and reaching standards of excellence, especially as the student body becomes increasingly more diverse in academic ability and preparation (Didriksson et als, 2008). Academics need systematic formation rather than intuitive pedagogical practices to offer quality teaching in changing and multicultural contexts. Regarding research, LA universities need to discuss important topics such as the kind of research that is needed in the region according to local needs rather than importing research that has been developed in totally different contexts. LA universities need therefore to invest more in the formation of researchers and in conducting relevant and pertinent research. All these issues should be of particular interest not only in universities but as part of a national and even regional policy.

An important aspect that needs to be addressed—which involves the relationship between the LA university and the state—is finance. Universities across the region, especially those that depend on state funding, struggle to secure some minimal resources in order to conduct the tasks of teaching and research in a proper way. As a result, universities financed by the state across the region experience a precariousness in terms of infrastructure, facilities, academic contracts and so on (López, 2003). It is difficult to meet the desired quality of both teaching and research if universities and their academics have to seek new forms of finance to survive.

The 'entrepreneurial university' (Slaughter & Leslie, 1997; Etzkowitz, 2004) has become apparent in LA but not in ways comparable to highly industrialized countries in which universities create knowledge to be consumed (Slaughter & Leslie, 1997; Clark, 1998; Slaughter & Rhoades, 2004), for example, through patents. Rather, in LA, universities are diversifying their incomes through the increase of student places in undergraduate programmes, and the creation of new campuses and postgraduate programmes. Academics, in turn, have supplemented their meagre salaries by offering their teaching services in these new programmes as well as supporting the creation of the 'consulting university', a university that sells professional services to the community (Arocena & Sutz, 2005).

State funding, nevertheless, inevitably involves tight processes of accountability these days. State universities need then to be open and work jointly with the state in order to justify the investment that is being made in order to reach standards of excellence in both teaching and research, even at the risk of the traditional idea of university autonomy—much prized in Latin America.

Conclusion

In this chapter, we have offered an historical overview of the LA university, identifying and analysing the main milestones that have configured its identity. Although we recognize great diversity across higher education systems in the region, we can see some crucial aspects around which LA universities have built their identities.

Throughout their history, LA universities have positioned themselves in tension with global processes of colonialism and imperialism on the one hand, and local oligarchy, on the other. LA universities have also shaped their identities by defying local processes of repression and global processes of both expansion and contraction. All these clashes have been guided by the need to construct and keep a sense of self-governance and autonomy *within* the university but, at the same time, have been projected *outside* the university in an attempt to change the socio-economic configuration of a country or context. In all these cases, students and academics have played key (sometimes revolutionary) roles that generate a permanent tension and interchange between structural forces and agentic responses.

Not forgetting the past and present of the LA university, we consider it is now time to look into the future and highlight the LA universities' role as institutions of relevant social knowledge for social learning (Marginson, 2015). There is a particular set of challenges that the LA universities have to address, namely, access, quality and social mobility. Although many more thousands of students have now access to universities—including first-generation students—in comparison with previous decades, only few have access to high quality universities. There is now a marked imbalance between elitist and selective universities—whose students have access to well-paid and prestigious jobs—and low quality mass universities (usually private universities).[8]

Governments, jointly with universities, need to work together to soften this imbalance and invest more effort and finances in order to improve the quality of those institutions where more vulnerable students are enrolled. Particular attention needs to be put into pedagogical processes and teaching practices to address diversity and inclusion. Also, on the part of the governments, a heightened regulatory regime needs to be established in order to prevent fraud and to guarantee that students—even in for-profit universities—are receiving education of demonstrably high quality. All of this means thinking seriously about new ways of teaching, research, and the relationship between these two tasks and, jointly with governments, planning and realizing new ways to reach excellence according to local and regional needs and global standards.

The future of the LA university will continue to be uncertain and probably, unpredictable. Although there are external global tensions that shape most universities around the world and tend to carry them towards a corporate model of university, there is, at the same time, a set of particular regional, national and local tensions in Latin America that reflect historical and cultural processes that are unique. The latter makes it difficult to glimpse the future of the LA university as a whole and perhaps just will allow the identification of particular cases or tendencies. Perhaps, we might speculate that, as in other matters in the region, the LA university will continue being crossed by a diversity of narratives of contradiction, inequality, the fight against hegemony and the hope for autonomy. And their main actors—students and academics—will be involved in new struggles to preserve these multiple identities and goals.

Acknowledgement: This work was supported by Conicyt-Chile, Fondecyt project 1170374 and PIA-CONICYT (Chile) Basal Funds for BF0003.

Notes

1. The creation of universities by separate decrees of the king and the Pope leads to certain controversy as to which was the first university in LA, whether the Universidad Santo Tomás de Aquino or the Universidad Mayor Nacional de San Marcos. Although the Universidad Santo Tomás de Aquino was established by the Pope in 1538, before the foundation of the Universidad Mayor Nacional de San Marcos, the former did not receive the required official recognition from the Spanish Crown until 1558, completing its legal authorization after San Marcos. The sequence of royal and pontifical authorizations, and the actual opening of these three universities, can be found in Levy (1986: 28).
2. Social responsibility took shape through what is called nowadays the 'third mission' of universities (additional to teaching and research), and was then referred to as 'university extension', which refers to 'concrete co-operation with deprived sectors in fields related with health, teaching, housing, legal advice and the like' (Arocena & Sutz, 2005: 576).
3. It is interesting to notice that this tradition persists, with the creation on new public universities to serve poor urban districts in Brazil, Argentina, and Venezuela and also in the legitimation discourse of new private universities, many of which claim to be serving the neediest populations excluded from elitist public universities.
4. Figures show that, for example, the number of undergraduate students at the UNAM increased from 106,000 in 1970 to 294,000 in 1980 (Mendoza, 2001).
5. The privatization of the higher education system was as well part of an explicit political agenda, especially in countries such as Chile, where it was implemented following neo-liberal recipes for policy reform with an emphasis on free market mechanisms.
6. It is not possible to give more details here about this situation, but, in general terms, primary and secondary students of lower classes tend to go to free public schools that, with few exceptions, offer poor quality education. As a consequence, these students are less prepared academically and usually obtain low scores in university examination tests. As a

result, they end up enrolling in less selective private universities or non-university tertiary institutions of higher education.

7. See the declaration in http://www.academica.mx/sites/default/files/final-declaration-encuentro_rankings.pdf
8. A tendency that is currently being experienced in several countries around the globe (Carnoy, Froumin, Loyalka & Tilak, 2014).

References

Acosta Silva, A. (2002). El Neointervencionismo estatal en la educación superior en América Latina. *Sociológica,* 17 (49), 43–72.

Acosta Silva, A. (2009). *Príncipes, burócratas y gerentes. El gobierno de las universidades públicas en México.* México, D. F.: ANUIES.

Albornoz, O. (1986). Dudas y dilemas. La educación superior latinoamericana. *Nueva Sociedad,* 84, 116–128.

Altbach, P. G. (2004). The costs and benefits of world-class universities. *Academe*, 90 (1), 20–23.

Altbach, P. G., & Salmi, J. (Eds.). (2011). *The road to academic excellence: The making of world-class research universities.* Washington, DC: World Bank Publications.

Arocena, R., & Sutz, J. (2005). Latin American Universities: from an original revolution to an uncertain transition. *Higher Education,* 50, 573–592.

Balbachevsky, E. (2015). The Latin American University Model and the Challenges Posed by the Reforms: Perspectives from the Academics. In W. Cummings & U. Teichler (Eds.) *The relevance of academic work in comparative perspective* (pp. 239–252). Dordrecht: Springer International Publishing.

Bellei, C., Cabalin, C., & Orellana, V. (2014). The 2011 Chilean student movement against neoliberal educational policies. *Studies in Higher Education*, 39 (3), 426–440.

Bernasconi, A. (2008). Is there a Latin American model of the university? *Comparative Education Review,* 52 (1), 27–52.

Bernasconi, A. (2012). Chile: The rise and decline of a student movement. *International Higher Education,* 66, 27–29.

Bernasconi, A. (2013). Are global rankings unfair to Latin American universities? *International Higher Education*, 72, 12–13.

Bernasconi, A. (2014). Policy path dependence of a research agenda: the case of Chile in the aftermath of the student revolt of 2011. *Studies in Higher Education*, 39 (8), 1405–1416.

Bodenheimer, S. (1971). Dependency and imperialism: The roots of Latin American underdevelopment. *Politics & Society*, 1 (3), 327–357.

Brunner, J. J. (2013). Latin American identity-dramatized. In E. Volek (Ed.), *Latin America writes back: Postmodernity in the periphery* (pp. 105–121). New York: Routledge.

Brunner, J. J., Balán, J., Courard, H., Cristián Cox, D., Durham, E. R., Fanelli, A. M. G., & Schwartzman, S. (1994). *Educación superior en América Latina: una agenda de problemas, políticas y debates en el umbral del año 2000.* Santiago: CEDES.

Carnoy, M., Froumin, I., Loyalka, P. K., & Tilak, J. B. (2014). The concept of public goods, the state, and higher education finance: a view from the BRICs. *Higher Education*, 68 (3), 359–378.

Clark, B. R. (1960). The cooling-out function in higher education. *American Journal of Sociology*, 65 (6), 569–576.

Clark, B. R. (1998). *Creating entrepreneurial universities: organizational pathways of transformation*. Oxford: Pergamon.

Clark, B. R. (2004). *Sustaining change in universities: Continuities in case studies and concepts*. Maidenhead, UK: Open University Press.

Connell, R. 2007. *Southern theory: The global dynamics of knowledge in Social Science*. Cambridge: Polity.

de Sousa Santos, B. 2014. *Epistemologies of the South: justice against epistemicide*. New York and

Didriksson et al

London: Routledge. Didriksson, A., Medina, E., Rojas, M., Bizzozero, J. & Hermo, J. (2008). Contexto global y regional de la educación superior en América Latina y el Caribe. In A. Gazzola & A. Didriksoon (Eds.), *Tendencias de la Educación superior en América Latina y el Caribe*, (pp. 21–54). Caracas: IESALC-UNESCO.

Easterly, W. (2001). The lost decades: developing countries' stagnation in spite of policy reform 1980–1998. *Journal of Economic Growth*, 6 (2), 135–157.

Espinoza, O., & González, L. (2012). Las protestas estudiantiles y sus implicancias para la gestión universitaria en Chile. In N. Fernández Lamarra (Ed.), *La Gestión Universitaria en América Latina* (pp. 245–281). Caaguazú: Ediciones de la Universidad Nacional de Caaguazú.

Etzkowitz, H. (2004). The evolution of the Entrepreneurial University. *International Journal of Technology and Globalisation*, 1 (1), 64–77.

García-Guadilla, C. (2003). Balance de la década de los '90 y reflexiones sobre las nuevas fuerzas de cambio en la educación superior. In M. Mollis (Ed.), *Las universidades en América Latina: ¿reformadas o alteradas? La Cosmética del Poder Financiero* (pp. 17–37). Buenos Aires: CLACSO.

Guzmán-Valenzuela, C., & Barnett, R. (2013a). Academic Fragilities in a marketised age: the case of Chile. *British Journal of Educational Studies*, 61 (2), 203–220.

Guzmán-Valenzuela, C., & Barnett, R. (2013b). Marketing time: evolving timescapes in academia. *Studies in Higher Education*, 38 (8), 1120–1134.

Guzmán-Valenzuela, C. (2016). Neoliberal discourses and the emergence of an agentic field: the Chilean student movement. In R. Brooks (editor) Student Politics and Protest (pp. 47-62). London: Routledge & SRHE.

Guzmán-Valenzuela (2017).The geopolitics of research in teaching and learning in the university in Latin America. *Scholarship of Teaching and Learning in the South* 1(1), 4-18.

Jiménez, E. (2007). La Historia de la Universidad en América Latina. *Revista de la Educación Superior*, XXXVI (1), 141, 169–178.

Keen, B., & Haynes, K. (2012). *A history of Latin America* (Vol. 2). Boston: Cengage Learning.

Kent, R. (1997). *Los temas críticos de la educación superior en América Latina*: Los años 90. Expansión privada, evaluación y posgrado. Vol. 2. Universidad Autónoma de Aguascalientes. Santiago: FLACSO.

Larraín, J. (2000). *Identity and modernity in Latin America*. Cambridge: Polity Press in association with Blackwell Publishers.

Levy, D. C. (1986). *Higher education and the state in Latin America: private challenges to public dominance*. Chicago: University of Chicago Press.

López, F. (2003). El impacto de la globalización y las políticas educativas en los sistemas de educación superior de América Latina y el Caribe. In M. Mollis (Ed.), *Las universidades en américa latina: ¿reformadas o alteradas? la cosmética del poder financiero. La cosmética del poder financiero* (pp. 39–58). Buenos Aires: CLACSO.

Marginson, S. (2015). The Landscape of Higher Education Research 1965–2015. Equality of Opportunity: The first fifty years. Keynote address at the SRHE 50th Anniversary Colloquium, 26 June 2015.

Marsiske, R. (2004). Historia de la autonomía universitaria en América Latina. P*erfiles Educativos,* XXVI, 106, 160–167.

Mendoza, J. (2001). *Los conflictos de la UNAM en el siglo XX.* Médico D. F.: Universidad Nacional autónoma de México Ediciones.

Mignolo, W. D. (2003). *Historias locales/diseños globales: colonialidad, conocimientos subalternos y pensamiento fronterizo* (Local histories / global designs: coloniality, subaltern knowledge and frontier thinking) (Vol. 18). Ediciones Akal.

Molesworth, M., Scullion, R., & Nixon, E. (Eds.) (2011). *The marketisation of higher education and the student as consumer*. Abingdon: Routledge.

OECD (2014). Education at a Glance 2014: OECD Indicators, OECD Publishing. Retrieved on February 20, 2015, from http://dx.doi.org/10.1787/eag-2014-en

Ordorika, I., Martínez, J., & Ramírez, R.M. (2012). La transformación de las formas de gobierno en el sistema universitario público mexicano: una asignatura pendiente. *Revista de la educación superior,* 40 (4), 29–49.

Petras, J. (1990). The metamorphosis of Latin America's intellectuals. *Latin American Perspectives*, 17, 102–112.

Quijano, A. (1993). Modernity, identity, and utopia in Latin America. *Boundary 2,* 20 (3), 140–155.

Rhoades, G., & Slaughter, S. (2006). Academic capitalism and the new economy: Privatization as shifting the target of public subsidy in higher education. In R. Rhoads & C. Torres (Eds.) *The university, state, and market: The political economy of globalization in the Americas* (pp. 103–140). Palo Alto, CA: Stanford University Press.

Salmi, J. (2009). *The challenge of establishing world class universities.* Washington, DC: The World Bank.

Saxonhouse, G. R., & Stern, R. M. (2003). The bubble and the lost decade. *The World Economy*, 26 (3), 267–281.

Slaughter, S. & Rhoades, G. (2004). Academic Capitalism and the New Economy. Markets, State and Higher Education. Baltimore, MD and London: Johns Hopkins University Press.

Slaughter, S., & Leslie, L. (1997). *Academic capitalism: politics, policies, and the entrepreneurial university*. Baltimore, MD and London: Johns Hopkins University Press.

Slaughter, S., & Leslie, L. (2001). Expanding and elaborating the concept of academic capitalism. *Organization*, 8 (2), 154–161.

Van Aken, M. (1971). University Reform before Cordoba. *The Hispanic American Historical Review*, 51 (3), 447–462.

Villanueva, E. (2010). Perspectivas de la educación superior en América Latina: construyendo futuros. *Perfiles Educativos*, XXXII (129), 86–101.

CHAPTER SIXTEEN

Towards an African University in Becoming

Positive Risk, Hope and Imagination

YUSEF WAGHID AND NURAAN DAVIDS

Introduction

The appointment of our university's first Black Vice-Chancellor in 2007 was largely viewed as a signal that the institution was serious about its commitment to transformation. His recent demise, however, has seen progressive voices raise—perhaps (un)warranted—concerns about the transformative vision of a leading African research institution being at risk. Similar expressions of fear and doubt continue to dominate the democratic psyche of post-apartheid South Africa seven months after Nelson Mandela's demise. And yet, as perhaps both these aforementioned individuals will testify, the capacity to transform is neither confined nor sustained through the ideas or practices of one person. Rather, not only is the vision of transformation not necessarily actualized by those who act towards it, but in fact only comes to fruition in the absence of those who are perceived to embody that vision. It would appear that in many respects, the realization of any vision necessitates a disjuncture between the vision and its actualization.

Universities, in its multiplex roles of social, political, epistemological and capital reform, are by their constitution expected to both symbolize and enact transformation. And like our institution, universities in South Africa continue to hanker towards this condition, called a transformed institution. Building on the notions of critique, hope and imagination in reference to the seminal thoughts of Derrida

(2004), Freire (2006) and Barnett (2013) respectively, we bring into contention this idea of a transformed university, for such a university would no longer be in a state of transformation. Instead, we argue that a transformative vision for an African research university should never be actualized, since its actualization would in fact put its capacity to think and transform anew at risk. We distinguish between two forms of risk: negative and positive risk. On the one hand, *negative* risk implies that the university aims to actualize and thus bring to completion its contrived vision—an idea which counteracts the possibility that institutional efforts to transform the institution are no longer required. *Positive* risk, on the other hand, offers a way of never actualizing the university as there is always more to do and hence more to unfold, that is, the university that is to be realized is only temporary with each act of transformation to be superseded by new forms of being. Historically advantaged universities in South Africa, for example, continue to debate transformation in terms of implementing equitable access criteria to students from both advantaged and disadvantaged backgrounds. Given the country's legacy of racial oppression, these debates remain couched in a language of race—and depending on one's vantage point, in terms of discrimination, or privilege. While previously marginalized groups are perceived to be offered preferential treatment, previously privileged groups stand accused of being counter-transformative. In this instance, the worth of transformative practices might not necessarily be shared by all—indeed, attempts at transformative practices at universities in South Africa have often been labelled as 'reverse racism'.

And so while it might not be possible to ensure that transformation speaks to all people in the same language, the understanding of transformation cannot be limited to its outcomes. Linking transformation to the actualization of outcomes would signify the end of transformation itself and thus the idea of taking positive risks will be circumvented. Instead, it has to be experienced in what it awakens in people, and hence society. Transformation, we contend, is made visible in the thinking that engenders the potential for perpetual new beginnings, and is therefore always in a state of transformation. To this end, transformation is not about transforming an institution; it is about transforming thinking, and ways of doing. Such a critical, hopeful and imaginative university is one that remains in becoming (Agamben, 1993), as it bears testimony and offers hope to the sphere of transformation that it aspires to see reflected in the society which it serves. This chapter, then, will commence with an exploration of how ongoing moves towards a transformed state might actually put the university at risk in terms of its own capacity to think differently (Giroux & Searls Giroux, 2004a; Giroux, 2007). This might offer new insight into particularly the South African university, which has continued to confuse demographic representivity with transformation (Teferra &

Altbach, 2004). We will argue that transformative practices, such as equitable access, are not actualized in terms of the number of previously disadvantaged students. Rather, it is actualized in the extent to which the university itself takes risks through self-critique, hope and imagination (Biesta, 2014)—all instances of positive risk-taking.

The university at risk

The role of higher education in public life continues to be a vigorously contested issue. In appealing to higher education to be morally engaged, not only with social issues but also with the pursuit of justice, Giroux and Searls Giroux (2004a) are tapping into what they view as the core purpose of higher education—that is, to serve democratic values by educating students as critical and engaged citizens. Their book, *Take back higher education*, calls on intellectuals to account, arguing that the ways those in the university articulate whom we represent and to whom we are responsible 'has drastic implications … for the kind of society in which we live' (2004a: 38). Indeed, educators must 'relat[e] their work to larger social issues … offering students knowledge, debate, and dialogue about pressing social problems' (2004a: 8–9). Their depiction of the university as agora—referring to an ancient Greek concept of political organization that, in the interest of democracy, pulls together private and public life—gives credence to their argument for the necessity for a distinct and tangible engagement between academic scholarship and civic capacities, participation and public commitment. On the one hand, Giroux and Searls Giroux (2004b: 30) are aware of counterarguments for the non-pursuit of social agency and responsibility within higher education. On the other hand, they remain steadfast in their contention that it is the very privilege and academic freedom that higher education has bestowed upon itself, which demands of higher education to prepare students to both understand and influence the larger educational forces that shape their lives (2004b: 30). For Giroux (2004), the call for the moral engagement of higher education is a self-explanatory one. Democracy, he argues, simply 'cannot function without educated citizens capable of being autonomous, making knowledgeable judgments, and bringing what they learn to bear on understanding and shaping civic culture' (2004). As such, says Giroux (2004), firstly, higher education cannot be separated from the imperatives of an inclusive democracy, and secondly, the crisis of higher education must be understood as part of the wider crisis of politics, power and culture.

Likewise, the perilous state of the university is lucidly highlighted in Henry Giroux's (2007: 2–3) *The university in chains* in which he contends that the promise of democratic education remains unfulfilled as it failed to engender a culture of questioning, critical engagement, and democratic politics and civic responsibility within the university. Unlike Bill Readings's (1996) *The university in ruins* that problematizes how the university has been transformed within a global neoliberal performative discourse of excellence and efficiency, Giroux (2007: 6) argues for a discourse of critique and possibility in an effort to unchain the university from an incessant assault on critical thinking and an all-embracing commitment to free-market fundamentalism. For him, the university is and will remain at risk unless it becomes a site of resistance against the growing forces of militarism, corporatism and right-wing political fundamentalism that compromises the place of the university to think in relation to other places where thought takes place (Giroux, 2007: 4). Put differently, the emancipatory transformative discourse of the university is put at risk because liberal notions of deliberation, critique and civic engagement are trumped by the forces of militarization and corporatization. As such, it is not only the emancipatory transformative discourse of the university, which is put at risk. If the university is at risk of not fulfilling its mandate of moral engagement, then it can be argued that the crisis is one of social justice, since as Giroux (2004) posits, higher education cannot be separated from the imperatives of an inclusive democracy.

And yet, for all the concerns over its uncriticality, its two features of education and youthful volatility have ensured that the contemporary university has not always remained impotent in the face of perceived unjust treatment of students, or in relation to greater societal issues. On the one hand, then, we have seen in London in 2010, 50,000 students and lecturers protesting against the coalition government's plans to raise the cap on tuition fees threefold and to impose cuts of 40% on teaching budgets (Spencer, 2010). On the other hand, the world has also watched the seven-week protests by students on the Tiananmen Square in 1989. More recently in 2013, as many as 3,000 Ukrainian students joined protests in the centre of Kiev against the government's abrupt move to freeze integration with the West and tilt towards Moscow (Danilova & Karmanau, 2013). Of course, given the spate of student protests across a number of North African states—culminating in what is commonly referred to as the 'Arab Spring'—the world is equally familiar with student protests, which started in 2010 in Tunisia, Egypt, Libya, Algeria, and continued in May 2014, when pro-Mohamed Morsi students protested at several universities across Egypt, resulting in clashes with security forces (Barsoum, 2014). So, what are the challenges faced by African universities? Are the risks encountered by African universities similar to that encountered by American universities, as highlighted through the lenses of Giroux and Searls Giroux? Or, are African universities as uncritical and as unwilling to engage in broader issues as their American counterparts?

The African university at risk

If we accept as Giroux and Searls Giroux (2004a) and Giroux (2007) does, that the emancipatory transformative discourse of the university is being put at risk by militarization and corporatization, then we might need to consider that the greatest risk facing the African university can be couched in a discourse of colonialism. Waghid (2011: 231), for example, argues that the university in Africa is put at risk because of instability between the failures, stagnation and regression instigated through colonialism that retarded the advancement of the university on the continent. Similarly, Teferra and Altbach (2003: 4) aptly posit that the influence of colonialism on the African university restricted students' access, academic freedom, and the Africanization of the curriculum. More significantly, conflict and war, dwindling financial resources to charge student fees, and most governments' intolerance of dissent, criticism and free expression of controversial views put the African university at risk (Teferra & Altbach, 2003: 11; Waghid, 2011: 237).

Considering that about 45% of the African population are living in poverty, 300 million people living in absolute poverty, more than 30 million people infected with HIV and AIDS, declining life expectancy levels in some countries, a rampant unemployment rate, major regional wars and massive displacement of people, the African university—regardless of being ontologically embedded in the developmental state—can no longer exclusively be concerned with development and nation-building to produce basic and scientific knowledge and form critical minds (Assié-Lumumba & Lumumba-Kasongo, 2011: 270). Given increasing unemployment, the 'brain drain' phenomenon and the persistent call to combat poverty and promote human well-being, the curricular emphasis on science and technology cannot just correspond to the preference of the global liberal economy (Assié-Lumumba & Lumumba-Kasongo, 2011: 270). Already more than a decade ago, arguments have been made that the African university should simultaneously retain its status as a community of reason through the construction of disciplinary knowledge or producing knowledge for its own sake, and fulfil its social mission in the process of nation-building and development—a matter of producing socially distributed knowledge in the quest to be responsive to the social, economic and political injustices that continue to plague the continent (Waghid, 2002). Similarly, strong arguments have been made that to avoid further putting the continent at risk, the African university should advance scientific knowledge for peace, human security, the environment, social and gender equality, individual and collective liberty, and rigorous research agendas for social progress (Assié-Lumumba & Lumumba-Kasongo, 2011: 283). Implicit in these arguments, however, is the assumption that universities on the African continent want to, and can indeed, act as agents of social restoration.

In exploring the restorative role of the university, we know, through the witnessing of protest action on Tahrir Square, or on the streets of Benghazi, that students have long played roles in some of the more momentous uprisings over the course of modern history (Sanborn & Thyne, 2011: 1). These uprisings, according to Sanborn and Thyne (2011: 2), appear to reveal that the more students pursue higher levels of education within contexts of social and economic insecurity and inequality, the more knowledgeable they become about the world around them, and the more, therefore, they seek to distinguish themselves with profitable skill sets, and are more likely to push for the political change, of which an education has made them aware. And yet, the type of uprisings as made visible through the Arab Spring has neither resulted in agora nor has it cultivated the type of community and moral engagement that allows the university to establish and extend meaningful and credible partnerships with civil society. Instead, the predominant higher education model in African universities, says Teferra (2006), remains one shaped by the former colonial powers—kept intact through non-indigenous languages of instruction. Moreover, coupled with debilitating financial constraints, African universities face tremendous challenges in pursuing any measure of autonomy when most public institutions depend on government subsidies for up to 90–95% of its income (Teferra, 2006). Likewise, issues of access, attrition, financial well-being, language of instruction and transformation continue to haunt higher education in South Africa.

The South African university at risk: (in)equality, access and exclusion

Echoing the post-apartheid trends at South African schools, the transformation agenda in higher education has needed to establish a single national system, through which to address the inheritance of racially, socially and economically segregated institutions. The new democratic South Africa was confronted with a legacy of 36 institutions—comprising of 17 historically white and 17 historically black universities, one mixed technikon (Technikon SA) and one mixed distance learning institution (UNISA or University of South Africa). Both the historically white and black universities included both English and Afrikaans mediums of instruction. And while the English-medium universities, according to Fiske and Ladd (2004: 204), used their connections with the business community to raise substantial private funds and thus minimize their dependence on the government, the Afrikaans-medium universities, starting with Stellenbosch (1918) and the University of Pretoria (1930), dedicated themselves to promoting the language and culture of Afrikaners prior to apartheid. Being isolated in terms of language and politics from the international community, explain Fiske and Ladd (2004: 205), meant that these universities were managed in authoritarian fashion and were almost totally dependent on the government for financial support and the funding of research.

A programme for the transformation of post-apartheid higher education is captured in the National Plan for Higher Education (NPHE; Ministry of Education, 2001). In terms of the NPHE, the key challenges facing the South African higher education system are: redressing past inequalities; transforming the higher education system to serve a new social order; meeting pressing national needs, and responding to new realities and opportunities (Ministry of Education, 2001: 4). The physical aspect of transformation manifested in the merging of particular institutions, thereby reducing the number of institutions from 36 to 23. Among the most important reasons for these mergers was the unification of the fragmented further and higher education systems inherited from the previous dispensation, and the need for the eradication of the profound inequalities and distortions of these education systems (Wyngaard & Kapp, 2004, in Arnolds, Stofile & Lillah, 2013: 3). Other reasons for the mergers, according to Mapasela and Hay (2005), include increasing student enrolments, especially from previously disadvantaged communities; meeting the national and global opportunities and challenges in terms of new technologies, research and training; and responding to the changing societal interests and needs as expressed in a transition from racial discrimination and oppression towards a democratic order.

Of course, as expected, these mergers have not been without serious resistance, as well as risk—which have included disparate organizational cultures and 'race' issues which manifested in diverse ways at different institutions (Arnolds, Stofile & Lillah, 2013: 3). Moreover, as noted in the NPHE (Ministry of Education, 2001), the opening up of access to higher education for black students at all institutions after 1994 has adversely impacted on student enrolments at the historically black institutions and, in particular, the historically black universities. Between 1993 and 1999, African student enrolments decreased from 49% to 33% in the historically black institutions and increased from 13% to 39% in the historically white institutions. The decline in enrolments, combined with a range of other factors, such as growing student debt, governance and management failures and general instability, has resulted in the rapid erosion of the sustainability of a number of historically black universities (Ministry of Education, 2001: 8). Two important factors need consideration. On the one hand, we note the exodus from historically black to historically white universities under the auspices of better facilities, more opportunities as well as the realization, that unlike historically black universities, historically white universities (English and Afrikaans-medium) enjoyed a certain measure of regard as among the best in Africa. Linked to this is that institutions, such as the universities of Cape Town, Witwatersrand, Natal and Rhodes, considered themselves as 'liberal' and in this sense, dissociated themselves from the interests of the state and viewed themselves as members of an international community of scholars (Fiske & Ladd, 2004: 203–204).

Given that most of the new entrants to the higher education system would be black students, such an expansion, explain Fiske and Ladd, would accomplish two important equity-related purposes: 'First, it would allow historically white institutions to transform themselves into integrated institutions without curtailing the number of white students they served. Second, expansion would facilitate an increase in both overall enrolment levels and the participation rate of black students, defined as the ratio of the number of black students enrolled in higher education to the age-appropriate black population' (2004: 210). On the other hand, instead of redressing the condition of disfavour apartheid bestowed on historically black universities, the programme of transformation of higher education has inadvertently widened the post-apartheid gaps between historically white and black universities. With greater demands for access from sectors of community previously not considered, historically white universities continue to enjoy the privilege of controlling student access via mechanisms of tuition fees, which in turn, has a direct impact on the quality of facilities, research and institutional support.

Like elsewhere on the African continent, the issue of financial means to access higher education remains a huge stumbling block for students in post-apartheid South Africa. In recognition that the desegregation of higher education was not enough to ensure access for historically excluded students, the Education White Paper 3—A Programme for the Transformation of the Higher Education System (Department of Education, 1997), which served as the basis of the NPHE (Ministry of Education, 2001)—was emphatic about the provision of a student aid scheme, namely the National Student Financial Aid Scheme (NSFAS). Not only, however, were these bursaries never adequately funded, explain Fiske and Ladd, but their effectiveness varied widely across institutions. Since the NSFAS only covered between 60% and 70% of the total cost of tuition fees, students who could not bridge the financial gap were forced to drop out—leading to a significant decline in the number of black students in universities (2004: 212–213).

Considered within the historical context of a highly unequal and discriminatory society, post-apartheid South Africa has achieved a number of significant goals in relation to its restructuring of higher education. Among these are the establishment of a national quality assurance framework and infrastructure, which comprises of policies, mechanisms and initiatives with respect to institutional audit, programme accreditation, quality promotion and capacity development; as well as increased and broadened participation within higher education to advance social equity and meet economic and social development needs (Badat, 2010: 40). These achievements, however, run the risk of being diminished by a growing number of challenges, which appear to be fuelling the erosion of—albeit historically disadvantaged—once thriving institutions. Significant challenges, as identified by Badat, include the issues of differentiation and diversity, which he argues, can make an immense contribution to the new socio-economic and educational goals and objectives of democratic South Africa; the deracializing and decolonizing of intellectual spaces; low postgraduate student enrolments and outputs, which are exacerbated by the fact that in 2010 only 32% of university academics possessed doctorates; and the challenge of cultivating a new generation of academics, constituted by not only blacks and women, in particular, but also by the intellectual and academic capabilities, necessary for transforming and developing South Africa's universities (2010: 41–45).

These accounts—manifested in inequality, access and exclusion—will continue to put South African universities at risk. Often this risk has been starkly exposed through student protests—most notably at historically black institutions—resulting in wanton acts of vandalism, burning of buildings, and worst, the temporary closure of universities. A recent incident (May 2014) showed violent clashes between students and riot police at the Cape Peninsula University of Technology's Bellville campus, as students protested about service delivery, facilities and fees (University World News, 2014). As Badat (2010: 42) explains, in locating higher education within a larger process of 'political democratisation, economic reconstruction and development, and redistributive social policies aimed at equity' (White Paper, 1997: 1.7), the White Paper emphasized a 'thick' notion of the responsiveness of higher education that incorporated its wider social purposes. As such, and increasingly, continues Badat, the 'trend has been to approach higher education and investments in universities from the perspective largely of the promotion of economic growth and the preparation of students for the labour market and as productive workers for the economy' (2010: 42–43). Such a trend, which as Giroux (2004) has repeatedly cautioned, will lead to silence about the relationship between education and democracy.

As is abundantly clear from the above discussion, social transformation cannot be enacted if universities are unable to combat the impediments of exclusion, lack of access and inequality. Added to these complexities is the issue of internal exclusion (Young, 2000)—whereby black students, although included at historically white universities, are excluded within the confines of an engendered institutional culture, which remains indifferent and averse to the social-academic experiences of these students. While South African universities, as accentuated by the NPHE, are aimed at producing students with 'enhanced cognitive capacities' and a commitment towards equitable redress, nation-building and global competitiveness, the performative aspirations, however, are not seen as militating against what universities ought to be—that is, institutions of critique, hope and imagination. And, even if the university were to enjoy wider access to black students, this would not mean that inclusion would have been realized. Inclusion itself can be both internal and external. Whereas external exclusion can be addressed through access, internal inclusion seems to be a bigger challenge for universities, especially given that students are procedurally (numerically) included yet remain excluded due to institutional constraints they encounter, for instance, due to a lack of institutional support to address their (black students') epistemological difficulties often compounded by teaching and learning.

If we now cast a critical eye over South African universities, where the groundwork has ostensibly been laid for increased participation, unbiased access and unfettered inclusion, particular questions have to be asked. Are the features of access and inclusion constitutive of transformation, and do they offer the social and intellectual spaces for critical democratic engagement? Or are higher numbers of black students at historically white universities mere symbols of what transformation ought to look like? Similarly, while Badat (2010: 40) commends South African higher education on its display and promise of knowledge production and dissemination, can this promise deliver in terms of contributing to social equity and justice? Asked more succinctly, can transformation in higher education attend to the development needs of an infant democracy?

Towards positive risk: critique, hope and imagination

Now that we have argued against the manifestation of negative risk as higher education, specifically in (South) Africa, endeavours to reconstitute its transformative agenda, it seems plausible to draw, firstly, on Derrida's notion of critique. The value of critique as an important positive risk that universities in Africa ought to pursue finds itself rightfully associated with 'thinking' that no longer lets itself to be determined by an obsession with privileging one form of knowledge over another, albeit knowledge of technoscience over ancestral beliefs and customs. As for Derrida, as it is for us, critique is a form of dissonance and questioning that is not dominated and intimidated by the power of privilege. 'This thinking must also unmask—an infinite task—all the ruses of end-orienting reason, the paths by which apparently disinterested research can find itself indirectly re-appropriated, reinvested by programs of all sorts' (Derrida, 2004: 148). This is basically always asking: 'What is at stake (in technology, the sciences, production and productivity)?' It is a kind of critique that allows us to take more positive risks, to deal openly with the radical incommensurability of the language games that constitute our society (including the traditions and customs of Africa's peoples) and invites new possibilities to emerge.

Critique is a matter of enhancing the possibility of dissent and diversity of interpretations; of complicating what is taken for granted, pointing to what has been overlooked in establishing identities; an active opening up of your own thought structures that is necessary for other ways to find an entrance (Burik, 2009: 301–304). Thus, critique is concerned with creating possibilities for dissent and diversity of interpretations, complicating the taken for granted and opening up to the other. Perhaps the possibility exists that we might just become critical, or, perhaps less critical, through our engagement with others and others' ways of knowing. And, African universities that are renowned to oppose dissent and difference would be genuinely transformed to take positive risks in their pursuit of cultivating critique. Taking positive risks involves taking risks with the possibility that more is yet to come and risk-taking remains an ongoing transformative pursuit.

Secondly, in the quest to enact critique, the possibility is always there that one might or might not achieve such a desirable and judicious outcome. Nevertheless, the hope that critique will be attained remains an aspiration in the mould Freire has advocated. Freire's educational philosophy has been very influential since he first authored *Pedagogy of the Oppressed* (1972) for which he set out in his later years to write an introduction to the twentieth anniversary edition of the book. It turned out to be a new book namely, *Pedagogy of Hope: Revisiting Pedagogy of the Oppressed* (1994)—wherein he reflected on the experience of writing *Pedagogy of the Oppressed*, on his thinking, as well as on reacting to criticism from other scholars. He extended his thinking on teachers and learners; teaching and learning; and teacher education and dedicated two works exclusively to these issues: *Pedagogy of Freedom: Ethics, Democracy and Civic Courage* (1998) and *Teachers as Cultural Workers: Letters to Those Who Dare Teach* (2005). As a critical point of departure for this chapter, we draw on Paulo Freire's argument that, 'The progressive must become critically inserted into pedagogical action and carry out policies consistent with an understanding of history as possibility' (Freire, 2004: 101). This means, that a progressive education, especially in a transformative context, should be rooted within a pedagogy of hope as an enabling epistemological framework of action.

The point about such an understanding of hope is the view that what can still be accounted for is politically and socially worthwhile an undertaking—a positive risk. To consider human action 'as possibility' is to bear in mind that nothing is insurmountable and incapable of being accounted for—an idea that makes the unexpected, incalculable, unknown worthwhile and hence a positive risk to undertake. In other words, to embark on a pedagogy of hope is in fact to take on a task where the unexpected, the improbable might not be unreasonable to aspire towards. This makes the risk so much more positive as there is then always more to encounter and experience without relinquishing the hope that the impossible might yet become possible with the very possibility that the impossible might also never be actualized. For African higher education to undertake a pedagogy of hope is to acknowledge that what is yet to come will always be in the making—where final blueprints and fulfilled aspirations work against the desirable effects of an encounter of the impossible.

Transformation in South African universities, for example, cannot only be understood in terms of equality, access and inclusion, because even when students are granted physical inclusion, they might still experience exclusion in terms of social and cultural ways of being. As such, they might not necessarily be able to articulate their own exclusion or voicelessness, because their transformation and that of the university have already been predefined in terms of practices of access. In South Africa, many universities have understood transformation as being in only that which is made visible—the changing of building names; the removal of effigies of apartheid stalwarts. This is neither transformation nor does it offer hope to those who remain abandoned within the discourse of transformation. Consequently, too many universities in (South) Africa have abandoned the hope that there is still more to come, more to know, and unexpected encounters that will inspire people to act anew.

Thirdly, Barnett offers an account of an imaginative and imagining university that breaks with the idea of the present-day entrepreneurial university, defined by its alliance to the corporate world of markets and performative targets. For Barnett, the latter university has succumbed to the narrow interests of corporatization, managerialism and knowledge capitalism. In a way, (re)imagining the university represents both a response to the entrepreneurial malaise that undergirds current understandings of the university and, an alternative conceptual plea to reconstitute the place of engagement, care, criticality, trust and responsibility in the university. In Derridian fashion, if the university were to prevent losing its soul and to 'perform its mysterious work' (2013: 156), it should work towards 'becoming' (2013: 155) a university that is yet to be imagined.

His idea of imagination vis-à-vis construing the university categorizes ideas of the university and elucidates conceptions of the university historically and contemporarily as well as its becoming, in particular, as it could become in the future. Most poignantly, the imaginative and imagining university is articulated within the parameters of 'criteria of adequacy', evoking the idea of the ecological university commensurate with what is public, wise, social, open and virtuous (2013: 144–145). On the one hand, for a university to be imaginative, it 'exudes actual innovative policies and strategies' (2013: 155) as it sets out to 'be sensitive to the potential callings of the wider world' (2013: 154). This connects the imaginative university to the world and one that enacts its responsibilities 'in and towards the world in aiding the wellbeing [and flourishing] of the world' (2013: 154). On the other hand, the imagining university is 'continually reflexive and gives itself to imaging its future ... for it is always becoming, in attempting to realize the imagining of itself' (2013: 155). The latter idea of the university establishes new assemblages of becoming as it opens new vectors of escape or lines of flight that may lead to its deterritorialization and reterritorialization of itself, continuously nurturing spaces for imagining (Deleuze & Guattari, 1987). At once, the imaginative and imagining university becomes dependent on the prevalence and nurturing of conditions such as conceptual spaciousness, trust, communicative openness, institutional self-criticality, social transactionality, conviviality, unfettered time and alterity (Barnett, 2013: 154) to work towards its fullest potential in promoting human and global well-being including its own well-being (2013: 146).

Thus, the imaginative and imagining university is a 'becoming-ecological-university' (2013: 144) that is connected to its aspirations to promote human flourishing and well-being, especially human understanding, transforming people's lives, forming self-sustaining communities and developing a self-critical society. In our own work we have argued for the notion of an African university that allows space for both reasoned argumentation and cultural voice and we are persuaded by the idea of an imaginative and imagining university that could be attentive to a call for the reasonable, culture-dependent aspirations of an African university. Such a university would not only become responsive to the well-being of Africa's peoples but would be suitably positioned to countenance the university's efforts to promote democracy, peace and human interdependence, particularly on the African continent (Waghid, 2014). Therefore, we are attracted to Barnett's call to think of the university 'to be fully imaginative of itself' (2013: 146).

Transformation as actualized in risk

Positive risk is not only a willingness to be imaginative; it involves abandoning any ideas of knowing beforehand who or what to expect—being simultaneously open to anything and nothing. As such, risk, states Biesta (2014), defines education. Through risk-taking, the possibility always exists that the individual might disrupt what she is about to encounter, because disruption, or engaging with the other, is an activity associated with taking a risk towards increasing imagination. To Biesta (2014: 1), education is a risk not because teachers might fail because of insufficient qualifications, or because students are not working hard enough. Education, he explains, is a risk because it involves encounters between human beings, and because human beings (students) are not objects to be moulded, but subjects of action and responsibility. To Biesta, taking the (positive) risk out of education means taking education out altogether (2014: 1).

For students to be educated means that they have to take the positive risk to encounter that which they have not encountered before. This means that they have to be willing to open themselves up to the pedagogical or lived experiences of others—that is, experiences that can provoke people to act anew, and be moved by the experiences of others. Unlike negative risk, which aims to actualize the performances of people to act anew, positive risk provokes people to act anew without the possibility that their performances in the act of transformation will be realized. Such transformative acts vis-à-vis negative risks will mark the end of education itself. Similarly, if South African universities—both historically black and white—wish to transform into that which best serves a socially just society,—then they have to be willing to act with a degree of risk-taking, and to engage imaginatively with new encounters. Only when South African universities take the risk of disrupting their respective legacies of historically white/privileged and historically black/disadvantaged, respectively, can we begin to talk about a transformation process in becoming. A transformation in becoming recognizes that transformation ceases in its actualization, because like Biesta's (2014) human beings, that are subjects of action and responsibility, rather than objects to be moulded, transformation is neither shaped by what is visible nor can it be moulded in line with a predetermined set of outcomes—such as in x number of students, or y number of female university academics. As a subjective experience, transformation lives in what is experienced and in what is encountered in the self, and in dialogue with others. Transformation, therefore, engenders the potential for perpetual new beginnings, and is therefore in itself always in a state of transformation, and always at risk of transforming, or not transforming. To this end, transformation is not about transforming an institution; it is about transforming thinking, and ways of doing. Such a critical, hopeful and imaginative university is one that remains in becoming (Agamben, 1993), as it bears testimony and offers hope to the sphere of transformation that it aspires to see reflected in the society which it serves.

In sum, a university that recognizes that its transformation is accounted for in its risk-taking is a university that can respond to Giroux and Searls Giroux's (2004a) to be morally engaged, not only with social issues but also with the pursuit of justice—because it recognizes that transformation is a subject of action and responsibility, which ceases to exist when the responsibility is perceived to be fulfilled. A university that is actualized in risk-taking, and therefore, always in becoming, can indeed be an agora—because it combines private action with public responsibility, perpetually geared at new beginnings.

To take the (positive) risk out of education, says Biesta (2014: 1), means to take education out completely. Stated differently, the absence of positive risk is the absence of education. By extension, then, if higher education does not take a positive risk, then it is in fact not educating. The two, therefore—education and risk—are mutually contingent. The contribution, then, of this chapter, is not to attempt to offer recommendations for the role and purpose of higher education in (South) Africa. And it is not to offer any insight into what transformation ought to look like, because transformation, as we have already begun to argue, neither has a particular look (of black students at historically white universities) nor a particular way of being or doing. Instead, the argument that we have submitted is that if a (South) African university hopes to transform itself from the oppressive legacies of colonialism and apartheid, it has to recognize two simultaneous histories, and therefore two processes of transformation. Firstly, to expect historically white universities to shift out of racial segregation towards integration seems to be a reasonable feature of a democratic society. And the focus, certainly in post-apartheid South Africa, has overwhelmingly been on previously marginalized groups gaining access to that which was previously inaccessible. What has not received much attention, however—and this is the second process—is what needs to happen at historically black universities. Thanks to apartheid, these universities have continually been hard-pressed to offer anything else but an unexceptional, at times dismal, educational experience. Throwing money at these universities is not going to address the massive deficiency in knowledge production, underpinned by poorly qualified academics, and poorer infrastructure.

Of course, the type of transformation needed at these institutions is indeed of a tangible kind—a very expensive one at that. But this is not the type of transformation needed to transform historically black and disadvantaged universities. Inasmuch as we might demand of historically white institutions to reconsider their policies on equity, access and participation, we also need to demand of historically black universities to move away from their own marginalization and oppression. This means, for example, that when students do not pass their courses, and complete their degree within the designated timeframe—due to poor attendance of classes, and a general lack of interest in their studies—that the university holds itself accountable by discontinuing funding to these students, and instead focus on students, who are in fact serious about their studies. Instead, it is common occurrence in South Africa—generally at the beginning of the academic year—for students, who have failed, and face the threat of exclusion, to hold entire institutions and other students to ransom through burning libraries, vandalizing public property and harassing those students who wish to attend class. The negative risk in excluding these students is outweighed by the positive risk of protecting the integrity and accountability of the university. Any idea of transforming higher education, so that it might transform society, requires measures of risks from all parts of higher education and society—and not only from those who were previously advantaged. The positive risk for higher education in (South) Africa is to accept its legacy of segregation, exclusion and oppression, and to re-signify a reimagined way of being. To continue to counter it through the removal of relics, building names and playing a numbers of game of black students and academics is neither a risk nor transformational, and therefore, not educational. Actualizing the aforementioned acts might not necessarily enhance transformation as such a risk is negative in the sense that measures have been achieved to ensure transformation. Yet, the negative risk to actualize transformation is to put transformation at risk as there should always be the potentiality that things are yet to come. Taking negative risks to actualize transformation might reduce the potentiality of transformation itself. Unless transformative practices are understood as that which happens in and through the educative process, the risk will always exist that (South) Africa never quite rids itself of the further risk of a society, which is inequitable and unjust.

Towards a conclusion

In this chapter we have argued that (South) African universities ought to be guided by positive risks that can counteract the institutional and perhaps societal malaises that have seemingly enveloped, and to a large extent, debilitated higher education discourses on the African continent—that is, exclusion, discrimination, inequitable access, violence and instability. Positive risk potentially promotes African universities' inclinations towards critique, hope and imaginative action. And, when proponents of a major African research university like ours articulate their concerns with the apparent negative risks in counteracting its deceased vice-chancellor's vision of a transformed higher education institution, they tend to ignore that substantive transformation is far more indelible and meaningful than the mere provision of procedural access to a diverse student population, changing quantitatively the number of black faces that perform academic work at the institution, and renaming the buildings in honour of anti-apartheid liberation activists. If transformation were to be ongoing and substantive, then universities should become higher education institutions endeared towards the cultivation of critique, hope and imagination—those inherent features of a positively risk-taking institution that invariably undermine the debilitating forces of oppression, marginalization and exclusion that seem to oppose institutional and societal changes on the continent.

References

Agamben, G. (1993). *The coming community: Theory out of bounds, Volume 1,* M. Hardt (trans.), Minneapolis, MN: University of Minnesota Press.
Arnolds, C. A., Stofile, R. N. & Lillah, R. (2013). Assessing the outcomes of the higher education mergers in South Africa: Implications for strategic management, *Acta Commercii* 13(1), Art. #175, 11 pages. http://dx.doi. org/10.4102/ac.v13i1.175
Assié-Lumumba, N. T. & Lumumba-Kasongo, T. (2011). The idea of the public university and the national project in Africa. In Rhoten, D. & Calhoun, C. (eds.) *Knowledge matters: The public mission of the research university.* New York: Columbia University Press, 251–289.
Badat, S. (2010). *The challenges of transformation in higher education and training institutions in South Africa.* Development Bank of Southern Africa.
Barnett, R. (2013). *Imagining the university.* New York: Routledge.
Barsoum, M. (2014). Cairo University engineering students begin strike to protest violence on campus. http://english.ahram.org.eg/NewsContent/1/64/97138/Egypt/Politics-/-Cairo-University-engineering-students-begin-strik.aspx [Accessed 26 May 2014].
Biesta, G.J.J. (2014) *The beautiful risk of education.* Boulder, CO: Paradigm Publishers.
Burik, S. (2009). Opening philosophy to the world: Derrida and education in philosophy, *Educational Theory*, 59(3): 297–312.
Danilova, M. & Karmanau, Y. (2013). Ukraine protests: *Students* join *demonstrations* in *Kiev* over EU deal. http://www.huffingtonpost.com/2013/11/26/ukraine-protests-eu-deal_n_4344308.html [Accessed 26 May 2014].
Deleuze, G. & Guattari, F. (1987). *A thousand plateaus: Capitalism and schizophrenia*, B. Massumi (trans.). Minneapolis, MN: University of Minnesota Press.
Department of Education (1997). *Education white paper 3: A programme for the transformation of higher education.* Pretoria: Republic of South Africa Government. Gazette, no. 386 (18207).
Derrida, J. (2004). *Eyes of the university: Right to philosophy 2*, J. Plug & others (trans.). Stanford, CA: Stanford University Press.
Fiske, E. B. & Ladd, H. F. (2004). *Equity: Education reform in post-apartheid South Africa.* Washington, DC: Brookings Institution Press.
Freire, P. (2004). *Pedagogy of indignation.* New York: Paradigm Publishers.
Freire, P. (2006). *Pedagogy of the oppressed.* New York: Continuum Publishing.
Giroux, H. A. (2004). An educator's reflections on the crisis in education and democracy in the US: An interview with Henry A. Giroux by Michael Alexander Pozo, 25 September 2004. www.dissidentvoice.org [Accessed 1 August 2014].
Giroux, H. A. (2007). *The university in chains: Confronting the military-industrial-academic complex.* Boulder and London: Paradigm Publishers.

Giroux, H. A. & Searls Giroux, S. (2004a). *Take back higher education: Race, youth, and the crisis of democracy the post-civil rights era.* New York: Palgrave Macmillan.

Giroux, H. A. & Searls Giroux, S. (2004b). Take Back Higher Education: Toward a democratic commons, *Tikkun*, 18(6): 28–32.

Mapasela, M. & Hay, H. R. (2005). Through the magnifying glass: A descriptive theoretical analysis of possible impact of the South African higher education policies on academic staff and their job satisfaction, *Higher Education*, 50: 111–128.

Ministry of Education (2001). *National plan for higher education in South Africa.* Pretoria: Ministry of Education.

Readings, B. (1996). *The university in ruins.* Cambridge, MA: Harvard University Press.

Sanborn, H. & Thyne, C. (2011). Learning democracy: Education and the fall of authoritarian regimes. vmi.academia.edu/HowardSanborn/Papers/1149456 [Accessed 19 October 2012].

Spencer, D. (2010). UK: *Violence* overshadows student fees *protests.* www.universityworldnews.com/article.php?story=20101113063427112 [Accessed 26 May 2014].

Teferra, D. (2006). Challenges of higher education in sub-Saharan Africa. Interview, Global University Network for Innovation. www.guninetwork.org › Resources › GUNi.Talks. [Accessed 4 August 2014].

Teferra, D. & Altbach, P.G. (2003). Trends and perspectives in African higher education. In Teferra, D. & Altbach, P.G. (eds.) *African higher education: An international reference handbook.* Bloomington, IN: Indiana University Press, 2–11.

Teferra, D. & Altbach, P.G. (2004). African higher education: Challenges for the 21st century. *Higher Education*, 47: 21–50.

University World News (2014). South Africa: Student *protest* turns *violent.* www.university-worldnews.com/article.php?story=20090508094607720 [Accessed 26 May 2014].

Waghid, Y. (2002). Rationality and the role of the university: a response to Philip Higgs. *South African Journal of Higher Education*, 16(2): 18–24.

Waghid, Y. (2011). Challenges for higher education in Africa, Ubuntu, and democratic justice. In Rhoten, D. & Calhoun, C. (eds.) *Knowledge matters: The public mission of the research university.* New York: Columbia University Press, 231–250.

Waghid, Y. (2014). *African philosophy of education reconsidered: On being human.* London: Routledge.

Young, I. M. (2000). *Inclusion and democracy.* Oxford: Oxford University Press.

PART FIVE

Knowledge and Research

Introduction

The modern university—effectively the university post-1850 or so—has increasingly been associated not just with knowledge but with the growth of knowledge. But this association with the growth of knowledge emerged with an axiom: that knowledge was of value in itself and was therefore to be pursued 'for its own sake'. This devotion to knowledge for its own sake came to constitute the 'academic dogma', as the American sociologist, Robert Nisbet, put it in 1971. It was simply an unspoken but universally accepted underpinning of the university. However, the impetus for Nisbet's reading lay in a shift in that this epistemic base for the university was already embarked on a turn towards useful knowledge—so, on Nisbet's further reading—constituting a 'degradation' of the academic dogma. Over the last fifty years, that turn has moved in several directions as universities have become central to the development of the knowledge society and 'cognitive capitalism'. Variously, universities are expected to ally themselves to knowledge that is produced in situ (so-called 'Mode 2 knowledge'; Gibbons et al., 1994), knowledge that has an 'impact' and knowledge that has an exchange value (and so can assist a university's income flow).

The first chapter in this part of our volume charts this story in some detail. In 'Citizenship and the University: The Consequences of Globalization', Gerard

Delanty shows how ideas of knowledge and ideas of the university have been intimately connected. *Both* the university and the kinds of knowledge with which it was associated were legitimated through ideas of emancipation and freedom. In this 'liberal' conception of the university, teaching and research formed a unity, in which knowledge was held to be an end in itself. This whole legitimation of the university has, though, quite quickly dissolved, as the university has come under the sway of instrumental reason, with the emergence of the global economy and the significance of the university thereto.

In this situation, some have declared the university either to be in ruins or dead. Others, such as Habermas and Gouldner, have sought to identify a new way of legitimizing the university, resurrecting in new forms earlier connections between the university, knowledge and reason. Yet others, such as Lyotard, have in effect denied that any kind of legitimation of the university is possible amid 'postmodernism', globalization, marketization and, most recently, digitization: knowledge, in particular, can no longer be bolstered by any 'grand narrative' except that of sheer 'performativity': the only criterion of valid knowledge lay in answer to the question 'What use is it?'

Questions arise, therefore, as to the extent of the globalization and economization of the university. For Delanty, there has been a tendency to 'exaggerate the instrumentalization of the university'. If so, there are perhaps spaces for new kinds of legitimation of the university, a possibility that Delanty pursues through the idea of the university as a space for the formation of three kinds of citizenship—at once cultural, social and technological. 'There are undoubtedly tensions between these dimensions of citizenship' and their discursive co-presence may constitute but one way in which the university can advance the public spheres.

The second chapter by Alberto Amaral, on 'Universities and the Knowledge Society Revisited', traces ways in which the above epistemic shifts have played out in the university itself. Significant is it that not only has the character of university knowledge changed but so too have universities themselves changed. Both academic knowledge and universities are now governed by the principle of instrumental reason. Universities have become organizations intent on 'driving up' their efficiency through the adoption of 'new public management' techniques, identifying possible income streams and so engaging in forms of 'academic capitalism' and entering pedagogic markets, with students being treated as customers. In all of this, academics' freedoms and powers are reduced, not least since their work conditions robs them of the space in which they can continue to offer critical voices.

These changes in the internal character of universities are exacerbated by global phenomena, including the emergence of 'cognitive capitalism', exacerbated by world rankings and symbolized by talk of 'world-class universities' and the emptiness of 'excellence'. The emergence of massive open online courses represents a coalescence of both the globalization of higher education and new disruptive digital technologies, and they herald a situation in which 'knowledge is necessary, but not sufficient, for success'.

How might this situation be understood? Are universities consigned only to adapting to the demands of a global, knowledge-based economy, finding their way in a privatization of the products of research? Intellectual property may well have even increased value, but it may be a heavily constrained value in certain kinds of markets.

The final chapter in this section is 'Parting Ways: Analogue People in a Digital University' by Robert Hassan, which analyses the effects of the computerization of the university. The suggestion here is that 'by embracing digital technology so rapidly and allowing it to permeate the university so comprehensively, we have unleashed a technological force—digitalization—that is radically at odds with what it is to be human [and which] conflicts with the analogue process and analogue technology that has been at the heart of the university system since Plato's Academy—that of writing and … reading'. These processes reduce knowledge to information and data and reduce understanding and possibilities for wisdom. Knowledge itself is analogue, with its human rhythms. 'Digital information', in contrast, 'has none of the temporal and physical constraints of print [or those] of our human brains'. 'Computers have no continuity in time and space that we can perceive in space and time'.

Thus, the assimilation of computers into universities has had and is having profound effects, both in the academic life of universities and in universities as organizations. In the academic life, computerization has dramatically affected processes of knowledge production and what it is to 'know'. Thinking, writing and (academic) communication change. This digitization of knowing is compounded by global academic capitalism which, in turn, has heightened demands for greater efficiency that computerization makes possible. 'This logic transforms our analogue time consciousness'.

Accordingly, the digital university poses major problems as to thinking, mind and criticality. It is not clear that such concepts have much purchase amid the instantaneity of 'network time'. Perhaps a first step is to realize that the assumption that 'the analogue human can function in the same way within the digital university' is 'a category mistake'. But more is necessary. The analogue human and human interaction have to be reclaimed: reading and writing are but 'conditions of possibility' for the safeguarding of universities as spaces for human thought, knowledge and understanding.

Ronald Barnett

References

Gibbons, M., Limoges, C., Nowotny, H., Schwartzman, S., Scott, P. and Trow, M. (1994). *The New Production of Knowledge: The Dynamics of Science and Research in Contemporary Societies.* London: Sage.

Nisbet, R. (1971). *The Degradation of the Academic Dogma: The University in America 1945–1970.* London: Heinemann.

CHAPTER SEVENTEEN

Citizenship and the University

The Consequences of Globalization

GERARD DELANTY

In this chapter, my aim is to look at how the debate on the university has been refracted through the main sociological theories of higher education and, on the basis of that review, will develop an understanding of the manner and possibilities for the university's role in relationship to citizenship. Hopefully, this will relativize some of the dire diagnoses of the current situation of higher education. The sociology of the university has been a neglected aspect of the history of sociology. Yet, most of the major sociologists and social theorists from those in the classical tradition such as Weber, Durkheim and Veblen and mid-century sociologists such as Parsons, Bell, Riesman and Shils, to the radical generation—Touraine, Gouldner, Habermas and Bourdieu—wrote extensively on it. In doing so they were not all necessarily working within the sociology of education but, from the broader perspective of social theory and the sociology of knowledge, saw higher education and more generally the institution of the university as central to a wider understanding of modernity. Too much of the debate on the university has been dominated by speculative and rather dismal work on the *idea* of the university.

More recently, some of this more pessimistic genre has become popular with the thesis of the postmodern university, beginning with Lyotard and reiterated by Bill Readings in an influential philosophical application of Lyotard's ideas. The postmodern theory of the university has been reflected in widespread concerns about the embracing of market values by the university under the condition of globalization. I shall try to demonstrate in this chapter that the sociological perspective offers an important appraisal of the university as an institution that marks major transformations within modernity. These works put into theoretical and historical perspective a wider view of the university as a resilient institution that both reflects and transforms the society of which it is a part. Thus rather than speak of the demise of the university as a result of the postmodern scenarios of the fragmentation of knowledge, the retreat of the state, the embracing of market values, or the impact of globalization, a sociological approach suggests a more differentiated view of the university. The chapter will show that the theme of citizen ship has been central to the conception of the university in modernity and much of this is still relevant to the current situation.

First I outline the major classical conceptions of the university in social theory; in the following section I discuss the idea of the university in radical social theory; next I turn to contemporary debates on the university and, finally, I offer an appraisal of the current situation of the university in light of these debates.

Social Theory and the University in Modernity

Since the Enlightenment, the university has been a central matter in many debates on the nature of modernity. From Kant and von Humboldt to Newman and Jaspers, much of this revolved around the question of academic freedom and the institutional underpinning of the unity of knowledge that was central to the Enlightenment project. If the Enlightenment promised progress through knowledge, the university was the institution in society that provided the space in which to make possible that goal. With Max Weber, the philosophical discourse of the university and the Enlightenment ideal of knowledge and science as an end is put on trial. Weber departed from the Enlightenment-influenced idea in one major respect: he did not think that knowledge had a self-evidently emancipatory function and he strenuously opposed the use of science for politics. The university suffered the same fate as knowledge under the conditions of advanced modernity and the total disenchantment of the world he believed accompanied modern rationalism, the result of which was the irreconcilable conflict between the realms of science, politics, ethics, and art.

In his famous lecture in 1918, 'Science as a Vocation' (*Wissenschaft als Beruf*), he discussed the role of the university professor in the disenchanted age of modern rationalization (Weber, 1948: 131). Weber lamented, but accepted with resignation, the inevitability of the disappearance of the Enlightenment university and the rise of the modern instrumental university. Less critically and in line with his value-neutral conception of science, he noted the separation of science and politics, for the conduct of science under the conditions of modernity allows no room for politics. [By 'science', Weber had in mind all systematic inquiry characteristic of universities. Ed.] Science is the product of a rationalized world devoid of personality while politics still offers some scope for personality and the recovery of charisma.

Weber was unambivalent in his commitment to 'ethical neutrality' for he believed that cultural values could not be judged. Knowledge might gain some power over them if it confined itself to neutral analysis. But even then it will be limited. As he put it in an essay on universities in 1908: 'The freedom of science exists in Germany within the limits of ecclesiastical and political acceptability. Outside these limits there is none' (Weber, 1973: 17; see also Shils, 1973). This was the basis of a view that won widespread support in later decades and is best represented by the German sociologist Helmut Schelsky's term 'solitude and freedom' (Schelsky, 1963). In *Einsamkeit und Freiheit*, a work never translated into English, Schelsky demonstrated, in what to some was unrealistic, the idea of an overarching and transcendent point of unity, which is to be found, he argued, in the 'solitude and freedom' of science and scholarship.

The Enlightenment model of the university believed the unity of knowledge rested on the unity of teaching and research. Much of the early sociology of the university recognized the breakup of this unified model of knowledge. For instance, Thorstein Veblen in his influential *The Higher Learning in America* (1962), first published in 1918, wrote about the decline of the liberal model of the university which becomes instead a place of research to which teaching is subordinated. This transition was marked by the creation of the PhD, as an attempt to usurp the German liberal humanist tradition of knowledge as an end by institutionalizing a research culture. Recognizing that the twentieth-century university would be different from that which preceded it, Veblen nevertheless held onto the Enlightenment humanistic understanding of knowledge as an end in itself. These theories were among the first intimations of the entry of the university into sociological consciousness.

In the 1960s and 1970s, when sociology as a discipline consolidated, several notable sociologists and from diverse perspectives contributed to the newly emerging interest in the university. Daniel Bell (1966) was one of the first to recognize the importance of the university for sociology, proposing the thesis that the university is a central part of the postindustrial society and in it a potentially emancipatory 'knowledge class' is to be found. For Bell, this class, essentially the intelligentsia, is composed of the scientific, the technological, the administrative, and the cultural. Since the postindustrial society depends to a great extent on the production of knowledge, the university will occupy a more important role than before. It would be inevitable that as the university becomes implicated in material production, it would also take on a political role. In his famous work *The Coming of the Postindustrial Society*, Bell defended the relevance of the traditional and the modern functions of the university. The function of the university, he argues

> is to relate to each other the modes of conscious inquiry: historical consciousness, which is the encounter with a tradition that can be tested against the present; methodological consciousness, which makes explicit the conceptual grounds of inquiry and its philosophical presuppositions; and individual self-consciousness which makes one aware of the sources of one's prejudgements, and allows one to re-create one's values through the disciplined study of the society. (Bell, 1974: 423)

In this respect, Bell identified an important feature of the university: it is one of the few locations in society where in face of specialization and differentiation, many modes of cognitive interaction are possible precisely as a result of its concentration of functions. For Edward Shils (1972), this role was inseparable from citizenship. He believed the university had made a major contribution to social and civic citizenship by providing society with some of its essential requirements, in particular a professional class.

For Parsons and Platt (1973) in *The American University*, the university is the key institution of the 'fiduciary' subsystem, which might be understood as the 'system of trust', and lies in the 'zone of interpenetration' between the cultural system and society. Influenced by functional theory and a liberal political ideology which predisposed them toward a largely harmonious view of society, they saw a complementarity in these functions and believed that the university did not have to compromise its role as the 'trustee of cognitive culture'.

The unity of the university for Parsons is not the unity of a legitimating idea but the functional unity of its structures with respect to the societal community. The two principal features of the American university are: '(1) that it, and with it the institutionalized cognitive complex, has become a differentiated part of a complex society and (2) that it has become upgraded in prestige and influence within the society to the point that some commentators describe it as the central institution in the society' (Parsons and Platt, 1973: 103). The key concept for Parsons and Platt is 'interpenetration', the process by which one subsystem affects another: the university is forced to occupy a zone between culture and society, and therefore must cut across these systems. But the imperatives of differentiation do not preclude the possibility of an overall integration.

This complementarity between differentiation and the possibility of integration is the central and unifying theme in Parsons's entire sociology of modernity

(Parsons, 1974). In the Parsonian framework this unity of purpose is reflected in the university's interpenetration into the domains of culture and society. Indeed, the very term cognitive rationality embodies both a cultural (cognitive) and a social (rationality) dimension, as Parsons and Platt point out (1973: 38). What is important in the Parsonian framework is that the university is still connected to the noncognitive structures of the cultural system, while being autonomous from the moral community at large. The complexity of the interrelationships that characterize the university prevents it from being the moral arbiter of society: the modern university cannot function as, they say, the 'Prince's conscience', as in the early modern university (Parsons and Platt, 1973: 47–50).

While Parsons and Platt argue that the primary core value of the university is cognitive rationality, they recognize that the university is increasingly becoming a certifier of professional competence within the occupational order. In Parsons's words: 'the university became the primary trustee of that phase of the cultural heritage of modern societies that was important for the grounding of professional competence' (Parsons, 1979: 91). In their framework, intellectuals, who have access to the mass media, are also important in their contribution to the 'general definition of the situation', with respect to the human condition as a whole and the status of the social sciences. The university, they argue, makes a major contribution to public knowledge which is central to modern society. The public, unlike professional knowledge producers, is concerned less with the problem of explanation than with the problem of meaning (Parsons and Platt, 1973: 279–82).

The American University was a product of disciplinary organized knowledge with politics kept outside. The role of the university was not to criticize or transform culture and morality but to pass on relatively intact a received tradition to future generations. Clearly this was an inherently conservative function. For Durkheim, indeed: 'the evolution of education always lags very substantially behind the general evolution of society as a whole'. He noted how, for instance, 'a great scientific movement was to be born in the sixteenth century and to be developed throughout the seventeenth and eighteenth centuries without making the slightest impact on the University before the beginning of the nineteenth' (Durkheim, 1977: 1964).

Radical Social Theory and the University

Cultural revolution in the Western world from the 1960s onward shattered the cultural framework which carried liberal education (Lipset, 1967). In this period the university becomes less a transmitter of culture than its transformer. In Germany, where de-nazification was a project led by the universities, this was particularly pronounced. What is striking about the revolutionary decades was the emergence of a cultural clash between bourgeois culture and mass culture. New cultural voices emerge: the women's movement, black and ethnic cultures, nationalist liberation movements, Marxism, and the postmodern avant-garde which sought to relink art and politics. As a result of the Vietnam War and the civil rights movement, the American university became a major political site, a factor enhanced by the academicization of Marxism. In the 1960s and 1970s, the countercultural impulse stemmed largely from the students, a contrast to the other great period of academic revolution—the 1790s and the opening decade of the nineteenth century—when it stemmed from the professors. This is expressed, for example, in a famous incident at Warwick University in 1970 and became the subject of the book edited by E. P. Thompson, *Warwick University Ltd*, when students, protesting about the lack of accountability in the university, occupied the administration and gained access to controversial information relating to what E. P. Thompson later called the 'industrial–intellectual oligarchy' (Thompson, 1970).

In a book entitled *Culture in the Plural*, published in 1974, Michel de Certeau discussed the embracing of democratic popular cultures by the university: 'The relation of culture to society has been transformed: culture is no longer reserved for a given milieu; it no longer belongs to certain professional specialities (teachers or liberal professions); nor is it any longer a stable entity defined by universally received codes' (de Certeau, 1997: 41). He believed the introduction of popular culture into the university was leading to the birth of the student worker and the wider abolition of the social divisions of labor. Though this socialism of the intellect and of labor was not to last, the politicization of the university was irreversible.

An important German debate on the university began in the late 1960s with contributions by Habermas. Habermas' (1969, 1971a, b) intervention concerned the question of democratization and cultural renewal. Rejecting attempts to define the university in terms of the culture of humanism, on the one side, and on the other, as a purely instrumental institution for providing technical knowledge, he defended the critical heritage of the university. Like many intellectuals on the left, he was aware that the older humanistic model of the university—the subject of Fritz Ringer's famous study (Ringer, 1969)—failed to offer resistance to fascism and consequently needed to recover its moral standing in society. Habermas emphasized the role of the university as an interpreter of a society's self-understanding and not just passing on its heritage in an unmediated manner: 'it belongs to the tasks of the university to transmit, interpret, and develop the cultural tradition of the society' (Habermas, 1971a: 2). However, Habermas believed the reform of the German university was compatible with the *Bildung* ideal of the older model insofar as this could be transformed into a more critical kind of self-reflection.

For Habermas, the university was also in danger of becoming dominated by the instrumental rationality of technology and capitalism. The alternative was democratization and the ending of the dualism of academic hierarchy and the administration of departments. In a later essay (Habermas, 1987), he argued that the critical role of the university has remained unrealized but to bring it to realization today will require the creation of a 'communication community'. For Habermas, like Parsons, the university is a 'bundle institution', that is, it is rooted in the life-world through the bundling of functions, such as research, general education, cultural self-understanding, the formation of public opinion, and the training of specialists: 'As long as this complex has not been completely torn apart, the idea of the university cannot be completely dead' (Habermas, 1987). But unlike Parsons, Habermas argued the unity of the university is not to be found in culture or in science but 'in the last analysis it is the communicative forms of scientific and scholarly argumentation that hold university learning processes in their various functions together' (Habermas, 1987). While the older humanistic conception of the university emphasized the professoriate as the guardians of culture, Habermas pointed out that it was the students who were now defending the university (Habermas, 1971b).

Habermas' theory of the university thus holds a central role in his wider social theory of modernity, seeing it as the site of critical and communicative reason. In his work on the public sphere, for instance, modernity is seen as the unfolding of communicative spaces and while many of these spaces have been feudalized or colonized by instrumental reason, the university has remained an important site of critique (Habermas, 1989, 1996). As is also evident in his other work from that period, *Knowledge and Human Interests* (Habermas, 1978), knowledge is a differentiated structure and is linked to society by its inseparable connection with cognitively specific human interests. But what links all the sciences together is not scientific rationality as such but the embeddedness of science in communication. Such a communicative understanding of the university allows us to speak of the 'idea' of the university with a major qualification: the 'idea' of the university does not necessarily derive from the university itself. As Habermas intimated, a 'new life can be breathed into the idea of the university only outside its walls' (Habermas, 1987).

This was also the position that Alain Touraine took. In *The May Movement*, Touraine (1971b) applied his sociology of action to the university. In the post-industrial society, knowledge is the key to the new struggles, he argued in *Post-Industrial Society* (1971a). The implication of this is that the university must decide whether it is to be allied to politics or to capital. Touraine believed the mode of knowledge produced by the university could be used to renew the cultural models and to lead to the creation of new social practices, a social theory that was elaborated in more abstract terms in *The SelfProduction of Society* (1977). He saw a new role for the university emerging as a reflection on society for the 'progress of knowledge is inseparable from the critical self-reflection of society on itself, on its intellectual operations as well as on its social and political organization' (Touraine, 1971a: 332). 'The university was and is, simultaneously, an instrument to reinforce the dominant scientific creation and a relatively independent center of criticism and cultural change' (Touraine, 1971a: 334). Seeing knowledge and politics as mediated in the cultural model of society, he criticized both the conservatism of the university and the offensive politics of the students.

A theme that becomes visible in the sociological writing on the university in this period is that the university is a site of cultural contestation. It is a relatively autonomous zone in society where major cultural conflicts are fought out over what might be broadly called 'cultural capital'. This is evident in the work of Riesman, Gouldner and Bourdieu. In *The Academic Revolution*, David Riesman and Christopher Jencks (1968) emphasized the rise of the academic profession which reached preeminence with the emergence of the student movement. In work published in 1980, *On Higher Education: The Academic Enterprise in an Era of Rising Student Consumerism*, Riesman explored the implications of this confrontation (Riesman, 1998). As a result of the emergence of student revolt, there was an inevitable decline in the power of the academic profession in an era of what he called 'student consumerism'.

In one of his most famous books, *The Future of Intellectuals and the Rise of the New Class*, Alvin Gouldner explored some of the contradictions of the university in postindustrial society (Gouldner, 1979). The argument was that intellectuals and the intelligentsia together formed a 'new class', a kind of 'cultural bourgeoisie', which is essentially contradictory since it is composed of two overlapping elements, the professions and the radical intellectuals. While both share a social existence in the production of knowledge, the former is embedded in the system of power and the latter is in opposition to it. In his view, education is more than just the 'ideological state apparatuses', as Althusser claimed (Althusser, 1971). Instead, he argued the university is a contradictory place in which the New Class may seek alliances with business or with apolitical culture or with political subversion. The university is, like the New Class itself, internally differentiated:

> To understand modern universities and colleges we need an openness to contradiction. For universities both reproduce and subvert the larger society. We must distinguish between the functions universities publicly promise to perform—the social goods they are chartered to produce—and certain of their actual consequences which, while commonly unintended, are not real: the production of dissent, deviance, and

the cultivation of an authority-subverting culture of critical discourse. (Gouldner, 1979: 45)

Gouldner's thesis is that the New Class, which is much more contradictory than the old class, does not control cultural capital such as knowledge. He believes there is enough empirical evidence to suggest that, in particular, in higher education power is loosened not tightened. Higher education thus becomes a major 'cosmopolitanizing influence' in modern society. In it there is a shift from causal to reflexive speech and a discourse emerges in which claims and utterances may not be justified by reference to a speaker's social status. As a result, all authority referring claims are potentially problematic (Gouldner, 1979: 3). However, as he put it elsewhere: 'The university's central problem is its failure as a community in which rational discourse about social worlds is possible. This was partly because rational discourse as such ceased to be its dominant value and was superseded by a quest for knowledge products and information products that could be sold for funding, prestige and power—rewards bestowed by the state and the larger society that is bent upon subverting rational discourse about itself' (Gouldner, 1979: 79). In sum, he argued universities foster a 'culture of critical discourse', so offering both cosmopolitanism and reflexivity.

In his extensive writings on education and the university, in books such as *Homo Academicus* (1988) and *The State Nobility* (1996), Bourdieu presents a view of the university as the paradigmatic site of cultural capital. Although Bourdieu's main studies on higher education are based on research conducted in the late 1960s and 1970s and are very specific to the French context, they provide a striking account of some general trends in the transformation of higher education. Sharing with Foucault the view that knowledge is power, Bourdieu maintains that knowledge is not primarily emancipatory but is socially located in contexts of power which are in essence classificatory, or cognitive, systems in which the different forms of capital circulate. Bourdieu's sociology of knowledge claims that cognitive structures shape, limit, and influence the production and circulation of knowledge in society. Consequently, some of the most important battles over cultural capital are fought out in the university. Education thus is a field in which the wider conflicts and sources of inequality in society are manifest. Inequality in economic capital and through the pursuit of distinction in cultural capital is very pronounced in education.

The expansion of education has not led to greater social equality, according to Bourdieu and Passeron in *Reproduction in Education, Society and Culture* (1977) and *The Inheritors* (1979). Participation in French higher education is predominantly middle and upper-middle class. Lying at the root of this position is a view of education as a form of cultural capital which can lead to economic capital but it is also something that is inherently a source of power in its own right. Education thus becomes a cultural field in which society selects individuals for positions of power and allocates status and prestige. Schools and universities are primarily institutions of selection. It is this functional selectivity that connects the university to society.

Bourdieu mentions in particular the struggle between three kinds of cultural capital that is fought out in the university. *Academic power* refers to the power of control over the administration of academic resources and the means of career influence. It is the power to preside over credentials and allocate status and as such it is a socially codified power. *Scientific power* is essentially the power that comes from research reputations based on scholarly publications. It is a matter of prestige deriving directly from knowledge as opposed to the status attached to honorific positions. *Intellectual power* (or 'intellectual renown') comes from the ability to influence public opinion. It can derive from academic power but it is more likely to stem from scientific power. In France, this is represented by membership of the *Académie Française*, writing reviews in the influential weeklies, or in publishing a book with a publisher read by the educated middle classes (Bourdieu, 1988: 78–9). The university thus can be examined as a site of struggle between these three fields of power and where different kinds of cultural capital collide.

There is no doubt that Bourdieu's studies on education and the university stress the autonomy that these institutions have won for themselves in their ability to create 'orders of classification'. However, there is relatively little in his analysis on the empancipatory struggles that other theorists have emphasized. Thus where Riesman saw a decline in 'faculty dominance', Bourdieu sees only the ascendancy of the professoriate and its consolidation as a 'state nobility'. Clearly in the current age of the 'postmodern university' this view of the academic profession is no longer tenable. Unlike the work of Riesman in the United States or Touraine in France or Habermas in Germany, Bourdieu ignored the wider social context, preferring to see the crisis as deriving from problems within French higher education. However, what remains of enduring importance in Bourdieu's work on the university is his account of cultural capital, which serves as a medium of exchange between the various kinds of power. In the context of the debate around the postmodern university this sense of the relative autonomy of the field of cultural capital is important.

The University in Contemporary Social Theory and Sociology

Despite their differences, the classical social theories of modernity, from Weber through Parsons, all took for granted certain assumptions about modernity, such as the relative autonomy of knowledge and the view that technology was contained by science. Such assumptions led them to a view of the university as an autonomous site in modern society. These assumptions were also present in modern social theory, such as in the theories of the university of Habermas and Bourdieu, and other figures in the radical tradition. However, in recent social theory—which is much more skeptical about the project of modernity—a corresponding uncertainty about the role of the university has become very pronounced amid a broader recognition of the transformation of scientific knowledge.

There are five main positions on the university in contemporary social theory: the liberal critique, the postmodern thesis, the reflexivity thesis, the globalization thesis, and the McDonaldization thesis.

The liberal critique

In essence, this is a conservative cultural critique and, although not sociological, is highly influential even within social science. It is primarily concerned with the university as a medium of cultural reproduction. The liberal idea of the university can be associated with the quite different positions of Allan Bloom (1987) and Russell Jacoby (1987). Bloom represents an old-fashioned conservative view of higher education as the preservation of tradition. He thus bemoans the attack on the traditional curriculum in the name of diversity. Jacoby, who represents a more radical liberal position, also attacks the arrival of cultural politics but not because of the greater value of the traditional canon: he regrets the decline of the public intellectual, who has disappeared from the university that has become the retreat of the specialist. Despite the different positions within this broad stance that derives from the neo-humanist tradition, the tendency is to see the university in crisis because of the decline of the autonomy of culture, be it the culture of critique or, in its more conservative version, the traditional culture of the canon.

The postmodern thesis

Theories that were to surface in the wake of Lyotard's theory of the university in *The Postmodern Condition* exaggerated the demise of the university as a result of 'material capital' invading the space of 'cultural capital' (Lyotard, 1984). In the postmodern informational society, Lyotard argued, the university suffers the same fate as the meta-narratives of modernity. Since there are no longer autonomous spaces, the university does not occupy a privileged site. Against Bourdieu's image of a resilient institution of modernity, Lyotard is more skeptical of the institutions of modernity such as the university's ability to offer possibilities for radical politics. He saw the university as based on a new unity by which the different kinds of knowledge are part of a universal principle of performativity. Universities, for Lyotard, are based on bounded discourses—such as the department, the faculty, the curriculum—and modern forms of legitimation, such as the lecture and professorial authority. Therefore, he did not see the university as central to politics, arguing instead that the postmodern condition is based on a different kind of politics, one of plurality and one that is located far from the jurisdiction of the state.

One implication of this is the postmodern thesis of the curriculum as a site of domination. Rejecting the neo-humanist ideal of the integration of teaching and research—which in different ways was accepted by Parsons and Habermas in their writings on the university—Lyotard sees teaching as counter-revolutionary while research can be emancipatory so long as it breaks from any criterion of legitimation. Unlike teaching, which he sees as under the control of the state, research can be subversive of all attempts to impose meta-narratives.

The reflexivity thesis

This reflexive thesis is best associated with the claim that there is a new mode of knowledge based on a more reflexive relationship between user and producer (Gibbons et al., 1984). As a Mode 2 paradigm around applied knowledge emerges, the university—which is caught up in the more hierarchical and disciplinary-based Mode 1 knowledge production—becomes, it is claimed, increasingly irrelevant to the post-Fordist economy in which techno-science is becoming more important. While offering a less dramatic theory of the decline of the university, an assumption of the obsolescence of the institutions of modernity is built into the argument. In more recent work by three of these authors, this prognosis is somewhat qualified (see Nowotny et al., 2001). In general, the point that lies behind this stance is that technical training, the provision of technical expertise and generally techno-science rather than basic science is what is important today, and universities are less equipped to deal with it, given that they are located in the nexus of basic knowledge characteristic of the humanities and experimental sciences.

The globalization thesis

This body of writing on the university draws attention to the instrumentalization of the university as it embraces market values and information technology, especially in the area of the online provision of higher education. Although the proponents of this thesis do not use the language of postmodernism, they share the view that the university, as a modern institution and servant of the nation-state, is embracing consumerism and, as it does so it loses its moral purpose in the global age. While e-programs are one dimension of the impact of globalization, another is in the area of techno-science. According to various authors, the university is far from irrelevant to capitalism, as the previous thesis would claim, but is in fact fully integrated into it and, as a new managerialism takes over the university, there is a resulting loss of academic freedom (Curie and Newson, 1998; Etzkowitz and Leydesdorff, 1997; Slaughter and Leslie, 1993). This thesis suggests that the university has become a major player in the global market and in information-based capitalism.

Slaughter and Leslie (1993) argue in a major study, *Academic Capitalism*, that the changes that took place in higher education in the 1980s and 1990s were as great as the changes that took place in the last quarter of the nineteenth century when the industrial revolution created the wealth that provided the base for higher education. But in the 1980s and 1990s, national systems of higher education were restructured in order to secure a greater share of global markets. The shift to 'academic capitalism' occurred because universities' search for extra funding coincided with the corporate quest for new products requiring a high input of scientific knowledge. So, rather than universities becoming irrelevant, they are becoming more and more central to capitalism in the provision of techno-science and the university has in fact strengthened its position by participating in the global expansion of capitalism. What in fact exists is a 'triple helix' of links between government, university, and industry, to use the term of Etzkowitz and Leydesdorff (1997).

These developments have led to a great deal of speculation about the emergence of global mega-universities, corporate universities, and even virtual universities (Miyoshi, 1998; Robins and Webster, 2002; Scott, 1998; Smith and Webster, 1997). Building on industry–university links established since the 1980s, it has frequently been noted, universities are also moving closer to digital degrees. The growth of vocational training, distance learning, and the move to make course curricula the property of the university are examples of how universities are reducing labor costs while expanding enrolment.

According to Bill Readings in a brilliant book, *The University in Ruins*, the university was created to legitimate and serve the nation-state in a historical mission to provide the nation-state with a cultural project (Readings, 1996). This project, which derived from the Enlightenment, is no longer relevant today since, he argues, the nation-state no longer exists. The university and the state are both modern creations and the fate of the former is inextricably linked to the latter, for globalization has put an end to the university of modernity as it has to the nation-state: 'The University no longer has to safeguard and propagate national culture, because the nation-state is no longer the major site at which capital reproduces itself' (Readings, 1996: 13). In place of defining a cultural project, the 'posthistorical' university is a 'ruined' institution, merely reproducing the corporate ideology of 'excellence' which commodifies all forms of knowledge. These accounts of the postmodern university thus portray it as nothing less than an enclave of global capitalism.

The McDonaldization thesis

The notion of the 'McUniversity' indicates the emergence of growing rationalization in the university along the lines of McDonaldization as in the Weberian theory of rationalization. In one version of the argument, new bureaucratic forms of university administration are taking shape diminishing the autonomy of academics and transforming the university into a Fordist organization for the mass production of higher education (Parker and Jary, 1995). Although not amounting to the end of the university, the idea of McUniversity indicates the arrival of a massified university in which education, professional organization, and research are standardized by neoliberal thinking. The McUniversity entails greater managerial power, structural centralization, increased student intake, the casualization of labor, and the elimination of inefficiency.

The Uses of the University: The University in the Knowledge Society

To what extent is the postmodern university a reality? Has the vision of the university in what might broadly be called modern social theory been rendered obsolete by developments that can be described as postmodernization: the penetration of market values into the university, the encroachment of globalization, the possibility of the virtual mega university, and the fragmentation of knowledge? Does the McUniversity offer some possibilities for the university to be a relevant institution? There is clearly much to suggest that the idea of the university in the older sociological theories of Weber, Parsons, Habermas, and Bourdieu has been undermined by recent developments and the liberal critique is at best a nostalgic plea for a lost modernity. Whether the assumptions of the older approaches are no longer valid is a different matter and must be soberly addressed.

First, there is a clear need for a historical contextualization of the university. The recent debates on the demise of the university tend to be based on a historically inaccurate view of earlier models of the university. While the augmented instrumentalization of the university by market values is an undeniable and probably irreversible development, it is by no means specific to the contemporary university. Universities have always been deeply involved in industry since the late nineteenth century. German universities since the middle of the nineteenth century were heavily involved in the technological innovations and American universities since the Land Grant Act became deeply embedded in the nascent industrial society.

Second, the globalization thesis exaggerates certain trends, especially relating to the impact of information and communication technologies. Assumptions of technological determinism underlie these notions of the mega-online university replacing all other kinds of higher education. There is no doubt that the delivery of higher education is moving to more and more mixed methods, which will include online delivery, and self-governance has been eroded by managerialism. However, current evidence is that the virtual university may be suffering the same fate as the wider virtual economy. The belief that online provision will solve the fiscal problem of widening participation is increasingly being doubted, as interactive learning is in fact expensive. Clearly, in the lower end of the market for academic produce, online delivery will not decline, and it may also be effective for certain kinds of training, but for most kinds of educational instruction, including much of vocational training, it will not be viable as the exclusive means of instruction. Moreover, it is a fundamental misunderstanding of the social impact of information and communication technologies to assume that they are revolutionary. Current sociological research reveals that in fact these technologies allow people to do what they have always done but in more diverse ways. In sum, technology has a differential impact on social relations.

Third, any sociologically informed account of the transformation of higher education today must recognize the diversity of universities. Much of the current debate tends to assume that American developments in academic capitalism are universally applicable. To an extent this can be generalized to the wider Anglo-American world, but it is highly questionable that it applies to, for instance, the European universities. Moreover, the great diversity within American higher education cannot be ignored. The European context is very different, simply because in most European countries the university is a public institution. Where the United States has been a market-dominated society, the European experience has on the whole given a stronger role to the state. Although this is less the case in the UK, the state tradition, as is reflected in Bourdieu's studies, is a striking feature of the European university tradition. The different state traditions in Europe have given the European university an extraordinary variety of institutional forms. While the economic exploitation of knowledge is becoming more and more globalized, science is still nationally organized and yet is globally interconnected. Nearly all the important organizations of science—*Centre National de Recherche*

Scientifique in France, the *Max-Planck-Gesellschaft* in Germany—are nationally funded. The persistence of national foundations for knowledge does not hinder the remarkable growth of global collaboration but makes it possible. In this respect an important consideration is the socalled 'Bologna Process' in Europe within which there is the expectation of a 'Europeanization' of higher education by 2010 along with a growing consciousness of the emergence of a European 'knowledge society'.

In sum, my argument is that the specter of the postmodern university tends to exaggerate the instrumentalization of the university by global forces and that there is not only a good deal of continuity with the older model of the university, but that much of the so-called instrumentalization is to be contextualized in a more differentiated analysis of the knowledge society where there are opportunities as well as dangers for the university.

Conclusion: Possibilities for Citizenship

Arising from a sense that knowledge is increasingly inseparable from democracy, I would like to conclude by exploring a particular dimension of the university in the knowledge society, namely that of citizenship.

First, the postmodern thesis that the turn from the state to the market fundamentally alters the historical purpose of the university can be challenged on the grounds that it exaggerates market developments. What the postmodern position neglects is that the university is still a major vehicle of *cultural citizenship*, especially in countries where civil society is weak, for example in China, as Calhoun has demonstrated, or in Iran and in numerous other examples (Calhoun, 1994). In Eastern Europe today, universities have a major role to play in reshaping societies. Universities throughout the world have been tremendously important in cultivating democratic values and in the extension of cultural citizenship, for example in bringing about a critical and reflexive awareness of issues relating to minorities, multiculturalism, human rights, feminism, and cultural heritage. While in the past much of the critical capacity of the university was subordinated to defining the cognitive structures of the nation-state, today the cultural mission of the university has extended into the broader domain of cosmopolitanism in the cultivation of post-national kinds of citizenship.

Second, in many countries higher education is central to *social citizenship*. In the UK, for instance, the question of widening participation in higher education is one of the main aims of government policy in the area of social citizenship. In the view of many critics, this has the disadvantage of a trade-off between the social question of widening participation and the cultural question of an overriding commitment to science. The defenders of liberal education make much of this, seeing only a loss in the cultural dimension. For good or for bad, higher education is being forced more and more to be an agent of social change. There is no sign of this abating and in fact the separation of mass education from research-based activities has for long been a feature of the American university. It is not implausible to suggest, following Parsons, that the university responds to integrative demands by undergoing differentiation. In this way it can achieve a degree of social integration while pursuing cultural goals. One of the best examples of the role of the university in extending social and cultural citizenship is the Open Society Foundation, funded by George Soros. Aside from being an interesting example of how globalization is not undermining higher education but supporting it, the Open Society Foundation testifies to the critical role higher education is playing in reconstituting civil society in postcommunist societies (see Dahrendorf, 2002).

Third, *technological citizenship* has become a new form of citizenship, going beyond social citizenship and, indeed also, cultural citizenship, and pertains to challenges to society that the new technologies are creating. In the context of the knowledge society the question of technological citizenship is especially important for the university to define a new identity for itself. Technology, especially technoscience, is shaping the world according to the dictates of global market forces and is one of the major societal discourses today in which rights and democracy are framed. As science is no longer exclusively based in the university, it is not far-fetched to propose that universities have an important role to play in linking technology to citizenship and bringing about a democratization of science and technology (Fuller, 1999).

There are undoubtedly tensions between these dimensions of citizenship. For instance, widening participation—the dimension of social citizenship—can undermine the cultural role of the university, but it can also enhance it. Perhaps it can be suggested that the term 'university' today means the interconnection of different societal discourses: cultural, social, and technological. While these are fragmented in the wider society, they are connected in the university. The university no longer has a monopoly over knowledge in the broad sense of education and nor does it exclusively define science. Yet, it is a vital institution in the public sphere, contributing to civil society and citizenship by connecting societal discourses. The public sphere today is part of the knowledge society in which knowledge is not only more widely available but is also more and more contested as increasing numbers of social actors are drawn into it. It is possible to see universities in the knowledge societies of the twenty-first century having the role of expanding public spheres as discursive sites in society where social interests engage with the specialized worlds of science and where national and global forces meet.

Note

This chapter is based on my *book Challenging Knowledge: The University in the Knowledge Society* (Buckingham: Open University Press, 2001).

References

Althusser, L. (1971). 'Ideology and the ideological state apparatus', in *Lenin and Philosophy and Other Essays*. London: New Left Books.

Bell, D. (1966). *Reforming of General Education: The Columbia College Experience and Its National Setting*. New York: Columbia University Press.

Bell, D. (1974). *The Coming of the Postindustrial Society*. London: Heinemann.

Bloom, A. (1987). *The Closing of the American Mind*. New York: Simon and Schuster.

Bourdieu, P. (1988). *Homo Academicus*. Cambridge: Polity Press.

Bourdieu, P. (1996). *The State Nobility*. Cambridge: Polity Press.

Bourdieu, P. and Passeron, J.-C. (1977). *Reproduction in Education, Society and Culture*. London: Sage.

Bourdieu, P. and Passeron, J.-C. (1979). *The Inheritors: French Students and Their Relation to Culture*. Chicago: University of Chicago Press.

Bourdieu, P., Passeron, J.-P. and de Saint Martin, M. (1992). *Academic Discourse: Linguistic Misunderstanding and Professorial Power*. Cambridge: Polity Press.

Calhoun, C. (1994). *Neither Gods nor Emperors: Students and the Struggle for Democracy in China*. Berkeley, CA: University of California Press.

Castoriadis, C. (1987). *The Imaginary Institution of Society*. Cambridge: Polity Press.

Curie, J. and Newson, J. (eds) (1998). *Universities and Globalization: Critical Perspectives*. London: Sage.

Dahrendorf, R. (2002). *Universities after Communism*. Hamburg: Korber-Stiftung.

de Certeau, M. (1997). *Culture in the Plural*. Minneapolis, MN: University of Minnesota Press.

Delanty, G. (1997). *Social Science: Beyond Realism and Constructivism*. Buckingham: Open University Press.

Delanty, G. (1999). *Social Theory in a Changing World: Conceptions of Modernity*. Cambridge: Polity Press.

Delanty, G. (2000a). Modernity and Postmodernity: Knowledge, Power and the Self. London: Sage.

Delanty, G. (2000b). *Citizenship in a Global Age: Culture, Politics, Society*. Buckingham: Open University Press.

Delanty, G. (2001). *Challenging Knowledge: The University in the Knowledge Society*. Buckingham: Open University Press.

Durkheim, E. (1957). *Professional Ethics and Civic Morals*. London: Routledge and Kegan Paul.

Durkheim, E. (1977). *The Evolution of Educational Thought*. London: Routledge and Kegan Paul.

Etzkowitz, H. and Leydesdorff, L. (eds) (1997). *Universities in the Global Economy: A Triple Helix of University Industry Government Relations*. London: Cassell Academic.

Fuller, S. (1999). *The Governance of Science*. Buckingham: Open University Press.

Gibbons, M., Limoges, C., Nowotny, H., Schwartzman, S., Scott, P. and Trow, M. (1984). *The New Production of Knowledge*. London: Sage.

Gouldner, A. (1979). *The Future of Intellectuals and the Rise of the New Class*. London: Macmillan.

Habermas, J. (1969). *Protestbewegnung und Hochschulenreform*. Frankfurt: Suhrkamp.

Habermas, J. (1971a). 'The university in a democracy: democratization of the university', in *Toward a Rational Society*. London: Heinemann.

Habermas, J. (1971b). 'Student protest in the Federal Republic of Germany', in *Toward a Rational Society*. London: Heinemann.

Habermas, J. (1978). *Knowledge and Human Interests*, 2nd edn. London: Heinemann.

Habermas, J. (1987). 'The idea of the university—learning processes', *New German Critique*, 41: 3–22.

Habermas, J. (1989). *The Structural Transformation of the Public Sphere*. Cambridge: Polity Press.

Habermas, J. (1996). *Between Facts and Norms: Contribution to a Discourse Theory of Democracy and Law*. Cambridge: Polity Press.

Jacoby, R. (1987). *The Last Intellectuals: American Culture in the Age of Academe*. New York: Basic Books.

Lazersfeld, P. and Wagner, T. (1958). *The Academic Mind: Social Scientists in a Time of Crisis*. Glencoe, IL: The Free Press.

Lipset, S. M. (ed.) (1967). *Student Politics*. New York: Basic Books.

Lyotard, J.-F. (1984). *The Postmodern Condition: A Report on Knowledge*. Manchester: Manchester University Press.

Miyoshi, M. (1998). '"Globalization", culture, and the university', in F. Jameson and M. Miyoshi (ed.), *The Cultures of Globalization*. Durham, NC: Duke University Press.

Nowotny, H., Scott, P. and Gibbons, M. (2001). *Re-thinking Science: Knowledge and the Public in an Age of Uncertainty*. Cambridge: Polity Press.

Parker, M. and Jary, D. (1995). 'The McUniversity: organization, management and academic subjectivity', *Organization*, 2 (2): 319–38.

Parsons, T. (1974). 'The university "bundle": a study of the balance between differentiation and integration', in N. Smelser and G. Almond (eds), *Public Higher Education in California: Growth, Structural Change, and Conflict*. Berkeley, CA: University of California Press.

Parsons, T. (1979). *Action Theory and the Human Condition*. New York: The Free Press.

Parsons, T. and Platt, G. (1973). *The American University*. Cambridge, MA: Harvard University Press.

Readings, B. (1996). *The University in Ruins*. Cambridge, MA: Harvard University Press.

Riesman, D. (1998). *On Higher Education: The Academic Enterprise in an Era of Rising Student Consumerism*. New Brunswick, NJ: Transaction Publishers.

Riesman, D. and Jencks, C. (1968). *The Academic Revolution*. New York: Doubleday.

Ringer, F. (1969). *The Decline of the German Mandarins: The German Academic Community, 1890–1933*. Cambridge, MA: Harvard University Press.

Robins, K. and Webster, F. (eds) (2002). *The Virtual University? Information, Markets and Management.* Oxford: Oxford University Press.
Schelsky, H. (1963). *Einsamkeit und Freiheit: Idee und Gestalt der deutschen Universitiit und ihrer Reformen.* Hamburg: Rowohlt.
Scott, P. (ed.) (1998). *The Globalization of Higher Education.* Buckingham: Open University Press.
Shils, E. (1972). 'The intellectuals and the powers: some perspectives for comparative analysis', in *The Intellectuals and the Powers and Other Essays.* Chicago: University of Chicago Press.
Shils, E. (1973). *Max Weber on Universities: The Power of the State and the Dignity of the Academic Calling in Imperial Germany.* Chicago: University of Chicago Press.
Shils, E. (1997). *The Calling of Higher Education: The Academic Ethic and Other Essays on Higher Education.* Chicago: University of Chicago Press.
Slaughter, S. and Leslie, L. (1993) *Academic Capitalism: Politics, Policies, and the Entrepreneurial University.* Baltimore, MD: Johns Hopkins University Press.
Smith, A. and Webster, F. (eds) (1997). *The Postmodern University?* Buckingham: Open University Press.
Thompson, E. P. (1970). *Warwick University Ltd.* Harmondsworth: Penguin.
Touraine, A. (1971a). *Post-Industrial Society.* New York: Random House.
Touraine, A. (1971b). *The May Movement: Revolt and Reform.* New York: Random House.
Touraine, A. (1977). *The Self-Production of Society.* Chicago: University of Chicago Press.
Veblen, T. (1962). *The Higher Learning in America.* New Haven, CT: Yale University Press.
Weber, M. (1948). 'Science as a vocation', in H. H. Gerth and C. Wright Mills (eds), *From Max Weber.* London: Routledge and Kegan Paul.
Weber, M. (1973[1908]). 'The alleged "academic freedom" of the German universities' (trans. Edward Shils). *Minerva*, 11.

CHAPTER EIGHTEEN

Universities and the Knowledge Society Revisited

ALBERTO AMARAL

Truth, therefore, and utility are here perfectly identical, and effects are of more value as pledges of truth than from the benefit they confer on man ... (I.24) There is a most intimate connection between the ways of human power and human knowledge ... and that which is most useful in practice is most correct in theory (II.4).

—FRANCIS BACON, *NOVUM ORGANUM* (1620)

Introduction

To think about the university of the future, it is useful to analyse the past, the origins of the university. What has been the evolution of the university since its already remote past? What ensures the extraordinary survival capacity of the university? Will present conditions still ensure that survival?

The old universities, rooted in medieval times, have revealed an unexpected capacity for survival, defying the passing of time and the profound changes of society. Kerr (1982) lists about 85 Western world institutions, founded before 1520, that still exist today under a recognisable form, performing similar functions, without interruption: the Catholic Church, the Parliaments of the Isle of Man, Iceland and Great Britain, some Swiss cantons and about 70 universities! (Van Vught, 1989: 51).

What are the extraordinary characteristics allowing the survival of these 70 universities while over the same period other institutions, apparently more powerful, have vanished? What are the peculiar organisational characteristics conferring universities this capacity of survival and adaptation to change? The answer to these questions lies with the fact that universities deal with knowledge. In universities "knowledge is discovered, preserved, refined, communicated and applied" (Clark, 1983a: 12).

The first characteristic is the predominance of the authority of "professional experts" who are the only well-qualified people to deal with knowledge. Therefore, professional autonomy is very important in higher education, its institutions being classified as "professional bureaucracies" (Mintzberg, 1979). The second characteristic is the concentration of the locus of power in the lower levels of the organisation, in its classrooms and laboratories, where professionals dominate. Universities are not a hierarchic organisation where the behaviour and working practices of the lower levels could be easily imposed top-down. The third characteristic is the great fragmentation of higher education institutions (Weick, 1976) into "chairs," laboratories, research centres, departments or faculties. Universities are considered "loosely coupled" systems (Weick, 1976), a characteristic reinforced because the loyalty of professional experts is given firstly to their fellow colleagues, in the same or other institutions, and only afterwards to the institution. The last characteristic is the large diffusion of power to make decisions. In a fragmented institution, where the production process is knowledge intensive, which favours decentralisation, the decision power is allocated to a large number of units and actors (Van Vught, 1989: 53–54).

These characteristics of higher education, put together, explain the great capacity of adaptation and survival of its institutions. Institutional fragmentation (Clark, 1983a) and organisational diversity make it easy to suppress, aggregate, divide or add new units or new knowledge areas without unsettling the institution. Universities are a unique organisational form due to the multiplicity of their missions and the absence of a unique form of absolute authority. For Allen (1988), "universities are really an organised anarchy, without being made illegitimate, immoral or ineffective."

These same characteristics allow higher education institutions to successfully oppose changes imposed from the outside. Cerych and Sabatier (1986) have examined reforms of higher education in several European countries to demonstrate how the lack of understanding by politicians of the characteristics of universities may frustrate these reforms.

The Emergence of the Knowledge Society

Over the last decades, universities all over the world have been confronted with pressures for change resulting from similar policy developments at the system level

(Samoff and Bidemi, 2006; Tilak, 2006). Impatience with academia's long-established norms and values, the pumping up of higher education's economic mission and purpose, the rise at institutional level of "New Managerialism" (Kogan, 2004), the "professionalisation" of university management, the increased weight and influence of external stakeholders, the imposition of evaluation of performance using criteria tied in with economic productivity, the promotion of "relevance" in both teaching and research, all represent central elements of the transformation of higher education in a globalised world.

New higher education policies promote changes of ideology and of values, and in the relationship between higher education institutions and the state and society (Amaral and Magalhães, 2003), which cannot be accommodated only by mere structural adjustments. The role of universities is becoming progressively tied with the economy or, as Guy Neave (1995) argues, the mission of the university is being redefined away from being an instrument for the distribution of wealth to becoming an instrument to supplement its generation.

As universities have always dealt with knowledge, what has changed? What changed is the emergence of knowledge as an increasingly important production factor, which is becoming dominant relative to the traditional ones—land, labour and capital. For Peter Drucker (1994), "Information is data endowed with relevance and purpose. Converting data into information thus requires knowledge" and he adds, "The new society will be a knowledge society. Knowledge will be its key resource and knowledge workers will be the dominant group in the workforce" (Drucker, 2001).

Knowledge has always played a role in the progress of mankind. Nico Stehr (2010) argues that some ancient societies (Israel and its law-like Torah-knowledge or Egypt where religious, astronomical and agrarian knowledge where the basis of authority) can be described as knowledge societies. In the long years before the Industrial Revolution (mid-18th century), the increase in economic output was due more to commercial progress than to technological progress (Mokyr, 2002). At the time "Even the best and brightest mechanics, farmers and chemists knew relatively little of what could be known about the fields of knowledge they sought to apply" (Mokyr, 2002: 4), which did not encourage a generation of sustained economic growth based on technological progress.

During the Industrial Revolution, knowledge started to be applied both to natural resources and to technology (Streckeisen, 2009) and "technology and science influenced one another in many ways and convolved, reinforcing and strengthening one another" (Mokyr, 2002: 7), which allowed for the early development of industry.

The beginning of the 20th century came with the "productivity revolution," Frederick W. Taylor being its mastermind. Taylor was responsible for the application of knowledge to factory work (Streckeisen, 2009) and he studied how work was performed and how this might affect worker productivity. His ideas are explained in the book *The Principles of Scientific Management*, published in 1909.

After the end of World War II new dramatic developments occurred, including new discoveries in areas such as microprocessors, satellites, antibiotics, bacteriology, etc. Progress in information technologies allowed for the growing use of statistics and the storage, treatment and transmission of huge masses of information, which resulted in a new revolution.

Robert E. Lane (1966) was the first author to use the term "knowledgeable society" in the meaning of a new society where common sense would be replaced by scientific reasoning, reducing the significance of politics. However, it was Peter Drucker, the author of *The Age of Discontinuity* (1969), who can be considered as pioneer and protagonist of the management revolution based on the application of knowledge to knowledge (Streckeisen, 2009: 184). Drucker refers to the "knowledge society" regarding "knowledge as central to modern society and as the foundation of its economy and social action" (Stehr, 2010), a term also used by Daniel Bell (1973) interchangeably with "post-industrial society."

The new society differs dramatically from the past and a new terminology has been coined including designations where the prefix "post" is extensively used: post-industrialism, post-capitalism, etc. originating what some have designated as a "post syndrome" of the social sciences (Gemperle and Streckeisen, 2007). The driving force of the new economy has become knowledge and services and knowledge-intensive products are replacing material and labour-intensive products. The work most individuals perform requires theoretical knowledge and the major resource of the post-industrial society is its well-educated workforce.

Initially there was an optimistic view of a future with improved life conditions, more interesting work placements and better employment conditions. However, since the 1980s, a more sceptical view started to emerge. In 1986, Ulrich Beck published *Risk Society. Towards a New Modernity*. In this book, Beck refers to a movement from pre-modernity to simple modernity as the industrial society replaced the traditional society and, more recently, to a new movement to "reflexive modernity." This new phase of modernity has to deal with the problems and risks resulting from the development of the industrial society, or how those risks can be "prevented, minimised, dramatised and channelled" (Beck, 1986: 19). It is important to notice that Beck uses "reflexive" in the sense of "reflex" rather than "reflection" as "the notion is about social development arising as a reflex to previous decisions or activities which give rise to unintended or even surprising consequences" (Aiken, 2000: 4). Beck, together with Giddens, argues that as humanity enters the new stage of modernity, reflexivity has become the main characteristic of society (Beck, Giddens and Lash, 1996).

Social sciences need to construct new concepts to understand the world dynamics at the beginning of the 21st century. Modernity has not vanished; what is new is that modernity has begun to modernise its own foundations. This is what it means to say modernity has become reflexive. It has become directed at itself, it is knowledge applied to knowledge.

Peter Streckeisen argues, "the theory of reflexive modernity bears a striking resemblance to Peter F. Drucker's (1993) ideas about the post-capitalist society … All three share the argument of reflexivity (that is, knowledge applied to knowledge), which is central to the new conventional wisdom" (Streckeisen, 2009: 184), although Giddens and Beck have a rather sceptical opinion while Drucker is far more optimist.

At this point it is interesting to analyse the Lisbon Strategy, as it aimed at building "the most dynamic and competitive knowledge-based economy in the world capable of sustainable economic growth with more and better jobs and greater social cohesion, and respect for the environment by 2010" (European Council, 2000). The Lisbon Strategy aimed at:

> … preparing the transition to a knowledge-based economy and society by better policies for the information society and R&D, as well as by stepping up the process of structural reform for competitiveness and innovation and by completing the internal market; modernising the European social model, investing in people and combating social exclusion; sustaining the healthy economic outlook and favourable growth prospects by applying an appropriate macro-economic policy mix. (European Council, 2000)

Unfortunately, the Lisbon Strategy was a failure and Europe is far from being a dynamic and competitive economy, producing more and better jobs. The replacement of "employment" with "employability," one of the buzzwords of the Bologna process, has contributed to the individualisation of social problems (Streckeisen, 2009) by making unemployment or poverty the responsibility of individual misconduct. Ulrich Beck (1983) considers that this individualisation of inequality has made irrelevant sociological concepts such as social class and estate.

Under the Lisbon Strategy, social problems derive from deficient knowledge, education and (occupational) training, being the responsibility of each individual to invest a percentage of his salary in long life education in order to remain employable. And Streckeisen further explains, "in order to limit unemployment, governments should not create jobs … rather they should provide incentives and sanctions so that the jobless either engage in further training to improve their 'employability', or accept jobs they might have turned down before" (Streckeisen, 2009: 186).

In the next paragraphs the impact of these changes on higher education institutions will be analysed.

Recent Changes

The observed trends include the introduction of a number of new instruments, such as using markets for public sector regulation, marketising higher education institutions including privatisation, reinforcing the executive leadership and weakening collegial governance, measuring institutional performance and financing via performance-based contracts, increasing institutional accountability and developing accreditation systems. Many of these changes can be seen as being influenced by the emergence of New Public Management (NPM). For Neave, these changes are the consequence that follows from "the rise to pre-eminence of Economics as the prime driving force in the higher education of non-totalitarian societies and very particularly those in Western Europe" (Neave, 2004: 131).

Market Regulation and New Public Management

Governments have been using markets as instruments of public regulation, while NPM invaded the universities, aiming at increasing their efficiency. Governments assumed that market-like competition was the solution to reform the sclerotic behaviour of public services, forcing them to increase their efficiency (Ball, 1998). Using economic incentives, governments forced institutions to compete in a higher education market driving "aside the values by which the universities of earlier generations were governed" (Bailey, 2008) and making them "quasi-commercial enterprises selling services in the knowledge industry to a wide range of purchasers" (G. Williams, 2004).

However, in general, markets are not good regulators of higher education, or of other services that like education produce significant externalities, i.e., benefits received by society beyond the individual private benefit. Society derives advantages from a well-educated and well-trained population, and this distinguishes education from a merely private good (Thys-Clément, 1995). As the market is a means of organising the exchange of goods and services based on price, additional social benefits (externalities) will tend to be ignored, or to be too little taken into account by market mechanisms. Many authors agree that total privatisation of higher education would not maximise social welfare (Dill, 1997; Rivlin, 1992; Thurow, 1996) and in a number of cases it was recognised that market regulation produced negative results.

Market failures show the shortcomings of markets, which occur when dealing with goods or services that show large externalities, their tendency to build monopolies or what are known as market imperfections (Van Vught, 1997), leading to inefficient market behaviour and opening the way to government regulation.

David Dill refers to insufficient information as one of the causes of "market failures." Consumers should make rational decisions, which imply good knowledge of the price and characteristics of goods and services to be purchased, including quality and price, as well as the market conditions. However, in many cases, the relevant information is not available (imperfect information) or the producer has more detailed knowledge than the consumer (asymmetric information).

For Dill, "students lack sufficient information about the quality of academic institutions or programs to make discriminating choices" (Dill, 1997: 180), and even if this kind of data were available, many students (or their families) would not use it. Students are rather uncertain about what a particular study programme offers in terms of education and future employment prospects, which results in psychological phenomena which form a "filter" or a mental framework through which students judge financial incentives in relation to their study choices (Vossensteyn and De Jong, 2005). This is what David Dill (1997: 181) calls the problem of immature consumers, "being (…) one rationale for the implementation of quasi-markets, rather than consumer-oriented markets, for the distribution of academic programs."

In a quasi-market, an agent (in general a public agent), acting on behalf of the clients, buys the goods or services that are then allocated to the final users (Cave and Kogan, 1990: 183). This monopsonistic purchaser should be more efficient than immature clients in dealing with producers of educational programmes (Dill, 1997: 178) to determine what is to be consumed and at what price. However, Lindsay and Rodgers (1998) question the use of quasi-markets as the student as client does not have an important role in the higher education market, on the one hand because he has no control over the money the university receives for his education, and on the other because he has only imperfect information as to the quality of each university.

Changes in Governance

Over the last decades, traditional university governance became a target of fierce criticism, and the multisecular tradition of collegial governance is today considered inefficient and corporative. Many governments have yielded to the temptation of improving university management "by a series of external interventions, implemented largely top-down, and drawn in the main from the management practices and reward systems of other kind of organisations" (Chris Duke, 1992). The

European Commission and supranational organisations such as the OECD and the World Bank strongly support changes that will replace the traditional collegial modes of university governance with "more efficient and effective" governance models.

The intrusion of the rhetoric and management practices of the private sector into higher education resulted in important changes in the operation of higher education institutions. Several authors have interpreted this phenomenon using concepts such as "managerialism" (Amaral, Magalhães and Santiago, 2003) "new managerialism" or "new public management" (Meek, 2003). Models were imported from the corporate world intended to change the slow, inefficient decision-making processes of academic collegiality. Government legislation was passed introducing substantial changes in university governance, aiming at giving institutions more efficient governance and management mechanisms. Decreasing collegiality and increasing concentration of power at the top level of the administration and the emergence of university boards with limited membership and strong external participation, representing the voice of society aimed to make institutions more responsive to the "external world" (Magalhães and Amaral, 2000).

Under NPM the public are clients of government, and administrators should seek to deliver services that satisfy clients. In higher education, too, students are to be seen as customers or clients while the academics were transformed into providers of educational services. Quality assurance systems and accountability measures, including extensive panels of performance indicators, were put in place to ensure that academic provision meets the client needs and expectations and the objectives and targets defined by the government.

As academics were transformed into service providers, they lost their aura of disinterestedness, and are no longer trusted to run their institutions. In 1974, Moodie and Eustace still argued that academics were the only people qualified to run complex organisations as universities (Moodie and Eustace, 1974) while the late Burton Clark considered that universities, running an activity strongly based on the development of the specialisms of different scientific areas, could only be efficiently run by professional experts in those areas (Clark, 1983b). All this is now gone and academics are viewed with suspicion as they might put their own interests above those of institutions and society.

Students as Consumers or Clients and Academics as Proletarians

The changes occurring in higher education have confronted students and academics with quite different fortunes. While academics are being downgraded from proud professionals into employees or work for hire, students have improved their fate and reinforced their institutional role, being transformed into clients or customers (Klemencic, 2012). Klemencic recognises that the autonomy of academics has suffered with performance measures while the student-centred learning paradigm has improved the autonomy of students. And she suggests that the two constituencies might increase their cooperation in governance matters.

The academic profession has lost attractiveness, as tenure became more restrictive or was even eliminated, an increasing number of part-time staff is being employed to teach students and more bureaucratic control is directed at supervising their activities. Performance-related salaries are a new step in the transformation of academics into employees. They were first proposed by Adam Smith to eliminate sloppy behaviour in academia: "… if his emoluments are to be precisely the same, whether he does, or does not perform some very laborious duty, it is certainly his interest … either to neglect it altogether, or, if he is subject to some authority … to perform it in as careless and slovenly a manner as that authority will permit" (Smith, 1776: 343).

The academy no longer enjoys great prestige on which higher education can build a successful claim to political autonomy (Scott, 1989). Unlike students, academics have not been directly represented in the Bologna process, which illuminates the relative political clout of the two university constituencies, and they have lost the traditional recognition of their capacity to run their own institutions.

Halsey refers to the gradual proletarianisation of the academic professions—an erosion of their relative class and status advantages (Halsey, 1992). The development of academic capitalism (Slaughter and Leslie, 1997) and institutional patent policies made faculty more like all other workers—less like university professionals and more like corporate professionals whose discoveries are considered work for hire, the property of the corporation, not the professional.

The influence of these transformations over the life of academics is visible when the time of academics is analysed (Barnett, 2008). The deterioration of the time of academics is a consequence of changes taking place in higher education, as academic time is becoming impregnated with the interests of the management, of economy, of efficiency and of output (2008, 10). And it results in the sacrifice of academic freedom and the reduction of the critical dimension of the university (Bailey, 2008: 5).

Competition, Rankings and Excellence Initiatives

Most national governments were not immune to the globalising pressures coming from the increasing popularity of international rankings of higher education institutions. The decision of the Ministers, in the 2009 Leuven and Louvain-la-Neuve Conference, to support multidimensional transparency tools, creating a classification of European universities (U-Map) to be followed by a ranking system (U-Multirank), with the enthusiastic support of the European Commission (Leuven communiqué, 2009), has contributed to create a context where institutions try to improve their classification or jump a few places in rankings. In the words of Robert Birnbaum, "many institutions across the globe are claiming either that they plan to become World Class Universities by a date certain, or else that they have already achieved this status" (Birnbaum, 2007).

In a number of European countries, governments are implementing policies to enhance the international competitiveness of universities and to promote their role "in the innovation system, economic development, knowledge-based economy and competitiveness of nation-state" (Tirronen et al., 2007). These developments show that some countries moved from the traditional view that "all national universities are of similar quality" to a new position that promotes a stratified system with a few research universities concentrating significant funding and a number of diversified institutions for provision of mass higher education, with limited research capacity.

Germany and France have launched "excellence initiatives" with substantial financial resources being used to create a small number of "world-class" universities capable of competing internationally for the best students and academics while Finland decided to create a "world-class" university through a merger of the Helsinki University of Technology with the Helsinki School of Economics and the University of Art and Design. In Denmark there was a top-down governmental decision merging a number of universities and research centres. In the Netherlands the three technical universities created a federation with support from the government. In the UK this process has been going for a number of years, using the research assessment exercises to concentrate research funds.

Disruptive New Technologies

Universities will also need to adapt to the impact of the communication technology revolution. Universities will have to develop ways to better handle fast increasing volumes of knowledge and to develop mechanisms for helping society to use and adapt to new knowledge. The impressive development of communication technologies has allowed institutions to deal simultaneously with very large numbers of students, creating possibilities that were not available in traditional e-learning systems. Quite recently MOOCs (massive open online courses) emerged as a new disruptive phenomenon in higher education.

Over the last few years there were heated debates about the role and future of MOOCs, and their effect over traditional modes of education. Some prophets of doom refer to MOOCs as a disruptive new technology that will affect higher education beyond recognition, leading to higher education without professors, only competencies. Others suggest that MOOCs will be just another fad, relegated to the start-up dustbin and soon forgotten.

Kyle Peck suggests that technologies will re-place, not replace higher education, meaning that higher education will be still there but the place of the professor will change, adapting to newer technologies. He argues that gathering information and developing understanding can be better done by technology rather than by attending classes. However, "The development of skills and attributes requires multiple opportunities to perform in front of a competent reviewer and solid assessments that provide comprehensive feedback to inform improvement. MOOCs can't do that, and that's what really matters. Knowledge is necessary, but not sufficient, for success" (Peck, 2014).

What Lies in the Future?

What kind of university will emerge under the influence of these changes? The development of the knowledge society will require well-educated populations which prompts the emergence of mass higher education systems in countries with still low participation rates, and a movement to universal higher education systems in countries with higher participation rates. Newer and more diversified institutions will be created all over the world and distance education will play a role without replacing more traditional education methodologies. And universities as such will survive due to their secular capacity to adapt to new conditions imposed by society.

Peter Streckeisen argues "the system of capitalist production does not consume only 'dead knowledge'; it cannot operate without the use of 'living knowledge', that is, the exploitation of the capacities and the skills of numberless jobholders" (2009: 194). In Europe, the universities remain the main producer of knowledge. The European Science and Research Commissioner, Janez Potočnik (European Commission, 2006), said that "universities are power-houses of knowledge generation" and "… they will need to adapt to the demands of a global, knowledge-based economy, just as other sectors of society and economy have to adapt."

In Europe, by promoting a student-centred learning paradigm, aiming at tuning education to short-term labour market needs, the Bologna process has developed a utilitarian view of higher education as a key element in a strategy of economic growth and competitiveness (Sin and Neave, 2014). Higher education institutions are under permanent pressure to supply the labour market with graduates having the skills necessary for the short-term needs of the economy, skills that change all the time and are to be evaluated as learning outcomes. And "this permanent demand to match skills requirements serves as a mechanism to limit the relative autonomy of the education system vis-à-vis capitalist production" (Streckeisen, 2009: 194).

The world is moving away from a pure Mertonian formulation considering science as open, communal, universal, disinterested and characterised by a sceptical habit of mind (Merton, 1942), which included a vision of knowledge as being free, universal and non-commercial (Slaughter and Rhoades, 2003). Slaughter and Rhoades argue that the development of academic capitalism and institutional patent policies are transforming what was "an academic public knowledge regime into an academic capitalist regime" (2003: 225), while the traditional idea of free and universal knowledge has been replaced by the idea that "rather than being shared, intellectual property is owned," with "the proliferation of conflict of interest language and rules [in intellectual property policies]" being an indication that disinterestedness no longer lives in academia.

Under the influence of corporate-led globalisation, the relative importance of knowledge for its own sake has declined relative to useful knowledge that may be used for improving the competitiveness of the economy. Institutions are under pressure to produce research that has direct relevance for economic competitiveness. Even if curiosity, the love of challenge and other pure epistemic motives have not completely disappeared as drivers of research, "economic interests, no matter how remote, have become increasingly important in driving and directing the growth of useful knowledge in the past century and a half" (Mokyr, 2002: 10), which apparently seems to make true the classical Baconian utopia, or the promotion of a research agenda improving the useful arts, meaning technology (2002).

The products of research are being privatised and patents protect its monopolistic use by companies, inhibiting "the free circulation and public use of scientific findings at the very moment when—thanks to new communication technologies and the internet—open and universal access to information and knowledge are easier to realize than ever before" (Streckeisen, 2009: 193).

The investments made by a number of countries to establish "research universities, capable of competing at world level", will create stratified national higher education systems and a stratified European Higher Education Area. This development will allow for clarification of the tertiary higher education, with a re-definition of what a university really is. This will create an elite group of traditional research universities, integrating a protected sector of fully autonomous and well-funded institutions, responsible for the traditional task of creating not new knowledge. As Guy Neave suggests, governments will create "a highly focused and selective 'Guardian Relationship' resurrected and built around a few highly performing establishments" (Neave, 2009).

Those elite research universities will coexist with a very large sector of higher education institutions, many of them teaching-only institutions, which will be responsible for mass higher education—less generously funded, not protected from strict regulation and from pressures to be relevant for the labour market. Or, in the words of Guy Neave, one will observe "the emergence in Europe's higher education systems of a 'temporarily protected' sector, consisting of highly performing research universities at the apex and at the base a 'market-driven' mass sector" (Neave, 2009). This large sector at the base will be the preferred tool for producing workers more directly to the labour market demands and will create space for preserving a protected research sector.

Conclusion

Unfortunately, in today's new brave world, I have to concur with Joel Mokyr:

> Economists today are usually bad philosophers. The age of giants trained in philosophy such as Adam Smith, Karl Marx, and John Stuart Mill, is long passed. For most people trained in economics, the simple idea that "more is better" derived from Benthamite utilitarian calculus seems to be enough. It is better to have more than less, and welfare comparisons are based on that axiom. Distributional issues are of course discussed, but often in terms that look at the effect of redistribution on the total size of the pie. (Mokyr, 2002: 18)

Despite some uncertainties about the role of markets in higher education, it seems unavoidable that the university will face their influence, at least as a rhetoric political device. Science and education will continue to contribute to the reproduction of an overall social order, i.e. the system of capitalist class relations (Streckeisen, 2009), where not only knowledge, but also knowledge about knowledge has value. Creating value means creating new knowledge and making sure its value will pay a return on invested capital. This is making intellectual property more important than physical property.

The expansion of higher education systems observed over the last decades has not changed the social reproduction mechanisms denounced by Bourdieu (Bourdieu and Passeron, 1970 and his colleagues. The investment made by some countries to create a few elite institutions will only continue to enhance those reproduction mechanisms relying upon the possession of a prestigious diploma.

Some characteristics of universities such as professional autonomy, absence of a hierarchic organisation or the diffusion or power to make decisions will continue to be contested, at least in those institutions removed from the top of rankings.

For Streckeisen, by claiming that social position depends on knowledge, that is, on investment in human capital by the individual, results in the individualisation of social problems, which contributes "to the legitimization of power and social inequality by invoking a principle of equal opportunities that Bourdieu and others have so convincingly deconstructed" (2009: 188).

In a New York debate organised by the Futures Project, Mala Singh argued that the presence of the market as a new ideological competitor was ousting the liberal-humanist discourse, and to avoid that higher education be "reduced to being the handmaiden of the economy" would require redefining the nature and social role of higher education institutions and "the terms of their insertion and functioning within the economy" (Singh, 2001: 9). Unfortunately, this would be much easier if economists were still good philosophers.

References

Aiken, M. (2000). Reflexive Modernisation and the Social Economy. *Studies in Social and Political Thought*, University of Sussex, March 2000, 2: 3–21.

Allen, M. (1988). *The Goals of Universities*, Milton Keynes: Open University Press.

Amaral, A. and Magalhães, A. (2003). The triple crisis of the university and its reinvention. *Higher Education*, 16.2: 239–253.

Amaral, A., Magalhães, A. and Santiago, R. (2003). The rise of academic managerialism in Portugal. In Amaral, A., Meek, V. L. and Larsen, I. (Eds.), *The Higher Education Managerial Revolution?* pp. 131–154, Dordrecht: Kluwer.

Ball, S. J. (1998). Big policies/small world: an introduction to international perspectives in education policy. *Comparative Education*, 34.2: 119–130.

Barnett, R. (2008). Being an academic in a time-impoverished age. In Amaral, A., Bleiklie, I. and Musselin, C. (Eds.), *From Governance to Identity*, pp. 7–17, Dordrecht: Springer.

Bailey, R. W. (2008). Is the University in Ruins? Discussion Paper number 2008–2, Institute for Economic Development Policy, University of Birmingham.

Beck, U. (1983). Jenseits von Stand und Klasse? Soziale Ungleichheiten, gesellschaftliche Individualisierungsprozesse und die Entstehung neuer Formationen und Identitäten. In Kreckel, R. (Ed.), *Soziale Ungleichheiten*, pp. 35–74, Göttingen: Schwartz.

Beck, U. (1986). *Risikogesellschaft: Auf dem Weg in eine andere Moderne*, Frankfurt: Surkamp Verlag.

Beck, U., Giddens, A. and Lash, S. (1996). *Reflexive Moderisierung: Eine Kontroverse*, Frankfurt: Taschenbuch.

Bell, D. (1973). *The Coming of Post-Industrial Society: A Venture in Social Forecasting*, New York: Basic Books.

Bourdieu, P. and Passeron, J. C. (1970). *La réproduction. Élements pour une théorie du système d'enseignment,* Paris: Minuit.

Cave, M. and Kogan, M. (1990). Some concluding observations. In Cave, M., Kogan, M. and Smith, R. (Eds.), *Output and Performance Measurements in Government—The State of the Art,* London: Jessica Kingsley Publishers.

Cerych, L. and Sabatier, P. (1986). *Great Expectations and Mixed Performance: the Implementation of Higher Education Reforms in Europe*, Trentham: Trentham Books.

Clark, B. R. (1983a). *The Higher Education System: Academic Organization in Cross National Perspective,* Berkeley: University of California Press.

Clark, B. R. (1983b). Governing the higher education system. In Shattock, M. (Ed.), *The Structure and Governance of Higher Education*, pp. 19–42, Guilford: Society for Research into Higher Education.

Dill, D. (1997). Higher education markets and public policy. *Higher Education Policy,* 10.3/4: 167–185.

Drucker, F. P. (1969). *The Age of Discontinuity. Guidelines to Our Changing Society,* New York: Harper & Row.

Drucker, F. P. (1993). *Post-Capitalist Society,* New York: Harper Business.

Drucker, F. P. (1994). The age of social transformation. *The Atlantic Monthly,* 274.5: 53–80.

Drucker, F. P. (2001). The next society, *The Economist,* 1 November 2001.

Duke, C. (1992). *The Learning University. Towards a New Paradigm?,* Buckingham: SHRE and Open Press University.

European Commission (2006). *Europe Needs Modernised Universities*, IP/06/592, Brussels, 10 May 2006.

European Council (2000). http://www.europarl.europa.eu/summits/lis1_en.htm

Gemperle, M. and Streckeisen, P. (Eds.) (2007). *Ein neues Zeitalter des Wissens? Kritische Breitäge zur Diskussion über die Wissensgesellschaft,* Zürich: Seismo.

Halsey, A. H. (1992). *Decline of Donnish Dominion: The British Academic Professions in the Twentieth Century*. Oxford: Clarendon Press.

Kerr, C. (1982). *The Uses of the University,* 3rd edn. Cambridge, MA: Harvard University Press.

Klemencic, M. (2012). The Changing Conceptions of Student Participation in Higher Education Governance in the EHEA. In Curaj, A., Scott, P., Vlasceanu, L. and Wilson, L. (Eds.), *European Higher Education at the Crossroads: Between the Bologna Process and National Reforms,* pp. 631–653, Dordrecht: Springer.

Kogan, M. (2004). Management and Evaluation in Higher Education, *UNESCO Forum Occasional Paper series, Paper No. 7*, Paris: UNESCO.

Lane, R. (1966). The decline of politics and ideology in a knowledgeable society. *American Sociological Review,* 31: 649–662.

Leuven communiqué (2009). http://europa.eu/rapid/press-release_IP-09-675_en.htm

Lindsay, G. and Rodgers, T. (1998). Market orientation in the UK higher education sector: the influence of the education reform process 1979–1993. *Quality in Higher Education,* 4.2: 159–171.

Magalhães, A. and Amaral, A. (2000). Portuguese higher education and the imaginary friend: the stakeholders role in institutional governance, *European Journal of Education*, 35.4: 439–448.

Meek, V. L. (2003). Introduction. In Amaral, A., Meek, V.L. and Larsen, I. (Eds), *The Higher Education Managerial Revolution?* pp. 1–29, Dordrecht: Kluwer.

Merton, B. K. (1942). *The normative structure of science*. Accessed 16/10/2017 at https://www.panarchy.org/merton/science.html

Mintzberg, H. (1979). *The Structuring of Organizations*, Englewood Cliffs: Prentice-Hall.

Mokyr, J. (2002). The Knowledge Society: Theoretical and Historical Underpinnings, paper presented at Ad Hoc Expert Group on Knowledge Systems, United Nations, New York, September 4–5.

Moodie, G. & Eustace, R. (1974). *Power and Authority in British Universities.* London: Allen and Unwin.

Neave, G. (1995). The stirring of the prince and the silence of the lambs: the changing assumptions beneath higher education policy, reform and society. In Dill, D. and Sporn, B. (Eds.), *Emerging Patterns of Social Demand and University Reform: Through a Glass Darkly*, pp. 54–71, Oxford: Pergamon Press.

Neave, G. (2004). Higher education policy as orthodoxy: being one tale of doxological drift, political intention and changing circumstances. In Teixeira, P., Jongbloed, B., Dill, D. and Amaral, A. (Eds.), *Markets in Higher Education: Rhetoric or Reality?*, pp. 127–160, Dordrecht: Kluwer Academic Publishers.

Neave, G. (2009). Institutional Autonomy 2010–2020. The Tale of the Elan—Two steps back to take one very large leap forward. In Kehm, B., Huisman, J. and Stensaker, B. (Eds.), *The European Higher Education Area: Perspectives on a Moving Target*, pp. 3–22, Rotterdam: Sense Publishers.

Peck, K. (2014). The evolving role of "Teacher" in a MOOCs and badges world, *The EvoLLLution, Illuminating the Lifelong Learning Movement,* retrieved 29.09.2014.

Rivlin, A. M. (1992). *Reviving the American Dream: The Economy, the States, and the Federal Government,* Washington, DC: The Brookings Institution.

Samoff, J. and Bidemi C. (2006). Influence:—direct, indirect and negotiated: the World Bank and Higher Education in Africa. In Neave, G. (Ed.), *Knowledge, Authority and Dissent: Critical Perspectives on Research into Higher Education and the Knowledge Society*, pp. 133–180, Paris: UNESCO.

Scott, P. (1989). The power of ideas. In Ball, C. and Eggins, H. (Eds.), *Higher Education into the 1990s: New Dimensions*, pp. 7–16, Buckingham: Society for Research into Higher Education and Open University Press.

Sin, C. and Neave, G. (2014). Employability deconstructed: perceptions of Bologna stakeholders. *Studies in Higher Education,* DOI: 10.1080/03075079.2014.977859.

Singh, M. (2001). Market Forces are Transforming Higher Education. En *Final Report of "Privileges Lost, Responsibilities Gained: Reconstructing Higher Education", A Global Symposium on the Future of Higher Education*, Columbia University Teachers College, June 14-15, 2001.

Slaughter, S. and Leslie, L. (1997). *Academic Capitalism: Politics, Policies and the Entrepreneurial University,* Baltimore: John Hopkins Press.

Slaughter, S. and Rhoades, G. (2003). Contested intellectual property: the role of the institution in the United States. In Amaral, A., Meek, V. L. and Larsen, I. (Eds.), *The Higher Education Managerial Revolution?*, pp. 203–228, Dordrecht: Kluwer.

Smith, Adam (1776). *An Inquiry into the Nature and Causes of the Wealth of Nations*, Vol. 2, 2nd edn, London: Strahan and Cadell.

Stehr, N. (2010). Theories of the information age, in historical developments and theoretical approaches in sociology, *Encyclopaedia of Life Support Systems*, UNESCO.

Streckeisen, P. (2009), Knowledge society—or contemporary capitalism's fanciest dress. *Analyse & Kritik*, 31.1: 181–197.

Thurow, L. C. (1996). *The Future of Capitalism: How Today's Economic Forces Shape Tomorrow's World*, New York: Morrow.

Thys-Clément, F. (1995). The crisis of university funding. *CRE-action*, 106.

Tilak, J. (2006). Higher education between the state and the market. In Neave, G. (Ed.), *Knowledge, Authority and Dissent: Critical Perspectives on Research into Higher Education and the Knowledge Society*, pp. 235–254, Paris: UNESCO.

Tirronen, J., Nokkala, T. and Hölttä, S. (2007). Consortium, federation and merger—strategic instruments of enhancing research capacity and competitiveness of universities, paper presented at the 2007 CHER Conference, 31 August–1 September, Dublin.

Van Vught, F. A. (1989). *Governmental Strategies and Innovation in Higher Education*, London: Jessica Kingsley Publishers.

Van Vught, F. A. (1997). Combining planning and the market: an analysis of the Government strategy towards higher education in the Netherlands. *Higher Education Policy*, 10.3/4: 211–224.

Vossensteyn, H. and De Jong, U. (2005). Student financing in the Netherlands: a behavioural economic perspective. In Teixeira, P., Johnstone, B., Rosa, M. J. and Vossensteyn, H. (Eds.), *A Fairer Deal? Cost-Sharing and Accessibility in Western Higher Education*, pp. 215–241, Dordrecht: Springer.

Weick, K. F. (1976). Educational organizations as loosely coupled systems. *Administrative Science Quarterly*, 21.1: 1–19.

Williams, G. (2004). The higher education market in the United Kingdom. In Teixeira, P., Jongbloed, B., Dill, D. and Amaral, A. (Eds.), *Markets in Higher Education. Rhetoric or Reality?*, pp. 241–270, Dordrecht: Kluwer.

CHAPTER NINETEEN

Parting Ways

Analogue People in a Digital University

ROBERT HASSAN

> The coming of 'academic capitalism' has been anticipated and praised for years; today it is here. Colleges and universities clamor greedily these days for pharmaceutical patents and ownership chunks of high-tech startups; they boast of being 'entrepreneurial'; they have rationalized and outsourced countless aspects of their operations in the search for cash; they fight their workers nearly as ferociously as a nineteenth-century railroad baron; and the richest among them have turned their endowments into in-house hedge funds.
>
> —THOMAS FRANK (2014)

Introduction

It is widely acknowledged that the university as an institution no longer corresponds—to the extent that it ever did—to the 'dreaming spires' epithet that 19th-century cultural critic Mathew Arnold coined to describe the 'sweet city' of Oxford. The romantic label has been used to distinguish that city's august university from its more demotic local realities, such as the Cowley car plant that has since 1912 been churning out classics like the Morris Oxford. Today, a high-tech and impressively automated Cowley produces the equally iconic Mini, but profits from this venture flow back to the plant's owners, BMW, in Germany. Neo-liberal globalization and the revolution in information technologies, has meant that in some important ways the university and the car factory have converged—and thus provide a useful template for how we can think about universities and their developmental trajectory in the 21st century.

Oxford and many other universities still have their spires and quads and gowns and much of the ancient impedimenta of learning—the materiality of difference, one may call it, of a place that appears as somehow special. Today there is very little 'dreaming', and much less quiet reflection occurring than there used to be. Out of bleak necessity, all universities now concern themselves more with calculation. And there is nothing special about it; it is the age-old calculation of profit and loss. It is the getting of grants, the attracting of paying students, the scrabbling for bequests, the begging from alumni, the streamlining and making as 'efficient' as possible every process, administrative as well as pedagogical, in order to be competitive and flexible. They constantly calculate, in other words, ways to survive.

Since the late-1980s the optimal route for achieving all this was to impersonate the standard business enterprise in order to find systems to become competitive not only locally, but globally also. And a great deal has been written subsequently about the 'neo-liberalization' of the university, where the institution was forced to be, or was sometimes created from scratch in order to be, a business. We see the tone of much of this in a book written for the UK context, Brown and Carasso's *Everything for Sale: The Marketisation of UK Higher Education* (2013). Its authors analyse the British experience (now globalized) where the university as a state-subsidized public service institution 'fell apart in the 1990s' to be reconstituted as 'a service provided by Adam Smith's invisible hand in which free markets decide how much is provided and who reaps the benefits …' (2013: xii).

The book is useful, but as its title indicates, it focuses on the narrow aspect, that is the commercialization process. As with similar research it overlooks a major element of what makes it all work: computerization. Without an understanding of the causes and effects of the digitalization process, we will not get a fuller picture of the root and branch transformation of the institution. Indeed, as I will argue here, we will miss the most important aspect of what digitalization brings—which is the creation of an alienating and socially destructive system that will, if not halted, bear little resemblance to the (quite different but related) traditional ideas of what constitutes a modern university developed by Wilhelm von Humboldt and John Henry Newman in the 19th century. I argue further, that through the unreflected upon drive to commercialize and computerize as much of the university as possible, we are committing, and every day reinforcing, a *category error* through the process. By this it is meant that by embracing digital technology so rapidly and allowing it to permeate the university so comprehensively, we have unleashed a technological force—digitalization—that is radically at odds with what it is to be human. In short, we have *misidentified* the computer as a technology and a logic that corresponds to what it is to be human. Humans are analogue creatures who evolved in an analogue world, and the logic of the digital, as we will see, is fundamentally antithetical to that. More particular to the argument, through networks of computers that colonize pedagogy and the processes of knowledge production, we create a logic of thinking and of knowing that conflicts with the analogue process and analogue technology that has been at the centre of the university system since Plato's Academy—that of writing, and its correlate, reading.

Speed of operation is of the essence in capitalist processes; it cuts costs, thereby making the product cheaper. Economists term it 'economies of scale'. It is the same in the university, but its administrators call it 'efficiency'. But the traditional university differs in that its product is supposed to be not 'things', but knowledge, theoretical and practical. This is knowledge acquired by students who graduate, and knowledge that disseminates into society as they enter the world as educated individuals. However, if we blend the need for speed with digital logic, and apply these to knowledge production, what we tend to get is not knowledge, but its provisional and raw and endlessly manipulable form, which is *information* (Hassan, 2003: 69–125). The argument I will develop below is that humans are analogue creatures that shaped their world—their tools and technologies especially—in ways that reflected their physical capacities and the rhythms and temporalities of the natural world they inhabited. Until very recently our analogue essence and the analogue worlds we constructed was something we barely considered in such terms because there was nothing to contrast it with. The inexorable rise of the digital furnishes such a contrast, and if we see that contrast as a fundamental contradiction, then much that is worrying and problematic stems from the category error we have made.

It is important that we complement the critique of the neo-liberal colonization of the university with an ontological perspective that goes to the heart of processes of cognition and the organization and dissemination of knowledge in space and time. The university as a social institution has been analogue from its very inception, reflecting as it did our relationship with the technologies of reading and writing, the rhythms of dialogue, the practice of pedagogy and the production of knowledge. Knowledge itself, as we have historically produced it, is analogue. It exists in the heads of people, in the contents and in the sharing and interpretation of what went into, and emerged from, print culture (Anderson, 1991: 53). It exists in the praxis upon which we shape and are shaped by society, and by its relationship to past, present and future. Analogue knowledge, moreover, has its own temporal rhythms, and because such knowledge is expressed through and by human beings, has its own physical and cognitive limits.

Information, by contrast, is the currency of digital logic and is fast becoming the currency of the university. Digital information is immaterial. It is code that resides in files and databases and is accessed by humans to be processed and modified and then returned to their electronic domains until required again for further processing and modification. Most importantly, digital information has none of the temporal and physical constraints of print, and none of the capacity constraints of our human brains. As 'users' we have, at best, only an abstracted relationship to a very recent technological process that has no parallel in human history.

In its quest for 'efficiency' and competitiveness, the university uses the very same digital-industrial methods as any other commodity-producer. It assumes that producing knowledge, enabling understanding and developing the fullest potential of our species and the societies we create may be achieved digitally and efficiently and with no loss of fidelity. Indeed the process is supposed to be enriched by computers. But this is transformation by, and widespread implementation of, an unproven technology. It expresses unwarranted faith in a digital logic that has been conceived and developed with very different purposes to that of the cultivation of the life of the mind and to the disinterested pursuit of ways of understanding the world. Accordingly, the humanist institution established to create and widely disseminate knowledge for the greater social benefit is mutating into a computer-driven information factory to feed the narrow needs of industry.

In his book *24/7*, Jonathan Crary writes that: 'To believe that there are any essential features that distinguish living beings from machines is, we are told by celebrated critics, naive and delusional' (2014: 13). It is my argument that it is the delusion that assumes that *we are alike* that constitutes the basis for the category error we made. And unless we recognize the essential difference between analogue and digital, between knowledge and information, and between human and machines, then the machines that appear to be tools that we control will become so dominant and powerful, that it is we who will have to increasingly adapt to them and their logic. We have in fact been adapting ourselves to computers since the 1980s.

Being analogue

The saying 'there are no straight lines in nature' expresses more than a high-school science debating point. It contains the wish or hope that there is more to humans and to nature than the 'reality' of mathematics and geometry as the arbiter of what is true and false. Immanuel Kant said something similar about us when he wrote about 'the crooked timber of humanity'. To consider ourselves as analogue goes to the heart of this view—and puts us firmly on the side of nature and humanity. Commonplace definitions of 'analogue' are dominated, predictably, by the technological, i.e., an analogue television or radio signal. The meanings that relate to humans are more interesting. For example, the Oxford Dictionary defines it as: 'a person or thing seen as comparable to another'. It is derived from the Greek analogon, meaning 'proportionate' or 'equivalent'. By taking this 'human' approach and adapting it to the work of computer theorist Charles Petzold, Silvia Estévez makes a valuable contribution by reminding us that in radical contrast to the digital environment that increasingly shapes our lives, we humans are in fact analogue beings. Predigital technologies were analogue also in that they were 'equivalent' to the organic, unfolding and durational processes of humans and their environments and 'whose operations simulated processes that people had seen in nature and in the functioning of their own bodies' (Estévez, 2009: 401). Even the first computers were analogue; with the very first, the Antikythera Machine from 100 BCE being modelled upon the recognized movements of the stars and the planets. Industrial-age machines that shaped the modern world were 'equivalent' to nature also in that the automobile, for example, was a reflection of the horse, or the steam engine replicated and surpassed the power of a bullock, or the airplane was mirrored in nature by the bird, and so on. Estévez goes on to note that such epoch-defining machines as automobiles, steam engines and airplanes express human-machine 'activity [that] crosses time and space in a visible way that allows us to grasp the link between a movement and its effect, the process, the continuity …' (Estévez, 2009: 402–403).

Digital machines are different. Their processes are invisible and their speed of operation means that we cannot register or grasp the connection between cause and effect. Indeed as computers became more widespread in the 1970s, they were initially viewed, as Arthur C. Clarke wrote, as a kind of 'magic', so unlike us did they seem in terms of what they appeared capable of (1973: 21). As analogue beings that use digital machines, we are disconnected from them in a way that goes deeper than Marx's theory of alienation from the industrial-age machine. We become more profoundly alienated precisely because, and to draw upon Estévez once more: 'we cannot see the continuity of movement crossing space and time to produce an effect [because] they [computers] do not function like something we can recognize in nature …' (2009: 402). What this suggests is the loss or diminution of what philosopher Arnold Gehlen termed the 'circle of action' (*handlungskreis*) (1980: 14), which expressed our ancient adaptation to technology use and which kept us linked with nature and in a kind of synchrony with its rhythms.

The non-recognition of digital logic in nature is a problem that has been identified by Gilles Deleuze. For him, computers were becoming the preeminent technology for what he termed 'societies of control'. Previously, 'machines [were] easily matched with each type of society'; they were mutually analogous, in other words (1992: 6). But computers represent a new 'mutation of capitalism' (1992) that displaces or makes digital analogue processes such as the clocks that 'paced' society, and the forms of analogue media (writing, print, books, television, etc.) that created cultures wherein (by analogy) humans could 'grasp the link between a movement and its effects, the process, the continuity' in space and time (Estévez, 2009: 402–403). Computers have no continuity or unfolding that we can perceive in space and time. Their speed of action is instantaneous and invisible, their processes infinitely both fractured and networked, with the latter rendering them incredibly powerful machines. Importantly, in their prime purpose of automation, computers function increasingly independently of human control, taking them outside of the ancient 'circle of action' with humans, and into an estranging and unseen realm that has no equivalent in nature and therefore no natural place for the analogue human. Indeed the innermost aim of digitality, from the time of Gottfried Leibniz, the inventor of binary code in the 1600s to the rise of modern computer science in the 1940s, was to replace the many elements of humans, especially in their modes of communication, that were viewed as unreliable and unpredictable and error-prone (Ashworth, 1996: 636; Bell, 1953: 123; Edwards, 1996: 43–75).

The technology of writing and its correlate reading are the analogue DNA of the university. The technology of writing emerged from nature and took its form from natural materials; the tool was born as sharpened stone, and its mark made on clay or tablet. The marks, in their earliest pictographic forms, which was the precursor of the alphabet, were representations of nature—of plants or animals or humans. Our ancestors used what was to hand to write and depicted what was familiar and readily understood to the reader. The modern practices of teaching and learning, of research and knowledge, all evolve from this basic and ancient practice. Too often, however, we fail to realize that we are expressing our analogue essence when we do this. Partly this has to do with the power of writing itself. For example, Walter Ong has argued that 'Writing is a technology that restructures thought' and with the development of writing and literacy, the technology 'takes possession of [human] consciousness' (1992: 293). Writing, it seems, is endowed with almost supernatural powers to such a degree that, as Ong observes, 'it tends to arrogate to itself supreme power by taking itself as normative for human expression and thought' (293).

Humans created writing and were in turn shaped by it (Culkin, 1967: 53). The context for this interaction was the analogue world of nature and our representations of nature. What this means is that the written word that is analogous to the spoken word reflected the capacities of humans and their physical and cognitive potentials as well as limits. For example, and with respect to the temporality of the process, reading and writing mirrored the constraints and capacities of our hand–eye functions: that is to say they are analogous with the fact that we can only read so fast, only write so fast, and only comprehend in time frames that have their limits, beyond which the process begins to break down (Hassan, 2012: 34). Again, like our lack of reflection on the concept of our 'being analogue', we tend not to consider that our fundamental capacities in reading and writing have been challenged by the advent of computers. Indeed we imagine, or are told, that our cognitive capacities and limitations are being enhanced and made more 'efficient' by them. As Theodore Roszak presciently tells it in his *The Cult of Information*, the high-pressure hype of the 'data merchants' from computer multinationals, backed by futurologists and industry consultants, established the initial bridgehead into the universities in the 1980s. There was no empirically demonstrable pedagogical need (then or now) for the blanket computerization and automation of schools, colleges and universities. The whole process was, argues Roszak, fundamentally about 'selling' (1986: 31). And for strategic reasons of perceived survivability, universities have been happy to buy.

The digital universe

Political economy can tell us much about how and why we find ourselves in a digital age with digital universities. The neo-liberalism that has triumphed across the world as both a mode of production and a political ideology has its roots in the 'crises of capitalism' that reached something of a climax in the 1970s. The crisis, as David Harvey argues, was essentially one of space and time in relation to the dynamics of capitalism. The old industrial and analogue mode of Fordism had reached a point of maturity in the developed countries where it was no longer able to expand easily into new areas of profitability (1989: 127–189). There were also too many national-economy and institutional-regulatory barriers to the free movement of capital. But as Harvey argues elsewhere, and drawing from Marx, 'every limit (to capital) is a barrier to be overcome' (2010: 47). The politics of neo-liberalism certainly pointed out the ways to the 'overcoming' of the crisis of capitalism—but it was information technologies that provided the means for it. Deregulation and productive efficiency (in every realm) were the watchwords for the process, and very quickly over the decades of the 1980s and 1990s the neo-liberal globalized world we live in today took shape.

Technologies of efficiency, primarily the networked computer, have carved out our digital world. In so doing, they have created another realm, a virtual space for a networked society—which was also a space and a society for capital to create, grow and colonize. In this new hyper-competitive age, hyper-flexibility was critical for business success. Analogue technologies tended to be inflexible and/or too slow—unless they themselves could be digitalized. And so the typewriter, for example, became the desktop computer; the fixed dial-telephone became a mobile digital device, and so on. Neo-liberal globalization is also a revolution in telecommunications, and this provides a good example of the cost-efficiency logic behind the analogue-to-digital transformation. Nicholas Baran describes how the analogue wave signal, the basis for radio, television and telephone telecommunications was 'the *natural* wave form of most natural phenomena such as sound and light' (1998: 124) (emphasis added). However, to network these communications through analogue means was expensive and slow by means of extensive patching and wiring. It is 'much more efficient', Baran adds, to transmit the signal in digital format, the simple on/off binary, whose discontinuous logic is antithetical to the analogue wave form (1998). This rationalizing of the communication process constitutes what Marshall McLuhan termed 'auto-amputation' (1964: 41–48), whereby direct human participation and equivalence begins to diminish, and the speed of the communication process begins to rise exponentially. Crucially, the innate human-technology analogue relationship is hardly recognized as something being lost because the ideology of efficiency has become so powerful that it is instead seen as positive and self-evidently so.

Indeed it should be remembered that the entire process of digitalization, across almost every register of life, was conducted as 'efficiency' and cost-effective measures, and with little or no reflection or consideration of any wider consequences. Technologies of efficiency not only created our converged digital universe, they also created what Hartmut Rosa, amongst others, has termed the (global) 'acceleration of the pace of life' where 'we do more things in less time' (2003: 49). Living in this new temporal context takes us beyond previous temporal experience, which was dominated objectively by the analogue clock and its rhythms. Living in the networked society is to live, to a growing degree, in what I have elsewhere termed 'network time' (2003: 225–241; 2014:3–16). This is the temporality of globalization, where the experience of 'acceleration' is on an open-ended trajectory that is limited only by levels of technological sophistication. This is time that supplants the analogue time of the clock and calendar and takes us to a form of temporal experience that we do not recognize in nature or in our analogue selves.

Information, as I said before, is the currency of this universe, and it is the staple means through which we live in it, through reading, writing and through the production and consumption of all kinds of digital content. But as analogue creatures from an analogue world, we adapt poorly to this unnatural environment because we have so little in common with it. The information we work with in network time is not neutral, something we shape or work interactively with, as in a 'circle of action'. In its network form it is separate from us and acts *upon* us. This is an effect of networked computer systems that was noticed as early as 1967 by Robert McBride in his book, *The Automated State*, who wrote that a computer *system* is very different from a singular, unattached computer. 'The system' he observes, 'begins not with equipment or even with people; it begins with the definition of a goal to be attained—a task to be accomplished'. Moreover, 'computer systems react actively to their environment. They do not wait for people to approach them with specific requests; they reach out to the environment …' (1967: 4). In other words, digital systems are programmed with the sole goal of instrumental efficiency, and then are let loose to 'reach out' to you and me to draw us into their logic and onto their unnatural, alienating and discontinuous paths.

This logic transforms our erstwhile analogue time consciousness in more specific ways through our exposure to the system's digital product. Bernard Stiegler has written insightfully about the nature of time and its digital production. He introduces the term 'temporal objects', which is a variant of my own 'network time', to describe how time becomes compressed and commodified and objectified in our networked lives. Drawing upon Edmund Husserl's phenomenology, Stiegler argues that in the digital universe, the saturation of media commodities such as film, music, television, YouTube, social media, etc., constitute a new relationship with time and transform how we distinguish and perceive past, present and future. For Stiegler, the pervasion of these real-time media products within the flows of the network disengages us from the perception of time, of différance in lived time, between what Husserl terms 'primary, secondary, and tertiary retention' (Stiegler, 1998: 17). The 'temporal objects' that constitute the form and shape of our networked lives are responsible for what Stiegler argues to be the synchronization of time consciousness with the temporality of the objects themselves (Hansen, 2004: 252). Time is thus constituted in a digital way that has radically different effects from that of the clock. Through connectivity, synchrony with the network 'objectifies' time from human experience in an equally radical way. For Stiegler, this is 'the expropriation of human time submitted to commodity-time' (2011: 27). Marx argues in *Capital* that commodities were alienated fetishes that we took to be real; Paul Virilio says something similar about network time: 'The virtual otherworld of cybernetics is … nothing more than the anachronism of another time in which critical space … merges with the critical instant of a fundamentally *uninhabitable* continuum' (2012: 17–18) (emphasis in original).

The important point to draw from all this is that once, and not so long ago, the 'tasks' or 'goals' of the university were ideally unspecific. They were generally oriented to the provision of public goods and services, and could evolve in a context where both science and technology and the arts and humanities could follow paths that were not mutually exclusive. Today 'efficiency' and commercialization are the major 'tasks to be accomplished' for the functioning and survival of the digital university.

The digital university (in network time)

In its relentlessly expanding digital mode, the future for the university could hardly be less auspicious. Efficiency, commercialization—with the corollary of temporal acceleration—all have migrated as colonizers from a neo-liberal post-Fordism whose logic views the university as merely another market, another space for accumulation, and another realm where computerization would be a key function in the achieving of its principal aims. That is not to say that the university should not respond in some fashion to wider social change. However, what has occurred is the degrading of the essential raison d'être of the university—which is the creation of a stable and organic context for the production of knowledge and debate and ethical and philosophical (as well as technical) expertise that all serve as public goods.

John Henry Newman's 1873 *Idea of the University* stressed the humanist value in the liberal education that he defined as the 'real cultivation of the mind' that is 'trained and formed to have a connected view or grasp of things' (1999: 235 & ix). Newman had his critics then and now, not least for being too 'otherworldly'. Nonetheless these quotes are representational of his approach and are generalizable as basic tenets. His 'cultivation' implies knowledge production on an organic and analogue temporal scale—which network time takes us beyond; and his 'connected view' of the diversity of human possibility is being replaced by the instrumentality of digital 'connections', networks, whose basic function is the intensification and acceleration of information. I will return to Newman's principles at the end of this essay.

As noted earlier, the commercialization of the university is a well-known aspect of the institution's transformation. However, the category error made in replacing our analogue essence with digital logic is hardly appreciated at all. Consequently, we rarely consider the social or cognitive or ontological effects of widespread computerization. For example, in the late-1990s, a report by the U.S. President's Information Technology Advisory Committee (PITAC) proffered what was in retrospect, a timid yet still ultimately ignored cautionary regarding the colonization of places of learning by networked computers:

> We know too little about the best ways to use computing and communications technology for effective teaching and learning, in particular, how to effectively use multimedia capabilities to create a richer, and more appealing learning experience. We need to better understand what aspects of learning can be effectively facilitated by technology and which aspects require traditional classroom interactions with the accompanying social and interactive contexts. We also need to determine the best ways to teach our citizens the powers and limitations of the new technologies and how to use these technologies effectively in their personal and professional lives. (1999: 1.3)

This Report went the way of most inconvenient advice to governments anywhere—it gathered dust. Too much was at stake (Roszak's 'selling') across much of western society to get in the way of 'progress' and the wonders of neo-liberal business practice pioneered by the new heroes such as Microsoft's Bill Gates. Thomas Frank captured this revolution-in-progress in his 2000 book, *One Market Under God*, which chronicled the new faith in 'markets and microchips' which were being seen as profoundly democratic and inclusive, and able to flatten 'hierarchies … and clusters of concentrated power' (82). As Frank relates it, the instrumental efficiency of computers was equated with egalitarianism and this helped to give them a popular appeal. Consequently, political and business elites eyed the universities as holdout 'clusters of concentrated power' that were ripe for reform, and where markets and microchips should enter—and enter they did.

Jump forward a generation and any counsel against the digitalization of teaching and learning is no longer even whistling in the wind. The logics of capitalist colonization, of economies of scale, and of 'efficiency' through the digitalization of every possible analogue process, have taken us to the threshold of an automated university. We see its leading edge today in the rapid spread of 'massive open online courses' or MOOCs. It's a development that the *Economist* (2012) predictably views as a force for democracy and excellence through the combination of markets and microchips. But this is a revolution dominated by entrepreneurial computer science professors from Stanford, MIT and elsewhere. By 2014, hundreds of thousands of students had signed up to a wide range of subjects in elite and non-elite universities, and not only in the United States. The vision is to 'improve productivity in higher education' through online lectures that may be seen potentially by millions of students in any part of the world with an Internet connection. Substituting a living and breathing analogical and dialogical lecture hall with a video link to a computer is seen as flexible and cost-effective because: 'Real-life lectures have no pause, rewind (or fast-forward) buttons; MOOCs let students learn at their own pace, typically with short, engaging videos, modelled on the hugely successful online lecturettes pioneered by TED, a non-profit organiser of upmarket mindfests' (Economist, 2012).

The motive force behind MOOCs is of course business and a nebulous 'efficiency'. And the rationalization of teaching and learning into 'lecturettes' comes from the assumptions of computer scientists who tend to see, as did 1940s 'human-computer symbiosis' guru J.C.R. Licklider, that computers are good at what humans are bad at: computers don't tire, they are more dependable, they don't endlessly digress, they are not 'opinionated', they don't have axes to grind, they can be re-programmed, and (most important) they don't constitute large recurrent costs in the form of salaries. Beyond the cost-saving rationale, the simplistic assumption is that we can replace analogue with digital with no loss of fidelity in teaching and learning. We are only at the beginning of the fully automated university. MOOCs need to be properly 'monetized' before it sweeps all before it. But the none-too-reassuring example of Amazon.com that went for years before making any money serves as a beacon of hope for the providers of software and for university managers.

Universities, as sites of ubiquitous computing, are moving decisively in the direction of automation with little consideration of the consequences beyond alleged efficiency gains. Indeed, the loss of the analogue rhythms of teaching and learning to their digital and accelerating non-equivalents involves the transformation of our relationship to print culture and analogue time in ways we consider even less. Reading and writing is still the core of any pedagogical and cognitive experience. However, digital hypertext, and screen reading more broadly, promotes skimming and the 'F pattern' of reading, whereas print encourages a deeper and sustained reading experience (Carr, 2010; Mikics, 2014). Indeed, fMRI scans show that the synaptic architecture of the brain changes rapidly when exposed to screen reading, with the neural connections becoming weaker (Carr, 2010: 141–143). Screen reading and writing engineers the brain in such a way as to be less attuned to concentration for long periods, and consequently less able to access the benefits of insight, of critical reflection and sedimented knowledge accumulation. Katherine Hayles, foremost theorist of digital writing, acknowledges this transformation (2010), but argues that screen reading is not going to disappear, and so we need to work out some way of adding it to our suite of cognitive processes, and hope that the benefits of print will somehow remain intact—despite the evidence of the neurological transformation caused by digital reading and writing.

We cannot afford to be as sanguine as Hayles. And we cannot afford to rely on the information supplied by digital fMRI technology alone; we must take our lead from what the university itself (used to) supply, which is analogue-based philosophy and analogue-aware theorizing that takes the analogue world and analogue human as its reference point. Through such a perspective, we can get insight into the consequences of the category error made by assuming ourselves to be compatible with digital logic. For example, in his essay 'The End of Temporality', Fredric Jameson makes the point that 'time governs the realm of interiority, in which both subjectivity and logic, the private and the epistemological, self-consciousness and desire are to be found' (2003: 697). Jameson speaks of the time of modernity, where the subjective time of experience and the objective time of the clock shaped and metered our thinking about our world. This time (or these times) is being lost in our postmodernity (or in our neo-liberal network society as I would term it). For Jameson, our 'postmodern generations are dispossessed (without even knowing it) of any differential sense of that deep time the first moderns sought to inscribe in their writing' (699). Jameson is describing the writing of literature, but that same logic of dispossession may be ascribed to anyone who reads, writes and seeks to learn in the accelerated environment of digital text network time. Instant information, Jameson tells us, suppresses the analogue space and time that constituted modernity (701). By so doing, it also suppresses the narrative and analogue-based time of the unfolding of history of past, present and future.

The network time of the university, moreover, suppresses the analogue being (narratively and historically constituted) that Paul Ricoeur, in his *Time and Narrative*, identifies as the locus of knowledge and knowledge production. Importantly, what Ricoeur terms the 'conditions of significance' of knowledge production become apparent only if we appreciate their 'conditions of possibility' (1998: 104). In other words, we take for granted, as if it is neutral, the technology of analogue writing used to produce knowledge. The technology of writing (and reading) is therefore not viewed as a 'condition of possibility', upon which knowledge is made possible. It is the same with temporality and our analogue essence; these too are 'conditions of possibility' that, to paraphrase Walter Ong, we take as the unreflected upon (and unchanging) bases for human thought and action (Ong, 1992: 293). However, digitalization has radically transformed these bases—literally under our noses. Only if we reflect upon these changes can we appreciate their 'condition of possibility' as the preconditions for knowledge production. It is a dripping irony (as well as profound contradiction) that the more we become immersed in the digital at the expense of the analogue, the less we will be able to reflect upon the new 'condition of significance' and what they actually mean. In short, until we appreciate the category error made in assuming that the analogue human can function in the same way within the digital university, we will be unable to render this transformation as problematic and therefore unable to see the root cause of the university malaise—which goes rather deeper than issues of 'efficiency' or profits or commercialization.

Some conclusions

I wrote earlier about the usefulness of the analogy of 'cultivation'—both of the mind and of the society of which it is part—as a way of thinking about the function and role of the community of the university. The analogue goes even deeper. Simone Weil, for example, in her book *The Need for Roots*, writes:

> To be rooted is perhaps the most important and least recognized need of the human soul. It is one of the hardest to define. A human being has roots by virtue of his real, active, and natural participation in the life of a community, which preserves in living shape certain particular treasures of the past and certain expectations for the future. This participation is a natural one [...]. Every human being needs to have multiple roots. It is necessary for him to draw well-nigh the whole of his moral, intellectual, and spiritual life by way of the environment of which he forms a natural part. (1952: 41)

Weil here expresses the totalizing nature of our analogue equivalence with nature, and how we have since the earliest times, knowingly or not, drawn almost everything we have from the relationship. Her concept of roots is clearly connected to the idea of cultivation that Newman argued must be the context for the training and development of the mind. The proportionality and equivalence of this relationship in the development of technology is (or has been) organic and evolutionary; but with any evolution or transformation there is loss and discontinuity that comes with gain and continuity. Much that is lost is either unlamented or unnoticed. Mark Oliver reflects upon what is lost through discontinuity in his *Buggy Life: Travels Through the Analogue Frontier*, which is a consideration of the eclipse of the horse-drawn cart by the train and automobile in 19th-century United States. He writes:

> A generation before, the pioneers had still known how to survive on the prairie by their own wits, but now that towns and the railway had brought easy access to goods and services, the young Americans quickly forgot how to use a knife in the pursuit and preparation of food. (2005: 4)

But loss can be sometimes consequential—or at least worth reflecting upon, because we can miss its wider import amid the excitement of seeming technological progress. Oliver reminds us that in this case, an ancient link with the natural world, of knife use, of hunting and of knowing about the provisioning of food was being lost; to be replaced by the commodified abstractions we live upon today. Perhaps this particular case does not matter so much. In our own time the frontier of the whole analogue world has been crossed by digital technology. The particular loss in the university is not of those analogue technologies that can evolve and/or disappear without profound consequence. We are losing the traditional analogue technologies of writing, print and reading to their digital non-equivalents. We are losing also the corollaries of reflective analysis, debate and exchange that are based on writing, print and reading—analogue technologies working in their own analogue time. These are the intellectual and cognitive technologies that created Ricoeur's 'conditions of possibility' from which has arisen everything that the university has given economy, culture and society in the form of public and civic goods. The 'conditions' are now increasingly digital, and their alien nature means that there is no natural place for the human. The 'possibilities' available to us are those that the computer, as McBride (1967: 4) tells us, comes preprogrammed with: its own 'definition of [the] goal to be attained—[the] task to be accomplished', and these are instrumental 'efficiency' through increasing speed.

The 'otherworldly' critique of the university, of the elitist 'dreaming spires', of 'tenured radicals' who won't live in the real world, of the arrogance of mediocrities who 'teach' because they can't 'do', and of the excoriation of the special pleading of the university that thinks itself somehow 'special' are commonplace in lazy media looking for a convenient scapegoat to jeer at, or for government policy circles seeking to make funding cuts. Often the response from those targets of such criticism is to either run from it, or to deflect it by conforming to the rhetoric of competition and 'efficiency' and thus accept that the university is indeed another kind of business that should sink or swim in the marketplace of students and of ideas of a 'useful' kind. Frequently these critiques are aimed directly at individuals who are seen to embody elitism, arrogance or otherworldliness. However, just as frequently, the institution gets conflated into the process. To target individuals is legitimate. There should be proper accountability and transparency over the actions and competence of individual academics, just like in any other institution. Humans are not so special in this context—*but the institution is*. This is not such a radical an idea. Religions, charities, art galleries, orchestras and so on attract a measure of protection (tax breaks, subsidies, etc.) because they are seen as somehow beyond the grubbiness of the marketplace and instrumentalized 'efficiency'. Universities were once included in this 'liberal' thinking and categorization. However, since the 1980s, their size and importance as potential markets and major profit centres has singled them out for inevitable colonization through commercialization.

We need to fight for the safeguarding of the university on this ostensibly unsafe ground. We need to argue that the university *is* special; indeed more special than we have hitherto imagined. And we need to do so not simply because the market will devalue critical reason and valourize instrumental reason; that is what capitalism has always done, wherever it functions. We need to because of the deeper category error made by replacing analogue with digital, humans with computers. Raimond Gaita, an Australian philosopher, has emphasized the special nature of the university, one where the individual is a mere carrier of an ethic:

> We must preserve the unworldly space in which university teachers are able to reveal to their students what it means, mostly deeply, to devote one's life to an academic vocation—to live an answer to Callicles. They will then reveal to their students, who will go into the world to live many kinds of lives, a value in their education that nourishes them more deeply than the kind of liberal education that many people praise. (2013)

The more universities are denied the analogue tools (and people as the bearer of these tools) that created the 'conditions of possibility', then the more we (and our children) are denied possible futures, futures that see beyond the instrumental and the 'efficient'. The cost of the loss of analogue tools and analogue structures is incalculable. What can be said with more precision is that if we do nothing then the computer-digital logic will continue to colonize our present, shape our future and neglect our past. Gaita's students will then go into the world—not to lead many different lives, but to lead increasingly narrowed lives, in an increasingly narrowed world with increasingly narrowed interests emerging from preprogrammed goals supplied for a fee by the university. This in itself would be bad enough. However, through our flawed assumptions regarding the nature of computers, we are not only erasing an ancient analogue institution, we estrange our analogue selves from each other through lives led increasingly through the portal of a screen. Perhaps most fundamentally of all, we become gradually disconnected from an analogue world of which we are fundamentally a part, and where we were once able to recognize ourselves, recognize each other and recognize nature within it.

References

Anderson, Benedict (1991). *Imagined Communities*. London: Verso.

Ashworth, W. J. (1996). 'Memory, Efficiency and Symbolic Analysis: Charles Babbage, John Herschel, and the Industrial Mind'. *Isis*, 87(4), 629–53.

Baran, Nicholas (1998). 'The Privatization of Telecommunication.' In *Capitalism and the Information Age*. McChesney, Robert; Meiksins Wood, Ellen; and Bellamy Foster, John (editors) pp.123-134.New York: Monthly Review Press.

Bell, Eric (1953). *Men of Mathematics*. Harmondsworth: Penguin.

Brown, Roger & Helen, Carasso (2013). *Everything for Sale: The Marketisation of UK Higher Education*. London: Routledge.

Carr, Nicholas (2010). *The Shallows: How the Internet is Changing the Way We Think, Read and Remember*. London: Atlantic Books.

Clarke, A. C. (1973). *Profiles of the Future*. New York: Harper and Row.

Crary, Jonathan (2014). *24/7*. London: Verso.

Culkin, John (1967). 'A Schoolman's Guide to Marshal McLuhan,' *The Saturday Review* http://www.unz.org/Pub/SaturdayRev-1967mar18-00051

Deleuze, Gilles (1992). 'Postscript on the Societies of Control,' *October* Vol. 59 (Winter), pp. 3–7.

Economist (2012). 'Learning New Lessons,' December 22nd Online: http://www.economist.com/news/international/21568738-online-courses-are-transforming-higher-education-creating-new-opportunities-best

Edwards, Paul N. (1996). *The Closed World: Computers and the Politics of Discourse in Cold War America.* Cambridge, Mass.MIT Press.

Estévez, Silvia (2009). 'Is Nostalgia Becoming Digital?,' *Social Identities* Vol. 15, No. 3, pp. 393–401.

Frank, Thomas (2000). *One Market Under God.* New York: Secker & Warburg.

Frank, Thomas (2014). 'Academy Fight Song,' *The Baffler* No. 23 http://www.thebaffler.com/salvos/academy-fight-song

Gaita, Raimond (2013). 'To Civilize the City?,' *Meanjin* Vol. 3, No. 4 http://meanjin.com.au/articles/post/to-civilise-the-city/

Gehlen, Arnold (1980). Man *in the Age of Technology*. Trans. Patricia Lipscomb. New York: Columbia University Press.

Hansen, Mark (2004). *New Philosophy for New Media*. Cambridge, Mass. MIT Press.

Harvey, David (1989). *The Condition of Postmodernity*. Oxford: Blackwell.

Harvey, David (2010). *The Enigma of Capital.* New York: Profile Books.

Hassan, Robert (2003). 'Network Time and the New Knowledge Epoch,' *Time & Society* Vo.12, No. 2/3. pp. 225–241

Hassan, Robert (2012). *Age of Distraction.* New York: Transaction Books.

Hayles, Katherine (2010). 'How We Read: Close, Hyper, Machine,' *ADE Bulletin* Vol. 150. www.mla.org/adefl_bulletin_d_ade_150_62.pdf

Jameson, Fredric (2003). 'The End of Temporality,' *Critical Inquiry* Vol. 29, No. 4 (Summer), pp. 695–718.

McBride, Robert (1967). *The Automated State: Computer Systems as a New Force in Society.* Philadelphia: Chilton.

McLuhan, Marshall (1964). *Understanding Media: The Extensions of Man.* London: Sphere Books.

Mikics, David (2014). *Slow Reading in a Hurried Age.* New York: Belknap Press.

Newman, John Henry (1999). *The Idea of a University.* Washington, DC: Regnery Publishing.

Oliver, Mark (2005). *Buggy Life: Travels through the Analogue Frontier.* Unpublished Thesis. University of California.

Ong, Walter (1992). *Orality and Literacy.* New York: Routledge.

President's Information Technology Advisory Committee (PITAC) (2000). 'Ten critical national challenge transformations.' www.ccic.gov/ac/report/

Ricoeur, Paul (1998). *Time and Narrative 1.* Chicago, IL: University of Chicago Press.

Rosa, Hartmut (2003). 'Social Acceleration' *Constellations* Vol. 10, No. 1, pp. 49–52.

Rosa, Hartmut (2014). *Social Acceleration: A New Theory of Modernity*. New York: Columbia University Press.
Roszak, Theodore (1986). *The Cult of Information*. Berkeley, CA: The University of California Press.
Stiegler, Bernard (1998). *Technics and Time 1: The Fault of Epimetheus*. Trans. R. Beardsworth & G. Collins. Stanford: Stanford University Press.
Stiegler, Bernard (2011). *For a New Critique of Political Economy*. Cambridge: Polity Press.
Virilio, Paul (2012). *The Great Accelerator*. Cambridge: Polity Press.
Weil, Simone (1952). *The Need for Roots*. London: Routledge and Kegan Paul.

PART SIX

Teaching and Students

Introduction

What large ideas might be drawn upon in order to do justice to the possibilities of universities so far as teaching is concerned? The question can be answered satisfactorily, if at all, only against a sense of the changes that teaching is undergoing. Those changes—exposed elsewhere in this volume—include the wide expectation that teaching should be directed to the student's acquisition of employment-related skills, of an increasingly systematic auditing of teaching, of the marketization of teaching such that students become 'customers' of the university and of an unduly narrow understanding of learning (with a vocabulary of learning 'outcomes' and learning 'gains'), as if worthwhile forms of human development can be tightly organized, predicted and measured. The chapters in this section build upon this horizon of profound changes to what counts as teaching and what it is to be a student, and offer suggestions as to ways forward.

The chapter by Martha Nussbaum, on 'Citizens of the World', notes that the very idea of worldly citizenship goes back at least as far as the Greeks and Romans: 'it was Diogenes the Cynic who coined the term "citizen of the world"'. 'This world citizenship does not ... require that we suspend criticism towards other individuals and cultures' but it does mean 'recognizing one another as fellow citizens in the community of reason'. 'What this means in higher education is that an attitude of mutual respect should be nourished both in the classroom itself and in its reading material'. In turn, this education 'requires transcending the inclination of both students and educators to define themselves primarily in terms of local group loyalties and identities'. This education must be 'a multicultural education ... that acquaints students with some fundamentals about the histories and cultures of many different groups'. This would be neither a curricula form of 'multiculturalism' nor an entry into cultural relativism. The students here would be exposed to difficult issues and challenged to work their way through. No less than the future of democracy is at stake.

The chapter by Paul Gibbs explores the matter of 'Trust in the University'. Gibbs observes that 'liberal education is dependent on a trusting relationship between the owner of the educational process and the recipient: one does not know what one is expected to receive, as it has to be jointly created'. However, trust has been marketized and distorted such that students come to trust that the education that they receive will deliver their assured success in the labour market. Students are rendered into customers, seeking certain kind of economic goods. In the process, the mutual trust of the pedagogical relationship—which 'involves offering up one's vulnerability to others'—is put in jeopardy. This is an 'empathic' form of trust and stands in stark contrast to the more utilitarian 'competence of trust'. Each is important to the pedagogical relationship but they are fundamentally different, and empathic trust is especially 'fragile'. There is a connection here, too, with 'self-trust' on the part of the student, which requires students to come to an understanding of themselves, which in turn requires 'reasoned argument and debate'. Ultimately, empathic moral trust has implications for the whole character of academic life.

In their chapter, 'The University as a Public Pedagogic Form', Jan Masschelein and Maarten Simons advance the idea of the university as 'a site for collective public study'. Such a university would offer a form of 'resistance' and offers an 'imaginative engagement' with the dominant ideologies of our age—as they concern higher education. Their analysis is situated especially against the 'production' conception of higher education being driven forward by the European Union and various of its agencies. Drawing on the character of the university in the Middle Ages, it is observed that the *universitas studii* had a distinctive form, that of collective, 'public', study. It involved a meeting, an encounter *with* texts and ideas and *through* others. 'These forms of university study are experiments', the outcome of which 'cannot be defined in advance'.

In this kind of pedagogy, 'students should not be merely regarded as those who stand to be informed by research ... but should be actively involved'. However, public study 'occurs precisely ... where knowledge or science leaves the context of disciplined research' so opening up 'another future through making collective thinking possible'. All this calls for a collective slowing-down and so resists the fast, personalized learning now emerging as the pedagogical default position. In this way, university study may again become 'a form of gathering that allows [discussion and shaping] of possible destinies and futures'.

In his chapter, 'Universities as Civic Spaces: In the Footsteps of Arendt and Jaspers', Jon Nixon continues the theme of learning and thinking together but places his discussion in the context of the relationship between the university and the state, and the spectre of totalitarian and authoritarian regimes. Against such a horizon, universities matter, as providers of civic spaces for collective thought and the works of Hannah Arendt and Karl Jaspers offer 'vital resources' for us today. Hannah Arendt saw a connection between thought and freedom, both being intimately connected with a public space in which differing points of view can engage and coexist. Complex matters of the relationship between solitude and thought arise here, with which Jaspers wrestled, for whom 'boundless communication' was the 'secret of becoming-human'. All of this matters, especially with the contemporary emergence of a democratic deficit. The university is on a cusp. It can choose to acquiesce in institutional processes that would either directly or indirectly close thought (in debate, in teaching and in the student experience) or 'can choose to provide spaces for thinking together about the collective problems that face us and the alternative futures that are open to us'. So conceived, universities can help in addressing global problems, that both call for collective solutions that run across disciplines and call too for 'thinking that is globally inter-connective'.

Ronald Barnett

CHAPTER TWENTY

Citizens of the World

MARTHA C. NUSSBAUM

> When anyone asked him where he came from, he said, "I am a citizen of the world."
> —DIOGENES LAERTIUS, *LIFE OF DIOGENES THE CYNIC*

Anna was a political science major at a large state university in the Midwest. Upon graduation, she went into business, getting a promising job with a large firm. After twelve years she had risen to a middle-management position. One day, her firm assigned her to the newly opened Beijing office.[1] What did she need to know, and how well did her education prepare her for success in her new role? In a middle-management position, Anna is working with both Chinese and American employees, both male and female. She needs to know how Chinese people think about work (and not to assume there is just one way); she needs to know how cooperative networks are formed, and what misunderstandings might arise in interactions between Chinese and American workers. Knowledge of recent Chinese history is important, since the disruptions of the Cultural Revolution still shape workers' attitudes. Anna also needs to consider her response to the recent policy of urging women to return to the home, and to associated practices of laying off women first. This means she should know something about Chinese gender relations, both in the Confucian tradition and more recently. She should probably know something about academic women's studies in the United States, which have influenced the women's studies movement in Chinese universities.

She certainly needs a more general view about human rights, and about to what extent it is either legitimate or wise to criticize another nation's ways of life. In the future, Anna may find herself dealing with problems of anti-African racism, and with recent government attempts to exclude immigrants who test positive for the human immunodeficiency virus. Doing this well will require her to know something about the history of Chinese attitudes about race and sexuality. It will also mean being able to keep her moral bearings even when she knows that the society around her will not accept her view.

The real-life Anna had only a small part of this preparation—some courses in world history, but none that dealt with the general issue of cultural variety and how to justify moral judgments in a context of diversity; none that dealt with the variety of understandings of gender roles or family structures; none that dealt with sexual diversity and its relationship to human rights. More importantly, she had no courses that prepared her for the shock of discovering that other places treated as natural what she found strange, and as strange what she found natural. Her imaginative capacity to enter into the lives of people of other nations had been blunted by lack of practice. The real-life Anna had a rough time getting settled in China, and the firm's dealings with its new context were not always very successful. A persistent and curious person, however, she stayed on and has made herself a good interpreter of cultural difference. She now plans to spend her life in Beijing, and she feels she is making a valuable contribution to the firm.

…

Asked where he came from, the ancient Greek Cynic philosopher Diogenes replied, "I am a citizen of the world." He meant by this that he refused to be defined simply by his local origins and group memberships, associations central to the self-image of a conventional Greek male; he insisted on defining himself in terms of more universal aspirations and concerns.[2] The Stoics who followed his lead developed his image of the *kosmopolitēs*, or world citizen, more fully, arguing that each of us dwells, in effect, in two communities—the local community of our birth, and the community of human argument and aspiration that "is truly great and truly common." It is the latter community that is, most fundamentally, the source of our moral and social obligations. With respect to fundamental moral values such as justice, "we should regard all human beings as our fellow citizens and local residents."[3] This attitude deeply influenced the subsequent philosophical and political tradition, especially as mediated through the writings of Cicero, who reworked it so as to allow a special degree of loyalty to one's own local region or group. Stoic ideas influenced the American republic through the writings of Thomas Paine, and also through Adam Smith and Immanuel Kant, who themselves influenced the Founders.[4] Later on, Stoic thought was a major formative influence on both Emerson and Thoreau.

...

The Idea of World Citizenship in Greek and Roman Antiquity

Contemporary debates about the curriculum frequently imply that the idea of a "multicultural" education is a new fad, with no antecedents in long-standing educational traditions. In fact, Socrates grew up in an Athens already influenced by such ideas in the fifth century B.C. Ethnographic writers such as the historian Herodotus examined the customs of distant countries, both in order to understand their ways of life and in order to attain a critical perspective on their own society. Herodotus took seriously the possibility that Egypt and Persia might have something to teach Athens about social values. A cross-cultural inquiry, he realized, may reveal that what we take to be natural and normal is merely parochial and habitual. One cultural group thinks that corpses must be buried; another, that they must be burnt; another that they must be left in the air to be plucked clean by the birds. Each is shocked by the practices of the other, and each, in the process, starts to realize that its habitual ways may not be the ways designed by nature for all times and persons.

Awareness of cultural difference gave rise to a rich and complex debate about whether our central moral and political values exist in the nature of things (by *phusis*), or merely by convention (*nomos*).[5] That Greek debate illustrates most of the positions now familiar in debates about cultural relativism and the source of moral norms. It also contains a crucial insight: if we should conclude that our norms are human and historical rather than immutable and eternal, it does not follow that the search for a rational justification of moral norms is futile.

In the conventional culture of fifth-century B.C. Athens, recognition that Athenian customs were not universal became a crucial precondition of Socratic searching. So long as young men were educated in the manner of Aristophanes' Old Education, an education stressing uncritical assimilation of traditional values, so long as they marched to school in rows and sang the old songs without discussion of alternatives, ethical questioning could not get going. Ethical inquiry requires a climate in which the young are encouraged to be critical of their habits and conventions; and such critical inquiry, in turn, requires awareness that life contains other possibilities.

...

Plato, writing in the early to mid-fourth century B.C., alludes frequently to the study of other cultures, especially those of Sparta, Crete, and Egypt. In his Republic, which alludes often to Spartan practices, the plan for an ideal city is plainly influenced by reflection about customs elsewhere. One particularly fascinating example of the way in which reflection about history and other cultures awakens critical reflection occurs in the fifth book of that work, where Plato's character Socrates produces the first serious argument known to us in the Western tradition for the equal education of women. Here Socrates begins by acknowledging that the idea of women receiving both physical and intellectual education equal to that of men will strike most Athenians as very weird and laughable. (Athenians who were interested in cultural comparison would know, however, that such ideas were not peculiar in Sparta, where women, less confined than at Athens, did receive extensive athletic training.)[6] But he then reminds Glaucon that many good things once seemed weird in just this way. For example, the unclothed public exercise that Athenians now prize as a norm of manliness once seemed foreign, and the heavy clothing that they think barbaric once seemed natural. However, he continues, when the practice of stripping for athletic contests had been in effect for some time, its advantages were clearly seen—and then "the appearance of absurdity ebbed away under the influence of reason's judgment about the best." So it is with women's education, Socrates argues. Right now it seems absurd, but once we realize that our conventions don't by themselves supply reasons for what we ought to do, we will be forced to ask ourselves whether we really do have good reasons for denying women the chance to develop their intellectual and physical capacities. Socrates argues that we find no such good reasons, and many good reasons why those capacities should be developed. Therefore, a comparative cultural study, by removing the false air of naturalness and inevitability that surrounds our practices, can make our society, a more truly reasonable one.

…

But it was Diogenes the Cynic who coined the term "citizen of the world." Diogenes (404–323 B.C.) led a life stripped off the usual protections that habit and status supply. Choosing exile from his own native city, he defiantly refused protection from the rich and powerful for fear of losing his freedom, and lived in poverty, famously choosing a tub set up in the marketplace as his "home" in order to indicate his disdain for convention and comfort. He connected poverty with independence of mind and speech, calling freedom of speech "the finest thing in human life."[7] Once, they say, Plato saw him washing some lettuce and said, "If you had paid court to Dionysius, you would not be washing lettuce."[8] Diogenes replied, "If you had washed lettuce, you would not have paid court to Dionysius." This freedom from subservience, he held, was essential to a philosophical life. "When someone reproached him for being an exile, he said that it was on that account that he came to be a philosopher."

...

Set in this context, the invitation to consider ourselves citizens of the world is the invitation to become, to a certain extent, philosophical exiles from our own ways of life, seeing them from the vantage point of the outsider and asking the questions an outsider is likely to ask about their meaning and function. Only this critical distance, Diogenes argued, makes one a philosopher. In other words, a stance of detachment from uncritical loyalty to one's own ways promotes the kind of evaluation that is truly reason based. When we see in how many different ways people can organize their lives we will recognize, he seems to think, what is deep and what is shallow in our own ways, and will consider that "the only real community is one that embraces the entire world." In other words, the true basis for human association is not the arbitrary or the merely habitual; it is that which we can defend as good for human beings—and Diogenes believes that these evaluations know no national boundaries.

...

The Stoic philosophers, over the next few centuries, made Diogenes' insight respectable and culturally fruitful.[9] They developed the idea of cross-cultural study and world citizenship much further in their own morally and philosophically rigorous way, making the concept of the "world citizen," *kosmou politēs*, a centerpiece of their educational program.[10] As Seneca writes, summarizing older Greek Stoic views, education should make us aware that each of us is a member of "two communities: one that is truly great and truly common ... in which we look neither to this comer nor to that, but measure the boundaries of our nation by the sun; the other, the one to which we have been assigned by birth." The accident of where one is born is just that, an accident; any human being might have been born in any nation. Recognizing this, we should not allow differences of nationality or class or ethnic membership or even gender to erect barriers between us and our fellow human beings. We should recognize humanity and its fundamental ingredients, reason and moral capacity—wherever it occurs, and give that community of humanity our first allegiance.

...

Stoics hold, then, that the good citizen is a "citizen of the world." They hold that thinking about humanity as it is realized in the whole world is valuable for self-knowledge: we see ourselves and our customs more clearly when we see our own ways in relation to those of other reasonable people. They insist, furthermore, that we really will be better able to solve our problems if we face them in this broader context, our imaginations unconstrained by narrow partisanship. No theme is deeper in Stoicism than the damage done by faction and local allegiances to the political life of a group. Stoic texts show repeatedly how easy it is for local or national identities and their associated hatreds to be manipulated by self-seeking individuals for their own gain—whereas reason is hard to fake, and its language is open to the critical scrutiny of all. Roman political life in Seneca's day was dominated by divisions of many kinds, from those of class and rank and ethnic origin to the division between parties at the public games and gladiatorial shows. Part of the self-education of the Stoic Roman emperor Marcus Aurelius, as he tells the reader of his *Meditations*, was "not to be a Green or Blue partisan at the races, or a supporter of the lightly armed or heavily armed gladiators at the Circus."[11] Politics is sabotaged again and again by these partisan loyalties, and by the search for honor and fame that accompanies them.

...

To be a citizen of the world, one does not, the Stoics stress, need to give up local affiliations, which can frequently be a source of great richness in life. They suggest instead that we think of ourselves as surrounded by a series of concentric circles.[12] The first one is drawn around the self; the next takes in one's immediate family; then follows the extended family; then, in order, one's neighbors or local group, one's fellow city-dwellers, one's fellow countrymen—and we can easily add to this list groups formed on the basis of ethnic, religious, linguistic, historical, professional, and gender identities. Beyond all these circles is the largest one, that of humanity as a whole. Our task as citizens of the world, and as educators who prepare people to be citizens of the world, will be to "draw the circles somehow toward the center," making all human beings like our fellow city-dwellers. In other words, we need not give up our special affections and identifications, whether national or ethnic or religious; but we should work to make all human beings part of our community of dialogue and concern, showing respect for the human wherever it occurs, and allowing that respect to constrain our national or local politics.

...

The Stoic, in fact, must be conversant with local differences, since knowledge of these is inextricably linked to our ability to discern and respect the dignity of humanity in each person. Stoics recognize love for what is near as a fundamental human trait, and a highly rational way to comport oneself as a citizen. If each parent has a special love for his or her own children, society will do better than if all parents try to have an equal love for all children. Much the same is true for citizenship of town or city or nation: each of us should take our stand where life has placed us, and devote to our immediate surroundings a special affection and attention. Stoics, then, do not want us to behave as if differences between male and female, or between African and Roman, are morally insignificant. These differences can and do enjoin special obligations that all of us should execute, since we should all do our duties in the life we happen to have, rather than imagining that we are beings without location or memory.

In school, ... it will be proper for us to spend a disproportionate amount of time mastering our native language and its literature. A human being who tried to learn all the world's languages would master none, and it seems reasonable for children to focus on one, or in some cases two, languages when they are small. On the other hand, it is also very important for students to understand what it is like to see the world through the perspective of another language, an experience that quickly shows that human complexity and rationality are not the monopoly of a single linguistic community.

This same point can be made about other aspects of culture that should figure in a higher education. In ethics, in historical knowledge, in knowledge of politics, in literary, artistic, and musical learning, we are all inclined to be parochial, taking our own habits for that which defines humanity. In these areas as in the case of language, it is reasonable to immerse oneself in a single tradition at an early age. But even then it is well to become acquainted with the facts of cultural variety, and this can be done very easily, for example through myths and stories that invite identification with people whose form of life is different from one's own. As education progresses, a more sophisticated grasp of human variety can show students that what is theirs is not better simply because it is familiar.

Since any living tradition is already a plurality and contains within itself aspects of resistance, criticism, and contestation, the appeal to reason frequently does not require us to take a stand outside the culture from which we begin. The Stoics are correct to find in all human beings the world over a capacity for critical searching and a love of truth. "Any soul is deprived of truth against its will," says Marcus Aurelius, quoting Plato. In this sense, any and every human tradition is a tradition of reason, and the transition from these more ordinary and intracultural exercises to a more global exercise of critical argument need not be an abrupt transition. Indeed, in the world today it is clear that internal critique very frequently takes the form of invoking what is found to be fine and just in other traditions.

People from diverse backgrounds sometimes have difficulty recognizing one another as fellow citizens in the community of reason. This is so, frequently, because actions and motives require, and do not always receive, a patient effort of interpretation. The task of world citizenship requires the would-be world citizen to become a sensitive and empathic interpreter. Education at all ages should cultivate the capacity for such interpreting. This aspect of the Stoic idea is developed most fully by Marcus Aurelius, who dealt with many different cultures in his role as emperor; he presents, in his *Meditations*, a poignantly personal account of his own efforts to be a good world citizen. "Accustom yourself not to be inattentive to what another person says, and as far as possible enter into his mind," he writes (6.53). … Given that Marcus routinely associated with people from every part of the Roman Empire, this idea imposes a daunting task of learning and understanding, which he confronts by reading a great deal of history and literature, and by studying closely the individual characters of those around him in the manner of a literary narrator. "Generally," he concludes, "one must first learn many things before one can judge another's action with understanding" (11.18).

…

World citizenship does not, and should not, require that we suspend criticism toward other individuals and cultures. Marcus continues to refer to his enemies as "deceitful and antisocial," expressing strong criticism of their conduct. The world citizen may be very critical of unjust actions or policies, and of the character of people who promote them. But at the same time Marcus refuses to think of the opponents as simply alien, as members of a different and inferior species. He refuses to criticize until he respects and understands. He carefully chooses images that reflect his desire to see them as close to him and similarly human. This careful scrutiny of the imagery and speech one uses when speaking about people who are different is one of the Stoic's central recommendations for the undoing of political hatred.

…

All parents know that it is possible to shape a child's attitudes toward other races and nationalities by the selection of stories one tells and by the way one speaks about other people in the home. There are few parents who do not seek to influence their children's views in these ways. Stoics propose, however, that the process of coming to recognize the humanity of all people should be a lifelong process, encompassing all levels of education—especially since, in a culture suffused with group hatred, one cannot rely on parents to perform this task.

What this means in higher education is that an attitude of mutual respect should be nourished both in the classroom itself and in its reading material.

Although in America we should have no sympathy with the outright censoring of reading material, we also make many selections as educators, both in assigning material and in presenting it for our students. Few of us, for example, would present anti-Semitic propaganda in a university classroom in a way that conveyed sympathy with the point of view expressed. The Stoic proposal is that we should seek out curricula that foster respect and mutual solidarity and correct the ignorance that is often an essential prop of hatred. This effort is perfectly compatible with maintaining freedom of speech and the openness of a genuinely critical and deliberative culture.

In our own time, few countries have been more rigidly divided, more corroded by group hatred, than South Africa. In spelling out its goals for society in its draft for the new Constitution, the African National Congress (ANC) recognized the need to address hatred through education, and specified the goal of education as the overcoming of these differences:

> Education shall be directed towards the development of the human personality and a sense of personal dignity, and shall aim at strengthening respect for human rights and fundamental freedoms and promoting understanding, tolerance and friendship amongst South Africans and between nations.[13]

Some of this language would have been new to Marcus Aurelius—and it would have been a good thing for Roman Stoics to have reflected more about the connections between the human dignity they prized and the political rights they frequently neglected. But the language of dignity, humanity, freedom, understanding, tolerance, and friendship would not have been strange to Marcus. (He speaks of his goal as "the idea of a Commonwealth with the same laws for all, governed on the basis of equality and free speech"; this goal is to be pursued with "beneficence, eager generosity, and optimism".) The ANC draft, like the Stoic norm of world citizenship, insists that understanding of various nations and groups is a goal for every citizen, not only for those who wish to affirm a minority identity. It insists that the goal of education should not be separation of one group from another, but respect, tolerance, and friendship—both within a nation and among nations. It insists that this goal should be fostered in a way that respects the dignity of humanity in each person and citizen.

Above all, education for world citizenship requires transcending the inclination of both students and educators to define themselves primarily in terms of local group loyalties and identities. World citizens will therefore not argue for the inclusion of cross-cultural study in a curriculum primarily on the grounds that it is a way in which members of minority groups can affirm such an identity. This approach, common though it is, is divisive and subversive of the aims of world community. This problem vexes many curricular debates. Frequently, groups who press for the recognition of their group think of their struggle as connected with goals of human respect and social justice. And yet their way of focusing their demands, because it neglects commonalities and portrays people as above all members of identity groups, tends to subvert the demand for equal respect and love, and even the demand for attention to diversity itself. As David Glidden, philosopher at the University of California at Riverside, expressed the point, "the ability to admire and love the diversity of human beings gets lost" when one bases the demand for inclusion on notions of local group identity. Why should one love or attend to a Hispanic fellow citizen, on this view, if one is oneself most fundamentally an Irish-American? Why should one care about India, if one defines oneself as above all an American? Only a human identity that transcends these divisions shows us why we should look at one another with respect across them.

World Citizenship in Contemporary Education

What would an education for world citizenship look like in a modern university curriculum? What should Anna, the future businesswoman in Beijing, learn as an undergraduate if she is to be prepared for her role? What should all students learn—since we all interact as citizens with issues and people from a wide variety of traditions?

This education must be a multicultural education, by which I mean one that acquaints students with some fundamentals about the histories and cultures of many different groups. These should include the major religious and cultural groups of each part of the world, and also ethnic and racial, social and sexual minorities within their own nation. Language learning, history, religious studies, and philosophy all play a role in pursuing these ideas. Awareness of cultural difference is essential in order to promote the respect for another that is the essential underpinning for dialogue. There are no surer sources of disdain than ignorance and the sense of the inevitable naturalness of one's own way. No liberal education can offer students adequate understanding of all they should know about the world; but a detailed understanding of one unfamiliar tradition and some rudiments about others will suffice to engender Socratic knowledge of one's own limitations. It would have helped Anna to have learned a great deal about China; but to have studied the culture of India would have been almost as valuable, since it would have showed her how to inquire and the limitations of her experience.

World citizens will legitimately devote more attention and time to their own region and its history, since it is above all in that sphere that they must operate. This need for local knowledge has important educational consequences. We would be absurdly misguided if we aimed at giving our students an equal knowledge of all histories and cultures, just as we would be if we attempted to provide a bit of knowledge of all languages. Besides the fact that this would produce a ridiculously superficial result, it would also fail in the task of giving students a detailed acquaintance with the local sphere in which most of their actions will be undertaken. Education at all levels, including higher education, should therefore strongly emphasize the history of American constitutional traditions and their background in the tradition of Western political philosophy. In a similar way, literary education should focus disproportionately on the literature of Anglo-American traditions which, however, are themselves highly complex and include the contributions of many different groups.

On the other hand, it is also extremely important that this material be presented in a way that reminds the student of the broader world of which the Western traditions are a part. This may be done with good educational results in the Western tradition courses themselves, where one can emphasize what is distinctive about this tradition through judicious and illuminating contrasts with developments elsewhere. But it must above all be done by the design of the curriculum as a whole, which should offer students the rudiments of knowledge about the major world traditions of thought and art, and the history that surrounds them, and, even more important, make them aware how much important material they do not know.

...

The world citizen must develop sympathetic understanding of distant cultures and of ethnic, racial, and religious minorities within her own. She must also develop an understanding of the history and variety of human ideas of gender and sexuality. As a citizen, one is called upon frequently to make judgments in controversial matters relating to sex and gender—whether as a judge, deciding a case that affects the civil rights of millions, or simply as a democratic voter, deciding, for example, whether to support a referendum like Colorado's Amendment 2, declared unconstitutional by the U.S. Supreme Court in 1996, which restricted the abilities of local communities to pass laws protecting the civil rights of gays and lesbians. To function well as a citizen today, one needs to be able to assess the arguments put forward on both sides; and to do so one needs an education that studies these issues. There are complex connections between cross-cultural study and the study of gender and sexuality. Cross-cultural study reveals many ways of organizing concepts of gender and sexuality; and thinking about gender and sex is essential to thinking critically about a culture. A good undergraduate education should prepare students to be informed and sensitive interpreters of these questions.

Building a curriculum for world citizenship has multiple aspects: the construction of basic required courses of a "multicultural" nature; the infusion of diverse perspectives throughout the curriculum; support for the development of more specialized elective courses in areas connected with human diversity; and, finally, attention to the teaching of foreign languages, a part of the multicultural story that has received too little emphasis.

Basic "diversity" requirements come in two varieties. There are elective requirements that allow the student to choose one or two courses from among a wide range of offerings. Such, for example, is the requirement at the University of Nevada at Reno, where students, in addition to completing a "World Civilizations" core course, must elect a course focusing on at least one area of human diversity outside the dominant culture of her own society. Areas included are the history and culture of non-Western peoples, the history and culture of minorities in the United States, women's studies, and the study of the varieties of human sexuality. Reno, like many institutions, cannot afford to hire new faculty to create integrative courses or to free existing faculty from many of their other commitments. Making a menu of what is on hand, and then giving students a choice from that menu, is these institutions' only option if they wish to diversify their curricula.

Such requirements can fulfill basic Socratic functions, showing students the possible narrowness and limitedness of their own perspective and inviting them to engage in critical reflection. And they can frequently impart methodological tools that will prove valuable in approaching another area of diversity. But this is not always the case: a student who has taken a course on American women writers of the nineteenth century is still likely to be in a weak position with respect to the sort of cultural diversity she will encounter if she finds herself in dialogue with people from China and the Middle East. Even a course in non-Western literature may leave the student blankly ignorant of non-Western history and religion. A student who has studied the history and literature of China may remain unaware of the variety and diversity of minorities within her own nation. It is odd and arbitrary to put all these different topics together in an area called "diversity" as if the grasp of any part of any one of them would somehow yield a person the breadth of learning that could be yielded only by some grasp of each area. This problem will be especially grave if, as at Reno, the courses listed as satisfying the "diversity" requirement are unrelated to one another by any common discussion about methodology, beyond the deliberations of the faculty group that put the requirement together in the first place. Such courses may not even produce a student who knows how to inquire about diversity in a new context.

...

For these many reasons, an amorphous elective diversity requirement does not adequately prepare students for the complex world they will confront. It is better than no diversity program at all, and it may well be the best that many institutions can do. But it does not provide sufficient direction to fulfill completely the goals of world citizenship.

...

For a university that is skeptical of the elective approach and can support a more ambitious undertaking, a more arduous, but potentially more satisfying, approach is to design a single basic "multicultural" course, or a small number of such courses, to acquaint all students with some basic conceptions and methods. A very successful example of such a course, in a non-elite institution with a mixed student body, is "American Pluralism and the Search for Equality," developed at the State University of New York at Buffalo in 1992. This course is required in addition to a two-semester world civilization sequence that provides basic instruction in non-Western religions and cultures. The pluralism course complements the primarily historical world civilization course by enhancing students' awareness of the many groups that make up their own nation, and of the struggle of each for respect and equality. Since these moral issues arise in the international context as well, reflection about them retrospectively enriches the other course.

John Meacham, a professor of psychology who is among its architects, enunciates several principles that contributed to the success of the Buffalo course and that should, in his view, guide the development of other such courses.

1. "*Design multicultural courses with broad content.*" The Buffalo course is designed to acquaint students with five categories of diversity: race, gender, ethnicity, social class, and religious sectarianism. Each section of the course must cover all five and must focus in depth on three. This approach gives the advantage of breadth and also ensures that students see one category in its relation to the others. Meacham argues persuasively that such a course contributes a deeper understanding of each of its topics than would a narrower course focusing on a single topic.
2. "*Base multicultural courses on faculty disciplinary expertise.*" Faculty staffing the course are drawn from ten different disciplines. Meacham comments: "For example, an intelligent discussion of affirmative action should be grounded at least in history, biology, law, economics, political science, psychology, and sociology." Nothing was included in the course that faculty were not equipped to teach expertly; and different faculty groups in different years approached the basic course plan differently, in accordance

with their preparation and training. This allowance for flexibility is very important. Interdisciplinary courses frequently falter if they lack a strong disciplinary base, and faculty cannot do a good job if they are asked to stretch far beyond their training.

3 "*Design programs for faculty development.*" Faculty should not be asked to teach material that lies to some extent outside their prior expertise without being given financial support for the time spent in retraining. Retraining involves time taken away from their course preparation in their own original areas, and also from the research that is an integral part of an active scholar's life. First-rate faculty will not choose to get involved in such new courses unless they are compensated for these sacrifices. It is standard practice to pay faculty summer salary for undertaking new course development projects. Where, in addition to retraining, the course will require extensive cooperation among faculty in different fields, such compensation is particularly important.

4 *Spend time reflecting about methodological and pedagogical issues.* Faculty drawn from literature, economics, political science, and philosophy will not intuitively approach a problem such as voting rights or affirmative action with the same set of questions in mind or the same standards of argument and inquiry. This heterogeneity is basically a good thing, since they can complement one another. But careful thought needs to be given to the methods and concerns that will be built into the course. How much, for example, will the course focus on general philosophical questions, such as the nature of rights and the contrast between relativism and universalism? How much empirical information about the history of the relevant issues will students be expected to master? How will quantitative analyses deriving from economics be presented, if at all? If these questions are not settled beforehand, the course will be a grab bag of issues, with no intellectual cohesion.

Faculty need to devote extra consideration to problems that arise when we approach issues on which people in our society have conflicting and strongly held views. Such issues—and these constitute most of the course—raise particular problems for classroom methodology. Here there is a particular need to be aware of the background and character of one's students and to design classroom methods to elicit the best sort of active critical participation. Buffalo students, Meacham argues, tend to be submissive and deferential. Faculty need to discourage them from simply following authority if the benefits of the course for citizenship are to be gained. In this course more than in others, then, instructors carefully withhold their own personal views, designing strategies for evenhanded classroom debate and not seeking to bring debate to a conclusion prematurely. As one instructor in the course said, it is important "to give students permission to be confused."

…

SUNY Buffalo faculty … publicize the course and discuss it in a variety of public media, focusing in particular on answering the criticism that such courses are "ideological." They articulate the relation of the course to the goals of democratic citizenship in a convincing way, satisfying the public that the effort contributes to public reasoning, not simply to the affirmation of various groups' identity. This is a legitimate area of public concern, and Buffalo has done more to address it than have many comparable institutions.

…

Some transformations involve the redesigning of a standard departmental course offering. At Brown University, a standard moral problems course has recently taken as its focus the feminist critique of pornography and related issues of free speech. In this way students learn to confront these divisive issues and learn basic facts about them while learning the techniques of philosophical analysis and debate. At Bentley College, Krishna Mallick offers a non-Western philosophy class, focusing on the philosophy of nonviolent resistance. At Harvard University, Amartya Sen offers a course called "Hunger and Famine." Standard topics in development economics are given a new twist, as students learn to think about the relationship of hunger to gender and also to democratic political institutions in areas of the world ranging from Africa to China to India. At the University of Chicago, historian David Cohen has developed a comparative course on war crimes that brings current events in Bosnia and Rwanda together with historical examples from many cultures.

…

Such integrative courses acknowledge that we are citizens of a world that is diverse through and through—whose moral problems prominently include the problems of women seeking to avoid violence, whose history does include a complex international history of both nonviolence and war, whose thought about hunger and agriculture must take cognizance of the unequal hunger of women and of the special circumstances of developing nations. This way of incorporating diversity has the advantage of relying on the disciplinary expertise of the instructor. Students who study Indian famines with Sen probably learn more that is important about India than will those who take a broad and general introduction to world civilization, although they will profit more from Sen's course if they have already had such an introduction. They will learn about religious and economic diversity in the process of thinking about hunger, but in a way that will be focused and made more vivid by being connected to a specific problem analyzed with rigor and detail. Such focused courses, taught by expert faculty, should be strongly encouraged, whatever else we also encourage.

In many institutions, however, there are few faculty available to teach such international courses, at least beyond the introductory level. If even the introductory level requires combining existing expertise with new interdisciplinary training, as the Buffalo course shows, the generation of more advanced elective courses integrating the perspective of world citizenship requires even more planning and institutional support. One particularly imaginative and successful example of a program for faculty development has recently been designed at St. Lawrence University. Called "Cultural Encounters: An Intercultural General Education," the program exemplifies the values of world citizenship both in its plan and in its execution. Cultural Encounters is a program containing courses at both the introductory and the more advanced levels. But its focus has been on redesigning disciplinary courses toward an emphasis on the student's encounter with a non-Western culture.

...

The program began when St. Lawrence received faculty and curriculum development grants from the Andrew Mellon Foundation and the Fund for the Improvement of Post-Secondary Education. In its initial phase, grants were given to a group of seventeen humanities faculty from different departments, enabling them to meet in a weekly seminar throughout the year, discussing common readings and eventually generating new courses, each in their separate disciplines. The course was informed from the beginning by three decisions. The first was to put philosophy at the heart of the matter, in the sense that all participants did a lot of serious discussing of issues of cultural relativism, along with whatever cross-cultural readings they also did. Grant Cornwell of Philosophy and Eve Stoddard of English, the two directors of the program, shared an orientation to the material that stressed the universal aspect of human needs and strivings and was critical of cultural relativism. They did not wish, however, to impose this perspective on the program as a whole; they wished to use the issue as a basis for faculty dialogue.

Cornwell and Stoddard's second decision was to focus on just two areas of diversity, by selecting two non-Western cultures, the cultures of India and Kenya. They decided to start from these two concrete areas in raising issues about ethnic and religious diversity, gender, race, and sexuality. They decided that they had a reasonable shot at understanding something of the history and traditions of these two places if they used the grant-supported faculty seminar to spend an entire year doing common research on each, but that they would have no chance at all of achieving responsible coverage if they cast their net more widely. Faculty in the group were drawn from philosophy, art history, anthropology, English, religious studies, biology, government, geology, economics, and Spanish.

The group's third decision was its most surprising. This was that all ten faculty involved should live for a month in the regions they studied, after a year of intensive seminar preparation, so that their teaching would be informed by a first-hand sense of what it was like to live the life of ordinary women and men in these countries. This undertaking was made financially possible because of the grant, and it proved to be the crucial point in the program. During each of the two visits, the group kept a public diary to exchange and refine views. It is clear that this experience permitted a level of insight into controversial issues such as female circumcision and population control that would not easily have been available from reading alone. It also infused the abstract readings with vividness and made the instructors feel that, for a brief time at least, they had been actual participants in the foreign culture.

At the same time, the group required that students who chose the Cultural Encounters "track," taking both introductory and advanced courses within the program, should have a foreign language requirement. If at all possible, they must live and study abroad for their junior year. Two-thirds of the students who go abroad go to Europe, the other third to Costa Rica, Kenya, India, and Japan. Not all the programs, then, directly support the intellectual aims of the Cultural Encounters course material. But even the apparently unrelated exposure to a European culture and its language indirectly serves the program's goals, since mastery of a foreign language and the ability to make oneself at home in a foreign culture are essential abilities of the world citizen, and build an understanding that can be used to approach a further and even more remote culture.

The Cultural Encounters program is a model of responsible teaching in several areas of human diversity. By design, it encompasses not only the encounter with a foreign culture but also related issues of gender, ethnic and religious pluralism, and sexuality, presenting issues of American pluralism in relation to those of global cultural diversity. Its interdisciplinary character ensures that these issues will be faced from many interlocking perspectives, including those of literary study and anthropology, long prominent in multicultural teaching, but also those of economics, biology, philosophy, and foreign language teaching. Where faculty are concerned, the program's focus on intensive training and dialogue and its demand for actual immersion in the culture sets it apart from many programs of this sort, as does its focus on foundational philosophical questions of relativism and universality. On the side of the student, the requirement to learn a foreign language and, where possible, to visit a foreign culture makes the "encounter" serious and prolonged, while critical discussion of basic issues about culture and values in the classroom ensures that the encounter will be conducted in the spirit of Socratic searching rather than of mere tourism and will prompt dialectical reflection on the beliefs and practices of the student's own culture while the student explores a foreign culture.

...

The Cultural Encounters program brings us back to the issues raised by the Stoics. Its designers firmly reject an approach to "multiculturalism" that conceives of it as a type of identity politics, in which the student receives the impression of a marketplace of cultures, each asserting its own claim. They insist on the importance of teaching that the imagination can cross cultural boundaries, and that cross-cultural understanding rests on the acknowledgment of certain common human needs and goals amid the many local differences that divide us. Like much of the ancient Greek tradition, beginning with Herodotus, Stoics suggest that the encounter with other cultures is an essential part of an examined life. Like that tradition, they believe that education must promote the ability to doubt the unqualified goodness of one's own ways, as we search for what is good in human life the world over.

Becoming a citizen of the world is often a lonely business. It is, in effect, a kind of exile—from the comfort of assured truths, from the warm nestling feeling of being surrounded by people who share one's convictions and passions. In the writings of Marcus Aurelius (as in those of his American followers Emerson and Thoreau) one sometimes feels a boundless loneliness, as if the removal of the props of habit and convention, the decision to trust no authority but moral reasoning, had left life bereft of a certain sort of warmth and security. If one begins life as a child who loves and trusts its parents, it is tempting to want to reconstruct citizenship along the same lines, finding in an idealized image of nation or leader a surrogate parent who will do our thinking for us. It is up to us, as educators, to show our students the beauty and interest of a life that is open to the whole world, that there is after all more joy in the kind of citizenship that questions than the kind that simply applauds, more fascination in the study of human beings in all their real variety and complexity than in the zealous pursuit of superficial stereotypes, more genuine love and friendship in the life of questioning and self-government than in submission to authority. We had better show them this, or the future of democracy in this nation and in the world is bleak.

Notes

1. "Anna" is a woman I interviewed in China. Her name has been changed.
2. All judgments about the Cynics are tentative, given the thinness of our information. The central source is Diogenes Laertius' *Lives of the Philosophers*. See B. Branham and M.-O. Goulet-Cazé, eds., *The Cynics* (Berkeley: University of California Press, 1996).
3. Plutarch, *On the Fortunes of Alexander* 329AB = SVF 1.262; see also Seneca, On Leisure 4.1.
4. For Paine, see *The Rights of Man*, pt. 2; for Smith, see "Of Universal Benevolence," in *The Theory of Moral Sentiments* (Indianapolis: Liberty Classica, 1982), vol. 6, pt. 2, p. 3, with special reference to Marcus Aurelius; for Kant, see *Perpetual Peace*, in Kant's *Political Writings*, ed. H. Reiss, trans. H. Nisbet, 2nd ed. (Cambridge: Cambridge University Press, 1991). For a discussion of Stoic ideas in Kant's political thought, see Martha C. Nussbaum, "Kant and Stoic Cosmopolitanism," *Journal of Political Philosophy* 5 (1997): 1–25.
5. See W. K. C. Guthrie, *History of Greek Philosophy*, vol. 3 (Cambridge: Cambridge University Press, 1969).
6. See Stephen Halliwell, *Plato: Republic V* (Warminster: Aris and Phillips, 1993).
7. The translation by R. D. Hicks in the Loeb Classical Library volume 2 of Diogenes Laertius is inadequate but gives the general idea. All citations here are from that *Life*, but the translations are mine.
8. Dionysius was the one-man ruler of Syracuse in Sicily whom Plato attempted, without success, to turn into a "philosopher-king."
9. The Stoic school had an extraordinarily long life and a very broad influence, extending from the late fourth century B.C. to the second century A.D. in both Athens and Rome.
10. Diogenes uses the single word *kosmopolitēs*, but Marcus Aurelius prefers the separated form.
11. See Marcus Aurelius, *Meditations*, trans. G. M. A. Grube (Indianapolis: Hackett, 1983).
12. The image is suggested in Cicero and is explicit in Hierocles, a Stoic of the first and second centuries A.D. (quoted here); it is probably older.
13. This is material from a draft written by the ANC for the new constitution; it was presented by Albie Sachs to a meeting on human rights at Harvard University in October 1993.

CHAPTER TWENTY-ONE

Trust in the University

PAUL GIBBS

Introduction

Trust has attracted the attention of higher education scholars in a number of forms and for a number of purposes. Gibbs (2007) has argued that consumers seek trustworthiness when they feel vulnerable and ignorant. This applies especially to universities, because higher education institutions need to help people to reach beyond the frontier of what is known, into the anxiety of what might be knowable. If students trust what universities say about facilitating choice and opportunities for their future, they are more inclined to take what universities propose as credible and worthy of participation. However, there is a loss of public trust, a trust resulting from a reasoned expectation that involves both confidence and reliance that these educational institutions are 'acting responsibly and for the common good' (Bird, 2013: 25). Indeed, Jameson has concluded that, in an era of marketisation focused mainly on competition, student demand and privatisation, in UK universities, there is a perceived 'loss of trust' (2012: 411), at least in Governments' rhetoric and its agencies of quality control. This is not a new observation. As early as 1992, Bok was seeking ways in which U.S. universities could go about restoring public trust; ten years later, O'Neill wrote of 'crises of trust' (2002: 45) and after another decade, Collini made reference to an 'erosion of trust' (2012: 108).

In this chapter, I discuss the nature of trust, both in institutions of higher education and the participants within them—students, faculty and other stakeholders—to explore it from the perspective of competence and empathy. I will argue that the level of trustworthiness a society ought to expect of its higher educational institutions sets them apart from other organisations, and when they fail to match such expectations, they lose the entitlement to support from their host community.

The market context

State-controlled universities, which introduced student fees, achieved significant market engagement through marketing programmes to distinguish themselves at a time of increasing demand and student numbers. Yet meeting this demand and securing their own financial futures is difficult in a marketplace that seeks diversity and hides under a homogeneity of quality and accountability. While it seems feasible for universities to retain the trust of the public and their constituted members, for many this trust has been lost, as indicated above, or at the very least has created a crisis for the edifying voice of higher education institutions. Evident in the shift from intrinsic trust in creating socially conscious leaders and their replacement by functionally skilful human resources, it is also manifest in universities' inability to provide a compelling argument for scholarship over an economic imperative in their rush to embrace a league table management mentality, adopting whatever metric they are dealt to demonstrate a willingness to be seen as accountable and compliant.

Certainly in the UK, they have not been helped by 'putting students at the centre' of higher education, in the sense of the students holding the funding. The government currently lends money to students to take on an often ill-informed responsibility at interest rates that encourage frivolousness, while taking away supportive central funding. With this shift comes 'engaging in professional marketing activities' (Veloutsou, Paton and Lewis, 2005: 279), perhaps in place of enriching the educational and the common good.

Universities have generally suffered a range of attacks on their sustainability. Significant changes in funding and shifts in priorities towards research that are practical rather than fundamental serve to increase interconnectivity with institutions outside the university (predominantly businesses). A global eagerness for increased participation has changed the structures of universities and the power relationships within them, with an expansion of communities of scholars to include 'market workers'. This economic rationalism is typified in the notion of 'new public management' in universities (e.g. Bleiklie, 1998; Ferlie, Musselin and

Andresani, 2008). This approach puts in place vertical line management hierarchies (and power relations) that cut across traditional forms of academic trust built on genuine academic leadership based on notions of collegiality. This is in tension with the professionalism implicit in the peer relationship at the cornerstone of modern science and journal knowledge systems, one of trust and a horizontal set of (power) relations.[1] This movement has had an unsettling effect on educational cultures, identities and workloads (Jawitz, 2009).

A consequence of this move to the market has been a marketisation of higher education (Gibbs, 2002; Molesworth, Scullion and Nixon, 2010; Hemsley-Brown, 2011; Gibbs, 2011), and an increasing emphasis by universities on how they promote themselves to potential students. Marketisation and its derivative, marketingisation, has put at risk the nature of education as a distinctive transformative process of the human condition by treating it, for the most part, as undifferentiated consumption. Universities have drawn their marketing from consumer markets best suited to selling chocolate bars, aspirins and supermarket discounts, albeit highly sophisticated and technical. Those that embrace the amorality of the market at a national or global level—that is, almost all—risk educational mission drift and loss of moral trust as they move away from an implicit trust in the development of a civil society to a world that supports and encourages individual goals, needs and satisfaction. These activities run the danger of displaying overwhelming consumerism (Naidoo and Jamieson, 2005).

The impact of these changes is summarised by Hassan, who observes:

> the commercialization of the university is primarily an economic and political process of transformation that has little if anything to do with education, knowledge production and the wellbeing of either staff or students. What is more, these changes are all being refracted through the prism of neo-liberal ideology. (2003: 77)

With consumerism changing students into customers (Molesworth, Scullion and Nixon, 2010; Woodall et al., 2014) and tutors into service providers (Guzmán-Valenzuela and Barnett, 2013), and with ever more vulnerable and naïve students being encouraged to enrol, the higher education market's ethos has become competition rather than sector collaboration. One consequence of such a change is that trust in the common good, once assumed of higher education (Giroux and Giroux, 2004; Carvalho and de Oliveira Mota, 2010), has been shaken by the uncertainty of the market and, as I will argue, needs to be re-built; not on the basis of competence in doing what is taken on trust, regardless of any implicit care for the transacting partner, but on empathetic trust where one considers a wider moral responsibly. The first can be actioned without caring about the person—one can trust the train ticket collector to check my ticket (competence), but not to care about me if I have lost my ticket or had it stolen and to trust me (empathetically) that I am telling the truth not to defraud the railways.

Trust in the university

The nature of liberal education and the ideal of emancipation through rational autonomy led to an evolving, enduring and empathetic delivery. Because it is transformative rather than for an economically defined purpose, liberal education is dependent on a trusting relationship between the owner of the educational process and the recipient; one does not know what one is expected to receive, as it has to be jointly created. In this sense, having trust in the hegemony of state control of education is to believe that it will not be used to exploit and manipulate recipients. A relationship of this nature, engaged in without enduring evidence of trust, is like that of authority: it may be cynically received because it appears to grant power, coercion and control to the party in whom trust has been vested. This may be manifest in forms of persuasion, manipulation of behaviour or psychological compulsion.

Trust has attracted some attention in the field of education. Tschannen-Moran and Hoy's (2000) study of schools is seminal, and in higher education Macfarlane (2009), and Carvalho and de Oliveira Mota (2010) have provided a review of the significance of trust within the university and the building of student institutional relationships. Furthermore, Gibbs (2007) has argued that consumers expect to be able to trust suppliers either to have their best interests, as the purchaser, as a core value or at least not to put their investment in the brand in jeopardy through poor feedback and publicity. This is particularly true of high-cost, poorly understood products such as electronic goods and services, where decision-making can make the purchaser feel vulnerable and ignorant, able to use the 'purchase' but not to understand its complexities or assess any performance claims. This applies especially to first-time attendees at university, because of these institutions' function in helping people reach beyond the frontier of what is known, to what might be knowable. Students having trust in a university has tangible benefits. As Fuller (2014) has speculated, the more one trusts one's educational environment, the more one is likely to participate and believe in the principles of meritocracy. If society trusts what universities say about how they can facilitate choice and opportunities for a student's future, students are more inclined to take what is proposed to them as credible and worthy of participation.

This Hobbesian relationship, where the more powerful party can change the notion of the relationship to one of reliance, fails Baier's test of moral trust where mutual reliance on the known circumstance of the trust relation is required of each party (1995: 120). That is, one knows more about an issue than another, but keeps quiet even when it is critical to the trusting relationship—such as being already married and undertaking a second. This is potentially broken in any form of centrally controlled curriculum, the idolatry of learning outcomes and where the structure of an institution alienates the tutor from the critical dialectic of education and turns her into an assessor of skills. Without openness and mutual respect, conflict emerges and the basis of trust dissolves into rancour and mistrust for all stakeholders in the provision of university higher education.

However, mutual trust need not be morally dependent on reciprocity, nor is it always rational or conscious. In its various forms it may be context-bound, power-ascribed or enduring (Fukuyama, 1986; Misztal, 1996). It is embedded in the contractualism of the social contract. It can have a short or long duration, for the length of the formal or tacit contract, or have its duration shortened by a failure to comply. Its intensity can be plotted as a continuum of checks and balances over time (Gibbs and Murphy, 2009), yet by nature is instrumental unless it seeks to be moral mutual trust. Then, a different teleological set of criteria needs to be considered. Moral mutual trust requires more than merely relying on others. It implies, according to Baier (1986: 235), that 'one leaves others the opportunity to harm one … and also shows one's confidence that they will not take it. Reasonable trust will require good grounds for such confidence in another's goodwill'. If moral trust is missing, contemplating even a small risk to an expected outcome—specifically in relation to a highly cherished aim—may prove intolerable.

This second form of mutual moral trust often involves offering up one's vulnerability to others on very limited information, in the belief that the relationship will not be exploited. It is an empathetic form of trust, derived from the Kantian categorical imperative which is based on duty regardless of consequences. Competence of trust, however, derives from Kant's less rigorous imperative, the hypothetical imperative, where the intent is not questioned but the utilitarian outcome is used to judge the worthiness of the act.

One of the ethical responsibilities of higher education is its role in revealing, for and with students, the nature of their desires for themselves and for the society to which they will contribute. For the purposes of this analysis, this mutual moral trust will be termed 'empathetic trust' and the hypothetical, utilitarian form of trusting only in the functional competency of parties, their skilfulness at activities, as 'competence of trust'. I am not drawing here an evaluative distinction between both forms of trust, as each is important to educational relationship. Yet I want to emphasise a difference and a requirement for both to be bases of educational institutional provision if they are to retain the more generalised trust in the indeterminate nature of educational provision. Who knows what students will learn, and can we trust that it will not be harmful to society in general?

Competence of trust

Competence of trust is based on the utilitarian premise of enlightened self-interest. It shares some of the outcomes of acts of empathetic trust, but only where benefit, immediate or deferred, accrues to the initiator of the act. Competence of trust differs from mere confidence for competence is a prerequisite for communication where trust is a condition of specific actions based on this confidence (Farini, 2012). Its value in fostering relationships is that it stands superficially in the place of empathetic trust and is only shown to be amoral when issues of personal benefit are confronted by acts of generosity to others. For example, to be considered as trust-competent, one would be capable of fulfilling an entrusted task such as giving correct travel directions to a stranger (also see Luhmann's (2000) distinction between confidence and trust). We need to believe that there is generally no malicious intent when the instructions are given and that, if they prove wrong, the giver was merely incompetent and not morally deceitful.

As Pettit (1995) observes, our reliance on the competence of trust is based on belief in the ultimately trustworthy disposition of the person in whom we trust. Should there be any erosion of the foundations upon which we build our assumptions of trust (for Pettit, loyalty, virtue and prudence), what settles for competence of trust will dilute any value attached to it. Pettit terms this trust deceit as 'the cunning of trust'.

Competence of trust is thus amoral and any argument made to express the relationship between student and academia in terms of competence leads it to be based on economic exchange (McMurtry, 1993). This leads to the calculative expediency of performativity rather than the discharge of a moral responsibility. It changes higher education from a mode of revealing, through trust based on unspecified obligation, to one where the economic exchange holds sway. The contractual model, at its core, redefines education not as the fusion of subject and object but in forms of instrumental competence that may deprive education of any teleological characteristics. From this position, the trust offer to higher education by its stakeholders is called into question, and more authoritarian controls are applied as trust in institutions is diluted, and accountability dominates.

Empathetic trust

Empathetic trust allows the socialised self to face the risk posed by the integration of others in a social context by virtue of having an authentic self. Ordinarily, this comportment towards others is based on a common experience of being-in-the-world. It is not ruled by the explicit embedding of specific durations, but is shown through a belief in the worth of others through trusting relationships. Empathetic trusting relationships endure the changing notion of self-ness and contribute to its revelation. Trusting in self or others is the essence of our autonomous everyday-ness and is central to a liberal educational ideal (Morgan, 1996). Those who betray this trust are socially vilified and its abuse in supporting academic hegemony or political expediency in education would seem morally indefensible. The employment rhetoric, which applies in reality only to certain professions, classes of degree and status of universities yet is presented as a universal consequence of any higher education experience, is one example; the loss of this trust amounts to betrayal, not disappointment.

Empathetic trust thus involves both the competence to undertake that which is entrusted by another party, the willingness to care for rather than harm that which is entrusted and an acceptance of one's own self-trustworthiness—that is, to trust in oneself to do such and such; to diet, to work all night or to be able to do, in the sense of confidence in one's ability. This definition can be shown to satisfy the necessary conditions for mutual empathy. It also has a resonance with the popular meaning of an empathetic emotional understanding between individuals, and is a more specific case of general respect as proposed by Williams (1973); it is more than the mere parade of trustworthiness (Baier, 1995). If perceived, this reduces the risk of trusting under complexity, for instance, when a first-time university student decides who to seek as advisor on his or her university choice.

Having refined the nation of trust, I will explore how this might be helpful in our understanding of the structural organisation of higher education. By looking for a balance between the forms of competence and empathetic trust, I investigate how some of its distinguishing features such as academic freedom, scholarly professionalism and student experience can be seen to offer the trustworthiness desired from the public, academics and students.

Public trust in higher education

Trust can act as a frame of reference that may be used to model the relationships of the higher education sector, including viewing it as a social institution. Within it, questions of the importance of self- and empathetic trust may be settled by the purpose of higher education. Certainly, in an educational framework, where the self has to expose its vulnerability to another, anything other than a moral duty of trusting care would potentially make the offer of education loaded and exploitative.

Tierney's (2006) work on academic organisational trust states that a 'cultural grammar of trust forces an analysis not only of structures but also the social contexts and histories in which these structures are embedded' (2006: 55). This grammar offers a framework to develop a notion of organisational trust culture built around notions of structure, environment and values, where formal–informal decision-making occurs in a perceptually complex and changing context over time. These perceptions determine the level and forms of trust offered and reflect the shared experience of the university. For Tierney, the shared experience offers a 'common interpretation of events, fosters shared interests in the organisation, allows for the communication of cultural facts, emerges from reciprocity and mutuality that are based in structures and beliefs, and cannot be summarized as rational' (2006: 64). This shared experience runs through different networks, formal and informal, and determines how the use of power is perceived and responded to. These shared experiences are framed by the universities' external environment, between constituents within the university, and between the formal and informal networks. The system reacts to this environmental irritation according to its own structures and notwithstanding the instability of the environment which is sometimes purposely not noticed by the system.

The notion of Public trust in universities and the trust that universities have a duty to create—in terms of a student experience—involves: competency in marketing of the university to its external environment; its own governance and quality assurance; and the reciprocity of its faculty trust, with its management and academic freedom. Competency trust alone would treat the students and academics as the means to an end of instrumental skill, well suited to explicit economic goals. This, however, is foolhardy and undermines trust in the university—not least because actually securing jobs for all or most of students is beyond a university's own competence. If higher education is to be more, and retain, a distinctive place in society, warranting the provision of resources, it must find time to empathise with the students in its academic community, nurturing them and engaging in helping them flourish as responsible citizens. This is a special, historical function and is the basis on which society allows them a degree of flexibility in the way they behave and the use they make of resources. To fail to do this would lead the public, government and students themselves to mistrust the privileges they are afforded. This is evident in the competency-only trust model of many for-profit universities where the economic self-interest of students and organisations dominates.

The interacting relationships of public trust involve State, university and student and society at large and while this model is simplistic, it captures the overlapping roles and illustrates how the nature of empathetic trust and self-trust can emerge at the level of both the social institution and the individual. This relationship is fragile and can be easily disrupted by deliberate ambiguity about the trustworthiness of the system to deliver what is required of it. If the state loses trust in its relationships with higher education, then the role of higher education in creatively questioning, and thus shaping, the nature of the state is in danger of being lost. The dialogue between higher education and state then becomes a one-way monologue of ideology delivered by the force of the financial rather than the intellectual.

Evidence for such a position is provided by Vidovich and Currie (2011) when considering the relationship between governance and trust in Australian universities. Building on the Tierney model mentioned earlier, they maintain that 'there is a need to examine the complex interrelationships between *external* and *internal environments*, between accumulating *economic* and *social capital* and between *structural* and *cultural* change in a context of globalisation' (2011: 54, *itals* in the original). Woelert and Yates (2014) come to similar conclusions, insofar as the imposition of metrics such that—to measure the activities involved in academic endeavour with the intent of increasing the visibility of accountability and competency—tends to reduce trust in the system. Such concerns are also shared by Maassen and Stensaker (2015) in the development of trust in international quality assurance. They argue that to rely on strong rational instrumental mechanisms might fail to secure the desired trust in the system, and that a diverse and flexible mechanism for building trust may be the way to deal with this complex problem.

The more explicit move to external accountability and a reduction of internal self-determination of higher education has been described by Trow (1996: 12) as 'a kind of mass degradation ceremony, involving the transformation of academic staff … into employees, mere organisational personnel'. This exchanges the acceptance of professional skills and reflective practice for a simpler control through the mechanism of competence-based models, favoured for their ease of audit and comparability. In terms of this chapter, it places competence of trust too far from that which gives it meaning: empathetic trust. The response from higher education cannot be whether or not to co-operate with the state's changes, but how to do so. Its task in such co-operation is how to retain its reputation for academic autonomy and excellence for its students while negotiating a stronger reputation with the state to secure future funding.

Gambetta's (1988: 229) analysis is penetrating on this point. He would acknowledge that an unwilling co-operation between higher education and state leads to loss of trust between parties and goes further, asserting that any knowledge of the coercion will reduce the trust that others have in this forced co-operation. This 'introduces an asymmetry which disposes of mutual trust and promotes instead power and resentment'. As Baier (1986: 241) observes, 'Trust is much easier to maintain than it is to get started and is never hard to destroy'. Bok's (1978: 33) analysis of the relationship between personal and institutional trust is illuminating on this point. She states, 'Trust in some degree of veracity functions as a foundation of relationships among human beings: when this trust shatters or wears away, institutions collapse' (*ibid*).

Academic offering and the student experience

The most comprehensive discussion of trust within the confines of academic teaching practices is provided by Curzon-Hobson. He argues that trust is a fundamental element in the pursuit of higher learning, for it is only through a sense of trust (a form of trust close to my term empathetic trust) that students will embrace an empowering experience of freedom, and the exercise of this freedom requires students and their teachers to take a risk:

> It challenges students to think and act according to their own perceptions without recourse to recitation or transcending ideals. This sense of freedom and the experience of risk is that which underpins students' projections to realise their unique potentiality. It requires a sensation of trust that is different from that which forms the bases of prescriptive accountability mechanisms, and is in fact marginalised by such practices. (Curzon-Hobson, 2002: 226)

Indeed, Carvalho and de Oliveira Mota (2010) identify what might be termed empathetic trust and loyalty in higher education institutes (HEIs) as a foundational premise for student engagement. The development of trust within educational institutions and the sector is important to the study of higher education, yet they claim 'research on HEIs has yet to include student trust as an antecedent of student loyalty' (2010: 146). Perhaps this is because, as Kovac and Kristiansen (2010: 276) add, 'it seems that researchers across specific disciplines are in agreement that trust is a theoretically and methodologically elusive, context-dependent, multi-level, discipline—as well as culturally and historically changeable—phenomenon".

Self-trusting

A feature of empathetic trust is the development of self-trust or confidence in students, going beyond the provision of pedagogical and research skills. It allows students to verify for themselves through critical analysis and appraisal if they are 'over-trusting' others because of their ascribed competency or status and to check that they are being treated with respect and honesty. It requires confidence in reflection and in the personal decision on what to accept as worthy of trust and respect. Self-trustworthiness is the basis of independently knowing one's world and being in that world. Lehrer (1997: 5) encapsulates this as being able to 'consider myself worthy of trust in what I accept and prefer'. Yet, as we have seen, Kovac and Kristiansen question the boundaries of such trust, suggesting that excessive trust 'might conflict with and sabotage the development of the basic learning processes, such as the ability of students to think critically' (2010: 277). This is evident when students cease to question what is offered to them in lectures, where they trust that what is covered in a course is all that is needed to master a subject or expect an examination to cover only what is presented through the course lectures, and seek to alleviate uncertainty rather than exploring it. In the UK, in 2015, there have been a number of such cases, for example at Exeter University.

Linking this work with the work of Hardin (2006) on the negative aspect of excess or blind trust, it can be argued that this overtrust is not misplaced trust, which can be resolved, but a trust where the dynamics of interpersonal trust draw either of the parties to the trust relationship into an uncomfortable exchange because of lack of appreciation of the full understanding of the relationship to the body of knowledge or lecture notes. Skinner et al. (2014) suggest that it is a 'dilemma from which it is difficult to extricate oneself; where the very nature of trust means that most of the options available as a response are neither viable nor attractive' (2014: 207). What seems to be an appropriate educational aim is to help identify and then to act to maintain a reasonable trust more in the trustworthy, not the untrustworthy.

Reflection, evaluation and monitoring are acts of autonomous thinkers of the type that liberal education, and indeed industry, claim to want. These reflective practices also contribute to self-belief, knowledge and truth, which differentiate the self from others. To trust in one's own ability to make decisions on one's own preference is central to liberal ideals of autonomous action. To be able to accept the responsibility that this implies, of constituting a reasoned world reality, facilitates the ontological integration of self. It encourages creativity, confidence and community through the negotiation of shared realities.

In building this reasoned network of preference and acceptances of 'truth', in the Heideggerian sense of everyday-ness of action, students reveal themselves both as self-trusting and as trustworthy people. To reach that position, they must be able to distinguish between their justified confidence in their competence in certain arenas, whether prepositional or of capacity, and where they are incompetent. Students are likely to retain their self-trustworthiness only while that which they hold as trustworthy maintains its social validity; they are able to argue rationally for what they hold to be true or to assimilate into what their community holds as truth. This revelation process, as we have seen, is interpreted by Tierney (2006) as a 'grammar of trust'.

Consider the example where a student entrusts another to do an essay. If the result achieves the dual objectives of acquiring the desired mark and maintaining the necessary level of security to prevent disclosure, has the transaction been morally trustworthy or has it been an act of trust competence? The same may apply to a tutor securing a level of examination success for a student cohort by structuring lectures in such a way that students are informed of the examination questions in advance. In both these cases, those engaged in the contract are satisfied and the trustee's trust proves justified. The morality of the actions may, however, seem indefensible while recognising personal trust is sometimes built on indefensible actions.

Higher education should encourage self-trust through reasoned argument and debate. For students to be prepared to risk the socially constructed self to a process of authentic discovery of truth demands mutual and empathetic trust. Students need to trust that if they stray too far from the commonality of experience they will not be expelled or vilified as eccentrics or charlatans. This leads to empathy and, in the educational context, it manifests itself in the *praxis* of critical being (Barnett, 1997). The recognition of the existence of the potential for such mutuality is held in the collective goodwill of all stakeholders of the institution and is (or, perhaps, ought to be) the basis of public trust in higher education institutions.

In relation to students, academics have a dependency relationship with them that requires empathetic trust to avoid the potential for exploitation of their vulnerability. In relation to the discipline, academics are trusted by their peers to share common goals that include: responsible conduct in research and authorship practices; no form of harassment; and the avoidance of conflict of interest, which erodes the fabric of trust on which worthwhile social interactions rely. A test of a profession's trust may take place when one of its numbers contravenes these principles. Is sanction dependent on incompetence assuming moral good intent or is it based on the competence deceit; of not being caught?

Professionalism

Turning now to academic trust, there has been a steady flow of recent higher education literature concerning the nature of academic professionalism, both for existing practitioners and for those entering the education occupation/vocation/profession (e.g. Holroyd, 2000; Nixon et al., 2001; Clegg, 2003; Nicoll and

Harrison, 2003; Macfarlane, 2004; Unwin, 2007; Kolsaker, 2008; Schuck et al., 2008; Cheng, 2009; Fitzmaurice, 2010; Tlili, 2010). As Unwin (2007) discusses, there are rapid changes and threats when the forces of the market, managerialism and greater accountability take hold. This echoes Nicoll and Harrison (2003), who conclude that 'the focus has been on teaching as a "technical" activity, defined as competence and reflective practice in a particular domain. This has obscured the social and discursive practices through which a very particular sort of teacher identity may be produced' (p. 24). Moreover, it places competency over empathetic trust, disrupting the balance in the vocation of higher education teaching and researching.

As seems appropriate if the term 'professional' is to have any meaning other than skilful when used in reference to academics, they have a duty to pursue the well-being of their students. From Nixon's (2010) perspective, as expressed in the opening sentence of his 2010 Hope University lecture, the 'ethics of academic practice is derived from our understanding of the ends and purposes of that practice' (p. 1). Nixon et al. (2001) have argued for the development of a new professionalism, framed not in 'terms of status and self-regulation, but in terms of values and practices' (p. 234), and '(T)he moral basis of the new professionalism lies, then, in our recognition of the freedom of all, academics included, to learn and to go on learning' (p. 237). This responsibility suggests that higher education practices should involve ethical behaviours as well as epistemological investigations and, I will later propose, require the exercise of ethical practical judgements in relation to others in the community. The virtue ethic approach has advocates within the higher education teaching literature.

Under the rubric of teaching with integrity, Macfarlane (2004) advocates practices of 'virtues compatible with reflective professionalism. This requires that the exercise of professional judgment is based on core moral virtues and conceived as a central duty to academic life' (pp. 127–128). Macfarlane identifies these as: respectfulness; sensitivity; pride; courage; fairness; openness; restraint; and collegiality. They require the professional to act with integrity and are achieved by a combination of qualities. He is clear that, within a changing context of higher education, making prudent choices is becoming ever more difficult. In conclusion, Macfarlane (2004) states that, despite the pressures, the community shares a vision of the moral virtues appropriate to teaching and suggests that encouraging 'their discussion and practice is probably the best way of ensuring that the forces that threaten to erode commitment to virtue are kept at bay' (p. 159). Fitzmaurice (2008) provides support for this proposition; she goes further to conclude that 'becoming a good academic practitioner is not just about mastery of techniques, approaches and methods but involves responsibility, professional intentions and ethical care' (p. 349). It requires empathetic trust!

However, as proposed, this professional relationship is currently in crisis and must adversely affect the nature of the other two relationships if it moves from empathy to expediency/competence. In relation to students, academics are authority figures and, in order to act in a professional sense, must not abuse the ascribed power. In relation to the discipline, the academics' personal integrity as scholars is tested by the tally of quality publications passing for academic achievement. Smith and Shoho (2007) found an inverse relationship between trust and academic rank, with professors being less trusting of their institutions than lower-ranking academics. This is clearly problematic if a culture of trust is to be developed.

In all professional relationships, academics will need to be trust-competent in at least two senses. First, they must be in possession of sufficient knowledge of the rules, procedures and consequences relevant to all those with an interest in their professional relationships. Second, they must be comprehensive and up to date in evaluating the full range of options before their students. However, they ought to encourage sufficient student scrutiny of what they say, thus they need to build a trust that transcends the comfort of a didactic relationship and favours one of critical engagement. The risk for tutors, however, is that challenging the customer-student proves uncomfortable, leaving him or her dissatisfied in not having answers provided. To achieve this, the relationship must also be grounded in empathetic trust. The cult of student satisfaction based on student experience might well work against the mission of an institution seeking to help students realise their potential, rather than realise a competency role model of an employable person.

These relationships demand that there must be a moral trustworthiness that stands behind this competent behaviour, giving motive and purpose to the role of the educator. In relation to the institution they are a duty of obligation, being trusted not to defame the reputation of the institution; indeed, more positively, they are trusted to enhance it. In return, the institution ought to be trusted to treat them with respect. Given this mutual empathetic trust, both parties are able to show goodwill to themselves and to the student. However, a form of organisational trust more akin to reliance may develop that can coexist with 'contrived and perpetuated inequality' (Baier, 1995: 131). In such a climate, claims of jointly held goals as the basis of mutual trust need to be treated with suspicion to avoid insidious betrayal, cloaked in the guise of long-term obligation or the immediacy of shared threat.

Given the competitive free market in which academic professionals are ever more frequently having to operate, it is difficult to see how empathetic trust in the sense of moral obligation could be allowed to predominate if not seen as a core ethical, as well as scholarly, competency. It seems to be only realisable in a profession with an ethic of service that is not corrupted by an overwhelming pressure to compete in the current marketplace, and is not an expression of power achieved by altering the cost and benefit options confronting the stakeholders. It cannot be developed by a regime of surveillance and examination through which the academic community exerts power over students.

Trust competence alone is a necessary but insufficient condition and, if treated as such, leads to a contracted output model of higher education rather than one of professional competence based on moral obligation. The development of empathetic trust is invoked in everyday contexts that commonly fall outside the rule-governed jurisdiction of codes of conduct. For example, the personal vulnerability involved in exposing what one does not know necessarily causes a state of uncertainty, only resolvable through self-trust. To nurture this goes beyond the professional competence of, say, the lawyer or the doctor, whose function is to reduce personal uncertainty. Credentials alone are not sufficient to establish the basis for empathetic trust to flourish. As McNamee (1997: 70) states, 'there are no rules to trust: it is almost a matter of volitional necessity'. Professional conduct in the sense of rule following will not increase the reputation of the higher educational professional: what will is a trusting disposition, and an atmosphere of trust in which it can thrive.

Academic freedom

The moral purpose of the academy has traditionally turned on the notion of academic freedom and tenure (De George, 2003) and both are under threat (Roepnack and Lewis, 2007). Tierney (2004) defines the concept:

> academic freedom pertains to the right of faculty to enjoy considerable autonomy in their research and teaching. The assumption is to search for truth without hindrance, and be able to report their findings regardless of what those finding may be. (p. 250)

We should go further, for the right to academic freedom is a right neither to indulge in unencumbered free speech nor to 'address people rudely or to assault them with chants and slogans. It is a right to present, refer to and argue for (or against) any claim or belief in an "appropriately academic manner"' (Barrow, 2009: 181). It is within the context of an institutional role and involves following as well as maintaining historic academic practices (rites) that distinguish the agent as being an academic in what is done, and the intent of those practices. These rituals include checking the evidence, not misrepresenting other peoples' views, seeking clarification and restraint in making claims, and arriving at well-argued conclusions in a transparent fashion. Such arguments need to be persuasive and compelling, but not manipulative, and should respect the vulnerability of others.

Scholarly behaviour including both competence and empathy, as suggested above, is a precondition, an obligation, before one can claim to be in an academic field. It is not anyone's right to be called an academic, whether by their own designation or by others. Claiming academic freedom turns on a set of trust obligations and places the academician as a role model for citizenry. As for Andreescu (2009), the main argument for academic freedom revolves around the role of the academic institution in society and the role of the individual to flourish as, in order 'to fulfil the role of cultivating the individual, of edifying him or her intellectually as well as morally, of helping him or her become an autonomous human being, academics need a considerable measure of freedom' (p. 509).

Concluding remarks—trust as the foundation of higher education

Trust has, in the main, been considered as a virtue of 'good' higher education between student, tutor and institution. In this chapter I have suggested a more nuanced notion of trust and proposed that a balance in the two forms of trust—competency and empathetic—can act as a frame of reference to model the relationships of the higher education sector, including viewing it as a social institution. Within it, there are opportunities to question the importance of self and one's contribution to society and this might well help settle the purpose of higher education and why it ought to have public trust. Certainly, in an educational framework where the self has to expose its vulnerability to another, anything other than a moral duty of trusting care would make the offer of education potentially loaded and exploitative.

The most important question for the future of higher education seems to be, 'can we trust those who control it to deliver anything other than competencies aimed at securing employment, thus placing education in the hands of the industrialist, or is there a role for the professional educationalist?' To hold someone accountable for their use of state-sponsored education in the sense of value (of money, citizenship and morality) requires a clear statement of the expected responsibility and output. A competence model of education has benefits for those who feel attracted to this economic expediency model. However, the appropriateness of such business comparisons is debatable and, even if valid, changes not only the process of becoming but the very nature of the autonomous individual.

I have suggested here that the competency notion of accountability in education through a cost benefit analysis, in its various forms, should complement but not dominate notions of the educated person. As a primary aim of higher education, it replaces moral trust with the amoral notion of competence of trust, which ultimately dilutes the moral dimension of higher education. The issue has to be addressed through an assessment of what we expect from our higher education institutions: quite simply, in what can we trust?

Note

1. I am grateful to M. Peters for drawing my attention to this point.

References

Andreescu, L. (2009). Foundations of academic freedom: Making new sense of some aging arguments. *Studies in Philosophy of Education,* 28: 499–515.

Baier, A. (1986). Trust and anti-trust. *Ethics,* 96: 231–261.

Baier, A. (1995). *Moral Prejudices: Essays on Ethics.* Cambridge: Harvard University Press.

Barnett, R. A. (1997). *Higher Education: A Critical Business.* Buckingham: SRHE and Open University Press.

Barrow, R. (2009). Academic freedom: Its nature extent and value. *British Journal of Educational Studies,* 57(2): 178–190.

Bird, S. J. (2013). *Public Trust and Institutions of Higher Learning: Implications for Professional Responsibility.* London: Portland Press, http://www.portlandpress.com/pp/books/online/wg86/086/0025/0860025.pdf

Bleiklie, I. (1998). Justifying the evaluative state: New public management ideals in higher education. *European Journal of Education,* 33(3): 299–316.

Bok, S. (1978). *Lying: Moral Choice in Public and Private Life.* Hassocks: Harvester.

Bok, D. (1992). Reclaiming the public trust. *Change,* 24(4): 12–19.

Carvalho, S. W. and de Oliveira Mota, M. (2010). The role of trust in creating value and student loyalty in relational exchanges between higher education institutions and their students. *Journal of Marketing for Higher Education,* 20(1): 145–165.

Cheng, M. (2009). Academics' professionalism and quality mechanisms: Challenges and tensions. *Quality in Higher Education,* 15(3): 193–205.

Clegg, S. (2003). Problematising ourselves: Continuing professional development in higher education. *International Journal for Academic Development,* 8(1): 37–50.

Collini, S. (2012). *What Are Universities for?* London: Penguin.

Curzon-Hobson, A. (2002). A pedagogy of trust in higher learning. *Teaching in Higher Education,* 7(3): 265–276.

De George, R. T. (2003). Ethics, academic freedom and academic tenure. *Journal of Academic Ethics,* 1: 1–11.

Farini, F (2012). Analyzing trust building in educational activities. *International Journal of Educational Research,* 53: 240–250.

Ferlie, E. Musselin, C. and Andresani, G. (2008). The steering of higher education systems: A public management perspective. *Higher Education,* 56: 325–348.
Fitzmaurice, M. (2008). Voices from within: Teaching in higher education as a moral practice. *Teaching in Higher Education,* 13(3): 341–352.
Fitzmaurice, M. (2010). Considering teaching in higher education as a practice. *Teaching in Higher Education,* 15(1): 45–55.
Fuller, C. (2014). Social capital and the role of trust in aspirations for higher education. *Educational Review,* 66(2): 131–147
Fukuyama, F. (1986). *Trust: The Social Virtues and the Creation of Prosperity.* London: Penguin.
Gambetta, D. (1988). Can we trust trust? In: D. Gambetta (ed.). *Trust: Making and Breaking Co-operative Relationships,* pp. 213–237. Oxford: Basil Blackwell.
Gibbs. P. (2002). From the invisible hand to the invisible handshake—Marketing higher education. *Research in Post and Higher Education,* 7(3): 323–335.
Gibbs, P. (2007). Does advertising pervert higher education? Is there a case for resistance? *Journal of Marketing for Higher Education,* 17(1): 3–11.
Gibbs, P. (2011). An Aristotelian model for ethical higher education marketing: The role of practical wisdom. *Journal of Marketing for Higher Education,* 21(2): 203–214.
Gibbs, P. and Murphy, P. (2009). Ethical marketing of higher education: What might be one to encourage its adoption? *Higher Education Management & Policy,* 21(3): 75–90.
Giroux, H., and Giroux, S. (2004). *Take Back Higher Education.* New York: Palgrave Macmillan.
Guzmán-Valenzuela, C. and Barnett, R. (2013). Marketing time: Evolving timescapes in academia. *Studies in Higher Education,* 38(8): 1120–1134.
Hardin, R. (2006). *Trust.* Cambridge: Polity.
Hassan, R. (2003). *The Chronoscopic Society: Globalization, Time and Knowledge in the Network Economy.* New York: Peter Lang.
Hemsley-Brown, J. (2011). Market, heal thyself: The challenges of a free marketing in higher education. *Journal of Marketing for Higher Education,* 21(2): 115–132.
Holroyd, C. (2000). Are assessors professional? Student assessment and the professionalism of academics. *Active Learning in Higher Education,* 1(1): 28–44.
Jameson, J. (2012). Leadership values, trust and negative capability: Managing the uncertainties of future English higher education. *Higher Education Quarterly,* 66(4): 391–414.
Jawitz, J. (2009). Academic identities and communities of practice in a professional discipline. *Teaching in Higher Education,* 14(3): 241–251.
Kolsaker, A. (2008). Academic professionalism in the managerialist era: A study of English universities. *Studies in Higher Education,* 33(5): 513–525.
Kovac, V. B. and, Kristiansen, A. (2010). Trusting trust in the context of higher education: The potential limits of the trust concept. *Power and Education,* 2(3): 276–287.
Lehrer, K. (1997). *Self-Trust: A Study of Reason, Knowledge, and Autonomy.* Oxford: Oxford University Press.
Luhmann, N. (2000). Familiarity, Confidence, Trust: Problems and Alternatives. In D. Gambetta (ed.) *Trust: Making and Breaking Cooperative Relations,* electronic edition, Department of Sociology, University of Oxford, chapter 6, pp. 94–107.

Macfarlane, B. (2004). *Teaching with Integrity: The Ethics of Higher Education Practice*. London: Routledge.
Macfarlane, B. (2009). A leap of faith: The role of trust in higher education teaching. *Nagoya Journal of Higher Education*, 9: 221–238.
McMurtry, J. (1993). Education and the market model. *Journal of the Philosophy of Education*, 25: 209–217.
McNamee, M. (1997). Rules, trust and professionalism, some cautionary notes. Paper delivered at *Philosophy of Education Society of Great Britain 31st Annual Conference*, April, Oxford.
Misztal, B. A. (1996). *Trust in Modern Societies*. Cambridge: Polity.
Molesworth, M., Scullion, R. and Nixon, E. (2010). *The Marketisation of Higher Education and the Student as Consumer*. London: Taylor & Francis.
Morgan, J. (1996). A defence of autonomy as an educational deal. *Journal of Philosophy of Education*, 30: 39–51.
Naidoo, R. and Jamieson, I. (2005). Empowering participants or corroding learning? Towards a research agenda on the impact of student consumerism in higher education. *Journal of Education Policy*, 20(3): 267–281.
Nicoll, K. and Harrison, R. (2003). Constructing the good teacher in higher education: The discursive work of standards. *Studies in Continuing Education*, 25(1): 23–35.
Nixon, J. (2010). Towards an ethics of academic practice: Recognition, hospitality, and 'rooted cosmopolitanism'. Hope Forum for Professional Ethics Lecture Series, http://www.hope.ac.uk/education-news/hfpe-lecture.html
Nixon, J., Marks, A., Rowland, S. and Walker, M. (2001). Towards a new academic professionalism: A manifesto of hope. *British Journal of Sociology of Education*, 22(2): 227–244.
O'Neill, O. (2002). *A Question of Trust*. The BBC Reith Lectures. Cambridge: Cambridge University Press.
Pettit, P. (1995). The cunning of trust. *Philosophy and Public Affairs*, 23: 202–225.
Roepnack, B. R. and Lewis, C. W. (2007). Academic freedom and academic tenure: Can they survive in the market place of ideas? *Journal of Academic Ethics*, 5: 221–232.
Schuck, S., Gordon, S. and Buchanan, J. (2008). What are we missing here? Problematising wisdoms on teaching quality and professionalism in higher education. *Teaching in Higher Education*, 13(5): 537–547.
Skinner, D., Dietz, G. and Weibel, A. (2014). The dark side of trust: When trust becomes a 'poisoned chalice'. *Organization*, 21(2): 206–224.
Smith, P. A. and Shoho, A. R. (2007). Higher education trust, rank and race: A conceptual and empirical analysis. *Innovation in Higher Education*, 32: 125–138.
Maassen, P. and Stensaker, B. (2015). A conceptualisation of available trust-building mechanisms for international quality assurance of higher education. *Journal of Higher Education Policy and Management*, 37(1): s30–s40
Tierney, W. V. (2004). The roots/routes of academic freedom and the role of the intellectual. *Cultural Studies, Critical Methodologies*, 4: 250–256.
Tierney, W. G. (2006). *Trust and the Public Good*. New York: Peter Langer.
Tlili, A. (2010). Exploring professionalism. *Journal of Further and Higher Education*, 34(1): 135–136.

Trow, M. (1996). Trust, markets and accountability in higher education: A Comparative Perspective. Seminar paper given at the SRHE Oxford, June.

Tschannen-Moran, M. and Hoy, W. K. (2000). Trust: A multidisciplinary analysis of the nature, meaning, and measurement of trust. *Review of Educational Research,* 70: 547–493.

Unwin, A. (2007). The professionalism of the higher education teacher: What's ICT got to do with it? *Teaching in Higher Education,* 12(3): 295–230.

Veloutsou, C., Paton, R. A. and Lewis, J. (2005). Consultation and the reliability of information sources pertaining to university selection. *International Journal of Educational Management,* 19(4): 160–171.

Vidovich, L. and Currie, J. (2011). Governance and trust in higher education. *Studies in Higher Education,* 36(1): 43–56.

Williams, B., (1973). *Problems of the Self.* Cambridge: Cambridge University Press.

Woelert, P. and Yates, L. (2014). Too little and too much trust: Performance measurement in Australian higher education. *Critical Studies in Education*, online: 26 August 2014.

Woodall, T., Hiller, A. and Resnick, S. (2014). Making sense of higher education: Students as consumers and the value of the university experience. *Studies in Higher Education,* 39(1): 48–67.

CHAPTER TWENTY-TWO

The University as a Public Pedagogic Form

JAN MASSCHELEIN AND MAARTEN SIMONS

It is one thing to complain or even mourn about the actual state of the university, but another thing to resist this present. As Isabelle Stengers suggests, such resistance is not about debunking or criticizing, it is rather about creating and reclaiming notions that can activate the possible and call for imaginative engagement instead of submission to the given definition of a state of affairs, even if this submission is in order to denounce it (Stengers 2005a). Following this suggestion, the brief notes below intend to reclaim the university as '*universitas studii*', thereby (re-)proposing or reclaiming both the notion of 'gathering' (*universitas*) and 'studium' (instead of *Bildung*) to approach the university as a site for collective public study. Let us note thereby that in English to reclaim means not only to recover, to obtain the return of, but also to bring again under cultivation, i.e. to re-invent. And let us add that we use the notions 'public' and 'collective' in a specific way. Public is not used to refer to issues of access ('open access') or funding and ownership (by a public agency or state-related authorities), and does not indicate a level or area that allows to discuss or act in the name of a public good (the 'public sphere'). Public study refers to the double movement of making something public and gathering a (thinking) public of students around something (see also Latour and Weibel, 2005). Making public in this sense is however not a kind of additional activity of moving beyond the closed walls of the university and students or professors reaching out for society and the broader public. Making public is what happens in the university—and for instance, in the lecture hall, the seminar but also a field trip—when a (silent) object becomes a (speaking) thing, and can be studied. Public is opposed here to private, at least when making private is understood as encompassing activities of appropriation and protection that define in advance ownership, proper usage, value or meaning. The notion of collective, in turn, implies the making public, but it is referring to an 'effective potential in the situation that exceeds both the individuals in the group and their aggregate number' (Massumi 2015, p. 83). Collective refers to the movement of thought that emerges when gathering around something, and attempting to make sense of something as (becoming) part of our common world. University study, we will argue, involves collective thinking in the sense that what is at stake in study and what becomes possible in terms of opening up a new future through studying always exceeds the given interests of individuals or groups and common grounds.

Our notes are organized in two parts. In the first, really brief, part we will sketch very roughly how the actual learning and research policies of the EU materializes in the European Higher Education Area and the European Research Area (Berlin Communiqué, 2003; European Commission, 2000). Being part of more global policies and governing regimes, the focus is on the development of European frameworks, standards, monitoring systems and funding structures that allow for flexibility and mobility of students and researchers, and on the support of institutional modernization to support mobile students and researchers (European Commission, 2003). These 'areas' at once shape and operate through the figures of the independent, personalized learner and the innovative, creative researcher. As figures, they symbolize a liberation from modern institutional settings. These figures understand themselves as entrepreneurs, and being involved in production (of competencies or knowledge), speculation (on profitable investment), calculation (of credits), accumulation (of competencies and publications) and capitalization (of innovations and learning outcomes). They require fast education and fast science, which is a requirement that the university cannot meet without being transformed in its heart or very existence since, as we will indicate, the university is crucially an arrangement that in various ways slows down. Or put otherwise, both the figure of the independent learner and the innovative creative researcher don't need the university but need stimulating, flexible and rewarding learning and research environments. In the second part, we suggest that the reaffirmation and reinvention of the *universitas studii* and the reclaiming of the notion of *studium* could offer a future to the university, because it does not orient the university to a personal(ized) or external ideal (e.g. 'Bildung') or an empty signifier ('excellence') but point to the importance of her pedagogic forms as working through problems in a way that is taking care of a shared future and doing justice to a shared world.

From there it can be clarified why universities in this sense are worthwhile to defend from a societal point of view (and not just from the viewpoint of independent learners or creative researchers).

Part One

Employability and excellence

While reading the current European discourses on the university (the various declarations and programmes and communications and policy papers) and looking at the various policy instruments (European Credit Transfer System, European Qualification Framework, Dublin Indicators, Key Performance Indicators, etc.) organizing the European Higher Education Area and the European Research Area, it is clear that the orientations of excellence and employability frame the role of universities in a particular way. What is at stake is the general mobilization and exploitation of resources in order to contribute to the growth of capital in its human, social, cultural and economic forms, and both at an individual and collective level. This is necessary, so we can hear and read, in order to maintain a competitive position within the global knowledge economy, to engage in the war on talent, but, importantly, also to deal with daunting societal challenges (European Commission, 2006, 2012). Opportunities for investment in human capital and to produce new knowledge are seen as the way to meet the demands of society (of individual learners, of the labour market, of social inclusion) and to deal with the future. The orientation towards excellence and employability defines research as the *production* of knowledge, education as the *production* of learning outcomes, and service as the *production* of impact on social and economic development (innovation). Excellence and employability might be empty signifiers, but they have an obvious strategic meaning. Lacking any external referent, the term excellence refers to the fact that a university/teacher/researcher is performing better than others measured on the basis of a set of performance indicators. Hence, the obsession with excellence is linked up with the 'dictates of comparison and optimisation'; the emphasis is on ongoing comparison in view of ongoing optimization (Bröckling, 2002). The basic assumption is that 'excellence emerges from competition' (European Commission, 2006, p. 9). In an analogue way, the orientation towards employability puts the learner into a position where she permanently and quickly has to calculate and recalculate her investments in human capital in view of expected market conditions and choices by other learners. The orientation towards excellence and employability actually changes the academic world at all levels—including the dispositions and ethos of the inhabitants of the university and the study practices. Indeed, the university of excellence and employability is a habitat which demands an entrepreneurial ethos of obedience or submission to a permanent 'quality' tribunal, its law of performance, comparison and improvement, and the dictates of continued (self-)competition and speeding up.

This reconfiguration of the university goes together with a changed condition of the mode of existence of academics and students, and gives birth to what we would like to call the figures of the 'independent learner' and the 'innovative researcher'. The independent learner is focused on the accumulation and recognition of her learning outcomes, and hence, she is concerned with his or her employability, while the researcher cultivates an orientation towards excellence in organizing his or her work as an academic business. It is beyond the scope of this chapter to elaborate on all the characteristics of these figures, so we will limit ourselves to two key aspects: acceleration and speculation.

Acceleration

It is fairly common knowledge that acceleration is a defining aspect of our capitalist society, and that the university in times of academic capitalism is both subject to increased acceleration and serves as a means of increasing the speed of society via innovation and development. But it is important to stress that speeding up university life is clearly only possible as long as we begin by looking at—and organizing—teaching, research and service in terms of productivity. This is precisely what seems to be happening today.

Learning is increasingly organized as a production process that leads to clearly defined learning outcomes, and when it focuses on these outputs as quantifiable figures, improving learning becomes synonymous with making it more efficient and effective. Fast learning becomes the ideal where the student as professional learner becomes the speed demon of higher education. Specific policy instruments and procedures, such as the European qualification framework, the ECTS file and the Europass Programm, exactly seek to enable this ideal. The student that follows ECTS-based programs, for instance, should be regarded as a person having his/her own learning style, and hence, in need of flexible trajectories in order to obtain the predefined learning outcomes. In the ECTS Users Guide, this student is baptized as the 'independent learner': 'An independent learner may accumulate the credits required for the achievement of a qualification through a variety of learning modes. She/he may acquire the required knowledge, skills and competence in formal, non-formal and informal contexts: this can be the result of an intentional decision or the outcome of different learning activities over time. The learner may select educational components without immediate orientation towards a formal qualification' (ECTS Users Guide 2015, p. 18). The student is someone whose learning process takes place independent of predefined curricula, an education setting, qualifications or even intentions, but the accumulated learning experiences and outcomes can always be recognized and verified. And many of the European frameworks have exactly the following objective: transforming the student into a learner, and making the learner independent from institutionalized forms of education. Clearly, this independency is only one side of the coin. He or she becomes dependent on newly arranged frames to, for instance, have her of his learning recognized and verified. For the independent learner, university education becomes organized as a collection of *personalized* learning trajectories to guarantee optimal learning gains (improvement), professors are asked to become professional teaching staff and to think of their teaching as the facilitation of the production of learning outcomes by the learners. Teaching is no longer considered as essential for, for instance, the movement of (collective) thought. Indeed as being equally 'autonomous' researchers, teachers (professors) are often tempted to take their teaching not too seriously or, when students start to complain, to invest extra time in efficient and effective teaching.

The situation is similar when it comes to research, where it becomes increasingly difficult to ignore that research is seen as a production process, with knowledge as the produced output, which is increasingly regarded as a commodity (to be protected, sold, etc.) and is clearly considered not only a way of looking or speaking about research, but also a way of organizing research. Project-based research seems to have almost become the norm, with its detailed formulation of work packages as production units and actually defining in advance the expected outputs. This approach maximizes the possible return for investors. Implicitly or explicitly, the logic of productivity functions as the guideline for the research. Research becomes something to be managed with the proletarization of the scholar as knowledge worker as its logical result. The innovative researcher finds herself faced with a division of labour that asks for coordination, negotiation and a lot of promises about fast outputs and outcomes.

But it is not just about fast education and fast research. The so-called 'service' or 'public' role of the university is also increasingly organized in terms of acceleration. This is expressed in the popular idea of (societal or public) impact, and draws upon an apparatus of indicators used to measure the impact. That apparatus is clearly not just measuring or valuing academic contributions post factum, but increasingly these indicators act as constitutive factors (elements) for what is considered valued service and what is not. The logic of acceleration, which in fact affects society as a whole, probably explains why there is no time at today's university; both students and professors are always busy, or rather, always involved in possible productive activities or projects. It is no surprise that multitasking has emerged as the highest virtue among these speed demons. The experience of 'no time' actually means that all of one's time is productive time, and hence, all time that is not yet defined or occupied is considered as a scarce resource to be exploited for acceleration and productivity.

Academic bubbles

Perhaps less obviously, but equally important, is that with the emergence of the accelerated and accelerating university we have created an arena for speculation. Despite the call for a permanent reality check that might lead to a focus on the employability of the student upon graduating, on innovation and development in research, on practical relevance and the impact on service activities, there has been an increased accumulation of 'imaginary' value or capital, that is, value or capital that is not real or not being used. Disconnected from so-called reality and utility, the permanent accumulation of value in learning, research and service becomes a goal in and of itself. In higher education, for instance, value is expressed in terms of (employable) competences. But competences refer to that which is assumed to enable someone to act or perform in a particular way in a particular context. Higher education learning, by being oriented towards these competences, is actually oriented towards an assumption. When we look at the detailed, carefully constructed and very long lists of competencies, it seems like we are re-entering the age of speculative philosophy. The professional learner who accumulates competences is someone who remains in a virtual state. And even worse, the value of what she has learned is subject to the law of supply and demand; the human capital in her portfolio does not have a stable value. There is no gold standard for education. The consequence is that the professional learner is not only asked to approach her learning as an investment, but also as a matter of speculation.

This is similar to what happens in research where publications and journals with citation indexes and impact factors just as patents are not only an indication of output, but actually the generally accepted currency for expressing academic value. Hence, we have academic speculation (including actual fraud) or at least a decisive concern for accumulation (or being cited). We should also not forget the complete disconnection between writing and actual reading, between making something public and actually gathering a (reading, thinking) public around something. The value of innovation has a similar logic. The focus on innovation, in fact, means that change has become a goal in itself. Competences, publications and innovations seem to have become the very bubbles of academic life.

In sum, together with the figure of the innovative researcher and independent learner, the need for acceleration and the requirement of speculation enter the university. In other words, as an academic or student it becomes increasingly difficult today not to look at speeding up and speculation as an important concern. However, it remains unclear why and whether the innovative researcher and independent learner actually need the university. Their mode of existence no longer seems to be linked to or interwoven with the university. Probably these figures still stay within or make use of the university as long as the university is functional, and hence, as long as the university is oriented towards excellence and employability. But little imagination is needed to notice that the independent learner and innovative researcher always look for other, more productive or enabling environments. The independent learner and innovative researcher have emancipated themselves from the university, and it is the university—now turned into a 'regular' working and learning environment—that is put in the position to indicate its added value for the learner and researcher.

But this is only one part of the story.

Part Two

In order to open a (different) future to the university, we suggest considering the possibility to become enlightened by another way of looking at what the university is by going back to its origin in the Middle Ages. Back then, the university was not just a sophisticated version of the cathedral school, nor an updated version of the ancient academy. Clearly, the *universitas studii* had a distinctive form. It was a concrete kind of gathering, association or assembly (that is indeed the meaning of *universitas*) where, in the case of the *universitas studii*, knowledge that previously was considered sacred and to be protected became profane, no longer protected and open for common use. The notion public refers to exactly this movement. The *universitas studii* takes place when something was made public and actually presented to a public, and hence, became subject to study. Again, the notion public does not just refer to an outside or out there. Instead, it refers to the act and practical arrangement of gathering where it becomes possible to study something, and therefore all kind of privatizing and protective claims are kept outside. Protections and gatekeepers were removed from the divine book and it became a secular book of study. But it is crucial to note that this happened *within* the actual (physical) assembly of students. Although the university clearly had its sources of inspiration, at the same time, it had a distinctive form as a *universitas studii*. At this point, it is important to stress that, from the very beginning, the university included a very specific form of *collective study*, which was often not initiated by people of wisdom who wanted to share their knowledge but by students themselves. More precisely, the *universitas* was established by those who wanted to become students, leaving the seclusion of the monastery to assemble in spaces, halls, rooms and sometimes simply meeting on a public bridge or a street corner.[1] In that sense, the establishment of a *universitas studii* was quite revolutionary because public study practices broke open existing knowledge circuits and related power hierarchies, allowing collective thinking to create an openness or a future.

As Emile Durkheim recalls, these associations articulated a general and intense *movement* of *intellectual concern and thirst for understanding* (Durkheim, 1904–1905, p. 63, translation ours, italics added). And being a student was less a role or position than a way of life. It was the notion of *studium* that was most used to indicate the 'pedagogical life' ('la vie pédagogique') that developed *within the space of these associations* (Durkheim, 1904–1905, p. 75, translation ours, italics added). Hence, these associations were not just about practices of initiation or socialization to become part of particular social, cultural, vocational or religious group and they were not about individual learning activities. The universities, then, were a new form of *scholé* of *public study enabling collective thought* (*studii* being the genitive singular of *studium*). And what they tried to protect (and later to license) was the right for study and the right to teach all over Europe (*licentia ubique docendi*), that is the right to communicate or share what is studied outside the encompassing reigns of the church, the state and the professional guilds (Ferruolo 1985, Rüegg 1992). And for that reason—and from the very beginning—the *universitas studii* was something to be stabilized, tamed or neutralized by church or state, or through their powerful alliance. But the gathering of *studium* and the student involved in collective thought remained throughout history a possible threat, the mark of revolt, or at least the time and place to open up a(nother) future.

Since to some extent all study can be said to be collective in the sense that it is always a *meeting* or encounter with others (texts, things, ideas, etc.), it is important to note that 'in the proposal of the notion of *studium*' 'collective' constitutively implies also other students. University study is never only about the future of individual students, but always about possible futures of our world departing from that world no longer to be self-evident. Moreover, it is important to not confound collective with community (or society—see Latour, 1993, p. 4) and to avoid approaching the collective thinking starting from the primacy of individual study (the image of a student in her/his study-room, absorbed by a book, or wandering through the library). *Studium*, however, is to be understood as constitutively collective.

Collective experiments

This is not a plea to replace our modern idea of the university with the classic *universitas*. It is about changing the perspective by focusing on public practices of study involved in collective thinking that are not often associated with the essence of a university. The focus here is on investigations and thinking done collectively and in public (and not on research done in the seclusion of the individual office or behind closed laboratory doors—which, in fact, don't really need the university). It means focusing on study within the assembly or *universitas* of students. These forms of university study are experiments in the sense that they always truly try to *meet with* the phenomenon (or text, or image). This therefore has to be made present simply and implies being in its company and, hence, the recognition that '*we* are not alone in the world' (Toby Nathan 2001), which might sound trivial but is in fact something 'we' ('humans') constantly seem to forget. Being not alone also meaning and implying that there are things, animals, plants, rivers, ghosts, causes, landscapes, ideas, etc. which are our companions in the strong sense (that we have to negotiate ways to live together with them). University study includes the attempt to understand what this meeting actually means through experimentation with description, explanation and narration. It is not just about knowledge production or transfer, but also about putting shared knowledge and what one commonly sees and thinks to the test. What happens is that the possibility to contribute to a new world opens up for the students through study. Experimental here refers minimally to the assumption or belief that the outcome of study is and cannot be defined in advance, and that the activity of study cannot be some planned, output-driven production process, but always implies a test or attempt.

Entering the university, and becoming a student, which also includes professors and researchers, means being open to an experimental life. This process is collective in the sense that students become witnesses to these attempts. For example, a professor who discusses issues refers to knowledge, but not without hesitation because there is always the chance that something will arise to cause hesitation (Stengers 2013). Clearly, today academics are trained to avoid hesitation, especially when standing in front of students. As part of public study, hesitations, however, indicate the attempt of carefully finding words and other meanings and articulate the process of collective thinking. Through interactions and as part of the public gatherings, an object is transformed into a thing, something that provokes thinking, and at that moment, the process of finding new descriptions, explanations and narratives can commence.

The test here not only refers to an adequate methodology that guarantees validity and reliability by defining in advance what should and what should not be taken into account. It also means thinking and performing research so that it can be shared, questioned, challenged without knowing the how and whom in advance. This in effect removes all sorts of *academic* protections, e.g. by established methods or disciplines, or at least questions these protections. Here the lecture, seminar and science laboratory—when they actually occur and enable collective thinking—are considered examples of a collective experiment. But without doubt, when we look at what goes on in university gatherings, unhindered by university ideas and ideals, other examples of public study begin to emerge. What happens in these contemporary forms of the *universitas* is that research is returned to the students (and professors), which allows university studies to be truly experimental again instead of merely productive, collective instead of merely protected and privatized. These so-called teaching and study activities should not be seen—as the fast researcher often does—as breaking or interrupting research productivity. To the contrary, research in the presence of students should be regarded as part of the intensification and publication process of research. Students should not be merely regarded as those who stand to be informed by the research (and publications), but should be actually involved from the very beginning. University study occurs in public forms of inquiry; students are involved *in actu*, and can partake in collective thinking, when studies are performed publicly.

Let us note, in passing, that it is striking that in many fields of thought and investigations many of the most important works consist, in fact to a rather large extent, of notes related to lectures or seminars (notes made by 'scholars' to prepare them or by others who attended them, books being often based on courses). As von Humboldt (1810) already suggested, research is therefore not so much moved through the contact with 'colleagues' but rather through it being part of what we want to call 'pedagogic forms'. University research is research that bears the mark of *studium*; it lives and grows by engaging a public of students and by collective movement of thought. This, in the words of von Humboldt, is operating in and for itself in these forms ('selbsttätig'). It is the public gathering itself (when it works) that has formative power, unfolding a movement of collective thought.

Inquiry and thinking not only require public exposition afterwards (as written publication or report), but precisely also *in actu*, and this is what happens in the lectures and seminars (when they actually happen) which in return make something happen to the public of students. Neither the writing of text nor its reading can simply replace the working of these pedagogic gatherings (think also about the gatherings around blackboards in mathematics and physics) which constitute forms that turn objects into public matter (bringing it into company as part of the collective thought which is always in the making) and gathers a public of students and scholars, that is, of learners and researchers turned into public figures. A public of students does not precede the event of gathering, but emerges in it. This gathering articulates, therefore, a movement of de-identification—*we are no disciples, no civil servants, no clergymen, but students and scholars.* This movement disturbs, questions or disrupts all kinds of stabilizations, fixations or crystallizations. It has no real beginning and no end, it occurs and 'takes/finds place' and implies that students and scholars are moving in a time of suspension (i.e. not simply a time of accumulation or re-production), that is the particular time of *studium* or of 'scholé'.

It is important to stress that the *universitas studii* always slowed things down. Being confronted with knowledge that has been made public (through presentation and discussion) implies that it was looking for a way to relate to that knowledge, to think in the presence of a new world that was becoming increasingly real via that very knowledge. What shows itself to students is something that can be named and discussed again, so that it becomes a challenge to do justice to something and to what it means for our future world. Slowing down was very much a consequence of the interruption of the usual ways of thinking, knowing and acting *within* the actual assembly of students. This probably helps to explain why the current acceleration processes and the capitalization of—and *on*—time are causing so much commotion; it touches at the heart of the university as the *universitas* of collective study. Unfortunately, today 'slowing down' is often perceived as an adagio embraced by sore losers.

University study—*studium*—is not the facilitation and support of personalized learning trajectories, but public study committed to collective thought. To be sure, public study is not simply the same as the collaborative meeting or conference with colleagues. It occurs precisely at the moment where *knowledge or science leaves the context of disciplined research.* Clearly, our (dear) colleagues often keep us in a context where the stakes and solutions are defined in advance. *Studium*, on the contrary, is about being exposed to something that is made public, that constitutes a studying public and opens up another future through making collective thinking possible.

The pedagogic forms are modes of encounter or gathering which are not based on a personalized understanding of subjectivity which would constitute them. It is, on the contrary, the forms that (are through and through technological and that) are making something happen that move us. Displacing some remarks from Isabelle Stengers we could say that pedagogic forms are particular modes of gathering: 'What the gathering achieves could perhaps be compared to what physicists describe as putting 'out of equilibrium', *out of [...] position* ... because the gathering makes present … something, a cause or thing, *which transforms our relation* to the stakes that have been put up' (2005b, 195, italics ours).

In this line, we can approach the university in the first place as a gathering or assembly which as a *collective-in-the-making* articulates a *movement of public thought* through unique *pedagogic forms* (such as the lecture, the seminar, the laboratory, but also fieldtrips) that, as technical devices, have the *power* to make things public and giving them the power to generate a thinking public. These technical devices (including texts, images, etc.) do not represent the world but refer to space-time conditions, to visual and auditory (sensual) conditions which allow a study of the world. They are therefore rather devices to make us think and be-in-form-ation, rather than devices to reproduce and recognize. It is not about personally owning thought or have knowledge or opinions, but about a movement of thought and about sustaining its unfolding. Which requires not to be true to oneself, but to that movement. The 'object of study' is not an object of knowledge to be acquired by individual subjects, but is what makes me/us think and what has to be searched for (Massumi 2015).

Careful vigilance

Study gatherings contribute to the creation of a future, not by producing learning outcomes or knowledge but by putting knowledge and science to a public test. This is a particular way of inserting ideas, objects or concepts into our shared world. What study achieves can be compared, as Isabelle Stengers notes, to an 'out of equilibrium' state that makes something appear that transforms our relation to what is at stake. The future here is not associated with an increase in knowledge or capital, or associated with progress, but with a fundamental uncertainty: 'we don't know what the future will look like', or 'we don't even know what we don't know'. The consequence of this is that we do not know whether, how and to what extent rational thought, our necessary abstractions and any new facts (and sometimes—e.g. genes—a new nature) that our science produces will affect our lives. This is exactly why we have to be remain vigilant. We should be careful, *faire attention*; the *universitas studii* are forms of association that allow us to be cautious, that is to take care, to 'regard' (see Illich about the early university as a 'tutor' of the text, Marin et al., 2017) and to pay attention and thus, to hesitate. *Studium* is 'to regard attentively', as one of the translations of the Latin sounds. This clearly implies that, *as students*, we slow down for what is at stake. We suspend the logic of investment, productivity and acceleration.

Slowing down is, thus, not simply embraced as an imperative to counter the imperative of speeding up. Slowing down is to be regarded as a consequence or an effect of collective study practices. This is not just some plea for slow science but for the renewal or reinvention of university study as collective public experiments; reinventing slow education instead of organizing fast learning tracks. When students get involved in collective study it allows them to find new or alternative futures rather than simply searching for predefined (learning and research) outcomes. Indeed, the assumption of collective study is that there is always something more important to be considered, that new issues may arise and that there are no fixed destinies and predefined futures. To phrase this in a more positive way: university study is a form of gathering that allows a discussion and shaping of possible destinies and futures.

This, then, would be one reason why society should offer the university a future. When you are involved in experimentation as a university student (or professor)—in lecture halls, labs, seminars or other pedagogic forms—one is always simultaneously being confronted with what matters and thus with new ways of organizing society. In other words, what opens up in study are possibilities to imagine new and shared futures. It clearly implies recognizing that university study is not confined to an institution that claims its name but is actually increasingly involved in taming and neutralizing the concept of study by framing it as a mode of fast, personalized learning. This is a trend we should resist! We should resist by recuperating time and space to allow for the creation of collective study practices that utilize both old and new tools.

If the work of the university study indeed resides in its possibility to invoke thinking by gathering people around an issue, the focus is thus on the art (the techniques), the artefacts, the architecture and the habitat. How to turn a text, a virus or a river into a cause for thinking? It is about an *art to give* the issue around which we gather the *power* to activate thinking, to give it 'a presence that transforms each protagonist's relations with his or her knowledge, hopes, … and memories, and allows the whole to generate what each one would have been unable to produce separately' (Stengers 2005c). To reclaim the university as *universitas studii* is about actually trying to develop or experiment with old and new techniques and practices in view of designing pedagogic forms that actually slow down, makes us vigilant and attentive and would allow us to look for creating futures rather than already define them in terms of 'outcomes' as if we would be clear about our futures. Instead of an innovation agenda or a new accountability and impact regime for universities, what is needed, being confronted with the new digital technologies and the actual learning policies, is a kind of research agenda, concentrated around *poles of attention* (instead of poles of excellence) and including a 'pedagogy' looking for *experimentation, invention and refinement of protocols and architectures for pedagogic forms that foster public collective study.*

Note

1. See for instance the study of Laurie on 'The Rise and Early Constitution of universities with a survey of medieval education' where he writes that 'university schools .... were *open to all* without restriction as *studia publica* or *generalia,* as opposed to more restricted ecclesiastical schools which were under a Rule' (Laurie 1887, 101; italics in original).

References

Berlin Communiqué (2003). *Realising the European Higher Education Area. Communiqué of ministers responsible for higher education*, Berlin, 19-09-2003

Bröckling, U. (2002). 'Diktat des Komparativs. Zur Anthropologie des "unternehmerischen Selbst"', in U. Bröckling & E., Horn, (Eds.), *Anthropologie der Arbeit* Tübingen: Gunter Narr. pp. 157–173.

Durkheim, E. (1904–1905). *L'évolution pédagogique en France (Cours pour les candidats à l'Agrégation prononcé en 1904-1905) Avec une introduction de Maurice Halbwachs*, 1938. Document produit en version numérique par Jean-Marie Tremblay: (http://classiques.uqac.ca/classiques/Durkheim_emile/evolution_ped_france/evolution_ped_france.html)

ECTS Users Guide (2015). Retrieved on 04/05/2016 from: http://ec.europa.eu/education/library/publications/2015/ects-users-guide_en.pdf

European Commission (2000, January). *Towards a European Research Area.* COM(2000) 6, Brussels.

European Commission (2003, February). *The role of the universities in the Europe of knowledge.* COM (2003) 58, Brussels.

European Commission (2006). *Delivering on the modernization agenda for universities: education, research and innovation.* COM (2006) 208, Brussels.

European Commission (2012). *Rethinking education: Investing in skills for better socio-economic outcomes.* Communication from the Commission (20.11.2012 COM(2012) 669). Brussels: European Commission.

Ferruolo, S. (1985). *The Origins of the University. The Schools of Paris and their Critics.* Stanford: Stanford University Press.

Latour, B. and Weibel, P. (eds) (2005). *Making Things Public. Atmospheres of Democracy.* London/Cambridge/Karlsruhe: MIT Press/ZKM.

Latour, B. (1993). *We have never been modern.* Cambridge: Harvard University Press.

Laurie, S. S. (1887). *The rise and early constitution of universities with a survey of medieval education.* New York: Appleton.

Marin, L., J. Masschelein & M. Simons (2017): Page, text and screen in the university: Revisiting the Illich hypothesis, Educational Philosophy and Theory, DOI: 10.1080/00131857.2017.1323624

Massumi, B. (2015). Collective Expression. A Radical Pragmatics. *Inflexions*. 8, 59–88.

Nathan, T. (2001). *Nous ne sommes pas seuls au monde. Les enjoux de l'ethnopsychiatrie*. Paris: Le Seuil.

Rüegg, W. (1992). 'Themes', in: H. De Ridder-Symoens (ed) *A History of the University in Europe. Vol.I. Universities in the Middle Ages*. Cambridge: Cambridge University Press, 3-34.

Stengers, I. (2013). *Une autre science est possible!* Paris: La Découverte.

Stengers, I. (2005a). Deleuze and Guattari's Last Enigmatic Message. *Angelaki. Journal of the Theoretical Humanities*. 10(2), 151–167.

Stengers, I. (2005b). Introductory notes on an ecology of practices. *Cultural Studies Review*. 11(1), 183–196.

Stengers, I. (2005c). The Cosmopolitical Proposal, In: B. Latour, P. Weibel (eds), *Making Things Public. Atmospheres of Democracy*, London/Cambridge/ Karlsruhe, MIT Press/ZKM, 994-1003.

von Humboldt, W. (1810). *On the internal and external organisation of the higher scientific institutions in Berlin*. Retrieved on 4.3.2015 from: http://germanhistorydocs.ghi-dc.org/sub_document.cfm?document_id=3642

CHAPTER TWENTY-THREE

Universities as Civic Spaces

In the Footsteps of Arendt and Jaspers

JON NIXON

... our thinking is truly discursive, running, as it were, from place to place, from one part of the world to another, through all kinds of conflicting views ...

—HANNAH ARENDT (1977, 242)

Between the state and the individual stand the institutions that comprise civil society. We take these institutions for granted, but they have been hard won and have in their time held their ground against the incursions of authoritarian states and rampant individualism. The university comprises one such institution that stands betwixt and between the corporate state and the isolated individual. It is a space in which we learn not only to think together but to think together about our shared world. To understand why the university matters is to understand why thinking matters: not thinking in its more specialised and refined forms but thinking as ordinary and commonplace. To think is to extend our mental reach, our communicative horizons, and our understanding of what constitutes our shared world. In pursuing these ideas I follow in the footsteps of two great public educators—Hannah Arendt and Karl Jaspers—both of whom hammered out their thinking on the tough anvil of 20th-century totalitarianism.

The spaces in between

One of the lessons to be learned from the history of the last century is that totalitarian regimes invariably seek dominance by destroying all existing associative and institutional bonds between people. Such regimes set about this task of total domination through what Hannah Arendt in *The Origins of Totalitarianism* termed 'mass atomization': a process whereby 'the completely isolated human being' is bound unconditionally and exclusively to the state 'without any other social ties to family, friends, comrades, or even mere acquaintances'. Because such ties—and the institutional contexts that frame them—bind human beings together in mutual care and obligation, they inevitably pose a direct threat to the 'atomized and individualized society' of the totalitarian state. Total domination requires total—that is, exclusive and unconditional—loyalty (Arendt, 1973, 323–324).

But the ties that bind human beings prove strangely resilient. In his extraordinary account of totalitarian society—*Life and Fate*—Vasily Grossman shows how all attempts to impose 'mass atomisation' falter in the face of what one of the characters in that great novel calls 'everyday human kindness': '[t]he kindness of an old woman carrying a piece of bread to a prisoner, the kindness of a soldier allowing a wounded enemy to drink from his water-flask, the kindness of youth towards age, the kindness of a peasant hiding an old Jew in his loft ... Even at the most terrible times ... this senseless, pathetic kindness remained scatted throughout life like atoms of radium' (Grossman, 2006, 391–392). Our sense of common humanity—of kinship one with another—can never be entirely extinguished. We reach out to one another, suggests Grossman, even when our reaching out is 'senseless, pathetic'—even when it puts us at incalculable risk and has no discernible significance.

Moreover, when totalitarian and authoritarian regimes are toppled—or simply implode—whatever remains of this 'everyday human kindness' forms the bedrock of social renewal. As Neil Harding (1992, 184) pointed out in the aftermath of the dissolution of the Soviet Union, '[c]ivil society began to emerge, reflecting and strengthening the public mood for freedom'. It did so 'through public meetings and demonstrations, an independent press, TV, and radio, and the emergence of interest groups, clubs, associations, and political groupings'. What defined these emergent social formations was their sense of shared purpose: people came together as free agents to express their opinions, to publish pamphlets and books, to play chess or read poems, to form political alliances ... and, so, the spaces began to open up.

Such spaces are inconceivable in an entirely 'atomized and individualized society'. They occupy the realm of what Craig Calhoun (1994) termed 'intermediate associations' that constitute 'the crucial defences both of distinctive identities imperilled by the normalisation of the mass, and of democracy against oligarchy' (p. 311). They are the spaces in between: spaces in which individuals are neither dissolved into a homogeneous mass nor atomised into a state of isolation. Within these spaces individuals associate with one another to pursue purposes the fulfilment of which is premised on the possibility of mutuality and reciprocity: purposes that relate, for example, to our care and well-being, to our growth through learning, to our need for cultural and artistic expression, and to our pleasure in simply being together. They are, in other words, spaces in which our association with one another is neither random nor indiscriminate but shaped by a sense of shared purpose.

Universities have historically provided these kinds of spaces. However, their defining purpose has always been—and continues to be—highly contested. That is partly because the debate about purposes has all too often collapsed into a debate about outcomes and outputs, as if universities were manufacturing plants dedicated solely to the production of academic qualifications, professional credentials, transferable knowledge and Nobel Prize winners. Of course, these outcomes and outputs matter. They are clear indicators of achievement. But the purpose of the university lies beyond any individual or group achievement regardless of how remarkable and praiseworthy such achievement might be. The purpose is to be found in the ongoing practice, and the practice—notwithstanding its ever increasing array of specialisations—is grounded in the commonality of human thought. To understand why universities matter we need to understand why thinking matters—and, as highlighted in the penultimate section of this chapter, why thinking matters *now*.

Enlarged mentality

Drawing on her hard-won understanding of totalitarianism, Arendt drew a sharp and uncompromising distinction between thinking and ideology: the former, as she saw it, being premised on freedom and *dissensus*, the latter on coercion and consensus. From this Arendtian perspective, thinking values heterogeneity and difference whereas ideology demands homogeneity and sameness. To think is to engage with the inescapable plurality of the human condition—a plurality that is an inevitable consequence of our freedom to act and an inevitable cause of our uncertainty regarding the outcomes of our actions. To submit to an ideology on the other hand is to embrace certainty at the expense of freedom and, in so doing, deny the plurality that defines our human condition.

Much of our thinking is conducted in solitude. But—argued Arendt (1978) in her final unfinished work—even solitary thinking involves a dialogical element or what she called 'the duality of the two-in-one'. On that basis, loneliness and solitude are very different states of mind: 'solitude is that human situation in which I keep myself company. Loneliness comes about when I am alone without being able to split up into the two-in-one, without being able to keep myself company' (I, 185–187). When we talk to ourselves we are thinking aloud, thereby carrying on a process that when internalised becomes solitary thinking and when externalised is manifest in the world of human affairs. In that sense thinking is Janus-faced, turning both inwards towards dialogue with oneself and outwards towards dialogue with others. But—and this is Arendt's crucial point—thinking is always dialogical.

In an earlier essay—first published in 1967 and written in response to the controversy following her coverage of the Eichmann trial—she had explained the dialogical nature of solitary thought in terms of what she called 'representative thinking': 'I form an opinion by considering a given issue from different viewpoints, by making present to my mind the standpoints of those who are absent; that is, I represent them.' She went on to argue that this process of representation 'does not blindly adopt the actual views of those who stand somewhere else'. Rather, it 'is a question … of being and thinking in my own identity where actually I am not'. Finally, she claimed that 'the more people's standpoints I have present in my mind while I am pondering a given issue, the better I can imagine how I would feel and think if I were in their place, the stronger will be my capacity for representative thinking and the more valid my final conclusions, my opinions' (Arendt, 1977, 241).

Such thinking, argued Arendt in her 1970 lectures on Kant's political philosophy, involves the imagination in that it 'makes the others present and thus moves potentially in a space which is public, open to all sides; in other words, it adopts the position of Kant's world citizen'. Imagination, for Arendt, is diametrically opposed to both fancy and ideology. Both deny the 'space which is public, open to all sides': in the case of fancy, by turning away from its externality; in the case of ideology, by violating its plurality. The imagination alone—drawing its inspiration from, and finding delight in, the plurality and specificity of the world—affirms that space through its willingness to reach out and view the world from other standpoints: 'To think with the enlarged mentality—that means you train your imagination to go visiting'. Whoever thinks in such a way, argued Arendt, 'adopts the position of Kant's world citizen' (Arendt, 1978, II, 257).

So, to think—even in isolation, even in *enforced* isolation—is to reach out to the world. Indeed, some of the most influential thinkers have done some of their most influential thinking while in prison: witness Dietrich Bonhoeffer, Antonio

Gramsci, Vaclav Havel, Rosa Luxemburg. (See Bonhoeffer, 2010; Gramsci, 1971; Havel, 1988; Luxemburg, 2004.) These and countless other political prisoners and prisoners of conscience have left a record of the human capacity to think beyond the confines of their own imprisonment. This is not to belittle the extreme deprivation suffered by political prisoners around the world, but merely to affirm Arendt's central insight: thinking—even in conditions of extreme deprivation—is always dialogical.

Boundless communication

For Arendt, the 'two-in-one' of solitary thinking and the activity of thinking together with others are mutually sustaining. Neither can survive without the other: dialogue with others requires self-reflection just as the 'two-in-one' of solitary thought relies on external stimuli. 'Even Socrates, so much in love with the market place, has', as she put it, 'to go home, where he will be alone, in solitude, in order to meet the other fellow' (Arendt, 1978, I, 189–190). It was because Arendt was convinced of the complementarity of dialogue with oneself and dialogue with others that she saw the risk of an exclusive absorption in solitary thinking. It was a risk that in her view Heidegger, her erstwhile mentor and lover, had failed to avoid: the Heidegger whom—in a handwritten journal entry dated July 1953—she famously characterised as a fox attempting to lure his prey into a trap from which he himself was unable to escape (Ludz, 2004, 304–305). Even when years later in a 1969 radio broadcast she sought to excuse Heidegger's Nazi past, she did so on the grounds that his residency in his own exclusive world of thought had made him a stranger to the wider world of human affairs (Ludz, 2004, 148–162). He had become trapped in his own closed and self-referential system.[1]

It was Karl Jaspers—her mentor and lifelong friend[2]—who was, for Arendt, one of the supreme exemplars of the 'citizen of the world'. Born in February 1883 and therefore almost twenty-three years older than Arendt, Jaspers was a man of seeming contradictions: an intensely private person who lived and flourished through his relationships with others; a German patriot who demanded that post-war Germany should acknowledge its own guilt and restore itself from the basis of that acknowledgement; a psychiatrist who rejected the psychiatric categories of mental disorder; a philosopher who sought to de-philosophise philosophy. He was also a loyal and resolute man who—unlike Heidegger—rejected the Nazi regime as morally abhorrent.[3]

Arendt saw beyond Jaspers' contradictions and deep reserve to his single-minded regard for others and his immense capacity for human communication. In an article published in 1957, she characterised him as someone for whom '[t]hinking becomes ... a kind of practice between men, not a performance of one individual in his self-chosen solitude'. Jaspers, she continued, was 'the first and only philosopher who has ever protested against solitude, to whom solitude has appeared "pernicious" and who has dared to question "all thoughts, all experiences, all contents" under this one aspect: "What do they signify for communication?"' (Arendt, 1970, 86). As she stated in the address she delivered at his memorial service in 1969, 'Jaspers exemplified in himself, as it were, a fusion of freedom, reason and communication' (Kohler and Saner, 1992, 685).

One of Jaspers' more influential—if slightly offbeat—ideas was what in his 1953 *The Origins and Goal of History*, he termed 'the Axial age': the period from 800 to 200 BC, during which—Jaspers conjectured—both religious and secular thought underwent a revolutionary surge that was to have a major and lasting impact on Western society. This was, as Jaspers interpreted it, a liminal period during which many of the enduring religions of the world emerged and the idea of democracy was born. His analysis of the causes, circumstances and contingencies that gave rise to 'the Axial age' is now of less significance than the implications of this periodisation for those with an interest in the beginnings of religious traditions and the ways in which those beginnings have played out through history over the last two millennia. Jaspers saw this periodisation as a pretext for reconciling diverse religious and secular traditions within a unified Europe whose new beginnings he traced back to 'the Axial age'—the historic axis, that is, upon which the world continues to turn.

For Jaspers, the significance of 'the Axial age', as he conceived it, was its '*summons to boundless communication*' (original emphasis, Jaspers, 1994, 387). If the great traditions of religion and culture thought turned on a common axis, then communication across and between religious and cultural divides was both possible and desirable. Jaspers was arguing that the meaning of 'the Axial age' in the here and now is more important than what he took to be its historical location in the period 800–200 BC. What it means for us existentially is that communication is a necessary condition for becoming human: 'This risking of boundless communication is once again the secret of becoming-human, not as it occurred in the inaccessible prehistoric past, but as it takes place within ourselves' (Jaspers, 1994, 387).

Care for the world

When we think, we think about 'something'. In thinking about that 'something', we distinguish it from other 'somethings'—and, in distinguishing between these various 'somethings', we each gain a sense of our 'self' as distinct from these 'somethings'. We begin to locate ourselves in the world and—in doing so—define ourselves in relation to others. We recognise ourselves through our recognition of others. It is this mesh of reciprocal recognition that constitutes what Arendt saw as our shared world: a world in which each of us is *both* a subjective 'I' that distinguishes and is distinct from others *and* an objective 'me' that is distinct from and distinguished by others.[4] 'The worldliness of living things', as she put it, 'means there is no subject that is not also an object and appears as such to somebody else, who guarantees its "objective" reality' (Arendt, 1978, I, 19).

So, thinking has volition. It requires proactive engagement rather than routinised response. This crucial distinction famously informed Arendt's judgement of Eichmann. The only notable characteristic she could detect in him 'was something entirely negative: it was not stupidity but *thoughtlessness*'. He had displayed a complete 'absence of thinking', which, as she disturbingly pointed out, 'is so ordinary an experience in our everyday life, where we have hardly the time, let alone the inclination, to *stop* and think'. His evil deeds were a result not of evil intent but of the complete absence of any intent whatsoever. So, the question, for Arendt, was: 'Could the activity of thinking as such, the habit of examining whatever happens to come to pass or to attract attention, regardless of results and specific content, could this activity be among the conditions that make men abstain from evil-doing or even actually "condition" them against it?' (original emphases, Arendt, 1978, I, 4–5).

Implicit in this question is a modest but highly significant claim regarding the ethics of thinking: although thinking may not guarantee right action, it might possibly guard against evildoing. For both Arendt and Jaspers, thinking was a moral imperative not because it provides a set of ready-made ethical precepts, but because it requires us to confront what is distinctive and unique in the world we inhabit and recognise the autonomy of those who inhabit it with us. To think is to care for the world—an idea that formed the basis of both Arendt's and Jaspers' ethical world view and helped shape Jaspers' path-breaking work in the field of psychotherapy. Visiting the International Art Exhibition in Cologne in 1912, he had been deeply influenced by the work of van Gogh. He saw in the texture of van Gogh's paintings—in, for example, the pattern, pace and intensity of brushstrokes—the need that the artist felt to depict reality through his expression of that reality. It was a reality hit head-on: an inter-subjective collision rather than a reality that one made prior sense of and then objectively depicted.

What Jaspers took from van Gogh was a deep scepticism regarding any form of therapeutic practice that categorised specific cases in relation to pre-specified categories: a scepticism that resulted in his becoming increasingly distanced from Freudian modes of analysis. His preferred approach to analysis was deeply inductive and grounded in an understanding of the particularities of each specific case. Jasper's intense 'seeing' of the immediacy of van Gogh's art played back into his thinking about intersubjectivity—about what it means to understand another human being. Human 'being'—the experience of being human—can only be understood in its irreducible specificity.

His way of seeing—and experiencing—particular works of art also contributed to what might be seen as his major conceptual contribution to philosophy: namely, his notion of 'limit situations'. Such situations, as he argued in the second volume of his three-volume *Philosophy* (Jaspers, 1969–1971), never change and present themselves as insurmountable and non-negotiable walls that constrain and limit us. When we look at the great works of van Gogh's middle period—for example, his 'Sower' of December 1882, his 'Weaver' of March 1884 or 'The Potato Eaters' of April 1885—we are faced with the 'limit situations' of the peasants whose working lives van Gogh was depicting. Among the 'limit situations' that Jaspers himself had to confront were the suicide of his brother, his own chronic ill-health and the rise of the Third Reich. These situations were non-negotiable. They were unavoidable 'facts of life'. They had to be acknowledged. Indeed, it was only by acknowledging them—by, as it were, staring reality in the face—that Jaspers was able to move forward. It was—he concluded—only by thinking through our particular 'limit situations' that we are able to identify openings, possibilities, opportunities.

Remaking the polity

Arendt and Jaspers valued thinking because they had witnessed the world topple into the meaningless void of totalitarianism—the void, that is, in which meaning is no longer the consequence of human volition but is whatever the totalitarian state requires it to be. We live in very different times, but the lure of what Arendt termed 'thoughtlessness' remains no less threatening. The threat no longer lies in what Sheldon S. Wolin (2010, xxi) terms 'classic totalitarianism'—in which '[t]he state was conceived as the main center of power, providing the leverage necessary for their mobilization and reconstruction of society'—but in what he terms 'inverted totalitarianism'. Here the state combines with other forms of power thereby encouraging 'a symbiotic relationship between traditional government and the system of "private" governance represented by the modern business corporation'.

As that 'symbiotic relationship' becomes established, 'the modern business corporation' spreads its net wider. It does so through a variety of mechanisms. Chief among these is the privatisation of the public and non-profit-making sector.

These systems-led mechanisms are supported by managerial cultures that have developed an orthodoxy of cost-effectiveness, efficiency and profitability. Those institutions and organisations that under 'classic totalitarianism' would have been crushed are now—more conveniently but no less deliberately—drawn into the ever widening net of unfettered, globalised capitalism. Civil society is no longer crushed but co-opted.

If the state is no longer the main centre of power, where does that power lie? Writing with specific reference to Europe, Tariq Ali (2015) locates it in what he terms 'the extreme centre'. This, he argues, now rules over large tracts of Europe and includes left, centre left, centre right and centre parties. This 'extreme centre' wages wars (on its own behalf or that of the United States), backs austerity measures (and where necessary imposes them) and defends widespread surveillance (ostensibly, as a defence against terrorism). Moreover, it neutralises any attempt to criticise—or even debate—these policies by claiming that 'there is no alternative': no alternative to wars in Iraq and Afghanistan; no alternative to cuts in public expenditure; no alternative to the covert monitoring of individuals and groups. Those with the temerity to question this claim are vilified as ideologues, fantasists or extremists.

This insistence on 'there is no alternative' has created a dangerous democratic deficit. Whole swathes of the electorate—young people in particular—see no point in voting in either local or general elections. This is partly because people no longer know where power lies, partly because they see very little to choose between the various political parties vying for office, and partly because they know they are disempowered. They neither feel that they are listened to nor trust the information that they are given. This feeling is not so much one of apathy—which is how it is so often described—as one of alienation: the sense of being excluded from all sources of power and influence. The danger under such circumstances is that people could—as they already have across large parts of Europe—shift very rapidly to the political right and embrace neo-fascist and explicitly fascist parties. That is the scale of the problem. Thinking matters—and matters *now*—because the spectre of 'thoughtlessness' yet again haunts us.

There is an urgent need for a remaking of the polity: a citizenry that can think across boundaries and cultural divides to new possibilities and emergent futures. These citizens of the future are already providing us with instances of enlarged mentality, boundless communication and care for the world. In doing so, they are also developing a new politics of participation and engagement. This emergent politics has found expression in a wide range of groupings, movements and networks: the *selmeyya*, *sebbab* and *shehuda* of the Egyptian Arab Spring; the *indignados* of Spain that inspired the worldwide Occupy movement; the locally based circles or assemblies of Spain's Podemos party; and the Greek 'Space for Dialogue for the Unity and Common Action of the Left' network that spawned the Syriza party. Such formations—notwithstanding their fluidity, extreme vulnerability and susceptibility to takeover—continue to expose the workings of 'inverted totalitarianism' and to challenge 'the extreme centre'.

Truly discursive

Universities may choose to ignore this emergent politics in the hope that it will go away. Or they may actively resist it through, for example, increased levels of surveillance, the continuing vetting of outside speakers and guest lecturers, and the further monitoring of course content. On the other hand, they can choose to provide spaces for thinking together about the collective problems that face us and the alternative futures that are open to us: spaces, that is, of enlarged mentality and boundless communication in which we learn—*together*—how to care for the world. So, how might universities set about that task? How might they create 'truly discursive' spaces: spaces in which, as Arendt puts it in the quotation that heads this chapter, thinking is able to run 'from place to place, from one part of the world to another, through all kinds of conflicting views'? (Arendt, 1977, 242).

One starting point would be to acknowledge the collective nature of the problems experienced within an increasingly globalised world. All the major problems we now face are collective problems—shared problems that can only be resolved collectively. Such problems are invariably both local and global. Waste, for example, confronts us on the doorstep and on the street as a 'litter' problem, but also presents a global problem in terms of how affluent nations manage the 'disposal' of their ever increasing effluence.[5] None of these collective problems can be understood—let alone addressed—through a single disciplinary or specialist lens. Nor can they be fully grasped by adopting a multidisciplinary approach whereby each discipline or specialism functions independently of the others. What is required is genuine transdisciplinary dialogue: ways of thinking across disciplinary divides and subject specialisms towards new forms of inter-connective enquiry. It is only through such transdisciplinary dialogue that the complex, collective problems we face can be fully—that is, collectively—addressed. Universities need to be at the forefront of developing the kinds of transdisciplinary frameworks and processes necessary for this collective endeavour.

They also need a renewed emphasis on the kinds of discursive practices that are indeterminate in their outcomes and require the careful balancing of divergent and sometimes diametrically opposed viewpoints. To think together in this way involves the kind of practical reasoning that Aristotle termed *phronesis*. Practical reasoning—or deliberation—cannot be reduced to a set of skills or competencies. It relies on dispositions or human qualities that can only be achieved through practice. We learn to think together—and converse together—through the activity of thinking and conversing together. This capacity to think across boundaries—to negotiate and persuade, to see things from the other's points of view, to understand the position from which one speaks—is indispensable in a world within which the local is rooted in the global and the global in the local. We need pedagogies that are grounded in the discursive, that allow for a wide diversity of discursive forums and that position learners not as unquestioning recipients of received knowledge but as questioning participants in their own learning. (See Nixon, 2012, for an elaboration of this line of argument.)

We also need pedagogies that enable the individual learner to gain a sense of her or his own vocation in life—the ethical direction of that life, its moral purpose and its unifying aspiration. Aristotle's term for this sense of purposefulness that can give unity to a human life was *telos*: the purpose that is implicit in—but always beyond—our prefigured ends. Unlike 'goals' or 'targets', purposes are articulated over time. Universities can provide the spaces in which the individual can begin to gain a clearer sense of the purpose—or moral trajectory—of her or his life. But in order to do so, they must focus not only on what has been achieved but on what might be achieved. Their task is to enable the learner to understand her or his own unique potential—the distinctive contribution that he or she might make in caring for the world. All education, notwithstanding its academic orientation, is vocational—not just in the sense of leading to a particular career pathway (although this is vitally important), but in the sense of knowing what we want to make of our lives.

Finally, we require pedagogies that speak to the particularity of the world we inhabit—a world characterised by what Ulrich Beck called (2006, 19) '*really existing cosmopolitanization*' (original emphasis). Cosmopolitanism, argued Beck, is not a conscious or voluntary choice of a particular value orientation, but 'a function of coerced choices or a side effect of unconscious decisions'. It is part of the human condition: an unavoidable 'fact of life'. We experience it at every level and in every context. That is why Kwame Anthony Appiah's (2005) notion of 'a tenable cosmopolitanism'—or 'rooted cosmopolitanism'—has such purchase: 'a cosmopolitanism with prospects must reconcile a kind of universalism with the legitimacy of at least some forms of partiality' (p. 223). A cosmopolitan outlook does not necessitate or even encourage an uprooting of affiliation and association from the partial to the universal, although it does necessarily involve shifts of perspective. 'Rooted cosmopolitanism' may be grounded in the particularities of local loyalty and community while branching out into the civic and flourishing within the broader interconnectivities of the global. There is a need for higher education practices that develop the cosmopolitan dispositions necessary for this rooting and flourishing: this recognition of the interdependency of the local and the global; this sense of the global-in-the-local and the local-in-the-global.

Conclusion

The past leaves us with more questions than answers. We cannot relive the past because the future is—and always has been—uncertain and unpredictable. To follow in the footsteps of Arendt and Jaspers is to acknowledge this uncertainty and unpredictability. Whatever similarities there may be between the 'classic totalitarianism' of the mid-20th century and the 'inverted totalitarianism' of the first quarter of the 21st century are of little significance compared with the radical differences between the world as experienced by Arendt, Jaspers and their contemporaries and the world we now inhabit. Nevertheless, they bequeathed us some of the vital resources necessary for understanding our 21st-century world and the seemingly insurmountable problems it presents. They are resources—I have argued—that we might draw on to imagine universities as civic spaces: spaces where we think together across disciplinary and specialist boundaries; where we think our way through collective problems to collective solutions; where we think about the shape and trajectory of our lives; and where our thinking is both globally inter-connective and deeply rooted in the particularities of affiliation and association.

Notes

1. That Heidegger nevertheless exerted a profound influence on Arendt is shown by the fact that in 1960 she wrote to him regarding the publication of her 1958 *The Human Condition* to say that '[i]f things had ever worked out properly between us … I would have asked you if I might dedicate it to you' (Ludz, 2004, 124). For a detailed study of Heidegger's influence on Arendt's political thinking, see Villa (1996).
2. I explore the lifelong friendship between Arendt and Jaspers in Chapter 5 of *Hannah Arendt and the Politics of Friendship*. (See Nixon, 2015, 85–107.)
3. Jaspers' attitude to Heidegger's Nazism differed markedly from that of Arendt. Although maintaining minimal contact with him, Jaspers remained highly critical of Heidegger. Arendt, on the other hand, sought his rehabilitation within the post-WWII academic community.
4. Arendt does not trace this line of argument back to its origins in Hegel. Axel Honneth (1995) very clearly does—and Paul Ricoeur (1992) in turn traces it back to Honneth.

5. Martha Nussbaum (2010, 80) includes the following in this category of collective problems: 'global warming; decent trade regulations; the protection of the environment and animal species; the future of nuclear energy and the dangers of nuclear weapons; the movement of labor and the establishment of decent labor standards; the protection of children from trafficking; sexual abuse and forced labor'.

References

Ali, T. (2015). *The Extreme Centre: A Warning*. London and Brooklyn: Verso

Appiah, K. A. (2005). *The Ethics of Identity*. Princeton: Princeton University Press

Arendt, H. (1970). *Men in Dark Times*. London: Jonathan Cape

Arendt, H. (1973). *The Origins of Totalitarianism*. New edition with added prefaces. San Diego, New York and London: Harcourt Brace and Company (Originally published in 1951)

Arendt, H. (1977). *Between Past and Future: Eight Exercises in Political Thought*. New York: Penguin Books (first published by Faber and Faber, 1961, and with additional material by Viking Press, 1968)

Arendt, H. (1978). *The Life of the Mind* (volumes I and II) San Diego, New York and London: Harcourt Inc.

Arendt, H. [1958] (1998). *The Human Condition*, 2nd edition. Chicago and London: The University of Chicago Press

Beck, U. (2006). *The Cosmopolitan Vision*. (trans. C. Cronin) Cambridge: Polity Press

Bonhoeffer, D. (2010). *Letters and Papers from Prison*. Dietrich Bonhoeffer Works, Volume 8 (trans I.Best, L.E. Dahill, R. Krauss and N. Lukes) Minneapolis: Fortress Press

Calhoun, C. (1994). Nationalism and civil society: democracy, diversity and self-determination, in C. Calhoun (ed) *Social Theory and the Politics of Identity*. Oxford, UK and Cambridge, MA: Blackwell, pp. 304–335

Gramsci, A. (1971). *Selections from the Prison Notebooks of Antonio Gramsci*. London: Lawrence and Wishart

Grossman, V. (2006). *Life and Fate* (trans. R. Chandler) London: Vintage Books. (Originally published in English in 1985)

Harding, N. (1992). The Marxist-Leninist detour, in J. Dunn (ed) *Democracy: The Unfinished Journey*, Oxford and New York: Oxford University Press, pp. 155–187

Havel, V. (1988). *Letters to Olga: June 1979-September 1982* (trans. P. Wilson) London: Faber and Faber

Honneth, A. (1995). *The Struggle for Recognition: the Moral Grammar of Social Conflicts* (trans. J. Anderson). Cambridge: Polity Press

Jaspers, K. (1994). *Basic Philosophical Writings* (ed. E. Erlich, L. H. Erlich and G. B. Pepper) Atlantic Heights, NJ: Humanities Press

Jaspers, K. (1953). *The Origins and Goal of History* (trans. M. Bullock) London: Routledge and Kegan Paul

Jaspers, K. (1969–1971). *Philosophy* (3 Volumes) (trans. E. B. Ashton) Chicago and London: University of Chicago Press

Kohler, L. and Saner, H. (eds.) (1992). *Hannah Arendt Karl Jaspers Correspondence 1926-1969* (trans. R. and R. Kimber) New York, San Diego, CA and London: Harcourt Jovanovich

Ludz, U. (ed) (2004). *Letters 1925-1975: Hannah Arendt and Martin Heidegger* (trans A. Shields) Orlando: Harcourt, Inc.

Luxemburg, R. (2004). The Junius pamphlet: the crisis in German social democracy, in Hudis, P. and Anderson, K. B. (eds) *The Rosa Luxemburg Reader*. New York: Monthly Review Press, pp. 312–341

Nixon, J. (2012). *Interpretive Pedagogies for Higher Education: Arendt, Berger, Said, Nussbaum and their Legacies*. London and New York: Bloomsbury

Nixon, J. (2015). *Hannah Arendt and the Politics of Friendship*. London and New York: Bloomsbury

Nussbaum, M. C. (2010). *Not for Profit: Why Democracy Needs the Humanities*. Princeton and Oxford: Princeton University Press

Ricoeur, P. (1992). *Oneself as Another* (trans. K. Blamey). Chicago and London: University of Chicago Press

Villa, D. (1996). *Arendt and Heidegger: the Fate of the Political*. Princeton: Princeton University Press

Wolin, S. S. (2010). *Democracy Incorporated: Managed Democracy and the Specter of Inverted Totalitarianism*. Princeton and Oxford: Princeton University Press

PART SEVEN

Possibilities

Introduction

There are now well over 25,000 universities in the world with the top 800 in the Times Higher Education World Ranking. From the mega open universities of India and Bangladesh with millions of students to small U.S. liberal arts colleges, the university is institutionally diverse as well as pervasive. The organizational form of the university has undergone rapid and continuing change since colonial times. Many of Europe's modern universities developed from medieval and early modern institutions increasing in number to some 200 in 1840. The number of universities worldwide increased spectacularly in the nineteenth century and exploded in number during the twentieth century, especially in the post-war period and after independence in former colonies. The university became a democratic institution of the modern state with the transition from elite to mass higher education beginning in the 1960s.

While the definition of the university varies across different countries, the form of the modern university has proved to be remarkably enduring. The *Humboldtisches Bildungsideal* developed by Humboldt with a group of reformers including Fichte and Scheleiermacher that founded the University of Berlin in 1810 was adopted in many parts of Europe and also in North America. While it was not the only model to emerge—the French model based on the *Grandes Écoles* and the residential nature of the Oxbridge model, for example, offered alternative forms, the Humboldtian university established itself as the classic form. The rise of the modern research university beginning in the nineteenth century in which teaching and research were combined in the search for truth was transformed after 1970 with the increasing realization that universities faced pressures of neoliberal globalization. One of the questions facing the university is whether the dominant model of the university—where teacher and research were combined, and universities pursued truth through independent and peer-reviewed disciplines under a form of autonomy from the state—can sustain itself. The democratization and era of global university expansion has already established a new vocationalism mixing liberal and vocational forms of education and detaching state-funded research from teaching, turning universities increasingly to fee-raising institutions responsible for self-funding of both teaching and research. This neoliberal alternative market model has distanced universities from social goods and its traditional welfare role of creating informed citizens and a cadre of leaders for the nation state. More and more the university recoils from its responsibilities within a democracy to emphasize its receptivity to world market competitive pressures for international students and for global rankings.

Starting from Bill Readings' work, Gary Rolfe discusses the idea of what he calls the "Paraversity" as "a subversive, virtual and barely visible community of dissensus that might exist alongside, and in parallel to, the corporate university" that involves a mission of undermining "the outcome-driven, target-based mission of the corporate university." The paraversity is more concerned with the social good and with "doing and being rather than with producing and acquiring". In short, the paraversity is process-oriented rather than a market institution that commodifies education.

In "The Platform University: The Destruction and Resurrection of Universities in the Auto-Industrial Age," Peter Murphy charts the transition from the mass postindustrial university to an auto-industrial institution where academic labor and professional activities are replaced through automation. Murphy predicts the automated industrial university will be platform-based and hi-tech. It will be smaller and more specialized focused on producing graduates for creative work and drawing on dispersed globally floating academics employed under different legal contracts. These auto-industrial universities will be cost-effective with streamlined bureaucracies.

Tom Bourner in his chapter writes of "The fully-functioning university" which emerges from three broad historical stages—medieval institutions, early modern institutions disengaged from the Church, and the development of the research-led university in Germany. In "every stage of its development the university has had the same three basic concerns: to provide for the higher education of students, to contribute to the advancement of knowledge, to benefit those beyond the walls of the university." Bourner examines this tripartite mission to argue for the full flowering of the fully-functioning university.

Rikke Toft Nørgård and Søren Smedegaard Ernst Bengtsen examine concepts of space and place to investigate "Academic citizenship beyond the campus." Taking their departure from Heidegger, they provide an ontological account of the meaning of a "placeful" university as a human construct that combines personal, academic, and societal value.

In "Do We Need an Academic Revolution to Create a Wiser World?" Nicholas Maxwell argues for the university as based on an approach to wisdom-inquiry, rather than knowledge inquiry, and discusses the necessary intellectual and institutional changes required to bring about such a revolution.

Michael A. Peters in his chapter discusses the Cosmopolitical University as a conception dating from Kant that can be described as a return to an earlier time—a revival of a line of development internal to the German research university—and the Postcolonial renewal of the university that represents an acknowledgment of the university as an institution figure large in colonialism. The Postcolonial University, then, originates outside the university tradition and functions not only as a correction to orientalism but also the retrieval and development of indigenous knowledges.

In the final chapter, Ronald Barnett writes of "The ecological university," as he argues "a university whose time has come." In a prophetic, farseeing and revelatory style, Barnett analyzes the conditions of the ecological university dedicated to a commitment and responsibility for all living things and their supporting ecosystems. His call, beyond sustainability, rests on identifying seven ecosystems of the university: the physical environment, social institutions, the economy, knowledge, culture, learning and human subjectivity that constitute an ecosophy of the university.

Michael A. Peters

CHAPTER TWENTY-FOUR

The Idea(l) of a Paraversity

GARY ROLFE

Introduction

There has been increasing recognition in both the academic and the popular UK press during the past decade that the university as an institution is undergoing profound changes, largely brought about by alterations in funding mechanisms and vastly increased student numbers.[1] Whilst some social commentators have welcomed these changes, a growing number of academics have complained that the university is in decline. Although many of these dissenters have produced long lists of what is wrong with the twenty-first century university, there have been few attempts to offer practical solutions.

Many of the complaints concern the shifting focus of academic priorities towards a corporate business ethos, resulting in a decline in academic standards. Some have argued that our universities are becoming little more than technical colleges in which the humanities and other non-vocational areas of study are being edged out, whilst others believe that the introduction of student fees has shifted the balance of power too far in favour of satisfying the 'customer'. Perhaps surprisingly, academics appear no longer to have very much influence over such matters, with Stefan Collini (2012) noting that their 'compelling and often devastating criticisms' have had no effect and have simply been ignored by policy makers. In the face of such powerlessness, responses to these changes include passive acquiescence, militant rhetoric and romantic nostalgia.

This chapter argues for a somewhat different response to the growing corporatization of the university, particularly in the UK. Drawing extensively on Bill Readings' book *The University in Ruins* (Readings 1996), I suggest that whilst we might have little influence over *what* we are compelled to do in the university, we still retain some control over *how* we go about it. Starting from Readings' injunction to 'dwell in the ruins' of the university, I outline a vision for what I refer to as the *Paraversity*, which I describe as a subversive, virtual and barely visible community of dissensus that might exist alongside, and in parallel to, the corporate university. The mission of the Paraversity is not to overthrow the corporate university, but neither should it be merely to add to the growing literature demanding that something must be done. Rather, it is a mission of active subversion, and in particular, of undermining the outcome-driven, target-based mission of the corporate university through the reintroduction of values and a focus on the means of education and research as more important than the ends.

The ruined university

It is generally agreed that the idea of the modern Enlightenment university has its origins in the founding of the University of Berlin in the early years of the nineteenth century, based on Friedrich Wilhelm von Humboldt's utopian vision to 'lay open the whole body of learning and expound both the principles and foundations of all knowledge' (Humboldt 1970). There is also widespread agreement that, two centuries later, the university is not what it used to be. In fact, there is evidence to suggest that the university has *never* been what it used to be. John Henry Newman, writing less than fifty years after the founding of the University of Berlin, was critical of this vision of the modern university which 'extracted of its members an acquaintance with every science under the sun' and which 'gave its degrees to any person who passed an examination'. For Newman (1992), the fundamental idea of the liberal university was that education should be an end in itself rather than a means to a practical or vocational outcome.

Gradually, however, the function of the university as producing a workforce trained to meet the increasingly technical needs of industrial society replaced the ideal of education for its own sake, leading Michael Oakeshott to observe in 1950 that 'Somehow or another the idea of a University in recent years has got mixed up with notions such as "higher education", "advanced training", "refresher courses for adults"—things admirable in themselves, but really very little to do with a university' (Oakeshott 2001). Newman's fear that universities would end up awarding degrees in any and every subject demanded by employers and their workforce to more or less anyone prepared to pay for them has finally come to pass, and arguably the only detail he got wrong was the need in all cases to pass an examination. And whilst the policy to open up our universities to all and sundry has been welcomed in some quarters as a move towards equal opportunities and greater democratization, critics suggest that it inevitably leads to lower standards and a corruption of the Enlightenment ideal of a broad liberal education.

Bill Readings (1996), echoing Oakeshott's sentiments, claimed that the university is in ruins. His concern was not only with the demands made on the university by a market-driven economy, but with the ways that those demands were being met. He noted that the modern university has become a corporate business organization in which important educational decisions are made by non-academic administrators, and in which students are customers and academics are encouraged to become entrepreneurs who sell their academic skills to the highest bidders.

Whether or not the university is thought to be ruined depends to a large extent on what it is considered to be *for*. If it is viewed as a corporate business which is forced to pay its way in a market economy, the university as an institution is more than holding its own and might even be said to be thriving. There is certainly no shortage of applicants, with few other businesses being in the fortunate position of having to turn customers away. And whilst there is fierce competition between universities, even those at the very bottom of the performance league tables are managing to meet their recruitment quotas. The university has therefore risen to the challenges and demands of late twentieth-century capitalist society to secure its position in a difficult financial climate where diminishing state investment has to be justified in terms of tangible output.

For Oakeshott (2001), however, the very fact of having to justify itself in this way at all is the beginning and the end of the problem since, in his words, 'a university is not a machine for achieving a particular purpose or producing a particular result; it is a manner of human activity'. At the moment when the purpose of the university changes from *being* or *doing* to *producing*, it is no longer a university. Thus:

> A university will have ceased to exist when its learning has denigrated into what is now called research, when its teaching has become mere instruction and occupies the whole of an undergraduate's time, and when those who come to be taught come, not in search of their intellectual fortune but with a vitality so unroused or so exhausted that they ... desire only a qualification for earning a living or a certificate to let them in on the exploitation of the world. (p. 117)

Somewhat ironically, Oakeshott's worst fears about the fate of the university have become its major selling points. Research is considered to be the primary function of the modern university and the yardstick against which academics are judged, teaching methods are becoming more technological and require less and less human contact, and vocationally oriented qualifications leading to highly paid jobs are the main attraction for potential students.

As the mission of the university becomes ever more concerned with production, attention is increasingly focussed on the smooth administration and measurement of its output. In the case of research, the product is the 'findings' paper and the unit of measurement is the impact factor of the peer-reviewed journal in which it is published, along with other more sophisticated metrics such as Eigenfactor scores and h-indices. As a consequence, the assessment of the 'quality' of the research output of university departments and individual researchers has become largely a matter of counting and accountancy, and growing numbers of administrators are being employed in order to facilitate the most cost-efficient translation of research grants into scores on the various measures and a high position in the league tables of research 'excellence'. Researchers are no longer called upon to account for their work according to academic criteria, but in terms of the numerical scores that their publications achieve. As Readings puts it, there has been a shift in the academy from accountability to accountancy, from qualitative academic judgement to a quantitative totting-up process.

High scores are not just indicators of research excellence, but also have a cash value in terms of attracting further grants for the institution and higher salaries for the individual researcher. Thus, the purpose of winning grants is less and less concerned with making a contribution to knowledge and practice through research and more and more with (quite literally) point scoring over colleagues and other universities. The cost to the individual, however, is that many researchers spend more time writing unsuccessful grant proposals, often for projects which they have no particular interest in or commitment to, than actually doing research. When they are successful in winning a bid, they are no longer intimately involved in all stages of the research project, but more often find themselves on a research production line as a specialized member of a large team, concerned with only a single element of the process such as the literature review or data analysis. Furthermore, their co-researchers are often regarded less as colleagues than as competitors.

In the case of the teaching role of the university, there has been a significant shift in recent years from the provision of education to the production of graduates. There are a number of reasons for this. The UK government is attempting to justify rises in student fees by placing greater emphasis on the student as a customer who is investing time and money in order to reap a financial benefit later in life.

As customers and investors, many of these students are seeking to purchase something more tangible than an education; what they want in exchange for their fees is a degree certificate that can be cashed in for a good job and a high salary. At a time when universities are quite literally being called to account for the public and consumer investment in them, education as an output is regarded as intangible, of limited exchange value and largely unmeasurable. In contrast, graduates can easily be counted and the numbers of 'good' degrees awarded by each university can be compared and ranked. This places students in a somewhat confusing position of being both the customer and the product of the university, and this ambivalent status is reflected in the ways that the 'quality' of the educational output is quantified.

In their role as *customers*, the experiences and levels of satisfaction of the students are sought through various polls and surveys, with the findings being used to rank universities, departments and, increasingly, individual members of staff. From the perspective of students as *products* of the university system, the quality of the teaching intervention is measured, as previously mentioned, in terms of attrition rates, proportions of good degrees awarded and the numbers of students gaining employment following graduation. The role of the teacher has therefore altered significantly in recent years to reflect these new priorities, and is now concerned with administering the student through the course as smoothly as possible towards a 'satisfactory' outcome for all concerned; that is, a 'good' degree for the student, a high satisfaction rating for the lecturer and an elevated position in the league tables for the university. In the jargon of the corporate business culture, keeping the customer satisfied is a 'win-win situation' for all concerned.

Some academics, particularly those younger ones who were themselves educated in the corporate university, have seen their careers thrive under this system and can presumably see little or no problem with it. Others, however, hark back to a golden age before the university was 'ruined' by the demands of commerce and industry. Readings refers to this attitude as romantic nostalgia, admitting that 'I am still inclined to introduce sentences that begin "In a *real* University …" into discussions with my colleagues, even though they know, and I know that they know, that no such institution has ever existed'.

Other academics adopt a stance of 'militant radicalism' against the corporate university, which Readings considers to be both inauthentic and futile. It is inauthentic because, for those who adopt it, it is a way of justifying and maintaining their place in the university by attempting to overthrow the very institution that defines and sustains them. And it is in any case futile because, as Readings points out, the university administrators will simply present any radicalism and rebellion as a selling point in order to attract a particular kind of student. The most common response to the ruination of the university, however, is simply to acquiesce and submit to the inevitability of a market-driven education system in which the customer is always right, even if it means awarding degrees in subjects such as brewing and distilling, ethical computer hacking, applied golf management or baking technology.[2]

For Readings, then, the university is in ruins, and for those of us who are dissatisfied with the status quo, neither the romantic nostalgic response of venerating those ruins as the *real* university nor the radical modernist response of sweeping them away or building over them will do. Rather, Readings tells us that we must adopt an 'institutional pragmatism'; like the inhabitants of some Italian city, we must simply 'dwell in the ruins', seeking 'neither to rebuild the Renaissance city-state nor to destroy its remnants and install rationally planned tower-blocks'. Readings advocates this as a positive response to the corporate values of the university, but he leaves us puzzling over quite what it means to 'dwell in the ruins' and how this might be achieved when those around us fail even to acknowledge that the modern corporate university *is* a ruin and continue to act as if it is a fully functional educational institution rather than, as its critics claim, a factory for producing graduates and research papers.

Readings does at least offer a partial and tentative way forward in his suggestion that we must build a 'community of dissensus' in which 'thought goes on alongside other thoughts, we think beside each other'. Thought must be regarded as a 'pure' activity, one that is undertaken as an end in itself rather than as a means of production. Thus, 'Thought does not function as an answer but as a *question*'. Unlike the corporate university, where the requirement to produce an outcome requires a consensus on what the product is and how it can best be manufactured, the production of thought is not tied to a common goal, it is not directed towards answering particular research questions or writing agreed-upon learning outcomes. Thus, when Readings advocates a community of dissensus, it should not be understood in negative terms as the opposite of a community of *consensus*, nor is it simply an outlet for the expression of dissent. To practice dissensus is to abandon the need and desire to arrive at a shared conclusion and to regard the purpose of thought (that is to say, the purpose of the university) as the generation and opening up of questions rather than the production of answers.

Towards the Paraversity

In the absence of any clear practical description of what such a community of thought might look like or how it might be brought into existence, I have elsewhere proposed the idea of the Paraversity (Rolfe 2013), which I describe as a subversive, virtual and barely visible community of dissensus that might exist alongside, and in parallel to, the corporate university. The Paraversity is both an idea and an ideal; a *utopia* (from the Greek—no such place) in the literal sense of the word, since it requires no physical presence, no buildings and no established faculty. However, if the idea(l) of the Paraversity is to develop beyond a utopian vision, it must present itself as a *practical utopia*, grounded in the economic and political realities of twenty-first-century higher education.

The Paraversity is therefore not intended as a radical *replacement* for the corporate university. Indeed, the Paraversity could not survive independently within a capitalist market economy where, as Readings tells us, 'Thought is non-productive labor, and hence does not show up on balance sheets except as waste'. Equally, however, the corporate university will not survive for much longer *as a university* without the Paraversity and its commitment to the non-productive labour of thought. The relationship between the corporate university and the Paraversity is therefore quite literally symbiotic, each living off and sustaining the other.

With no realistic prospect of overthrowing the corporate university, the only alternative is to subvert it, literally to change its direction or influence it from below. To subvert is not to destroy, it is not a revolutionary call to bring down the system; it is not, as Readings puts it, a cynical demand for the abolition of the university as a way of defining and maintaining our place in it. It is not an attempt to sweep away the old and build something new in its place, but simply a productive and authentic attempt to dwell in the ruins, as Readings puts it, 'without alibis'. To subvert the corporate university is, quietly but surely, to bend its trajectory away from production and back to process, away from quantity and back to quality, away from accountancy and back to accountability. Subversion can only happen from within; it can only be practised alongside and in parallel to our contracted employment and this, as we shall see, is no easy matter.

The university without discipline(s)

The idea of the Paraversity, then, is the ideal of a subversive community of thought running in parallel with the corporate university, populated by academics with a foot in each camp. However, subverting the idea of a university as a factory for the production of information, knowledge, research findings, publications, graduates and, ultimately, hard cash, towards the ideal of a community of thinkers who agree only that there is no need to agree, necessarily entails a rethinking of the idea of community in terms of how it is both conceived and structured. Readings points out that, currently, the university community is built around academic disciplines and founded on the myth of 'communicative transparency'.

A discipline is thus a community which shares and communicates a set of common goals and a common agreement on the methods for achieving them, as well as a mechanism for policing its boundaries in order to exclude goals, methods and academics that are considered to fall outside the discipline. It is, according to Readings, 'a community whose dialogue is about nothing, in the sense that no issues for dispute are engaged. There are no differends [a term which he borrows from Lyotard], no radical and incommensurable differences, only arguments as to the exact nature of what it is that we agree on'. Any attempt to subvert the idea of the corporate university by reconfiguring the disciplines will therefore have only a superficial effect, as will the move to bring about greater unity through interdisciplinarity.

For Readings, the loosening of disciplinary structures should not be done in order to create *new* disciplines, nor even to encourage more communication *between* disciplines, but is rather an opportunity to call permanently into question the very notion of disciplinarity. Thus, 'instead of a new interdisciplinary space that will once and for all reunify the University, I have attempted to propose a shifting disciplinary structure that holds open the question of whether and how thoughts fit together'. The Paraversity, then, is neither interdisciplinary nor transdisciplinary; rather, it is *adisciplinary* in both senses of the word, and requires a structure that disregards the disciplinary boundaries of the corporate university along with the disciplinary practices through which those boundaries are traditionally enforced.

The organizational and managerial structure of the corporate university can be imagined as a tree, with a central administrative trunk to which are attached the large boughs of the various faculties or colleges, the smaller branches of departments and schools, the twigs of individual academics and the buds and leaves of students. The trunk provides a firm and rigid structure to a managerial hierarchy and regulates communication between boughs and branches, buds and leaves. Deleuze and Guattari (1987) contrast this 'arborescent' structure with the rhizome, which is a botanical term for a root system that spreads horizontally beneath the ground by sending out roots and shoots from its nodes. Rhizomatic organizations are therefore underground systems, connecting and intermeshing unseen and unbeknownst to those living and working on the surface.

Rhizomatic structures cannot be externally imposed on an organization since 'any point … can be connected to anything other, *and must be*' (Deleuze and Guattari 1987, my emphasis). Rhizomes are therefore self-organizing and heterogeneous, and develop in unplanned and unforeseen ways. The imperative of a rhizomatic organization is simply to connect in as many ways as possible, to form alliances across disciplines and specialisms. The image of the rhizome illustrates perfectly the way that the Paraversity structures itself. Unlike the arborescent university, there is no central trunk, no command system and no preconfigured lines of communication: 'the rhizome is an acentred, nonhierarchical, nonsignifying system without a General and without an organizing memory or central automation, defined solely by a circulation of states' (Deleuze and Guattari 1987).

Deleuze and Guattari further suggest that different organizational arrangements encourage different linguistic structures and different ways of thinking. Thus, hierarchical treelike organizational structures necessarily produce treelike or arborescent thinking in which channels of communication are pre-established and tightly regulated and where traditional lines of thought result in traditional and predictable outcomes and solutions. Arborescent thinking produces only 'tracings' of what has gone before. As Deleuze and Guattari explain: 'The tree imposes the verb "to be," but the fabric of the rhizome is the conjunction, "and ... and ... and ..."'.

Whereas arborescent thinkers tend to favour denotative and authoritative language games (A *is* B, C *is* the correct answer, D *is* the right thing to do), rhizomatic thinkers 'know how to move between things, establish a logic of the AND, overthrow ontology, do away with foundations, nullify endings and beginnings. They know how to practice pragmatics'. Rhizomatic thinking produces maps rather than tracings, and maps are oriented towards the future, towards what Deleuze and Guattari term 'an experiment in contact with the real'. This vision of a way of thinking that considers A *and* B (*and* C *and* D *and* ...) to be a more fruitful approach to research and scholarship than A *is* B resonates with Readings' call for an institutional pragmatism and a community of dissensus which seeks to keep questions alive rather than closing them down with definitive 'correct' answers.

The Paraversity can therefore be imagined as a rhizomatic organization, that is, a network of scholars without hierarchies and without 'Generals', in which individual thinkers are free to connect with any and all other individuals to form temporary or semi-permanent 'assemblages' (Deleuze and Guattari 1987) for specific purposes. Deleuze and Guattari refer to the individual nodes of the rhizome as 'little machines' to emphasize the fact that we should look for function rather than meaning in the workings of rhizomatic organizations.

The metaphor of the 'little machine' offers a useful and powerful image for how to behave in the Paraversity. Rather than cogs in the large corporate university machine, it is more productive to act as far as possible as individual little machines, each connecting freely to other little machines as appropriate for specific purposes, characterized not by what we do but by the manner in which we do it. Deleuze and Guattari tell us that little machines (people, books, scientific apparatus, and so on) are defined by which other little machines they reach out and form assemblages with rather than by any essential features (A *and* B rather than A *is* B). If I form an assemblage with books and scientific apparatus, I temporarily become a little research machine; if I form an assemblage with one or more students, I become a little teaching and learning machine. Because the Paraversity allows and encourages me to form assemblages with each and every other little machine, I am not bound to the trunk of the arborescent university but can jump freely between boughs, branches, twigs and leaves.

The fourth mission

I have suggested that members of the Paraversity must, out of necessity, pursue parallel academic pathways. On the one hand, we must practise what Readings called institutional pragmatism. It is unrealistic and untenable to attempt to overthrow the corporate mission of the university; we are paid employees with a contractual obligation to publish papers and produce graduates and we must, of course, continue to do so. But we must do so subversively, that is to say, by attempting to undermine the values and practices of the corporate university from within; to bend them as far as we are able without breaking them. As Gros (2014) observes, 'subversion is not a matter of opposing but of evading, deflecting, altering with exaggeration …'.

If I wish to subvert the mission of the corporate university, it is important to begin with a clear understanding of what that mission is and what purpose it serves. When American universities first began to publish their mission statements in the 1930s, they were broad and lofty expressions of social and educational aspirations and expectations. As the practice spread to Canada, the UK and the rest of the world in the ensuing decades, it met with growing opposition from the academic community. Writing in 1950, Michael Oakeshott complained:

> it would be necessary for a university to advertise itself as pursuing a particular purpose only if it were talking to people so ignorant that they had to be spoken to in baby language, or if it were so little confident of its power to embrace those who came to it that it had to call attention to incidental charms. (Oakeshott 2001, p. 106)

The promotion by the university of its 'incidental charms' and extramural attractions has grown considerably in the intervening sixty years, with Stefan Collini recently likening the university mission statement to 'an advertising brochure for an upmarket health club' (Collini 2012).

Scott (2006) points out that 'today's mission statements are often based on the triad (twentieth-century) mission of the university: teaching, research and public service'. I suggested earlier that when operationalized for the twenty-first-century corporate university, the teaching mission can be stated as scoring highly on student satisfaction surveys, employability and other metrics, and the research mission is concerned with maximizing grant income and publications in 'high impact' journals (and, in countries where it is relevant, scoring highly on government-initiated research assessment exercises). The roots of the so-called 'third mission' of public service can be traced back to both the French and German universities of the early nineteenth century, and tends to be interpreted differently in countries across the world. In the UK in the twenty-first century, the third mission has often been cynically distorted into an opportunity for making as much money as possible from industry and businesses through entrepreneurship and 'knowledge exploitation'.

The extent to which mission statements are being increasingly corporatized in this way can be seen in the example of my own university. In 1993, its teaching mission was stated simply as 'to provide ... all branches of a liberal education' (cited in Maskell and Robinson 2001, p. ii). In its *Strategic Plan 2009–14*, this was rewritten as to 'deliver an outstanding student experience, with teaching of the highest quality that produces graduates equipped for distinguished personal and professional achievement'. Of course, few universities aspire any longer to providing a broad liberal education; the focus nowadays is narrow and vocational. However, what is most notable about the above mission statement is firstly that there is no mention of education whatsoever, nor indeed of learning, and secondly that it is written in the language of business and industry, with an emphasis on *delivering* an experience and *producing* graduates[3].

The research mission of my university, as with many others, has refocused the expectations on academics from *being* researchers to *producing* outputs, and when I hear the word 'research' spoken in academic settings nowadays, it is almost always being used as a noun rather than a verb. Stefan Collini tells an amusing story to illustrate what is now the rather outdated view that research is something that we do rather than something we produce. He recounts how, when a newly appointed vice chancellor at his university wanted to come and see him at work, he asked himself just what 'carrying on with my research' might mean:

> Should I be correcting the proofs of my latest publication, or be discussing my exciting new 'findings' with one of my colleagues, or be on the point of filling in a large grant application? Finally, I realised that if I was supposed to represent 'research in the humanities' it was clear what I ought to be doing: I ought to be sitting alone reading a book. (Collini 2012, p. 147)

Although Collini was writing specifically about the humanities, the argument for a return to research as an intellectual activity of learning and discovery rather than a formulaic means for the production of information is just as relevant to engineering and the pure sciences. Indeed, the idea that reading the published work of others can inspire new ideas and new knowledge is increasingly considered to be an anachronism for the very simple reason that ideas and knowledge have been replaced by information as the currency of the research community. Whereas the purpose of research was once concerned with learning, it is now to produce and disseminate information and data, and reading books therefore has little or no role to play in the research mission of the corporate university. And as Oakeshott (2001) pointed out, 'a university will have ceased to exist when its learning has denigrated into what is now called research'.

If the teaching and research missions of the university have changed significantly during the past half-century, the 'third mission' of public service is now all but unrecognizable. The Robbins Report into higher education in the UK, published in 1963, identified one of the roles of the university as 'the transmission of a common culture and common standards of citizenship', such that 'Universities and colleges have an important role to play in the general cultural life of the communities in which they are situated' (Robbins 1963).

By the 1990s, talk of the cultural benefits to the community had been replaced by economic ones, and the UK government was promoting universities as 'dynamos of growth' and 'major agents of economic growth' (Department of Trade and Industry 2000), with the White Paper *The Future of Higher Education* urging two-way partnerships with local businesses (Department for Education and Skills 2003). As Roper (2005) observed, 'the third mission has evolved from serving the community, to extending and reaching out to it, to engaging it in bi-directional relationships and interactions', with my own university echoing government rhetoric by stating in 2009 that its mission was to be 'a powerhouse for growth in the regional economy'.

The wording of my university's corporate mission was modified slightly when the last strategic plan was updated in 2014. As noted above, the word 'education' has been inserted and 'powerhouse for growth' has been removed, along with one or two other issues which I highlighted in my previous critique of its mission statement (Rolfe 2013). Whilst it is to be hoped that these changes are more than merely cosmetic, if I wish more fundamentally to influence this corporate mission, it is not enough simply to campaign for a change in the wording; to subvert the mission is not to rewrite it but to counter it through my actions.

I have suggested that my membership of the Paraversity is defined not by *what* I do but by *how* I do it and, more importantly, by my way of *being* in the university. Oakeshott (2001) suggests that 'the distinctive mark of a university [is] a place where [the student] has the opportunity of education *in conversation* with his teachers, his fellows and himself'. If research and teaching are each concerned with the scholarly pursuit of learning, then the mission of the Paraversity is not with student satisfaction, producing graduates, research inputs and outputs and growing the economy, but quite simply with what Oakeshott refers to as developing 'the manners of conversation' in order that we might learn together.

With this in mind, I will conclude this chapter by outlining a fourth mission, the mission of the Paraversity, which is concerned with establishing a foundation of values and relationships which constitute the 'manners of conversation' necessary to construct a community of dissensus amidst the ruins of the old Enlightenment university. The fourth mission, then, is quite simply the mission to undermine and subvert the other three. As I have pointed out above, the purpose of subversion is not to destroy the university mission but rather to shift its focus away from production and back to process. In any case, I cannot simply ignore the missions of teaching, research and service, but neither would I wish to. What I can do, however, is to add *value* to them by adding *values*, to add *quality* by challenging the pursuit of *quantity*, and to install academic *accountability* as the main criterion by which my work is judged by rejecting economic *accountancy*.

The fourth mission can be conveniently divided into three somewhat notional categories which suggest how I might *be* in the university rather than what I *produce*; how I might conduct myself in relation to the institution in which I am employed, to my colleagues, and to the discipline and practice of scholarship. It is, in other words, a rough guide to academic manners.

Be good

The first and possibly the most subversive act is simply to *be good* in every sense of the word. Being good in this context is concerned with knowing how to behave at the institutional level, with doing the right thing rather than doing the corporate thing. It is an invitation to practice values-based scholarship, that is, scholarship based on a belief in the intrinsic values of teaching, research and service, and to value the processes and products of academic work against criteria of quality rather than quantity. Clearly, I cannot completely ignore the outcome-driven agenda of the corporate university and I must still meet my largely quantitative and financial contractual obligations, even if only to a limited extent, but I can nevertheless do so with integrity and on my own terms.

For example, I can separate the ends of my corporate obligations from the means by which those ends are achieved. I can satisfy my university's demand for grant income by applying only for small grants for action research and collaborative enquiries with a clear and practical outcome in a local setting; by only conducting studies that have personal meaning for me, which have a sound ethical basis, and which are small enough for all those involved to feel fully involved in the work. I can satisfy my university's demand for outputs by publishing my work in journals where it is likely to be read by practitioners and others beyond the narrow bounds of the academic community who are likely to act on the findings rather than merely cite them in their own papers. I can satisfy my university's demand for higher degree classifications and 'satisfied' students by attempting to engage them in meaningful educational experiences rather than by spoon-feeding them facts and teaching only what is required to pass the course assignments.

In each of these examples, I am doing what I need in order to address the outcomes of the corporate university, but attempting to subvert the process by striving to incorporate values, quality and accountability into my academic practice. A more extreme subversive strategy would be to reject both the means *and* the ends of the corporate university in favour of pursuing my own agenda. In my own case, rather than apply for grants to carry out funded research projects, I work directly with healthcare practitioners in the 'real world' outside the university by helping them to research their own practice and publish their own findings.

Similar partnerships and working practices have been developed across a wide range of academic disciplines, including the arts, the professions, industry and commerce. For example, action research originated in industrial settings and continues to be deployed in factories, schools, hospitals and other workplaces. More recently, so-called 'Mode 2 knowledge production' (Gibbons et al., 1994) shifted the primary location for scientific discovery out of the university laboratory and into the workplace. Mode 2 knowledge production has profound implications for the corporate university, since it distributes the production and ownership of knowledge and information across a broad range of participants in the research process beyond university academics. In each of these cases, the academic members of the research teams are arguably driven more by the desire to 'be good' than to meet the corporate goals set for them by their universities.

However, the practice of being good in the sense of introducing values and quality back into academic practice entails that we are also good in the performative sense. The simplest and easiest way of meeting the corporate ends of the university is to address those ends directly; for example, the easiest way of maximizing the pass-rate for an assignment is to coach the students through it by providing them with the relevant information and requiring them to spend their time writing practice answers. Meeting these corporate ends through educational means rather than by coaching is more difficult and demands extra effort and a greater ability to teach. Furthermore, if we work towards our own ends rather than those of the university, as in the above examples, we must meet them to an exceptionally high standard if we are to satisfy our managers. Being good in the moral and professional sense therefore requires that we are also very good at what we do.

Be collegiate

Bill Readings observed twenty years ago that 'Anyone who has spent any time at all in a University knows that it is not a model community, that few communities are more petty or vicious than University faculties' (Readings 1996). Recent changes to the mission of the corporate university have served to intensify an already competitive environment, with the metrics employed to measure the outputs of individual academics fostering a combative element which has resulted in regular disputes between academic 'colleagues' about whose names will appear on research papers, the order in which they will appear, who 'owns' the papers for assessment purposes and who should be named as principal investigator on research bids.

In addition to this jostling for position in the research hierarchy, the corporate management structure of the university has opened up other areas for competition. Administrative roles, many of which were formerly considered by academics to be somewhat onerous distractions from their real work of teaching and research, and which colleagues took in turns for fixed periods as a way of serving the department and the university, are increasingly presented as alternative career pathways and are subsequently hotly contested. Furthermore, academics are also coming into conflict with career administrators who, as Readings points out, are increasingly assuming areas of responsibility and making important decisions previously taken by academics.

This is not simply an issue of power, since many of the metrics against which my 'performance' as an academic is measured are now completely outside my sphere of influence and rely on decisions made by professional administrators with little or no academic training or experience. Furthermore, the master–apprentice relationship between academics and students has been distorted by the market into a purchaser–provider contract in which money is exchanged for goods and services. As a result, teaching is now regarded by some academics as something to be avoided, and student contact is seen as a distraction from the 'real' work of research rather than as a collegial practice of learning together.

A return to true collegiality is therefore an important element in the subversion of the corporate mission. It is, of course, impossible to dismantle the existing managerial and administrative hierarchy, but we can nevertheless undermine it by building an underground rhizomatic network which recognizes our status as individual little machines rather than merely cogs in the large corporate machine.

We must 'decentre' our hierarchical relationships with fellow academics, administrators, managers and students, and learn to think together rather than imposing and being imposed upon through existing arborescent power structures.

Be radical

The word 'radical' has two quite distinct meanings, both of which are important for the Paraversity. The original meaning, which is reflected in the Latin *radix*, invites us to look to our roots, to rethink and reconsider what it means to be an academic. However, the more populist usage of the word is to describe a significant and innovative departure from the usual or traditional. We must consider, therefore, how we might, at the same time, instigate an innovative departure from tradition whilst remaining true to our roots in the Enlightenment university. This is the conundrum which faces us in the Paraversity, and which is summarized by Readings' instruction to 'dwell in the ruins'.

There is no simple answer to this question, and it is the responsibility of each of us to find our own way, bearing in mind that those of us who are dissatisfied with the mission of the corporate university probably did not originally decide to become academics in order to spend our time coaching students through exams, writing endless and often unsuccessful grant applications, engaging in 'knowledge exploitation' and helping our universities to become 'powerhouses for growth'.

Conclusion

There can be little doubt that the idea of what a university is and what it is for has changed significantly over the past two or three decades. The advocates of these changes point to the benefits of a greater engagement with the world of commerce and industry beyond the ivory tower, along with the provision of access to higher education for a far greater proportion of the population than previously. However, whilst critics broadly welcome these moves, they point out that the benefits come at a cost. The university has, partly out of necessity, become corporatized; in Readings' words 'the University is not just *like* a corporation; it *is* a corporation. Students … are not *like* customers; they *are* customers' (Readings 1996). Whilst this shift has significantly affected what the university does, the most profound effects have been on the way that it goes about doing it. In a nutshell, the mission of the university has shifted from process to product; the university has changed from being a place where things *happen* to a place where things are *produced*.

I believe that there is little that can realistically be done to reverse this trend. In Lyotard's words, we must produce or disappear. However, it is still possible to have some small influence over what we produce and a greater influence over how we produce it. For those of us who cannot, in all good faith, continue as cogs in the university machine, our best hope is to find a way to dwell in the ruins of what the university has become. I have suggested in this chapter that we can most effectively do this by subverting the corporate mission of production and accountancy with a 'fourth mission' based on the intrinsic value and values of education as a way of learning together. Michael Oakeshott, writing in the 1950s, claimed that:

> Education is not acquiring a stock of ready-made ideas, images, sentiments, beliefs and so forth; it is learning to look, to listen, to think, to feel, to imagine, to believe, to understand, to choose and to wish. (Oakeshott 2001)

Education is concerned with doing and being rather than with producing and acquiring; it is a process rather than a product. It cannot be commoditized and it cannot be measured or counted. Whatever it is that the corporate university thinks it is engaged in manufacturing and selling, it is not education. The university is being ruined, but there is still an opportunity for those who care about education to do something about it.

Notes

1. Although written from a UK perspective, I believe that this chapter speaks to similar issues in universities across the world.
2. These are all examples of actual degrees currently offered by UK universities.
3. Since first drawing attention to this in my book *The University in Dissent* (Rolfe 2013), my university has slightly changed the wording of its teaching mission to include the word 'education'. It has also omitted the words 'powerhouse for growth' from its 'third mission' (see below).

References

Collini, S. (2012). *What Are Universities For?* Penguin Books, London

Deleuze, G. and Guattari, F. (1987). *A Thousand Plateaus.* University of Minnesota Press, Minneapolis

Department for Education and Skills. (2003). *The Future of Higher Education: Creating Opportunity, Releasing Potential, Achieving Excellence.* The Stationery Office, London

Department of Trade and Industry. (2000). *Excellence and Opportunity: A Science and Innovation Policy for the 21st Century*. Office of Science and Technology, London

Gibbons, M., Limoges, C., Nowotny, H., Schwartzman, S., Scott, P., and Trow, M. (1994). *The New Production of Knowledge: The Dynamics of Science and Research in Contemporary Societies*. Sage, London

Gros, F. (2014). *A Philosophy of Walking*. Verso, London

Humboldt, F. W. von (1970). 'On the Spirit and Organizational Framework of Intellectual Institutions in Berlin'. *Minerva*, 8, 242–67

Maskell, D. and Robinson, I. (2001). *The New Idea of a University*. Haven Books, London

Newman, J. H. (1992). *The Idea of a University*. University of Notre-Dame Press, Indiana

Oakeshott, M. (2001). *The Voice of Liberal Learning*, Liberty Fund, Indianapolis

Readings, B. (1996). *The University in Ruins*. Harvard University Press, Cambridge, MA

Robbins, Lord (1963). *Higher Education: Report of the Committee Appointed by the Prime Minister under the Chairmanship of Lord Robbins*. HMSO, London

Rolfe, G. (2013). *The University in Dissent*. Routledge, London

Roper, C. D. (2005). *Extension, Outreach, Knowledge Transfer, Technology Transfer: What Is It that We Do—Officially?* http://www.leadershipeducators.org/Resources/Documents/Conferences/Wilmington/roper.pdf

Scott, J. (2006). 'The Mission of the University: Medieval to Postmodern Transformations'. *Journal of Higher Education*, 77, 1, 1–39

CHAPTER TWENTY-FIVE

The Platform University

The Destruction and Resurrection of Universities in the Auto-Industrial Age

PETER MURPHY

From exhilaration to enervation

Right across the OECD (Organisation for Economic Co-operation and Development), the prevailing model of the university, the mass post-industrial university, is in deep trouble. It took off in 1970. Today, it is an educational, research, fiscal, and careers-enhancing failure. It is consumed by wasteful bureaucracies, pointless functions, grossly inflated costs, falling research output, diminishing discovery, chronic dropout rates, and a poor return on student investment.[1] Degrees are of diminishing value; university graduates increasingly end up in low-level service occupations. The post-industrial university has few, if any, means of reversing this. Yet more confronting still than the creeping entropy of these ageing institutions are the epic structural changes that are percolating under the surface of contemporary economies. In the past two centuries, leading societies have moved through agrarian, industrial and post-industrial stages. Each stage involved large-scale structural change. Today, post-industrialism is being supplanted by auto-industrialism.[2]

Auto-industrialism entails the replacement of human labour, notably office work, with a mix of computerization, automation and robotics. Where post-industrialism expanded office work, auto-industrialism is shrinking it. Computer algorithms are increasingly performing routine office-and-sales as well as para-professional operations, reducing the need for white-collar employees. All social institutions including universities are starting to be affected by this. As auto-industrialism expands, the post-industrial knowledge economy is being demolished.[3] As office-and-sales work and mid-tier jobs are computerized, the market for the post-industrial university is disappearing along with its rationale. So what will replace it? The universities of the mid-term-future, arguably, will look like high-tech versions of a medieval or an eighteenth-century university. They will be smaller, more cost-effective, platform-based and technology-driven. They will focus on preparing graduates for creative work rather than routine work. Mostly, micro-campuses only will exist. Administration will be automated. Salaried employment will shrink. Academics will be geographically dispersed, mobile and organized in legal partnerships.

None of this change is being driven by universities themselves. It is being wrought almost exclusively from the outside. It is large-scale, long-term, big-picture social change. A new wave of creative destruction is descending on advanced economies. The last time such a wave happened, in the 1970s, the distinctive generation of post-industrial organizations started to appear. These employed then growing numbers of mid-level white-collar 'knowledge workers' engaged in information processing in offices. Corporate back-offices, government departments, and the health and education sectors expanded as post-industrialism spread. The post-industrial era today is in its twilight phase. In its place, we are seeing the rise of the auto-industrial era. The latter is marked by office-and-sales automation and the growing application of robotics, self-service computerization, and self-regulating sensor technology to all aspects of industry, work, goods, services and government.

The technologies involved in this are not new ones. Robotics and artificial intelligence go back to the 1950s and 1960s. But these have merged with post-industrial computing and information technology and advances in cheap sensor technology. This techno-fusion is generating a classic Schumpeterian wave of creative destruction. What is being destroyed is routine work of all kinds including large numbers of office and para-professional jobs done by graduates. The average cost of an Australian government department face-to-face customer transaction is $16.90. By post it is $12.79; by telephone $6.60; and online $0.40.[4] Computerization is irresistible given such comparative costs. This is especially so when customer satisfaction with online transactions is high.[5]

Universities led the post-industrial wave of change. In the emerging auto-industrial age, they are lagging institutions. Many of today's universities were created in the post-industrial era and most universities came to subscribe to the assumptions of post-industrialism.[6] Those assumptions are now being scuttled. This has left present-day universities behaving like foot-draggers as the world around them is being subtly but powerfully reshaped by auto-industrialism. This is reminiscent of manufacturing industries four decades ago in advanced economies. Manufacturing declined. Blue-collar work shrank. The converse of this was an expansion of higher education accompanied by the promise of extra and better jobs. These were jobs in the 'knowledge economy'. In 1970, advanced economies were on the cusp of the information age. Today, the established knowledge economy is in a state of entropy—and so are the universities.

Higher education went through a period of exhilaration in the 1970s. It rode a subsequent great wave of expansion. This continued to the mid-2000s in all the OECD countries. Three percent of nineteen-year olds were enrolled in university in 1970. By 2005, that figure was anywhere between thirty percent and forty percent, depending on the country. Even then, proselytizers pressed for fifty percent or more of nineteen-year olds to enter higher education. Three years later, in 2008, as global stagnation set in, the intoxication ended. The state of irrational exuberance was over. For the first time in forty years, governments and individuals started to rethink the seemingly endless investments in higher education. Sceptics started to ask: is this really worth the money? Attention began to turn to the advantages of 'not going to university'.[7] Universities are counter-cyclical institutions; enrolment rises when economies shrink.[8] Yet after 2008, the opposite happened. U.S. tertiary enrolment (2011–2015) declined 13 percent. In the UK (2011–2013) it declined 8 percent.[9] Between 2010 and 2013, enrolment per capita dropped in the Czech Republic, Hungary, Israel, Ireland, Italy, New Zealand, Poland, Portugal, the Republic of Korea and Sweden. It was static in France, Japan and Spain.[10] At the same time, embryonic alternatives to campus-based, classroom-centred universities began to appear, notably competency-based degrees. These are degrees that are built on autodidactic learning (using the vast resources of the Internet). This learning, in turn, is assessed by independent degree-granting authorities.

Is university worth the money?

Forty years of higher education intoxication masked the fact that decade after decade the post-industrial university failed to meet every one of its self-proclaimed benchmarks. Its performance was mediocre. As time passed, this performance got progressively poorer. The mass university hid its failures behind rhetoric, bluster and money. In 1970, higher education was a small genteel sector and a barely noticed line-item in national budgets. Then the expansion began. It did so amidst inflated claims about the economic benefits of knowledge and human capital.[11] Government money began to flow to universities in unprecedented amounts. As the money flowed, universities turned themselves into lobbies. They struck a Faustian bargain with the state. They accepted regulation in exchange for subsidization. They gave up being collegial institutions and became procedural bureaucracies.[12]

Higher education grew by growing administration. In 1970, 40 percent of university income went to central administration. In 2010, the figure was 70 percent.[13] The major achievement of the post-industrial university was to expand its executive organization. Rules, controls, policies, processes, templates and administered services mushroomed; the resources allocated to departmental teaching and research shrivelled. What resulted, it was claimed, was the growth of society's 'human capital'. Universities supposedly delivered an increasingly educated workforce that met growing employer demand for qualified labour. This claim was invariably accompanied by the proposition that more and more individuals from low-income backgrounds attended university. In short, universities claimed that they were the key to economic prosperity and social equity. The trouble was that none of that was true.

The standard picture across the OECD is that 25 percent of entrants drop out of university and 25 percent of graduates never in their lifetime work in a job that requires a degree.[14] Forty percent of university students learn little while at university.[15] Today, employer demand for graduates is decreasing.[16] Higher education costs continue rising. University liquidity is declining.[17] The 'graduate premium' (what a university graduate on average can earn over and above a high school graduate) over time has shrunk. It was 235 percent in 1950, 121 percent in 1982, 115 percent in 1997 and 113 percent in 2006.[18] Meanwhile, the perennial source of university reputation, research, has waned. Universities today spend four times (in real terms) what they did on research in 1960 for the same research output per academic.[19] Similarly, the price of a degree is three to four times (in real terms) what it was in the mid-1950s.[20] Inflation-adjusted academic salaries are virtually unchanged from the 1970s.[21] What has made universities expensive is administration. Post-industrial universities turned themselves into large, costly bureaucracies.

To meet escalating administrative costs, universities have had to constantly grow revenue. Revenue growth can be achieved in several ways. In the century before 1970, the universities relied principally on market and gift income. After 1970, they became aggressive rent-seekers. They turned to the state for income. They convinced governments to subsidize student places at university. Governments were eager to do so. They instituted subsidies ranging from forty percent to one hundred percent of the cost of university places. The rationale was that university education was expensive and subsidies would help students from low-income backgrounds attend university. Subsidization however achieved the opposite of this. A university education today is much more costly for someone of modest means than it was five decades ago. Real costs have risen three- to fourfold. Even with subsidies, university places are 2.5 times as expensive as they were fifty years ago.[22] As with other public goods like health, government subsidies have one effect only: they drive up costs and prices.

The number of students at university increased dramatically after 1970. Vice chancellors spoke glowingly of the many students who were 'first in their family at university'. Yet the proportion of students attending university from the lowest income quartile did not change at all after 1970. The vast expenditure on higher education and access programmes had zero impact on relative social opportunity across four decades. The absolute numbers of persons from the low socio-economic quartile increased at university but only because the absolute numbers from all quartiles increased. The claim that universities contributed to social equality was bogus.[23] What they did contribute to, rather, was the post-industrialization of society, beginning with the institution of the university.

Tectonic structural change

Post-industrialization represented a tectonic shift in employment structure. In the 1970s and 1980s, across the OECD, manufacturing industries declined. Factories were shuttered or relocated aboard. Middle-income blue-collar work shrank. The question followed: what could replace these jobs? The answer was white-collar 'knowledge work'. Universities and colleges, it was reasoned, would educate the 'knowledge workers' of the future. How did that pan out? As noted, today at least a quarter of graduates never work in a job that requires a degree. As the size of the university sector grew, so did the numbers of graduates working as taxi drivers.[24] Human capital economics assumed that education determines economic outcomes. If anything the reverse is the case. As numbers at universities expanded, the gap between graduate salaries and median income shrank. So also did the number of middle-income salaried jobs.

From 1970 to 1990, the post-industrial script outwardly looked credible. The classic industrial middle tier of skilled work shrivelled while low-income service work, middle-income administrative-and-sales work and high-income high-tier professional work grew. From their inception eight centuries prior, the primary role of universities was to educate professionals—beginning with doctors, lawyers and priests. After 1970, universities re-geared themselves to educate a white-collar workforce that social engineers wagered would replace mid-tier skilled industrial work. On the surface the post-industrial expansion of government, health and education seemed to vindicate this bet. But under the surface, another contrary story began to take shape. This centred on the phenomenon of 'job polarization'.[25] This development began to crystallize in 1990. It was first noticed analytically in 2003.[26] Job polarization means the shrinking of middle-tier middle-income work relative to low-income service work and high-income high-end professional work. This is a function of technology. Manual and office work are both affected. Computerization today is eliminating routine administrative, service and retail work at an accelerating pace. Robots are replacing machine operators, assembly and production workers, miners and wharf labour. The classic mid-tier of occupations is shrinking. At the same time, demand for low-skill service work (in security, cleaning, care and hospitality) that requires manual dexterity has grown—along with the demand for high-skill abstract labour involving elements of interpretation, invention, judgement and creativity.

As a result of job polarization, the second half of the post-industrial era (the period between 1990 and 2010) started to generate an employment structure that looks like the opposite of what post-industrialization was supposed to achieve. The effects of this incipient reversal have become clearer over time. Graduate employment in low-skill service occupations has grown. The premium received by the 30+ percent of young adults getting degrees has shrunk. Median income in most advanced economies has flattened. In contrast, the career income of the 10 percent of the young adult population who now undertake some kind of postgraduate degree has increased.[27] The percentage of the population in 2005 getting PhDs was about twice the percentage of the population getting undergraduate degrees in 1955. Large numbers today might attend university but the principal beneficiary of this higher education is the small postgraduate class whose labour is abstract. This is reflected in job polarization. Demand (as expressed in income) continues to grow for that 10 percent of work that leans heavily on calculation, interpretation, judgement, problem-solving, reflexivity, coordination, ingenuity, resourcefulness, imagination, originality, innovation or creativity.[28] In the meantime, the demand for qualified mid-tier salaried employment undertaking tasks that are well defined, organized into clear analytical steps, demarcated, recurring and methodical is shrinking. Machines are replacing people in these roles.

Where post-industrialism eviscerated manufacturing work in advanced economies, auto-industrial technologies are eliminating routine work.[29] This includes routine manual, office, sales, service and para-professional work.[30] As this technology wave unfolds over the next ten and twenty years, much existing routine mid-tier pink collar, white collar and ancillary-professional work will disappear. As such, the need for the mass post-industrial university is being eliminated. The world of 'the office' and the 'sales department' staffed by middle-income workers with generic university degrees, doing defined repetitive tasks, is collapsing.

Computerization and automation are replacing these kinds of employees.[31] Thirty to forty percent of current occupations will be very significantly affected by computerization and automation in the next ten years. In effect a net fifteen to twenty percent of current jobs will disappear. The era of large-scale routine knowledge work is powering down. This change is occurring persistently on a large scale and over the long term. As manufacturing work in the 1970s was automated and off-shored, routine office and para-professional work is similarly being automated and off-shored. This will break the back of the mass post-industrial university.

The auto-industrial future

The post-industrial university is facing extinction. This will be a drawn-out process like the extinction of the earlier industrial-era discursive university was. But it will happen. Prospective students are thinking harder about the worth of going to university or college. They are more often considering the option of going straight from high school into the workforce.[32] This is in no small measure because the post-industrial promise of mid-tier incomes for graduates is not being fulfilled as routine office, sales and para-professional work is automated. The trend began as noted in 1990 and is accelerating. By 2035, few mid-tier 'knowledge jobs' will be left. Whether for society this means structural unemployment or underemployment or else different kinds of employment, or rather different kinds of occupation, at this point in time is unclear. Demand for manually dextrous service work that robots (yet) cannot do and for high-end abstract professional labour foreseeably will be sustained. There is also the long-term trend to generate income from capital rather than labour. This shift is progressively reshaping the nature of labour markets and social and political behaviours. It began in the 1950s. It accelerated in the 1970s and it looks as though it will persist, deepen and intensify in the foreseeable future. This means that if there is a future expansion of mid-tier occupations these will be sourced from the self-employed workforce. Entrepreneurial nous will substitute for labour skills. Salaried work will decline and capital work will increase.

Larger firms are caught up in this *zeitgeist* as well. Around 2010 a new hiring preference began to crystallize.[33] Employers increasingly are looking for digital know-how, agility, creativity, entrepreneurship, problem-solving and negotiating ability.[34] The post-industrial universities on the whole have been poor at cultivating these kinds of abilities. This is often not for want of trying yet efforts tend not to be matched by outcomes. This is because of a systemic cultural problem. Post-industrialism demanded a workforce orientated to routine detailed step-by-step process and procedure. The cognitive frame for this was analytic and the emotional frame was controlling. The post-industrial university was permeated by an analytic-controlling spirit that discounted traits like creativity, initiative and agility. This is now proving self-defeating. Take the example of 'training'. This is a favourite concept of the academic-bureaucratic class that runs the post-industrial universities. This class thinks of universities as a logical-methodical procedural training ground. It is hardly surprising then that, in 2015, 84 percent of students in the United Kingdom expected to receive 'formal training' when they began work. Yet, wisely, only 28 percent of British employers provide such training.[35] Self-starting behaviours not trained responses have value in the auto-industrial age. This is an era where self-management rather than direction is at a premium.

In 2015, 20 percent of contemporary UK university students said they wanted to work for a large company and 34 percent for a medium-sized company. Yet the logic of the auto-industrial age favours small start-up companies, partnerships and sole proprietorships.[36] Most net new employment is now generated by small businesses less than five years old with less than 250 staff and especially those with less than 50 staff.[37] Yet only 6 percent of British students said they wanted to run their own business and only 10 percent wished to work for a start-up company.[38] This conflicts directly with the social fact that income from capital work is growing relative to income from wages and salaries.[39] The desires of UK students in 2015 are unsurprising given that the broader post-industrial university culture is hostile to entrepreneurialism and self-ignition of any kind.[40] Auto-industrialism favours self-starters and those with broad, flexible, agile talents. Transdisciplinary abilities are sought after.[41] Such talents are related to creative abilities. Both take what is set apart and fuse it together.[42] The auto-industrial era favours syntheses of business, science, technology and the arts. Yet these syntheses are at odds with the mentality of the post-industrial universities. Attempts to create transdisciplinary programmes and degrees in the post-industrial decades typically failed.[43] Even when academic rhetoric supported them, the DNA of universities repelled them.

The post-industrial universities developed as bureaucratic institutions. This means that they are rigid. They have little agility. This follows the pattern of once-successful but now-failed large companies.[44] These organizations typically operate with an eighteen-month time horizon. They are operationally focused and fiercely controlling. They fixate on detailed implementation and disciplined execution. However big-picture innovation—five, seven and ten years out—is beyond them. So when it is required they wither or collapse. The post-industrial university is similar. It is capable of delivering in a proficient procedural manner discipline-based courses. It does this on a large scale in a repetitive template-style manner where learning is principally a kind of regurgitation and self-organization is depreciated. The surrounding institutional culture emphasizes standardization, normalization, sequencing and scheduling. This fits neatly with methodical, analytically structured, procedurally organized routine bureaucratic office and para-professional work. Creativity has little role to play in this context; likewise, entrepreneurship, problem-solving and negotiating.

A handful of tough undergraduate programmes like biomedicine, economics, engineering, logistics and political science still produce high-end problem-solving professionals. But these are the exception to the rule. Most post-industrial university programmes are tacitly tailored to mid-tier knowledge work whose purpose is not to solve problems but to progress claims and demands through procedures. The result is that the prevailing university model favours process and system and tacitly discourages invention, adaptation, resourcefulness or ingenuity. This is understandable considering the kind of synthesizing cognition required for inventive functions. It is the opposite of the compartmentalizing, classing, partitioning and slotting mentality that prevails in mid-tier routine work.[45] As this work declines, the need for the type of mass university that serviced it is in decline. In short, in the auto-industrial age, the post-industrial university is redundant. It has outlived its function.

The platform university

Post-industrial universities are caught in a pincer movement. Auto-industrialism is eliminating mid-tier knowledge work while declining productivity is shrinking the tax base of the major economies. The result is diminishing demand for university qualifications, declining public subsidies for universities and growing consumer resistance to overpriced higher education. The post-industrial model of the university is broken. As auto-industrialism spreads, this broken model will be replaced. Every age—from the agrarian to the post-industrial—creates its own kind of university in its own image. The auto-industrial age will do the same.

Accordingly, we can expect the auto-industrial university to mimic key aspects of the auto-industrial ethos. These include intensified automation, expanded digital supply and coordination, reduced physical capital, increased reliance on rental assets, growth in the importance of small business, sole proprietorships and partnerships, a greater social and economic focus on DIY activity (including autodidactic learning and autotelic enterprise), and a shift from salaried work to capital work.[46] If we assume that these are key emergent social building blocks, it is possible then to create a hypothetical model of the auto-industrial university. This model has seven key features:

(1) The auto-industrial university will be smaller in size. Thirty percent (or more) of nineteen-year olds do not need to go to university. No more than ten to fifteen percent of nineteen-year olds clearly benefit from university study.[47] For the others, the intellectual and material return on their investment is mediocre, non-existent or negative.
(2) The auto-industrial university will focus on creativity rather than knowledge. It will emphasize experimentation, originality, ingenuity, creation, imagination, inventiveness, initiative, enterprise and resourcefulness.
(3) The auto-industrial university will be embedded in a social world where many more individuals exit high school straight into the workforce. Contemporary employers are increasingly less concerned with someone's qualifications and more concerned with a person's capacity for problem-solving, digital invention, analogizing imagination and the like; or else their reliability and character.
(4) The means of organizing the auto-industrial university are platforms of the kind developed in the contemporary 'sharing economy'.[48]
(5) The auto-industrial university will be less physical than the post-industrial university. It will operate with micro-campuses, using with algorithmic (automated) administration, online lectures and discussions, and non-campus 'third places' for tutorials and meet-ups. Assessment of autodidactic learning will replace a portion (perhaps eventually a substantial portion) of classroom teaching.[49]
(6) There is no reason any longer for academics or students to have a fixed geographical location. Digital technology dispenses with the need for this.
(7) Digital platforms will enable academic partnerships to form in place of the existing employment contract between an academic employee and employer.[50] Treating academics as salaried employees allowed the capture of post-industrial universities by a bureaucratic academic management class. Basing universities on legal partnerships of academics would reverse this. The result would be closer to the self-governing corporation of scholars of the medieval university than the procedural Fordism and command economies of the post-industrial universities.

What is primarily required for the emergence of the auto-industrial university is an effective digital platform that allows self-organized contractually mediated groups of academics to create degrees that enrol fee-paying students. The platform is the software and hardware combination that performs business functions for the academic groups. Such a platform would algorithmically deliver financial, human resources and student services. A platform of this kind would service multiple academic groups. These contractual communities of scholars (CCSs) would agree partnership terms. They would teach, research and deliver major sequences of study; examine and certify autodidactic competency-based learning; and govern themselves consistent with their partnership responsibilities.[51] Individual academics could freely move from one CCS to another. They would no longer be tied to the soil of those baronial estates otherwise known as campuses. Like their medieval counterparts, the platform university would be in significant measure a virtual and mobile institution.[52] It would be principally an institution of the mind dedicated to the discovery of all things interesting. Like their medieval forebears, the teachers and researchers of the CCSs would use domestic houses and 'third spaces' for discussion, classes and research.[53] Lectures would be delivered online. Generic labs would be owned by third-party vendors and rented by CCSs as needed as would other kinds of facilities.[54] Specialist labs, notably those that are externally funded, would be CCS assets. Some CCSs could well develop a large asset base.

An individual CCS would typically support a major sequence of studies. Multiple majors compose degrees and multiple degrees form the basis of universities. A federated combination of CCSs would constitute a university for the purpose of degree-granting. This involves a more complex organization than the aggregation of sole traders to provide 'shared ride' or 'B-n-B' services.[55] Yet it is foreseeably achievable within a platform structure. It would require however something akin to a federative contractual system. This has implications not just for the university sector but for other sectors dominated by high-end professionals who work best in small organizational units but who need (for certain purposes) to be able to coordinate in order to deliver services on a large scale.[56] Given the competitive nature of global markets, it is likely that several platforms at least would service the majority of the world's CCSs and their respective degree-and-university federations. The entry and exit of academics into CCS partnerships would function like a person today entering and exiting a law firm or an accountancy partnership. CCSs in their turn would contractually enter into (and exit) partnership agreements in order to co-create degree-and-university federations. This mechanism would enable them to co-deliver degrees through federative cooperation with other CCSs.[57] Each CCS would elect a limited-term Head to oversee the business affairs of the partnership. Each CCS would be a distributed community with its members located in dispersed locations. The expectations and duties of members would be defined by the clear and simple means of a partnership contract rather than the cumbersome, often-arbitrary and ever-shifting policy imperatives of the post-industrial university.[58]

The economics of the CCS type of university would also be simple. Student fee income would come to the CCS partnerships. The platforms would take 20 percent of that income for the algorithmic administration, micro-campus and space-rental services that they would provide. This returns to the eighteenth-century model where the modern university began. In that model, academics (not central administrations) received fees directly from students.[59] The academics then turned over 20 percent of income they earned to the central administration of their university for the services that it performed for them. Today, as noted, central administrations absorb 70 percent of university income. This is the sole reason for the crippling costs of contemporary higher education. The platform university would automate administration, eliminate the academic-bureaucratic class, jettison the multitude of non-academic and pseudo-academic functions of the post-industrial university, and rent facilities instead of investing in physical campuses that are a half-or-less utilized across the year.

There is no good reason why university administration, services and facilities should cost more than 20 percent of income. Arguably, in many cases, it could be significantly less than 20 percent. The algorithmic administration, micro-campus, space-rental model of a university would at the very minimum halve the current costs of running a university, and very possibly reduce costs up to fourfold, returning universities to the cost and price levels of the first half of the twentieth century. The core functions of universities that focus on the classic model of departmental teaching and research are not inherently expensive. They require only minimal administration to enrol, progress and exit students, and deliver routine payroll, finance, HR and technology services for academic staff. The first step in future cost-effectiveness is to strip away the panoply of pointless non-academic functions that the post-industrial university became fixated on. The platform university in concept is a functionally simple operation that is underpinned by sophisticated automation and straightforward elegant professional partnership contracts. A federative mechanism is its principal point of complexity.

Post-industrial universities are heavily regulated. This allows them to function as a *de facto* monopoly. They collectively enjoy the protections of formidable barriers of entry provided by state certification while pretending that they compete with each other. As has been long understood, regulation benefits the industry not the consumer.[60] The function of regulation is to enforce industry norms. The effect of this is to discourage defiant entrants, especially those intent on re-configuring an industry. A well-financed platform would obviate this in the short term by providing the financial capacity to undertake prolonged and obstructive certification processes. A key factor though is not just undertaking regulatory accreditation but being able to automate the evidence gathering required by such processes.

That is, it is essential to successful university platforms to be able to algorithmically demonstrate compliance with regulatory 'standards' (academic qualifications, student–staff ratios, degree completions, casual-to-continuing staff ratios, etc.) in multiple jurisdictions. That said, in the long term, the ultimate rationale of automated accreditation is to reduce industry rules and regulation to a minimum. The prime growth industry of post-industrial societies was regulation. Accordingly, compliance costs today have expanded to upwards of 12 to 15 percent of the gross domestic product (GDP) in major economies.[61] This is what a lot of back-room mid-tier white collar work amounts to. As this kind of work in the future disappears, as it is automated, the tacit social demand for regulation will also de facto disappear. Regulatory auditing was post-industrial 'make work'. As such 'make work' is automated, the opportunity will present itself for the de-regulation of hyper-regulated industries, including higher education.

Conclusion

Developing university platforms financed by venture capital is functionally no different from John D. Rockefeller and Marshall Field underwriting the creation of the University of Chicago. Its time has come. The many dysfunctions of the contemporary post-industrial university are a symptom of a broken model. Belief in the existing model has withered. Yet while models are important along with belief and motivation, social transformation is not simply or even mostly a matter of design or desire. It arises from the larger dynamic systems that shape the world. Industry and its technologies is one of these systems. Modern economies and societies are industrial. As generations of technologies evolve and advance, societies respond and adapt. Across time, different types of industrialism have formed, dissipated and reformed. Today major economies are entering one of the periodic phases of dissipation and reformation. The post-industrial age is terminating. The auto-industrial age is emerging. The effects of this are beginning to touch all social domains including higher education.

Universities were the key signifying institution of the post-industrial era. As the power of post-industrialism has ebbed, a different kind of industrialism has gradually gelled. With this, the symbolic potency of universities has declined. The search is on for an alternate model of the university. The post-industrial university has outlived its usefulness. With a different form of industrialism comes different technology, expectations, markets, cognitive styles, types of work and modes of social cooperation and coordination. What was once the leading organization of its time is now a legacy institution; its energy has given way to entropy. Somewhere just over the horizon, a new beginning for one of the oldest of all social institutions is being hatched.

Notes

1. Murphy, 2015.
2. Murphy, 2017.
3. Deloitte, 2014; Frey & Osborne, 2013, 2015; Autor & Dorn, 2013.
4. Deloitte Access Economics, 2015, Table 3.1.
5. Deloitte Access Economics, 2015, Table 4.1.
6. These included the UK's 'plate-glass' and Australia's 'gum-tree' universities founded in the 1960s. These were followed in both countries by the 'new' universities created by converting polytechnic institutions, teaching colleges, colleges of advanced education, and art colleges into universities in the 1990s.
7. Google Trends shows a sharp upswing since 2008 of Internet searching on phrases like 'do not go to university', 'don't go to university', 'is university worth it' and 'don't go to college'.
8. For example: 138,000 US bachelor degrees were awarded in 1931; in 1939, 186,000.
9. UK HE numbers: 2,496,645 (2011–2012), 2,299,355 (2013–2014); US HE numbers: 21,016,126 (2010), 20,994,113 (2011), 20,642,819 (2012), 19,105,651 (2013), 18,948,521 (2014), 18,592,605 (2015). Data sources: UK Higher Education Statistics Agency, US National Center for Education Statistics and US National Student Clearinghouse Research Center (NSCRC).
10. Data source: UNESCO http://data.uis.unesco.org/
11. Murphy, 2015, 69–79.
12. Murphy, 2014.
13. Murphy, 2015, 110, 129, 217, 224, 231.
14. The Accenture Strategy 2015 U.K. University Graduate Employment Survey (Barea & Vasudeva, 2015) indicated that 60 percent of the sample group of 2013 and 2014 graduates in the workforce self-reported that they were employed in jobs that did not require a degree or else were underemployed. The survey pointed to the difference between the expectations of final year 2015 students and the employment realities of the 2013 and 2014 graduates. Eighty-four percent expect to earn £19,000+ in their first job; 75 percent do. Seventy-two percent expect to find full-time work; 58 percent do.
15. On a 5-step scale, 4 percent and 17 percent of Australian graduates perform at the lowest two adult literacy levels; 6 percent and 22 percent perform at the lowest two adult numeracy levels. Norton, 2014, Figure 29.
16. Catherine Livingstone, President of the Business Council of Australia proposed there be fewer university graduates (Gilmore and Knott, 2014).
17. In the UK the number of 'liquidity days' (i.e. days for which a university cash reserves cover their expenditure) is forecast to decline from 120 days in 2012–2013 to eighty days in 2016–2017. Johnes, 2015 based on Higher Education Funding Council for England Financial, Health of the Higher Education Sector: 2013–2014 to 2016–2017 Forecasts.
18. Murphy, 2015, 192–193, 214.

19. Murphy, 2015, 73–74, 257.
20. Murphy, 2015, 187–190.
21. Murphy, 2015, 115.
22. Murphy, 2015, 186–187.
23. Murphy, 2015, 184–186.
24. Murphy, 2015, 170.
25. Autor & Dorn, 2013; Autor, Katz & Kearney, 2006.
26. Goos & Manning, 2003; Autor, Levy & Murnane, 2003.
27. Murphy, 2015, 197–198.
28. Does this favour or disfavour the humanities? As universities expanded in the post-industrial era, enrolment in the humanities and social sciences declined. The big decline occurred in the 1970s and 1980s (Murphy, 2015, 43). The effect of auto-industrialism is likely to be a net real decrease in undergraduate enrolment relative to population and an increase in emphasis on sub-disciplines that have a strong mathematical-calculation-metrical-figurative-design-pattern-analytics base. The critical-textual-typographical thread of the classic twentieth-century humanities, already in decline, arguably will decline further.
29. Frey & Osborne, 2013, 2015.
30. Autor, Katz & Kearney, 2006; Autor & Dorn, 2013.
31. Frey & Osborne's research for Deloitte (2014) on the UK workforce in the next ten to twenty years projects a large decline in white-collar office, retail and service jobs (figure 2). In 2001–2013 in London, the number of library assistants, sales occupations, record assistants, travel agents, counter staff, PAs and secretaries, and bookkeepers declined sharply (figure 4).
32. The reluctance of qualified individuals to go to university is growing (e.g. Cavendish, 2015) as is the advice 'not to university' from those who are qualified, successful and sceptical of the value of their degrees (e.g. The Investor, 2012).
33. Kern, 2010.
34. Deloitte, 2014, figure 12; Kern, 2010.
35. Barea & Vasudeva, 2015, 5.
36. 14.7 percent of the UK workforce is sole proprietors; in Australia, it is 9 percent. 11 percent of the U.S. workforce is sole proprietors working more than fifteen hours a week with most working more than thirty-five hours a week; another 7 percent work less than fifteen hours a week. (Johnson, 2013; MBO Partners, 2014; Committee for Economic Development of Australia, 2015, 180.) This is a contented workforce. Fifteen percent of U.S. sole proprietors who work more than fifteen hours a week earn an income of $100,000 or more a year. (MBO Partners, 2014, 4, 5, 8, 12.)
37. Stangler, 2010, figures 3–5.
38. Accenture, 2015.
39. This trend is reflected in the rise in the numbers and income of sole proprietors. In the United States, in 1995, there were 16,423,000 sole proprietor tax returns lodged. In 2012, the number was 23,426,000, an increase of 42 percent in 18 years. Over the same period, the population of the United States increased by 22 percent only. The total business receipts of sole traders grew from $807 billion to $1301 billion, outpacing inflation by 7 percent. Data source: Internal Revenue Service (IRS) Sole Proprietorship Returns 1996 and 2012.

40. In the United States, nearly half of 800 surveyed young registered voters said that they hoped to start a business of their own someday. This included 58 percent of African-American and 64 percent of Latino respondents. Kristen Soltis Anderson, 2014.
41. From 1970 to 2000, demand for IT specialists boomed. Then the IT bubble burst. Today, where the professional market flourishes is not in traditional IT roles but in hybrid IT-business-organizational roles (Miller, 2011; Glover, 2011).
42. See e.g. Christensen, Dyer & Gregersen, 2011, 41–64.
43. This is not a reference to the normal process of intellectual discipline creation where one research discipline (e.g. biology) merges with another discipline (e.g. chemistry). But rather to the efforts of university institutions to have multiple non-adjacent disciplines coexist together in common teaching or scholarly programs.
44. Christensen, Dyer & Gregersen, 2011, 31; Foster & Kaplan, 2001.
45. On the synthetic nature of creative cognition, see Murphy, 2012, 73–99.
46. Murphy, 2017.
47. Murphy, 2015, 192–201.
48. Examples of the many and expanding contemporary 'sharing economy' or 'collaborative economy' platforms include AirBnB, Uber, Lyft, eBay, Taskrabbit, Redbeacon, Techshop, Heal, Cohealo, Feastly, Munchery, Prosper and Shareable. Terms such as 'sharing' or 'collaborative' are not though adequate to describe the phenomenon.
49. This echoes the university distance-education model that dates back to the 1870s (Nasseh, 1997). Learning materials were packaged and mailed to off-campus students who then, in significant part, proceeded auto-didactically.
50. A legal partnership is an association of two or more persons who are engaged in an enterprise in which profits and losses are shared proportionally. Partnership incubation would be a big development for the digital platforms. Today these mainly connect peers with peers or sole traders with customers.
51. The understanding of rights, responsibilities and obligations is essential in legal partnerships. This is something that academic employees often have a poor grasp of; in that sense, a partnership with others, with mutual responsibility for assets and liabilities, would be different, and arguably better, than academic employment arrangements currently existing. The conventional ceiling on partnership numbers is often around 20, a good maximum size also for a functioning academic group.
52. Rait, 1912, 9, 15.
53. 'Third spaces' is the term coined by the urban sociologist Ray Oldenburg, 1989, for spaces that have neither the attributes of 'home' nor 'workplace'.
54. The renting of physical assets and third-party services typifies contemporary start-up businesses (Taneja, 2015). These concentrate on designing products, the core intellectual aspect of their business. The post-industrial university, ironically, did the reverse. It marginalised intellectual activity for all kinds of non-academic and pseudo-academic pursuits.
55. In the case of 'bed-and-breakfast' services (e.g. Airbnb or Tujia) or ridesharing transport services (such as Uber or Lyft), the digital platform provides a transaction medium between an owner-operator and a customer. In contrast, universities have to mediate not only between the service provider and the student but also between academic peers whose interactions generate teaching degrees and research activity. Research archive platforms such as Academia.edu (established in 2008 and with 26 million registered users in October

2015) demonstrate the potential of digital platforms to facilitate academic peer exchange. Departmental peer organization represents a further (future) step in the development of platform sophistication.

56. Between 2003 and 2012, the U.S. population grew 8 percent while the number of partnerships reporting to the IRS rose 42 percent from 2,375,375 in 2003 to 3,388,561 in 2012; net income grew 258 percent from $301,398,218,000 in 2003 to $777,924,476,000 in 2012, outpacing inflation by 100 percent. Data source: Internal Revenue Service (IRS) Partnership Returns 2003 and 2012.
57. A full-service university would be constituted by up to 40 CCSs, 800 academics and a ceiling of 12,000 full-time equivalent students, though 4,000–8,000 FTE students would be optimal.
58. The academic partnership contract would cover decision-making, contributions to the partnership, salaries, what happens in the event of death or disability, dispute resolution, and the dissolution of or exit from the partnership.
59. The term used in German-speaking countries in the eighteenth century for the lecturer who received income from students was *Privatdozent.* Immanuel Kant (1724–1804) became a *Privatdozent* at the University of Königsberg in 1755. Kant spent fifteen years lecturing in this capacity. He was a witty and popular lecturer, and taught a wide variety of disciplines and subjects including physics, mathematics, moral philosophy, logic, metaphysics, rational theology, pedagogy, fortifications and physical geography. The scope of this teaching is almost inconceivable in the post-industrial university. It was only in 1770 that Kant was appointed as a salaried professor of the university.
60. George Stigler (1971) described the 'capture' of regulatory agencies by their industries.
61. Murphy, 2015, 94; Deloitte Access Economics, 2014.

References

Accenture. 2015. 'Majority of 2015 UK Graduates Feel Prepared for the Workforce, but 60 Percent of Recent Graduates in Work Are Underemployed, Accenture Study Finds', *Accenture News Release*, July 7.

Anderson, K. S. 2014. 'Conservative Ideas Are Our Biggest Strength with Young Americans', *National Review Online*, August 24.

Autor, D. H., Levy, L. & Murnane, R. L. 2003. 'The Skill Content of Recent Technological Change: An Empirical Exploration', *Quarterly Journal of Economics*, 118:4, 1279–333.

Autor, D., Katz, L. F. & Kearney, M. S. 2006. 'The Polarization of the U.S. Labor Market', *American Economic Review Papers and Proceedings*, 96:2, 189–194.

Autor, D. & Dorn, D. 2013. 'The Growth of Low-Skill Service Jobs and the Polarization of the U.S. Labor Market', *American Economic Review*, 103:5, 1553–1597.

Barea, D. & Vasudeva, P. 2015. *Will Today's Graduates Want to Work for You? Reshaping Your Talent Supply Chain to Drive Growth*, London, Accenture Strategy.

Cavendish, L. 2015. 'My Son Doesn't Want to Go to University', *The Telegraph*, July 14.

Christensen, C. M., Dyer, J., Gregersen, H. 2011. *The Innovator's DNA.* Cambridge, MA, Harvard Business Review Press.

Committee for Economic Development of Australia. 2015. *Australia's Future Workforce?* June.

Deloitte. 2014. *London Futures: Agiletown: The Relentless March of Technology and London's Response*, November.

Deloitte Access Economics. 2014. *Building the Lucky Country: Business Imperatives for a Prosperous Australia.* Canberra.

Deloitte Access Economics. 2015. *Digital Government Transformation.* Canberra.

Foster, R. N. & Kaplan, S. 2001. *Creative Destruction.* New York, Random House.

Frey, C. B. & Osborne, M. 2013. *The Future of Employment: How Susceptible Are Jobs to Computerisation?* Oxford Martin School, Oxford University, September 17.

Frey, C. B. & Osborne, M. 2015. *Technology at Work: The Future of Innovation and Employment*, Oxford Martin School, February 2015.

Glover, J. 2011. 'Investigating "Hybrid" Jobs in IT: A "Third Way" Skills Set?', *Bcs.Org*, January.

Goos, M. & Manning, A. 2003. 'Lousy and Lovely Jobs: The Rising Polarization of Work in Britain', London School of Economics, *Center for Economic Performance Discussion Papers*, No. DP0604.

The Investor. 2012. 'University Has Become an Unaffordable Luxury', *The Monevator*, January 31.

Johnes, J. 2015. 'Hard Evidence: Are Universities Strapped for Cash?', *The Conversation*, July 29, 2015.

Johnson, W. 2013. 'Independent Work May Be Inevitable', *Harvard Business Review*, February 19.

Kern, F. 2010. 'What Chief Executives Really Want', *Bloomberg Businessweek*, May 19.

MBO Partners. 2014. *State of Independence in America*, Virginia, MBO Partners.

Miller, R. 2011. 'Lots of IT Job Growth Despite Fewer IT Jobs', *IT Knowledge Exchange*, May 23.

Murphy, P. 2012. The Collective Imagination: The Creative Spirit of Free Societies, London, Routledge.

Murphy, P. 2014. 'Discovery and Delivery: Time Schemas and the Bureaucratic University' in R. Barnett, C. Guzmán-Valenzuela, O. H. Ylijok & P. Gibbs (eds). *Time and Temporality in the University*, London, Routledge, 137–153.

Murphy, P. 2015. *Universities and Innovation Economies: The Creative Wasteland of Post-Industrial Society*, London, Routledge.

Murphy, P. 2017. *Auto-Industrialism: DIY Capitalism and the Rise of the Auto-Industrial Society*, Sage, London.

Nasseh, B. 1997. 'A Brief History of Distance Education', www.seniornet.org.

Norton, A. 2014. *Mapping Australian Higher Education 2014-15*, Melbourne, Grattan Institute.

Oldenburg, R. 1989. *The Great Good Place*, New York, Parragon Books.

Rait, R. S. 1912. *Life in the Medieval University*, London, Cambridge University Press.

Stangler, D. 2010. *High-Growth Firms and the Future of the American Economy*, Kansas City, Kaufman Foundation for Entrepreneurship, March.

Stigler, G. J. 1971. 'The Theory of Economic Regulation', *Bell Journal of Economics and Management Science*, 2:1, 3–21.

Taneja, H. 2015. 'Why Startups Are More Successful than Ever at Unbundling Incumbents', *Harvard Business Review*, June 18.

CHAPTER TWENTY-SIX

The Fully-Functioning University[1]

TOM BOURNER

Introduction

This chapter is about what it means to be a fully-functioning university in the early decades of the 21st century. It is an important issue because rapid growth in the number of university students and growth in the number and size of universities raise questions about dilution of the university concept. It is important, too, because increasing diversification of the range of institutions referred to as universities prompts concern about fragmentation of the university idea. And it is important because rapid change within universities leads to the question: how much can a university change and still be a university?

The last century has seen an unprecedented increase in the number and size of universities, and the rate of increase has accelerated in the last 20 years. Worldwide, the number of universities has risen as economic development is associated with an increase in the proportion of the population receiving a university education. Continuing world economic growth means that the global expansion of universities is unabated. In Britain, recent decades have seen the age-participation rate for 18- and 19-year olds more than double, with plans for it to rise further. This has been accompanied by a corresponding rise in both the number and average size of universities. Does growth in the number and size of universities signal increasing relevance of the university concept or is it evidence that it is being watered down?

Growth in the number of universities has been accompanied by widening in the range of institutions that carry the name 'university'. This is exemplified by rebadging the polytechnics in Britain as universities in the 1990s. The heterogeneity has been exacerbated by strategic decisions in some institutions to specialise in particular fields and find niche markets. Is such diversification a sign that the notion of a university is splitting apart? How far can an institution specialise and still remain a university?

The last three decades have brought enormous changes to universities. It would not be difficult to make the case that universities have experienced more change in this period than in any other 30-year period in their long history. Here, for example, are a dozen major changes experienced by British universities in recent decades:

1. Introduction of fees and government-backed loans for university students.
2. Widening of the curriculum to include transferable skills and reflective learning.
3. Huge increase in the range of subjects available for study at university (including student-selected fields of study on some courses of independent study and self-managed learning).
4. Modularisation of many courses in higher education.
5. Semesterisation of much of higher education.
6. Changes in teaching and learning methods (for example, growth in project-work, group work, resource-based learning, problem-based learning, enquiry-based learning, etc.).
7. Development of new courses and qualifications. For example, professional doctorates were largely unknown in British universities in the early 1990s and now most British universities offer one or more professional doctorate programmes.
8. Growing concern with league tables.
9. 'Third leg' funding for university involvement with business and the community.
10. Increase in the student–staff ratio.
11. Emergence of e-learning (with associated developments such as 'managed online learning environments').
12. Training for university teachers.

It would not be difficult to find another dozen changes to compete with that list in terms of significance for the university.[2] The transformation of universities in recent decades has not been confined to Britain. In the United States it started earlier and proceeded more quickly—see Clark Kerr's (1991) *The Great*

Transformation in Higher Education, 1960–80. Arguably, university transformation has been a global phenomenon.

Background and approach

The university seems to be a remarkably timeless institution; it can serve as symbol of our medieval past or our knowledge-based present age. But what does it mean to be a university?

It is tempting to look for an answer to this question in the endeavours of British universities at the current time. The problem with this approach is the danger of focusing on current concerns and thereby mistaking the wood for the trees. Even if we try to answer the question on the basis of the values and beliefs expressed in the practices of universities within living memory we are not much better off. Moreover, even a very senior academic with 40 years of working experience in universities will have witnessed no more than 5 per cent of the history of the western university—with nothing to suggest this is a typical 5 per cent and much to suggest it is not.

Concern about what it means to be a university is not new. Perhaps the most famous statement is Newman's *The Idea of a University* published in 1852. Such answers tend to be context-bound in time and place and in the concerns at issue. For example, Newman's tract was written when British universities were under threat from the idea of the 'research university' originating in Germany. An alternative approach would be to identify what originally brought the universities into existence and the reason(s) why. This too presents a problem, since the origins of the earliest universities in Western Europe are obscure. It is difficult even to date the establishment of the earliest universities with any confidence.

> It is hard, even for the modern world, to realize that many things had no founder or fixed date of beginning but instead 'just grew', arising slowly and silently without definite record. This explains why, in spite of the work of all the researches … the beginnings of the oldest universities are obscure. … (Haskins, 2002: 4)

For this reason this chapter adopts a different approach again: it looks for an answer amongst the university aims and objectives that have endured across all the stages of the development of the Western university. This enquiry has been aided by the timely publication of the four volumes of *The History of the European University in Europe* (spanning the Middle Ages to the present time) sponsored by the Standing Conference of Rectors, Presidents and Vice-Chancellors of the European Universities, now European University Association (EUA).

Institutions that have been referred to as universities go back for millennia outside Western Europe. However, there is a good measure of agreement that the history of the modern Western university has its origins in the Middle Ages. For example:

> The medieval university was essentially an indigenous product of western Europe. … Centres of higher education such as the philosophical schools of Athens, dating from the fourth century B. C., the law school of Beirut which flourished between the early third and mid-sixth century, or the imperial university of Constantinople, founded in 425 and functioning intermittently until 1453, may have anticipated the medieval universities in some respects, for example in terms of embryonic organization and the emergence of regular courses of study. But collectively the distinguishing features of the medieval university seem to have been nowhere reproduced in previous institutional form; and there does not appear to be any organic continuity between the universities which evolved towards the end of the twelfth century and the Greek, Graeco-Roman, Byzantine or Arabic schools. (Cobban, 1975: 21–22)
>
> All advanced civilizations have needed higher education to train their ruling, priestly, military and other service elites, but only in medieval Europe did an institution recognizable as a university arise … Only in Europe from the twelfth century onwards did an autonomous, permanent, corporate institution of higher learning emerge and survive, in varying forms, down to the present day. (Perkin, 1997: 3)

The backdrop of this chapter is the western university that originated in Europe's Middle Ages. At centre stage, however, is the national system of universities in England. It is a system that has its roots in the 12th century and has an unbroken history to the present day. This is the perspective from which university development has been viewed.

Three broad stages can be discerned in the development of the university. The first was the medieval university that lasted until the end of the 15th century. The western university of the Middle Ages started as an institution of the Latin Church, no less than a cathedral or a monastery. Most of the earliest universities of Europe that emerged in the 12th and 13th centuries had their origins in these cathedral schools (Pedersen, 1997). Their teachers were in Holy Orders, all instruction took place in Latin, the mother tongue of the Latin Church, students accused of crimes were tried in ecclesiastical courts as clerics-in-training rather than civil courts[3] and their primary purpose was to provide an education that would prepare students for service to the Latin Church[4]. It was an institution run by clerics primarily to serve the needs of the Church.

The second stage was triggered by disengagement of the university from the Latin Church and lasted until relatively recent times. The university acquired a large measure of independence. Income from endowments and the fees of students from well-heeled and well-connected families meant that the post-medieval universities had sufficient financial autonomy to give them considerable discretion to follow their own destinies. In this stage the university curriculum became less Church-focused and more student-focused. The range of university subjects expanded and university education became a more liberal one.

The third stage has its origins in the development of the research-led university in Germany in the 19th century. It is characterised by increased emphasis on the advancement of knowledge, by the admission of empirical knowledge into the university and by subject specialisation. The university in this stage is sometimes known as the Humboldtian university in recognition of the role played by Wilhelm von Humboldt in conceiving it and then acting as midwife to its birth in early 19th-century Prussia. In this stage, a subject-focused education replaced the more student-focused education of stage 2. The heyday of the Humboldtian university was the high years of the 20th century and it was increasingly challenged in the latter part of the 20th century.

We are looking to answer the question 'What does it mean to be a university?' by identifying what is common about the endeavours of universities across all the stages of development of the western university. To answer this question it is necessary to look more closely at the university in each of its stages.

Stages in the development of the Western university

Stage 1: The medieval university

Most of the earliest universities emerged out of the leading cathedral schools of medieval Europe. In 1079 the Pope issued a papal degree instructing all cathedrals to establish schools for the training of the clergy. The highest level of education in these schools provided a preparation for service in the Latin Church by preparing students for the priesthood. The primary work of the priesthood was to contribute to the salvation of the immortal souls of Christendom. Through the pastoral role of the priesthood they would also serve to comfort the distressed in an age with much to cause distress.

These universities played an important part in the advancement of spiritual knowledge through dissemination of the word of God as they prepared students for clerical vocations. They necessarily engaged in scholarship because priests had a crucial role to play in the interpretation and reinterpretation of Holy Scripture to meet the needs of changing times. What was new, however, was when the Latin Church gave these institutions the task of accumulating such secular knowledge from Islamic and Byzantine countries as could be reconciled with the

Holy Scripture of the Latin Church. The emergence of this role at this time needs some explanation.

In the 9th and 10th centuries Latin Europe had been under frequent attack from the Vikings from the north and invaders from the east such as the Magyars. These forces kept Latin Europe from settling down into a stable political pattern. Their attacks were always capable of disturbing any fragile balance of power that emerged. Consequently, Latin Europe was a turbulent place as the political ambitions of the secular rulers often found military expression. In these war-torn times, churchmen were dependent on the secular rulers for their safety and for the continuation of their work. The Latin Church was most concerned with defence and the protection of Latin Christianity from the more prosperous and more powerful religious empires of Islam and Byzantium. In the 8th century Islamic invaders had invaded Latin Christendom and advanced almost to Paris before partially retreating. Their occupation of most of Spain in the 9th and 10th centuries was a constant reminder of the military and spiritual threat to Latin Europe and the Latin Church. According to the medieval scholar Richard Southern:

> The first thing that stands out in this period is the inferiority of western Europe to its Greek and Moslem neighbours. … Both Greek and Islamic systems were immensely richer, more powerful, and intellectually more sophisticated than that of western Europe. The West was the poor relation of Byzantium, making, after the manner of poor relations, strident claims to a superiority which was derisory by any objective test. … Western Christendom was a beleaguered citadel which only survived because its greatest enemy, Islam, had reached the end of its lines of communication, and its lesser enemies (the Slavs, the Hungarians and the Vikings) were organised only for raids and plunder. (Southern, 1970: 27)

The situation changed in the 11th century. Attacks on Latin Europe from the Vikings abated following the conversion to Christianity of Scandinavian countries. Attacks from the east abated following the conversion of countries of eastern Europe. Without the destabilising effects of these attacks Europe settled down politically and militarily. Political stability was followed by economic expansion and relative prosperity. These conditions provided an environment in which the influence of the Church could grow. Freed of anxiety about their immediate futures, the people of Europe were able to contemplate their longer term futures in an afterlife: they could turn their attention from survival of their mortal bodies to the future of their immortal souls. Moreover, the new rulers sought legitimacy for their conquests, a legitimacy the Church could confer.

As a consequence, the Latin Church grew bigger, richer and more powerful. By 1077 the growing power of the Church over secular rulers was symbolised by the abasement of the ruler of Latin Europe's largest territory, the Holy Roman

Emperor, before the Pope at Canossa. In England, by the time of the Domesday Book in 1086, the Latin Church already controlled a fifth of the kingdom's resources.

In the second half of the 11th century the Latin Church was preparing itself to confront the threat of Islam. The first crusade of the Latin Church in 1095 is one manifestation of this. Another manifestation was the attitude of the Catholic Church to the knowledge held by Islam. The Latin Church needed an explanation for the spectacular success of Islam in the four centuries up the 11th century. What had Islam got that had made it so successful? It could not be superior spiritual knowledge, a superior faith; that was an unacceptable conclusion for any Christian Church. It was much more acceptable to the Church to believe that it was superior secular knowledge.

The Church wanted Islam's secular knowledge for Latin Europe. It particularly wanted the practical and scientific knowledge and the thinking that underpinned that knowledge. There were additional reasons for this. First and foremost, if Latin Christendom and the Latin Church only survived because Islam 'had reached the end of its lines of communication' (*ibid*) then Latin Christendom was in mortal danger from advances in practical and scientific knowledge that might extend those lines of communication.

Second, there was increasing contact with Islam through pilgrimages to the Holy Land. This revealed how much more prosperous were the countries of Islam and Byzantium. It became clearer that the Latin Church was the poor relation. Its churches were impoverished by comparison with the churches of Byzantium and the mosques of Islam. The Latin Church recognised the contribution of secular knowledge to the power and prosperity of Islam and Byzantium and it wished to share in that power and prosperity.

Third, the phrases 'knowledge is power' and 'know thy enemy' express a significant element in preparations to confront Islam. The knowledge that the Church wanted, however, was potentially dangerous as it contained the unchristian ideas of Islam. The problem that faced the leaders of the Latin Church was how to make available to western Christendom such of that knowledge as was consistent with the teachings of the Christian Church. Who could be entrusted with this difficult task? It had to be clerics. It had to be learned clerics. And it had to be clerics who were expert in the interpretation of Christian scripture. All considerations pointed to those clerics who were responsible for the preparation of students for the priesthood. For the most part they were to be found in the leading Cathedral Schools of Europe.

So, in summary, the emergent universities of the medieval period, first and foremost existed to serve the needs of the Church by preparing students for the priesthood. They were also for advancing knowledge through the dissemination of spiritual knowledge, scholarship (primarily the interpretation of Christian scripture) and the accumulation of secular knowledge from the dangerous worlds of Islam and Byzantium.

Over time, however, the medieval university became more than just a church-based institution; it became concerned with developing a range of professions and sometimes even resisting the authority of the Latin Church and challenging the will of the Pope in Rome. These developments are addressed in the next section.

Development of the medieval university

One of the earliest developments in the new universities of medieval Europe was the absorption of the higher education of the other main learned professions of the Middle Ages, i.e. law and medicine, as higher faculties within the university. These faculties were responsible for further study by those who had achieved the arts-based first degree.

Why would the Latin Church want the training of lawyers and doctors to be within Church-controlled institutions rather than outside? It ensured that the leading practitioners of the other main learned professions fully understood Christian teachings and would practice within a framework of Christian teaching. The Latin Church wanted influence over not only the political life of western Christendom but also over the personal and professional lives of Western Christians. It saw the control of education as being an integral part of its remit. Fully independent colleges of medicine and law could have challenged its pronouncements and affected its authority. It wanted to be in a position to be able to rule on what was true and what was untrue in all significant areas of human life.

But why should the leading learned professions of medicine and law wish to align themselves with the institutions of higher education provided by the Church? The professions of law and medicine were based on bodies of received knowledge and locating their education within institutions sanctified by God gave status and authority to these teachings and their practitioners. The Latin Church was responsible for nearly all the primary and secondary education on which any professional education would depend. Moreover, as the power of the Latin Church grew, it made pragmatic sense for these learned professions to locate themselves within the institutional power of the Church rather than outside it.

The result was that eventually, the archetypal structure of a medieval university emerged comprising a Faculty of Arts together with higher faculties of law, medicine and theology. The emergence of these higher faculties was a significant development for three main reasons.

First, it implied the development of academic specialisation as a higher form of learning. Some students would continue their studies in these faculties after they had completed their studies in the Arts Faculty. The term 'superior' faculties conveys their relative position in the medieval universities.

Second, it recognised the importance of academic scholarship. The Islamic countries of the Middle East had acquired the learning of classical antiquity. The Latin Church gave to its institutions of highest learning the task of reconciling the secular knowledge held in the countries of the Middle East with the teachings of the Latin Church. This was a major task of interpretation and scholarship. Gradually *interpretation* became more important than merely *disseminating* knowledge within universities. Consequently, scholarship, the application of reason to text for the purpose of interpretation, played a more prominent part in the activities of universities. Scholarship demanded new skills. Those who aspired to join the ranks of university teachers would need to demonstrate the ability to interpret the approved texts and defend their interpretations. In order to graduate from the superior faculties the students engaged in 'disputations' to defend their interpretations against challenge. It became increasingly apparent that the practical and scientific knowledge of the countries of the Middle East were underpinned by the thinking of classical antiquity. Consequently, the range of approved texts widened to include many more texts from antiquity. For the most part, the knowledge of classical antiquity became available via translations from the Arabic via the countries of the Middle East.

Third, it encouraged and enabled the universities to serve the educational needs of a wider range of professions. This was a significant part of the process by which the universities ceased to be part of the Latin Church.

In the later years of the Middle Ages, the 14th and 15th centuries, 'service to the Church' was a less uplifting vision for universities. Corruption in the Latin Church undermined its moral authority. 'Service to the Church' may have promised a comfortable calling for potential students in the later Middle Ages, but for the university as an institution it was a less compelling aspiration.

At a more practical level, as the moral authority of the Latin Church declined, student numbers fell and universities encountered financial difficulties. Green (1974) writes of Oxford at the end of the medieval period:

> In the fifteenth century the university entered into … a period of contraction. Its numbers apparently fell from 1,500 to 1000; only 27 men took the masters' degree in 1456-7. Contemporary letters complained of the shortage of students, teachers and endowments … Once, the university exclaimed somewhat rhetorically in 1430, 'she was famous in the world: students flooded to her from every nation: then she abounded with men learned in every art and science; her schools were not dilapidated nor her inns empty.' The university it was urged in a letter to the Duke of Gloucester, pleading for his patronage," is reduced to the greatest misery. Lectures have ceased and a complete ruin of education is imminent." (Green, 1974: 31)

The fall in student numbers encouraged the universities to reassess their priorities. A number of other factors contributed to the outcome of this reassessment.

- The emergence of the nation state in Europe also created the need for more learned people. They were needed to administer the structures of the state, to conduct relations with other nation states and their expertise was often needed to settle disputes. Sometimes the emergent nation states needed the support of the most learned to escape the dominance of the Church of Rome. For example, when Henry VIII wanted a divorce he needed to challenge the legal interpretation of the papal experts. Thomas Cranmer sought assistance from the universities in finding an interpretation of the legal situation that would support the King. The Church no longer had a monopoly of the power of knowledge. The secular authorities of the new nation state courted the universities as sources of educated people for its various employments.
- The attentions the emergent nation state paid to the universities were reciprocated. The rise of the power of secular authorities of the new nation state relative to the power of the Church led universities to court the influence of the State.
- Through endowments and other gifts, the universities, or the colleges that comprised the universities, had become less financially dependent on the Church. This gave them greater power to choose the focus of their endeavours.
- The sons of the relatively wealthy comprised an increasing proportion of the student population. This enabled fees to be charged at levels that supported the financial independence of the university.
- As the social composition of the student body changed, an increasing number of university students saw their futures outside the Church. In the earliest days of the university, students entered the university to prepare for a vocation in a priesthood based on poverty and obedience. Why did students enrol in the university at the close of the Middle Ages? There were still those who aspired to employment in the priesthood. But a growing number found employment in teaching, fuelled by the growth in literacy and fuelling the growth in literacy, often as private tutors in relatively wealthy families. Also, a growing number aspired to work in the increasing range of employments available from the secular authorities of the new nation state. And some aspired to no employment at all save that of gentlemen.

All these factors served to diminish the extent to which universities saw their main role as serving the Church. Taken together, they gave rise to the second great epoch in the history of the university.

Stage 2: The early modern university: a university for scholars and gentlemen

During the medieval period many colleges were supported through benefaction or gift of endowment. As the medieval period progressed, the Church encouraged the gift of endowments to establish churches, monasteries, schools and colleges of clerics to pray for the souls of the benefactors. It was believed that such charity would reduce the time the soul spent in purgatory and also reduce the likelihood of everlasting damnation. It also financed the establishment of the institutions of the Church. The institutions were run by clerics and the clerics were obedient to the Church.

The danger of this arrangement became apparent when the clergy ceased to obey the church in Rome. The medieval period ended with disenchantment with the Roman Church and rise of the nation state which generated competing claims on the loyalty of the universities. In England, this is exemplified by the break between Henry VIII and Rome.

The universities of this period provided an education for students with a variety of employment aspirations—cleric, teacher, lawyer, medic, administrator or even none at all. What sort of education would serve students in all these vocations? The answer was a *broad* knowledge, the development of good manners and social graces and the cultivation of moral decency, nicely captured in the expression 'Manners makyth man'. In this epoch the highest aspiration of the university was to produce gentlemen of integrity who would grace any profession.

The university of the 15th and 16th centuries developed leaders for high office in the nation state. It sought to develop people who would hold high office with honour. And it acted as a civilising influence in what was still a barbarous age:

> If learning decay, which of wild men maketh civil; of blockish and rakish persons, wise and goodly counsellors; and of evil men, good and godly Christians; what shall we look for else than barbarism and tumult? (The Duke of Somerset, quoted in Brooke and Highfield, 1988: 137)

An indication of the growing role of university graduates in governing the new nation state can be found in their increasing numbers in the House of Commons. In 1563 there were 67 and in 1593, only three decades later, there were 160 (Curtis, 1959: 59).

In the medieval university it had been the Church that determined what constituted academic knowledge. The post-medieval university took over that role from the Church and had a much more liberal view of the boundaries of academic knowledge. It legitimised new knowledge by recognising new subjects. The range of subjects taught increased significantly in this period.

With the rise of the nation state Church patronage of the universities was increasingly replaced by royal patronage. Through royal patronage, new colleges were established and regius chairs endowed. The new patron sought to have a say in what students were taught, but the financial independence of the universities limited the practical impact of this. This freedom also helped to broaden the university curriculum. The term 'liberal education' came to replace the term 'the liberal arts' in describing a university education. Compared with the medieval university the students had more freedom in what they studied, as did their tutors.

Some of the students abused the freedom, as did some of the academics. Some students engaged in wild living and stories of their escapades reached the parents of perspective students. Consequently, many opted instead for private tuition and the Grand Tour as ways of achieving the aims of a higher education in the 18th century: a broad education, good manners and the cultivation of personal integrity. The end of the 18th century was subsequently represented as the nadir of the university in terms of the higher education of its students. This was the judgement of those in the 19th century who were advancing a new (Humboldtian) agenda for higher education. With the success of the Humboldtian revolution this view became the conventional wisdom. It was in their interests to portray the pre-Humboldtian university as approaching death through decay. For example:

> By the eighteenth century universities everywhere were in the doldrums, confined to the training of priests or pastors, a few civil servants, and those gentry too poor to educate their sons by private tutors and the increasingly popular 'grand tour' of the Continent. ... most universities in eighteenth century Europe were moribund, with idle professors ... despised by the intellectuals of the Enlightenment. In England the historian of the Roman empire Edward Gibbon described his student days at Oxford as 'the fourteen months the most idle and unprofitable of my whole life,' and his teachers, 'the monks of Magdalen,' as 'decent, easy men who supinely enjoyed the gifts of the founder.' In Germany civil servants and politicians seriously discussed whether universities did more harm and good and ought to be abolished. (Perkin, 1997: 14, 15)

Recently, the higher education of the universities of the 18th century has undergone rehabilitation. For example:

> ... it was possible for a young gentleman ... who knew how to use his tutor, his college library and such university lectures as were on offer, to take away from the university a useful grounding in classical literature, moral philosophy and political philosophy, natural history, perhaps a smattering of medicine, and even some theology ... It must be added that it was equally possible for a young scallywag to come away from the university with a BA and precious little else except some advanced skills in drinking and driving a coach and pair. We have no way of knowing what the proportion of these last were ... (Leedham-Green, 1996: 120)

A reasonable conclusion is that the university of the second stage provided an unrivalled opportunity for students who wished to study, and for those who wished to play it provided an unrivalled opportunity for that too.

In this second stage, there was a change in the balance of subjects in the universities with the humanities steadily gaining ground. However, the epistemological basis of learning in the university remained the same—reason applied to approved texts. The main difference was that the range of approved texts widened significantly from those prescribed by the Church to those prescribed by a more humanistic spirit. In this period 'virtue' replaced 'piety' as the highest value of the university. With its roots in scholasticism and the growing strength of the humanities it was difficult for empirical knowledge to gain entry to the university. The scientific revolution of the 17th century did not cause a revolution in the universities until much later, and when it did it ushered in stage 3 of the development of the university. It arrived in the form of Wilhelm von Humboldt (1767–1835).

Stage 3: The Humboldtian university

As Minister of Education in the Prussia in the early years of the 19th century, Humboldt was given the task of building a system of higher education for the Prussian state and its people. According to Humboldt, the purpose of a university is not to serve the needs of the students; instead, the purpose of both students and staff within a university is to serve the advancement of knowledge. Humboldt intended that the fruits of the research would be available to the nation state:

> The stimulus for this development stemmed from Napoleon's military defeat of Prussia in 1806. Smarting over the loss of the university of Halle, which was situated in territory forfeited to Napoleon, a new system of higher education was formulated to assist the rebuilding of the demoralised Prussian state.
>
> This task of modernising the older universities and the creation of new universities was assigned to Humboldt. Through his efforts as minister for education, a university was established at Berlin in 1810-12, the primary objective of which was to create knowledge. (Noble, 1994: 6)

Humboldt's Prussian universities were viewed as successful and envied in other countries. They attracted students and scholars from across the world. The universities that were established subsequently (most of the universities that exist in the world today) tended to follow the model of the research-led university created by Humboldt.

The issue was less clear in the universities that pre-dated Berlin University. Those universities, like Oxford and Cambridge, had their own rituals, beliefs and values. It had taken centuries to transform institutions whose primary role was as seminaries for the Latin Church into institutions whose primary role was to serve the purposes of the students. Moreover, the ordering of the priorities of these universities was embedded in traditions, structures and practices that were difficult to shift.

For most of these institutions, the intellectual history of the 19th century was one of a battle between those who attached primary importance to the education of students and those who attached it to research. In the end, the Humboldtian vision of the research-led university triumphed, but not until the early 20th century.

The Humboldtian university sought the advancement of knowledge. Coming so soon after the scientific revolution it saw the advancement of knowledge in terms of the *accumulation* of knowledge. To that end it invited the empirical sciences into the university. The Humboldtian university valued research as the intentional creation of new knowledge, it valued the dissemination of newly minted knowledge and it valued scholarship as the reinterpretation of the existing map of knowledge, particularly in the light of the latest contributions of new knowledge.

The purpose of the higher education of students in the Humboldtian university was to *serve* the advancement of knowledge. This included the dissemination of recent additions to knowledge to the students of the university. It included the development of the students' critical faculties, their ability to test ideas, assertions and evidence as the means by which claims to new knowledge could be evaluated. And it included the development of a questioning attitude as the by-product of well-honed critical faculties.

The emphasis on research and scholarship within the Humboldtian university gave rise to the charge that universities were becoming 'ivory towers' divorced from the concerns of the rest of society. This is unfair to the Humboldtian university, as the advancement of knowledge was seen as a road to greater human material well-being. It sought to enlarge the pool of knowledge from which all could freely draw. This would lead to increased human mastery of the physical world, promising improvement of the human condition, including the eventual eradication of poverty and disease. And the development of the capacity to test ideas, assertions and evidence would help active citizens to recognise those who would mislead through error or deceit.

The third stage of the development of the university, the Humboldtian university, was unchallenged until the latter part of the 20th century. That challenge is addressed in the next section.

Discussion and conclusions

What can we conclude from this summary of the main endeavours of the university in each of its developmental stages to answer the question, 'What does it mean to be a university?' The first conclusion is that in every stage of its development the university has had the same three basic concerns: to provide for the higher education of students, to contribute to the advancement of knowledge, to benefit those beyond the walls of the university. Table 1 summarises the main focus of each of these concerns in the three stages of the development of the university.

Table 1: Main focus of endeavours in the main stages of the western university.

	Stage 1: The medieval university	**Stage 2: The early modern university**	**Stage 3: The Humboldtian university**
Advancement of knowledge	Accumulating knowledge from Islam and Classical Antiquity and scholarly interpretation of texts approved by the Latin Church	Enlarging the domain of academic knowledge by opening up new fields of enquiry beyond that prescribed by the Latin Church, particularly in classical studies and the humanities more generally	Enlarging the domain of academic knowledge through research and the recognition of empirical knowledge
The higher education of students	Preparing students for service within the Latin Church	Providing an education fit for godly gentlemen, including an introduction to the finest thoughts of civilisation since classical antiquity	Developing critical faculties and their application to the latest knowledge in academic subjects
Service to those beyond the walls of the university	Serving the Latin Church including contributing to the salvation of the immortal souls of Christendom	Contributing to the civilisation of those who would hold high office in the learned professions and the young nation state	Contributing to improving the human condition through greater understanding and control of the world in which we live

Source: Author. (2008). The fully functioning university. *Higher Education Review, 40*(2), 3–23.

It is reasonable to conclude that to warrant the name 'university' it is necessary that an institution perform all three of these roles: the advancement of knowledge, the higher education of students and service to the wider society beyond the university. It seems that the notion of the *tripartite* mission of the university is deeply grounded in the history of the university in each of the stages of its development.

A second conclusion is that in each of the stages of the development of the university one part of the mission has dominated the other two. How did the dominance of one part of the mission impact on the other two parts in each of the three stages of the development of the university?

In the medieval university the dominant part was service. The medieval university directly served the Latin Church and was thereby dedicated to the salvation of the immortal souls of Christendom. That was the main way it served those beyond the walls of the university. What sort of higher education of students was provided by the medieval university? A higher education that supported the university's primary purpose of serving the Church. The particular forms that the advancement of knowledge took in the medieval university were such as would support the university's primary purpose of serving the Church—dissemination of the Word of God, interpretation of Holy Scripture (i.e. scholarship) and the accumulation of such secular knowledge as could be reconciled with Christian scripture.

In the second great epoch of university development, with universities financially independent of the Latin Church, the dominant purpose of the university was the higher education of students. In this stage, universities contributed to the advancement of knowledge by legitimising new fields of academic study; this was the age when the humanities gained entry to the university. Relaxation of Church-based constraints allowed the fellows of the university more freedom to indulge their own interests in the pursuit of knowledge. Freed of the requirement to study subjects that supported service to the Church, there was increasing interest in humanistic enquiry. The goal of higher education was to develop godly gentlemen, men of virtue. How did universities of the second stage benefit those beyond the walls of the university? They developed leaders for the new nation state and the learned professions and they were a civilising influence in what was still a barbaric age.

The third stage of the development of the university is the Humboldtian university when the advancement of knowledge became the dominant part of the university mission. Consequently, the nature of a university education changed, with an emphasis on the dissemination of new knowledge and the development of critical faculties. Likewise, the 'service' part of the university mission was interpreted in ways that reflected that new dominance, with an emphasis on the enlargement of the pool of knowledge from which we can all draw, increasing mastery of the physical world and the development of critical faculties to expose those who would seek to control through deception.

As the tripartite mission of the university has been dominated by each part in turn, the other two parts have taken on new forms that serve the dominant part. This implies another significant conclusion: the way that each part of the mission of the university has been expressed has been very different in each of the three epochs of the development of the university. This suggests that there may be many more options in the ways that each of the three parts of the mission can be expressed than are currently imagined by minds still dominated by the Humboldtian paradigm.

The tripartite mission in the 21st century

The last decades of the 20th century saw a further change in the relative position of the three parts. The 'advancement of knowledge' which was dominant for most of the 20th century has been challenged by increasing weight attached to 'the higher education of students' and 'service to those beyond the university'. Much evidence is available to support this contention. Three examples should suffice. First, we now have three streams of funding corresponding to the three parts of the tripartite mission. Second, universities now produce 'mission statements' to make explicit their priorities. Until the 1980s, university mission statements were unnecessary since their purpose was self-evidently the advancement of knowledge. Inspection of the current mission statements of a range of universities reveals a varying mixture of the three parts of the tripartite mission. Third, the admission in the early 1990s of the polytechnics and some colleges into the university fold doubled the number of universities; the polytechnics had been created to give more emphasis to the education of students who would follow a range of professional employments and to serve local and regional communities. A reasonable conclusion is that in these early decades of the 21st century the three parts of the university mission are more evenly balanced than in the 20th century when the Humboldtian ideal dominated universities.

In the last few decades, universities have experienced pressure to demonstrate gains in all three fields of endeavour. This pressure was accompanied by increasing measurement of performance in each domain. It resulted in increasing prioritisation by universities *within* each domain of endeavour. They have focused on 'research' within the domain of the 'advancement of knowledge', on 'teaching' within the domain of 'the higher education of students' and on 'knowledge transfer' (or whichever aspect represents government's current main concern) within the domain of 'service to those beyond the university'. Consequently, the tripartite mission of the university is sometimes described in terms of 'research', 'teaching' and 'knowledge transfer'. This prioritisation *within* each of the parts of the tripartite mission is a strategy for ensuring the achievement of all three parts of the mission of a university. But it is only one strategy for so doing and it flows from a particular interpretation of the tripartite mission inherited from the most recent (Humboldtian) stage in its development.

So what does it mean to be a university in the 21st century? It means what it has always meant: the advancement of knowledge, the higher education of students and service to those beyond the university's walls. These three ingredients can be recognised in all the stages of its development since the Middle Ages. This implies that the so-called 'tripartite mission' of the university has a sound historical pedigree.

Etched across this continuity has been a pattern of change as first one then another part of the tripartite mission has dominated the other two. Dominance by one part has meant that the other parts have been interpreted in ways that serve the dominant part. Consequently, each stage of the development of the university has displayed distinctive characteristics. A summary table of these can be found in the appendix, which displays the stages in terms of 'ideal forms'. Dominance by one part means that the other two parts are expressed in ways that serve the dominant part. It means that the other two parts are valued insofar as they serve the dominant part. A university cannot function fully in terms of the tripartite mission if two parts are constrained the serve the third. A prerequisite for a *fully-functioning* university is that each of the three parts of the tripartite mission is valued in its own right.

For most of the 20th century the 'advancement of knowledge' has dominated universities and they were able to align the 'higher education' and 'service' parts of the mission to serve that part. In recent decades its dominance has been challenged by the pressures on universities to pay increasing attention to 'the higher education of students' and 'service to those beyond the university' as goals *in their own right*. In the first decades of the 21st century we have moved out of stage 3, the Humboldtian stage, in the development of the university to a post-Humboldtian position where the three parts of the university mission have become more evenly weighted. Universities increasingly feel pulled in three different directions and for many within universities this is an uncomfortable experience.

The danger of increased prioritisation within each field of endeavour is that the advancement of knowledge will be seen as *synonymous* with research, service to those beyond the university will be seen as *synonymous* with the current views on 'reach-out' and the higher education of students will be seen as *synonymous* with teaching.

Nostalgia is sometimes expressed for the high years of the 20th century when the Humboldtian flame burned brightest in the universities of Britain (and the rest of the world). From the longer historical perspective, the Humboldtian university is but one stage in the development of the university and its focus on the advancement of knowledge seems excessively narrow. The broadening of the university curriculum in recent decades and the growing engagement of universities with business and social communities recognises that the other two parts of the university mission have value in their own right. This can be viewed as the defining feature of the post-Humboldtian university. So long as the universities pursue all three parts of the university mission, it is reasonable to view growth in the number and size of universities as evidence of the growing relevance of universities rather than dilution of the historical meaning of the university concept.

How much can a university change and still be a university? The university is a very old institution which has seen massive changes in its long history. The environment of the university has changed so much that it has had to adapt to survive and thrive. Clearly change per se is not inimical to the university concept. Indeed, the university concept would seem to *require* institutional change to preserve the tripartite mission or to realise it more fully. However, to specialise in any one part to the exclusion of the others is to become a different sort of institution: a research institute, a college of tertiary education or a charitable foundation. To give up on any one is to give up on part of what it means to be a university in any historically meaningful sense. This is what limits the extent of specialisation within the university.

Institutions that most fully express the tripartite mission and express each of the three parts most fully deserve the name university. The Humboldtian university, as interpreted in the 20th century, was dominated by the advancement of knowledge and the other parts of the university were valued as they served that purpose. The post-Humboldtian university of the 21st century that values each of the three parts in its own right represents significant progress towards the flowering of a truly fully-functioning university.

Notes

1 "This chapter is a revised version of an article with the same title published in *Higher Education Review* (40 [2]: 26–46). It was followed by two articles, co-authored with Linda Heath and Asher Rospigliosi, that look at implications of the fully-functioning university concept, published in the same journal: 'The fully-functioning university and its higher education' (45 [2]: 5–25) and 'The fully-functioning university and its contribution to the advancement of knowledge' (48[2]: 51–70)."

2. For example, (1) emergence of work-based learning, (2) rising proportion of students living at home, (3) increase in the proportion of students who work part-time during their 'full-time' studies, (4) rise of 'performance' indicators, (5) the filtering down of research 'training' from PhDs into Masters and then many undergraduate degrees, (6) the decline in the incidence of tutorial and tutor-led discussion in small groups, (7) growth of managerialism in academic leadership, (8) requirement that all universities produce university strategies, (9) increasing government involvement in university policies and practices, (10) the research

assessment exercises and their impacts, (11) arrival in universities of business practices, (12) legitimisation of 'mode 2' knowledge within the academy.

3. This could be a major source of resentment by the townsfolk where universities were located and resulted in conflict between 'town and gown'.
4. This did not mean, of course, that all those who enrolled at such institutions became clerics any more than all the students who nowadays enrol on engineering degrees go on to become engineers; many become managers, maths teachers, accountants, etc.

References

Brooke, C and Highfield, R (1988). *Oxford and Cambridge*, Cambridge: Cambridge University Press

Cobban, A (1975). *The Medieval Universities: Their Development and Organisation*, London: Methuen

Curtis, M (1959). *Oxford and Cambridge in Transition 1558-1642*, Oxford: Clarendon Press

Green, V (1974). *A History of Oxford University*, London: Batsford

Haskins, C (2002). *The Rise of Universities* (2nd edn), Ithaca (USA): Cornell University Press

Kerr, C (1991). *The Great Transformation in Higher Education, 1960-80.* New York: State of New York Press.

Leedham-Green, E (1996). *A Concise History of the University of Cambridge*, Cambridge: Cambridge University Press

Newman, J (1852). *The Idea of a University*, London: Longman

Noble, K (1994). *Changing Doctoral Degrees*, Buckingham: Society for Research into Higher Education and Open University Press

Pedersen, O (1997). *The First Universities: Studium Generale and the Origins of University Education in Europe*, Cambridge: Cambridge University Press

Perkin, H (1997). 'History of Universities' in *The History of Higher Education* (2nd edn) edited by Goodchild, L and Weschler, H, Boston (USA): Pearson

Ridder-Symoens, H de (ed) (1992). *Universities in the Middle Ages* (Vol. 1 of 'A History of the University in Europe'), Cambridge: Cambridge University Press

Ridder-Symoens, H de (ed.) (1996). *Universities in Early Modern Europe (1500-1800)* (Vol. 2 of 'A History of the University in Europe'), Cambridge: Cambridge University Press

Rüegg, W (ed.) (2004). *Universities in the Nineteenth and Early Twentieth Centuries (1800-1945)* (Vol. 3 of 'A History of the University in Europe'), Cambridge: Cambridge University Press

Rüegg, W. (ed.) (2011). *Universities Since 1945* (Vol. 4 of *A History of the University in Europe)* Cambridge: Cambridge University Press.

Southern, R (1970). *Western Society and Church in the Middle Ages*, London: Penguin

Appendix 26.1: The main stages in the development of the western university: Key characteristics

	Stage 1 **The medieval university**	Stage 2 **The early modern university**	**Stage 3** **The Humboldtian university**
Approximate period	Early 12th century to late 15th century	Early 16th century to mid-19th century	Mid-19th century to late 20th century
Dominant mission	Service to Latin Church and the people of Latin Christendom	Higher education of the students	Advancement of knowledge
Highest value	Piety	Virtue	Knowledge
Focus	Church-focused	Student-focused	Subject-focused
Metaphor	*Apprenticeship* for servants of the Latin Church	*Finishing school* for gentlemen	*Seed-bed*[1] for researchers
Highest aim of higher education	To develop pious clerics	To develop godly and civilised gentlemen	To develop critical scholars
Generic learning outcomes	Knowledge of Holy Scripture Mastery of the liberal arts Piety	Breadth of knowledge (including classical studies) Good manners & social graces Virtue	Latest knowledge Well-honed critical faculties Questioning attitude
Focus of the curriculum	Holy Scripture	Humanities through classical studies	Subject-specific
Main form of patronage	The Church	The Crown	The State
Religious affiliation	Latin Church	National Church	Secular
Dominant subject	Theology	Classical studies	Science
Dominant epistemology	Reason applied to texts approved by the Latin Church	Reason applied to an enlarged range of texts	Empirical knowledge
Ascendant intellectual paradigm	Scholasticism	Humanism	Empiricism

Source: Author. (2008). The fully functioning university. *Higher Education Review, 40*(2), 3–23.

[1] The word seminar comes from the Latin *seminarium*, i.e. seed-bed.

CHAPTER TWENTY-SEVEN

Academic Citizenship beyond the Campus

A Call for the Placeful University

RIKKE TOFT NØRGÅRD AND SØREN SMEDEGAARD ERNST BENGTSEN

Introduction: beyond the campus

In this article, we promote the concept of academic citizenship and argue that it contains a powerful but often overlooked potential of personal, academic and societal value. In common discourse, academic citizenship often refers to the element of service universities are expected to provide for the wider society they are placed in. This can concern the societal relevance of specific types of courses and degrees, or it may be about how civil society in general can draw from the universities as resources of knowledge and expertise. However, this chapter is not concerned with discussing to what extent the university should be seen as in service of civil society, or the other way around for that matter. Instead, the chapter aims at exploring what we may benefit from the understanding of a *mutual engagement* between universities and the surrounding society—and is advanced using Paulo Freire's (2013) term of 'integration'. We understand academic citizenship as the intertwining of participation in, engagement between, and mutual responsibility of, universities and society. Here, we are building on the description of the virtuous academic citizen as outlined by Nixon (2008) and Macfarlane (2007), emphasising virtues such as engagement, care, loyalty, collegiality and benevolence, which implies a mutual obligation between universities and society. In other contexts, the term academic citizenship might refer to how students and staff should behave within academia, listing guidelines and suggestions for good student behaviour and honour codes. By drawing on Macfarlane's (2007) and Nixon's (2008) work we move from such guides and honour codes towards fundamental moral virtues and obligations on a deeper value-based level. Where Macfarlane (2007) and Nixon (2008) mainly take a moral perspective to the idea of academic citizenship, we wish to supplement this with *ontological* meaning. Thus, our aim is, on the background of already existing theories and understandings of academic citizenship, to develop a new concept that, on the one hand, moves away from the idea of service towards a focus on mutual engagement and integration, and, on the other, fuses the already existing work on the moral responsibilities of academia with a focus on the ontological conditions that enable such forms of responsibility in the first place. Where the moral dimensions of Macfarlane and Nixon refer to the development of specific virtues and a range of moral obligations for students, teachers and intellectual leaders (the people *in* the university), the ontological dimension in this chapter refers to the 'being of places' and, ultimately, the 'being of universities'—the moral obligations for universities *themselves*.

Following from this, academic citizenship implies a mutual bond of interest, care and responsibility *beyond the secluded campus*. In this way, different academic planes are merged in academic citizenship—professional, personal and public. This intertwining of societal and academic potential in academic citizenship has been overlooked due to a tendency to separate individuals in higher education from the places they are part of through a disconnect between citizenship and university. This possible schism emerges from the fact that educational institutions today are often seen as more or less abstract and secluded spaces withdrawn from the surrounding world, entailing the call for more market-oriented and commodified universities, as critically discussed by Readings (1996), Barnett (2004, 2011, 2013), Land (2004), Watson (2013), Solberg and Hansen (2015), Biesta (2006, 2013) and Filippakou and Williams (2015). In this article, we argue that universities must offer spaces where citizenship can develop and let academics dwell—a placeful university. To grasp academic citizenship at the placeful university, we link theories of space and place (Casey, 1997; Creswell, 2004, Heidegger, 2000, 2001, 2011; Tuan, 1977) with theories of institutional being, value and becoming in education (Barnett, 2007, 2011; Barnett & Coate, 2006; Biesta, 2006; Dall'Alba, 2013; Dall'Alba & Barnacle, 2007; Macfarlane, 2007; Nixon, 2008; Temple, 2014a). Instead of viewing academic place as disconnected from everyday surrounding societal life and value, we argue for a societally rooted concept of higher education—*for a placeful university and academic citizenship beyond the campus.*

On this view, education springs from the interactions and experiences of people and places; from experiences of belonging, dwelling, ownership and responsibility in relation to interactions between university, people and society. As such, the concepts of place and academic citizenship provide an opportunity to reimagine the possibilities of the university to reconnect with people and society. In this chapter, we address primarily stakeholders *within* the university, or, to put it more evocatively, so-called 'institutions-makers', 'managers', 'wardens', 'stewards' and other 'intellectual leaders' (Macfarlane, 2012) of the university who have stakes in building, maintaining and improving research, teaching, learning, and living milieus and environments at universities.

Space, spatiality and place

For a university to be meaningful, to be more than a space of traversal where bodies go to access knowledge or get an education, we need to rethink what academic citizenship and being a university might entail and signify. We must think beyond the physical spatiality of the campus and establish a notion of the *placeful university* (our term). But, to enable this, we need to make a distinction between 'spaces for traversal' and 'places for dwelling'. In his seminal book *Space and place*, Yi-Fu Tuan draws this distinction, arguing that space is characterised by temporal-physical traversal (from one place to another), while place is characterised by the embodied experience of inhabitation (Tuan, 1977). For Tuan, space and place are codependent, since place requires space in order to be a place, and space requires places to go to and from in order to be space. Furthermore, spaces are without social connections; they are without value or meaning imbued through human participation. Thus, space is more or less abstract (Tuan, 1977, pp. 164–165). Place, on the other hand, emerges from human experience and connection. Place emerges out of space, imbued with significance, belonging and commitment (pp. 164–165).

This initial distinction between spaces of traversal and places of inhabitation is developed and refined in Edward Casey's *The fate of place—a philosophical history* (1997). Here, it is clarified how space itself is not completely neutral, abstract or value-free, but also something 'made'. The spatial layout constitutes us, as we constitute it. Space is always in the process of 'placing' us as we are engaged in place-making (Casey, 1997). Space organises experience through its layout and, thus, impacts the way we experience and are able to make place. In this way, space and place are interwoven and entangled, but that does not make them identical or interchangeable. Space and place stand in a relation to each other that shares similarities with Casey's (1997) distinction between biological 'flesh body' and experiential 'lived body'. Like biological and experiential body, the one does not precede the other, but they are not the same; they have different structures. In this way, the architectural university campus (spatial layout) and the lived placeful university (experiential layout) are interwoven. Furthermore, when people have the university as a place, they carry the university within them beyond the spatial layout of the campus. Likewise, they bring their living self to the campus and thus transform the architectural campus. Consequently, place is interdependent on the structures, values and voices people pick up as they settle into the university—as cleaning lady, professor, student, technical supporter or lecturer. We step into place through our lived body and the places we dwell in impacts our experience and lifeworld:

> This much is true for place: we are immersed in it and could not do without it. To be at all—to exist in any way—is to be somewhere, and to be somewhere is to be in some kind of place. (Casey, 1997, p. ix)

Thus, a central question becomes whether the university is only framed and enacted as spatial layout for fleshy bodies (sitting in lecture halls, going to the bathroom, eating at the canteen and working in offices)? That is, if the university is regarded purely as an architectural campus structure? Or, conversely, is the university only framed and enacted as an experiential place for lived bodies (constructing discourse, partaking in sociocultural activities, enacting academic identity and building knowledge)? That is, if the university is regarded purely as a theoretical conceptual structure? The challenge is to enable academic citizenship and the placeful university to emerge beyond both concept and campus as sites of our academic being and becomings. Places are what surround us, and what we inhabit (Merleau-Ponty, 2002, p. 161) and dwell in (Heidegger, 2001). As pointed out by Temple: '[T]he physical resources of the institution, the buildings in which they are held, and the land on which they are built are (…) critical to institutional success' (2014a, p. xxi). In this way, Temple underlines this important relation between physical and intellectual spaces, maybe even the intimate bond between building and thought.

This argument is in line with Heidegger's distinction between building and dwelling, where 'building' is understood as a means to support man's 'dwelling' (Heidegger, 2001, p. 144). However, the buildings, and the process of building itself, are important in the way that the 'word bauen (…) means at the same time to cherish and protect, to preserve and care for (…)' (Heidegger, 2001, p. 145), in that '[b]uilding as dwelling unfolds into the building' (Heidegger, 2001, p. 146). This means that specific, built spaces, such as campus areas and buildings, are central sites that can or cannot invite dwelling within education.

As such, architects and designers of academic space, as well as stakeholders, decision-makers and frontrunners of that space, must safeguard that the university as spatial layout promotes academic virtues, place-making and dwelling. As Buchanan argues in 'Human dignity and human rights: Toward a human-centered framework for design': 'design is fundamentally grounded in human dignity and human rights [...] We should consider what we mean by human dignity and how all of the products that we make either succeed or fail to support and advance human dignity' (2006, p. 302). Consequently, a close connection between built space and experienced place emerges in education as a potential site for human dignity. A university campus is not just a composition for containing academic life, making sure that people do not get wet during lectures or have office space to work in. It is a site engraved with certain ethical and ideological implications; it emanates certain values, calls for certain forms of participation and speaks to us in a certain 'voice' (Buchanan, 2006; Nixon, 2008). As such, the university is a certain offer of experience:

> All of the products of design are offers of experience. If we have designed well, then our offers sustain and enhance human dignity. If we are given the opportunity to design a product that, in the quiet of our soul, we believe will diminish human rights, then our responsibility as designers is clear. While we may design such a product [or space] that meets technical standards of quality, it is a product that we should avoid. (Buchanan, 2006, p. 305)

The university is a layout for human experience. Students, technical staff, visiting family, professors, guest lecturers or someone taking a stroll in the university park are all occupying and travelling the space of the university. For many, it remains a spatial layout where university 'space has no trodden paths and signposts. It has no fixed patterns of established human meaning' (Tuan, 1977, p. 54). Their personal places lie elsewhere, and the campus remains a space for traversal. They do not connect with, dwell or feel addressed by the voice, values and experience of the university.

Becoming a place

Taking central theories of space and place (Casey, 1997; Creswell, 2004; Tuan, 1977) as a point of departure, we argue that often the university traditionally has been occupied with developing and improving physical academic (work) spaces for staff and students, but has not necessarily viewed such work spaces as places for academic virtues and dwelling in the Heideggerian sense, in which a more fundamental sense and experience of being and belonging is made possible.

Rather than considering the university as physical architectural spatiality (concrete) or imagined articulated space (concept), it might be fruitful to approach the university as place, considering the ways people may dwell within institutional settings, bringing values, concerns and forms of engagement of a broader societal character into the academic context, and vice versa. The university space/place is a particular form of invitation that supports and promotes particular beings and becomings in education while stifling and preventing others. In this way, following Creswell and Tuan, a space becomes a potential place through the invitations we build into it (designed place) and the ways we interact with and experience it (lived place):

> [P]lace is also a way of seeing, knowing and understanding the world. When we look at the world as a world of places, we see different things. We see attachments and connections between people and places. We see worlds of meaning and experience [...] To think of an area of the world as rich and complicated interplay of people and the environment—as a place—is to free us from thinking of it as facts and figures. (Creswell, 2004, p. 11)

Such places are always also an emplacing of people, meanings and things (Gieryn, 2000). How education is to be experienced—as submission or empowerment, dismissal or invitation, engagement or dislocation—is something to consider whenever we build spaces that could be potential places for future dwelling (Gieryn, 2000).

Consequently, a concrete/conceptual university can invite or reject dwelling through its built-in visions and enterprises, emerging from the values, views and virtues of those who envisioned it. If place-making people at the university have visions and enterprises for their academic places that do not correlate with the university as concrete/conceptual space, it will attempt to disempower or debar such attempts. Universities are, in this way, place-holders of specific doings, knowings and beings in education—welcoming towards certain forms and unwelcoming towards others. In this perspective, we argue that stakeholders, decision makers and intellectual frontrunners within the university carefully consider with what vision they design their institutions and whether this design promotes academic dwelling and citizenship.

This implies that whoever exerts power over the placeful university, and how it can be transformed into material and imagined academic places for dwelling, also influences which values, views and visions become prevalent in the fostering of academic citizenship. If people's place-making activities are not recognised by the 'institution-maker', they may come to experience themselves as homeless at the university and in education: 'To be without a place of one's own—*persona non locata*—is to be almost non-existent, as studies of the homeless imply' (Gieryn, 2000, p. 482). Consequently, education at the university is meaningful to the extent that we can be there, dwell in it, have a sense of (co) ownership of it and feel agency in relation to it.

This connects to notions of academic authenticity, linking the individual lifeworld to academic practice (Barnett, 2007; Batchelor, 2008) and, maybe especially important in this context, to notions of academic authenticity that link academic practice with virtues (Macfarlane, 2007; Nixon, 2008). It unites or gathers, in the Heideggerian sense, academia and the social lifeworld of the broader society.

Being in education

As argued by Rømer (2010, 2011), Bengtsen (2014), Aaen and Nørgård (2015), Temple (2014a), Beyes and Michels (2014) and Masschelein (2011), academic contexts are lived contexts, embodied and inhabited—education is *taking place* through the life and being there of university and academics. To examine this further, we draw on Heidegger's understanding of the 'Dasein' ('Being-there') to visualise universities as sites for such a 'taking-place-ness' (our term). We suggest that Heidegger's notion of the 'Dasein' can be used not only to describe individuals' ontological voices, as done by Batchelor (2006, 2008) and Barnett (2004, 2007), but that the ontological voice of the *placeful university* itself should be further explored and heard. This way, education itself should be seen as having a 'Dasein', a 'being *there*', as an 'In-der-Welt-Sein' (a Being-in-the-World) (Heidegger, 2000, p. 78). When we speak of the university as a place and not merely a space, we speak of it as a place where people, with Heidegger's term, 'dwell' (Heidegger, 2000, p. 80, 2001, p. 143ff.). It is not an empty container to be filled with the conceptual spirit or concrete flesh of the people occupying these spaces (Aaen & Nørgård, 2015). The university itself is a force of being, and by dwelling there we become 'absorbed' (Heidegger, 2000) into this being. Accordingly, the university is not just a space we occupy in a specific time span during the day, while we teach or attend classes, continue our research projects and maintain and develop the infrastructure of our department or faculty. Rather, the university becomes part of our broader lifeworld.

The university is not merely a human, or sociocultural, construct, but a placeful form of being, tangible and forceful. The university can be a 'charming place'. For Harman (2005) it is important that we understand that the 'Dasein' of places is just as powerful and relevant a form of being as the authenticity of people. Harman does not use the term 'authenticity' to describe the 'Dasein' of places, but the term 'charm'. He admits that he simply

> can think of no better technical term than *charm*. This word should be heard with overtones of witchcraft rather than those of social skills. What is at issue is not some sort of people-pleasing faculty in things, but a sort of magic charm or elixir (...). (2005)

In similar terms, Lingis argues that places are not something we construct discursively or socially, at least not primarily, but forces that also construct and influence *us*. As Lingis writes, we

> are not grasping the carpentry of things in their appearances nor subjectively fabricating images of them, but find ourselves caught up in their images, their shadows, their reflections, [and] halos (...) We find ourselves among them and carried on by them (...). (1998, p. 101)

Following Harman and Lingis, we argue that 'charm' and 'allure' are central constituents of 'placeful-ness' (our term) within the university. When we become caught up in the charm and allure of the placeful university itself, we adapt to local shared values and interaction emerging from the centre of the participation that springs from placeful qualia and place-making potentialities of a specific place (Toft and Nørgård, in press). More concretely, this entails, as Macfarlane suggests (Macfarlane, 2012), that for people to be able to dwell within the university, and not merely occupy its space, they must be 'enabled' (Macfarlane, 2012, p. 96ff.) to dwell there; to have access to resources, be supported, feel encouraged in their projects, and be drawn into worthwhile and collaborative connections. As Temple (2014b) points out, the connectedness between success in academic collaboration and the spatial environments where such collaboration are anchored can be very subtle. By quoting Sailer and colleagues, Temple underlines that it is 'inherently difficult to disentangle which behaviours stem from which influence [because] both spatial and organisational influences appear to have shaped the structures and evolution of academic collaboration networks' (Temple, 2014b, p. 3). As Macfarlane (2007, 2012) points out, this calls for intellectual and moral leadership.

Places for dwelling

As we see pointed out in the works of Biesta (2006, 2013), there is a focus on the existential and ethical projects that underlie people's engagement with the university. A similar perspective on education is found in Nixon (2008) and Macfarlane

(2007) who in different ways highlight that certain virtues are necessary within academic practice to foster creative and innovative academic places. In line with Nixon (2008), Macfarlane (2007), Filippakou and Williams (2015) and Temple (2014a), we see the placeful university as constituting an inextricable link between individuals and the surrounding society. Dialogue, so essential to all forms of learning in education (Freire, 2013), must essentially be democratic, empathic and participatory to be 'dialogical'. In this way, what could be labelled 'dialogical dwelling' incorporates some of the main tenets of academic practice: honesty, compassion, collaboration and care in carrying out our work at the university (Macfarlane, 2007; Nixon, 2008), all of which require a sense of belonging and authenticity.

To give deeper conceptual meaning to this notion, we draw on Heidegger in arguing that the placeful university is characterised by a 'Mitsein'—a 'We', or a 'Being-with-Others' (Heidegger, 2000, p. 149). As Heidegger writes, the 'Dasein' discloses itself as a 'Mitsein' where '[o]thers are encountered *environmentally*' (Heidegger, 2000, p. 155), and 'the world is always the one I share with Others. The world of Dasein is a with-world [Mitwelt]. Being-in is *Being-with*-Others' (p. 155). Furthermore, Dall'Alba and Barnacle (2007) stress the point that the university is an arena for *meaning*-making, and meaning-making happens exactly because of the underlying link between academia and society in general; they are conjoined in the placeful university.

Such academic places, fused with values and ideals, hopes and fears, are, as Vogel (1994) points out, 'fragile' places and constitute a 'fragile we'. Heidegger's 'Mitsein' is seen by Vogel as having an ethical dimension, because '[w]e coexist authentically and so form an "authentic We" when each feels that he belongs to a common project yet encourages the others to pursue the project in a way that attests to their own individuality' (Vogel, 1994, p. 79). However, as Vogel underlines, '[e]very "authentic We" is fragile because it is composed of self-responsible members who live at the boundary of this membership' (1994, p. 79). Following Vogel's interpretation of Heidegger, we argue that the placeful university can be seen as a 'Mitsein', or a 'We'—but a fragile 'We', as the common project of the placeful university is never ultimately fixed or settled. This means, paraphrasing Dall'Alba's (2013) argument, that academic places themselves must develop the capacity to care, which is a central qualia for the 'Dasein-with' in Heidegger (2000, p. 157). A university inviting academic citizenship should foster not only persons who care but also *places that care*—places that are welcoming rather than excluding and invite place-making and dwelling rather than directing towards a specific use or being rigid and inflexible towards the creativity and playfulness of place-making university staff and students. In line with Harman, we suggest that universities should become more attentive to their 'carnal plasma' (2005, p. 173), that is, the way that each place is 'obsessed' by being *some*thing and not *any*thing (Harman,

2005, p. 139). This is, we argue, the ethics of the placeful university—a responsibility evoked by drawing people together, fostering dwelling, inviting for joint place-making and invoking care, collaboration and connectedness.

Integrating academic citizenship

Focusing on core values and virtues that cling to and emanate from academic places, we argue that the above can help us give new meaning to the term academic citizenship. Academic citizenship at the placeful university expresses 'total engagement (…) eternal dialogue between man and man, between man and the world' (Harman, 2005, p. 139). Thus, we stretch Macfarlane's (2007, p. 160ff.) point that universities should recover their academic citizenship as not only a service to, but also through *engagement with*, the public and argue that education, maybe even academia, could take place outside the institution and within public arenas. With our understanding of academic citizenship, the university is something we carry with us and has a place in us, as the university carries us and has a place for us. Paraphrasing Heidegger again, we argue that the placeful university is 'authentic—that is, something of its own' (2000, p. 68) in its spatio-ontological being. This is a placeful university beyond the campus that integrates critical academic practice with societal values, facilitating academic being and belonging. Consequently, we argue that the university as a virtuous *place* is necessarily a place of 'Mitdasein' and 'Führsorge', which includes Heidegger's description of the kind of solicitude where one may:

> *leap ahead* [of the other person in contrast to *leaping in* for him] (…) in his existential potentiality-for-Being, not in order to take away his 'care' but rather to give it back to him authentically as such for the first time. This kind of solicitude pertains essentially to authentic care—that is, to the existence of the Other, not to a *'what'* with which he is concerned; it helps the Other to become transparent to himself *in* his care and to become *free for* it. Solicitude proves to be a state of Dasein's Being—one which, in accordance with its different possibilities, is bound up with its Being towards the world of its concern, and likewise with its authentic Being towards itself. (Heidegger, 2000, pp. 158–159, emphasis in the original)

The purpose of the university of the future is to let itself be inhabited and used by the people living around, outside and within it. In line with Heidegger's notion of authenticity, we should not view the university of the future as a place where problems are to be solved for people or society, but as a place where challenges, potentials and issues of real importance become visible to people and society in a critical and compassionate light. This means that the 'solicitude' of the university of the future should not be understood as a tool for society to redeem it (or for it to redeem society), but as a means to 'sober up' and become aware of more fundamental challenges. This calls for action from the current university-makers. More attention should be given to the 'worldhood' of the university. How do we create and engage environments at the university where society as an existentiale seeps into the university as an institution? How do we speak *from*, rather than *about*, society *within* the university?

The university beyond the campus

However, placeful-ness and dialogue is not often found in public discourse on the university. When the university is seen from the perspective of society, or when society is seen from the perspective of universities, either party describes the other in terms of what Heidegger calls 'das Man' ('the they') (2000, p. 163). Heidegger describes 'das Man' as the 'neuter' (2000, p. 164) and the 'nobody' (2000, p. 166), exemplified by what happens when we generalise without taking pains to authentically promote a critical and compassionate understanding of a matter or a person. When this happens, 'the real dictatorship of the "they" is unfolded' (Heidegger, 2000, p. 164). In this context, 'das Man' equals the persistent and often tacit understanding of the university as a spatial campus and secluded architectural structure containing abstract knowledge.

This means that a challenge lies ahead concerning the inclusion and integration of society, people and university into each other. Academic citizenship occurs when the university becomes a place where the 'they' is being dissolved (Heidegger, 2000, p. 168)—when university, society and people are nested within each other. As such, the placeful university moves beyond the campus to take place as academic *citizenship* embracing its worldhood and its Being-in-the-world ('In-der-Welt-Sein'). In this way, the notion of the 'Mitsein' ('Being-with'), we argue, should apply to our conception of universities as well: they must acknowledge that they are in the world *with* the world, that is, surrounding society, which consists of, among many other things, other institutions, citizens, companies, organisations, communities, private individual projects, concerns, etc. Going a step further, the university is not merely an institution among others, but a *place* among other places. In this light, the 'Mitsein' ('Being-with') of the university shows to be a *togetherness of places*. This implies that the university does not *leap in for* society (Heidegger, 2000, pp. 158–159), trying to please it as the 'hand that feeds it'. Society is no longer a phenomenon or existentiale outside the university. Rather, the university *leaps ahead of* society (Heidegger, 2000, pp. 158–159), which means using its placeful-ness as a means of integration between critical being and societal value.

As such, the definition of the university as a placeful being that invites, supports and promotes academic citizenship means that our notion of the 'public' sphere must also be rethought. As Barnett points out, '[w]e seem to be in an age of multiple and fragmented publics; and to say this is almost to imply that the notion of public is dissolving' (2015, p. 26). However, as Barnett further argues, this should not diminish the idea and possibility of the 'public student' (Barnett, 2015, p. 23), and it is important 'to continue to search for a public; even for a global public. This very search may even help to bring about the connection—between higher education and the public domain—that it seeks' (Barnett, 2015, p. 27). Here, Barnett implies that the very search itself influences the creation of a public place within the university, but also, we argue, the creation of the placeful university beyond the campus and within the public.

Such public-academic places should consist not only of virtues in an ethical sense, but also, as Barnett suggests in one of his earlier works, of 'epistemic virtues' (2007, p. 104), which include 'connections between interest in understanding the world, on the one hand, and human virtues, on the other hand' (p. 104). This is why we do not only call attention to the interplay between conceptual and concrete dimensions of the placeful university, but also to the values, virtues and visions for the becoming and being of place. Furthermore, rather than placing the responsibility for such places to happen on teachers and students, as Barnett does in his own work (Barnett, 2004, 2007), we argue the other way around that the responsibility, and the virtues needed to live up to such a responsibility, lies just as much within the *placeful university* as it does within the *place-making person*. To have people express virtuous academic citizenship we need a *virtuous university*.

That the university itself can be virtuous, and manifest the virtue of guardianship that Macfarlane (2007, p. 118) links to academics (people, not places), becomes meaningful if we apply Heidegger's (2000, p. 171) notion of the 'clearing' ('Lichtung') together with Casey's (1997) notion of 'becoming a place' to the placeful-ness of the university. Participating in making such a 'clearing', and thereby letting placeful-ness 'disclose itself' as Heidegger describes it (2000, p. 171), calls for action from the frontrunners, decision makers and place-makers within the university. It is a call to participate in the transformation of spaces into places, to make university spaces porous to society and people, to invite for, promote and participate in the becoming of place within the university (Casey, 1997).

Whereas it would be traditional to link Heidegger's notion of authenticity, Barnett's notion of responsibility and Freire's notion of integration to persons, we wish to stretch that link to universities as well. In this way, a university can be an inauthentic, irresponsible and enclosed space that shuts its gates to protect itself and contain the people within, or it can be placeful, emanating dialogue, authenticity and integration and dissolving its boundaries to become permeable for what is inside and outside of it. That is, the placeful university is public in the Freirean sense, where university and society integrate into one another. Following Nixon, we argue that the placeful university 'constitute a kind of buffer zone between the crude forces of personal self-interest and the impersonal interests of the state' (Nixon, 2008, p. 129). Here, Nixon echoes Freire's call for integration of the public and the private sphere in a way that enlightens and creates moments of disruption for both spheres. It is also a call for the university 'to become virtuous institutions committed to creating and sustaining relationships based on the virtues of truthfulness, respect, authenticity, and magnanimity' (Nixon, 2008, p. 130).

Despite agreeing with Nixon's call, we argue that it goes the other way around as well: how do we engage the public in the university? How do we make the public see the epistemic, societal and ethical resources being strengthened and further developed through education? This is not a classical 'Catch-22' dilemma between the mode 1 and mode 2 university (Barnett, 2004), but a genuine wish to invite for places that are ongoing dialogues between institutional and societal spheres. To achieve this, we argue for promoting open and democratic public-academic places. This hinges on, as Scott underlines, that we rethink and reimagine the meaning of the public, which 'is now close to being regarded as a boo-word' (2015, p. 41). From what we have argued in the above, we suggest that 'academic citizenship' should be seen as a core virtue for such an endeavour. We argue further that academic citizenship is not something that is acquired at a general level, but a virtue that emerges from the placeful university offering public engagements in the university and academic engagements in society—a placeful university where integration, dwelling and dialogue prevail. Paraphrasing Vogel's (1994) point about the 'fragile we' of the Heideggerian 'Mitsein' ('Being-with'), we might also say that an authentic public placeful university does not emerge in spite of, but exactly because of, its self-exposure and environmental fragility; the placeful university risks itself, making itself exposed to the judgement and meanings of its inhabitants.

Conclusion: academic citizenship in placeful universities

In this chapter, we have argued for the placeful university; the university as virtuous placeful-ness in the sense that it 'integrates' (Freire, 2013) the private, professional and social spheres of persons and society. It invites people and society to take place and dwell. This integration gives new meaning to the term 'public', which changes from being a neutral *spatiality* to critical, value-saturated and academic placeful-ness of co-belonging between people, society and university. At the placeful university, academic citizenship emerges through dialogical integration and 'Mitsein' in the critically open bond between university and society as they are *in* and *for* each other—not only economically or morally, but ontologically as well.

Academic citizenship is, as we have pointed out, at the same time an ethical, epistemic and ontological virtue. What we know, what we do and who we are as academics in society co-constitute the virtue of academic citizenship. Having academic citizenship implies the formation of public place within the university and academic place within society. This is done authentically when the university offers itself as a means and springboard for social issues and activities in order for them to become critically visible and aware of themselves and the inherent opportunities within them, *rather than* when the university offers to solve or judge the challenges within society. However, 'means' does not in this context connote a passive and indifferent offering of oneself (as the idea of 'service' might critically be understood), but rather an engaged, responsible and dialogical solicitude. Offering the placeful university to a societal endeavour must always take the form of dialogical integration. That entails designing universities that allow for openness, dialogue, mutual integration, joint responsibility and care—*a placeful university for academic citizenship beyond the campus*. This argument hinges on the pressing need for institution-makers—stakeholders, decision makers and front-runners—to acknowledge their central role in building, maintaining and developing the placeful university that promotes academic citizenship, place-making and dwelling. Places for academic dwelling grow out of the environmental work and care for academics that are such a central part of the responsibility of institution-makers. Ultimately, this means that the notion of place and dwelling at the university must be rethought—not only to include classrooms, lecture theatres, libraries, canteens, lounge areas and hallways as spaces to occupy, but to think of them as places to *be for the lived body*: part of the lifeworlds of students and staff. From this, new words and worlds for placeful-ness and academic citizenship must be forged to invite, support and promote the place-making, dwelling and citizenship of the university being as it grows out of its concrete confined campus shell.

Disclosure statement
No potential conflict of interest was reported by the authors.

References

Aaen, J. H., & Nørgård, R. T. (2015). Participatory academic communities: A transdisciplinary perspective on participation in education beyond the institution. In C. M. Reestorff, C. Stage, J. L. Stephensen, L. Fabian, J. Fritsch, K. Samson, et al. (Eds.), *Conjunctions. Transdisciplinary journal of cultural participation*, Special issue on Participation across, between an beyond disciplines and institutions (pp. 67–98). Aarhus: The State and University Library Aarhus.

Barnett, R. (2004). Learning for an unknown future. *Higher Education Research & Development, 23*(3), 247–260.

Barnett, R. (2007). *A will to learn. Being a student in an age of uncertainty*. Berkshire: Open University Press.

Barnett, R. (2011). *Being a university*. London: Routledge.

Barnett, R. (2013). Imagining the university. London: Routledge.

Barnett, R. (2015). In search of a public: Higher education in a global age. In O. Filippakou & G. Williams (Eds.), *Higher education as a public good. Critical perspectives on theory, policy and practice* (pp. 15–28). New York, NY: Peter Lang.

Barnett, R., & Coate, K. (2006). *Engaging the curriculum in higher education*. Berkshire: The Open University Press.

Batchelor, D. (2006). Vulnerable voices: An examination of the concept of vulnerability in relation to student voice. *Educational Philosophy and Theory, 38*(6), 787–800.

Batchelor, D. (2008). Have students got a voice? In R. Barnett & R. Di Napoli (Eds.), *Changing identities in higher education. Voicing perspectives* (pp. 40–54). London: Routledge.

Bengtsen, S. E. (2014). Into the heart of things: Defrosting educational theory. In P. Gibbs & R. Barnett (Eds.), *Thinking about higher education* (pp. 175–191). Switzerland: Springer International.

Beyes, T., & Michels, C. (2014). Performing university space: Multiplicity, relationality, affect. In P. Temple (Ed.), *The physical university. Contours of space and place in higher education* (pp. 15–33). London: Routledge.

Biesta, G. J. J. (2006). *Beyond learning. Democratic education for a human future*. Boulder, CO: Paradigm.

Biesta, G. J. J. (2013). *The beautiful risk of education*. Boulder, CO: Paradigm.

Buchanan, R. (2006). Human dignity and human rights: Thoughts on the principles of human-centered design. In A. Bennett (Ed.), *Design studies* (pp. 300–305). New York, NY: Princeton Architectural Press.

Casey, E. S. (1997). *The fate of place—a philosophical history*. Berkeley, CA: University of California Press.

Creswell, T. (2004). *Place—a short introduction*. Oxford: Blackwell.

Dall'Alba, G. (2013). Re-imagining the university. Developing a capacity to care. In R. Barnett (Ed.), *The future university. Ideas and possibilities* (pp. 112–122). New York, NY: Routledge.

Dall'Alba, G., & Barnacle, R. (2007). An ontological turn for higher education. *Studies in Higher Education, 32*(6), 679–691.
Filippakou, O., & Williams, G. (2015). *Higher education as a public good. Critical perspectives on theory, policy and practice*. New York, NY: Peter Lang.
Freire, P. (2013). *Education for critical consciousness*. London: Bloomsbury.
Gieryn, T. F. (2000). A space for place in sociology. *Annual Review of Sociology, 26*, 463–496.
Harman, G. (2005). *Guerrilla metaphysics. Phenomenology and the carpentry of things*. Chicago, IL: Open Court.
Heidegger, M. (2000). *Being and time*. (J. Macquarrie and E. Robinson, Trans.). Oxford: Blackwell.
Heidegger, M. (2001). *Poetry, language, thought*. (A. Hofstaadter, Trans.). New York, NY: HarperCollins.
Heidegger, M. (2011). *Basic writings. Martin Heidegger*. London: Routledge.
Land, R. (2004). *Educational development. Discourse, identity and practice*. Berkshire: Open University Press.
Lingis, A. (1998). *The imperative*. Bloomington, IN: Indiana University Press.
Macfarlane, B. (2007). *The academic citizen: The virtue of service in university life*. London: Routledge.
Macfarlane, B. (2012). *Intellectual leadership in higher education. Renewing the role of the university professor*. London: Routledge.
Masschelein, J. (2011). Experimentum scholae. The world once more … but not (yet) finished. *Studies in Philosophy of Education, 30*, 529–535.
Merleau-Ponty, M. (2002). *Phenomenology of perception*. (C. Smith, Trans.). London: Routledge.
Nixon, J. (2008). *Towards the virtuous university. The moral bases of academic practice*. New York, NY: Routledge.
Readings, B. (1996). *The university in ruins*. Cambridge, MA: Harvard University Press.
Rømer, T. A. (2010). The educational thing. *Studies in Philosophy of Education, 30*(5), 499–506.
Rømer, T. A. (2011). *Uddannelse i spænding.* Åbenhjertighedens, *påmindelsens og tilsynekomstens pædagogik*. Aarhus: Klim.
Scott, P. (2015). Higher education, the public good and the public interest. In O. Filippakou & G. Williams (Eds.), *Higher education as a public good. Critical perspectives on theory, policy and practice* (pp. 41–58). New York, NY: Peter Lang.
Solberg, M., & Hansen, F. T. (2015). On academic bildung in higher education. A Scandinavian approach. In T. Fossland, H. Mathiasen, & M. Solberg (Eds.), *Academic bildung in net-based higher education* (pp. 28–54). London: Routledge.
Temple, P. (Ed.). (2014a). *The physical university. Contours of space and place in higher education*. London: Routledge.
Temple, P. (2014b). Space, place and university effectiveness. In P. Temple (Ed.), *The physical university. Contours of space and place in higher education* (pp. 3–13). London: Routledge.
Toft, H., & Nørgård, R. T. (in press). Pla(y)ceskabelse. Når børn og robotteknologi mødes. In P. K. Fridorff-Jens, J. J. Hansen, R. Hachmann, L. Buus, I. M. F. Christensen, C. Dalsgaard et al. (Eds.), *Læring og Medier*. Special issue on Robots.

Tuan, Y. (1977). *Space and place—the perspective of experience*. Minneapolis, MN: The University of Minnesota Press.

Vogel, L. (1994). *The fragile "we". Ethical implications of Heidegger's being and time*. Evanston, IL: Northwestern University Press.

Watson, D. (2013). *The question of conscience. Higher education and personal responsibility*. London: IOE Press.

CHAPTER TWENTY-EIGHT

Do We Need an Academic Revolution to Create a Wiser World?

NICHOLAS MAXWELL

Introduction

We urgently need to bring about a revolution in academic inquiry, one that transforms knowledge-inquiry into what may be called *wisdom-inquiry*. This revolution, were it to occur, would help humanity make progress towards as good a world as possible. Wisdom-inquiry gives intellectual priority to articulating problems of living, including global problems, and proposing and critically assessing possible solutions—possible actions, policies, political programmes. It actively seeks to promote public education about what our problems are, and what we need to do about them. It seeks to discover how problematic aims of social, political and economic endeavours may be improved. It includes a virtual government that seeks to discover what the actual government ought to be doing. In these and other ways, wisdom-inquiry would be actively and rationally engaged in helping humanity make progress towards a better world. Academia as it exists at present, dominated by knowledge-inquiry, cannot engage in these vitally necessary activities, or can only do so in a restricted, ineffective fashion. There are strong grounds for holding that wisdom-inquiry would dramatically enhance the capacity of humanity to make progress towards a better, wiser world.

Our Grave Global Problems

Our future looks grim. We are confronted by grave global problems which show every sign of intensifying in the future. Millions, possibly billions, of people may suffer and die prematurely from disaster as a result.

There is the problem of rapid population growth. A few years ago it was thought that the world's population might level off at something like ten billion by the middle of the century. Now it is thought there may be as many as eleven billion people by the end of the century. There is the problem of habitat destruction and increasingly rapid extinction of species. We are living in a period of mass extinctions, only this time the cause is us. There is the problem of vast inequalities of wealth and power around the globe—inequalities that have in some respects being increasing in the last few decades. There is the problem of the spread of modern armaments, conventional, chemical, biological and nuclear. And on top of that, there is our proclivity for war, our record of war, and the increasingly lethal character of war: something like twelve million people killed in wars in the 19th century, around one hundred million in the 20th century—and we have not been doing too well so far in this century. There is the problem of pollution of earth, sea and air. And most serious of all, there are the impending threats of climate change. As the population goes up way beyond what one imagines the earth can sustain, the capacity of the earth to support and feed people goes down as climate change decreases habitable land as a result of drought and flooding, food production is threatened, people attempt to migrate *en masse*, and all the conditions likely to provoke war and devastation come to prevail.

The Role of Universities

One might well hope that universities would be actively and effectively engaged in helping humanity learn how to tackle these grave global problems that threaten to engulf us in disaster. It turns out that, quite to the contrary, universities are in part responsible for the genesis of these problems. They are even the *cause* of these impending disasters—in one perfectly legitimate sense of "cause."[1]

Universities have long been dominated by a view that I shall call *knowledge-inquiry*. According to knowledge-inquiry, the proper way for academia to help promote human welfare is, in the first instance, to acquire knowledge. First, knowledge and technological know-how are to be acquired; then, secondarily, they can be applied to help solve social problems.

Knowledge-inquiry is, however, damagingly irrational in a wholesale fashion when judged from the standpoint of helping to promote human welfare. It is this structural irrationality of our universities that is a key factor in the genesis of our current global problems, and in our present incapacity to solve them.

In order to solve our global problems we need, fundamentally, to *act* in new, more cooperatively rational ways. In order to put a stop to population growth, we need to make birth control available to everyone, and we need to create economies, societies and cultures such that inducements to have lots of children disappear. In order to put a stop to war, we need to discover how to resolve, or cope with, our conflicts without resorting to war. In order to end habitat destruction and extinction of species, we need to change agriculture and development. And in order to put a stop to global warming, insofar as we can, we need to change production of electricity, transport, industry and agriculture so that CO_2 emissions go down to zero. In every case, it is what we *do*, or refrain from doing, that counts. Insofar as knowledge and technology are relevant, is it what these enable us to do that solves our problems.

Thus, a kind of academic inquiry rationally devoted to helping humanity tackle global problems would give absolute intellectual priority to the twin tasks of (1) articulating the problems of living that need to be solved, and (2) proposing and critically assessing possible and actual *actions* from the standpoint of their capacity to resolve global problems. Academia would have, as its basic task, to engage in and promote cooperatively rational tackling of conflicts and problems of living. The pursuit of knowledge and technological know-how would emerge out of and feed back into the central and fundamental intellectual task of promoting increasingly cooperatively rational tackling of problems of living in politics, industry, commerce, finance, agriculture, the media, the law, education, international relations and other areas of personal, social, institutional and global life.

But universities that put knowledge-inquiry into practice can do none of this. Knowledge-inquiry demands that only those considerations relevant to the acquisition of knowledge can enter the intellectual domain of inquiry: evidence, factual claims to knowledge, theory, logic. Proposed solutions to problems of living, including global problems—political actions, policies, political and economic programmes, ways of living, philosophies of life—have no place within knowledge-inquiry because they do not constitute even potential contributions to knowledge. Vital intellectual activities associated with solving problems of living are either excluded from academia altogether, or are pushed to the periphery and marginalized.

Knowledge-inquiry does not just fail to do what most needs to be done to help humanity learn how to solve global problems. Even worse, perhaps, the astonishing intellectual success of scientific and technological research pursued within the framework of knowledge-inquiry has been a key factor in the genesis of our global problems in the first place.

Modern science and technology have of course been of great benefit to humanity. They have made the modern world possible. But, in making possible modern medicine and hygiene, modern industry and agriculture, modern armaments, they have also made possible population growth, habitat destruction and extinction of species, the lethal character of modern war, and climate change. But science and technology are not themselves to blame. Rather, what is to blame is science and technology *pursued in a way which is dissociated from a more fundamental concern with our problems of living and what to do about them.* What is to blame, in other words, is science and technology pursued within the framework of knowledge-inquiry. If, during the past two or three centuries, academia had given priority to helping humanity learn how to tackle problems of living in increasingly cooperatively rational ways, we might have learned how to deal with incipient global problems long ago, before they became too serious. It is the astonishing intellectual success of modern scientific and technological research *pursued within the framework of knowledge-inquiry* that is the key factor in the genesis of our global problems—and the key factor in our current incapacity to solve them.

All this ought to have been an obvious outcome, long ago. Scientific knowledge and technological know-how vastly increase our power to act—for some of us, at least. In the absence of wisdom, this enhanced power to act, bequeathed to us by science, can be expected to have all sorts of beneficial consequences—as indeed it has. But it ought also to be expected that it will have all sorts of harmful consequences as well, either unintended and unforeseen, as in environmental damage (initially), or intentionally, in war and terrorism.

As long as we did not have modern science, lack of wisdom did not matter too much. We lacked the power to do too much damage to ourselves and the planet. Now that we have modern science, wisdom has become, not a private luxury, but a public necessity.

As a matter of supreme urgency, we need to bring about an intellectual-institutional revolution in our universities so that they become rationally organized and devoted to helping us create a wiser world.

From Knowledge to Wisdom

For nearly 40 years now I have argued, in a steady stream of books, articles and lectures, that we urgently need to transform universities around the world so that come to seek and promote wisdom, and do not just acquire knowledge, as they do, by and large, at present.[2] Since this argument is readily available, in great detail, and in summary, I will here now only briefly indicate how the argument goes—already sketched in the previous section. I will then spell out 23 implications the argument has for changes that need to be made to universities and academic inquiry. I then indicate how and why these changes really would make a difference to the capacity of universities to help humanity create a wiser world, and I conclude by considering a number of developments in universities in the last few years that can be regarded as steps towards the kind of inquiry we really need.

I distinguish two kinds of inquiry which I call "knowledge-inquiry" (indicated above) and "wisdom-inquiry." Both kinds of inquiry take helping to promote human welfare—helping people realize what is of value in life—to be the fundamental (social or humanitarian) aim of inquiry. Knowledge-inquiry holds that the proper way to do this is for academia in the first instance to pursue the intellectual aim of knowledge. First, knowledge is to be acquired; then it can be applied to help solve social problems. This is the conception and kind of inquiry we have inherited from the past. Even though not everything that goes on in universities conforms precisely to its edicts, it nevertheless still dominates academia today. But it is, I argue, profoundly and damagingly irrational. Wisdom-inquiry is what emerges when knowledge-inquiry is modified just sufficiently to remove its rationality defects. According to wisdom-inquiry, the intellectual and social (or humanitarian) aims of academia are one and the same: to seek and promote wisdom—wisdom being the active endeavour and capacity to realize what is of value in life, for oneself and others, wisdom thus including knowledge, technological know-how and understanding, but much else besides.

The notion of rationality that we require for this argument appeals to the idea that there is some rather ill-defined set of rules, methods or strategies which, if put into practice, give us a best chance, other things being equal, of solving our problems, realizing our desirable aims. The rules of reason don't guarantee success, and don't tell us precisely what to do—they tell us, rather, what to attempt. They are meta-methods: they presuppose that we can already implement many methods in successfully performing many actions, solving many problems, realizing many aims, and they tell us how best to marshal these successful actions in order to solve new problems, and realize hitherto unrealized aims.

I have two arguments. The first appeals to a problem-solving conception of rationality; the second employs and develops an aim pursuing conception.

Here is the first argument.

Four elementary, wholly uncontroversial rules of reason are the following:

(1) Articulate, and try to improve the articulation of, the problem to be solved.
(2) Propose and critically assess possible solutions.[3]

(3) If the problem to be solved is especially difficult, break it up into easier-to-solve, preliminary, specialized, subordinate problems, in an attempt to work gradually towards the solution to the basic problem to be solved.
(4) But in this case ensure that basic and specialized problem-solving interact with one another, so that each influences the other.[4]

Any problem-solving endeavour which persistently violates just one of these rules is severely irrational, and will suffer as a result. Knowledge-inquiry is so seriously irrational that it violates, not just one, but *three* of these rules.

Knowledge-inquiry puts rule (3) into practice—at least as far as problems of knowledge are concerned. And indeed, a striking feature of academia today is that specialization is rampant. Specialized disciplines divide again, again and again into ever more specialized sub-sub-disciplines. But knowledge-inquiry violates rules (1), (2) and (4). Granted that the basic aim is to help promote human welfare then the basic problems that academia, dominated by knowledge-inquiry, needs to try to help solve are problems of living. Implementing the first two rules thus involves (1) articulating, and improving the articulation of, problems of living, and (2) proposing and critically assessing possible solutions—possible and actual actions, policies, political programmes, etc. But, given knowledge-inquiry, these activities are excluded from the intellectual domain of academia on the grounds that they do not contribute to knowledge (and might even subvert knowledge). Instead of occupying centre stage, they are banished altogether or, at best, marginalized. Once rules (1) and (2) are violated, rule (4) is violated as well, since rule (4) requires rules (1) and (2) to be implemented.

The gross, structural irrationality of knowledge-inquiry—so extreme that it amounts to *three* of the four most elementary rules of reason one can conceive of being permanently violated—is no mere formal matter. Failure to put rules (1), (2) and (4) into practice means that universities fail to do what they most need to do to help humanity learn how to tackle our current grave global problems. Furthermore, it is the extraordinarily successful solving of specialized problems of knowledge dissociated from a more fundamental concern for problems of living—because of the failure to put rules (1), (2) and (4) into academic practice—which has led modern scientific and technological research to be the key factor in the genesis of our global problems in the first place. It is hardly too much to say that our failure to learn how to solve global problems is due to the gross irrationality of academic inquiry, encapsulated in its failure to implement the elementary rules of reason (1), (2) and (4).

Wisdom-inquiry (first version) arises as a result of knowledge-inquiry being modified just sufficiently to ensure that all four rules of reason are built into the intellectual-institutional structure of academic inquiry and universities. The social sciences and humanities need to change quite fundamentally so that they give intellectual priority to (1) articulating problems of living, and (2) proposing and critically assessing possible solutions. Social science is not, fundamentally, *science*, or the pursuit of *knowledge*. It has, rather, the task of promoting increasingly cooperatively rational tackling of problems of living in the real world. The relationship between social inquiry and natural science needs to change. The former is

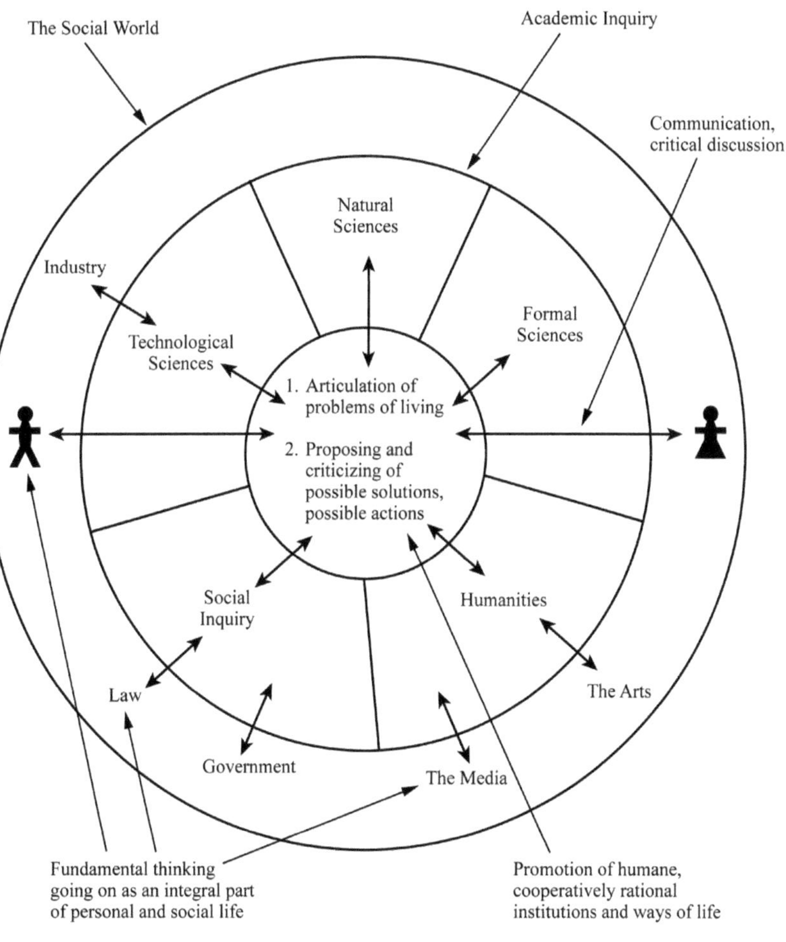

Diagram 28.1: Problem-Solving Version of Wisdom-Inquiry.
Source: Author (2015).

intellectually more fundamental than the latter. The whole relationship between academic inquiry and society needs to change. A basic task of academia is not to *study* society, but to encourage and promote cooperatively rational tackling of problems of living as an integral part of personal, social, institutional and global life. As I have said on more than one occasion, wisdom-inquiry academia needs to do openly for the public what civil services are supposed to do in secret for governments: see diagram 28.1.

So much for the summary of the first argument. The second argument builds on and develops the first one.

It may be asked: if it is right that academia violates three of the four most elementary rules of reason conceivable, how and when did this state of affairs arise? It goes back to the 18th century Enlightenment. The *philosophes* of the French Enlightenment, Voltaire, Diderot and the rest, had the magnificent idea that it might be possible to learn from scientific progress how to achieve social progress towards an enlightened world. They did what they could to put this idea into practice in their lives. But in developing the idea intellectually, they made a series of blunders, and it is these blunders that we are suffering from today.

In order to develop the Enlightenment idea, three steps need to be got right.

(1) The progress-achieving methods of natural science must be correctly characterized.
(2) These methods must be appropriately generalized so that they become potentially fruitfully applicable to any worthwhile, problematic human endeavour, and not just to science.
(3) These generalized, progress-achieving methods must then be got into the fabric of personal and social life, into our other social endeavours besides science, and above all into the endeavour to make progress towards as good a world as possible.

The *philosophes* got all three steps wrong. They thought (1) natural science makes progress by assessing claims to knowledge impartially and exclusively by means of evidence. This *standard empiricist* conception of scientific method did not need much generalization because the *philosophes* thought that step (3) involved applying scientific method to the task of improving *knowledge* of the social world. Knowledge of the social world first needs to be acquired; then it can be applied to help humanity make progress towards a better world. They set about creating the social sciences: psychology, economics, sociology and the rest. These were developed throughout the 19th century, often outside universities, and built into academia in the early 20th century. The outcome is what we have today: knowledge-inquiry.

But if the above three steps had been implemented correctly, the outcome would have been very different. Let us take the three steps in turn.

Step (1). It is false that science proceeds by assessing claims to knowledge by means of evidence alone. In physics, a new theory, in order to be accepted, must (i) be sufficiently empirically successful, and (ii) sufficiently *unified.* Endlessly many disunified rival theories can always be concocted to fit the evidence even better than the accepted theory, but these never get considered for a moment. This persistent rejection of empirically more successful, disunified rivals means that physics accepts implicitly a metaphysical (i.e. untestable) thesis about the world, independent of (or even against) the evidence, which asserts at least: the universe is such that no seriously disunified theory is true. There is, in other words, some kind of underlying unity in nature.

This implicit metaphysical presupposition is both influential and problematic. It needs to be made explicit so that it can be critically assessed and, we may hope, improved. In order to facilitate its improvement, we need to represent it in the form of a hierarchy of assumptions, and associated methods, assumptions becoming progressively less and less substantial and so more and more likely to be true, and more nearly such that their truth is required for science to be possible at all, as we go up the hierarchy: see diagram 28.2. The assumption at the top, at level 7, is: the universe is such that we can acquire some knowledge of our immediate circumstances. We will never want to reject that conjectural assumption, even if we have no reason to hold it to be true. From level 6 to level 2, that thesis is accepted which best accords with the thesis above. The thesis at level 3 is chosen to do the best justice to the most empirically progressive research programme of theoretical physics.

All this may be reformulated in terms of aims. The aim of theoretical physics is not truth per se; rather, it is truth *presupposed to be explanatory*—explanatory truth, in other words. Because this aim is profoundly problematic, we need to represent it in the form of a hierarchy of aims, and associated methods, aims becoming less and less specific and problematic, as we go up the hierarchy.

As physics advances, and knowledge improves, aims and methods, low down in the hierarchy, improve as well. There is something like positive feedback between improving scientific knowledge, and improving aims and methods—improving knowledge about how to improve knowledge. According to this conception of science, which I have called *aim-oriented empiricism*, this positive feedback feature is the nub of scientific rationality. It helps explain the explosive growth in scientific knowledge and understanding. For, even though most scientists pay at least lip service to the orthodox standard empiricist view that evidence alone decides what theories are accepted and rejected, physics in practice, in a somewhat implicit way,

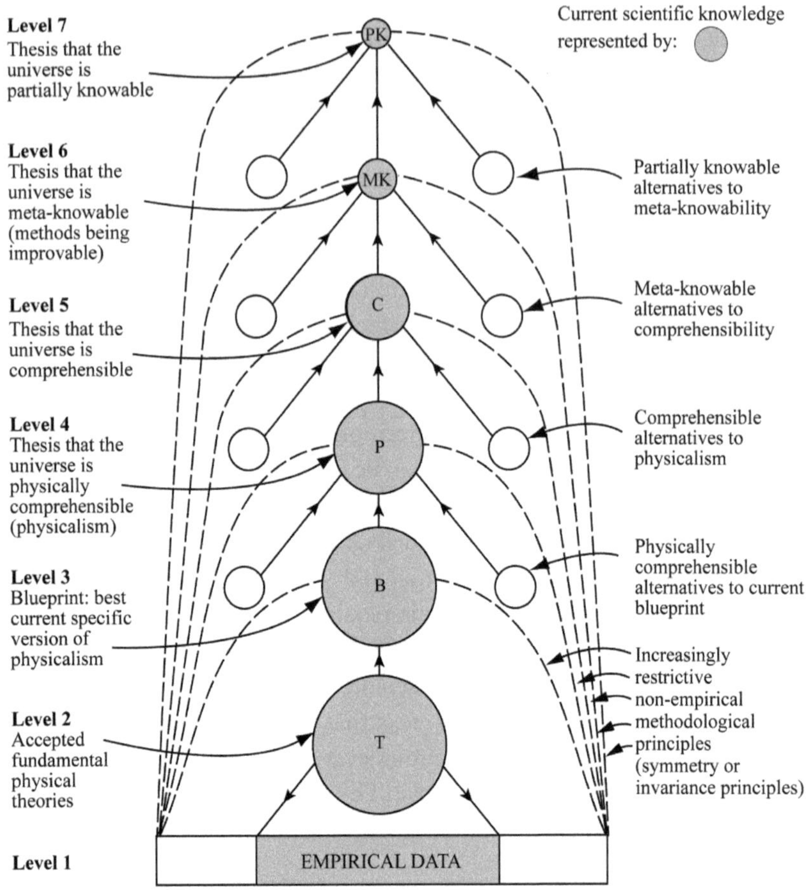

Diagram 28.2: Aim-Oriented Empiricism.
Source: Author (2015).

has put something like aim-oriented empiricist view into practice. If it had not done, we would still be stuck with Aristotelian science.[5]

Correcting the first step, then, involves rejecting the orthodox standard empiricist conception of science, and adopting and implementing aim-oriented empiricism instead as constituting the correct progress-achieving methods of science.

Step (2) involves generalizing aim-oriented empiricism to form *aim-oriented rationality*, a conception of rationality especially fruitful when aims are problematic or misrepresented, as they often are. Aim-oriented rationality requires us to represent problematic aims in the form of a hierarchy of aims, and associated methods, on analogy with aim-oriented empiricism, so that we create a framework of relatively unproblematic aims and methods, high up in the hierarchy, within which much more problematic and contested aims, and associated methods, may be improved as we seek to resolve conflicts, and act.[6]

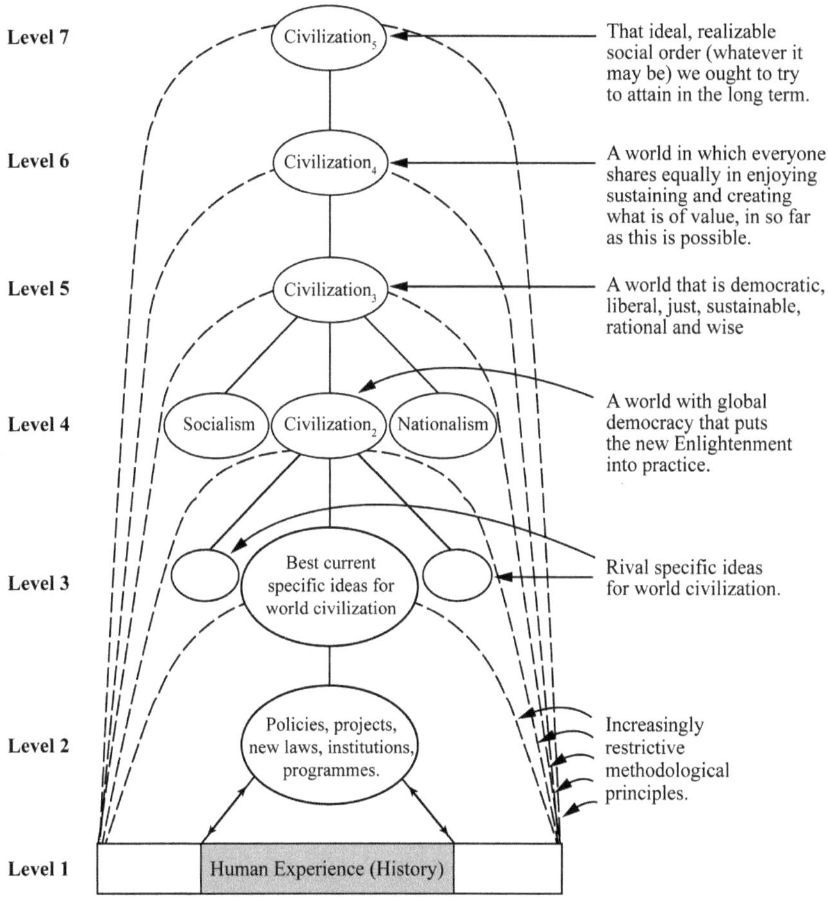

Diagram 28.3: Aim-Oriented Rationality Applied to the Task of Creating a Wiser World.
Source: Author (2015).

Step (3) consists in the vital, momentous and long-term task of getting aim-oriented rationality adopted and implemented in personal and social life. Progress-achieving methods, which have proved to be so astonishingly successful in natural science, need to be got into all our other worthwhile social and institutional endeavours with problematic aims: government, industry, agriculture, the economy, finance, international relations, the media, the law, education, marriage and personal life.

The proper, primary task of social inquiry and the humanities is to work out how this is to be done, in a multitude of social contexts, and help people do it. This means that social inquiry is not primarily social *science*, or devoted to the pursuit of *knowledge* of social phenomena: rather, the various branches of social inquiry and the humanities need to be pursued, and conceived of, as *social methodology* or *social philosophy*. What philosophy of science is to science within the framework of aim-oriented empiricism—that part of the scientific endeavour which seeks to articulate and improve the aims and methods of science—so social inquiry and the humanities are to the social world. Their task is to articulate and help improve problematic aims of diverse social endeavours.

Above all, their task is to help the great social-moral-political endeavour to make progress towards as good a world as possible (insofar as it exists) to put aim-oriented rationality into practice: see diagram 28.3.

The outcome of correcting the three blunders of the Enlightenment in the ways indicated would be *wisdom-inquiry*, a kind of academic inquiry very different from what we have at present. The basic aim of wisdom-inquiry (as I have already remarked) is to seek and promote, not just knowledge, but rather wisdom—wisdom being the active endeavour and capacity to realize what is of value in life, for oneself and others, "realize" meaning both "apprehend" or "experience" and "create" or "make real," wisdom-inquiry doing better justice to both aspects of inquiry (inquiry pursued for its own sake, and inquiry pursued in order to realize other ends).[7]

Unfortunately, despite the fact that this argument, very briefly summarized here, has been spelled out in detail in the literature for over 40 years at the time of writing, there is little awareness of the urgent need to transform academia in the way I have indicated. It is not just that social inquiry is still pursued primarily as social *science*. The very idea that we need to develop social *methodology* is still almost entirely unknown. The profound importance of building aim-oriented rationality into the fabric of social life is not appreciated. Even worse, the very concept of aim-oriented rationality is still largely unknown.

Our grave global problems, our threatening future, stare us in the face. Everyone appreciates that we humans, above all, are the species that learns. And yet, mysteriously, it has not yet dawned on humanity—or even on experts in the field—that we urgently need to learn how to tackle our grave global problems more intelligently, effectively and humanely than we have managed to do so far, and for that our institutions of learning need to be well designed, rationally designed and devoted to the task. It has not dawned on those whose job it is to concern themselves about these matters that our institutions of learning, above all our universities, are an intellectual and rationality disaster when judged from this standpoint, it being vital for the future of humanity that we put right the structural intellectual-institutional defects that at present plague academia, inherited from the blunders of the Enlightenment.

From Knowledge-Inquiry to Wisdom-Inquiry

Here is a list of 23 intellectual and institutional changes that need to be made to academia if knowledge-inquiry is to become wisdom-inquiry. All but the last three follow from the requirement that knowledge-inquiry be modified so as to implement elementary standards of problem-solving and aim-pursuing rationality.

1. There needs to be a change in the basic intellectual *aim* of inquiry, from the growth of knowledge to the growth of wisdom—wisdom being taken to be the capacity to realize what is of value in life, for oneself and others, and thus including knowledge, understanding and technological know-how (but much else besides).
2. There needs to be a change in the nature of academic *problems*, so that problems of living are included, as well as problems of knowledge—the former being treated as intellectually more fundamental than the latter.
3. There needs to be a change in the nature of academic *ideas*, so that proposals for action are included as well as claims to knowledge—the former, again, being treated as intellectually more fundamental than the latter.
4. There needs to be a change in what constitutes intellectual *progress*, so that progress-in-ideas-relevant-to-achieving-a-more-civilized-world is included as well as progress in knowledge, the former being indeed intellectually fundamental.
5. There needs to be a change in the idea as to where inquiry, at its most fundamental, is located. It is not esoteric theoretical physics, but rather the thinking we engage in as we seek to achieve what is of value in life. Academic thought is a (vital) adjunct to what really matters, personal and social thought active in life.
6. There needs to be a dramatic change in the nature of social inquiry (reflecting points 1 to 5). Economics, politics, sociology, and so on, are not, fundamentally, *sciences*, and do not, fundamentally, have the task of improving knowledge about social phenomena. Instead, their task is threefold. First, it is to articulate problems of living, and propose and critically assess possible solutions, possible actions or policies, from the standpoint of their capacity, if implemented, to promote wiser ways of

living. Second, it is to promote such cooperatively rational tackling of problems of living throughout the social world. And third, at a more basic and long-term level, it is to help build the hierarchical structure of aims and methods of aim-oriented rationality into personal, institutional and global life, thus creating frameworks within which progressive improvement of personal and social life aims-and-methods becomes possible. These three tasks are undertaken in order to promote cooperative tackling of problems of living—but also in order to enhance empathic or "personalistic" understanding between people as something of value in its own right. Acquiring knowledge of social phenomena is a vital but subordinate activity, engaged in to facilitate the above three fundamental pursuits.

7. Natural science needs to change, so that it includes at least three levels of discussion: evidence, theory and research aims. Discussion of aims needs to bring together scientific, metaphysical and evaluative consideration in an attempt to discover the most desirable and realizable research aims. It needs to influence, and be influenced by, exploration of problems of living undertaken by social inquiry and the humanities, and the public.
8. There needs to be a dramatic change in the relationship between social inquiry and natural science, so that social inquiry becomes intellectually more fundamental from the standpoint of tackling problems of living and promoting wisdom. Social inquiry influences choice of research aims for the natural and technological sciences, and is, of course, in turn influenced by the results of such research. (Social inquiry also, of course, conducts empirical research, in order to improve our understanding of what our problems of living are, and in order to assess policy ideas whenever possible.)
9. The current emphasis on specialized research needs to change so that sustained discussion and tackling of broad, global problems that cut across academic specialities is included, both influencing and being influenced by, specialized research.
10. Academia needs to include sustained imaginative and critical exploration of possible futures, for each country, and for humanity as a whole, policy and research implications being discussed as well.
11. The way in which academic inquiry as a whole is related to the rest of the human world needs to change dramatically. Instead of being intellectually dissociated from the rest of society, academic inquiry needs to be communicating with, learning from, teaching and arguing with the rest of society—in such a way as to promote cooperative rationality and social wisdom. Academia needs to have just sufficient power to retain its independence from the pressures of government, industry, the military and

public opinion, but no more. Academia becomes a kind of civil service for the public, doing openly and independently what actual civil services are supposed to do in secret for governments.

12. There needs to be a change in the role that political and religious ideas, works of art, expressions of feelings, desires and values have within rational inquiry. Instead of being excluded, they need to be explicitly included and critically assessed, as possible indications and revelations of what is of value, and as unmasking of fraudulent values in satire and parody, vital ingredients of wisdom.
13. There need to be changes in education so that, for example, seminars devoted to the cooperative, imaginative and critical discussion of problems of living are at the heart of all education from five-year-olds onwards. Politics, which cannot be taught by knowledge-inquiry, becomes central to wisdom-inquiry, political creeds and actions being subjected to imaginative and critical scrutiny.
14. There need to be changes in the aims, priorities and character of pure science and scholarship, so that it is the curiosity, the seeing and searching, the knowing and understanding of individual persons that ultimately matters, the more impersonal, esoteric, purely intellectual aspects of science and scholarship being means to this end. Social inquiry needs to give intellectual priority to helping empathic understanding between people to flourish (as indicated in 6 above).
15. There need to be changes in the way mathematics is understood, pursued and taught. Mathematics is not a branch of knowledge at all. Rather, it is concerned to explore problematic *possibilities*, and to develop, systematize and unify problem-solving methods.
16 Literature needs to be put close to the heart of rational inquiry, in that it explores imaginatively our most profound problems of living and aids personalistic understanding in life by enhancing our ability to enter imaginatively into the problems and lives of others.
17. Philosophy needs to change so that it ceases to be just another specialized discipline and becomes instead that aspect of inquiry as a whole that is concerned with our most general and fundamental problems—those problems that cut across all disciplinary boundaries. Philosophy needs to become again what it was for Socrates: the attempt to devote reason to the growth of wisdom in life.
18. Academic contributions need to be written in as simple, lucid, jargon-free a way as possible, so that academic work is as accessible as possible across specialities and to non-academics.

19. There needs to be a change in views about what constitute academic contributions, so that publications which promote (or have the potential to promote) public understanding as to what our problems of living are and what we need to do about them are included, in addition to contributions addressed primarily to the academic community.
20. Every university needs to create a seminar or symposium devoted to the sustained discussion of fundamental problems that cut across all conventional academic boundaries, global problems of living being included as well as problems of knowledge and understanding.

In addition, the following three institutional innovations ought also to be made to help wisdom-inquiry to flourish:

21. Natural science needs to create committees, in the public eye, and manned by scientists and non-scientists alike, concerned to highlight and discuss failures of the priorities of research to respond to the interests of those whose needs are the greatest—the poor of the earth—as a result of the inevitable tendency of research priorities to reflect the interests of those who pay for science, and the interests of scientists themselves.
22. Every national university system needs to include a national shadow government, seeking to do, virtually, free of the constraints of power, what the actual national government ought to be doing. The hope would be that virtual and actual governments would learn from each other.
23. The world's universities need to include a virtual world government which seeks to do what an actual elected world government ought to do, if it existed. The virtual world government would also have the task of working out how an actual democratically elected world government might be created.

Conclusion

Our only hope of solving our problems successfully lies in tackling them *democratically*. This in turn requires that a majority of people on earth have a good understanding of what our problems are, and what we need to do about them. Democratically elected governments are unlikely to be able to do what is required if the people who elect them do not understand what our problems are, and what we need to do to resolve them. This in turn requires that we have in existence institutions of learning rationally devoted to helping humanity come to understand what our problems are, and what needs to be done to solve them. It is just this that we do not have at present. Instead, we have institutions of learning devoted to the pursuit of *knowledge*. But it is knowledge and technological know-how, and the power that these engender, in the absence of wisdom, that have made possible the creation of our current global problems.

We urgently need to bring about a revolution in our schools and universities so that they come to seek and promote wisdom by rational means. Almost every branch and aspect of academic inquiry needs to change.

This revolution—intellectual, institutional and cultural—if it ever comes about, will be comparable in its long-term impact to that of the Renaissance, the scientific revolution or the Enlightenment. The outcome will be traditions and institutions of learning rationally designed to help us realize what is of value in life. There are a few scattered signs that this intellectual revolution, from knowledge to wisdom, is already under way. It will need, however, much wider cooperative support—from scientists, scholars, students, research councils, university administrators, vice chancellors, teachers, the media and the general public—if it is to become anything more than what it is at present, a fragmentary and often impotent movement of protest and opposition, often at odds with itself, exercising little influence on the main body of academic work. I can hardly imagine any more important work for anyone associated with academia than, in teaching, learning and research, to help promote this revolution.

Notes

1. It may be objected that it is not *science* that is the cause of global problems but rather the things that we *do*, made possible by science and technology. This is obviously correct. But it is also correct to say that scientific and technological progress *is* the cause. The meaning of "cause" is ambiguous. By "the cause" of event E we may mean something like "the most obvious observable events preceding E that figure in the common sense explanation for the occurrence of E." In this sense, human actions (made possible by science) are the cause of such things as people being killed in war, destruction of tropical rainforests. On the other hand, by the "cause" of E we may mean "that prior change in the environment of E which led to the occurrence of E, and without which E would not have occurred." If we put the 21st and 20th century into the context of human history, then it is entirely correct to say that, in this sense, scientific and technological progress is the cause of our distinctive current global disasters: what has changed, what is new, is scientific knowledge and technological know-how, not human nature. Give a group of chimpanzees rifles and teach them how to use them and in one sense, of course, the cause of the subsequent demise of the group would be the actions of the chimpanzees. But in another obvious sense, the cause would be the sudden availability and use of rifles—the new, lethal technology. Yet again, from the standpoint of theoretical physics, "the cause" of E might be interpreted to mean something like "the physical state of affairs prior to E, throughout a sufficiently large spatial region

surrounding the place where E occurs." In this third sense, the sun continuing to shine is as much a part of the cause of war and pollution as human action or human science and technology. In short, if by the cause of an event we mean that prior change which led to that event occurring, and without which the event would not have occurred (the second of the above three senses), then it is the advent of modern science and technology that has *caused* all our current global crises. It is not that people became greedier or more wicked in the 19th and 20th centuries; nor is it that the new economic system of capitalism is responsible, as some historians and economists would have us believe (science plus communism would have done the trick just as well—even better, in fact, as the record of the Soviet Union reveals, in connection with environmental degradation, for example). The crucial factor is the creation and immense success of modern science and technology.

2. The argument was first expounded in Maxwell (1976). It received a much more detailed exposition in Maxwell (1984; 2nd ed., 2007), and was further developed in Maxwell (2004; 2014a; 2014b; 2016b; 2017a; 2017b). Summaries of the argument are given in Maxwell (1980; 1992; 2000; 2007; 2009; 2012).
3. "the one method of all rational discussion ... is that of stating one's problem clearly and examining its various proposed possible solutions critically" Popper (1959, p. 16). Popper was too opposed to specialization to emphasize rule (3); he did not see that the evils of overspecialization can be counteracted by implementing rule (4). For a discussion of Popper's opposition to specialization, see Maxwell (2016a).
4. For a more detailed discussion of methods of rational problem-solving, see Maxwell (1984, ch. 4).
5. For a very much more detailed exposition and defence of aim-oriented empiricism, see Maxwell (1984, chs. 5 and 9, or 2nd ed., chs. 5, 9, and 14; 1998; 2004; 2005; 2013; 2016b; 2017a; 2017b). It was first expounded in Maxwell (1974).
6. I here tread a path parallel to the one trod by Popper, when he generalized his falsificationist conception of scientific method—see Popper (1959, 1963)—to form *critical rationalism*, which Popper then applied to social and political problems, above all in his masterpiece, Popper (1962). Thus Popper declares "inter-subjective *testing* is merely a very important aspect of the more general idea of inter-subjective *criticism*, or in other words, of the idea of mutual rational control by critical discussion" Popper (1959, p. 44, n *1).
7. For much more detailed expositions of the argument for wisdom-inquiry (or "the philosophy of wisdom" as I have called wisdom-inquiry in the past), see Maxwell (1976; 1980; 1984; 1998; 2004; 2014a; 2014b; 2016b; 2017a; 2017b).

References

Maxwell, N., 1974, The Rationality of Scientific Discovery, Part I: The Traditional Rationality Problem, *Philosophy of Science*, vol. 41, pp. 123–153.

—— 1976, *What's Wrong With Science?* Bran's Head Books, Hayes, Middlesex (2nd ed., Pentire Press, 2009).

—— 1980, Science, Reason, Knowledge and Wisdom: A Critique of Specialism, *Inquiry*, vol. 23, pp. 19–81.

—— 1984, *From Knowledge to Wisdom: A Revolution in the Aims and Methods of Science*, Blackwell, Oxford (2nd ed., revised and extended, Pentire Press, 2007).

—— 1992, What Kind of Inquiry Can Best Help Us Create a Good World? *Science, Technology and Human Values*, vol. 17, pp. 205–227.

—— 1998, *The Comprehensibility of the Universe: A New Conception of Science*, Clarendon Press, Oxford.

—— 2000, Can Humanity Learn to become Civilized? The Crisis of Science without Civilization, *Journal of Applied Philosophy*, vol. 17, pp. 29–44.

—— 2004, *Is Science Neurotic?*, Imperial College Press, London.

—— 2005, Popper, Kuhn, Lakatos and Aim-Oriented Empiricism, *Philosophia*, vol. 32, nos. 1–4, pp. 181–239.

—— 2007, From Knowledge to Wisdom: The Need for an Academic Revolution, *London Review of Education*, vol. 5, no. 2, pp. 97–115.

—— 2009, How Can Life of Value Best Flourish in the Real World? in *Science and the Pursuit of Wisdom: Studies in the Philosophy of Nicholas Maxwell*, ed. L. McHenry, Ontos Verlag, Frankfurt, pp. 1–56.

—— 2012, The Menace of Science without Civilization: From Knowledge to Wisdom (Text of Keynote Lecture given in Warsaw 20 May 2011), *Dialogue and Universalism*, no. 3, 2012, pp. 39–63.

—— 2013, Has Science Established that the Cosmos is Physically Comprehensible? *Recent Advances in* Cosmology, ed. Travena, A and Soen, B. Nova Publishers Inc, New York, Chapter One, pp. 1–56.

—— 2014a, *How Universities Can Help Create a Wiser World: The Urgent Need for an Academic Revolution*, Imprint Academic, Exeter.

—— 2014b, *Global Philosophy*, Imprint Academic, Exeter.

—— 2016a, Popper's Paradoxical Pursuit of Natural Philosophy, in *Cambridge Companion to Popper*, ed. J. Shearmur and G. Stokes, Cambridge University Press; available online at http://philpapers.org/archive/ MAXPPP.1.doc.

—— 2016b, *Two Great Problems of Learning: Science and Civilization*, Rounded Globe, ebook available free at https://roundedglobe.com/books/61539716-6ed9-4df5-89fa-8fdd5ec80df8/Two%20Great%20Problems%20of%20Learning:%20Science%20and%20Civilization/

—— 2017a, U*nderstanding Scientific Progress*, Paragon House, Saint Paul, Minnesota.

—— 2017b, *In Praise of Natural Philosophy: A Revolution for Thought and Life*, McGill-Queen's University Press, Montreal, Quebec.

Popper, K., 1959, *The Logic of Scientific Discovery*, Hutchinson, London.

—— 1962, *The Open Society and Its Enemies*, Routledge and Kegan Paul, London.

—— 1963, *Conjectures and Refutations*, Routledge and Kegan Paul, London.

CHAPTER TWENTY-NINE

Renewing the Idea of the University

The Cosmopolitan and Postcolonial Projects

MICHAEL A. PETERS

Introduction

This essay explores the discourse concerning the Idea of the University and its moral ideals to ask in face of the neoliberal Onslaught: is there life after the death of the liberal university? I refer to these ideals as "ends" in the traditional Kantian sense. I also use the term to refer to "ends" more elliptically and metaphorically to refer to the discourse that addresses itself to the "end of the University" (as we know it), that is, an institution no longer tied to the historical mission and a specific moral and cultural set of ideals of the Humboldtian or Newmanian university expressed in the concept of *Bildung* or Catholic theology. Many contemporary scholars, for example, now talk of the "post-historical" university and discuss its various neoliberal formations as the "entrepreneurial," "enterprise," or "innovation." The post-historical university institutes a break with the past and with the tradition of the Idea of the University in terms of moral, aesthetic, and epistemological criteria. Most often, this break with the past, and therefore with the Idea of the University, is considered in terms of its new economic mission imposed by neoliberal policies. Sometimes, much less often, the break is seen in *positive* terms as a means of encouraging a different kind of institution that cannot simply be reduced to neoliberal criteria and at the same time signals a departure from the liberal discourse to express a new set of ideals such as "ecological," "open," "digital," or "creative."

The "ends" of the university refers to both the moral ideals that characterize the Idea of the University as well as the discourse that expresses these ideals and the attendant anxiety that the institution is being permanently separated from them. One question that emerges around "the new" is whether it represents a genuine departure or rather an accommodation of new ideas within the discourse referred to as the Idea of the University. I examine two moments of renewal of the university: the cosmopolitan, a renewal from within the tradition and discourse; and, postcolonial, a renewal from outside the tradition. The former is a Kantian moment based on a cosmopolitanism that, in the best sense, may substitute or offer a lead for forms of internationalization and globalization; the latter originates in a critique of the Western tradition and therefore of the Idea of the University, often emphasizing its blind rationalism, its culture-bound moral ideas, its Orientalism, and the false universalism of European civilizational ideas.

The Cosmopolitan University

Moral Cosmopolitanism

To talk of the cosmopolitan university is immediately to invoke a globally oriented institution that aims at the cultivation of globally minded citizens. In short, it is oriented to the cultivation of cosmopolitan citizens rather than national citizens. The idea of "citizen of the world," though vague, has been characterized by a set of political values that has been an enduring feature of Western political thinking forming the basis for international law. Indeed, the root of the word first used in 1614 to mean "citizen of the world" derives from the Greek *kosmopolites* (*kosmos* "world," *polites* meaning "citizen," and *polis* meaning "city"). "Cosmopolitanism" with a first recorded use in 1828 registers the idea that there is a *single moral community* based on the idea of freedom and thus in the early twenty-first century is also seen as a major theoretical buttress to the concept of universal human rights that transcend all national, cultural, and state boundaries.

While the Greeks had a concept of "cosmopolitanism" that issued from the Sophists against the form of political culture advocated by Plato and Aristotle which was wedded to the city and its citizens, and later took a Stoic form that was popular with early Christianity, its modern form emerged with the Enlightenment and was associated first with Erasmus' humanism and with the development of natural law doctrine. Pauline Kleingeld (2006) argues

> The historical context of the philosophical resurgence of cosmopolitanism during the Enlightenment is made up of many factors: the increasing rise of capitalism and world-wide trade and its theoretical reflections; the reality of ever expanding empires whose reach extended across the globe; the voyages around the world and the anthropological so-called "discoveries" facilitated through these; the renewed interest in Hellenistic philosophy; and the emergence of a notion of human rights and a philosophical focus on human reason.

Kleingeld (2006) documents the way in which the impulse of cosmopolitanism was strongest in the late eighteenth century both feeding and growing out of the 1789 declaration of human rights. While Montesquieu, Voltaire, Diderot, Addison, Hume, and Jefferson all saw themselves as cosmopolitans, it was Kant (1970) who defended and popularized the idea that human beings belong to a single moral community sharing the characteristics of freedom, equality, and autonomy that grounded the concept and legitimacy of law.

Moral cosmopolitanism, therefore, had a parallel in political philosophy based on a concept of law that applied to all States. Thus, Kant in *Perpetual Peace* (1795) argues for a concept of moral cosmopolitanism based on universal law which States would observe even though he rejected a strong notion of world government in favor of a loose federation. In Section II of Perpetual Peace, he adumbrates the principles—"three definitive articles"—that are required to establish peace (against the natural state of war) beginning with the republican civic constitution, a federation of free States, and the law of world citizenship is said to be limited to conditions of "universal hospitality" where "Hospitality means the right of a stranger not to be treated as an enemy when he arrives in the land of another."

Political Cosmopolitanism

On this initial formulation, the "cosmopolitan university" is an extension of a set of cosmopolitan values and ideals that constitutes the Western political tradition and acts to both inform and develop that set of values embedded in the concept of human rights. As a first formulation, the cosmopolitan university might be said to be devoted to the cultivation of global citizens and to expanding the concept of human rights as a universal framework for the resolution of world problems.

The notion of "citizen of the world" or "global citizens," in its oldest incarnation, is associated with ideas of cosmopolitanism. But the capacity of cosmopolitans to proclaim the idea of a moral community and to travel has always been dependent on the capacity of states to guarantee safety and movement. Yet Bowden (2003) points out an obvious contradiction confronting the idea of cosmopolitan global citizenship:

> For cosmopolitan advocates of global citizenship there is an inescapable dilemma that is still to be addressed with any degree of satisfaction. If cosmopolites embrace and advocate only Western liberal-democratic values at the expense of non-Western values, then they are not truly multicultural pluralist cosmopolitans at all. Rather, they are (at best) cultural imperialists, perpetuating the Western Enlightenment's long history of universalism-cum-imperialism. On the other hand, if repelled by this prospect, cosmopolitans instead embrace cultural pluralism, that is, if they embrace all (or a broad range of) values, then it may very well be the case that they lack any, as Pagden suggests. And as Arendt rightly points out, as nothing more than human beings in general they lose all significance. (p. 360)

Bowden's (2003) formulation avoids the fact that ideas that spring from one locality can take on universal significance as in science, the adoption of universal number systems and also the ideology of human rights. Cosmopolitan values that transcend all national, cultural, and state boundaries are generally considered an essential component of cultivating cosmopolitan perspectives of globally minded citizens but what kind of cosmopolitan values? What kind of globally minded citizen? In contemporary discourse, cosmopolitanism is often referred to under the term globalization and includes economic (neoliberal) cosmopolitanism, political cosmopolitanism, and cosmopolitan law, based on a form of moral universalism.

Economic Cosmopolitanism

Besides moral and political (or legal) cosmopolitanism, there is also a form of *economic cosmopolitanism* associated with the work of Adam Smith who sought to diminish the role of politics in the economic realm. Said to date from Quesnay, the notion of economic cosmopolitanism has been promoted strongly in the twentieth century by Friedrich Hayek and Milton Friedman, and taken up in a particular form of neoliberalism that now characterizes the doctrine of "free trade" and the World Trade Organization.

For all three accounts, as Thomas Pogge notes, there is, first, an assumption of *individualism*—the unit of analysis is the individual rather than the State or some other entity; second, the assumption of *universality*, and finally, an assumption of *generality*: "the primary concern for the individual is extended to all humanity" (Bowden, 2003: 354).

There are then three forms of contemporary cosmopolitanism: Kantian moral cosmopolitanism represented by the discourse of human rights and, perhaps, institutionally by the United Nations; Kantian political cosmopolitanism represented by the likes of Habermas, Rawls, Beitz and Pogge and cosmopolitanism democracy, argued by Held; and finally, economic cosmopolitanism currently best exemplified by a form of neoliberal "free trade." Furthermore, each of these concepts of cosmopolitanism informs competing projects of political integration in transnational spaces influencing university institutions. More precisely, within those projects are ideas influencing the type of globally minded citizens to be cultivated by universities.

Comparing the Cosmopolitanisms

The problem is that there are competing and contradictory forces at work among these different forms. For example, neoliberal cosmopolitanism assumes citizens as consumers. This perspective assumes that "cosmopolitanism" is only a type of global commodity subordinated to the demands of capital. Students are considered consumers in transnational spaces, while university institutions provide narratives and expectations of "world citizenship" where cosmopolitan experiences and consumption become one and the same. Neoliberalism assumes a world unbounded in which nation states operate exclusively under the logic of the economic activity of supranational spaces. In these circumstances, international students are considered a mere reflection of the erosion of boundaries and frontiers but also part of an ambivalent reality dominated by economic rationalities and perspectives.

The cosmopolitan values that dominate this concept are clear: the values of consumerism in transnational spaces and the promotion of a tourisitic attitude. Cosmopolitan refers to a specific type of traveler, the one that is able to choose where to be and to live without subjecting his or her own cultural values to the exchange and test of their host culture. In other words, universal values like freedom of movement are part of an image of cosmopolitan citizen but they are restricted to those able to purchase and afford movement. Habermas (2003) points out some of the problems of the assumptions made by the advocates of this project, especially given the consideration of the potentially unintended consequences of a project articulated primordially in economic terms that creates forms of social integration of segments of the global academic population while encouraging forms of exclusion and marginalization for vast segments of the world population.

The attempt to cultivate globally minded citizens subordinated to this neoliberal kind of cosmopolitanism is characterized by empty and nihilistic forms of political practices. Subtle feelings and growing sensibilities toward unfamiliar spaces become void/sterile. In other words, this is the cultivation of a type of cosmopolitan citizenship that does not demand any kind of *responsibility* or awareness toward others, toward their cultures, languages, and traditions. Consequently, it cultivates perspectives that ignore that exclusion for most of the people in this planet is still operating through the government of spaces and territories, and over a large array of cosmopolitan experiences and differences.

Moreover, strategies of internationalization of higher education subordinated to the primacy of this form of cosmopolitical cosmopolitan vision of the university not only ignore the social and political roles that universities have played through time but are unable to enhance education experiences through the cultivation of cosmopolitan perspectives about the diversity and the preservation of the diversity of knowledges, languages and cultures. Appadurai (1996: 24) notes that "diversity is a particular organization of difference. The question is what kind of organization?" It is possible to argue that, if we are going to speak of a cosmopolitical project of the university, we also must refer to the way in which the "economy of diversity" is made manifest in the curriculum and generally managed in the academy.

We could assume that difference is managed in the academy according to the type of policies applied by the type of cosmopolitical project that generates those political practices. It may be that the official discourse of the university on internationalization is one of an essentially empty nature driven by a competitive global strategy with little awareness of broader educational goals or purposes. For instance, to state the goal of promoting globally minded citizens when it is used as a marketing tool, or to enunciate diversity by simply asserting the recruitment of students of color, international students, or scholars as if diversity is a good in itself.

Alternative ideas of the cosmopolitan university are possible. For instance, Kantian moral and legal cosmopolitanism are two projects that still have potential as alternative projects of social integration. Both projects refer to the construction of democratic universes based on the construction of supranational political formations that point to the silence aspect of a project based on the idea of a cosmopolitan citizen as a consumer of markets: "markets, unlike political entities cannot be democratized" (Habermas, 2003: 95). Alternatives are necessary if we take into consideration the inability of cosmopolitical concepts of university informed by neoliberalism to address two critical aspects for the future development of universities.

Because the liberal arts remain quintessentially cosmopolitan, they provide a space for the cultivation of a specific cosmopolitan habitus of research and inquiry. However, this is only possible today with humanities that are able to escape traditional frameworks of reference. Thus the humanities must be able to escape their local origins and trajectories and broaden their accounts to take in the radical pluralism existing as part of a new globalism recognizing the claims of local autonomy made by first peoples, indigenous peoples, substate cultural minorities, international religious movements, youth cultures, gender groups, and all sorts of political associations (Peters, 2007: 8).

The idea is that the creation of a habitus of research cultivates a cosmopolitan perspective rather than be merely a vocational and professional training of graduate students. The care and cultivation of habits of research and inquiry is based on the cultivation of a specific type of "cosmopolitan self." Thus the cosmopolitan perspective is the object of post-humanistic pedagogies that focus on projects of organization of difference that cultivate a perspective that seriously engages with the values of diversity. First, the quality of the academic experience is tied to the creation of ecologies for organizing diversity: a culture of diversity, rather than "cultural diversity" as it appears in university mission statements. It is dependent on political administrative practices, the management of diversity that allows the creation of an institutional climate "that is actually hospitable to diversity: one which puts diversity at the center of the curriculum and the demographics of the university, rather than at its statistical or conceptual margin." Without a "conscious commitment to the mutual value of intellectual and cultural university," it is not possible to create a "habitus where diversity is at the heart of the apparatus itself" (Appadurai, 1996: 26).

The potential of the modern university as a part of a democratic project will examine cosmopolitan political practices, looking for a humanistic view of cosmopolitanism, such as the one explicitly adopted by Derrida (2001): recuperating ancient concepts of friendship, the ethics of hospitality, forgiveness, and the gift, the invitation that outlines his account of responsibility to the other. Only in these instance will projects of internationalization of higher education also include places of critical resistance, and dissidence, (as well as intercultural understanding and cultural empathy) against cosmopolitanization processes, and cosmopolitan political practices made under the claim of universal humanism or one culture, a claim of universal superiority characteristic of fundamentalist movements.

The cosmopolitan renewal of the university is a renewal from within the tradition and discourse based on the Kantian moments of cosmopolitanism that, in the best sense, may substitute or offer a lead for forms of internationalization, globalization, and democracy where the university begins to explore its responsibilities to global civil society, to the promotion of global democratic forms, and to the project of the global citizen that is based on moral and political imperatives.

The Postcolonial University

The postcolonial university represents a renewal from *outside* the tradition. It originates in a critique of the Western tradition and the Idea of the University in its colonizing form that emphasizes its role in the processes of colonization based on an instrumental concept of "scientific" and universal Western and a set of European civilizational ideas. Where the cosmopolitan university calls for a deepening of the tradition in accordance with Kantian ideals, the postcolonial university calls for a critique of the university as an instrument of colonizing power and an action perspective to redress historical subjugation of indigenous knowledge systems.

Often the term "postcolonial" is reserved for a discourse or academic discipline that purports to explain the deleterious effects of power in imperial and colonial relationships including cultural legacies. Postcolonial studies thus takes its place with other disciplines within the academy to analyze the politics of knowledge in terms of power relationships that dominated the colonial university system including questions of elite formations, identity and the construction of the colonial subject, and the formation of the canon. Mostly this approach is a form of literary or cultural studies culminating in postcolonial theory or "criticism" inspired by Frantz Fanon, Aime Cesaire, Léopold Sédar Senghor and later developed by Edward Said, Gayatri Chakravorty Spivak, Dipesh Chakrabarty, Derek Gregory, and others.

Margaret Kohn (2012) provides an explanation:

> From the perspective of world-systems theory, the economic exploitation of the periphery does not necessarily require direct political or military domination. In a similar vein, contemporary literary theorists have drawn attention to practices of representation that reproduce a logic of subordination that endures even after former colonies gain independence. The field of postcolonial studies was influenced by Edward Said's path-breaking book Orientalism. In Orientalism, Said applied Michel Foucault's technique of discourse analysis to the production of knowledge about the Middle East. The term orientalism described a structured set of concepts, assumptions, and discursive practices that were used to produce, interpret, and evaluate knowledge about non-European peoples. (1979)

Kohn (2012) suggests that "Orientalism" functions as a specific field of study, a set of Western practices that is used to depict Others that manages European anxieties, and a mode of exercising authority by classifying and creating knowledge. Following Spivak's (1988) "Can the Subaltern Speak?", one can broaden the notion of Orientalism to questions of representation more broadly to understand questions of power in the contemporary academy. These aspects of postcolonial theory remain largely at the level of critique providing resources for a counter-narrative to European imperial narratives that have dominated the last 600 years. These resources provide us with the means for deconstructing a literary text, revealing the problematics of colonial identity, and even recording anti-colonial resistance. As such, they provide the conceptual means for a critique of the colonial university in its main function of training elite formations. Achille Mbembe suggests that "postcolonial studies" and "postcolonial theory" is characterized by its heterogeneity being derived "both from anti-colonial and anti-imperialist struggles on the one hand, and from the heritage of Western philosophy and of the disciplines that constitute the European humanities on the other."

Clearly, the postcolonial university takes different forms. First, it is possible to talk of the *reassertion* of the precolonial "university" of the classical civilizations that were colonized where a Western modernist credo was substituted for civilizational cultural ideals. Second, we can talk of the protection, development, and adaptation of indigenous knowledges and universities. In a positive recuperative movement, the world's indigenous peoples are preserving their languages and local traditional knowledges and wisdoms in medicine, studies of local flora and fauna, spirituality and mythologies, and traditional arts and crafts as a theoretical and value basis to approach the future. Some seek a kind of integration with values and approaches of Western science and humanities; others look to establishing specialist indigenous institutions. Third, we can mention the growth of postcolonial studies, scholars, and scholarship within the Western university as yet a form of literary and cultural criticism confined to the humanities but with the potential to have further curriculum power effects. In this regard we might also register the growing force of "Why is my curriculum White?" and similar campaigns.[1] The issue was first raised in this sense by a video made by UCL (University College London) students who propose responses to this question pointing out the lack of awareness that the curriculum is white comprised of "white ideas" by "white authors" and is a result of colonialism that has normalized whiteness and made blackness invisible. As I commented, "This is a fundamental educational challenge that has not been addressed by the educational establishment, nor by the majority of philosophers including philosophers of education. Racism rarely figures on philosophy of education conference agendas and papers discussing the ethics of education that tend to talk in general and abstract terms neglecting issues of race or gender" (Peters, 2015).

Finally, we can mention the critique of, and defense against, the most recent round of neoliberalization and spread of U.S. and other Western universities in the Global South. All of these initiatives and developments have the power to contest and disrupt the neoliberal cosmopolitan model, limiting its expansion at the periphery and paring back its neoliberal project of "internationalization" by substituting its own developing university education alternatives.

Some of these options are essentially *defensive* strategies; others are tied to curriculum change and innovation proceeding from the critique of westernization, ethnocentrism, and what Derrida calls the metaphysics of "logocentrism"—arguably a philosophical platform from which all initiatives take root. Derrida is, perhaps, the foremost philosopher of the humanities and of its place in the university

(Peters, 2016). Over the long period of his career, he was concerned with the fate, status, place, and contribution of the humanities. Through his deconstructive readings and writings, he has done much not only to reinvent the Western tradition by attending closely to those texts that constitute it, but also he has redefined its procedures and protocols, questioning and commenting upon the relationship between commentary and interpretation, the practice of quotation, the delimitation of a work and its singularity, its signature, and its context—the whole form of life of literary culture, together with textual practices and conventions that shape it. From his very early work, he has occupied a marginal in-between space—simultaneously, textual, literary, philosophical, and political—a space that permitted him a freedom to question, to speculate, and to draw new limits to humanitas. Derrida has demonstrated his power to reconceptualize and to reimagine the humanities in the space of the contemporary university around the reimagining of tasks for the new humanities (Trifonas & Peters, 2005).

The postcolonial university takes two main forms and in each case the result is a reassertion of cultural values and identity: the first is the reassertion of the cultural values of the ancient centers of learning that now are grafted onto the modern university form, which has become a truly global institution; the second is the reassertion of cultural values that comes with the first experimentations of the indigenous university. In both cases, the motivation in part comes from an awareness and critique of Western colonialism and the multiple ways that universities from European powers became a means of social control as well as knowledge production. Said's Orientalism, based on Foucault politics of exclusion, provides a general theoretical model to analyze and understand the university as a locus for the circulation of cultural power and power/knowledge. The late twentieth and early twenty-first centuries saw the first developments of the indigenous university by African, Māori, Inuit, and South American tribes who embrace as a first principle the critique of the Western university both as a form of knowledge colonialism and as a form of knowledge as commodity under neoliberalism. There are some 3,000 indigenous peoples who are becoming organized and pursuing the cultural ideals of their peoples with a greater awareness of the marriage and differences of traditional and Western scientific knowledge. With the colonized great civilizations in Asia and parts of Africa, the new constellations represent the conscious and deliberate reconstruction of institutions of higher education that embody traditional values often within the neoliberal global organizational forms. Scholars have remarked on the rise of Confucius Institutes and Arab universities that embrace Muslim ideas in philosophy, science, and theology.

The cosmopolitan university attempts to account for cultural difference within the Western university as the institution becomes global and enters into new global networks and consortia that also involve non-Western members. On the other hand, the postcolonial university, as yet in its infancy, is beginning to understand the significance of the assertion of cultural identity in a global world and is moving quickly to establish its own institutions. In both cases, these new forms offer greater hope for difference and cultural self-determination than either the prospect for moral reconstruction or reform of the neoliberal university. Curiously, the Idea of the University may yet be further developed in an intercultural phase, especially where humanistic values are strongest as they are in Confucian cultures of East Asia.

The Māori Example: Māori case

Often the effect of colonization has been to create subjects divided against themselves (Fanon, 1967), although this process was/is two-sided as Mika (2012) acknowledges in the case of Māori:

> Many Māori writers note that "knowledge", in one way or another, engages with Māori in either problematic ways or else presents itself as a given in various areas of Māori existence. The conundrum of Western knowledge for Māori is often represented in hitherto untraversed areas: Elizabeth McKinley (2005), for instance, explores the '... production of historical knowledge of "Māori women"' (p. 482) by science, and emphasises how Māori women scientists deal with this immediate inscription by scientific knowledge; Royal (2009), speaking directly about knowledge, unearths that it has "found expression" (p. 5) in such domains as health, and could play a large role in the "creative industries" (ibid.). Thus, in Māori writing there is both resistance to, and possibility for, aspects of "knowledge."

What this passages raises is the crucial question of language—in this case te reo Māori—and its colonization as only one example briefly elaborated in the space remaining that points to the complexity of issues of philosophy, language, and identity within the university, and the role of the university as first colonizer and then enabler of indigenous language and culture.

There are some 125,000 speakers of Māori (21% of all Māori; 3% of New Zealand) with some 50,000 fluent speakers, many over 65 years. Only since the 1960s has an understanding of the linguistic diversity of the Pacific area emerged: 4,000 languages are spoken in the region, most of them in Melanesia where 2 million people speak one-quarter of the world's languages (Mühlhäusler, 1996: 9). As Derrida (1999: 14) comments: "What is identity, this concept of which the transparent identity to itself is always dogmatically presupposed by so many debates on monoculturalism or multiculturalism, nationality, citizenship, and, in general, belonging?" In other words, what are the philosophical connections between linguistic group, native language, and identity? How does the denial or subjugation of the language impact on selfhood? (Anaru, 2011; Ngaha, 2011).

The history of te reo Māori from colonization to autonomy can be represented schematically in eight phases:

1. Prehistory: Māori language from Eastern Polynesia: predominant oral language with local dialects and symbolic meanings preserved in carvings, weaving, and material design;
2. Te reo Māori as language of first contact when in 1769 the H.M.S. Endeavour sailed into Poverty Bay and marked a period of sustained contact between two cultures and two languages, English and te reo Māori and the beginning of NZ English with loan words and borrowings of Māori words based on names of fauna and flora and place names;
3. Alphabetization: Te Reo Māori as a written language: in 1814 Samuel Marsden establishes first Mission attempts to write down the language, to systematize it, and to import new concepts of literacy and numeracy with rapid learning by Māori;
4. Progressive Colonization (1840–1880) with open language borrowings, the first printings of Māori (first book in 1815 and first Māori newspaper—*Te Karere o Niu Tireni*—in 1842);
5. Recolonization (1880–1970): Māori as a declining language based on reestablishing ties with Britain and resistance to Māori as an "imperfect vehicle for thinking" based on the liberal dictum of "one language, one nation";
6. Decolonization and Revitalization (1970–2000) with political seeds of change in the early 1970s and the emergence of Ngā Tamatoa (The Young Warriors), Victoria University's Te Reo Māori Society (Professor Hirinui Mead), and Te Huinga Rangatahi (the New Zealand Māori Students' Association), Māori language week introduced in 1975, the first Māori-owned Māori-language radio station (Te Reo-o-P neke) opened in 1983, the first k hanga reo (preschool language nest) opened in Lower Hutt in 1982, kura kaupapa, a system of primary schooling in a Māori-language environment developed in the 1980s, and Māori being made an official language of New Zealand under the Māori Language Act 1987.
7. In 1989, the Waitangi Tribunal recommended that te reo Māori should be restored to its proper place by making it an official language of New Zealand with the right to use it on any public occasion, in the Courts, in dealing with Government Departments, with local authorities, and with all public bodies.

8. Language Autonomy: In the period since the end of 2000 there have been massive and cumulative changes with the growth of Māori language development in the education system, in government, and in all the media. Moreover, te reo Māori is the major force that has made New Zealand English distinctive with Māori word passing into common parlance and the adoption of Māori Language Strategy. Much of this "autonomy" is the legacy of the development of Māori Studies departments.

The first Māori Studies department in New Zealand higher education was established in the 1970s. Sir Sidney (Hirini) Moko Haerewa Mead completed his PhD in 1968 and became the first Professor of Māori Studies at Victoria University of Wellington in 1977. Dr. Ranginui Walker took up a temporary lectureship in the Anthropology Department at Auckland University in 1967, where he completed his PhD in 1970. In 1986, Dr. Walker was appointed associate professor of Māori Studies in the Anthropology Department at Auckland University. In 1993, he was appointed professor and head of department in Māori Studies.[2]

In less than 180 years of European contact with the metropolitan language, English, *te reo Māori* has suffered a massive depletion. Measures affecting the ecology of *te reo Māori* have included the introduction of a new *lingua franca*, and its selection as the official language; the introduction of new media, especially writing and print technologies; the introduction of "hostile" education policies; and the sanctioning of foreign naming practices. Accordingly, *te reo Māori* has endured a dramatic reduction in the size of its speech community and profound changes in its language structures, domains, and functions. The full extent and direction of these changes have yet to be understood in detail.

While, for instance, we know that *te reo Māori* as an oral language was reduced to English alphabetic and syllabic forms and Māori culture, therefore, exposed to writing and print technologies early in the colonizing process, we do not know the wider implications of these changes, the deeper effects of the shift from acoustics to optics, from sound to visualization, in Māori as primarily an oral culture. Not only did the missionaries fail to create literacy in Māori—the main use of literacy was in letter writing rather than in reading—but in their desire to christianize Māori through reading the "divine" word, failed also to equip them to negotiate their rights, land purchase, confiscation and dispossession, an area that really mattered to them.

The history of this policy can be seen in a number of clearly discernible successive phases: an "assimilationist" approach to race relations which predominated up until the late 1950s; a focus on a policy of "integration" implicitly based on a notion of "cultural deprivation" during the 1960s and early 1970s; followed by a transitional period where emphasis was shifted from "cultural deprivation" and "the problem of the Māori child" to a concept of "cultural difference" which emphasized *pakeha* tolerance of *non-pakeha* culture; and, finally, an attempt to formulate a "multicultural" policy with the attendant notion that "cultural diversity" should be valued. Most recently, there have been some signs that we are moving into a policy era of "biculturalism," mostly as a result of Māori initiatives, with the introduction of total immersion schools at all levels where education is *by* Māori, *for* Māori, and *in* Māori, and with a number of bicultural schools. Whether these policies succeed is, however, another matter (Peters & Marshall, 1988).

Te reo Māori emerges as "autonomous" as the seventh stage might be construed in the following senses: as the language form of culture upon which other forms depend—a precondition for other cultural-symbolic forms (*independence*); in the sense of the language of *cultural self-determination* in relation to tribal solidarity and enhanced linguistic use; in the sense of the language of *political self-determination*; legal claims before the Waitangi Tribunal for historical redress against the Crown; as a cultural validation and historical contribution to the *phenomenology of racialized discourse* and race as a founding category of colonialism; and as a *language of cultural possibility* in new media, new writing, and new philosophy. In part, language autonomy concerns the heart of the culture and its distinctive cultural collective forms that provide the basis for trans-tribal political identity and challenges to successive governments concerning historical redress of lands, forests, fisheries, and other taonga (treasures). Te reo Māori also contains the seeds for articulating Māori philosophy and the symbolic means for sustaining self-determination, especially in the "post-settlement" phase when the Waitangi Tribunal legal process is complete and all the historical claims have been heard.

The role of the university in promoting these senses has been mixed but generally progressive since the 1990s indicating just how recent the colonial effects of the university have been and how close or how far away we still are to making a robust assessment of the monolingual, monocultural, and monological nature of the Western university. Te Whare Wananga o Awanuirangi,[3] one of three Maopri "universities," has been denied the title "indigenous university."

Conclusions

Drawing all of the threads together I should start by reminding the reader of the beginning problem—that is, Is there life after the death of the university?—and the postcolonial and cosmopolitan universities as possible responses. I explained why they might usefully be thought of together: both responses are connected philosophically and historically. The first response represents an attempt to find a way forward by returning to the roots of the Kantian tradition to find a serviceable notion of cosmopolitanism that cannot be corrupted or reduced by a solely economic instrumentalism but rather is committed to principles of social justice in the name of a global civil society and the project of global citizenship. The second response also grows out of the tradition but acts as a therapeutic philosophy to remind us that the university institution played an essential role in the process of colonization (and neoliberal globalization) both in terms of administrative reason (after Weber) subjugating and denying indigenous knowledge while training an indigenous elite in Western culture, and in turn of economic reason helping to extract the colonial surplus for the mother country.

From the beginning, Western knowledge was a double-edged sword that taught the principles of Western philosophy and science (and to that extent also often the means of liberation) but also introduced forms that aided the sampling and capitalist exploitation of natural resources and peoples in the colonies in Africa, Latin America, and Oceania. University education in the colonizing process perpetuated the culture of the dominant colonizing group helping to build capacity, markets, and labor through professional training. This process of university education, it is claimed, often led to forms of cultural assimilation that works through consent and a process of internal colonization. Universities as colonial institutions acted as cultural filters to extend economic exploitation of the colony absorbing indigenous society into the metropole by stripping the colonized away from their indigenous learning cultures and their cultural identities.

What motivates this essay is the idea that two sources of renewal of the Idea of the University come from both within the tradition *and* from outside it. Kantian and other forms of cosmopolitanism provide a model of globalization/internationalization of universities that has a deeper moral code than the practice of neoliberal export higher education such as values of respect and tolerance for and of the Other and a commitment to intercultural understanding. In one sense it might be argued that this provides the social infrastructure for the Kantian notion of citizenship at the supranational level. The force for renewal from outside the tradition is perhaps more complex because it originates in two sources: the renewal of the notion of the university and its organizational form in terms of premodern traditional indigenous knowledge systems and the revival of ancient centers of learning mostly constituted within the great religious civilizations. What shape the "postcolonial" university will take is a matter of cultural invention and hybridization. Both sets of processes offer future forms very different from the modern university as it evolved in Europe. These twin sources of renewal may save the university from itself.

Notes

1. See https://www.facebook.com/events/977925202236883/ and http://www.nus.org.uk/en/news/why-is-my-curriculum-white/.
2. I regarded Ranganui Walker as one of my academic Kaumatua (elders) when I was at the University of Auckland during the period 1992–2005. He confided in me that the colonial process of setting up Māori Studies at the University of Auckland resulted in the Senate initially throwing out the concept of Māori cultural studies for want of a literary tradition, Māori being based on an oral culture (see Walker, R., 1999).
3. See http://www.wananga.ac.nz/

References

Anaru, N. A. (2011). "A Critical Analysis of the Impact of Colonisation on the Māori Language through an Examination of Political Theory" Unpub MA, Auckland University of Technology.

Appadurai, A. (1996). 'Diversity and disciplinarity as cultural artifacts' In C. Nelson and D. P. Gaonkar (eds.), *Disciplinarity and Dissent in Cultural Studies.* New York: Routledge.

Bowden, B. (2003). The perils of global citizenship, *Citizenship Studies*, 4:3, 349–362.

Derrida, J. (1999). *Monolingualism of the Other; or, the Prosthesis of Origin.* Trans. Patrick Mensah. Stanford: Stanford University Press.

Derrida, J. (2001). *On Cosmopolitanism and Forgiveness.* New York: Routledge.

Fanon, F. (1967, Orig. 1952). *Black Skin, White Masks*, trans. Charles Lam Markmann. New York: Grove Press.

Habermas, J. (2003). Toward a cosmopolitan Europe, *Journal of Democracy*, 14:4, 86–100.

Kant, I. (1970). *Perpetual Peace*, trans. W. Hastie (Edinburgh: T&T Clark, 1891) in Kant's Political Writings, ed. Hans Reiss, trans. H. Nisbett. Cambridge: Cambridge University Press.

Kleingeld, P. (2006). Cosmopolitanism. Stanford Encyclopedia of Philosophy, at http://plato.stanford.edu/entries/cosmopolitanism/

Kohn, M., "Colonialism", *The Stanford Encyclopedia of Philosophy* (Spring 2014 Edition), Edward N. Zalta (ed.), http://plato.stanford.edu/archives/spr2014/entries/colonialism

McKinley, E. (2005). Brown Bodies, White Coats: Postcolonialism, Māori women and science, *Discourse: Studies in the Cultural Politics of Education*, 26:4, 481–496.

Mika, Carl Te Hira (2012). Overcoming 'Being' in Favour of Knowledge: The fixing effect of 'mātauranga,' *Educational Philosophy and Theory*, 44:10, 1080–1092.

Mühlhäusler, P. (1996). *Linguistic Ecology: Language Change and Linguistic Imperialism in the Pacific Region.* London: Routledge.

Ngaha, A. B. (2011). "Te Reo, a language for Māori alone? An investigation into the relationship between the Māori language and Māori identity" Unpub. PhD, University of Auckland.

Peters, M. A. (2007). The humanities in deconstruction: raising the question of the post-colonial university, *Access: Critical Perspectives on Communication, Cultural & Policy Studies*, 26:1, 1–11.

Peters, M. A. (2015). Why is my curriculum white? *Educational Philosophy and Theory*, 47:7, 641–646.

Peters, M. A. (2016). The Postcolonial University, *Linguistic and Philosophical Investigations*, 15: 77–89.

Peters, M. A., & Marshall, J. (1988). Te Reo O Te Tai Tokerau: Community Evaluation, Empowerment and Opportunities for Oral Māori Language Reproduction. In: *Report of the Royal Commission on Social Policy, Te Kamihana A Te Karauna Me Nga A Hautanga-A-Iwi*, April, Vol. III, Part Two, *Future Directions*, Wellington, Government Printer: 703–744.

Said, E. (1979). *Orientalism*. New York: Vintage.

Spivak, G. (1988). 'Can the Subaltern Speak?' In C. Nelson and L. Grossberg (eds.), *Marxism and the Interpretation of Culture*, Urbana: University of Illinois Press, pp. 271–313.

Trifonis, P. & Peters, M. A. (2005) Deconstructing Derrida: Tasks for the New Humanities. New York: Palgrave Macmillan US.

Waitangi Tribunal. (1989). *Te reo Māori report: Wai 11* (2nd Ed). Wellington: GP Publications.

Walker, R. (1999). The development of Maori studies in tertiary education in Aotearoa/New Zealand, In M. A. Peters, R. Horrocks, B. Opie & R. Walker (Eds.), *After the disciplines: The emergence of cultural studies* (pp. 187-198). Westport, CN: Bergin & Garvey.

CHAPTER THIRTY

The Ecological University—A University Whose Time Has Come

RONALD BARNETT

Introduction

The ecological university is a university whose time has come. In near-invisible guises, it is already with us, if only to an embryonic extent. But it will not wait its calling. It is willing itself forward already.

That, at least, is the thesis I wish to advance here. In order to do that, I wish to distinguish between the idea of the sustainable university and the ecological university; to identify seven ecosystems of which the university is part and towards which, therefore, the university has responsibilities to assist the thriving of those ecosystems; to draw upon recent developments in 'assemblage theory' so as to fill out the idea of an ecology as an assemblage; and to offer examples of what it is to be an ecological university in relation to each of the seven ecosystems.

Beyond sustainability

Understandably, there is much concern these days with the matter of sustainability. The concept of sustainability has come to the fore doubtless as a result of two considerations: first, that the natural environment is degrading and, second, that humanity has a responsibility to ensure that its interactions are sustaining the environment rather than impairing it. The second of these considerations by no means follows from the first. It requires additional premises even to begin to substantiate it. One would be that humanity has itself—even if unwittingly—acted so as to bring about massive changes to the natural environment that are of concern. Another is that humanity has the capacity to alter the course of events in the natural environment. And yet another is that if humanity can act so as to limit or, even better, halt the degradation of the environment, it should do so.

Linked to this whole way of thinking are theories and frameworks of understanding. These include a sense, first, that the world is composed of interacting ecosystems, second that—all things being equal—these ecosystems have properties that allow them to be self-sustaining, and third that humanity has interfered with the natural order of these ecosystems, albeit largely unwittingly.

In this context, it is evident that there is a particular equivocation that attaches to the concept of sustainability. On the one hand, it invokes an interest in the natural environment having a level of order and replicability such that it is self-sustaining. On the other hand, it invokes a concern that the actions of humanity, in interacting with the natural environment, are guided by a concern for sustainability such that its actions are themselves sustainable. The first is that of an *exterior sustainability* while the second is that of an *interior sustainability*.

What does all this have to do with the university? A first response is that both forms of sustainability apply to today's university. *Exterior* sustainability is evident in universities happily subscribing to the self-designation, *the sustainable university*. These are universities that wish to 'integrate higher education into the wider societal context of sustainability' (Sterling, Maxey and Luna, 2014: 19). Such universities are wanting to attune themselves to the global ecological concerns and they look for opportunities—in their curricula, their research activities and their interactions with communities—to orient themselves towards sustainability. *Interior* sustainability is on the cusp of entering universities in an interest in 'sustainable leadership'. At present, the phrase is present in relation to schools (Hargreaves and Fink, 2012), the central concern being that of a leadership that is self-sustaining and which, for instance, is not dependent on individuals. We can hypothesise that it will not be long before this sense of sustainability will find its way into universities.

There are, though, two larger senses in which these reflections about sustainability link to universities. The first is that of interconnectedness. As remarked, a concern for sustainability has its place against a sensitivity towards humanity as residing within—and being active in—ecologies. The 'trope' of the ecological has become almost strident in its ubiquity. Widening from an identification of ecology with the natural environment, ecosystems are now being spotted in human activities and institutions. Knowledge, learning systems and the business world are but some of the fields which are portrayed as ecologies, a cardinal point being the interconnectedness of entities that constitute the fields in question. It might be also observed that these themes of the ecological and interconnectedness are themselves but elements in a much broader sensitivity, indications of which are surely to be found in concepts such as 'assemblage', 'rhizome', 'web', 'network' and so forth. This large theme of interconnectedness hints, too, at fragility, openness and possibilities. We shall return to these considerations.

Sustainability has a second intimation of significance here. Especially in its connections with ecology, a value element imposes itself. To speak of ecologies is not only to raise matters about ways in which actions can help to sustain them but it is also to suggest a responsibility in that direction. To bring into play the idea of ecology is to invoke an *ecological spirit*. It is to insert a plea to the effect that humanity cannot be immune from an ethical responsibility in attending to the repercussions of its actions. More positively, it is to imply that effort should be expended so as to *sustain* the ecologies in question.

Both of these aspects of the theme of sustainability come into play here, in relation to the university. On the one hand, the theme of sustainability invites considerations of the many ecologies with which the university is interconnected. It invites a *relational* understanding of the university. On the other hand, it intimates that here may lie a space in which it is legitimate to talk of the university having responsibilities. Not merely is the university implicated in various ecologies but it also has responsibilities towards sustaining those ecologies, whichever they may be.

These remarks have admittedly been rather schematic. And I shall take this schematic nature of my remarks a step further. I have been exploring—albeit in a rather abstract way—connections between the concept of sustainability and the university. And I have been indicating that there are connections between the two that repay attention. There is value in placing the concepts of university and sustainability together. But I want, even in these very schematic remarks, to suggest that there is a fundamental limitation in the idea of sustainability in this context.

Sustainability as a concept begins to do work when there is a concern about the fragility or even the impairment of an ecology. We may point to knowledge or learning systems or social institutions or culture or the economy and speak of these regions as ecosystems and so move to the suggestion that the university has a responsibility towards their sustainability (whatever that might mean). But this is to limit the idea of the university unduly. For the regions in question, being regions of humanity, are susceptible to infinite development and even advancement. Values can legitimately come into play here. Questions can be posed as to the ways in which a human ecosystem can be taken forward and so strengthened. Doubtless there will be ineradicable dispute as to what is to count as strengthened. And the strengthening of the knowledge ecology—for example, through the enlargement of the public understanding of complex matters—is quite different from the strengthening of the learning ecology, which has a necessarily personal aspect. Understandable reservations of this kind can, however, be overplayed not least since the very theme of ecology gains much of its traction—as observed—from a sense of ecological *impairment* (either actual or potential).

The ecological imaginary—as we may term it, after Taylor (2004)—has taken hold as a worldwide dimension of the lifeworld precisely out of a dual sense both that ecologies in which humanity is embedded are damaged and even liable not to be able to sustain themselves *and* that humanity has the wherewithal and a responsibility to do it what it can to repair those damaged ecologies. The trope of the ecological, in short, is itself party to a dual value orientation, a dual value orientation that arises out of empirical readings of the world. Facts and values are intertwined in this imaginary.

As such, an overtight connection between the ecological spirit and the theme of sustainability is unduly to limit the ethical range that might come into view. For sustainability expresses a concern with the capacities of a system—including any kind of social system—to sustain itself. Sustainability is intimately connected, it may be observed, with the autopoietic tendencies in systems, and the ways in which such self-reproducing systems may be impaired. But the question arises: once those autopoietic capacities have been restored, what then? For human systems, is that it? Is the very notion of sustainability at all helpful here? Is it not more fruitful to open the way to thinking about ways in which, say, the university can go on being developed and strengthened and even improved?

With these very schematic remarks, questions and observations on the limited nature of sustainability, let us move directly to the matter of the university and the concept of the ecological.

The university and its seven ecosystems

The university has its being amid multiple ecologies. In addressing the general matter of ecology, Guattari identified three ecological registers, those of the environment, social relations and human subjectivity. Each of these is evidently in play, so far as the university is concerned but we need to supplement this list for the university is implicated in at least four further ecological registers, those of the economy, knowledge, learning and culture. After all, we may understand each of those latter four regions as an ecosystem of its own, around which arise—in turn for each of them—questions of its sustainability, its impairment, ways in which its malfunctioning might be restored, and its future possibilities. We have, therefore, no less than seven ecosystems in which the university is necessarily implicated, those of the physical environment, social institutions (I transpose here Guattari's 'social relations'), the economy, knowledge, culture, learning and human subjectivity. This total ecological space—with its regions, and its ethical dimensions—opens to an 'ecosophy' (to use Guattari's (2005) term) of the university. An ecosophy here is nothing short of a general and systematic inquiry into, and concern with, the ecological embeddedness of the university.

These seven ecosystems of the university are themselves interconnected and, just as with the notion of ecology conventionally understood, there are interplays with values and human concerns. Drawing on a distinction in Delanda's (2013: 10) philosophy of society (which itself draws on Deleuze and Guattari), there are here present *relationships of interiority* (and in the embeddedness of the university with any one of its six ecological registers) and there are *relationships of exteriority* (in the interconnections between and amongst those seven ecological registers as they implicate the university). Particular issues arise—practical issues, policy issues—both as to how the university might disport itself in any of the seven ecologies in which it moves *and* in relation to its movements more broadly across those registers as they interconnect with each other.

For example, a university might wish to develop its strategy of internationalisation. Immediately, five of our seven ecologies, those five of knowledge, culture, social institutions, the economy and human subjectivity are implicated. And, in turn, in being so implicated, the five ecologies will impinge upon each other. A drive to encourage the enrolment of more international students will raise questions as to what is to count as knowledge, given the different ways of knowing that may accompany students as they arrive from different regions of the world. The presence of and intermingling of students from across the world, not least with students in the host institution, will have repercussions for human subjectivity. Questions can arise as to the economic value that attaches to international students, both while and even after their studies. Manifestly, too, the presence on campus of students from perhaps one hundred countries or more poses nice questions about inter-culturality, about the intensity of those students' cultural scripts and the rights of those students to be heard in their own cultural voices.

But why, it may be pressed, draw here on the notion of 'ecologies'? In what ways are the zones picked out here 'ecologies'? They are ecologies in the ways identified earlier. There are present discrete regions, each with its own interior set of relationships and each with its own 'autopoietic' tendencies towards self-reproduction. In each case, however (the economy, knowledge, culture, social institutions and so on), the zone in question is susceptible to being impaired in some way.

For example, we may speak here of a pedagogical or a learning ecology. There is a network of pedagogical relationships amongst the students and the total (learning) environment. It is an ecology that is liable to be impaired by the presence of international students. (Of course, it can also be enhanced, a matter we shall come to in a moment.) It can be impaired, for instance, where incoming international students and students in the host community fail properly to interact or where the international students prefer to remain in their 'home' communities and rarely engage with other students. It can be impaired where the tutors in the host institution neglect the 'cultural scripts' (Welikala and Watkins, 2008) accompanying the international students, and so diminish those students' preparedness to engage with the learning situations into which they are placed.

These seven ecologies of the university, it is apparent, possess their own spaces, but those are fuzzy spaces, overlapping and always moving, with and against each other. There is complexity here, a complexity of manifold forms weaving in and out, and always liable to be destabilised. Each ecology is itself a 'multiplicity' (Deleuze and Guattari, 2007), opening and closing, moving, interacting, intermeshing with other ecologies. 'Sustainability' takes on a challenging character. Just what is it to 'sustain' the pedagogical and learning ecology under these circumstances? But, as intimated, if the universities' ecologies can be impaired, so perhaps they can also be enhanced, or strengthened, or made more robust? Or perhaps other vocabularies are called for? More delight, mystery, beauty, wonder? How might such considerations gain traction? For that, we need another kind of opening.

Three ecological planes

The university, it may be observed, moves on three planes (Barnett, 2016):

1. *The university as institution—the university as idea*. These two regions are not on different levels but on the same level. Certainly, ever since its modern foundation (at the end of the eighteenth and beginning of the nineteenth century in Germany), the idea of the university and the university as institution have informed each other. Ideas of the university, variously as a space of reason, as a place of research, as an 'open university' and as an 'entrepreneurial university', have influenced the development of the university as an institution and vice versa. Practical developments—for example, the digital revolution, globalisation and the move to 'performativity'—have given impetus to ideas of the university.

2. *An individual university in its own time and space—the possibilities in front of a university.* A university has its contemporary being in its own time and space, with its history behind it; and this is a space with a configuration that is unique to a particular university. In turn, a particular university will have before it a set of possibilities, perhaps even yet not imagined, that are also unique to it.
3. *The singulars that constitute a university—the universals or large concepts through which the university might be understood.* As well as there being an infinite set of singulars—its artefacts, resources, persons, activities and projects—that characterise a university, so we also understand an institution as an institution through an array of universal concepts. This conceptual terrain is always on the move. Many fear that it is shrinking as, globally, the university comes to be understood through concepts such as research, students-as-customers, entrepreneurialism and knowledge transfer having supplanted concepts such as reason, critique, dialogue, objectivity, truth and rationality. Famously, postmodernism was identified as 'an incredulity towards metanarratives' (Lyotard, 1984). But, in fact, far from being incredulous, this terrain of universal concepts is all the time widening, as concepts such as internationalisation, civic engagement, the idea of 'public' (the university's public role, its 'public' benefits and its relationship to the 'public sphere'), equity, democracy, social justice and citizenship come into view with others (well-being, wisdom, virtue, and sustainability not far behind).

We may picture these three planes in the following way:

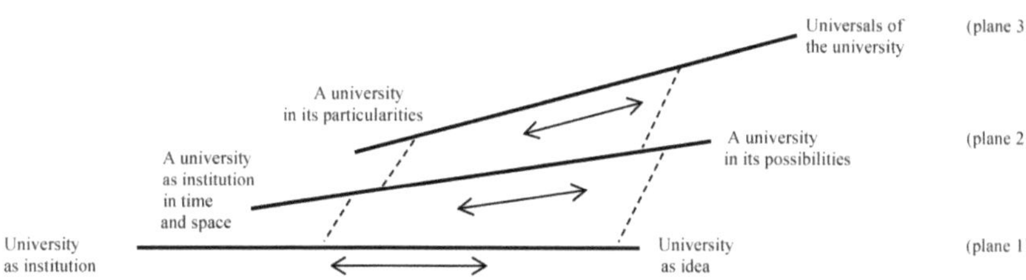

Figure 30.1: Three Planes of the University and Their Interconnections.
Source: Ronald Barnett, Routledge (2016: 55).

The ecological aspect is at work on all three planes of the university. As intimated, the university is implicated in seven ecosystems—those of the physical environment, social institutions, the economy, knowledge, culture, learning and human subjectivity. *On plane one*, all are to be found immediately as components of the university as an institution. We can naturally enquire, in the most general terms, into the swirling of the university with, in turn, each of these seven ecosystems. For example, in which ways, in the twenty-first century, does the university impinge upon knowledge as an ecosystem? Is it *widening* that ecosystem and making it more robust, helping its circulation in the public sphere, by broadening public understanding of and public involvement in, the circulation of knowledge and knowledge-intensive matters? Or is it *limiting* the knowledge ecology, through focusing on science, technology and commercial aplications and the support that the university could be said to be giving to the emergence of academic capitalism (Slaughter and Rhoades, 2004) and to cognitive capitalism (Boutang, 2011)?

On plane two, we can ask a parallel set of questions about a single university. To what extent is a particular university focusing its attentions on the marketing of its knowledge wares? To what extent is it working in the interests of the corporate sector? In short, is it biasing, distorting or impairing knowledge as an ecosystem? To such questions attach temporal horizons. Each university can critically reflect on its past (an older university may reflect somewhat ruefully on the ways in which a century of more ago that it continuously reached out into the public realm, widening the public understanding of science through its public lectures). It can critically reflect on the pattern of its knowledge activities and consider the extent to which they serve the interests of the corporate sector and neglect the public realm. And it can imaginatively construe the possibilities ahead of it, in expanding the public sphere in illuminating controversial issues.

On plane three, we can look forensically at the particulars of university life, and look in turn at their place in the university's ecosystems. For instance, we can peer into the ecosystem of human subjectivities and inquire into the extent human subjectivities within the university are being malformed or shaped unduly, so as to limit human experiences (whether of students or of the faculty). It may be, for example, that pedagogic relations or research dispositions are being marketised and so distorted.

It will be observed that each of these pools of ecological movements resides at the left-hand end of one of our three planes; it might be termed the *ontological* end of each plane, concerned with aspects of the university's *being in the world*. And this is to be expected, insofar as the university has its ecological dimensions, that they are to be found in the here-and-now and in the manifest being of the university in the world. But what of the right-hand end of our three planes: does the university exhibit any ecological tendencies or aspects *there*? On the right-hand end, it will be recalled, reside concepts and ideas of the university, and barely glimpsed possibilities of the university. The ecological aspect is here too, but in less immediate ways. Here enters, to use a term we used earlier, *the ecological spirit*. For here are the university's possibilities, the spaces to become itself in different ways, and to understand itself anew. Armed with an ecological spirit, new options are liable to present themselves, conceptually and practically, and for the university in general in the twenty-first century and for any particular university. Infused with an ecological spirit, possibilities may open that herald new ideas about and new forms of the university. Less new 'lines of flight' (Deleuze and Guattari, 2007; Guattari, 2016), these would amount to *trajectories of ecological becoming* for the university.

The university—just an assemblage?

Provocative here is assemblage theory, as suggested by Deleuze and Guattari (2007) and as further developed by DeLanda (2013). Assemblages have two kinds of components: material and expressive. And we may observe that universities as assemblages have both material and expressive components. For example, they have physical resources, technologies, financial resources and so forth, so constituting their material components. They also have expressive properties. Immediately, these are evident in the symbolic events of universities (their degree ceremonies, their lectures and seminars, their characteristic modes of communication) but they are also evident in the modes of expression and language giving rise to their intellectual fields.

Assemblages possess relations of interiority and relations of exteriority. Through their *relations of interiority*, the components of an assemblage relate to each other internally, and so the assemblage takes on its own identity. We have seen this working on two planes, those of the university in general (in national and global systems of higher education) and in relation to an individual university. At each of these levels, we can inquire into the specificity of the university as a single institution and as a system, a specificity that arises out of its components and their relationships. But the university possesses also *relations of exteriority*. In such relations, a component of a university—say, a research centre—could be detached and plugged into another, and take up a different configuration in that other assemblage. It is partly through such relations of exteriority, in which its component parts have real and potential differential interactions with the wider world, that a university possesses powers of 'emergence'.

A university also possesses tendencies towards both 'territorialisation' and 'deterritorialisation' (to draw on other terms from Deleuze and Guattari, and as developed by Delanda). Territorialisation is a process that stabilises the university while deterritorialisation is a process that *destabilises* it. We can see both processes at work in relation to the university, both within the university and in its relationships with the wider society. The university is prone to processes of deterritorialisation: internally, its departments may clash, its research and teaching processes may become antagonistic towards each other, and especially under market conditions, students and faculty may develop pedagogical relationships with a high degree of tension. Externally, a university may be prone to being destabilised in its income flows (international students from India may suddenly choose instead to enrol in other countries), a nation's economy may falter if its universities are not producing the requisite 'skills' and a society's culture may be weakened if a university focuses its attention mainly on so-called STEM disciplines and repudiates the humanities and care-oriented dispositions. And all the time, the university will engage in processes of territorialisation, aimed at securing regions of stability in its activities.

How does the idea of the ecological university come into play here, in relation to the university considered as an assemblage? It does so in a number of ways. Firstly, the idea of the university as an assemblage can now be extended to embrace our depiction of the university as implicated in seven ecosystems. Each of those seven ecosystems can be understood to be regions of the university as an assemblage. Questions can then be asked about the processes of territorialisation and deterritorialisation at work, in the interconnections between the university and each of the seven ecosystems in which it moves.

For example, with regard to the *knowledge ecosystem*, to what extent is the university assisting stronger interconnections between intellectual fields or, to the contrary, to what extent is it weakening those potential cross-linkages? Is it involved, unwittingly to be sure, in processes of epistemological territorialisation or of epistemological deterritorialisation? With regard to the *learning ecology*, we can ask to what extent a university enables its students to make connections across all of their life-wide learning, so helping them to strengthen and become more reflective about their own personal learning ecologies (cf Wals, 2015; Jackson, 2016).

Value judgements do not enter here, it should observed, in a straightforward way. Processes of deterritorialisation may have either deleterious or beneficial effects. After all, splitting of, and antagonisms between and within, intellectual fields may open opportunities for new insights and new discoveries. Relationships might form anew between disciplines hitherto some way apart from each other, so opening lines of inquiry and research programmes that turn out to be highly fruitful. Connected here are, in DeLanda's terminology, processes of coding and decoding, 'processes which consolidate and rigidify the identity of the assemblage or, on the contrary, allow the assemblage a certain latitude for more flexible operation while benefiting from genetic or linguistic resources' (ibid: 19).

Just networked?

It might be felt that a helpful term here is the term made famous by Castells (1997), that of 'network'. The ecological university is manifestly a networked university, not least being interconnected with—or networked with—its seven ecosystems. Further, the fluidity of networks, as suggested by Castells, is clearly apposite here. The ecological university is a 'space of flows' and may even, in its global reach and dynamism, be understood as flows of space. Its epistemological manoeuvrings have an impact not just on the knowledge ecosystem but on, for example, the ecosystems of the economy and social institutions and even that of culture. We can conduct a formal inquiry into, say, two major and leading multi-faculty universities even in the same city, to try to form some understanding of the differences in the 'flows' in this sense in which they are involved. Their cultural, economic and epistemological currents may turn out to be quite different. We may want to characterise those currents as *warm* and *cool*, as fast or slow-moving, and as varying in their local, national and global ranges.

So the ecological university is necessarily and manifestly a networked university. But there are two problems with the metaphor of network. Firstly, in the hands of Castells at least, and notwithstanding his language of flows and spaces, the metaphor has undue rigidity. For example, the idea of 'nodes' is helpful in alerting us, here, to the ways in which some universities (characteristically but by no means only in the North and the West) have become major nodes of knowledge creation and also (and just as importantly) of knowledge transmission. But the rigidity implied, not least by the diagrams, of those nodes, being fixed both as centres of knowledge creation and knowledge transmission is misleading. Very recently, for instance, the world has witnessed the rise of universities in Asia, especially in China. Subservient receptive nodes can become—and relatively quickly too—primary creative nodes. So the idea of networks needs to be interpreted as having considerable flexibility and openness; and allowing for changes in the total network of universities and university systems.

The second point is that the idea of networks is liable to appear to be value-neutral. It opens just to an examination of the linkages that, say, the university has, both across the global academic world and to other institutions and organisations in the wider society. The idea can be nuanced. We could inquire into the networks that a university has within the deep institutional structures undergirding it. Whether it knows it or not, whether it cares or not, the university IS networked, digitally, economically, politically, culturally and so on. But we can also inquire into the networks that a university self-willingly pursues. Characteristically, universities form partnerships with like universities across the world; these cognitive birds of a feather are testifying to the process of flocking together.

But, beyond such value-neutral inquiries, the idea of the network can take on value-laden aspects, and legitimately so. For questions can be asked about the character of a university's networking. To what extent are its networked relationships entered into in anything approaching an ethical comportment? Does the university have an eye on the ethical implications of its networking with pharmaceutical companies, or its partnerships with local corporations in developing student housing, or its partnerships with private 'learning' organisations as it sets up new programmes for its students who are learning at a distance?

But there, at that point, the ethical dimension falters. For a network is ethically neutral in itself, in a way that an ecosystem is not. The very idea of an ecosystem points to a complex entity—with self-reproducing powers—that has a value. If impaired, or if, worse still, an ecosystem was to be robbed of its energies and fade away, then the world—the term implies—would be worse off. The ascription of 'ecosystem' is one that is, *ipso facto*, value-laden.

Becoming ecological

The ecological university, it may be said, then, is a university that is not merely networked but is a university that takes its networks seriously. It does not merely, for instance, engage with the knowledge ecosystem but does so in ways that help to sustain it and, moreover, to enhance it. It embraces many knowledge*s*, it puts its debates into the public sphere, it engages with the debates of the wider world, it brings the wider world into its campuses (with invited guests from all walks of life) and it does so in a spirit of disputatious openness. It abides by the tacit rules of academic discourse and demonstrates in public its upholding of those rules. Of course, difficult questions arise: should speakers from the wider world who represent unpalatable positions be given a hearing? But that it has a debate—even a fractious debate—about such matters is illustrative of its attentiveness to its responsibilities in furthering (here) the knowledge ecology.

To put the point directly, the networked university is not necessarily an ecological university but the ecological university is *necessarily* a networked university. Some universities are intent on extracting what they can from their environments, typically to enlarge their income streams. They are—the word can be used—exploitative universities. They are networked but they are not ecological universities. Other universities, however, are seized with a mission to deploy their resources so as to aid humanity. This may play out especially in some ecosystems rather than others: a university's *ecological profile* may be somewhat skewed, as a result.

Building on our analysis, a university's ecological profile may be plotted along two axes, as it were. On one axis—say the vertical axis—sits the seven ecosystems while the other axis—say the horizontal axis—is testimony to the range of the university in each of the seven ecosystems; its *ecological space*. In relation to the engagement of a university in each one of the seven ecosystems, we can inquire into its presence nationally, regionally and globally. And so a particular *ecological footprint* forms for each university (cf Hoyer, 2012). More, this grid could be deployed to show the ecological footprint not just of individual universities but of whole higher education systems. A country in one region of the world could be compared with a country in another part of the world, for the extent to which and the ways in which its universities could characteristically be said to ecological. Opening here, therefore, is both the possibility of and a need for a kind of 'geophilosophy' of the university in its being ecologically attuned (cf Hroch, 2016).

The coming of the ecological university

The ecological university has come amongst us (Barnett, 2018), at least in its softer guises. The modern university is heavily networked and increasingly takes its networking seriously. It is with us and yet unrecognised. And this presence is unavoidable. It is part of the university in the twenty-first century as an assemblage. It will be recalled that an assemblage contains both material and expressive components; and so it is with the university. Increasingly across the world, whether newly born or ancient, universities are coming to be reflexive about their stances towards the world, their value positions and their primary goals. Many are joining global associations—such as the Talloires Group or the GUNI collective—that are manifestly taking up value-impregnated stances, wishing to have a positive impact in engaging with their communities, both local and global (cf Watson et al., 2011).

And yet, the full coming of the ecological university is still ahead; but it is assuredly not far away. The world presumes increasingly upon its universities. They are extraordinary unrealised repositories not only of cognitive and technological resources but of other resources barely understood. There are two kinds of resources that are especially pertinent to our inquiry here. They are, firstly, 'living-with' resources. These are resources that enable humanity to live with itself, to live with difference, to live with strangeness. The university accomplishes this feat through its (Habermassian-like) regulative rules of rational discourse. These rules give participants boundaries but also pause. They supply a self-monitoring mechanism for quiet but rigorous engagement.

The other resource pertinent here is that the university can assist in the widening of human understanding. It can enable society to become more a rational society. The Internet age is already furthering this possibility, with universities not merely putting their knowledge wares into 'open access' circulation but even inviting the world actively to share in debates and even in refining the databases being generated through particular projects and ventures. 'Citizen scientists' and the 'university without walls' are but testimony to the ways in which some universities and some research centres are reaching out to multiple publics and so widening the public sphere. In teaching, too, we are seeing imaginative ways—drawing on the interactive possibilities of new communication technologies—of putting classes in touch with each other across continents.

That the world has an expanding array of apparently intractable problems which the university is well-placed to address has been a long-running theme. 'The university of wisdom' (as we may glimpse in the work of Nicholas Maxwell (2007 and here, chapter 28) is one that attends to and helps to identify the matters that are of most value to the world and then assists in addressing those matters. And such a university of wisdom is assuredly also an ecological university. But the ecological university will be most fully present us when it is self-consciously aware of the seven ecosystems through which and in which it has its being, and does all within its resources and powers to enhance the well-being of those ecosystems.

This is a university surely soon to be amongst us; and, as implied, we can already see—in many universities across the world—embryonic instances of just such a university. The world is calling the ecological university forward. It needs universities to assist it, and it is giving space to universities to reach out in manifold ways, in and across the seven ecosystems of academic life. An infinite 'lines of flight' are opening up.

Each university, therefore, has ecological options before it. And some—the great multi-faculty universities of the world—will have more ecological options than smaller specialist institutions. But each university has before it the potential to become an ecological university in its own manner, across ecosystems of its choosing, and to a greater degree locally, nationally and globally.

Conclusions

The ecological university is just before us. It is before us, in that it is impending; it is just arriving. But it is also before us in that embryonic instances of the ecological university can be identified, and in all of the seven ecosystems identified here. Around the world, universities can be seen stretching themselves out in various trajectories of flight, working to develop one or more of the seven ecosystems in which universities are willy-nilly implicated.

Variously, universities can be seen to be contributing to the knowledge ecology by advancing the public understanding of and critical engagement with issues, contributing to the learning ecology by assisting students with their life-wide learning, contributing to the economic ecology by finding ways through the public–private antimonies, contributing to the ecology of the physical environment by turning themselves into 'green campuses', contributing to the ecology of culture by hosting all manner of cultural and transcultural events, contributing to the ecology of social institutions by working collaboratively with the wider civic community, and contributing to the ecology of human subjectivity by having a care for all those who come into contact with it, not only its staff and students but all others as well.

At present, these developments are happening sporadically. Not yet evident is a university that adopts the self-attribution of an ecological university, and which strides out, developing a strategic mission in that way. It takes a careful look at itself and becomes a 'corporate agent' (List and Pettit, 2011), intent on working ecologically. It looks in turn at its resources (material, human, financial, expressive) and assesses how that panoply of resources—unique to each university—opens opportunities in each of the seven ecosystems. Note that this conspectus is not to give the world straightforwardly what it wants. To the contrary, this ecological university—being corporately agentic—works out for itself its own possibilities and its own *modus vivendi* in each of the seven ecosystems, and so derives its own singular ecological footprint for and by itself. The ecological university becomes its own collective institutional person.

References

Barnett, R (2016). *Understanding the University: Institution, Idea, Possibilities.* Abingdon and New York: Routledge.

Barnett, R (2018). *The Ecological University: A Feasible Utopia.* London and New York: Routledge.

Boutang, Y-M (2011). *Cognitive Capitalism.* Cambridge: Polity.

Castells, M (1997). *The Rise of the Network Society. Volume 1 of The Information Age: Economy, Society and Culture.* Malden, MA and Oxford: Blackwell.

DeLanda, M (2013/2006). *A New Philosophy of Society: Assemblage Theory and Social Complexity.* London and New York: Bloomsbury.

Deleuze, G and Guattari, F (2007/1987). *A Thousand Plateaus: Capitalism and Schizophrenia.* London and New York: Continuum.

Guattari, F (2005/1989). *The Three Ecologies.* London and New York: Continuum.

Guattari, F (2016). *Lines of Flight: For Another World of Possibilities.* London and New York: Bloomsbury.

Hargreaves, A and Fink, D (2012). *Sustainable Leadership.* London: John Wiley.

Hoyer, K G (2012). 'Ecophilosophy and the Environmental Debate', in Bhaskar, R, Hoyer, K G and Naess, P (eds) *Ecophilosophy in a World of Crisis: Critical realism and the Nordic contributions.* Abingdon and New York: Routledge.

Hroch, P (2016). 'Deleuze, Guattari, and Environmental Pedagogy and Politics: *Ritournelles* for a Planet-Yet-To-Come', in Carlin, M and Wallin, J (eds) *Deleuze and Guattari, Politics and Education: For a People-Yet-To-Come.* London and New York: Bloomsbury.

Jackson, N (2016). *Exploring Learning Ecologies.* Betchworth: Chalk Mountain.

List, C and Pettit, P (2011). *Group Agency: The Possibility, Design and Status of Corporate Agents.* Oxford: University of Oxford.

Lyotard, J-C (1984). *The Postmodern Condition: A Report on Knowledge.* Manchester: University of Manchester.

Maxwell, N (2007/1984). *From Knowledge to Wisdom: A Revolution in the Aims and Methods of Science* (2nd ed). Oxford and New York: Blackwell.

Slaughter, S and Rhoades, G (2004). Academic Capitalism and the New Economy: Markets, State and Higher Education. Baltimore: Johns Hopkins.

Sterling, S, Maxey, L and Luna, H (2014). *The Sustainable University: Progress and Prospects.* Abingdon and New York: Routledge.

Taylor, C (2004). *Modern Social Imaginaries.* Durham, NC: Public Planet Books, Duke University,

Wals, A (2015). *Beyond Unreasonable Doubt: Education and Learning for Socio-ecological Sustainability in the Anthropocene.* Wageningen: Wageningen University.

Watson, D, Hollister, R M, Stroud, S E, and Babcok, E (2011). *The Engaged University: International Perspectives on Civic Engagement.* London and New York: Routledge.

Welikala, T C and Watkins, C (2008). *Improving Intercultural Learning Experiences in Higher Education: Responding to Cultural Scripts for Learning.* London: Institute of Education.

Contributor Biographies

Alberto Amaral, a former rector of Porto University, is at present the chair of the administration council of the Portuguese Quality Agency. His latest books are 'Cross-Border Higher Education and Quality Assurance. Commerce, the Service Directive and Governing Higher Education' and 'European Policy Implementation and Higher Education. Analysing the Bologna Process'.

N'Dri Thérèse Assié-Lumumba is Professor of African, African Diaspora and Comparative/International Education at Cornell University in the Africana Studies and Research Center. She is past President of the Comparative and International Education Society (CIES), a Fellow of the World Academy of Art and Science, is currently Distinguished Visiting Professor in the Faculty of Education at the University of Johannesburg (South Africa), and Extraordinary Professor in Education Policy Studies at Stellenbosch University (South Africa). She has published extensively on various topics of education, especially higher education.

Jana Bacevic works on social theory and politics of knowledge production. She has a PhD in anthropology and is presently doing one in sociology at the University of Cambridge. Previously, she was a lecturer at the Central European University and Marie Curie fellow at the University of Aarhus.

Ronald Barnett is Emeritus Professor of Higher Education at University College London Institute of Education. He is past-Chair of the Society for Research into Higher Education (SRHE), has won the inaugural prize of the European Association for Educational Research for his 'outstanding contribution to Higher Education Research, Policy and Practice', and is a Fellow of the Academy of Social Sciences, the SRHE and the Higher Education Academy (HEA). His books include—most recently—a trilogy on the university, *Being a University* (2011), *Imagining the University* (2013), and *Understanding the University* (2016).

Søren S. E. Bengtsen is Associate Professor at the Centre for Teaching Development and Digital Media, Aarhus University, Denmark. His main areas of research include doctoral education, higher education, and educational philosophy. His most recent book *Doctoral Supervision. Organization and Dialogue* was published in 2016.

Andrés Bernasconi is Associate Professor and Vice-Dean at the School of Education of the Pontificia Universidad Católica de Chile, where he also heads the higher education research program at the Center for Research on Educational Policy and Practice (http://www.ceppe.cl/).

Tom Bourner is Emeritus Professor of personal and professional development at Brighton University, where he was Head of Research at Brighton Business School. Before that, he headed the Management Development Research Unit, publishing over 100 articles in academic journals and more than a dozen books. He was also a committed teacher being featured in the Times Higher Education's 'Star Turn' series.

Brendan Cantwell is Assistant Professor of Higher, Adult, and Lifelong Education at Michigan State University. His work addresses the political economy of higher education. Brendan is co-editor (with Ilkka Kauppinen) of *Academic Capitalism in the Age of Globalization.*

Nuraan Davids, PhD, is Senior Lecturer in the Faculty of Education at Stellenbosch University. Her recent books include *Ethical dimensions of Muslim education* (with Yusef Waghid), and *Educational leadership-in-becoming: On the potential of leadership in action* (with Yusef Waghid).

Gerard Delanty, Professor of Sociology and Social & Political Thought, Sussex University, Brighton, UK, is the author of various books, which include *Inventing Europe*, *Formations of European Modernity: A Historical and Political Sociology of Europe*, and *The Cosmopolitan Imagination: The Renewal of Critical Social Theory*. His email address is g.delanty@sussex.ac.uk

Paul Gibbs is Professor of Education at Middlesex University. His interests include the marketing of higher education and a pedagogy of contentment and despair.

Henry A. Giroux currently holds the McMaster University Chair for Scholarship in the Public Interest in the English and Cultural Studies Department. His most recent books are *Dangerous Thinking in the Age of the New Authoritarianism* (2015) and (co-authored with Brad Evans), *Disposable Futures: The Seduction of Violence in the Age of Spectacle* (2015), and *America at War with Itself* (2016). His website is www.henryagiroux.com.

Dr. Carolina Guzmán-Valenzuela is a researcher at the Centre for Advanced Research in Education at the University of Chile. She is the principal investigator (and leader) of various competitive nationally-funded research projects focused on the impact of global transformations on the contemporary university and also on university teaching-learning processes.

Robert Hassan is Associate Professor and Head of the Media and Communication Program at the University of Melbourne. His most recent book, *Philosophy of Media*, was published in 2016.

Richard Heraud is a doctoral student at the University of Waikato, where he is researching how the concept of innovation is understood in education.

Dr. Jane Knight, Ontario Institute for Studies in Education, University of Toronto and Ali Mazrui Centre for Higher Education Studies, University of Johannesburg, focuses her research on the international dimension of higher education at the institutional, national, regional, and international levels. Her work in over 70 countries with universities, governments, and UN agencies helps to bring a comparative, development and international perspective to her research, teaching, and policy work.

Janja Komljenovic is Marie Curie Research Fellow at the University of Bristol, UK. Her research is in processes of market-making and marketization focusing on the higher education sector. She is particularly interested in the diversity and complexity of markets in and around universities, including the variety of actors who have entered the sector, their strategies, ways of working, and consequences for higher education and societies at large.

Marek Kwiek is Professor and UNESCO Chair in Institutional Research and Higher Education Policy, University of Poznan, Poland. His research interests include university governance, the welfare state, the academic profession, and academic entrepreneurialism. He is the author of *Knowledge Production in European Universities: States, Markets, and Academic Entrepreneurialism* (2013) and an editorial board member of *Higher Education Quarterly*, *European Educational Research Journal*, *British Educational Research Journal*, and *European Journal of Higher Education*.

Simon Marginson is Professor of International Higher Education at the UCL Institute of Education at University College London. He is Director of the ESRC/HEFCE Centre for Global Higher Education, and joint Editor-in-Chief of the journal 'Higher Education', and author of '*The Dream is Over: The Crisis of Clark Kerr's California Idea of Higher Education*' (2016).

Jan Masschelein teaches philosophy of education and is Director of the Laboratory for Education and Society at Leuven University. He co-authored (with Maarten Simons): *Globale Immunität: Ein kleine Kartographie des Europaischen Bildungsraum* (2005); *Jenseits der Exzellenz. Eine kleine Morphologie der Welt-Universität* (2010) and *In defence of the school. A public issue* (2013).

Nicholas Maxwell is Emeritus Reader at UCL, where he taught philosophy of science for 30 years. His work is primarily devoted to arguing that a more rigorous academic inquiry, one that seeks and promotes wisdom instead of simply acquiring knowledge, is needed. He has published ten books on this theme as of the spring of 2017.

Peter Murphy is Adjunct Professor in Humanities and Social Sciences at La Trobe University and Research Fellow in the Cairns Institute at James Cook University. His books include *The Collective Imagination* and *Universities and Innovation Economies*.

Jon Nixon is Honorary Professor at The Education University of Hong Kong. Recently authored books include *Hannah Arendt and the Politics of Friendship* (2015), *Interpretive Pedagogies for Higher Education: Arendt, Berger, Said, Nussbaum and their Legacies* (2012), and *Higher Education and the Public Good* (2011).

Rikke Toft Nørgård is Associate Professor, PhD, at the Centre for Teaching Development and Digital Media, Aarhus University, Denmark. Her research focuses on the intersections of design thinking, critical pedagogy, and educational technologies at the future university. Recent publications within this area include 'Participatory Academic Communities' (2015) and 'Open-Ended Education' (2016).

Martha C. Nussbaum is Ernst Freund Distinguished Service Professor of Law and Ethics at the University of Chicago, appointed in the Law School and the Philosophy Department. She is the winner of the 2016 Kyoto Prize in the area of Thought and Ethics. Her most recent book is *Anger and Forgiveness* (2016).

Thorsten Nybom is Professor of history at Örebro University, and Visiting Professor at Humboldt University Berlin and UC Berkeley. He has published a number of articles and books on university history during the last 25 years.

Michael A. Peters is Professor in the Wilf Malcolm Institute for Educational Research at Waikato University, Emeritus Professor at the University of Illinois at Urbana–Champaign, and Professorial Fellow at James Cook University. He is the executive editor of *Educational Philosophy and Theory* and founding editor of several other journals, including the *Open Review of Educational Research* and *The Video Journal of Education and Pedagogy*. His interests are in education, philosophy, and social policy, and he has written over sixty books, including most recently *The Global Financial Crisis and The Restructuring of Education* (2015) and *Paulo Freire: The Global Legacy* (2015), both with Tina Besley.

Susan L. Robertson is Professor of Sociology of Education, University of Bristol, UK. Her research is engaged with understanding transformations of the state and education as a result of global, regional, and national projects and processes. Susan is founding Director of the Centre for Globalisation, Education and Social Futures, and is founding co-editor of the journal *Globalisation, Societies and Education*. She has published widely in international journals. Recent books include *Public Private Partnerships in Education*, and *Privatisation, Education and Social Justice*.

Sarah Robinson is Associate Professor at the Centre for Teaching Development and Digital Media at Aarhus University in Denmark. Sarah is an educational anthropologist whose research interests span from policy in practice and curriculum reform to enterprise education and the role of the entrepreneurial university.

Dr. Francine Rochford is Senior Lecturer at La Trobe University in Australia. Her work on the law and policy of higher education includes her doctorate, dealing with the *Liability of the University in Negligence* (2001) and many articles and book chapters dealing with aspects of the law and policy of higher education, and particularly the relationship between a university and its students.

Gary Rolfe is Emeritus Professor at Swansea University with 30 years of experience in practitioner education. Gary's latest book, *The University in Dissent*, examines the rise of the corporate university and explores strategies for meeting the challenges to the provision of authentic education.

Peter Scott is Professor of Higher Education Studies at the UCL Institute of Education. He is a member of the Academia Europaea and the Academy of

Social Sciences. His books include *The Meanings of Mass Higher Education*; *The New Production of Knowledge: Science and Research in Contemporary Societies* (with five other co-authors); and the forthcoming *New Languages and Landscapes of Higher Education* (with two co-editors).

Wesley Shumar is Professor and Department Head in the Department of Anthropology at Drexel University in Philadelphia, PA, USA. Wes is an educational anthropologist whose research has had two main foci—online educational communities and cultural change in higher education.

Maarten Simons is Professor of Educational Policy and Theory at Leuven University. He has co-authored (with Jan Masschelein) *Globale Immunität. Ein kleine Kartographie des Europaischen Bildungsraum* (2005); *Jenseits der Exzellenz: Eine kleine Morphologie der Welt-Universität* (2010); and *In defence of the school: A public issue* (2013).

Sheila Slaughter is Louise McBee Professor of Higher Education at the University of Georgia. She writes about academic capitalism and the marketization of higher education. Her recent work may be accessed at: http://ihe.uga.edu/people/profiles/faculty/core/sheila-slaughter

Nicolas Standaert is Professor of Sinology at the University of Leuven (Belgium). He has published widely on Sino-European cultural contacts in the seventeenth and eighteenth centuries.

Joanna Tidy is based in the Department of Politics, University of Sheffield (UK). Her work is interdisciplinary but situated within international relations. She also has a background in law. Joanna's interest in the global politics of higher education draws on these areas and is animated by her commitment, as an educator, to the worth of education beyond its ascribed market value.

Dr. Jussi Välimaa is Professor in Higher Education Studies at the University of Jyväskylä, Finland. He is responsible for leading the research focus area 'Educational Systems and Society' and the higher education research team at the Finnish Institute for Educational Research. His own research covers topics from academic work and disciplinary cultures to the relationship between higher education and society. He is joint editor-in-chief of the journal Higher Education.

Yusef Waghid is Distinguished Professor of Philosophy of Education at Stellenbosch University in South Africa. He is the author of *African philosophy of education reconsidered: On being human* (2014).

Subject Index

NB: *Main entries are in boldface. Entries in the notes to chapters are in italics. Terms associated with particular authors or having emblematic status appear in quotation marks.*

A

'Academic capitalism' **55–77**, 300, 330, 345, 361, 364, 370
Academic community 262, 419, 554
Academic freedom 7, 27, 29–31, 33, 87, 89, 97, 137, 149–50, 240, 243, 246–47, 258–59, 297, 303, 330, 345, 360, 419, **426–27**
  see also Autonomy, university; Freedom
Academic inquiry
  See Inquiry
Academic mobility 99
Academic profession 24, 340, 423
Academic staff 73, 84, 159, 167, 360, 385, 413, 419, 462, 467, 492–93, 502, 513, 525, 533, 535, 555, 584
Academy 565
Access 166, 315, 317, 319, 322, 325
Accountability 138–39, 141, 150, 228, 253, 255, 360, 417, 420, 468, 471, 477–78
Administration
  See Management
Afghanistan 455
Africa 219, 226, **270–291**, **311–327**
Agency 45
Agriculture 158
Algeria 284–85, 314
Analogue essence 370–85
Angola 286
Anthropology 409
Anxiety 413
Arabic 276
Architecture 168
Argentina 295, 297–300, *306*
Argumentation 323, 390, 403, 423, 426
Arts 60, 243, 478, 490, 563
Asia 81, 85, 219

Assemblage 32, 323, 473, 575–76, 583, 587
Audit culture 24, 389
Audit 80, 141, 420
Australia 84, 124, 137–38, 142, 146, 150, 199, 201, 204, *211–12*, 219, *496–97*
Austria 225
Authenticity 417, 531, 533–34
Authoritarianism 448
Authority 415
Automation 462
Autonomy, university 27, 33, 64, 81, 142, 209, 233, 240, 243, 245, 247–49, 255, 270, 293, 295–97, 299, 303–05, 342, 364, 366
Autopoiesis 578–79

B

Bangladesh 461
Barbarism 18
Becoming 322
Being 325, 528, 531–32, 582
  Academic 531
  Critical 533
Belarus 227
Bildung 19, 79–80, **81–82**, 172, 183, 217, 259, 338, 432–33, 558
Biology 158, 409
Biomedical sciences 67, 491
Bolivia 299
Bologna process 25, 171–72, 184, 218, **223–30**, 255–56, 348, 357, 361, 363
Books 438–39, 475
Bosnia 407
Brazil 206, *211*, 296, 298, 300–03, *306*
Brunei 199–200, *212*
Burundi 279
Business studies 68–69, 88

C

California Master Plan 119–21
Cameroon 286
Campus 525–26
Canada 124, 127, 129, 199, 201, 203, 205–06, *211–12*, 474
Capital 339
  Cultural 96, 127, 294, 340–42
Capitalism 3, 141, 144, 345, 375–76, 384, 455, 467, 560
  'Academic' 4, 18
  Cognitive 4, 9, 11
  Global 25
  Knowledge 322
Care 424, 427, 449
Charm 530
Chile 199, 205, *211–12*, 238, 271, 298–302, *306*
China 111, 199–200, 206, *211*, 287, 348, 393–94, 404, 585
Christianity 276–77, 559
Church 157, 439, 462, 504, 507, 509–11, 514–16, *520*
Citations 437
Citizens 455, 462, 559, 562
Citizen scientists 588
Citizenship 18–19, 37, 89, 101, 183, 210–211, 234–35, 249, 281–82, 330, 334, 336, **348–49**, 389, 419, 462, 568, 581
  Academic 522–535
  World **393–411**, 559–60, 562, 572
Civic society 122, 240, 244, 248, 414, **447–459**, 522
Civilisation 405
  Western 564
Classical studies 515
Climate change 144
'Cognitive capitalism' 86, 329–30
Collegiality 479
Colombia 205, *212*, 295, 298, 300–02
Colonialization 270–72, 277, 293, 302, 325, 564, 567–69 Knowledge 567
Confidence 417
Commercialization 96, 100, 115–17, 136, 143, 379, 382, 414
Commodification 4, 8, 74, 83–85, 115, 481

Communication 5, 456
Communicative processes 339
Community 145, 383, 401, 458, 471–72, 559–60
  Speech 570
Communities of scholars 493
Compact 180–81
  See also Social contract
Competence 413–14, 437
Competition 8, 25, 56, 60, 64, 69–70, 116–17, 127, 131, 140, 210, 255, 257, 361, 363, 412, 434–35, 479
Complexity 418
Compliance 26
Computerization 376, 379, 385
Congo 279, 283, 286
Consumerism 344, 414
Control 375
Conversation 476–77
Cordoba movement 270, 296–97
'Corporate agent' 589
Corporate sector 582
Cosmopolitanism 457, **559–64**, 572
  Economic 561–62
  Moral 559–560
  Neoliberal 562
  Political 560–61
  See also University, the cosmopolitan
Costa Rica 205, *212*, 300, 409
Countries
  See under individual countries
Courses
  See Curricula
Creativity 79, 86, 140, 168, 491
Crisis
  See University, Crisis of
Criteria of adequacy 11
Critical argument 399–400
Critical inquiry 395
Criticality 44, 46
Critical thinking 37, 43, 49, 422
Critique 321, 326, 343, 346
Cuba 294, 296–97, 300
'Cultural scripts' 579–80
Culture 3, 46, 90, 240, 245, 248, 255, 279, 282, 336–41, 343, 345, 348, 390, 399, 401, 409–10, 476, 559, 564–65, 571, 579–81, 585, 589
  Counter 338
  Cross 403
  Maori 568–71
  Multi 404
  Oral 570
  See also Capital, cultural; Knowledge, culture
'Culture of Critical Discourse' 341, 401
Cultures 102, 115, 402–03, 405, 563
Curricula 87, 99, 105–06, 108, 114, 136, 143, 246, 259–60, 274, 343–44, 401, 403–04, 502, 505, *520*, 563–64, 566
Cyprus 195
Czech Republic 485

D

Dasein 528–31
Degrees 114, 194, 470, 487–88, 493, *498*
Democracy 18–19, 37, 40, 45–47, 50–51, 208, 271, 297, 313, 316, 319–20, 323, 338, 348, 380, 391, 407, 449, 452, 462, 467, 530, 554, 564, 581
  Post- 136–37, 142, 150
Denmark 129, 224, 234–8, **239–241**, 242, 245, 247, 255, 362
Depth 9–10
'Deterritorialization' 323, 583–84
Dialogue 472, 532
Dictatorships 271, 294, 298
Digital revolution 4–5, 97, 158–61, 167, 371, 379, 383, 580, 585, 587
  See also Information and communication technologies
Dignity 401, 526
Disciplines 47, 69, 114, 263, 277, 289, 337, 405, 408, 421, 471–72, 511, 544, 584

Displacement 163–64, 167, 169
Dispute 472
'Dissensus' 3, 462, 470
Diversity 147, 394, 404–05, 408, 413, 420, 563–64
Doctoral programmes 226
Dominican Republic 298
Dutch 165

E

Ecological footprint 587, 589
Ecology 158, 230, 564, 578, 580
 See also Ecosystems
Economics 407, 409, 491, 546, 551
Economy 61, 79, 89, 245, 276, 319, 355–56, 364, 366, 579–81, 584–85, 589
'Ecosophy' 463, 579
Ecosystems 9, 463, 575–77, **578–582**, 585–86, 588
Ecuador 295, 299
Efficiency 25
Egypt 275, 314, 395–96, 455
Elites 233
El Salvador 298–300
Emancipation 47, 89, 314, 330, 334, 341, 415
Emergence 13, 583
Empathy 390, 413–418, 423–24, 426, 530, 564
Empiricism 546–47
 'Aim-oriented' 547
Employability 303, 357, 434–35, 438, 475
Endowments 63
Engagement 12, 581
Engineering 60, 67–71, 491, *520*
England 185, 209, 229, 255, 257, 507
 See also United Kingdom
English 165, 276, 302, 316, 409
Enlightenment, the 157, 216, 334–35, 345, 466–67, 546, 559–61
Enterprise 147
Entrepreneurialism 19, 65, 73, 86, 139, 228, 435, 467, 489, 581
Entrepreneurship 79–81, 88–89, 91, 433, 475
 see also University, the entrepreneurial
Environment 540, 589
Equality 119, 125, 128, 131, 234, 237–38, 315, 322, 341, 396, 487, 560
 See also Inequality
Equal opportunities 237–38, 467
 See also Social mobility
Equity 145–46, 320, 325, 581
Ethical dimension 12, 242
Ethical range 578
Ethiopia 275–76, 279
Ethnicity 397, 409
Europe 25, 57–59, 67, 70, 79, 83–85, 105, 124, 129, 156, 158–59, 165, 171–73, **174–91**, 193, 202–03, 209, 217, 222, 228–29, 253, 277, 294, 347–48, 354, 409, 439, 452, 455, 461, 503–04
 Latin 506
European civilization 564–65
European University Association 207, 223, 256, 503
European Higher Education Area 227–28, 364, 433
European Research Area 159, 433
European Union 18, 25, 55–77, 194, 201, 204–09, *211–12*, 218, 222–24, 262, 390
Examinations 423
 'Excellence' 3, 9, 24–25, 120, 145, 162, 263, 273, 304–05, 346, 433–35, 438, 468
External ideas 8, 10–11

F

Facts 578
Faculty
 See Academic staff
Fascism 338
Feasibility 5–6
Fees, student 21, 47, 68–70, 127, 184, 238, 298, 301, 314, 318, 413, 465, 468, 502, 504

Feminism 348
Finland 234–38, 240–245, 247–48, 362
Fluidity 585
Fragility 534, 577
France 27, 68–69, 158, *186*, 220–21, 224–25, 277, 280, 294, 348, 362, 461, 475, 485
Freedom 10, 45–46, 96, 330, 391, 401, 421, 424, 512, 516, 559–60, 562
  see also Academic freedom
French 165
Friendship 564
Funding 72, 138

G

Gender 397, 403, 408–09, 563, 566
General Agreement on Tariffs and Trade (GATT) 192–93, 208, *211*
General Agreement on Trade in Services (GATS) 192, 209–10, 284, 288
Generosity 417
Geology 409
Geophilosophy 587
German 165
Germany 59, 68–70, 73, 79, 129, 158, 183, *186*, 197–98, 217, 220, 222, 224–25, 249, 253, 256, 279, 335, 337–38, 347–48, 362, 462, 475, 503, 512, 580
Ghana 286
Global economy 85, 95, 330
  See also Knowledge economy
Globalization 9, 96, 99, 145, 147, 160–61, 172, 180, 184, 228, 260, 271, 283–84, 288, 298, 300, 329–30, 333–34, 344, 6346–47, 355, 361, 364, 420, 455, 493, 559, 564, 580
God 275
Governance 24–25, 29, 41, 45, 137, 139, 145, 150, 208, 240–43, 247, 258, 270, 292, 296, 317, 358, 360, 419–20, 454
Government 58, *519*, 554
Graduates 462, 469, 474–75, 483, 486
Great Britain
  See United Kingdom
Greece 72, 225, 228, 456
Greenland 227
Guatamala 299
Guilds 439
GUNI collective 587

H

Haiti 299
Health 158
Hermeneutics 164–65
Higher education 27, 32, 37, 40–75, 44, 46–47, 49, 60–61, 85, 99, 113, 208, 221, 237, 244, 252–53, 262, 274, 277, 281, 283–84, 313, 318–19, 342, 349, 361, 403, 416, 419–20, 458, 495, 502, 515–18
  Crisis of
    See University, crisis of
  European 216–232
  Public 230
    See also Public
  Purposes 313
  Vocational 221
Higher education institutions 112, 254, 354, 365–66
Higher education policy 303
Higher education systems 236, 258, 269, 298, 317–18, 363, 365, 554, 587
History 399, 408
Honduras 299
Hong Kong 205, *212*
Hope 271, 321–22, 326
Hospitality 560, 564
Human being 454
  See also Being; Humanity
Human capital 59–60, 119, 121–22, 130, 281, 283, 366, 434, 485–87
Humanism 338, 559
Humanities 24, 41, 60, 67, 299, 408, 465, 475, *497*, 513, 515, 545, 550, 552, 563, 566–67, 584

Humanity 242, 397–98, 400, 539–42, 544, 550–52, 554, 576, 578, 586–87
Human resources 63
Human rights 394, 401, 406, 559–61
Humboldtian model 27, 217, 254, 512, 517–18
See also University, the Humboldtian
Hungary 484

I

Iceland 205, *212*, 234–35, 353
'Ideological state apparatuses' 340
Ideologies 13, 41, 59, 73
Ideology 87, 103, 258–59, 263, 293, 336, 346, 355, 366, 377, 407, 419, 449, 561
Identity 24, 565, 567–68, 579
Imaginaries 89, 322
Imagination 74, 271, 313, 326, 432, 437–38, 450, 458, 581
Impact 437
Impairment 577–78
Imperialism 293–94, 297
Inclusiveness 147
Inclusion 322
Incommensurability 472
India 206, *211*, 402, 407–09, 461, 584
Indigenous peoples 563, 565–68
Individualism 561
Indonesia 206
Industry 142, 347, 478
Inequality 28, 41, 49–50, 96–97, 123–28, 130, 317, 319, 341, 357, 425, 540
See also Equality
Information 261, 347, 355, 377–78, 455, 476, 478
Information and communication technologies 115, 289, 344, 347, 370–71, 376
See also Digital revolution
Innovation 145, 147, 171, 255, 260, 435, 437
Inquiry 541, 544–45, 550–53, 564
See also Knowledge-inquiry; Wisdom-inquiry
Institutional autonomy
See Autonomy, university
'Integration' 522, 533–34
Integrity 424
Intellectual fields 584
Intellectuals 44–46, 335, 337–8, 340
See also Public intellectuals
Intelligentsia 340
Interculturality 102, 579
Interdisciplinarity 159, 166, 406, 408–09, 472
Internal ideas 8, 10–11
International Association of Universities 275
Internationalization 96, **99–119**, 175, 248, 263–64, 300, 559, 563–64, 566, 572, 579, 581
International students
See under Students
Internet
See under Digital revolution
Iran 348, 395, 455
Irrationality 541, 543–44
Ireland 72, 485
Islam 275–76, 286
Israel 29–32, 205, *212*, 485
Italy 217, 224–25, 228, 280, 485
'Ivory tower' 21–22, 26–27, 30, 33–34, 480, 514

J

Japan 59. 124, 197, 205, *211–12*, 409, 485
Journals 414, 437, 478–79
Justice
see Social Justice

K

Kenya 274, 286, 408–09
Knowledge 2, 10, 26, 47, 82, 84, 89–91, 95, 97, 99, 137, 139–41, 144, 158–59, 163, 166, 168, 240, 244, 255, 257, 261, 320, 329–330, 334–35, 339, 341, 343–44,

349, 353, 355–56, 362–64, 365–66, 372, 375, 390, 393, 403, 420, 422, 442–43, 463, 471, 476, 478, 507, 514, *520*, 522, **542–47**, 550, 555, 565, 568, 579–80
Advancement of 515, 517–18
Broad 511
Circuits of 55–56, 62, 65, 70–71
Indigenous 566, 572
'Mode 2' 260, 329, 344, 478, *520*, 534
Politics of 565
Power/ 567
Public 337
Self 398
Socialist 9
Spiritual 508
Traditional 566
Knowledge capitalism
See Capitalism, knowledge
'Knowledge class' 335
Knowledge constellations 55
Knowledge creation 585
Knowledge culture 163
Knowledge ecology 578–79, 582, 585–86, 588
Knowledge economy 9, 64–65, 71, 85–86, 100, 113, 131, **139–141**, 178, 269, 357, 362, 434, 485
Knowledge exploitation 475, 480
'Knowledge-inquiry' 539–41, 543–46, 551, 553
Knowledge institutions 304
Knowledge production 85, 90, 161, 176, 262, 274, 287, 340, 372–73, 379, 382, 434, 436, 440, 478
Knowledges 586
Knowledge society 79, 253, 348–49, **353–366**
Knowledge systems 414, 572, 584
Knowledge transfer 62, 517, 581, 585

L

Laboratory 441, 478
Labour market 96, 123, 178, 319, 363–65, 434
Languages 158, 165, 399, 402, 409, 568–70
Latin 276, 443
Latin America 57, 218, 226, 270
Law 508
Leadership 358, *519*
League tables
See Rankings
Learner 457
Learner engagement 79
Learning 5, 79, 83, 85, 90–91, 106–07, 113–15, 210, 276–77, 379–80, 389, 399, 435, 467, 474–76, 486, 502, 513, 524, 550, 555, 572, 579, 581
Autodidactic 485
Distance 286, *498*
e- 502
Fast 435
Higher 287–89, 421, 508
Independent 435–36, 438
Institutions of 555
Life-long 159, 242, 258
Life-wide 584, 588–89
Personal 444
Processes 339
Self-directed 89, 121
Socialist 6
Student-centred 363
Virtual 107
Work-based *519*
Learning ecology 580, 584, 588
Learning outcomes 416, 434–35, 470
Learning style 435
Lecturers
See Academic staff
Lectures 380, 423, 441, 444
Online 492–93
Legitimation crisis 79
Legitimacy 2, 182
Liberal education 217, 233, 379, 402, 414, 422, 475, 512
Liberalisation
See Marketisation 288
Liberia 286
Library 326, 439, 535

Libya 314
Liechtenstein 205, *212*
Life 399, 410, 468, 539, 542, 549, 552–54
Life sciences 67, 158
Lifeworld 339, 535, 578
'Lines of flight' 10, 323, 583, 588
Literature 158, 382, 399, 403, 553
Living
See Life

M

Malawi 286
Malaysia 199–201, 206, *212*
Mali 284
Management 25, 62–65, 72, 135, 241–42, 249, 355, 359, 419, 479–80, 492, 494
Managerialism 322, 345, 347, 355, 360, *519*
Managers 26, 30, 33, 555
Maori
See Culture, Maori
Market 150, 206, *306*, 348, 359, 365–66, 379, 384
See also Markets
Market economy 48, 71, 84, 122, 141, 144, 462, 467
Market ethos 139, 470
Market failure 71
Marketization 21, 74, 84–85, 97, 136, 144, 209, 256, 260, 288, 330, 358, 389–90, 412–14, 419, 582
Market, labour
See Labour Market
Markets 5–6, 8, 10, 37–40, 56–57, 60, 69–71, 73, 80, 136, 193–94, 333, 371, 380, 425, 502
Quasi- 65, 127, 178–79, 185, 359
Marxism 338
Mass higher education 82, 85, 119, 138, 181, 184–85, 220–21, 258, 298–9, 301, 346, 349, 362, 461
See also Universities, mass
Mathematics 157–58, 373, 441, *520*, 553
Mauritius 205, *212*
Measurement 164
Medicine 67, 158–59, 238, 508, 512, 542
Medieval universities
See Universities, medieval
Meritocracy 128, 415
Metaphor 156, 163, 165, 168, 585
Metaphysics 547
Metrics 420
Mexico 199–200, 205, *212*, 294–98, 301
Middle Ages 216, 390, 438, 445, 503–05, **507–11**, 518
Mind 2, 373, 396
Mission statements 145, 147–48, 474, 476–77, 479, 517
Mobility 108, 129, 131
Modernity 219, 342–43, 356
Modular programmes 502
MOOCs 100, 102, 259, 362–63, 380–81
Morality 405, 423, 428
Morocco 275–76, 280, 284
Mozambique 286
Multiculturality 114, 348, 402, 405, 409–10, 568
Multidisciplinarity 159, 456
Multiplicity 580
Multiversity 119
Mutuality 449

N

Nation 282, 345
Nationality 397, 568
Nation state
See State, nation
Nature 374, 547, 575–76
Nazism 458
Neoliberalism 3–4, 8, 18, 22–24, 26, 28, 32–34, 40, 55, 57, 62, 74, 81, 84, 86, 124, 147, 172, 247, 249, 274, 300, 346, 370–72, 376–80, 382, 462, 558, 562–63, 566–67, 572
Neoliberal institutions 65
See also State, the neoliberal

Netherlands, the 222, 225–26, 255
Networks 97, 127, 158–59, 164, 379, 419, 568, 577, 585, 587
'Network society' 155, 158, 160, 162, 167, 169, 377
'New Class' 340
New public management 18, 63, 137–38, 149, 176, 185, 243, 255, 260, 294, 330, 358, 360, 413
New Zealand 84–85, 199, 201, 205, *211–12*, 219, 485, 568–69
Nicaragua 299
Nigeria 286, 288
Nobel Prizes 449
Nodes 164–65, **585**
Non-completion rates 483, 486
Nomadic practices 166
Nordic countries 127, 129, 131, 222, **233–251**
Norway 65, 205, *212*, 234–38, **244–245**, 247–48
North-South relationships 270, 294, 320

O

OECD 56, 123, 125, 179, 210, 237–39, 295, 298, 360, 483, 486–87
Oligarchy 294
Oman 111
Ontology 523
Open access 587
Openness 322, 586
Opportunity 125–27
Optimism 6, 8, 10–11
Orientalism 216, 218, 559, 565, 567
Other, the 161

P

Pakistan 205, *212*
Palestine 30–32
Panama 205, *212*, 295, 299
Paraguay 205, 212, 295, 299
'Paraversity' 465, **470–80**
Participation 146, 297, 318, 325, 347–48
Patents 66, 71
Pedagogical relationships 5, 390, 425, 580, 582, 584
Pedagogy 45–46, 51, 91, 159, 259, 304, 321, 372, 376, 441, 443–45, 457
See also Teaching
Pedagogy of hope 321–22, 406
Performance indicators *519*
Performance management 4, 139, 145, 148, 355
Performativity 2, 8, 25, 344, 580
Peru 199, 205, *212*, 295, 297, 299
Pessimism 4, 8, 10
Pharmaceutical industry 140, 586
Pharmacy 158
PhD
See Doctoral programmes
Philosophy 81, 158, 382, 397, 408, 454, 512, 553, 566, 568, 570
Western 566, 572
Physics 67, 69, 158, 165, 441, 547, 551, *555*
Place 159–60, 168, 524, 530, 535
Poland 485
Politics 245, 335, 339, 551
Polytechnics 83, 221–22, 502, 517
Portugal 72, 279, 296, 485
Postcolonialism 274, 276, 284
'Postindustrial society' 335, 339, 256, 487–90, 493
Postmodernism 159, 262, 330, 334, 344
Postmodernity 382
Possibilities 581–82
Post-political era 144, 148, 150
Poverty 396
Power 25–26, 41, 44, 47–48, 341–42, 366, 420, 443–44, 479, 505, 527, 565, 567
Private good 260–61
Privatization 100, 269, 274, 284–85, 412
Problems 541
Productivity 25
Professionalism 414, 423–26, 487

Professions 338, 478, 487, 509, 515
Professoriate 339
 See also Academic staff
Profile, ecological 586
Progress 546
Proletarianisation 361, 436
Psychology 546
Public 3, 166, 208, 288, 322, **432–445**, 469, 534–35, 555, 581
Publications 95, 109, 437
Public good 37, 40, 42–43, 47, 258, 260, 270, 283, 287, 289, 412
Public goods 379, 487
Public intellectuals 31, 45, 343
Publics 45, 588
Public service 24, 176, 185, 248, 436, 474–75
Public space 45, 390–91
Public sphere 31, 40, 44, 46, 137, 339, 349, 586, 588
Public understanding 582, 588

Q

Quadrivium 157
Quality 100, 104, 108, 111, 162, 225, *306*, 318, 360, 477–78
Quality assurance 412, 419
Questioning 410

R

Race 408, 566
Racism 566
Rankings 61, 85, 95, 100, 116, 162, 219, 263, 300, 302, 330, 361–62, 366, 413, 467
Rationality 41, 341, 542–43, 547, 552–54, *556*, 559
 'Aim-oriented' 548–50
 Cognitive 337
 Instrumental 45, 339
Rational society 587
Reading 372, 375, 377, 381–82, 384
Reason 2, 3, 10, 216, 384, 390, 395, 398–99, 416, 422, **543–44**, 553
 Administration 572
 Community of 399
 Economic 572
 Instrumental 330, 384
 Public 407
 Space of 9
Reflexivity 344, 356–57
Regulation 209
Relationality 577, 583
Relativism, cultural 390, 406, 408
Religion 285, 296, 404–05, 409
Renaissance 158, 164, 470
Repression 299
Republic of Korea 205, *212*, 485
Research 18, 21, 58, 61, 69–70, 73, 81–82, 85, 89, 95, 106–08, 113, 115, 135, 139–43, 149, 157, 163–64, 166, 180, 209, 240, 242, 245–46, 252–53, 255, 257, 260–64, 270, 289, 302, 304, 330, 344, 364, 390, 424, 435–36, 440, 442, 444, 462, 467–68, 474–79, 486, 494, 524, 541–42, 552, 554, 564, 581–84, 588
 Basic 140
Research capability 269
Research community 476
Researchers 167, 433, 438, 475, 493
Research evaluation *519–520*
Research findings 471, 475
Research funding 111, 261
Research policy 261–63
Research system 260
Resistance 26
Respect 402
Responsibility 3, 7, 43–46, 48, 105, 228, 230, 245, 297, 323, 462, 479–80, 522–23, 533–34, 562, 575, 577
Reterritorialization 323
Rhizome 472–73, 479, 577

Risk 71, 312, 314, 316, 320, 324–26, 534
Robbins Report 119–21, 476
Robotics 484, 488–89
Russia 73, 206, 211, 448
Rwanda 279, 286, 407

S

Saudi Arabia 206
Scandinavia 79, 81, 88, 91, 123, 220, 225, 229
Scholarship 105–06, 335, 413, 442, 477, 505, 509, 514, 553, 555
Science 60–61, 65, 68, 70–71, 82, 113–14, 157, 159, 163, 168, 243, 263, 285, 302, 315, 320, 334–35, 347, 349, 365, 379, 390, 414, 442–44, 490, *520*, 542, **546–49**, 551–54, *555*, 567
  Entrepreneurial 66
  Western 566, 572
Science policy 261–62
Self 82, 161, 398, 410, 417–18, 422, 564
Seminars 444
Service to society 107, 115, 425, 477, **515–18**
Sierra Leone 280, 286
Signifiers, empty 434
Singapore 111, 199, 206, 212
Skills 584
Social class 96, 286, 357, 397
Social contract 186, 416
Social good 37, 85
Social goods 59, 462
  See also Public good
Social justice 7, 10, 38, 47–48, 51, 59, 80, 119, 320, 402, 572
Social mobility 96, 120–21, 301
Social sciences 60–61, 67, 69, 83, 299, 311, 357, 545, 550
  See also Sociology
Society 242, 244, 246, 419, 427, 432, 448, 579–80, 585, 589
Sociology 335, 341–42, 546, 551
  See also Social sciences
South, the 566
South Africa 167, *211*, 279, 311–12, **316–327**, 401
South Sudan 286
Soviet Union
  See Russia
Space 159–60, 167–68, 449, 524, 526, 562–63, 581
  See also Public space
'Space of flows' 585
Space-time 443
Spain 72, 228, 296, 455–56, 485
Spanish 409
Speech 396
Speed 444
Spin-offs 71
Spirit
  Ecological 577, 583
Spirituality 277
Staff
  See Academic staff
Standards 465, 467
State, the 48, 55, 57, 64, 66, 73, 85, 120, 150, 157, 178, 180, 184, 210, 235, 241, 247, 255, 270, 282, 344, 347, 415, 419–20, 447, 462, 510
  Nation 181–82, 184, 238, 248–49, 260, 348
  The neoliberal 55, 65, 71
  The welfare 175, **177–182**, 184–86, 234, 248
States 96, 299
STEM disciplines 11, 60, 66–67, 69–70, 584
Student debt 317
Student enrolment 284–85
Student experience 391, 419, 475
Student mobility 107, 112
Student numbers 465, 510
Student protest 271, 296, 297, 300, 314, 316, 340, 469
Student retention 303
Students 37, 41–43, 45, 50–51, 59, 67, 69, 72, 84–85, 87, 90, 107, 157, 159–60,

166–67, 178, 184, 249, 253–54, 298, 305, 318, 325–26, 339–40, 359–61, 372, 380–81, 385, 390, 401, 404, 413, 415, 419–20, 423, 425, 432–33, 439, 441–42, 444, 468–69, 474, 478, 480, 487, 494, 501, 504, 507–10, 512–15, 523, 526, 533, 535, 555, 562–63, 566, 584
Black 317–20, 326
Disadvantaged 313
Fee-paying 492
International 68, 71, 73, 105–06, 112, 238, 562, 580, 584
Postgraduate 319
Prospective 489
Students as customers 4, 42, 84, 178, 258, 260, 340, 389, 465, 467, 469, 581
Student housing 586
Student satisfaction 425, 475, 478
Student, the 403, 438, 440, 476, *498*, 525
Student trust 423
Study 439
Stupidity 453
Subjectivity 24, 581, 589
See also Identity; Self
Subjects
See Disciplines; also see under particular disciplines
Superficiality 9–10
Surveillance 426, 455–56
Sustainability 145, 413, 540, **576–77, 580–81**
Sweden 198, *234–38*, **245–247**, 254, 264, 485
Switzerland 205, *212*, 255, 353

T

Talloires Group 587
Tanzania 283, 286
Teachers
See Academic staff
Teaching 79, 81, 85, 95, 107, 110, 113–14, 136, 139, 141, 149, 157, 159, 164, 180, 242–43, 263, 304, 330, 344, 391, 409, 424, 435–36, 441, 467–68, 474–77, 479, 492, 494, 502, 510, 524, 555
Teaching load 143
Technology 61, 82, 113, 343, 347, 349, 363, 374, 379, 383, 488, 490, 495, 542, *555*
Digital 492
See also Digital era; Information and communication technologies
Technology transfer 61, 66–68, 71
Territorialisation 583–84
Theology 158, 508, 512, *520*, 558
Thinking 163, 320, 324, 372, 391, 447, 449–50, 452
See also Thought
Third mission 57, 139, 143, 242, 246, *306*, 475–76
Thought 436, 470, 551
Thoughtlessness 453, 455
Tiananmen Square 314
Time 361, **377–78**, 381, 581
Totalitarianism 448, 454–55, 458
Training 564–65, 572
Transdisciplinarity 159, 456, 472, 490
Transformations 23, 318, 320, 324–26, 343, 361, 371, 382, 502, 555
Transgressivity 95
Triple helix 139–40, 260, 345
Trivium 157
Trust 38, 254, 323, **413–428**
Truth 43, 82, 135, 144, 158–59, 399, 422, 547
Truthfulness 9
Tuition
See Fees
Tunisia 280, 314
Turkey 205, *212*

U

Uganda 286
Understanding 161, 165, 399, 543, 551, 576, 587
United Arab Emirates 206

United Kingdom 24, 56, 68–69, 83–84, 96, 111, 120–131, 146, 148, 158, *186*, 208, 217–18, 222, 224–26, 276–77, 279, 301, 347, 362, 474–76, *481*, 490, *496–97*, 502–03, 518
United Nations 195, 211, 561
UNESCO 283, 299, 302, *496*
United States 18, 24, 27, 30–32, 37–38, 41–43, 47, 50–51, 55–77, 82–85, 96, 111, 120–131, 137, 142, 150, 195, 199–200, 202–05, 207, 209, *211–12*, 218–20, 226, 228, 254, 261, 264, 277, 279, 282, 288, 294, 297, 301, 338, 349, 380, 393, 401, 455, 474–75, *497–98*, 502, 566
Universality 165–66, 406, 457, 560–61, 564, 581
Universitas 438
Universities 24, 33, 42, 55, 60, 63, 65, 83, 85, 90, 95–97, 99, 104–05, 137, 141, 155–56, 176, 242, 257, 311, 316, 330, 363, 371, 412, 434, 449, 456, **461**, 469, 486–87, 495, 502, 507, 510–11, 524, 527, 530, 532, 540, 555, 562–63, 566, 571, 585
  Auto-industrial 462, **491–92**
  Corporate 345, 462
  Cosmopolitan 12
  Crisis of 137
  Ecological 12
  See also University, the ecological
  Elite 126
  European 172
  Exploitative 586
  For-profit 6, 100, 115, 125, 287, 419
  of Culture 12
  Ivy League 125, 127–28, 130
  Land Grant 217
  Mass 305, 485, 491
  Medieval 281–82, *445*, 461–62, 484, 493, 509, 515
  See also University, medieval
  Mega 345–46
  Networked 162
  Open 297
  Paris 183
  Post-industrial 490–91
  Public 286, 293, 298, 301, 304
  Private 284–86, 288, 298, 301, *306–07*
  Research 72–73, 185, 257, 287, 362, 462
  Russell Group 126
  Socialist 12
  State
  See Universities, public
  Teaching 303
  Under siege 25, 32
  Virtual 102, 108, 345
    See also University, the virtual
Universities (named)
  Adelaide 146
  Ahfad University for Women 274
  Al-Azhar 275–76
  Al-Feteh 280
  Amherst College 259
  Ashesi University College 290#
  Auckland 570
  Australian National University 146
  Bamako 284
  Bentley College 407
  Bergen 245
  Berlin 27, 81, 183, 461, 466, 513
  Brown 407
  California 121, 128, 402
    Berkeley 257, 264
  Cambridge 125, 130, 219, 259, 276, 462, 513
  Cape Town 279, 318
  Charles Darwin 146
  Chicago 121, 407, 495
  Curtin 147
  de Lima
  Exeter 422
  Ez-Zitouna 280
  Flinders 144, 146
  German University of Technology 111
  Griffith 146
  Harvard 65, 128, 180, 219, 257, 259, 407
  Helsinki 242, 362
  Illinois 23, 28–30

Islamic Sciences of Constantine 285
James Cook 146
Karawiyyinn 275, 280
La Trobe 146
Leuven 166
Liberia
Massachusetts Institute of Technology (MIT) 259, 264, 380
Melbourne 146
Mayor Nacional de San Marcos *306*
Missouri 166
Monash 146
Murdoch 146
Natal 318
Nazarbeyev 111
Nevada 404
New South Wales 146
New York 111, 405–08
Norwegian University of Science and Technology 245
Oberta de Catalunya 167
Open University of Tanzania
Oslo 245
Oxford 125, 127, 130, 276, 282, 371, 462, 509, 513
Paris 280
Pretoria 279, 316
Princeton 50, 128, 276
Queensland University of Technology 147
Rhodes 318
Royal Melbourne Institute of Technology 147
St Lawrence 408
Santo Tomás de Aquino *306*
Sciences Po 127
Singapore University of Science and Technology 111
Sino-British 111
Sorbonne 276
South Africa (UNISA) 284, 316
South Australia 147
Stanford 128, 380
Stellenbosch 316
Swarthmore College 259
Sydney 146
Tromso 245
UNAM *306*
University College London 566
University of Technology, Sydney 147
Uppsala 264
Venda 279
The Victoria University of Wellington
Western Australia 146
Wharton 128
Witwatersrand 279, 318
Xi'an Jiaotang Liverpool University 111
Yale 65, 128, 276
Zimbabwe Open University 284

University 27, 32, 88–89, 96–97, 119–20, 122, 130, 159–60, 166, 336, 349, 384, 419, 438, 440, 447, 463, 468, 478, 503, 508, 510, 516, 524–25, 532, 554, 566, 571, 576–77
Being a 21, 502, 505, 514, 517, 523–24, 526, 531
Crisis of 313–14, 343
Death of 571
Global 462
History of 81
Idea of 1, 5, 7, 12, 28, 33, 81, 99, 186, 233, 274, 284, 333, 339, 364, 467, 480, 501, 519, 558–59, 564, 568, 580
See also University as idea
Ideas of 11, 13, 330, 466, 582
Medieval 157, 461, 492, **505–511**, 515–16, *520*
See also Universities, medieval
Postmodern 346
Purpose of 470, 513
The African 311–327
The colonial 565, 572
The cosmopolitan 463, **559–564**, 571
The corporate 4, 466, 469–70, 472, 475, 477–80
The digital 382
The ecological 9, 162, 322, 463, **577–589**

The engaged 9
The Enlightenment 480, 555
The entrepreneurial 1, 9, 10, 19, **78–94**, 140, 178, 221, 228, 260, 304, 322, 370, 558
The European 179, 216, **216–232**, 220, **252–267**
The fully-functioning 502–21
The Humboldtian 176, 178, 182–83, 233, 462, 505, **513–516**, 519, *520*, 558
See also Humboldtian model
The indigenous 571
The imagining 323
The instrumental 334
The international 117
The liberal 466, 558
The marketized 300
The modern 86, 564
The neoliberal 19, 25, 90
The networked **155–169**, 585
The Newmanian 558
The Nordic **233–251**
The open 9, 12
The placeful 523
The platform 483–496
The post-colonial 564–68, 571
The post-historical 558
The post-industrial 483, 494–95
The postmodern 348
The public 9, 162, 178
The research 177, 463, 505, 514
The socialist 11
The sustainable 75
The virtual 347
The Western 503, 505, 566–67, 571
World 162–63
University as idea 2, 7, 10, 515, 580–81
See also University, idea of
University as institution 2, 7, 10–11, 142, 333, 370, 372, 418, 427, 447, 465, 467, 484, 562, 58
University education 572
University 'in Ruins' 314, 466, 469, 480–81
University life 163
University mission 519
University of wisdom 588
University without walls 588
Uruguay 205, *212*, 299
Utilitarianism 390, 416
Utopia 13

V

Value 81, **84**, 87, 90–91, 124, 139, 143, 147, 244, 263, 329, 365, 427, 437, 457, 477, 550, 577, 579, 588
Hierarchy of 127, 549
Values 40, 44, 96, 142, 145, 149, 166, 246, 261–62, 333, 355, 410, 474, 477–78, 513, 527, 533, 553, 560–61, 577–78
Cosmopolitan 562
Cultural 567
Market 346
Value ladenness 586
Value judgements 584
Value positions 587
Value statements 147–48
Venezuala 295, 300
Vietnam 199–201, 212
Virtue 417, 424, 513, 516, *520*, 534–35, 581
Virtues 8, 526, 533
Virtuousness 322

W

Web **158–59**, 577
Welfare society 235, 239
Welfare state
See State, the welfare
Well-being 10, 289, 323, 414, 449, 581
Of world 12
Wisdom 9, 12, 322, 463, 542, 545, 550–53, 581
'Wisdom-inquiry' 539, 543, 545, 550–51, 553, *556*
Wissenschaft 217

Women 407
World 373
World Bank 283, 299, 360
'World-class' universities 3, 9, 24, 95, 109, 287, 300, 302, 330, 362
World Trade Organization (WTO) 192–94, 206, *211*, 284
Writing 372, 375, 377, 381–82, 384, 571

Z

Zambia 286
Zimbabwe 274, 286

Name Index

A

Aaen, J 528
Abrahamsson, P 235
Ackers, L 64
Acosta Silva, A 294, 298–301
Agamben, G 312, 324
Aghion, P 140
Aiken, M 356
Ainley, P 85
Ajayi, J 275, 279–80
Albornoz, O 294, 298, 301
Aldrich, H 177
Alestalo, M 235
Alexander, F 70
Ali, T 455
Allen, M 354
Altbach, P 100, 147, 287, 294, 313, 315
Althusser, L 340
Amaral, A 178, 355, 360
Anderson, B 372
Andreescu, L 427
Andresani, G 414
Anaru, N 569
Appadurai, A 563–64
Appiah, K 457
Apple, M 79
Arendt, H 51, 391, 447–51, 453–54, *458*
Aristotle 457, 559
Arnold, M 370k
Arnolds, C 317
Aronowitz, S 52
Arora, A 282
Aroncena, R 294–96, 304, *306*
Arum, R 129
Arum, S 102
Ash, M G 27, 30
Ashby, E 282
Ashenden, D 138
Ashworth, W 375
Assié-Lumumba, N 267, 273–291, 315
Autor, D *497*
Avery, C 126

B

Bacevic, J 18
Badat, S 319
Badiou, A 52
Baert, P 31
Baier, A 415–16, 418, 420, 425
Bailey, R 358, 361
Bakhurst, D 7
Balan, J 287
Balbachevsky, E 302
Ball, S 25, 358
Baran, N 377
Barea, D *497*
Barkawi, T 22
Barnabe, F 139
Banacle, R 523, 530
Barnett, R 1, 3, 5, 9, 11, 21, 25, 77–79, 81, 162, 301, 312, 322–23, 361, 414, 423, 463, 523, 528, 533–34, 580–81, 587
Barr, N 176
Barrow, R 426
Barsoum, M 314
Batchelor, D 528
Bauman, Z 44, 51–52
Becher, T 176
Beck, U 356–57, 457
Becker, G 59, 121–22
Belei, C 301
Ben-David, J 186
Bell, D 333, 335–36, 356
Bell, E 375
Bengtsen, S 463, 528
Bentele, K 125
Berlin, I 219
Bernasconi, A 270, 293, 296, 300–02
Besley, T 4
Beyes, T 528
Bhagwati, J 196
Bieler, A 58
Biesta, G 79, 313, 323–25, 523, 529
Birnbaum, R 362
Bladh, A 244, 247–49
Blanden, J 129
Bleiklie, I 413
Blenker, P 88–89
Bloom, A 343
Blum, D 78
Blyth, M 181
Boden, R *91*
Bodenheimer, S 293
Boehm, A 107
Bohr, N 219
Bok, D 2, 412, 421
Boliver, V 126–27
Bonaccorsi, A 178
Bonhoeffer, D 450
Booth, J 31
Borgen, N 126
Bourdieu, P 33, 81, 89, 122, 340–43, 347, 365–66
Bourner, T 462–63
Bousquet, M 63
Boutang, Y M 11, 582
Bowden, B 561
Bradwell, P 6
Brand, J 130
Branham, B *411*
Blum, D 78
Brennan, J 184
Breschi, S 62
Briggs, A 221
Brinkman, P 59
Britez, R 5
Brockling, U 434
Brown, R 371
Brunner, J 294, 300
Bruno, J 59
Brunson, N 177
Buchanan, R 526
Buraway, M 21
Burik, S 321
Bush, V 181
Butler, J 31
Byon, J 141

C

Cabalin, C 301
Calhoun, C 287, 349, 448
Campbell, J 180
Canaan, J 22, 85
Cantisano Terra, B 139
Cantwell, B 18, 56–57, 64, 72–73
Carasso, H 371
Carnoy. M *307*
Carr, N 381
Carrigan, M 31
Carvalho, T 25, 414–15, 421
Casey, E 523–26, 533
Castells, M 95, 158, 160–61, 585
Castles, F 181
Cave, M 359
Cerych, L 354
Chaker, M 69
Cheng, M 424
Chomsky, N 41, 52
Christiansen, C *498*
Ciancanelli, P *91*
Clark, B R 1, 9, 57, 86, 228, 281, 301, 303, 354, 360
Clarke, A C 374
Clegg, S 423
Coaldrake, P 138
Coate, K 523
Cobban, A 504
Coetzee, J 141
Cohen, D 407
Collini, S 412, 465, 475
Connell, R 294
Cook, C 24
Cope, J 88
Considine, M 138
Corak, M 126, 129
Coser, L 219
Crary, J 373
Creswell, T 523, 526–27
Crook, R 109
Crosier, D 223
Culkin, J 375
Currie, J 345, 420
Curtis, M 511
Curzon-Hobson, A 421
Cusmano, L 62

D

Dahrendorf, R 349
Dale, S 130
Dall'Alba, G 523, 530
Danilova, M 314
Daraio, C 178
Daunton, L 24
Davies, H 201, 208
Davies, S 127, 149
Davis,G 138
Deardoff, D 105
de Boer, H 139
de Certeau, M 160–61, 167–68, 338
Deem, R 26, 63
De George, R 426
De Jong, U 359
DeLanda, M 579, 583–84
Delanty, G 21, 179, 182, 330
Deleuze, G 10, 323, 374, 472–73, 580, 583
Dembéle, M 273
de Oliveira Mota, M 414–15, 421
Deresiewicz, W 130
Derrida, J 3, 7, 312, 320, 322, 564, 566–68
De Sousa Santos, B 294
De Ville, F 203
Dewatripont, M 140
Dewey, J 38, 82, 91
de Wit, H 102–04
Didriksson
Djelic, J-L 177, 180
Dill, D 358–59
Diogenes 393–94, 396–97, *411*
Dilthey, W 165
Doherty, T 22
Domatob, J 281
Dorf, M 30
Dooley, L 139

Dorling, D 123
Dorn, D *497*
Dreyfus, H 88–89
Drucker, P 355–56
Drykek, J 179
Duke, C 359
Durkheim, E 333, 337, 439
Dyer, J *498*
Dzulkifli, A 103

E

Easterly, W 299
Edwards, C 88
Edwards, P 375
Egron-Polak, E 110
Ehrenberg, R 68
Ertl, H 60
Esping-Andersen, G 234
Espinoza, W 301
Esterman, T 64
Estévez, S 374–75
Etzkowitz, H 87, 139–40, 301, 304, 345
Eustace, R 360
Evans, G 136
Experton, W 282

F

Fagerlind, I 243, 247
Fanon, F 568
Farini, F 417
Ferlie, E 413
Ferruolo, S 439
Fichte, J *186*, 461
Filippakou, O 523, 530
Fink, D 576
Finkelstein, J 63
Fish, S 22, 31
Fiske, E 316–18
Fitzmaurice, M 424
Flaherty, C 30
Flores, F 88–89
Foster, R *498*
Foucault, M 24, 122–23, 341, 567
Frank, T 380
Freeman, J 177
Freese, J 32
Freire, P 312, 321, 522, 530, 533–34
Freud, S 453
Frey, C *497*
Friedman, M 561
Froumin, I *307*
Fukuyama, F 416
Fuller, C 415
Fuller, S 349
Fulton, D 29
Fung, A 47

G

Gaita, R 137, 385
Gambetta, D 420
Garcia-Guadilla, C 298–99
Gartner, S 127
Gehlen, A 374
Geiger, R 130
Geiysztor, A 217
Gemperle, M 356
Gerhardt, C 139
Geuna, A 71
Gibb, A 88
Gibbons, M 95, 329, 343
Gibbs, P 90, 414–16
Gietzen, G 6
Giddens, A 356–57
Gieryn, T 527
Gill, B 64
Ginder, S 64
Giroux, H A 4, 18, , 51, 312–15, 324, 414
Glaister, K 149
Glidden, D 402
Glover, J *498*
Goma, G 275, 279–80
Gonzaléz, L 301

Goos, M *497*
Gorman, P 148
Gornall, L 24
Gornitzka, A 65, 176, 185
Gordon, G 24
Gouldner, A 330, 333, 340
Goulet-Cazé *411*
Gramsci, A 451
Green, A 182
Green, V 509
Greenwood, D 91
Gregersen, H *498*
Greve, B 185
Grossman, V 448
Grewal, D S 158
Gros, F 474
Guattari, F 10, 323, 472–73, 578–80, 583
Guédon, J-C 167
Guthrie, W K C *411*
Guzmán-Valenzuela, C 270, 301–02, 414

H

Habermas, J 3, 90, 178, *186*, 330, 333, 338–39, 342–43, 346, 561–62, 587
Hale, T 177
Halfmann, W 25
Halsey, A H 361
Hanley, C 124–25
Hanney, M 176
Hannan, M 177
Hardin, R 422
Harding, N 448
Hargreaves, A 78, 576
Harjes, T 70
Harman, G 528, 530–31
Harrison, R 424
Harvey, D 376
Haskins, C 503
Hassan, R 414
Hassane, M 276
Hartley, M 145–46, 148
Haug, W 84
Havel, V 451
Hayek, F von 17
Hay, C 194
Hay, H 317
Hayek, F 561
Hayles, K 381
Haynes, K 294
Hays, J 180
Hazelkorn, E 116
Heath, L *519*
Hegel, G *458*
Heidegger, M 219, 422, 451, *458*, 463, 523, 525–26, 530–33
Held, D 177, 180–81
Hemsley-Brown, J 414
Hennessy, P 122
Higgs, P 282
Hoble, E A 24
Hollander, E 51
Hollinger, D 30
Holroyd, C 423
Honneth, A *458*
Horn, H 195
Hoxby, C 126
Hoy, W 415
Hoyer, K 587
Hroch, P 587
Hudson, R 110
Hudzik, J 102
Huisman, J 111
Hurrelmann, A 175–76
Husserl, E 378

I

Illich, I 164, 443

J

Jacoby, R 343
Jary, D 346

Jaspers, K 1, 79, 178, *186*, 334, 391, 447, 451–53, *458*
Jameson, F 382
Jamieson, I 4, 414
Jawitz, J 414
Jencks, C 340, 342
Jessop, B 195
Jiménez, E 293, 295
Johnes, J *496*
Johnson, A 275, 279–80
Johnson, P 143
Johnstone, D 282
Judt, T 40, 52
Jurgenson, N 86

K

Kane, O 276
Kant, I 2, 334, 373, 394, 416, 450, 463, *499*, 559, 561, 564–65, 572
Kaplan, S *498*
Karmanau, Y 314
Katz, L *497*
Kaul, I 287
Kauppinen, I 73
Kavanagh, M 63
Kearney, M *497*
Keeling, R 226
Keen, B 294
Kehm, B 24
Kelly-Reid, J 64
Kelsey, J 138, 199
Kent, R 300
Kern, F *497*
Kerr, C 1, 119, 150, 353, 502
Kettunen, P 135
Keynes, M 181
Kleingold, P 559–60
Knapp, L 64
Knight, J 96, 99–118
Kogan, M 176, 359
Kohler, L 452
Kohn, M 565
Kolsaker, A 424
Komljenovic, J 172, 195, 203
Koshy, P 146
Kouvo, A 235
Kovac, V 421–22
Kristiansen, A 421–22
Krueger, A 130
Kuder, M 114
Kuhnle, S 235
Kweik, M 81–82, 172

L

Labaree, D 83
Ladd, H 316–18
Lakens, M 91
Lam, A 139
Lamumba-Kasongo, T 315
Land, R 523
Lanmans, S 166
Laredo, P 57
Larrain, J 293, 295
Larsen, I 65
Lash, S 356
Latour, B 432, 439
Laurie, S 445
Leathwood, C 25
Leedham-Green, E 512
Le Grand, J 57
Lehrer, K 422
Leibfried, S 175–76, 181
Leigh Scott, D 52
Lemaitre, G 165
Leslie, L 57, 59, 85, 87, 301, 304, 345, 361
Levy, D 293, 296, *306*, *497*
Lewis, C 426
Lewis, J 413
Leydesdorff, L 345
Lightman, A 165
Lillah, R 317
Lin, K 235
Lindsay, G 359
Lingis, A 529

Link, A 61
Lipset, S 337
List, C 589
Liu, T-C 5
López, F 304
Loyalka, P *307*
Lucas, L 63
Ludz, U 451
Lulat, Y 275
Luhmann, N 417
Lundvall, B 79
Luna, H 576
Lupton, G 139
Luxemburg, R 451
Lyotard, J-F 2, 333, 343–44, 472, 481, 581

M

Maassen, P 176, 185, 223, 420
Macan, T 148
Macfarlane, B 415, 424, 522–24, 528–31
MacIntyre 3
Magalhaes, A 355, 360
Makdisi, G 217
Mallick, K 407
Mann, M 61
Manning, A *497*
Mapasela, M 317
March, J 177
Marchetti, J 206
Marginson, S 9, 57, 79, 86, 96, 138, 305
Marin, L 443
Marques, J 87
Marsiske, R 296
Martin, B 71
Martin, R 206
Martinez, J 294, 300
Marx, K 378
Maskell, D 475
Masschelein, J 3, 162–63, 167, 390, 528
Massumi, B 433, 443
Maxey, L 576
Maxwell, J C 165
Maxwell, N 5, 9, 463, *556*
Mayson, S 138
Mazrui, A 273, 276, 288
Maxwell, N 588
Mazza, C 176, 178
Mbembe, A 565
McBride, R 384
McClelland, C *186*
McGettigan, A 84–85
McGrew, A 177, 180–81
McKenna, B 22
McKinley, E 568
McLauchlan, L 25, 87
McLuhan, M 377
McMahon W 59
McMurtry, J 417
McNamee, M 426
McPherson, M 72
Meacham, J 405–06
Meek, V 360
Menand, L 137
Mendoza, J *306*
Meriac, J 148
Merleau-Ponty, M 525
Merton, R 364
Mettler, S 125, 128–29
Michels, C 528
Mignolo, W 294
Mikics, D 381
Miller, E 64
Milman, O 143
Mincer, J 121
Minogue, K 1
Mintzberg, H 354
Mishra, R 180
Misztal, B 416
Miyoshi, M 345
Moberly, W 8
Mok, K 63
Mokyr, J 355, 364–65
Molesworth, M 300, 414
Moodie, G 360
Morphew, C 145, 148
Morris, J 149

Morton, A 58
Moses, I 137
Mountford-Zindars, A 126
Muche, F 226
Murphy, P 79, 86, 137, 416, 462, *496–99*
Murname, R *497*
Musselin, C 413
Myant, M 209
Myrsiades, K 4

N

Naidoo, R 4, 414
Nasseh, B *498*
Nathan, T 440
Neave, G 148–49, 183, 355, 358, 363, 365
Negrao, J 283
Neuvonen-Rauhala, M 236
Newfield, C 84
Newman, J H 1, 233, 334, 371, 379, 383, 466–67, 503
Newson, J 345
Newton, I 165
Nichol, G 53
Nicoll, K 423–24
Nisbet, R 329
Nixon, E 300, 414, 534
Nixon, J 5, 391, 423–24, 457, 522–23, 526, 528–30
Noble, K 513
Nokkala, T 64, 244, 247–49
Norgard, R 528–29
Norton, A *496*
Nowotny, H 95, 343
Nussbaum, M 389, *459*
Nybom, J 172–73, 233, *267*

O

Oakeshott, M 466–68, 474, 477, 481
Obinger, H 181
O'Boyle, L 81
O'Brien, R 209
Odin, J 103
Oldenburg, R *498*
Oliver, M 383
Olmedo, A 34
Olsen, J 177, 223
Olssen, M 23, 135–36
Olukoshi, A 288
Ondercin, D J 5–6
O'Neill, O 412
Ong, A 85
Ong, W 375, 382
Ordorika, I 294, 300
O'Reilly, C 139
Orellana, V 301
Ortega y Gasset, J 178
Orwell, G 37
Osbourne, M *497*
Owen, M 144/

P

Packham, D 136
Paine, T 394, *411*
Palier, B 185
Paradeise, C 176, 178
Parker, J 8
Parker, M 346
Parry, G 121
Parsons, T 333, 336–37, 339, 342–43, 346
Parveva, T 223
Passeron, J-C 341, 365
Paton, R 413
Peck, J 23, 28
Peck, K 363
Pedersen, O 217, 504
Pelkmans, J 203
Perkin, H 504, 512
Perkmann, M 142–43, 146
Pestieau, P 181, 185
Peters, M A 5–6, 9, 23, 79, 86, 135–36, 563, 566–67
Petras, J 294

Pettit, P 417, 589
Phillips, K 141
Philpott, K 139
Pierson, P 182
Piketty, T 120, 122–23, 125, 129–30
Pinheiro, R 184
Pittaway, L 88
Plato 396, 399, 559
Platt, G 336–37
Pogge, T 561
Popper, K 219, *556*
Posecznick, A 25
Potocnik, J 363
Prado, S 127
Pusser, B 63, 233

Q

Quack, S 177, 180
Quijano, A 294

R

Radder, H 25
Rait, R *498*
Ramirez, R 294, 300
Rawls, J 561
Raza, W 203
Read, B 25
Readings, B 2, 3, 8, 21, 182, 314, 333, 345–46, 462, 466–67, 469–70, 472, 479, 523
Reeves, M 8
Reichert, S 225
Reid, I 4
Riesman, D 333, 340, 342
Reiss, H *411*
Ren, Y 235
Rhoades, G 4, 22, 57, 59, 61, 64, 72, 85, 301, 304, 364, 582
Rhoten, D 287
Ricoeur, P 382, *458*
Riddiford, M 135
Ringer, F *186*, 338
Ritzen, J 229/
Ritzer, G 86
Rivera, L 128
Rivlin, A 358
Robertson, S 155, 172
Robbins, L Lord 476
  See also Robbins Report
Robins, K 345
Robinson, I 475
Robinson, S 19, 89
Rochford, F 96–97
Rodgers, T 359
Rodrigues, C 135
Roepnack, B 426
Rolfe, G 462, 470, 476
Roper, C 476
Rosa, H 377
Rospigliosi, A *519*
Roszak, T 380
Rothblatt, S 179, 217, *267*
Ruegg, W 27, 171–72, 439
Ruggie, J 180–81

S

Sabatier, P 354
Sabbagh, D 126
Sadlak, J 27
Saez, E 123
Said, E 45–46, 53, 565, 567
Salaita, S 23, 28, 30–33
Salmi, J 294
Sam, C 87
Sanborn, H 16
Saner, H 452
Santiago, R 25
Sarewitz, D 148
Sarrico, C 149–50
Sauvé, P 205–07, *212*
Scapens, R 149
Schapiro, M 72

Schapper, J 138
Scharpf, F 180
Schelling, F 186
Scheiermacher, F *186*, 461
Schelsky, H 335
Scherrard, J 207
Schmidt, V 180
Scotchmer, S 140
Schultz, T 121
Schuster, J 63
Scott, J 474
Scott, P 8, 95, 172, 184, 361, 534
Scullion, R 300, 414
Searls Giroux, S 312–13, 315, 324, 414
Seeleib-Kaiser, M 181
Sen, A 407
Sennett, R 51
Shane, S 88
Shattock, M 138, 178
Shavit, Y 129
Shils, E 333, 335–36
Shoho, A 425
Shore, C 25, 80, 85, 87, 90
Shumar, W 19, 22, 78, 85–86
Siles-Brugge, G 202–03, 210
Simons, M 3, 162–63, 390
Sin, C 363
Singh, M 365
Skinner, D 422
Slaughter, A-M 177
Slaughter, S 4, 18, 22, 56, 61, 63, 72, 85–87, 301, 304, 345, 361, 364, 582
Smith, A 345, 361, *365*, 394, *411*
Smith, P 425
Soares, J 128, 130
Socrates 395–96, 451
Southern, R 506
Spencer, D 314
Spinosa, C 88–89
Spivak, G 565
Sporn, B 64
Springer, S 36
Standaert, N 97
Stangler, D *497*
Stanton, P 149
Stehr, N 355–56
Stein, J 140
Stengers, I 432, 440, 442, 444
Stensaker, B 248, 420
Sterling, S 576
Stiegler, B 378
Stigler, G 498
Stiglitz, J 123–25, 176, 201, 207
Stofile, R 317
Streckeisen, P 355–57, 363–64, 365–66
Sutz, J 294–95, 304, *306*
Stromquist, G 243, 247
Swank, D 181
Swyngedouw, E 136, 139, 144
Sy, J 276

T

Tallis, R 4
Tauch, C 225, 578
Taylor, B J 57, 70
Taylor, F 355
Teferra, D 313, 315–16
Teichler, U 24, 186
Temple, P 523, 525–26, 529–30
ter Bogt, H 149
Tholen, G 127
Thomas, S 63
Thompson, E P 338
Thurow, L 358
Thyne, C 316
Thys-Clément, F 358
Tidy, J 172
Tierney, W 419, 423, 426
Tilak, J *307*
Toft Norgard, R 463, 529
Touraine, A 333, 339–40, 342
Trifonas, P 567
Trounson, A 141
Trow, M 420
Tschannen-Moran, M 415
Tuan, Y 523–24, 526–27
Tuerk, E 197
Turner, R 22

U

Ullman, C 78
Unz, R 128

V

Vabo, A 245
Valimaa, J 172, 184, 233–251
Van Aken, M 296
van Apeldoorn, B 58
van de Water, J 102
van der Wende, M 102
van der Sijde, P 87
Van Vught, F 148, 353–54, 359
Vasudeva, P *497*
Veblen, T 335
Veluotsou, C 413
Venkatararam, S 88
Venugopal, R 23
Verschaffel, B 160–61, 168
Vidovich, L 420
Villa, D *458*
Villaneuva, F 298–99
Virilio, P 378
Vogel, L 530, 534
von Humboldt, W 171, 180, 182, *186*, 371, 441, 461, 466, 505, 513
Vossenesteyn, H 359
Vrielink, J 141–42

W

Wachter, B 225
Waghid, Y 282, 315
Walker, R 570, 572, *573*
Watkins, C 580
Watson, D 9, 523, 587
Watts, R 138
Weber, M 178, 334–35, 342, 346
Webster, A 139
Webster, F 345
Weibel, P 432
Weick, K 354
Weil, S 383
Weiss, M 186
Welikala, T 580
Weymans, W 159
Whitchurch, C 24
Wilkins, S 111
Williams, B 4, 418
Williams, G 178, 358, 523, 530
Wilson, T 145
Wisman, J 125
Wittgenstein, L 219
Wittrock, B 81–82, 177, 179, 183, 217
Wodajo, M 279
Woelert, P 420
Wolff, R P 1
Wolin, S 454
Wright, S 25, 80, 85, *90–91*
Wright Mills, C 44, 47, 51, 53

X

Xie, Y 130

Y

Yates, L 420
Yliojoki, O-H 135, 136, 146, 184
Young, I 319
Young, K 180
Young, S 149

Z

Zeleza, P 288
Zhuang, L 112
Ziman, J 181
Zimmerman, D 139
Zusman, A 137

GLOBAL STUDIES IN EDUCATION

A.C. (Tina) Besley, Michael A. Peters,
Cameron McCarthy, Fazal Rizvi
General Editors

Global Studies in Education is a book series that addresses the implications of the powerful dynamics associated with globalization for re-conceptualizing educational theory, policy and practice. The general orientation of the series is interdisciplinary. It welcomes conceptual, empirical and critical studies that explore the dynamics of the rapidly changing global processes, connectivities and imagination, and how these are reshaping issues of knowledge creation and management and economic and political institutions, leading to new social identities and cultural formations associated with education.

We are particularly interested in manuscripts that offer: a) new theoretical, and methodological, approaches to the study of globalization and its impact on education; b) ethnographic case studies or textual/discourse based analyses that examine the cultural identity experiences of youth and educators inside and outside of educational institutions; c) studies of education policy processes that address the impact and operation of global agencies and networks; d) analyses of the nature and scope of transnational flows of capital, people and ideas and how these are affecting educational processes; e) studies of shifts in knowledge and media formations, and how these point to new conceptions of educational processes; f) exploration of global economic, social and educational inequalities and social movements promoting ethical renewal.

For additional information about this series or for the submission of manuscripts, please contact one of the series editors:

A.C. (Tina) Besley: t.besley@waikato.ac.nz
Cameron McCarthy: cmccart1@illinois.edu
Michael A. Peters: mpeters@waikato.ac.nz
Fazal Rizvi: frizvi@unimelb.edu.au

To order other books in this series, please contact our Customer Service Department:
(800) 770-LANG (within the U.S.)
(212) 647-7706 (outside the U.S.)
(212) 647-7707 FAX

Or browse online by series:
www.peterlang.com